The Color Encyclopedia of GARDEN PLANTS

The Color Encyclopedia of GARDEN PLANTS

Annuals • Perennials

ALLAN M. ARMITAGE

TIMBER PRESS
PORTLAND • LONDON

All photographs, except those of *Cleome* 'Linde Armstrong' (page 118, by Linda Askey) and *Clitoria ternatea* (page 121, by Meg Green), are by Allan M. Armitage.

Originally published by Timber Press in separate volumes: *Armitage's Garden Perennials* (2000) and *Armitage's Garden Annuals* (2004).

Published in 2009 by Timber Press, Inc.
The Haseltine Building
133 S.W. Second Avenue, Suite 450
Portland, Oregon 97204-3527
www.timberpress.com

2 The Quadrant
135 Salusbury Road
London NW6 6RJ
www.timberpress.co.uk

ISBN-13: 978-1-60469-119-1

Printed in China

A catalog record for this book is available from the Library of Congress.

Armitage's GARDEN ANNUALS

A Color Encyclopedia

ALLAN M. ARMITAGE

TIMBER PRESS
PORTLAND • LONDON

Contents

Preface

SOME THOUGHTS OF THE AUTHOR

Gardening is anything but staid and steady. When you talk with people who enjoy gardening, they are often so excited they can hardly stand still. They want to get out there and put a pond in their yard, or learn how to put in a stone wall, or build a path. They get dirty and downright exuberant when a particular plant or weed is discussed. Put gardeners together in a garden, and if they drink (which most do), they have to sip and walk at the same time. The most conservative people, who would never ask a stranger for the time of day, do not hesitate to ask a gardener for a piece of a plant they're lusting for. Vibrant, exciting, and changing—but hardly dignified.

On plant preferences

There are those who are collectors—their passions run to hydrangeas, daylilies, or iris. In general, they are in the minority, which is just as well; they are rather boring. I mean, how many daylilies can be described in a single sitting? (Answer: 67.) Most gardeners enjoy all plants if they perform well for them, although to be sure, we have many "woody camps" and an equal number of "herbaceous camps." As for me, I love them all. Annuals, perennials, shrubs, trees, bulbs, and ferns, who cares, as long as they look good.

On annuals

Nothing has changed faster in the last decade than the development, distribution, and use of annuals. In 1995, the predominant group of annuals were bedding plants such as petunias, marigolds, and alyssum. They were the engine that supplied most of the annual color in gardens. Today, those plants are still popular, but the volume of newcomers like angelonia, cuphea, verbena, and coleus has quadrupled as these genera become more available to the gardening public. Add bacopa, duranta, osteospermum, and stictocardia to the mix, and to be sure, we're not in Kansas anymore. However, while the genera keep appearing, the number of species of annuals within that category is often limited to one or two, and in many of these new genera, there may be only a handful of cultivars. The large number of cultivars of bedding plants like petunias and impatiens, by contrast, mirrors their longevity and popularity. Without doubt, some of the less common material shown in this book will be commonplace in five years, providing additional diversity each year.

On plant names

Most gardeners would be astonished at the amount of time and effort that goes into making a new cultivar of plant. From hybridizing, selection, propagation, distribution, promotion, and marketing—not to mention the tedious jobs of removing viruses and the tissue culturing needed for some material—the outlay of time and money is significant. Yet isn't it amazing how many annuals (and perennials) are so poorly labeled? Labels are often missing, or too small for anyone over forty to read, or simply state "4-inch annual," and on and on. What is the point of going through such an expensive, time-consuming practice when retailers accept such shoddy labels? The losers, of course, are the gardeners, who seldom know what they are buying, and furthermore will be unable to purchase the same thing next year. And what a mess is created when the same plant is sold under two, three, or even four different names! We are a patient lot, we gardeners, but not stupid. Get your labels cleaned up, and we will come back for more. Make it simple to buy the product, and then get out of our way.

On new plants

A lady named Rachel walked into our greenhouse, which was overflowing with new and colorful exotic plants. She selected two plants and approached me to pay. I told her that they were research plants and not for sale, and, with great disappointment, she turned to put them back. However, her selected plants caught my eye, and I was floored! Believing she had the entire contents of the greenhouse from which to choose, she had picked up a 4-inch pot of 'Better Boy' tomato and a 6-inch pot of Leyland cypress! Uncommonly common plants when surrounded by such beauty. I asked her why she had chosen these (after all, I figured I was making the world a better place), and she looked me straight in the eye and said, "That's all I recognized." Now, thanks to Rachel, I keep all this new stuff in perspective. They will soon be recognizable, but until then, there are some lovely new geraniums I'd be happy to share with you.

About the book

I wrote this book because people, including myself, love pictures. It is designed to provide well-researched and useful information, but in this book, the text supports the images shown. It was created as a complement to my larger annual book, *Armitage's Manual of Annuals, Biennials, and Half-Hardy Perennials*; in that book, the information is far more specific and in-depth, and the images support the text. Between the two, you'll learn everything you ever wanted to know about annuals but were afraid to ask.

It was also written to complement another wonderful color book, *Armitage's Garden Perennials*. With the two together, you can have your own photo-library of more than 2800 images, and some good reading to boot. I hope you enjoy yourself, enjoy your reading, and enjoy your garden.

ACKNOWLEDGMENTS

Thanks to Stephanie Anderson, who helped with the incredible job of image management, and to Judy Laushman, who read over the text and provided insightful comments. And without doubt, the book is far better because of my editor, Franni Bertolino Farrell.

PART ONE

Armitage's Garden Annuals A to Z

Abelmoschus

I first heard of *Abelmoschus* in a botany class in Canada, where we students were provided with various cooked vegetables to examine, identify, and taste. I looked at this long mucus-covered green thing in front of me and, after gagging on the taste, I was told it was a favorite vegetable for soups. It was called okra. No wonder there are so few tins of Campbell's in our pantry. And what kind of a name is abelmoschus anyway? If nobody can pronounce it, how in the world will anyone buy it for the garden?

Of course, the definition of conservative can generally be found in the dictionary under "Canadian cuisine," so when I moved to the South, I became far more tolerant of weird things like okra and grits. I tried okra again, and they . . . well, they were as slimy and awful as I remembered. However, when I had more opportunity to reexamine the ornamental members of the genus, I found some neat plants hidden in that long name (pronounced "a bel *mos* kus"). And, believe it or not, ornamental forms of okra are among my favorites.

While I can drive by a field of corn and hardly notice it, a field of okra (*Abelmoschus esculentus*) is another matter. At least I slow down, because the plants can be as tall as a man and the flowers are always ornamental. Fields

Abelmoschus moschatus 'Pacific Scarlet'

Abelmoschus esculentus 'Little Lucy'

Abelmoschus esculentus 'Okrazilla'

Abelmoschus manihot

Abelmoschus manihot 'Cream Cup'

of okra are one thing, but who wants a 5' tall, prickly plant with slimy fruit in the garden anyway? Well, let me introduce you to the fat fruit of an ornamental form called 'Okrazilla', a name only its creator, Ralph Cramer, could think of. As hard as it was for me to get used to the idea, these are used in bouquets and floral arrangements. And I may add, people are always impressed once they learn what they are. Wouldn't you be? With the introduction of ornamental forms, the gardener now has some choice. A dwarf form such as 'Little Lucy' (only about 2' tall) has something for Canadians and Southerners alike, gorgeous cut-leaved bronze leaves, handsome flowers, and edible fruit. The genus belongs to the mallow family, so expect some damage from Japanese beetles and thrips. Full sun.

If the idea of ornamental vegetables is appealing, an even brighter member is aibika, *Abelmoschus manihot*. These are similar to okra and are cultivated extensively in the lowlands of Melanesia as nutritious leafy vegetables. The flowers are also beautiful, making it a candidate for both the flower garden or kitchen garden. Ornamental forms can be up to 3' tall; one such, 'Cream Cup', provides stunning creamy yellow flowers with a purple eye on spineless plants. Full sun.

If planting veggies is not up your alley and other colors are called for, why not try musk mallow (*Abelmoschus moschatus*)? The common name comes from the fact that the seeds smell somewhat musky. Other common names are muskdana and ambrette, and plants are grown in India for seed exports, mainly to Europe, for use as an aromatic oil. Drug manufacturers are also introducing new herbal drugs containing ambrette for medicinal use. Odor and oil aside, the cultivated forms of the plant provide flowers in red and pink, and continue to bloom all season. As with all members of the genus, flowers persist only a day or two, but so many are formed, it does not seem to matter. Much shorter than *A. manihot*, they may be used as bedding plants or simply to provide some interest in containers or the front of the garden. Two of my favorites are 'Pacific Light Pink' and 'Pacific Scarlet'. Full sun.

Abutilon

FLOWERING MAPLE, CHINESE LANTERN

The flowering maple has been a favorite for a long time. It had its heyday in Great-grandmother's front hall or parlor, where it was much better known as the parlor maple (the maple name refers to the shape of the leaves). Sadly, as the parlor went the way of the smoking jacket, parlor maples all but disappeared from horticulture. They have come back,

Abutilon ×*hybridum* 'Bella Deep Coral'

MORE ☞

however, and showy abutilons can now be found in containers and gardens from Tampa to Toronto. Dozens of cultivars are sold, but mail order and the Internet are the best sources for flowering maples today. Availability in garden centers and nurseries is still limited.

Many species exist in this interesting group of plants, and the most common are generally listed under *Abutilon ×hybridum*, or common flowering maple. They come in an array of colors; if you find a good source of these plants, you may find them under their correct names, however, names like "Red" or "Yellow" are not infrequent. In general, the hybrids are 1–2½' tall and are better suited to containers or baskets than to the garden proper. I also enjoy some of

Abutilon ×hybridum Bella Hybrids

Abutilon theophrasti 'Salmon'

Abutilon ×hybridum 'Souvenir de Bonn'

Abutilon ×hybridum 'Savitzii'

Abutilon pictum 'Thompsonii', flowers

the newer flowering forms such as the Bella Hybrids, available in yellow and deep coral among other colors.

One likely parent of the hybrids is *Abutilon theophrasti*, known as velvet leaf. However, it is apparent that Tinkerbell has been spreading pixie dust over the leaves of some of the hybrids, and variegation patterns seem endless. Tall plants with exquisite eye-catching foliage may be found in 'Souvenir de Bonn', stunning almost-white foliage with green centers is seen in 'Savitzii', and leaves splashed with yellow are the norm in Thompson's flowering maple, *Abutilon pictum* 'Thompsonii'. The orange flowers on the variegated forms are handsome, but it is the foliage that catches the eye.

Not to be outdone are the pendulous forms, represented mainly by trailing maple, *Abutilon megapotamicum*. The flowers are tubular, pendulous, and generally in red and yellow. The most common form is 'Variegatum', in which the leaves are splashed with yellow, and I also enjoy 'Melon Delight', with its obvious trailing maple in its blood. Exceptional for containers and hanging baskets.

All abutilons tolerate full sun in the North; a little afternoon shade in the South is appreciated, especially with the highly variegated forms. Some of the larger-leaved forms will wilt in hot sun but come back fresh in the evening.

Abutilon pictum 'Thompsonii', foliage

Abutilon megapotamicum 'Variegatum'

Abutilon megapotamicum 'Melon Delight'

Acalypha

Acalyphas are schizophrenic. The flowers of chenille plant (*Acalypha hispida*) are in long braids, whereas those of copperleaf (*A. wilkesiana*) are hardly noticed at all. Some plants bear large leaves in an array of incredible (some may say gaudy) colors, while others bear thin, twisted leaves in muted tones. Regardless, plants have found their way to the garden, and containers and baskets of acalyphas are seen more and more on porches and patios in North American gardens.

The prettiest of all is probably chenille plant, historically a gift plant, and its long-flowered relatives. Sold for the long tassels of pink to red flowers, plants are also grown for the attractive heart-shaped leaves. Try it in large hanging baskets in morning sun, afternoon shade. Trailing red tail, *Acalypha reptans*, has shorter flowers and is not quite as showy but may be tougher and can be used as a groundcover. The best is probably the pink-flowered 'Summer Love'.

Chenille plant may be the prettiest, but it is not the toughest for the long-

MORE ☞

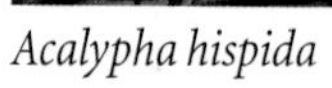

Acalypha hispida

Acalypha hispida, basket

Acalypha reptans

Acalypha reptans 'Summer Love'

Acalypha wilkesiana 'Copperleaf' with lantana

Acalypha wilkesiana 'Kona Coast'

Acalypha wilkesiana 'Bourbon Street'

Acalypha godseffiana 'Heterophylla'

Acalypha godseffiana 'Tricolor'

MORE ☞

season rigors of our gardens. My bet for tough goes to the foliage forms whose flowers are secondary. These are found mainly in the cultivars of copperleaf, whose splashes of color are eye-popping. They are dressed for the costume party, bedecked in colors that Ralph Lauren could not have dreamed up. In containers, they provide the pizzazz. 'Copperleaf' is a handsome plant well suited to containers, and 'Bourbon Street', with its copper and pink leaves, really made our containers at the University of Georgia look good. For simplicity, the bright green and yellow leaves of 'Kona Coast' are hard to beat.

While the leaves of some copperleaf plants are large and colorful, others are more like long pliant needles. I notice the expressions of people as I try to explain (unsuccessfully) the subtly variegated beauty of the plant known as 'Heterophylla', a selection of *Acalypha godseffiana*. The twisted leaves can be thought of as many things, but seldom is beautiful mentioned. However, the multicolored 'Tricolor', with similar ghoulish leaves and habit but far more colorful, evokes more sympathy, if not love. Of course, I think they are both must-have plants.

None of the cultivars is easy to find at your garden shop, however, many are available through mail-order sources. Full sun.

Acmella oleracea

TOOTHACHE PLANT, EYEBALL PLANT

Here is a plant with something for everyone. From the gardener's perspective, where else can you find eyeballs staring back at you as you putter around the place? From the herbalist's point of view, this plant is chock-full of medicinal goodies, and claims of its benefits can be found all over the Internet. It is best known for its numbing effect on the mouth and gums, and thus became known as toothache plant. In the event of a toothache, chew on the flower bud, and relief from pain will be almost instantaneous, probably lasting at least until you can get to the dentist. The flower buds are said to provide the most sensations, and in the name of learning, I make my students sample various plant parts. The sensation of numbness and the production of saliva occur within thirty seconds and, while not pretty, it is the only time I can get my students to salivate over my class. None of the literature I have read shows any danger from this sport, but by all means, try it first before introducing your neighbor to its medicinal virtues. By the way, slugs seem to like it as well—maybe that's where slug slime comes from.

Acmella oleracea

Acmella oleracea 'Peek-A-Boo'

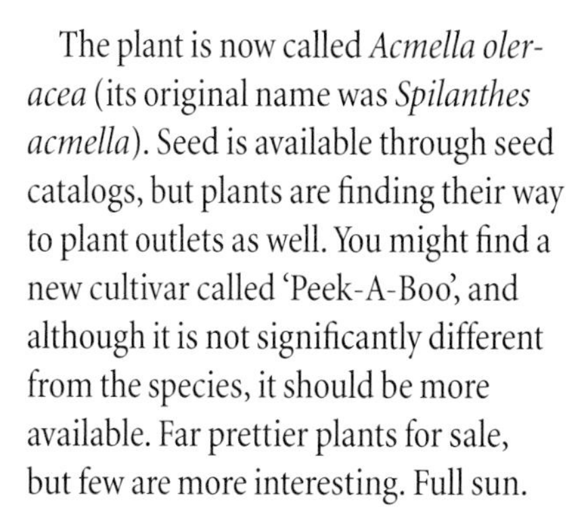

The plant is now called *Acmella oleracea* (its original name was *Spilanthes acmella*). Seed is available through seed catalogs, but plants are finding their way to plant outlets as well. You might find a new cultivar called 'Peek-A-Boo', and although it is not significantly different from the species, it should be more available. Far prettier plants for sale, but few are more interesting. Full sun.

Agastache

GIANT HYSSOP

It may be argued that *Agastache* does not belong in a book about annuals, that many species can be grown as perennials at least to zone 5. However, plants grow rapidly and flower profusely in a single season (a characteristic unbefitting a self-respecting perennial), so that they can be enjoyed as annuals or perennials. In the Armitage garden (zone 7b), I find most agastaches persist for only two or three years. Regardless, these culinary herbs all provide a fragrance of anise, some gently fleeting and others highly pungent.

By the way, I don't want to get into plant pronunciation . . . however, people hesitate to say this genus because it doesn't seem to "sound right." Most Americans pronounce the name "*ah* ga

Agastache foeniculum

Agastache foeniculum 'Honey Bee Blue'

Agastache foeniculum 'Honey Bee White'

MORE ☞

stash," I prefer the British "ah *gas* ta key." I realize this makes me sound like a plant snob, but the real reason I prefer it is that it helps me spell the darn thing correctly. Both are just fine, and fulfill the Armitage Axiom of Plant Pronunciation, "Get the syllables in the right order, and fire away."

Many of the agastaches available to the gardener are hybrids, and offered as such. The nomenclature of some of the cultivars is either unknown or mixed up, so I will mention some of my favorites and attempt to put some parentage with them.

I think some of the best plants are associated with *Agastache foeniculum*, anise hyssop. These tough plants are easy to grow from seed but will be 3–4' tall. The cultivars 'Honey Bee Blue' and

Agastache foeniculum 'Golden Jubilee'

Agastache urticifolia 'Licorice Blue'

Agastache austromontana 'Pink Pop'

'Honey Bee White' are exceptional performers but grow no taller than 2½'. I am also most impressed with 'Golden Jubilee', whose golden yellow foliage looks good all season and contrasts well with the purple flowers. And if you can find some 'Licorice Blue', likely a selection of the nettle hyssop, *A. urticifolia*, you will be rewarded with an abundance of long-stemmed cut flowers for the vase.

If color is the goal, sit tight because breeders are really going to town. Gardeners are still excited about one of the earlier ornamental forms of *Agastache barberi*, called 'Tutti Frutti', and while I have seen it look good here and there, I always thought the name was more exciting than the plant. However, I am really impressed with the endless flowers on 'Pink Pop' (probably a selection of *A. austromontana*) and the big rosy purple blooms of the hybrid 'Hazy Days'. But even those fine colors didn't prepare me for the wonderful golden flowers found in the selections of *A. aurantiaca*. It is tough to walk by 'Navajo Sunset', which grows 2–3' tall and is covered with flowers all summer, without stopping for a moment. Its partner 'Apricot Sprite', which also causes knee-lock, differs by being a little shorter but is equally lovely.

Most of these plants are likely hardy to zone 6, but who cares? Enjoy them for a year or two. Full sun.

Agastache barberi 'Tutti Frutti'

Agastache 'Hazy Days'

Agastache aurantiaca 'Navajo Sunset'

Agastache aurantiaca 'Apricot Sprite'

Ageratum houstonianum, garden

Ageratum houstonianum 'Artist Blue'

Ageratum houstonianum 'Pacific Pink'

Ageratum houstonianum climbing stairs

Ageratum houstonianum 'Leilani'

Ageratum houstonianum

FLOSS FLOWER

Walkways, driveways, and garden paths have been lined with an abundance of floss flower for decades, and this old-fashioned bedding plant has really not changed a great deal over the years. Having said that, however, I can't think of a more beautiful use for this plant than the one I saw at the Isle of Mainau in southern Germany, where old stone stairs became so much more inviting in partnership with the floss flowers planted there. And the borders at the Butchart Gardens in British Columbia seemed to come into focus as the ageratum begged you to follow. Most of us can't reproduce such scenes, but they provide inspiration.

I tell my students that to help remember the name for *Ageratum houstonianum*, they should think about the city in Texas. However, while that is an effective mnemonic device, the species was named for a Scotsman, William Houston, who was a plant collector in South America.

A good deal of breeding has occurred in recent years. Ageratum is undergoing a transformation to include new colors for the garden and can also be highly useful as cut flowers, if the right cultivars are chosen. They occur in the common shade of lavender, but 'Artist Blue' is anything but common. Rose, pink ('Pacific Pink'), and white are quite popular. The best cultivar for the garden, as opposed to the garden edge, is 'Blue Horizon', which provides an upright habit, loads of flowers, and stems strong enough to be cut and brought inside. Professional cut flower growers thought it was so good that the plant was recognized as the Fresh Cut Flower of the Year by the Association of Specialty Cut Flower Growers in 2003. Compared to the standard edging form 'Blue Danube', the contrast is obvious. 'Leilani' is about halfway between the two in size and provides a choice between the tall and the short. Full sun in the North, afternoon shade in the South.

Alcea rosea

HOLLYHOCK

I can't seem to write about this species without dredging up bad memories of bad plants in a bad garden in Montreal where I grew up. That really isn't fair, because as I have gotten older, cultivars have gotten better, and heck, why should memories of a few Japanese beetles and a little rust disease ruin my youthful reminiscences? One thing that has not changed, however, is that people still love hollyhocks, warts and all.

MORE ☞

Ageratum houstonianum 'Blue Horizon' with *A. h.* 'Blue Danube' as edging

Alcea rosea 'Barnyard Red'

Alcea rosea, bicolor form

Alcea rosea 'Indian Spring'

Alcea rosea 'Nigrita'

Alcea rosea 'Nigra'

Alcea rosea 'Chaters Purple'

Most plants are simply raised by putting seeds in prepared soil, although started plants can be purchased and may be worth the extra dollars. Plants are technically biennials with plenty of cold tolerance, and although they may come back occasionally in the spring, or a few seeds may sprout, it is best to treat them as annuals. Many named cultivars have been selected; however, most people totally forget what the labels said and are really only interested in the flower color anyway. Plants produce a wide range of flowers, including singles in many colors, although old-fashioned reds, like 'Barnyard Red', and bicolors, in which the center is a different color than the rest of the flower, seem the easiest to find. One of the best single hollyhocks, 'Indian Spring', consists of flowers in a riot of color. They grow 4–6' tall on strong, stout stems. An "in" color that never seems to fade from a gardener's consciousness is black or deep purple, and both 'Nigrita' and 'Nigra' are "in."

Want a little weirder, try the doubles. Some excellent eye-poppers can be seen around gardens; I particularly like the Chaters series (a series is a group of similar plants that usually differ in flower color only), and 'Chaters Purple' is tough to beat. Of course, a little dose of reality may be needed here. Most hollyhocks in most parts of the country are filet to bugs, beetles, and assorted fungi. The doubles are no better than the singles; in fact, the extra layers of petals simply seem to provide more meeting places for the beetles. If Japanese beetles are not a problem (careful of earwigs too), then plant a bunch of hollyhocks; if the pests arrive at the same time as the flowers open, get the bricks ready and start clapping. Certain chemicals are also quite useful, simply be careful. Full sun.

Alocasia

ELEPHANT EAR, TARO

Regardless of what the "experts" tell you, there are no easily visible differences between this genus, *Colocasia*, and *Xanthosoma*. I have visited taxonomists, studied books, and talked with aroidites (plants belong to the family Araceae), who say that simply looking at the plant, even if in flower, will not tell you if a certain cultivar is an alocasia or a colocasia. It drives me crazy not to be able to tell you to look at the petals, or stamens, or leaves to make a determination, but the only place these genera consistently differ is the ovary, and the way in which the

Alcea rosea with Japanese beetles

Alocasia macrorrhiza, Australia

MORE ☞

ovules are held there. In my book on annuals (*Armitage's Manual of Annuals, Biennials, and Half-Hardy Perennials*), I stated, "[Leaves] are always peltate in *Colocasia* but less so in *Alocasia*." In fact, leaves usually start out peltate in *Alocasia* but may change to normal attachment. The reason for this long-winded introduction is that the cultivars I mention probably belong to the genus listed, but then again they may not. The bottom line: as a gardener, it doesn't matter; if you want to be a taxonomist, meet me in the lab.

My, but how these plants have been embraced. Ten years ago, gardeners outside the Gulf States would have been hard-pressed to find any alocasias for sale. While they are surely not common today, they are no longer rare, and a few cultivars have become downright familiar. *Alocasia macrorrhiza*, with its enormous leaves, is one of those easier-to-find species. Some gardeners feel that these are "plants for the South," however, the large stand at the marvelous Allen Centennial Gardens on the Madison campus of the University of Wisconsin amply states the distance this tropical has traveled.

Alocasias are beautiful to behold, but holding is all you should do. All parts are poisonous, and eating is expressly forbidden. If you wish to test this statement, expect painful irritation of lips, mouth, tongue, and throat after chewing as well as difficulty in speaking. After that, probably nausea and diarrhea, delirium, and, finally, death. Ho hum, just another engaging plant for our gardens.

The choices of *Alocasia* are numerous, but only a few are easily found at the garden center. Alongside the big-leaved *Alocasia macrorrhiza*, you may find its variegated selection, *A. macrorrhiza* 'Variegata', with no two leaves seemingly the same. Both of these, but particularly the variegated form, tolerate some shade and still keep their color. Three or four extraordinary species may sometimes be found in the garden center, but mostly they reside in conservatories and botanical gardens. The leaves of copper alocasia, *A. cuprea*, remind me of burnished metal, the veins making a wonderful contrast to the rest of the wide leaf. The arrow-shaped dark purple leaves of the long-lobed alocasia, *A. longiloba*, are quite spectacular, while the big, bold shiny purple sheen of *A. plumbea* 'Metallica' makes the Armitage garden more exotic than ever. And the clean green and white lines of *A.* ×*amazonica*, usually known as green velvet, seem perfect in every way. However, do not fret if you cannot find such species for the garden; they are present in many of the hybrids, and these are becoming more readily available every year.

Alocasia macrorrhiza, University of Wisconsin

Alocasia macrorrhiza 'Variegata'

Alocasia longiloba

Alocasia cuprea

Alocasia 'African Mask'

Alocasia plumbea 'Metallica'

Alocasia 'Polly'

MORE ☞

I would not hazard a guess as to which hybrid I see the most, but 'African Mask' must be up there with the leaders. Plants go under a number of names; it's real name is *Alocasia micholitziana* var. *maxkowskii*, but I dare you to say that ten times. A few others have similar looks. I love the habit and leaf color of 'Polly', which is a dwarfer form with dark velvet leaves and obvious white to silver venation; it is quite spectacular. As a young or mature plant, it is my first choice. 'Frydek' is fabulous, with wonderfully velvety looking leaves; they are similar to those of 'Polly' but thinner, and with veins of light yellow rather than white. And how can you not enjoy the large smokey leaves of 'Corazon', the immense black foliage of 'Black Magic', or the white-veined dark leaves of 'Fantasy'? The only cultivar I have trouble falling in love with is the speckled thing known as 'Hilo Beauty', which is offered as an alocasia, a colocasia, and even as a caladium. I am alone, of course, as this is one of the best-selling tropicals on the market. To each his own.

In late fall, cut the foliage back when it starts to decline (around 40°F) and dig the tuberous rootstalk. If a heated cold

Alocasia ×*amazonica*

Alocasia 'Frydek'

Alocasia 'Corazon'

Alocasia 'Hilo Beauty'

Alocasia 'Black Magic'

Alocasia 'Fantasy'

frame or greenhouse is available, pot up the root and keep it around 40–50°F. If plants are to be enjoyed in a conservatory or greenhouse during the winter, be prepared to heat the structure to about 70°F. If no overwintering facility is available, enjoy their beauty during the season, and save your money for next year.

Full sun in the North, afternoon shade in the South, and reasonably good drainage: they are not bog plants like some species of *Colocasia*.

Alonsoa

MASK FLOWER

I first saw a diminutive plant of this genus in a greenhouse in Denmark, then a second species in a garden in England, where every plant seems to look its best. Small salmon to coral flowers were all over the 1' tall plants. They were cute, flowered heavily, and looked terrific in a container. I had to have some, and finally found some seeds, which I proceeded to sow. Not a month later, I spied the species I first encountered in England, in orange-red this time, in a container at North Hill, in southern Vermont, the extraordinary garden of Wayne Winterrowd and Joe Eck. If those fine gardeners were using it, well, then, maybe I wasn't so far off after all.

The plants were mask flowers, which is a simpler and far more user-friendly way of saying *Alonsoa meridionalis* or

MORE ☞

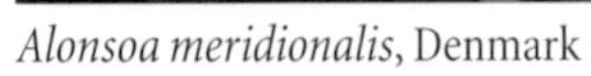

Alonsoa meridionalis, Denmark

Alonsoa warscewiczii, Vermont

Alonsoa warscewiczii, red form

Alonsoa warscewiczii, England

Alpinia zerumbet 'Variegata', Georgia

Alpinia zerumbet 'Variegata', University of Wisconsin

A. warscewiczii. The latter is perhaps a little easier to grow and may flower more profusely, but the former, although more shrubby, is also worth a try. There are not a lot of choices; plants come in pink, red, and salmon-coral, but probably others can be found with a little effort. They are not particularly happy in hot weather, but even if they melt out by July in the South or August in the North, they will have provided a few months of pleasure. Best in containers. Full sun in the North, afternoon shade in the South.

Alpinia zerumbet

GINGER LILY

The rise in popularity of tropical plants in the landscape should not be considered surprising when one understands that most annuals, such as impatiens and begonias, are from the tropics. However, the rise in demand for annuals like *Alocasia*, *Kaempferia*, and ginger lilies has been nothing short of remarkable. One of the first plants to be used by landscapers and gardeners was the variegated ginger lily, *Alpinia zerumbet* 'Variegata'.

I have always enjoyed ginger lily in my garden because it tolerates shade but grows well in full sun. The promise of flowers is an empty one in most temperate gardens; it simply is not warm enough for long enough, but temperatures that hover around 80°F are excellent for foliage growth. The big leaves all arise from the ground (no main stem) and are streaked in yellow and green. The amount of streaking differs on every leaf, and the leaves are brighter (i.e., more yellow) in the sun than in the shade.

They are particularly useful in areas of heavy foot or road traffic; they are tough, colorful, and essentially maintenance-free. Gardeners in the North and West tend to shy away from plants that have "ginger" as part of their name, in

MORE ☞

the belief that they have insufficient heat. Get over it, plants will be smaller in the North but can still be quite stunning, and this is one of the easier ones to try. Full sun.

Alternanthera

CALICO PLANT

In certain American cities, the appreciation of ornamental plants is a way of life, in both the private and public sectors. People in these cities expect their parks not only to be clean and safe but also to be well landscaped. Walking down Atlanta's Peachtree Street, I see a kaleidoscope of colorful beds in front of apartments and malls. If I can get to Montreal, I wander into Westmount Park, to glory in one of the finest floral clocks in the land. Boston, Vancouver, New York, Portland, and Seattle are all known as plant-friendly places for the public. City planners and park planners complement private landscapers and architects in such cities, and we live better because of them.

It is interesting that one of the most common plants used in planted beds is seldom seen in home gardens. The most common of the public plants is *Alternanthera ficoidea*, joseph's coat, because of its short, formal meatball-like habit, bright colors, and lack of maintenance needs. Growing no more than 9" tall and often clad in chartreuse foliage, these plants are the fences of formal beds, the cultivar 'Fizzy' being the best example. Wherever tight designs are called for, be they formal beds at Wisley in England, or the purple backgrounds on floral clocks, *Alternanthera ficoidea* and its short-statured relatives are planted. Numerous colors are available, but chartreuse and purple are the main ones employed by the garden designer.

Not all alternantheras are the strict domain of the professional, however, and

Alternanthera ficoidea, chartreuse form

Alternanthera dentata var. *rubiginosa* 'Wave Hill'

Alternanthera ficoidea 'Fizzy'

Alternanthera ficoidea, floral clock

a few new stars have appeared in recent years. The most common is 'Wave Hill', an upright purple form that can grow 3–4' tall. Likely a selection of *Alternanthera dentata* var. *rubiginosa*, the plant maintains its shiny purple color all season. Its only drawback is that it may be a little too large and aggressive for many gardeners. If that is the case, don't be bashful; whack it off at the knees, and it will branch and return rapidly. A shorter selection, sporting similar dark purple foliage and perhaps even shinier, is 'Gail's Choice', selected by Gail Kahle in Plano, Texas. We have had the two plants side by side at the University of Georgia Trial Gardens and 'Gail's Choice' is shorter and slower to take off, but that is not a bad thing. She can also be clipped if needed. A recent introduction to the world of darkness is 'Purple Knight', but

Alternanthera ficoidea, formal bedding

Alternanthera dentata 'Gail's Choice'

Alternanthera dentata 'Gail's Choice', container

MORE ☞

Alternanthera dentata 'Purple Knight'

it is not quite as dark as the other two, nor does it bear the same luster.

Two wonderful colorful but low-growing hybrids have been developed. 'Red Runner' is a bronzy red with relatively large leaves, but 'Red Threads' is even better, with its fabulous thin red leaves. The name joseph's coat refers to the fact that many colors were apparent on the leaves, but the demand for monochrome floral designs led growers to produce few of the old-fashioned multicolored forms. However, with the appearance of 'Party Time' and its upright habit, three-colored leaves, and vigorous growth, gaudy is back! It differs from others in the genus by being more open in habit (not a great choice for a floral design), but it also performs better and is more colorful in shade. In sun, the pink fades, some damage occurs to the tips of the leaves, and the plant color is far more subdued. Full sun for most, partial shade for 'Party Time'.

Alternanthera 'Red Runner'

Alternanthera 'Red Threads'

Alternanthera 'Party Time'

Amaranthus

AMARANTH

If all the amaranths were put in a line, the genus would win the Halloween prize in the plant world, hands down! Perhaps that is why there is such a love-hate relationship with these wonderfully weird plants: you love to see them, just not in your own garden. I am the same way—I admire, I gush, I look twice—but always I am looking in public gardens, arboreta, or conservatories. Are we a little too timid?

Then again, maybe not. Fire-engine red has nothing on the color of some of the tall amaranths, and they can be seen from miles away. I always enjoy traveling to Ontario, and to the Royal Botanical Gardens, located between Hamilton and Burlington. Someone there has his or her act together and is not afraid of bright colors. I remember walking a path and spying large stoplights of color, beckoning me to come closer. They dominated everything around them and were perfectly sited to draw me like a magnet. They were plants of 'Early Splendor', and they were a warning of the brightness yet to come. As I rounded another corner, I had to shield my eyes as I came face to face with 'Molten Fire'. Their spectacular color made even the yellow celosias brighter. The color of 'Illumination' is a little more subdued but not much. Still a 55-mph plant, and still brightens up the flowers around it. But somebody really got into the sauce when they thought that 'Perfecta', sometimes known as 'Splendens Perfecta', would win a lot of

Amaranthus 'Illumination'

Amaranthus caudatus, British Columbia

Amaranthus caudatus, Ontario

MORE ☞

friends. Truly a clown at the circus, but impossible to ignore and even harder not to enjoy, the plant has been dubbed the summer poinsettia.

I admit to enjoying the show that amaranths provide. And, just when the red has strained the eyeballs a little too much, I find relief in one of my favorites, 'Aurora'. In Rastafarian dreadlocks of gold, these plants look like they just emerged from a good drenching at the end of the rainbow.

Most cultivars just mentioned probably belong to *Amaranthus tricolor*; however, the taxonomy of the genus is being debated, and species may be lumped or split in the future. The flowers of most are rather forgettable; it is the colored bracts that provide the show. But not all the amaranths are so endowed; a few, such as *A. hypochondriacus* (prince's feather) and *A. cruentus* have marvelously colored flowers. 'Prince's Feather' is used both as a cultivar and common name for the 4–6' tall plants, which seem to flow as they flower, while the wheat color of the thousands of small flowers on 'Hot Biscuits' proves that not all amaranths are red.

If plant people were to come up with their favorites, it is likely that the tassel flower (*Amaranthus caudatus*), also known by the macabre name of love-lies-bleeding, would be on a few lists. The flowers are similar to those of chenille plant (*Acalypha hispida*) but thinner and longer, and appear to be arranged in small knots down the tassels. In the Butchart Gardens in British Columbia, crowds were gathered, cameras were blazing, and people just wanted to know what it was. It was also impressive in mixed gardens in southern Germany and was on steroids in Hamilton, Ontario. For those with weaker constitutions, 'Viridis' is a far more subdued form of this bleeding plant, with green rather than red tassels. Quite excellent if

Amaranthus 'Perfecta'

Amaranthus 'Aurora'

Amaranthus 'Hot Biscuits'

Amaranthus caudatus Towers Mix

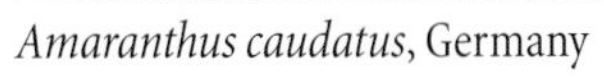

Amaranthus caudatus, Germany

Amaranthus caudatus 'Viridis'

Amaranthus 'Molten Fire'

MORE ☞

provided with a dark background: plants tend to get lost when placed with other greens. And last but not least in this group of amaranths, I came across Towers Mix, red and green weapons on stems, each of which would shame a good shillelagh. Awful, but like a car wreck, it is hard to ignore.

All amaranths have their great moments, but like the meteors they are, they crash and burn with regularity. Don't expect them to be spectacular all season, and although the flowers persist for a long time, once they have peaked, they are toast. Since all are raised from seed, replanting halfway through the season is a good way to keep the meteors coming. Fertilize heavily, as a tremendous amount of growth must be nurtured in a short period of time. Full sun.

Anagallis monellii

BLUE PIMPERNEL

I always enjoy a good planting of blue pimpernel (*Anagallis monellii*); the wonderful color always tickles my fancy.

Amaranthus 'Early Splendor'

Anagallis monellii 'Skylover' with pulmonaria

Amaranthus 'Prince's Feather'

Anagallis monellii 'Skylover', garden bed

Maybe because it is not the easiest plant to grow (at least not in the Armitage garden) or maybe it is simply supposed to make us smile. After all, the genus name comes from the Greek, *anagelao* ("to laugh") and was suggested as a tonic against sadness. This should be mandatory viewing on Monday mornings.

In the garden, blue pimpernel is best used in containers and baskets, although I have seen it peeking from beneath pulmonarias as well as growing vigorously in a landscape bed. Plants are far more suited to cooler summers than to hot, and do better for a longer period of time in a Duluth summer compared to an Athens summer. In hot weather, they look beautiful in May, okay in June, then struggle and proceed to the compost bin. They may end up in the same place in Seattle or Fargo, but they will take their own good time getting there.

Few cultivars have been selected. 'Skylover' and 'Blue Light' seem to be the most available; I believe that more purple is apparent in the former, but not a great deal of difference exists between them. Full sun in the North, afternoon shade in the South.

Anagallis monellii 'Blue Light'

Angelica

People always enjoy seeing angelica in gardens, but I am not sure why. It may be their sheer size (they pump themselves up to 6' in height), their great balls of flowers, their stately seed heads, or just that the name is so much fun to say. Regardless, they hold people's attention when they are in their glory, even though their glory is often short-lived. They are technically perennials, but they frequently disappear after flowering, or persist for no more than two years.

The best known of this group is wild parsnip, *Angelica archangelica*, whose

Angelica archangelica, stems

Angelica gigas

MORE ☞

very name conjures up images of a Raphael painting, or Michelangelo's frescoed ceiling in the Sistine Chapel. The stems and petioles of wild parsnip can be candied and eaten, and young shoots can be prepared like asparagus. However, most of us are more interested in the towering architectural plant than the vegetable. It looks rather like an interesting weed for a long time, until the huge globose heads of white flowers appear in late summer; then it is difficult to ignore. And even after flowering, the seed heads hold attention. However, if the seeds are allowed to form, there is little chance of the plant returning the next spring. Cut them off if you must, but you are missing a big part of the big show.

The other neat plant in this group has darker leaves and stems, gets up to a reasonable height, if not quite as tall as wild parsnip, and produces rosy purple flowers. This purple parsnip is *Angelica gigas*, and to many it is a better behaved and more civilized candidate for the garden. Quite lovely seed heads are also produced later in the season. But let's be honest, these plants are more than a little on the wild side, and they are not for the high-heeled gardener. In general, they will be making good compost after fruiting. And good compost is always in demand. Full sun.

Angelica archangelica

Angelonia angustifolia

ANGEL FLOWER, SUMMER SNAPDRAGON

A superb and highly popular plant, and a perfect choice for containers or the garden. Plants stand upright throughout most of the season, although in warm areas, they may need a little cutting back to keep them from falling over. In less than five years, this plant went from obscurity to sitting beside petunias on the retail bench. I like the name summer snapdragon because in most areas of the country, snapdragons look best when the weather is cool and decline in the heat. Not this one!

Angelonia angustifolia is available in

Angelica gigas, fruit

Angelonia angustifolia 'Purple'

Angelonia angustifolia 'Light Blue'

Angelonia angustifolia 'Blue Pacific'

Angelonia angustifolia 'Angel Face Bicolor'

Angelonia angustifolia 'Angel Mist Lavender Pink'

Angelonia angustifolia 'Carita Rose'

MORE ☞

Angelonia angustifolia 'Angel Mist Lavender Improved'

Angelonia angustifolia 'Carita Purple'

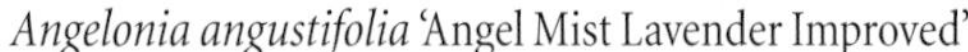

numerous solid colors as well as one or two bicolor forms. I love them in containers, where they can complement other plants, and I find that container planting results in shorter plants, often a good thing for today's vigorous cultivars. They are also prized as cut flowers because of their spike-like habit. Flowers will begin to fall off after a few days, but by then the party will be over and the guests will have gone home.

A number of cultivars have been bred, but from the gardener's perspective, there are only small differences in height and flower size. Older cultivars were simply named for the color, e.g. 'Light Blue' or 'Purple', but today look for cultivars with names like 'Blue Pacific' and series with names such as Angel Mist, Angel Face, and Carita. 'Angel Mist Lavender Pink' fills containers to overflowing, and 'Angel Mist Lavender Improved' is always a hit, particularly when planted in combination with yellow everlastings. Larger-flowered forms like 'Angel Face Bicolor' are impressive, as is the newcomer, the Carita series, amply demonstrated by 'Carita Rose' and 'Carita Purple'.

All do well in full sun, and should be fed lightly. Overfertility results in too many leaves, weak stems, and few flowers. In general, a pinch when planted is helpful to make the plants branch, but if they become too tall later on, do not hesitate to cut them back. They will reflower in about two weeks.

Anisodontea ×*hypomadara* 'Elegant Lady'

Anisodontea

AFRICAN MALLOW

The mallow family is rich in ornamental members, including hibiscus and lavatera, not to mention functional crops like cotton and okra. The few gardenworthy members are essentially woody shrubs, and in a single season they will produce woody stems with substantial girth. The stems, however, are not why we place them in the garden; rather it is the 1" wide, outward-facing bright rose to pink flowers that provide the charm. In their native habitat (Cape area of South Africa), they remain evergreen, flowering from early spring to fall.

Most plants available today are hybrids (*Anisodontea ×hypomadara*) and may go under such names as 'Elegant Lady'. Occasionally Cape mallow (*A. capensis*) can be found in garden centers; plants are similar, bearing smaller light lavender flowers, and are perfect as upright standards.

Plants should be pinched at least twice for best success: once when they are purchased, and again in early summer. This allows for better branching, reduced height, and additional flowers. At Athens we have been growing African mallow in containers for the last few years, and they do well until late summer, when they start falling apart. Since their native habitat is essentially Mediterranean, the combination of heat, water, and high humidity result in too much stress, but the early season growth is handsome. Northern gardeners will have fewer problems. Full sun; avoid wet feet but provide moisture as needed.

Antirrhinum

SNAPDRAGON

The snapdragon has long been a favorite, and its "snapping" flowers are common sights everywhere gardeners till the soil. The genus name comes from the

Anisodontea capensis, standard

Antirrhinum majus 'Liberty Bronze'

Antirrhinum majus 'Solstice Purple'

Antirrhinum majus 'Tahiti Mix'

Antirrhinum majus 'Tahiti Plum'

MORE ☞

Antirrhinum majus 'Sonnet Pink'

Antirrhinum majus Rocket series

Antirrhinum 'Chandelier Rose Pink'

Antirrhinum majus 'Liberty Yellow'

Antirrhinum 'Chandelier White'

Antirrhinum 'Chandelier Lemon' with bracteantha

Greek *anti* ("opposite") and *rhis* ("snout"), referring to the lopsided petals, which give the flower its common name. Next time you are in the midst of a few snapdragons, do what I do when I am teaching. Pull the flower off, align it so the "lip" of the flower is at the bottom, then hold the "cheeks" between your thumb and forefinger. Squeeze gently, and you will soon have the dragon snapping, not to mention the kids squealing. People age six to ninety-six love to see the dragon snap. Unfortunately for the snapper, some flowers on certain cultivars have been bred to be much wider, with a less obvious lip. This group of cultivars, referred to as butterfly types, are quite handsome, but they don't provide near the fun.

All snaps prefer cool weather and look their best in cool seasons. Where summers are cool, they may be a popular summer bedding plant, but where summers are hot, such as in the South, they are best planted in the fall and enjoyed as greenery in the winter and as early color the next season. In all areas, they are also effective if planted in mid to late summer and enjoyed until hard frosts reduce their beauty.

Tall forms are generally used as cut flowers and may be seen grown by the acre by commercial growers. These are mainly represented by the popular Rocket snapdragons, which may be bought in seed packages every spring. These may grow 4' in height, however; medium forms (2½–3' tall) do not topple nearly as easily and still give a bold upright look to the garden. Numerous medium forms have been bred, but one of the best is the Liberty group, available in many colors. 'Liberty Bronze' and 'Liberty Yellow' are tough to beat. The Sonnets are similar, and 'Sonnet Pink' is one of the best. A shorter group yet (2–2½') is seen in plants such as the Solstice group, also colorfully represented and a little earlier to flower than the Libertys. 'Solstice Purple' is but one of the many colors of this popular garden plant. Finally, the shortest snaps (1–1½' tall) can be found when the Tahiti group is planted. They are still upright but are the most compact group and easy to use in mixed gardens. 'Tahiti Plum' is outstanding.

And more good news for snap lovers. In recent years, trailing snapdragons have been developed. These hybrids work particularly well in containers but also in the front of a garden. I have looked at dozens of these plants, and the Chandelier series is one of the prettiest. 'Chandelier Rose Pink' has done well in the garden, and 'Chandelier Lemon' and 'Chandelier White' are wonderful in mixed containers. As much as I am pleased with the ability of the trailing forms to tolerate hot weather, they are still snapdragons and flower well for only as long as the cool weather holds up. However, the trailing forms are a little more heat-tolerant and well worth searching out.

Full sun, cool weather for all selections; good drainage for the trailing forms is essential.

Arctotis

AFRICAN DAISY

Native to South Africa, this daisy is among the most beautiful and most underused flowers in American gardens. Hardly anyone has heard of it, let alone grows it! I have seen a beautiful planting of African daisies, deep rose in color, growing by a Long Island greenhouse, flowering away all summer, but hardly anyone knew what it was and fewer bought them. One can simply credit the paucity of plants to a lack of availability, or perhaps it is because the average American garden climate is not particularly conducive to the plants. Regardless, it is a waste of good garden space to put in marigolds when you could try some African daisies.

Arctotis ×*hybrida* 'Flame'

Arctotis ×*hybrida* 'China Rose'

Arctotis ×*hybrida* 'Silver Pink'

MORE ☞

If plants can be found in garden centers, they will be hybrids, often with related species, but also with related genera, such as *Venidium*. In general, plants will be labeled as *Arctotis* ×*hybrida*, with a melange of parents in their background. The hybrids have produced a magnificent array of hues, at least one of which will fit into any garden scheme. Some of the most colorful flowers belong to the Harlequin hybrids, which are usually sold by the flower color, such as 'Flame' and 'Mahogany'. All are compact with large colorful flowers. For a rose-colored flower, I search out 'China Rose', while 'Midnight Red' would satisfy my dark side, if I had one. But dark colors aren't always welcome in a garden, which is perhaps why my eye always goes to the

Arctotis ×*hybrida*, by greenhouse, Long Island

Arctotis ×*hybrida* 'Mahogany'

Arctotis ×*hybrida* 'Midnight Red'

Arctotis ×*hybrida* 'Sunset Gold'

Arctotis ×*hybrida* 'Zulu Prince'

Argemone platyceras

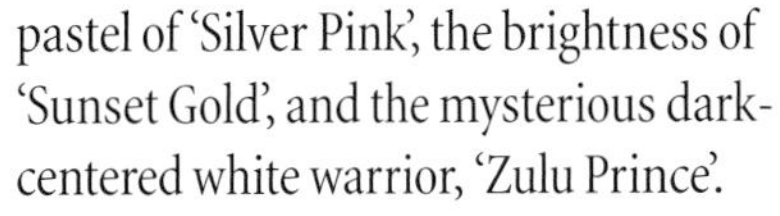

pastel of 'Silver Pink', the brightness of 'Sunset Gold', and the mysterious dark-centered white warrior, 'Zulu Prince'.

Plants prefer cool-temperate climes, and I have trouble growing them in the South. In the Northeast and upper Midwest plants grow far better, and in the Northwest, they are almost at home. If they are stressed, they will almost certainly go dormant and can perish, even before the onset of winter. They are all best placed in raised beds, on hillsides, or in containers, to enhance drainage. Full sun.

Argemone

PRICKLY POPPY

These plants are like kids' birthday parties: they are much better at other people's houses. In this case, other people's gardens. I include this group because sometimes ignorance is not bliss. The beautiful flowers, usually white in those that can be purchased, belie the true nature of the plant. The common name is not a misnomer, and even the species that are less prickly are not particularly user-friendly.

But to be fair, "One man's ceiling is another man's floor," and such plants will always have some followers. Having grown the plant in Athens, I can vouch for a few things: The flowers are large and beautiful, and the plants, depending on species, aren't going to kill you. I admit to enjoying our western native, *Argemone polyanthemos*, as much for the blue-green foliage as for the flowers, but, if truth be told, any plant with a common name of cowboy's fried egg deserves to be grown somewhere. A more spiny cousin, with prickly fruit and foliage, is *A. platyceras*, the crested poppy, which grows 4–5' tall and can be quite intimidating.

Have fun with this group of poppies; they don't do well in gardens with high heat and humidity but are worth some pain in other parts of the country. Full sun.

Argyranthemum

MARGUERITE DAISY

What a taxonomic mess this group of plants has turned out to be. So many species, so much hybridization—it is a taxonomist's nightmare and a gardener's dream. The marguerites have long been cultivated, but in the last decade or so, breeders in Europe and Australia have crossed and recrossed the various

MORE ☞

Argemone platyceras, fruit

Argemone polyanthemos

species to obtain some rather spectacular, if confused, plants. Since most of us don't care what they are as long as they perform in our gardens, the "argys" have become quite popular.

The main species that make up this group include the yellow-flowering *Argyranthemum maderense*, which is seldom seen as a garden plant. Its single flowers are handsome, but its popularity is limited mainly to the plant breeder. The silver-leaved, white-flowered *A. foeniculaceum* is a beautiful species in its own right, and in containers or in the ground, it is tough to beat. I can think of no prettier plant when it is well grown. Unfortunately, most of the well-grown ones I have seen were on the West Coast or in Australia or England. A few cultivars are occasionally offered, but 'Vera' (with white flowers) and 'Roseum' (a pink form) are all I see.

Argyranthemum frutescens is the "original" marguerite daisy and is distinguished by the somewhat domed flowers available in many colors. Many forms have been bred, but their popularity is diminishing in direct proportion to

Argyranthemum maderense

Argyranthemum frutescens 'Sugar and Ice'

Argyranthemum frutescens 'Mary Wooten'

Argyranthemum foeniculaceum

Argyranthemum foeniculaceum 'Vera'

Argyranthemum foeniculaceum 'Roseum'

Argyranthemum frutescens 'Vancouver'

Argyranthemum hybrids, vista in California

Argyranthemum hybrids, Mainau, Germany

Argyranthemum hybrids, out of flower

Argyranthemum 'Summer Eyes'

MORE ☞

the rise in popularity of the hybrids. One of the cultivars I most enjoy is 'Sugar and Ice', whose domed white flowers were even whiter when I spied it growing through some zinnias. 'Mary Wooten' is not as clean a white as 'Sugar and Ice', but this old-fashioned selection throws out many flowers. For pink flowers, I would choose 'Vancouver'.

However, it is the hybrids, which possess a few genes of each of the species just mentioned, that people are growing. In coastal California, they are incredible most of the year, while containers of salmon-colored argys on an extraordinary railing at the garden at Mainau in southern Germany were fabulous. Argys are beautiful to be sure but not without some serious limitations. The limita-

Argyranthemum 'Butterfly'

Argyranthemum 'Midas Gold'

Argyranthemum 'Comet Pink'

Argyranthemum 'Summer Stars Pink'

tions are simply that they require relatively cool temperatures (45–55°F) to initiate flowers well. Since plants are produced in early spring in controlled temperature greenhouses, they are offered to the consumer in full flower. They will remain in flower in the spring; however, when temperatures start rising during the summer months, plants flower sparsely, and the result is a handsome, but not particularly welcome, small green shrub. Wonderful foliage, but no flowers! This is less a problem in areas of cool summer temperatures and high elevations.

Argyranthemum 'Comet White'

As is the case for all general statements, there are exceptions. Even in the heat of a Georgia summer, 'Butterfly' flowered its head off. An older cultivar, but still the best on the market for long term flowering in the heat. Almost as good in heat is 'Midas Gold', with its much lighter flowers; in combination with fan flower it can look good all season. Many cultivars have been developed, and some of those that have caught my eye include 'Summer Eyes' and 'Comet White' for good white flowers, but pink flowers also abound in this group. 'Comet Pink' is an outstanding plant, compact and with relatively good summer flowering; 'Summer Stars Pink' has beautiful foliage but is shy of flowering once the heat arrives. I have always enjoyed the form and flower color of 'Summer Melody', one of numerous argys bred in eastern Australia by Mal Morgan. Compact and handsome, perfect in a container. Many more cultivars have been bred, and many more are yet to appear; they are beautiful, simply be aware that for most of them, you will be enjoying more foliage than flowers during the summer. If the fall is sufficiently long before frost, flowers will reappear along with the cooler weather. Full sun.

Asarina

CLIMBING, CREEPING, TRAILING SNAPDRAGON

Several genera have borrowed the name snapdragon. The snapdragon is *Antirrhinum*, the summer snapdragon is *Angelonia*, and there is also a genus in which the flowers resemble snapdragons but whose habit is decidedly un-snapdragon-like. That genus is *Asarina*. At least these three all start with the same letter.

Although the flowers resemble those of the true snapdragon, all species are rather rangy, and some will climb if support is provided. However, the creeping snapdragon, *Asarina procumbens*, wants to scramble over rocks or out of containers and has no climbing tendencies at all. But it is a marvelous plant, with its gray foliage and creamy white flowers. Plants are hardy to about zone 6 and are particularly effective when drainage is excellent. The trailing snapdragon, *A. antirrhiniflora*, will climb but prefers to send out long stems that trail about the ground. The best choice for this species is 'Red Dragon', with deep red flowers on light green foliage.

The most fun, however, has to be with the climbers, which can scale tall

Argyranthemum 'Summer Melody'

Asarina procumbens

MORE ☞

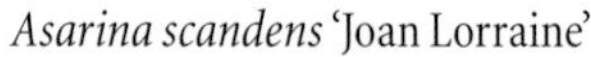

Asarina scandens 'Joan Lorraine'

Asarina scandens 'Mystic Pink'

Asarina antirrhiniflora 'Red Dragon'

Asarina scandens 'Jewel Purple'

buildings and jump wide canyons. Not really, but they do grow quite rapidly. The most common is the climbing snapdragon, *Asarina scandens*, which twines around the supporting trellis or netting. I place them at the base of a fence tacked with some woven wire. The wire is almost invisible when the plants are not on it but is an easy structure for the stems to get around. Most cultivars are seed-propagated, and some people direct sow the seed into the ground once the soil warms up. Several seed selections are out there; one of the more common is Jewel Mix, the favorite being 'Jewel Purple', while 'Joan Lorraine' provides many small deep purple flowers on a massive vine. The Mystic series is also grown; it seems that 'Mystic Pink' is one of the most prolific. They all want to flower in spring and, when summers are cool, will continue on and off throughout the season. In areas of hot summers, plants often grow rampantly, covering fences and trees, but flower again only as the weather cools down. Full sun.

Asclepias

MILKWEED

Ask a corn or wheat farmer about the ornamental value of milkweed, and he will think you are either crazy or just plain stupid. As a college student, I drove a large spray rig through the agricultural fields of southwestern Ontario, simply trying to keep the milkweed and other weeds under control. The cost for the equipment and the chemicals and the loss of production attributable to this weed did not endear it to anybody. So imagine my surprise when some-

Asclepias curassavica, flowers

Asclepias linaria

Asclepias curassavica 'Silky Scarlet'

MORE ☞

body talked about an ornamental milkweed!

However, stupidity aside, several annual species truly are spectacular. Without a doubt, the colors of the flowers of blood flower, *Asclepias curassavica*, will make you stop for a second look, and maybe a third and fourth as well if you look closely at the flower structure. The flowers are orange and red and sit atop the green foliage. If a stem or flower is broken, they will exude a milky sap that is best kept off your skin, as some people are quite sensitive to it. In a grouping of a dozen or more plants, blood flower is difficult not to notice. Unfortunately, all members of the genus are magnets for aphids, so don't be upset if an aphid or two come to dinner: by planting asclepias, you opened a five-star restaurant and invited a few guests. A stream of water from the hose usually persuades them to find other fare. A number of cultivars are available, some, such as 'Deep Red' and 'Silky Scarlet', quite similar to the species. The Silky series also includes 'Silky Gold', a handsome golden-yellow form that people seem equally to enjoy. The fruit is upright, skinny, and also handsome. Open them up and have fun with silky seeds.

A few interesting species are grown more for the fruit than the flower. I found a stand of *Asclepias linaria* in Tucson, Arizona, with light green needle-like leaves and all sorts of bladder-like fruit. I thought that maybe this genus is special after all. However, it was while walking through Christchurch Botanical Garden in New Zealand that I first spied the swan plant, *A. physocarpa*. I looked at the weird inflated fruit, squinted a few times and yes, I could tell it was a swan dangling amidst the leaves. It is difficult to imagine that the rather nondescript clusters of green-white flowers could create such a strange seed

Asclepias curassavica

Asclepias curassavica 'Deep Red'

Asclepias curassavica with aphids

Asclepias curassavica 'Silky Gold'

Asclepias physocarpa, fruit

Asclepias physocarpa, flowers

Asystasia gangetica, flowers

vessel. Plants are native to South Africa, so I enjoyed the sight and doubted I would find them again. But I was not the only one to enjoy it, as I keep seeing it in gardens in America. The City of Swan Plants award probably goes to Washington, D.C., where great gardens, great plants, and great plantspeople abound. This plant can be found in the Smithsonian's wonderful Ripley Garden as well as in the expansive Green Spring Gardens Park, across the river in Alexandria, Virginia. It obviously reseeds, and the early start allows for 4–5' tall plants with many flowers and many swans. Perhaps it will soon be viewed as a noxious weed in the greater D.C. area, but I expect that it will be grown here and there for many years. Seed must be purchased, but if you are in and around our nation's capital, I suspect you can collect a few seeds there. Full sun.

Asystasia gangetica

GANGES PRIMROSE

Other than landscapers in Florida and the Gulf Coast, I would bet that ninety-nine people out of a hundred have never seen or heard of Ganges primrose, *Asystasia gangetica*. I rather enjoy this rampant, somewhat sprawling member of the acanthus family, which provides handsome rosy pink flowers with a white eye. Flowers can cover up the plant when conditions are right. However, therein lies the problem. The right conditions are not easy to provide in most parts of the country. Plants like it warm, no problem; reasonable drainage, again, no problem. However, plants flower only under conditions of warm temperatures and reasonably long nights (short days) likely more than twelve hours long. The beginning of long nights occurs in the fall, but in the North, temperatures are falling and are usually too chilly to sustain flowering

MORE ☞

Asystasia gangetica

Ballota pseudodictamnus

Ballota pseudodictamnus, white-flowered form

for any length of time. Even in Athens, Georgia, flowers occur only early in the spring and late in the fall, around mid October, and the show is short-lived there as well. However, let us not get too serious about the plant's shortcomings. The growth and foliage in the garden are outstanding, and plants can be used in containers and as greenery in the garden. Heat and humidity are no problem, and while it appears to be a thug, it is a wimp when temperatures fall below freezing for any length of time.

A yellow-flowering cultivar occurs, but I have not been able to find it.
Full sun.

Ballota

HOREHOUND

It is hard to keep a straight face when telling a friend that you just purchased a horehound. As tenuous as that conversation would be even with a fellow gardener, try broaching the subject at a Tupperware party or with your football friends. However, horehounds have their use in the garden, if not as a topic of conversation. They are used more in Europe than in the United States and have never gained the popularity of, say, lamb's ears in America.

The common horehound, *Ballota pseudodictamnus*, is a marvelous little gray-leaved plant that functions as a foil for stronger colors and looks terrific in containers. The whorled hairy leaves are the best feature of the plant; in bloom, the dozens of small pink or white coleus-like flowers actually detract from the look of the plant. Plants are tender, being native to southern Greece, however, they have been known to return as far north as zone 6.

The black horehound, *Ballota nigra*, has started to colonize parts of the Northeast and Northwest but is not yet easy to find elsewhere. Plants are more upright, somewhat shrubby and less

Ballota nigra 'Variegata'

useful than the previous hound. The common form is 'Variegata', a fine improvement on the species. Best in containers or the front of the garden. Full sun to partial shade.

Barleria cristata

PHILIPPINE VIOLET

Philippine violets should be grown more, of that there is little doubt. They are not violets at all, and perhaps the common name conjures up the sight of weedy violets taking over the garden. Philippine violet, *Barleria cristata*, belongs to the acanthus family and is not even native to the Philippines but rather to India and Myanmar. Plants stand upright, and in the UGA Trial Gardens are about 2–3' in height. They are absolutely undemanding in culture, providing handsome foliage throughout the summer. The drawback for some gardeners is that they don't flower until late summer or fall, but that is a blessing rather than a fault. We don't need more spring and summer flowers, of those we have plenty. Fall flowers are always welcome, particularly when the gardening fervor has subsided. Another blessing is that *Barleria*, in general, is extremely tolerant of drought, and in these times of water restrictions, now so common in much of the country, their popularity should improve. Full sun.

Barleria cristata

Basella alba

MALABAR SPINACH

What an interesting plant, what a shame it is seen so seldom. I recently came across this fascinating vine at the Ripley Garden in Washington, D.C. In this must-see garden, horticulturist Janet Draper has planted all sorts of extraordinary plants and made a Mecca in the middle of Washington pavement. There, scrambling up posts and pillars, was this weird purple-leaved vine, *Basella alba*. This twiner produces long spikes of white flowers in the axils of the leaves and small purple fruit; the common name comes from the heart-shaped leaves, which can be prepared and eaten like spinach. *Basella* thrives in heat that would otherwise be the demise of spinach. Since plants are raised from seed, a good deal of variability may occur. The most handsome form is

Barleria cristata, flowers

Basella alba 'Rubra'

MORE ☞

Basella alba

'Rubra', with darker green leaves and red to rose flowers. In tropical countries, they are grown as a vegetable (like our pole beans) and used in the same way as spinach. Full sun.

Begonia

What an unbelievable genus: on the one hand dismissed as boring by gardeners who know of little except the wax begonia, on the other hand loved for the eye-catching flowers of the tuberous forms or the exciting foliage of the rex types. And begonias attract another segment of the gardening population: those who collect cultivars and species like stamps, a hobby that is fulfilling and frustrating at the same time. With a genus of over 900 species and an untold number of cultivars and varieties, begonia collectors will never reach the finish line, but what fun they will have trying to get there.

I have seen but a fraction of the known begonias; however, I must try to filter even those few to whittle the number down. This is, of course, impossible but necessary. I have cubbyholed the cultivated forms into four main groups, and then added an assortment of lesser known species that I feel have great potential for the bold gardener. The unfortunate reality, however, is that many of the finest forms are not easily available and must be aggressively sought out through plant associations or mail-order sources. But what else is new? Start with a few easy ones, and if the begonia bug starts to itch, enjoy the scratching. The four main groups, from a gardener's point of view, are angel wing begonias (*Begonia coccinea* and hybrids), rex begonias (*B. rex-cultorum*), tuberous begonias (*B. tuberhybrida*), and wax begonias (*B. sempervirens-cultorum*).

The angel wing begonias, among the oldest "parlor" plants in gardening, have been arching over plants on coffee tables and in conservatories and greenhouses for years. Only recently, however, has this group made inroads into the great "common folk" of the gardening public, and now the floodgates are open for

Begonia coccinea 'Maribel Pink Shades'

Begonia coccinea 'Torch'

Begonia coccinea 'Dragon Wing Red'

Begonia rex-cultorum 'Persian Swirl'

Begonia rex-cultorum 'Lalomie'

Begonia rex-cultorum 'Connie Boswell'

Begonia rex-cultorum 'Good and Plenty'

Begonia rex-cultorum 'Escargot'

Begonia tuberhybrida, red and orange mix

Begonia tuberhybrida 'Chanson'

MORE ☞

Begonia coccinea 'Dragon Wing Pink'

Begonia rex-cultorum 'New York'

Begonia sempervirens-cultorum 'Ambassador Rose'

Begonia sempervirens-cultorum Cocktail series

Begonia tuberhybrida 'Non-Stop'

Begonia tuberhybrida 'Illumination Salmon Pink'

Begonia tuberhybrida 'Spirit'

Begonia sempervirens-cultorum behind fence

garden experimentation. Most cultivars are hidden in mail-order nurseries and are not as easily accessible as they should be, but that will change as more are hybridized for general garden and container use. I have enjoyed the Maribel series, particularly 'Maribel Pink Shades', and other seed-propagated strains, such as the red-flowered 'Torch'. However, the angel wings became a mainstay of the public with the introduction of the now famous Dragon Wing series. 'Dragon Wing Red' was the original plant and was hanging about in greenhouses for years before some brilliant person at Ball Seed Company thought that the time was right for something other than a wax begonia. Plants performed well throughout the country, mainly in baskets, and became a highly sought-after item. This was followed by 'Dragon Wing Pink', a lovely plant but less in demand as it is not quite of the same vigor as the red. They are best for containers and baskets. Full sun or partial shade.

The rex group is where the gardening public has really made demands upon the begonia, pulling the beautiful "foliage" plants of the 1950s into the gardens of the twenty-first century. As I travel around public and private gardens, I see more of these plants appearing every year. It is the boom in container gardening that has been the impetus for the demand, and now I see marvelous plants like 'New York', 'Persian Swirl', 'Lalomie', and 'Fireworks' beautifying areas in the Missouri Botanical Garden, or the gorgeous 'Connie Boswell' flourishing in containers in Virginia's Green Spring Gardens Park. And who would have thought that a plant like 'Good and Plenty' would find itself plunged into a pot at the Chicago Botanic Garden? These old-fashioned plants have also spawned one of the neatest begonias in recent times, the nautilus-leaved 'Escargot'. People cannot help themselves—

MORE ☞

oohs and aahs are common language when this plant is on display. Partial shade, at least in the afternoon.

Planting the tubers of tuberous begonias in the small greenhouse at school was an annual event for me as a high school teacher in Montreal, accomplished on 1 March each year. With water and a little heat, these dried-up old things would expand into leaves and flowers in a couple of months' time, ready to be hung in baskets outdoors. I suppose there were many named cultivars, but we just called them red, yellow, etc. That was enough for me then and, to go by the tags of most tuberous begonias

Begonia rex-cultorum 'Fireworks'

Begonia sempervirens-cultorum, Michigan State University

Begonia semperviren-cultorum 'Brandy' with purple fountain grass

sold today, still seems to be the case.

However, marvelous cultivars like 'Non-Stop' were developed from seed and became highly popular for landscapers and gardeners alike. Since then, 'Chanson', 'Illumination', and 'Spirit' have become available to the greenhouse operator. Tuberous begonias, however, differ from other forms in that they disdain hot weather and are seldom seen in the southern half of the country. Regardless of where they are grown, they need consistent moisture and partial shade. They are at their best in the Northeast and Northwest, but gosh, they are still worth a try in other parts of the country, at least on 1 March.

I have been trialing and growing wax begonias for so many years I don't even know where to begin. One place I won't begin, however, is to make apologies for this bedding plant. Plants like wax begonias are so good, so diverse in color, so easy, and so carefree that their success has bred a backlash. Perhaps they aren't new but neither are antiques, and nobody seems to tire of those. There are literally dozens of series and hundreds of named cultivars. Some have larger flowers than others; the leaves of some are bronze, while others are green. In the landscape, they are planted in mixes of colors, forming great mounds of colored cones; in public areas, they may be fenced off from curious dogs and gum-wrappers. Although breeders have spent

Begonia sempervirens-cultorum 'Vodka'

Begonia sempervirens-cultorum 'Party Flair'

Begonia sempervirens-cultorum 'Espresso Rose'

Begonia sempervirens-cultorum 'Encore Light Pink'

Begonia sempervirens-cultorum 'Pink Avalanche'

MORE ☞

their lives improving the plants, providing subtle colors with fanciful names, all too often the gardener is facing a generic label that reads nothing more than "Red Begonia," and it is likely that named cultivars can be found more easily in good garden centers than in the box stores. Probably the only series that has reached the consciousness of the general public and one of the most popular is the Cocktail series, available by the drink. For example, 'Vodka' is a handsome rose-red begonia, 'Whiskey' is white, etc. One of the prettiest uses for 'Brandy' was at the East Lansing, Michigan, home of Will Carlson, one of this country's leading floriculturists, where he had interplanted clouds of purple fountain grass through great swaths of those pink flowers. Other rose-pink cultivars include 'Ambassador Rose', the large-flowered 'Party Flair', and one of the best per-

Begonia sempervirens-cultorum 'Olympic Light Pink'

Begonia sempervirens-cultorum 'Doublet Pink'

Begonia sempervirens-cultorum 'Kaylen'

Begonia fuchsioides

formers in the UGA Trial Gardens, 'Espresso Rose'. Pinks are everywhere; one of my favorites is 'Olympic Light Pink', although 'Encore Light Pink' and 'Pink Avalanche' are just as handsome. 'Senator White' provides hundreds of flowers to contrast with the reds, roses, pinks, and bicolors available in the spring. A number of researchers are looking for more cold-hardy forms of wax begonia; 'Kaylen' has wonderful bronze foliage and rosy pink flowers, hardy to zone 7b. All wax begonias are equally at home in full sun or partial shade. Double flowers have been bred in almost all ornamentals, so why not wax begonias? The Doublet series was so outstanding, it earned a Classic City Award from the UGA Trial Gardens. 'Doublet Pink' and 'Doublet Rose' are among the best.

The trend toward container gardening has allowed closer examination of the outdoor qualities of some little-known begonia species, and a few are leaving the obscurity of the greenhouse conservatory to find their way to gardens around the country. Some are best grown for the foliage, as flowers tend to be formed in winter conditions in the greenhouse; others have handsome flowers in the garden as well. Because of the huge number of species, there is no outdoor testing program for begonia species anywhere; however, gardeners always try to stretch their plant horizons. I have seen some winners (and a few losers) as I travel, and in my own garden.

I think that the small-flowered fuchsia begonia, *Begonia fuchsioides*, has great potential to be a star. The flowers are somewhat similar to those of fuchsia, and the margins of the clean foliage are often flushed with red in the spring. Flowers come in rose-pink and red, and although they are less than 1" across, many are formed. Partial shade. I have also recently discovered the joys of the shield begonia, *B. popenoei*, whose large, light green rounded leaves look like shields advancing over an imaginary battlefield. I grew this under the shade of large trees in Athens, and although I never saw any flowers, the foliage was magnificent throughout the season. Apparently, the flowers are quite impressive in the greenhouse, but probably

MORE ☞

Begonia sempervirens-cultorum 'Senator White'

Begonia sempervirens-cultorum 'Doublet Rose'

Begonia popenoei

Begonia serratipetala

Begonia pedatifida

most gardeners won't see them. Who needs them? Partial shade.

One of the common greenhouse species that surprised me was the tooth-petaled *Begonia serratipetala*, whose deeply cut dark olive-green leaves, flushed with white or pink spots, are the main reason for including it. Occasionally, however, a few rose-pink to red flowers may also appear. Terrific in combination with other plants, in the garden or in a container. Heavy to partial shade. I was introduced to a new rhizotomous begonia, *B. pedatifida*, which has reveled in the dry, shady conditions of the Armitage garden. Plants just keep on growing and growing, with no concern for the abuse of a southeastern summer, finally discoloring a little in late fall. Supposedly, it produces white flowers, but it has not flowered for me. Its performance, vigor, and lack of insects and diseases have made me take notice anyway. Heavy to partial shade.

Bellis perennis

ENGLISH DAISY

A great deal of breeding of this English lawn weed has occurred, with the zenith of hybridization in the early to mid

Bellis perennis 'Pomponette White'

Bellis perennis 'Medicis White'

Bellis perennis 'Radar Rose'

Bellis perennis 'Chevreuse Rose'

1990s. They started out their lives as tiny but pretty weeds and in some cases have evolved into handsome colorful bedding plants available in a wide range of colors. The breeders have certainly left their mark; some of these poor little flowers appear as if they have been pumping iron. Single, fluffy, and doubled, they have been given no respite.

But to be honest, I still like these little guys. As do many other people. Pastel

Bellis perennis 'Carpet Rose'

Bellis perennis, Harrogate, England

Bellis perennis, Palmerston North, New Zealand

MORE ☞

mixes have colored the feet of Leyland cypress in England and brightened up parks in Palmerston North, New Zealand. This is not just a weed anymore! The individual colors are brilliant. I enjoy the whites in 'Pomponette White' and 'Medicis White', while 'Carpet Red' and 'Radar Red' provide the garden with wonderful red flavors. 'Carpet Rose' and 'Radar Rose' are also colorful, but I must stop there in my enthusiasm. I can't bring myself to love the dumpy 'Chevreuse Rose'.

English daisies do not tolerate heat and in much of the country, they will do poorly after 15 July. In areas of moderate winters, such as the Southeast, they can be planted in the fall with pansies; however, expect some foliar damage and 10 to 30 percent death if temperatures fall below 10°F for any length of time. Fall plantings at the UGA Trial Gardens in Athens have not been sufficiently outstanding to allow recommendation for fall planting even in that area. Further north, plants persist longer into the summer and should be planted when the nasturtiums and Iceland poppies go in the ground in early spring. Full sun.

Bellis perennis 'Carpet Red'

Bellis perennis 'Radar Red'

Bidens

BEGGAR'S TICK, PITCHFORKS

The common names are in themselves wonderful but so are the plants, which are used mainly in baskets but also as brighteners and fillers in gardens. Everybody calls the plant bidens—I can't recall anyone asking how the pitchforks look in the basket; however, the fruit are tick-like and beggar's tick has a certain ring to it. Dozens of species exist, most native to North America and many listed as weeds in various books on flora of the United States. However, unless you are digging weeds in the pasture, there is very little choice in what is available for the garden.

The only species easily found in most outlets is fennel-leaf tick, *Bidens ferulifolia*, with fennel-like foliage and bright yellow flowers. Although the species is native to Arizona, plants have the reputation of being cool lovers, and make no mistake about it, they look better and persist longer in areas of cool summers. I have seen fabulous baskets in northern Europe and Portland, Oregon, blooming their heads off in late August, and long sad, stringy plants in Houston at the same time of year. Although most older cultivars shine only in cool climes, all is not lost for the warm-summer gardeners. From our heat trials in Athens, I can recommend 'Peter's Gold Carpet' for its compact habit, which when temperatures heat up, continues to provide a good deal of flower power. I have also been impressed with 'Smiley', a cultivar which looked a little shabby in the heat but recovered well in late summer and fall. These all look the same from afar, so be sure to check the label carefully when purchasing those pitchforks.

One or two others of those dozens of species are finding their way into gardens; however, they still have a long way to go before competing with the cultivars for attention. *Bidens heterophylla* has narrow leaves and light yellow to almost white flowers. Not recommended except in the coolest of summers, otherwise, it is a weed. A tall upright species is nodding beggar's tick, *B. cernua*,

Bidens ferulifolia, basket

Bidens ferulifolia, mixed basket

Bidens heterophylla

Bidens cernua

MORE ☞

which if planted in a cool area can make quite an impressive showing. Plants, however, may self-sow, and you might be cursing those beggar's ticks for a long time. Full sun.

Brachycome iberidifolia

SWAN RIVER DAISY

The Swan River runs through Perth, Australia, and empties into Fremantle on the Southern Indian Ocean. Flora in the area include eucalyptus and fan flower (*Scaevola*), and rounding any corner on any spring day, one may come across beautiful plants of the ever-present Swan River daisy (*Brachycome iberidifolia*). Bringing the "brachys" out of the wilds of Australia and domesticating them for the containers of Chicago

Bidens ferulifolia 'Peter's Gold Carpet'

Brachycome iberidifolia, Perth, Australia

Bidens ferulifolia 'Smiley'

Brachycome 'Mini Yellow'

has been a challenge, but they have made a nice, if not eye-popping, addition to North American gardens. Plants generally grow no more than 1' in height and, if well grown, are covered with small single daisies. The common color in nature is lavender, but breeders have produced pink, rose, and yellow in small- and large-flowered forms. High temperatures are no problem, but they prefer areas of low humidity for best growth. Outstanding plantings are found in San Diego and high-altitude areas; more searching is needed to find picturesque plants in the Southeast and Midwest. Such areas may see poor flowering and disease problems, causing dieback and black leaves in the summer.

I see more and more hybrid brachys being used in combination with trailing snapdragons and pansies or other cool-loving plants. Hybridization has not only produced some beautiful material, but the additional hybrid vigor has

Brachycome 'Billabong Moonlight'

Brachycome 'Mauve Delight'

Brachycome 'Lilac Mist'

Brachycome 'Petite Delight', *B.* 'Mini Yellow'

MORE ☞

resulted in plants being successfully gardened in more areas of the country. I particularly enjoy the small-flowered forms such as 'Lilac Mist' and 'Petite Delight', both with lavender-blue flowers, and 'Lemon Drop', an excellent yellow-flowered cultivar. However, if bigger flowers are desirable, try the marvelous Billabong series, the best being 'Billabong Moonlight', with perfect light yellow flowers. 'Mini Yellow' provides some fine yellow hues but tends to fade later in the summer. In the world of retailing, bigger is perceived as better, and breeders went to work on creating larger flowers. The result was been plants with gaudy chrysanthemum-like blossoms such as 'Jumbo Mauve' and 'Mauve Delight', both beautiful on the retail bench but not as weather-tolerant in the garden as the small-flowered forms.

All brachys are better in containers than in the ground. Full sun or afternoon shade is recommended.

Brachycome 'Jumbo Mauve'

Bracteantha bracteata 'Nullabor Spectrum'

Bracteantha bracteata 'Bright Bikini'

Bracteantha bracteata

STRAWFLOWER

This fine Australian plant is experiencing a renaissance, and new cultivars are making significant inroads in North American gardens. It is a wonderful plant to put in the garden for no other reason than to enjoy the texture of the flowers; my goodness, they really do feel like straw. Kids love them, and so do people who want to cut flowers from their garden. The more established name for this everlasting plant was *Helichrysum*. Plants are still listed as such, so don't be confused when you can't find *Bracteantha* in the catalog index. Of course, if confusion is your thing, look up strawflower and you may find other genera as well, but this is the one you want.

The actual strawflower from eastern Australia does not reside in the garden centers or florists, but the hybrids are tougher and more weather-tolerant for North American gardens anyway. Plants such as 'Nullabor Spectrum' look quite at home beside lantana or other sun lovers, while 'Florabella Yellow' freely performed in a container, as witnessed one sunny morning in southern California.

The Chico series was one of the first compact groups of plants that provided a mixture of colors and good garden performance. The Bikini series was popular for many years, for the bright colors of cultivars like 'Bright Bikini', which stop people in their tracks, and the clean colors in 'Bikini White'. 'Golden Beauty' provided free-flowering plants, but the flowers were a little small and the plants a little big. But they certainly provided months of color. The big breakthrough for good garden strawflowers occurred with the Florabella series. Colors include bright yellow, brilliant gold, and a subdued lemon. Excellent flower size and good performance, although perhaps a little lanky and tall for some gardeners.

Dwarfer forms have been introduced,

Bracteantha bracteata 'Florabella Yellow'

Bracteantha bracteata 'Bikini White'

Bracteantha bracteata Chico series

Bracteantha bracteata 'Golden Beauty'

Bracteantha bracteata 'Dreamtime Antique Shades'

Bracteantha bracteata 'Sundaze Pink'

MORE ☞

providing good flower size, persistent flowering, and more compact plants. I have been impressed with the Sundaze series, particularly 'Sundaze Lemon Yellow' and 'Sundaze Pink', both of which garnered high grades in our trials. As well, the Dreamtime series was impressive and a favorite of many passers-by, displaying unfettered growing and flowering. 'Dreamtime Antique Shades' was superb.

All the strawflowers are native to hot, dry areas, and while heat is not a problem, high humidity and summer rain can be. Place in full sun in as well drained a location as possible. Hillsides, raised beds, or containers come to mind.

Bracteantha bracteata 'Sundaze Lemon Yellow'

Brassica, Beta

If you live in an area of mild winters, you may miss the snowballs and the skating, but having flowers in the winter may help to stem your disappointment. In such areas, pansies, pinks, and snapdragons are often planted in the fall to provide color throughout the fall and winter and burst into even more color in early spring. And one of the plants that bursts the most is ornamental kale, *Brassica oleracea.*

Some people suggest that kale is rather boring, simply taking up space in an otherwise barren winter landscape. Not so, as witnessed by the scene in McDonough, Georgia, where kale became the presents under the Christmas tree, and when you see a bed of multicolored foliage in the winter sun, that bed is hardly boring. Many fine series and cultivars of kale have been devel-

Bracteantha bracteata 'Florabella Gold'

Bracteantha bracteata 'Florabella Lemon'

Brassica oleracea, Christmas in McDonough, Georgia

Brassica oleracea Tokyo series

Brassica oleracea 'White Sparrow', diseased centers

Brassica oleracea 'White Feather'

MORE ☞

Brassica oleracea var. *botrytis* (cauliflower)

Beta vulgaris 'Bright Lights'

Brassica ×*hybrida* (mustard) and *Petroselinum crispum* (parsley) in mixed bed

oped. The most common are the "cabbage" forms, which include the Tokyo series in a mixture of rose, red, and white, but some of the single colors are outstanding. Not all is perfect in kale paradise, however, and after particularly cold weather or heavy cold rains, the insides of white-centered plants often turn brown, such as was the case with 'White Sparrow'. If the cabbage forms are your choice, go with darker colors such as 'Rose Bouquet' and 'Red Chidori'. They do not show the damage and are unbeatable for weather tolerance; even when it snows or rains, the centers of the plants appear unblemished. But as bold as those incurled forms are, I am particularly impressed with the leafier kinds. I think the Peacock series is one of the most outstanding, and the Feather series also earns its name. 'White Feather' pro-

Brassica oleracea 'Peacock White'

Brassica oleracea in flower

Brassica oleracea 'Rose Bouquet'

Brassica oleracea 'Peacock Red'

MORE ☞

vides color, form, and creativity that all gardeners can count on.

One of the characteristics of any plant is that it wants to flower. When plants in the mustard family flower in the spring, it is referred to as bolting. Some people like the yellow flowers; I am not one of them. To me, they signify the end of the planting, and if I am not too lazy, I will remove them at that time. Research has shown that the leafy forms (Peacock, Feather series) bolt later than the cabbage forms. If you dislike the flowers, planting the leafy forms provides a few extra weeks of enjoyment.

Last thing: regardless of where one lives, if heavy snow cover is normal, these are useful only in the fall until several hard frosts. Perhaps in early spring, they may also provide some color prior to spring planting. Even in Athens, Georgia, if temperatures fall below 20°F for an extended length of time, plants turn into cabbage soup. Try a few, the worst that can happen is a few months of color where no color existed, regardless of how long they provide it. And if they die, you won't have to worry about those crummy flowers. Full sun.

There is no lack of creativity among gardeners in using other closely related veggies. Gardeners do not live by kale alone, so why not try some of the colorful chards (*Beta vulgaris*)? 'Ruby Red' is

Brassica oleracea 'Red Chidori'

Beta vulgaris 'Ruby Red'

Brassica ×hybrida 'Redbor'

Brassica ×hybrida 'Red Giant'

a favorite, but the winner in popularity among chards is 'Bright Lights', with stems of yellow, red, or orange. Not even mustard plants are immune from landscape beds, often incorporated in a winter bed with parsley as a companion. The ornamental mustards (*Brassica* ×*hybrida*) have been increasingly popular, I have always admired the frilled leaves of 'Redbor', growing from containers of lettuce. The biggest of them all is probably 'Red Giant', which towers over everything else in the winter garden in Georgia. And not to be left out or outdone, a creative vegetable gardener even puts cauliflower in hanging baskets. Nothing is sacred anymore.

Breynia nivosa

SNOW BUSH

Not a whole lot of snow bushes can be found in landscapes these days, although when I do see a planting or two, I wish availability was wider. Snow bush (*Breynia nivosa*) grows rapidly in its native environment and is often used as a hedge in some parts of the world. Passing by the hedge provides an insight as to its popularity, with deep hues of red, pink, white, and green all interspersed. However, where it is annual, which is most of this country, the length of the growing season provides insufficient time for such grandeur. We have to content ourselves with interesting specimen plants, which can be grown among other annuals or perennials. The plumage is brilliant in the spring but tends to fade a little in the heat.

I very much like what this plant can do in the landscape, but to be frank, I seldom see them for sale in the Midwest or Southeast, so it is difficult to run out and plant a specimen, let alone a hedge. All is not lost, however. Good growers like Denise Smith of GardenSmith in Jefferson, Georgia, and Mark Terkanian at Natchez Trace in Kosciusko, Mississippi, keep producing beautiful specimens in the hope that gardeners and landscapers will enjoy it as much as they do. I think we should give these people a break, and purchase some of these orphans. I have seen a few cultivars listed, but mostly it is the species that can be found. There are no flowers to speak of, plants are grown entirely for the zigzag stems and colorful foliage. Full sun.

Breynia nivosa, hedge

Breynia nivosa, flowers

Breynia nivosa with erigeron

Browallia

BUSH VIOLET

Browallia was a favorite in Grandmother's garden but is not grown very much in her granddaughter's garden. This is probably because this is truly an "old English" plant, having been brought over by the colonists and then benefitted by the huge popularity of English gardens and English garden literature in the 1950s and '60s. The common form (*Browallia speciosa*) produces abundant violet-blue flowers on 1' tall plants, and they combine well in containers with many plants, including 'Limelight' helichrysum. A number of cultivars are

MORE ☞

Browallia speciosa 'Daniella'

Browallia speciosa 'Blue Bells'

Browallia speciosa

Browallia speciosa 'Marine Bells'

available, mostly in the blue-lavender-violet spectrum. I have seen good-looking plants of 'Marine Bells' in the University of Minnesota arboretum, and 'Blue Bells' looked terrific in the Royal Botanical Gardens in Ontario. In Athens, plants seldom look good after 15 July, pointing out the lack of tolerance of warm temperatures. In containers at the Butchart Gardens in Victoria, British Columbia, 'Daniella' called for attention, but in Cincinnati, they needed to be put out of their misery in early August. That plants do better in one area of the country than they do in another is true of almost all species, to deny it is to have never traveled. However, this is simply a problem of timing. In all areas, they look better in cool gardens, so southern gardeners should plant them early in the season and enjoy them for a few months, or place small plants out in early August to be enjoyed all fall. I hope this plant comes back in popularity, as I enjoy seeing it; it simply won't get to the Armitage garden until later in the season. Full sun in the North, partial shade in the South.

Brugmansia

ANGEL'S TRUMPET

What was once a plant seen only in the tropics or in the tropical conservatory is now being sold across the country. What

Brugmansia sanguinea

Brugmansia arborea

Brugmansia ×candida 'Double White'

Brugmansia aurea

was once looked upon as a sloppy shrub is now being viewed as a magnificent architectural feature. I was fortunate to see natural groves in travels to South and Central America, and coming across maikoa, *Brugmansia arborea*, or red angel's trumpet, *B. sanguinea*, was indeed a rush! And, while they may not be 20' tall in our gardens, they can look equally impressive at home. Plants can be placed in the garden but will also look beautiful in large containers.

Angel's trumpet is a common name for plants in this genus as well as those in *Datura* (which see), but *Brugmansia* is certainly the more impressive of the

Brugmansia ×candida

MORE ☞

two. All the many species and cultivars residing under this name produce quite beautiful pendulous flowers, most single but a few doubles as well. Plants should be considered annuals in most places in the country, but that should not deter even cool-summer gardeners, as they can grow 4–5' in a single year. Some gardeners as far north as zone 7 may have them overwinter occasionally, but they should not be counted on as being perennial north of zone 8.

Brugmansia ×*insignis*, white form

I have planted *Brugmansia versicolor*, the ever-changing angel's trumpet, in Athens, and people are always confused as they notice that the unopened flowers appear yellow then bloom into a rich salmon color and fade to white. But confused or not, they come back for a second look. And the golden angel's trumpet, *B. aurea*, with its large leaves and handsome yellow flowers, looks as good in Wisconsin as it does in Miami. Normally, the abundant flowers of *B.* ×*candida* open slightly yellow then turn white, but this hybrid also provides some double flowers, such as in 'Double White'. But most of the time, when you go shopping for these things at your local retailer, you will simply find the label stating "White" or "Orange," or other flower color. These are probably hybrids of B ×*insignis*, and they are perfectly fine plants to purchase. In specialty catalogs,

Brugmansia versicolor

Brugmansia ×*insignis*, orange form

Brugmansia 'Charles Grimaldi'

Brugmansia 'Sunset'

Brugmansia 'Snowbank'

the correct names for the plants will be listed, and if possible, spend your money on a hybrid like 'Charles Grimaldi', with abundant and large salmon-pink flowers. Absolutely one of the best of these superlative plants.

And for those who belong to the ABG (Anything But Green) group, the variegated form, sometimes sold as 'Sunset', is all right, but you will go head over heels for 'Snowbank', a newer form with a much stronger variegation pattern.

Oh yes, I nearly forgot. These plants are poisonous. If you ingest large amounts of leaves, flowers, or fruits, you may suffer from hallucinations, dry mouth, muscle weakness, increased blood pressure and pulse, fever, dilated pupils, and paralysis. They are not as bad as chewing on datura, but try to restrain yourself. Full sun; take cuttings in the fall if you wish to overwinter a favorite form.

Caladium

I never used to be much of a fan of caladiums (either selections of or hybrids involving *Caladium bicolor*), but the more I see them, the more they grow on me. They come in many colors, from busy patterns of red to beautiful bright white forms. The key to caladium performance is not to plant the corms too early; they will simply sit in the ground until it

MORE ☞

warms up. The foliage will emerge eventually, but it is heat that these plants love, without which, forget it! Of course, buying plants already leafed out makes great sense if you want quicker success, and if summers don't last long. I don't remember a lot of caladium tubers being planted where I grew up in Montreal; by the time it was warm enough for sprouting, fall was the next day.

Brilliant is a pretty good description for some of the cultivars out there. The large pastel pink leaves of 'Fannie Munson' are outstanding, and the tricolor palette of 'Fire Chief' also catches the eye. However, perhaps because caladiums prefer shady conditions, the cooler white and off-white shades suit my fancy more. They simply seem to brighten up that

Caladium 'Fannie Munson'

Caladium bicolor 'Gingerbread'

Caladium bicolor 'White Queen'

Caladium bicolor 'Candidum'

shade a little, and I find myself drawn toward them. 'Gingerbread' is a little busy, but the smaller leaves and the flecking pattern on the off-white leaves are at least cute, if not handsome. I saw a planting of 'White Queen' at Longwood Gardens, towering over some red begonias, and the contrast was spectacular. However, I must be boring, as I would have the all-white foliage of 'Candidum' in the Armitage garden any day of the week. The leaves go with any color, and the shade in the garden almost disappears.

To overwinter caladiums, dig them out after the leaves begin to decline in the fall. Place the tubers in dry peat moss and place in an area that doesn't freeze. Replant in containers or in the ground when the soil warms up the next spring. Partial to heavy shade.

Calendula officinalis

POT MARIGOLD

In Montreal, pot marigolds (*Calendula officinalis*) were a summer staple; they were planted in the spring and continued to grow well throughout the summer. Often people tired of them before the calendulas tired of the people. However, the further south one moves, the more difficulty one has in growing this as a summer annual. Pot marigolds (so called because they were often brought into the house, and they looked like a marigold) flower in spring to early summer in much of the country and tend to struggle by mid July. Seed is easily purchased and can be started indoors so plants can go out early, even before the last frost occurs, assuming they have

Caladium bicolor 'Fire Chief'

Calendula officinalis 'Bon Bon Yellow'

Calendula officinalis 'Bon Bon Orange'

Calendula officinalis 'Mandarin Orange'

MORE ☞

been placed outside for a few days and nights to be hardened off. Otherwise start seed in the ground as temperatures warm up, or plant started material in April or May.

Many fine cultivars have been bred, some for bedding, some for cut flowers, and all quite colorful. Probably the dwarf forms, such as the Bon Bon series, have garnered the most attention; particularly striking are large drifts of 'Bon Bon Orange' and 'Bon Bon Yellow' in the landscape (honestly, I don't make these names up!). A planting of 'Mandarin Orange' often includes a few yellow flowers in the seed package, but that is not all bad. 'Indian Prince' is taller, with orange flowers with a distinct if not overwhelming red center. The undersides are also tinged red, making it a favorite with designers. Mixtures are popular; Gitano Mix provided a nice complement to plants of lavender at the Auckland Botanical Garden. Propagate from seed, full sun.

Calendula officinalis with sweet alyssum

Calendula officinalis 'Indian Prince'

Calendula officinalis Gitano Mix

Calibrachoa ×hybrida

TRAILING PETUNIA

Confusion reigned when the trailing petunia (*Calibrachoa ×hybrida*) was first introduced to the market in the early 1990s. Everybody thought it was a petunia: it looked like a petunia, smelled like a petunia, and even grew like a petunia, but no such luck, we all had to learn how to say calibrachoa instead. Actually when they are growing side by side, it is pretty easy to tell most "calis" from most petunias; calibrachoa's leaves and flowers are both significantly smaller. Regardless of their name, these plants with the petunia-like flowers grow rapidly, generally sitting about 4–6" tall and blanketing the ground like a groundcover. At Athens, we use them to complement the entrance to the UGA Trial Gardens. Flowers are plentiful in the spring and fall, and in areas such as the Midwest and Northeast, plants will flower well all season. They are exceptional for hanging baskets and quite at home spilling out of the base of mixed containers.

They are reliably hardy in zone 7 but should be treated as annuals elsewhere. In zone 7b and warmer, leaving plants in the ground over the winter provides unbelievable color in early spring. Some exceptional colors have been bred; five years ago nobody had even heard of this

Calibrachoa ×hybrida 'Million Bells Cherry Pink'

Calibrachoa ×hybrida 'Starlet Rose'

Calibrachoa ×hybrida 'Lirica Showers Blue'

Calibrachoa ×hybrida 'Terra Cotta'

MORE ☞

plant, and now there are almost too many out there to keep track of—all are starting to look the same. But here are a few you might want to experiment with in your basket, container, or garden.

The two most recognized series names are Million Bells and Lirica Showers, both of which offer numerous colors. I have been particularly impressed with the performance of 'Million Bells Cherry Red' and 'Million Bells Cherry Pink'. For blue flowers, I would probably recommend 'Lirica Showers Blue', and for white, no doubt it would be 'Lirica Showers Pure White'; many more are available in the series and are equally good. Other hybrids continue to appear; we have trialed the Colorburst series, exempli-

Calibrachoa ×hybrida vs petunia

Calibrachoa ×hybrida 'Million Bells Cherry Red'

Calibrachoa ×hybrida 'Lirica Showers Pure White'

Calibrachoa ×hybrida 'Colorburst Violet'

fied by 'Colorburst Violet', as well as the Starlet series, nicely shown by the early spring flowering of 'Starlet Rose'. However, the color that has taken the garden world by storm is 'Terra Cotta'. I have seen it trialed from Georgia to California and photographed it across the country, but the overflowing basket in a garden on Long Island, New York, showed why it has become so popular. An outstanding color, used to perfection. Full sun.

Callistephus chinensis

CHINA ASTER

There need be no confusion about the aster name among gardeners. The China aster (*Callistephus chinensis*) is an annual, flowers all season, and generally produces one to three flowering stems. The genus *Aster* (*Aster* spp.) is perennial, flowers mainly in the fall, and produces dozens of flowering stems. That part of the common name is the same is simply because the flowers are similar. China asters are an important cut flower in the world's flower-producing countries. Rows upon rows of flowers in bud, such as the Matsumoto series shown here, are harvested every day. Flowers of the Meteor series and others provide good vase life after cutting and are used by arrangers to make vibrant statements on their own or as companions in a mixed bouquet.

Callistephus chinensis Matsumoto series, cut flower field

Callistephus chinensis 'Matador Salmon Pink'

Callistephus chinensis Meteor series, cut flowers

Callistephus chinensis 'Blue Ribbon'

MORE ☞

However, who said cut flowers cannot also make fine garden plants? People incorporate China asters in their gardens or containers to provide color and to cut a few flowers to bring in as needed. There are some disease problems with China asters, but for the most part, the flowering plants and the cut stems provide great pleasure. For flowers similar to those used by commercial growers, one of the Matador series, such as 'Matador Salmon Pink', provides good stem length but is not so tall as to flop over, a common problem with the large-flowered forms. Some mixes (Pommex series) provide pompon-like flowers and are easily grown in the flower garden. They can be purchased as seeds or as started plants and planted in the spring, then again in mid summer, for best succession of bloom. Recently, there has been greater garden demand for these flowers, and more dwarf material has steadily become available. 'Blue Ribbon' can be used in containers or the garden, and the small ball-like flowers of the Pompom series, like 'Pompom Red and White', are quite spectacular, if a little gaudy. I really am not a fan of "dog-eared" flowers like those in the Ballet series, but some gardeners really enjoy that frizzy look. As for me, I will take the Astoria series any day and plant them everywhere. The mix is awesome, and as

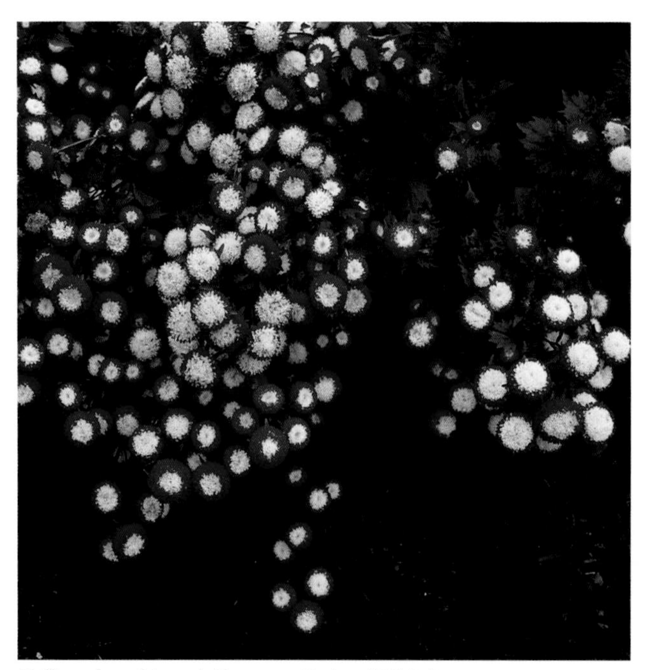
Callistephus chinensis 'Pompom Red and White'

Callistephus chinensis Ballet series

Callistephus chinensis Astoria series

Callistephus chinensis 'Astoria Deep Blue'

single colors, they are all lovely, my favorite being 'Astoria Deep Blue'.

Not everything is perfect in Camelot. China asters often look terrible by mid to late summer; if so, pull them out and replace with additional plantlets or seeds for fall enjoyment. This is not difficult to do but does take time and effort. They also have a history of being plagued by aster yellows. This virus is spread by aphids and other insects and results in leaves turning yellow and the general demise of the plant. Cut flower growers usually screen their plantings to eliminate the carriers, but we simple gardeners put up with these things only if we like the plant enough. Few other plants in the garden are susceptible to aster yellows, and if you see the problem, there is no cure. While I am no fan of yellows, that does not deter me from planting China asters every now and then. Full sun.

Callistephus chinensis Pommex series

Canavalia gladiata

SWORD BEAN

I learned long ago that there are two groups of people I will hear from when presenting a lecture: members of a hardy plant society (any state) and master gardeners (ditto). That is why I try to be prepared for anything, because as sure as day turns to night, I will get questions that people have gunnysacked for years, just waiting to ask the "expert." But always, I learn from them. And how I enjoy interacting with such enthusiasm.

One day, in such an interaction, Jose Tallent, a master gardener in Georgia, brought me a huge green pod from a vine and asked if I knew what it was. I did not, but I was intrigued: the thing could have been used as a lethal weapon in the wrong hands. The experts in tropical vines checked references, scratched their heads for a while, and then came up with sword bean, *Canavalia gladiata*, well known in Africa and Asia, where it is grown as a legume for animal feed and human consumption. When Jose give me the pod, the pink-claret seeds within were just waiting to be sown. Like Jack, I tossed the seeds out, and once warm temperatures arrived, away my magical beanstalk climbed. Now, I don't want to tell you that this vine can in any way compete with the beauty of clematis or passion flower, but it was, well, neat. It climbed by tendrils and formed many heart-shaped leaves on a robust vine. In the summer, small rosy pink pea flowers occurred, which were handsome even if not particularly overwhelming. Even the fruit that Jose originally brought me was not particularly eye-catching, being as green as the leaves and hardly noticeable until pointed out.

Canavalia gladiata, seeds

Canavalia gladiata

MORE ☞

But oh my, once they were pointed out, their size became obvious, and whenever I toured people around the garden, I would scramble to the fence and harvest a pod. And just like Jose, I would ask, "Do you know what this is?"

The seeds mature in the fall and can be kept in a jar on your desk. Wait until the soil warms up, then sow them in the ground; doing so earlier will not gain any time. This is a plant for plantspeople; it will not excite those who have eyes only for the brightest. Full sun.

Canna ×*generalis*

CANNA LILY

Where did all these cannas come from? It used to be that canna lilies (*Canna* ×*generalis*) were fillers, green leaves and red flowers, maybe one or two with yellow blooms or with burnished leaf

Canavalia gladiata, flowers

Canna ×*generalis*, leaf in border

Canavalia gladiata, fruit

Canna ×*generalis* 'Tropicanna', in water

color. Those are becoming collectors' plants; today the choices of flower and foliage colors put cannas right up there with petunias and impatiens in their diversity. They have become popular because in zone 7 and warmer, most are comfortably hardy. And in the rest of the country, they grow vigorously enough that they can "strut their stuff" as far north as Nome. Every time I visit growers and breeders, I discover new cultivars of cannas, and it seems gardeners have also started to embrace these marvelous plants. And creativity is not dead—even if the plants don't flower, designers use the foliage alone as feature in a mixed border. And how many plants do you know that can grow in normal garden soils and be equally at home immersed in water? More and more water gardeners are using the handsome foliage of cannas to brighten up their wet spots, from bogs to ponds.

Canna ×*generalis* 'Erebus', in water

Canna ×*generalis* 'Tropical Red'

Canna ×*generalis* 'Tropical Yellow'

Canna ×*generalis* 'Bugle Boy'

MORE ☞

But like any other plant out there, they are not plastic and are bothered by some serious insect pests. Leaf rollers cause the leaf to roll around itself like a rolled tongue, but unfortunately, it can't unroll. The other bugaboo is Japanese beetles, who like to savor cannas as much as hibiscus, although some cultivars appear less susceptible than others. Both can cause severe disfigurement. One can spray chemicals, but that is generally a losing battle. The leaf rollers can be unrolled, and the beetles, depending on population density, can be picked off and disposed of. If you're defeated by dense populations, at least remove the flowers; they are the primary target. If they become too much of a frustration, don't plant any more cannas.

But if you do, what a choice you have! As wonderful as the big cannas are, breeders are also concentrating more on shorter forms. The Tropical series consists of relatively short cultivars and should not to be confused with 'Tropicanna', a much larger cultivar. 'Tropical Red' and 'Tropical Rose' are obviously shorter than "normal" cannas and have been excellent plants for containers and smaller gardens, but 'Tropical Yellow' is to die for. In Georgia, we placed it in a mixed container, and it flashed its bright smile all season. And while I still enjoy the flowers and functionality of green-

Canna ×generalis 'Tropical Rose'

Canna ×generalis 'King Humbert'

Canna ×generalis 'Liberty Scarlet'

Canna ×generalis 'Perkeo'

Canna ×generalis 'Cleopatra', flowers

leaved cultivars such as 'Bugle Boy' and 'Perkeo', they are taking a backseat to the multicolored foliage cultivars.

Dark foliage is always desirable, and there is nothing wrong with the old-fashioned 'King Humbert'; however, gardeners also have choices, from the Liberty series, like 'Liberty Scarlet', to the orange-flowered, almost black 'Australia'. If that is too much darkness, 'Cleopatra' provides some purple striping on the broad green leaves along with interesting speckled bicolor flowers. But for real brightness, the perennial favorite 'Bengal Tiger' brightens up landscapes regardless of where it is planted. Other variegated forms include 'Kansas City' and 'Stuttgart'. The former is difficult to find, and the latter is terrific if you want a canna where sunshine is limited. 'Stuttgart' performs far better with afternoon shade; it burns up in full-sun gardens.

The sight of 'Panache' always elicits differing opinions. The long sword-like leaves are different from most others, and while the flowers don't blow anyone away, a second look is always in order to appreciate the subtle color. I always include 'Pink Sunburst' in my recommendations because, like Baby Bear's bed, it is not too big and not too small, and has wonderful colored foliage and handsome flowers. It simply works, and works well. However, as I am always asked what canna brings the most com-

Canna ×*generalis* 'Kansas City'

Canna ×*generalis* 'Panache'

Canna ×*generalis* 'Cleopatra', foliage

Canna ×*generalis* 'Pink Sunburst'

MORE ☞

ments in the garden, I must come clean and tell you more about 'Tropicanna'. Big, bold, and beautiful, the dark multicolored leaves simply radiate and become the center of attention. The flowers are orange—pretty enough, but absolutely unnecessary to complete this marvelous cultivar. Find it, buy it, grow it.

Full sun for all but 'Stuttgart'. Dig up roots after the first frost, cut off all foliage, and store in a 35–40°F place, like a garage area. If perennial, divide every three years or so. Wet soils are better than dry.

Canna ×generalis 'Bengal Tiger'

Canna ×generalis 'Australia'

Canna ×generalis 'Stuttgart'

Canna ×generalis 'Tropicanna'

Capsicum annuum

ORNAMENTAL PEPPER

I love it when high school students tour the UGA Trial Gardens, especially when both girls and boys are in the group. When I point out the ornamental peppers (*Capsicum annuum*), all I need to say is, "These are very hot, anybody want to try one?" Saying that is like putting a red cape in front of a bull, and these young bulls would probably be smart enough not to charge, except for the presence of the bull-ettes. Invariably, the girls elbow the boys a little, and soon one or two bulls will have to show the herd that they are up to the task. And the peppers are indeed hot! And how those bulls sweat. Between the girls, the peppers, and the *Acmella* (which see), these guys don't stand a chance.

Ornamental peppers are easy to use in the garden, seldom growing more than 1' tall. I have seen individual plants in a patio container to whole populations lining a walkway at Longwood Gardens. They bear white flowers, which give way

Capsicum annuum 'Holiday Flame'

Capsicum annuum 'Medusa'

Capsicum annuum 'Explosive Ember'

Capsicum annuum 'Treasures Red'

MORE ☞

to green or white fruit and usually mature to bright colors. Occasionally, plants with variegated leaves, such as 'Jigsaw', are chosen, but they don't have the vigor or joie de vivre of the others. The fruit are the best part, and they can be long and narrow, rounded, and might be purple, red, or orange. I am biased; I do not much like the squat rounded fruit of 'Fireworks' and other selections, or the fat stuff I see on cultivars like 'Korona'. Interesting but no subtlety. 'Treasures Red' provides lots of color, and the fruit are getting a little closer to my taste (although not to my tongue). My favorites have to be the long narrow forms, like the incredibly abundant 'Explosive Ignite', which matures to a bright red in the fall, and 'Holiday Flame', an older cultivar but still with excellent eye appeal.

Some recent releases to gardeners have made me a solid pepperite, particularly with 'Medusa' and 'Chilly Chili' (an All-America Selection in 2002); both provide abundant fruit and are easy to look at and ridiculously easy to grow. Along with the fruit, some purple-leaved

Capsicum annuum 'Korana'

Capsicum annuum 'Explosive Ignite'

Capsicum annuum 'Chilly Chili'

Capsicum annuum 'Masquerade'

forms have also emerged as winners. A favorite for many is 'Masquerade' with dark fruit and dark green leaves, but the winner of this beauty contest has to be 'Explosive Ember' with seemingly hundreds of purple peppers clothed in bronze foliage. Everybody loves this one. Full sun, eat at your own risk.

Cardiospermum halicacabum

LOVE-IN-A-PUFF

Love truly takes on many faces, but finding love inside a puffy fruit has to be one of the more creative forms. Some of the early names of flowers must have been coined by frustrated nearsighted old men—how else can you explain names like love-in-a-puff (*Cardiospermum*), love-in-a-mist (*Nigella*), and love-lies-bleeding (*Amaranthus*)? Talk about finding love in all the wrong places! But love-in-a-puff, at least, makes a little sense; break open the puffy fruit, and look at the seed. Each black seed has a white heart shape

MORE ☞

Capsicum annuum 'Jigsaw'

Capsicum annuum 'Fireworks'

Cardiospermum halicacabum, seeds

Cardiospermum halicacabum

Cardiospermum halicacabum, fruit

on the outside. Plants look best growing through other plants, although they are quite happy on arbors and fences.

The white flowers of *Cardiospermum halicacabum* are tiny and uninteresting, but the fruit inflates as it grows and after a while, puffs are all over the place. Later the fruit dries to an unattractive brown color, but then you know the seeds are ready to be studied or gathered for next year's crop. Simply a fun plant, and no other reason is needed to grow this vine. Full sun.

Caryopteris incana

BLUE MIST SPIREA

Ninety-five percent of the caryopteris plants in gardens are the perennial hybrid, *Caryopteris* ×*clandonensis*, but if you get lucky, you might find some seed or starters of the annual form, *C. incana*. This has been one of my favorite plants for years, but seeds and plants have almost disappeared because of the popularity of its perennial cousin. It differs from the common perennial by being more upright and single-stemmed, with clusters of blue flowers surrounding the stem. They are used as fresh flowers from the garden, combining well in the vase with other cuts.

Plants can be planted quite densely, and a fine display will be had by about late June. More flowers result in full sun, but afternoon shade is also tolerated, at least in the South.

Caryopteris incana, flowers

Caryopteris incana

Caryopteris incana, arrangement with celosia, statice, and white loosestrife

Catananche

CUPID'S DART

Only one species, *Catananche caerulea*, is common in gardens, although many are known. Plants prefer cool weather and are more often seen in the Northeast and Northwest than elsewhere. They produce thin stems topped with lavender flowers bearing a darker eye, the target of Cupid's dart. Supposedly, plants were used in those ubiquitous love potions of yesteryear, thus the common name. Quite beautiful, but they can become leggy and a little weedy at times, particularly in the heat of the summer.

Catananche caespitosa is a yellow-flowered species, best for rock gardens or containers. Both prefer full sun and good drainage.

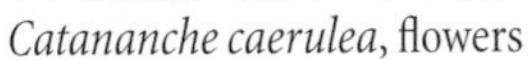

Catananche caerulea, flowers

Catananche caespitosa

Catananche caerulea

Catharanthus roseus

VINCA

From an almost unrecognizable small flowering plant on the island of Madagascar, vinca (or Madagascar periwinkle) has been reinvented by plant breeders into a bigger, bolder, and more vigorous plant. Gardeners now can chose from dozens of cultivars, in an astonishing array of flower colors and flower sizes.

Most gardeners, when eyeing the sun-loving, heat-seeking flowers, refer to these plants (*Catharanthus roseus*) as vinca, but no one should get this mixed up with perennial vinca (*Vinca* spp.). This vinca is sold as a bedding plant and became popular when its tolerance to heat, humidity, and full sun were combined with outstanding new flower colors. Plants look good in the garden, in a container, and even as an edging to large beds and walkways. They seldom grow more than 1' tall and are covered with flowers from June to frost.

However, their popularity declined in recent years because of their susceptibility to root rots associated with overwatering. If you are overzealous in over-

Catharanthus roseus, edging

Catharanthus roseus 'Bourbon Street'

Catharanthus roseus 'Heat Wave White'

Catharanthus roseus 'Icy Pink Cooler'

Catharanthus roseus 'Caribbean Lavender'

head watering, or the bed is in a low area, these are not the plants for you. One of the few good things about times of drought is that many plants suffer far fewer fungal problems, and vinca is certainly one of them. It is unfortunate that a good plant suffered because of poor gardening practices, but this is not the first example, nor will it be the last.

Given a few brains, most gardeners can succeed easily with these plants, even under normal rainfall. Don't include them near the in-ground sprinkling system you use on your turf in the middle of the night. Don't plant them where the rain does not drain well, and provide full sun. Then get out of the way.

The change in flower size and shape over the past fifteen years has been nothing short of spectacular. Cultivars such as 'Bourbon Street' and 'Orchid Stardust' have obvious eyes in the flowers and are quite eye-catching themselves. White is always in fashion; 'Heat Wave White' provides clean color, while 'Icy Pink Cooler' adds that hint of pink. Pinks and lavenders are well represented in the land of vincas, and I have always enjoyed 'Pacifica Pink' and 'Tropicana

Catharanthus roseus 'Pacifica Pink'

Catharanthus roseus 'Tropicana Bright Eye'

Catharanthus roseus 'Tropicana Rose'

Catharanthus roseus 'Pacifica Red'

MORE ☞

Bright Eye', as well as 'Caribbean Lavender', all of which sport off-color centers. Some of the brightest flowers occur on 'Tropicana Rose', whose white eye contracts wonderfully with the rose petals. Years ago, I was struck by the true red of 'Pacifia Red', one of the very best red-colored flowers available to the gardener. Great then, still great today. Full sun, good drainage.

Celosia

COCKSCOMB

So much diversity in flower, habit, and use can be found in this genus that it will never go away. As a cut flower, plants are

Catharanthus roseus, UGA Trial Gardens

Celosia argentea var. *cristata* Jewel Box Mix

Catharanthus roseus 'Orchid Stardust'

Celosia argentea var. *cristata* 'Bicolor Chief'

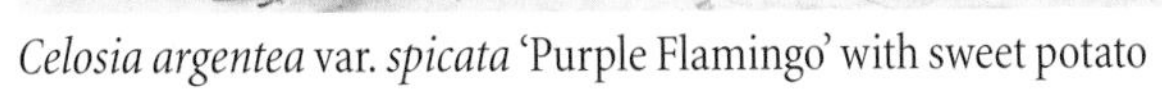

Celosia argentea var. *spicata* 'Purple Flamingo' with sweet potato

Celosia argentea var. *spicata* 'Cramers' Amazon'

Celosia argentea, cut flower field

MORE ☞

Celosia argentea var. *cristata* 'Amigo Mahogany Red'

Celosia argentea var. *plumosa* Castle series

Celosia argentea var. *cristata* 'Prestige Scarlet'

Celosia argentea var. *plumosa* Sparkler series

Celosia argentea var. *cristata* 'Red Chief'

Celosia argentea var. *plumosa* 'Apricot Brandy'

rowed out like corn and appear in bouquets and as single stems throughout the country. Gardeners have never had a major love affair with *Celosia argentea* but not for lack of visibility of the plant. Although not as popular as petunias or geraniums, celosias have been aggressively hybridized to keep plants new and fresh, resulting in their continued visibility in public places and retail outlets. This is a good thing, because while bedding plants in general have lost some of their luster, celosia continues to reinvent itself. One of the ways the genus remains in the crosshairs of landscapers and gardeners is in its multitude of forms. Like begonias, they wear many different costumes, all of which can be welcome in the garden.

The cockscomb look (var. *cristata*) is the form easiest to hate. Colored brains always come to my mind when I teach these plants, but who is to account for taste? What had to have started out as a joke among breeders ("I can make a shorter, uglier celosia than you, wanna bet?") resulted in a startling transfiguration of quite a nice plant. I can think of many adjectives for 'Amigo Mahogany Red', but "subtle" would not be one of them. Each large colored brain squatting on the plants of Jewel Box Mix persists most of the summer, so one can relive *The Hunchback of Notre Dame* remakes every day. But to be fair, I am likely in the minority in my aversion to this group, because more just keep on coming. But at least they are getting better. I have come to enjoy the upright flowers of 'Prestige Scarlet' and believed they would also make fine cut flowers. But when I was introduced to the mother of all cut flowers in celosia, the Chief series, I realized the cut flower market had already been taken. In the garden, they really are awesome, producing large clubs so in case anyone attacks you in the garden, you have a ready-made defensive weapon. All sorts of colors may be had, but if a picture is worth a thousand words, looking at 'Red Chief' and 'Bicolor Chief' can substitute for an essay. When they are taken out of the garden and teamed with goldenrod or other bright flowers, put on your shades and duck for cover.

Celosia argentea var. *spicata* 'Purple Flamingo'

Celosia argentea var. *spicata* 'Venezuela'

Celosia argentea var. *cristata* 'Scarlet Chief', arrangement with goldenrod

Celosia argentea var. *plumosa* 'New Look'

MORE ☞

A relatively recent group, wheat celosia (var. *spicata*), is often seen in parks and botanic gardens. Tall and stately, wheat celosias can be impressive in the background or surrounded by other plants at their legs. The purple-leaved, purple-flowered form 'Purple Flamingo', outstanding in its own right, is tough enough to anchor a corner of the UGA campus in concert with 'Margarita' sweet potato. The drawback of this cultivar is that it does not flower until fall and can reseed with gusto. Season-long flowering, however, is the norm for 'Flamingo Feather', and seeing it towering over other celosias puts its height in perspective. 'Cramers' Amazon' is a popular tall cut flower form and for those who like this form but don't have space for such

Celosia argentea var. *spicata* 'Flamingo Feather'

Celosia argentea var. *plumosa* 'Century Red'

Celosia 'Enterprise Dark Pink'

Celosia 'Punky Red'

monsters, 'Venezuela' can work in containers or in gardens.

Competing for the honor of best known is the plume celosia group (var. *plumosa*), whose flowers look like the plumes of gladiators. This is my favorite by far, and some outstanding breeding has been concentrated in this form. Gardeners can choose short plants, such as the 9–12" tall Castle series; 'Castle Yellow' is an outstanding performer. The ever-popular 'New Look' is a little taller. Plants are taller but the feathery look is a little muted in the Sparkler series; however, several fine colors are available in the mix. If the traditional feather look is important, it is impossible to overlook the knock-your-socks-off color of 'Century Red'. Its color combined with its compact habit makes it an easy choice when bright colors are demanded. And when taller forms are wanted, surely 'Apricot Brandy' should appear on a gardener's wish list. An All-America Selection in 1981, plants have stood the test of time. And still celosias change, exemplified by the mix of wheat and feather blood in such new hybrid cultivars as 'Enterprise Dark Pink' and 'Punky Red'. Never a dull moment! Full sun, deadhead in mid summer.

Centaurea cyanus, flowers

Centaurea

BACHELOR'S BUTTONS, CORNFLOWER

By placing a blue-flowered daisy in his label, the single Victorian gentleman signaled his marital status, and plants became known as bachelor's buttons. This same flower was also an inhabitant of cornfields, and cornflowers have become blue sentries at the edge of many of our roadways in this country. The sultan of Constantinople enjoyed the sweet smell of one species' flowers, and one of our lesser-known American natives is also a member of this fine genus of plants. However, not all species are appreciated and even fewer are grown consistently in our gardens.

The common blue of bachelor's buttons (*Centaurea cyanus*) is underappreciated, but flowers look right at home in gardens or containers. They are also useful as fillers in arrangements. There are some choices in colors; I am fond of Florence Mix, which sports a wide diversity of colors. 'Garnet' is one example of single colors becoming more available; this one provides dark colors for the garden plan.

Centaurea moschata 'The Bride'

MORE ☞

The American basket flower (*Centaurea americana*) is hardly seen in North American gardens, although it is produced as a cut flower by growers around the world. The plants can grow to about 4' in height. The flower of the most common cultivar, 'Jolly Joker', starts out as long, thick hair-like strands, seemingly straining to get out of their case, and opens to a large, bushy pink flower. A great deal of fun to grow, but don't expect it to be well behaved.

Sweet sultan (*Centaurea moschata*) has an ephemeral sweet fragrance that requires nose-to-flower contact. The common Imperialis series produces a potpourri of colors on 2' tall plants and is especially useful for bouquets. I also enjoy the white form called 'The Bride'. Sweet sultans prefer cool summers and perform better in the North than in the South.

Centaurea cyanus 'Garnet'

Centaurea americana 'Jolly Joker', opening bud

Centaurea americana 'Jolly Joker'

Centaurea moschata Imperialis series, as cut flowers

Centaurea cyanus Florence Mix

All members of the genus are grown from seed, which can be sown after threat of frost. Deadhead for most persistent performance, and, if needed, sow again in mid summer for fall flowering. Full sun to afternoon shade.

Cerinthe major

HONEYWORT

Honeywort (*Cerinthe major*) has such a weird flower, it is small wonder that so few people grow it. It is difficult to describe the small pendent purple and black flower; I mean, come on, how many people really want purple and black as part of their floral display? But to those of you who must have the newest and the weirdest: this fascinating plant should definitely be on your short list.

The gray-green leaves are waxy and thick, and plants are relatively drought-tolerant; however, high humidity and wetness are not to their liking. The flowers lean over the foliage and don't really contrast well, and for me at least, tend to get lost. But believe it or not, some people think they make good cut stems. I have also tried the yellow form, 'Aurea', whose flowers are a lot more likeable and more reliable as well. Still a tough plant to keep alive throughout the sea-

MORE ☞

Cerinthe major

Cerinthe major

Cerinthe major 'Aurea'

son in areas of warm, humid summers, but I'd grow it again. A great plant to check out the plant knowledge of your know-it-all gardener friend. Full sun, good drainage.

Chrysanthemum

Only a few species remain in this once glorious genus, and the ones we are able to put our hands on are all annuals. Often, purchasing seeds from a good seed catalog is the sole means of finding plants. While they are not well known to gardeners in North America, many of the plants originated as European weeds. All these mums prefer cool summers, and in areas of warm, humid summers, it may be necessary to replant in mid summer for all-season performance.

Tricolor daisy (*Chrysanthemum carinatum*) seems to be the most difficult to

Chrysanthemum carinatum 'Polar Skies'

Chrysanthemum segetum

Chrysanthemum coronarium 'Primrose Gem'

Chrysanthemum segetum 'Prado'

Chrysanthemum segetum 'Eastern Star'

find, and this three-colored flower remains rather obscure. However, some cultivars are breaking through the garden ranks, and I find 'Polar Skies', a handsome white-flowered form, quite lovely. Crown daisy (*C. coronarium*) has ferny leaves and usually bears yellow flowers. The best selection is 'Primrose Gem', with dozens of small double light yellow flowers.

Lastly, in our search for the true chrysanthemum, let us not overlook the best one of all and discover what a corn marigold (*Chrysanthemum segetum*) really looks like. What it really looks like is a common yellow daisy with handsome dark green dissected leaves. The smaller darker center contrasts with the lighter yellow rays. However, there are enough boring yellows out there, and I prefer 'Prado' for its much more contrastive flower center. Excellent performer as well. 'Eastern Star' is the most unusual in that the only trace of yellow surrounds the center. Quite beautiful.

Full sun in the North, afternoon shade is tolerated in the South. All purchased from seed. Deadheading is beneficial. Reseed in the summer for fall flowers.

Chrysocephalum apiculatum

NULLABOR BUTTONS, GOLDEN BUTTONS

Here is a plant that definitely needs to be grown to be appreciated. To see this plant in a container at the garden store is to walk right past it, but that would be a mistake. Nullabor buttons (*Chrysocephalum apiculatum*) is native to the Nullabor Plain in Australia, indicating a tolerance for heat and drought. I was impressed with the plant when I first saw it growing in eastern Australia, so I brought some home and grew it out in Athens. I was not disappointed.

Buy it for a sunny, difficult spot; it will

Chrysocephalum apiculatum, Australia

reward you with aggressive, but not invasive, growth, and with dozens upon dozens of small button-like yellow flowers that just keep on appearing. Plants tolerate conditions from Minneapolis to Miami and are as at home in the ground

MORE ☞

as in a container, where they are not so tamed that they look like marigolds.

Hopefully, there will be a pot of this stuff at the garden center to walk by, and if there is, stop and buy. Full sun.

Cirsium japonicum

JAPANESE THISTLE

The very word "thistle" is a major turnoff to most gardeners; however, as thistles go, the Japanese thistle (*Cirsium japonicum*) isn't all bad. I am sure that such a powerful endorsement may not result in everyone searching for seed, but for some of you, additional information may be useful.

Plants are prickly, to be sure, but not nearly as bad as most other thistles that come to mind, in particular Canada

Chrysocephalum apiculatum, UGA Trial Gardens

Cirsium japonicum 'White Beauty'

Cirsium japonicum 'Rose Beauty'

Cirsium japonicum 'Pink Beauty'

thistle or Scotch thistle. These grow only about 2' tall, and the long-lasting cut flowers are colorful and quite useful in arrangements. The only cultivars I am aware of are in the Beauty series, appearing in rose, pink, or white. 'Rose Beauty' is the best of the three; 'White Beauty' is fair at best. Full sun.

Clarkia amoena

SATIN FLOWER

Having wandered through landscapes and gardens all over this country and a few above the 45th parallel as well, I can honestly say that less than one percent of that buying public purchase satin flowers with the idea of enjoying them outdoors. That is not to say satin flowers are ugly—in fact, well over half the people who regularly purchase cut flowers in the grocery store or florist buy satin flowers. So they must be grown somewhere. And they are, in greenhouses around the country and in fields in the Northwest and occasionally in the Northeast. However, there are a few problems.

Satin flower (*Clarkia amoena*), also known as godetia, loves cool, dry conditions. In eastern gardens, heat usually gets to them by mid June to early July and they tend to stretch and get floppy. I love their understated beauty but have come to terms with the fact that, outside coastal California and the Far North, I will have to enjoy them as amputees, not as the entire plant.

Of course, the more the challenge, the more we want the plant in the garden. Satin Mix contains a number of handsome pastel colors including 'Satin Pink' and is sometimes available in seed packets in the spring. The best series by far is the Grace series, used by cut flower growers because of the wonderful colors and uniform habit. I especially enjoy 'Grace Rose Pink' and 'Grace Salmon Red'. Not particularly creative names, but quite spectacular plants. Full sun, excellent drainage.

Cleome

SPIDER FLOWER

Grandmother's garden would never have been without a few spider flowers (*Cleome hassleriana*) partly because they

MORE ☞

Clarkia amoena 'Grace Rose Pink'

Clarkia amoena 'Satin Pink'

Clarkia amoena 'Grace Salmon Red'

were so common at the time and also because they self-seeded everywhere and never disappeared. Plants were a bit of a nuisance, and kind of leggy, and okay, they fell apart halfway through the summer, and yes, they did self-sow, but still, the flowers were quite lovely in their detail, and Grandma did like them.

Some of the older cultivars are still around today. 'White Spider', a selection of *Cleome marshallii*, is still occasionally seen but never caught on in garden circles. It was the Queen series, among the first named cultivars of *C. hassleriana*, that people flocked to. The series included the muted 'Pink Queen', the violent 'Violet Queen', and the handsome 'Purple Queen'. These were the mainstays along with 'Helen Campbell', a fine tall white form. All were grown from seed and were wonderfully simple plants to include in the garden. However, over the years, it seems people started tiring of them, and they became less noticeable in our gardens.

However, in the early 2000s, the interest in spider flower was reinvigorated by the introduction of two new cleomes. The

Cleome hassleriana, flower

Cleome marshallii 'White Spider'

Cleome hassleriana 'Pink Queen'

Cleome hassleriana 'Violet Queen'

Sparkler series is a hybrid that provides outstanding performance and colors. It is shorter than the common forms but certainly cannot be considered dwarf. 'Sparkler Blush' is my favorite, with its pink and white flowers, and in combination with 'Sparkler White' makes quite a show. 'Sparkler Rose' is among the most eye-catching; it is impossible to walk by it, in combination with other plants like mealy-cup sage (*Salvia farinacea*), without stopping. Plants produce few viable seed, and the self-sowing problems are of little concern. However, in warm-summer climates, plants still pooped out by mid summer.

At the same time, a new entry in the cleome game came to market under the name 'Linde Armstrong'. This dwarf (<18" tall) plant is named for two wonderful Charlotte gardeners, Linde Wilson and Ann Armstrong, who promoted its charms. The bright rose-colored flowers are beautiful, and plants look outstanding in the garden or in mixed containers. Plants begin blooming in May, and while most cleomes fall apart by mid to late summer, 'Linde Armstrong' continues to flower until frost. If needed, she can be

Cleome hassleriana 'Purple Queen'

Cleome 'Sparkler Blush', *C.* 'Sparkler White'

Cleome hassleriana 'Helen Campbell'

Cleome 'Linde Armstrong'

MORE ☞

Cleome 'Linde Armstrong', flowers

Cleome 'Linde Armstrong', container

Cleome 'Sparkler Rose'

given a haircut to rejuvenate the plants. This plant is grown from cuttings, seedlings will be similar but will not be 'Linde Armstrong'. All cleomes prefer full sun.

Clerodendrum

A large number of species reside in the genus, but all are on the periphery of gardeners' consciousness, unless, as one or two are prone to do, they have become noxious weeds. The harlequin glory bower (*Clerodendrum trichotomum*) is hardy as far north as New York and as beautiful as the fruit can be, plants can

Clerodendrum trichotomum, calyces and fruit

Clerodendrum speciosissimum

Clerodendrum ugandense

MORE ☞

spread rapidly by underground suckers and soon get out of control. The same can be said for shrubby glory bower, *C. bungei*, which for some people is a treasure, for others a smelly obnoxious weed.

Most of the plants in this genus are interesting but usually disappointing in the garden. The only garden annuals worth trying, and even that is debatable, are the showy clerodendrum and the blue butterfly bush. I have seen the former, *Clerodendrum speciosissimum*, in full red regalia in outdoor containers, but plants are at their best if protected from the elements. The red flowers knock your socks off, and if you can find a pot or two, try them on a protected patio. The other plant I have long been fascinated with is the blue butterfly bush (*C. ugandense*), which grows reasonably

Clerodendrum bungei

Clerodendrum ugandense

quickly in the garden. The handsome blue and white flowers that are formed truly are beautiful, but unfortunately, the plant has a sprawling habit and doesn't flower consistently. Keep it within arm's reach: it is a plant for a container near where people gather, so the flowers can be admired, even though there may not be many of them. Certainly worth growing, but may not be worth the time or expense in subsequent years. Full sun.

Clitoria ternatea

BUTTERFLY PEA VINE

What a beautiful vine, how little used it is. It's common name needs to become far more common, for this is a terrific plant. The butterfly pea vine (*Clitoria ternatea*) hails from the island of Ternate, one of the Molucca Islands in Indonesia, an interesting but absolutely useless piece of plant trivia. Plants grow rapidly and climb by tendrils, which allow them to scramble up walls or through shrubs. The handsome foliage consists of five leaflets per leaf, but it is the dark blue flowers that are so outstanding. After flowering, long thin pods form, which should be saved for next year's crop. Plant the seeds after the threat of frost, and sit back and enjoy this fine import from Ternate. Full sun.

Cobaea scandens

CUP AND SAUCER VINE

Another marvelous annual vine that can fill an arbor or clamber through a shrub. The cup and saucer vine (*Cobaea scandens*) is well named, with a well-defined cup and saucer dancing on the vine. Soak the seeds overnight, then sow them in the ground after frost is no longer a problem; starting any earlier is simply a waste of time. Otherwise start them in containers about two weeks before the last frost-free date. Plants grow quickly and can easily reach 10–15' in a season.

In general, the lavender-flowered

Cobaea scandens

Clitoria ternatea, flower

Clitoria ternatea

MORE ☞

Cobaea scandens 'Alba'

Coleus 'Dip't in Wine'

Coleus 'Alabama Sunset'

species itself is as good as any cultivar, and cultivars are few and far between anyway. The only other choice I have seen is 'Alba', whose white flowers tend to discolor as they age. Collect seeds in the fall. Full sun.

Coleus

Coleus, coleus everywhere, and more on their way: if one plant exemplifies the explosion of specialty annuals in North America, it has to be coleus. Actually, the real name for coleus is *Solenostemon*

Coleus 'Aurora'

Coleus 'Copper'

Coleus 'Velvet Lime'

Coleus, container

MORE ☞

Coleus 'Solar Morning Mist'

Coleus 'Solar Flare'

Coleus Stained Glass series

Coleus 'Kiwi Fern'

Coleus 'Flirting Skirts'

Coleus 'Ducksfoot'

scutellarioides, but no self-respecting gardeners are going to allow the whims of taxonomists to tongue-tie them, so *Solenostemon* will be bandied about the hallways of herbaria but seldom heard in the real world.

It wasn't so long ago that everyone believed that shade was a necessity for successful coleus garden performance; however, in the last ten years that myth has been soundly put to rest. Plants tolerate shade to be sure, but with the myriad of new cultivars, most selections do better in full sun. Coleus were born to be in containers, the larger and more chaotic the better. A row of containers containing red canna lilies embraced with 'Dip't in Wine' is impressive in Madison, Wisconsin, while a planting of 'Copper' is set off wonderfully by the base of creeping zinnia in Athens, Georgia. I can picture 'Alabama Sunset', one of the most popular coleus throughout the country, dominating a pendulous planting of perennial vinca, and I relish the memory of datura at the base of a wild planting of random colei. One of my favorite combinations was a container of 'Aurora' and ageratum interplanted in the garden, but the blend of verbena with the new 'Velvet Lime' was equally stunning. What fun these containers are, and how easy.

So many cultivars have been released lately that a coffeetable book of coleus images could easily be produced, but I'll contain myself and offer just a few. The Solar series, introduced by George Griffith of Gainesville, Florida, has to be one of my favorites, including such breakthrough plants as the deeply colored 'Solar Eclipse', and the bright 'Solar Flare', which is one of the few cultivars I recommend for the shade (it grows in a shady bed in the Armitage garden). And some of the largest most eye-popping

Coleus 'Solar Eclipse'

Coleus 'Diane's Gold'

Coleus 'Pineapple'

Coleus 'Amazon'

Coleus 'Daredevil'

MORE ☞

leaves were introduced with 'Solar Morning Mist'. You can't go too far wrong in bringing some Solar power home to the garden.

For plain fun, you might want to try the beautiful Stained Glass series, all of which provide vibrant colors, and for no other reason than plain fun, try the multicolored rounded leaves of 'Flirting Skirts'(aka 'Hurricane Jenni') and 'Diane's Gold', or the sensational 'Kiwi Fern'. All are novelties, all will bring many smiles and many comments, good and bad.

For more muted colors in the yellow and green hues, I have always found 'Pineapple' and 'Amazon' to be very effective. They are used en masse in many landscapes. Many coleus such as 'Daredevil' are big and bodacious (>3' tall and wide); others have a wonderful mounded habit. Many compact forms can be found, but probably the most popular of these medicine balls is the Ducksfoot series, with duckfoot-like foliage. 'Ducksfoot' makes a wonderful hanging basket in the Missouri Botanical Garden, but its cousin, 'Ducksfoot Purple', is equally beautiful in the landscape in Georgia. Another dark-leaved form that continues to impress is 'Merlot', almost as good as the wine and far better for you.

The series that helped start the coleus revolution was selected over ten years ago and named the Sunlover series. If available, they provide wonderful colors and a little history as well. Some you may still find are the chartreuse 'Gay's Delight', the muted orange of 'Rustic

Coleus 'Ducksfoot Purple'

Coleus 'Gay's Delight', *C.* 'Rustic Orange'

Coleus 'Merlot'

Coleus 'Rustic Orange'

Orange', the strikingly beautiful variegation of 'Collin's Gold', and the large yet handsome 'Freckles'. Part of the beginning, certainly not the end of the coleus phenomenon. Full sun for most; shade is tolerated for all, but colors will not be as vibrant.

Colocasia

ELEPHANT EAR

This introductory sentence is nearly identical to the one you read under the genus *Alocasia*: regardless of what the "experts" tell you, there are no easily visible differences between this genus, *Alocasia*, and *Xanthosoma* (see further discussion under *Alocasia*). The reason for mentioning this again is that the cultivars I cite probably belong to *Colocasia*, but then again they may not.

The common elephant ear (*Colocasia*

Coleus 'Collin's Gold'

Colocasia esculenta

Coleus 'Freckles'

Colocasia esculenta 'Nancy's Revenge' (top)

MORE ☞

Colocasia esculenta with bananas

Colocasia esculenta 'Black Magic', landscape

esculenta) is well known in the South. The immense fluted leaves provide an architectural feature that is difficult to ignore. Plants are highly tolerant of different soil conditions; they put up well with drought but also can be planted in a bog. They are used in containers, where they behave themselves reasonably well, but I have seen them locked in battle for supremacy with tropical bananas in a residential neighborhood. It was a violent sight.

The gardener has numerous choices, not all easily found but obtainable through reputable mail-order sources. I occasionally see the white and green leaves of 'Chicago Harlequin', which seems to be less stuck in conservatories and public gardens than it once was. The petioles are magnificent as well. Another interesting form is 'Nancy's Revenge'; it too is difficult to describe, but I have little doubt that Nancy McDaniels of Florida, after whom the plant was named, is often asked just what she was avenging. The form I see the most, however, is 'Black Magic' (aka 'Jet Black Wonder') and for good reason. Although the leaves may unfold green, they mature to jet black and remain that way throughout the season. In bold landscapes or at the top of the Armitage driveway, this is a winner. Another handsome form is *Colocasia antiquorum* 'Illustris', whose purple and green pointed leaves look good in

MORE ☞

Colocasia esculenta 'Chicago Harlequin'

Colocasia esculenta 'Black Magic'

Colocasia antiquorum 'Illustris'

Colocasia antiquorum 'Illustris', foliage

containers or in the ground. It contrasts yet blends in with many ornamental annuals and perennials.

Overwinter *Colocasia* by digging the large tuber after temperatures dip into the mid 30s; remove the foliage, and put the tuber in sphagnum moss in a garage or other area that stays above freezing. Full sun for the species, afternoon shade for the cultivars.

Consolida

LARKSPUR

Larkspur is a mainstay for cut flower growers, particularly in the West, where it is grown by the acre for fresh and dried stems. Most larkspurs grown today are hybrids of two or three species. The characteristics that make it so appealing to growers can be taken advantage of by gardeners as well. Larkspurs are easy to grow: simply throw some seed out in the spring in the North, in the fall in the South, and get out of the way. Viewed as a single stem, one can see that the flowers are similar to those of delphinium, right to the spur, and plants are thus known as the annual delphinium. Seldom, however, do larkspurs grow as a single stem; rather, they reseed and crowd each other for attention. Double-flowered forms in pastels and pinks, lavender-purple flowers, and pastel pinks to white flowers are all possible from a single seed package picked up at the garden center. Larkspurs are cool lovers, and in the heat and humidity of the summer, they can decline rapidly. Replant in late June or early July if flowers are desired all season. If reseeding is a problem, cut down the plants before they produce fruit. But I bet you have a neighbor or two who would love to receive some of those seeds, so they too can bring in cut flowers next spring. Full sun, cool season.

Consolida 'Alba'

Consolida, flowers

Consolida, double-flowered forms

Convolvulus

BINDWEED

Say the words "morning glory" and "bindweed" in the same sentence, and many gardeners will run away in fear. Fear of reseeding, fear of rapacious weeds, and fear of the unknown are the reasons for turning tail. With the true morning glory (*Ipomoea*, which see), plants can become a terrible nuisance, but not so with ornamentals of this genus. While bindweed is a member of this genus, nobody in their right mind would plant it in a garden. A number of species are considered perennial, mainly the very silvery silverbush, *Convolvulus cneorum*, although hardiness south of zone 7 is questionable.

The popularity of some of the excellent annuals is not large, but they are gaining ground little by little. I think the prettiest is a selection of trailing morning glory, *Convolvulus sabatius*. 'Baby Moon' produces dozens of light blue flowers and can fill a container or brighten up the edges of a walkway. Its cousin 'Full Moon' is similar in habit but has darker flowers. Both are superb plants during the cooler days of spring and fall but may have difficulties in mid summer.

Some of the showiest plants are known as the annual morning glory, *Convolvulus tricolor*. The tricolor refers to the wild coloration of the flowers on

Convolvulus cneorum

Convolvulus sabatius 'Baby Moon', container

Convolvulus sabatius 'Baby Moon', garden

Convolvulus sabatius 'Full Moon'

MORE ☞

the short sprawling stems. The Ensign series includes two of the showiest plants, 'Blue Ensign' and 'Red Ensign'. The flashy flowers have one color in the outside and another in the eye, with a contrasting hue in the middle. They are excellent in containers or sprawling through the garden. Full sun.

Coreopsis

TICKSEED, CALLIOPSIS

Only one species in this large genus is worthy of being tucked into this annual book, and it is the colorful annual tickseed, *Coreopsis tinctoria*. All the other perennial species are much better known by gardeners, and as a result this wonderful plant from the south and central United States has been ignored. But a comeback has occurred with the greater interest in natives, meadow gardening, and lawn-free gardens. Meadows throughout the land feature calliopsis and other meadow-type plants like cosmos. There, as in other "wild" gardens, calliopsis seems most at home, romping around hand in hand with other fancy-free flowers. The footloose characteristic

Convolvulus tricolor 'Blue Ensign'

Coreopsis tinctoria with nasturtiums

Convolvulus tricolor 'Red Ensign'

Coreopsis tinctoria, narrow petals

is nowhere more wonderful than in the helter-skelter garden once tended by Monet at Giverny, which today is historically correct and a perfect study in chaotic brilliance. Because this plant is most at home in a meadow garden or

MORE 

Coreopsis tinctoria, red centers

Coreopsis tinctoria, wildflower mix

Coreopsis tinctoria, Giverny

where it can do its own thing, it is often found in native flower mixtures or from meadow-in-a-can companies. They are at their best when temperatures are cooler and are often found in the company of cosmos and nasturtiums.

All plants are raised from seed, and the diversity, even in a single seed package, is startling. The common golden color, often with a dark center, can give way to rounded flowers with a much larger red center and to wild, weird, and wonderful narrow-petaled red forms, a wonderful surprise one year in the Armitage garden. Full sun; ignore them until they need to be cut back. Allow them to seed and plants will come back the next year.

Cosmos

This underappreciated plant does most anything most anywhere for most anybody. Why it is not in everyone's garden is beyond me, it simply works. As a meadow and "wild" plant, tall cosmos (*Cosmos bipinnatus*) is easy on the eyes and cavorts with plants of all descriptions. The sulphur cosmos (*C. sulphureus*) is outstanding in the garden, and what more can I say about a flower that smells just like chocolate, which is a fact when you stick your nose in the flower of *C. atrosanguineus*?

Cosmos bipinnatus 'Versailles Pink'

Cosmos bipinnatus 'Sonata Pink'

Cosmos bipinnatus, wildflower mix

Cosmos bipinnatus 'Versailles White'

Cosmos bipinnatus 'Sonata White'

Cosmos bipinnatus 'Seashell'

Cosmos bipinnatus Early Sensation Mix

Cosmos bipinnatus 'Loveliness'

Cosmos bipinnatus 'Daydream'

Cosmos sulphureus 'Cosmic Orange'

MORE ☞

Tall cosmos, native to the southern United States and Mexico, dominates wildflower mixes, and in trials, its performance dwarfs that of others in the row. Wildflower plantings are fine, but the plant has been significantly improved to provide even more colorful flowers and lower maintenance. The Versailles series is a mainstay, and my goodness, was I blown away at the white garden outside Giverny, where 'Versailles White' and white flowering tobacco made people literally stop and stare. 'Versailles Pink' is no slouch either, and the combination of the two immediately elevates one to "professional designer." An equally beautiful group is the Sonata series, slightly shorter than the Versailles but just as useful. In combination with a light green background such as a cutleaf sambucus, 'Sonata White' is even whiter and lights up the shrub as well. 'Sonata Pink' is almost ball-shaped, with dozens of clear pink flowers top-

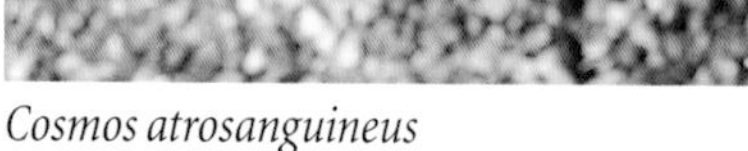

Cosmos atrosanguineus

Cosmos sulphureus 'Polidor'

Cosmos sulphureus 'Diablo'

ping the ferny foliage. Both series are no-brainers.

Other choices are available in this species. Early Sensation Mix is taller and a bit more weedy but excellent as cut flowers from the garden. And for novelty, gardeners can choose from the beautiful bicolored 'Daydream' and the different and statuesque 'Seashell' with its fluted petals. And wouldn't you know it, breeders just couldn't leave well enough alone, they created a double form. And even I, the curmudgeon of double flowers, have to admit that 'Loveliness' is just that.

The sulphur cosmos may not be quite as beautiful, but the number of flowers on a plant is astounding. The flowers of 'Cosmic Orange' are almost double and sit on compact plants that don't fall over. I recall coming across an entire bed of 'Diablo' in a landscape in Georgia, and the flowers just went on and on. As impressive as that was, I also loved approaching a bright planting of 'Polidor' lining a path, and then as I was beside them, admiring the contrast in combination with other plantings. Excellent.

And for the sheer hell of it, plant some chocolate cosmos one year. The somber dark purple flowers are quite different from the happy-face flowers of the previous species, and although performance doesn't come close to those, who cares when you can go to the candy store every time you put your nose near it? Non-fattening as well. Plant them in a container where you don't have to bend too far to inhale.

Full sun, good drainage. If plants begin to decline in the summer, resow the seeds directly into the beds, in and among plants already there. The second planting will keep you in color the rest of the year.

Cosmos sulphureus 'Polidor' with white sweet alyssum

Cuphea pallida

Cuphea

This group of plants is fast becoming a garden mainstay, for several reasons, not the least of which is the wonderful diversity exhibited in the genus. The purple cuphea (*Cuphea pallida*) has not really caught on yet but is quite marvelous, with its purple flowers filling the plant. Unlike most members of this genus, it is better in the cool Northwest than the warm Southeast. While we may not be cuphea connoisseurs, most of us have tried a plant or two of Mexican heather (*C. hyssopifolia*). The mounding plants with their pastel flowers have been attractive if not memorable. However, plants of 'Charmar Pink' are always full of flowers, even in the brutal heat of a southern summer, and the shrubby 'Allyson' still enjoys popularity. They are tough and resilient.

Those adjectives could describe most of the species because all work well under rather stressful conditions. Small-flowered but floriferous hybrids are also appearing, such as 'Twinkle Pink', which has filled containers all summer. Most of us are also well aware of the toughness of the cigar flower (*Cuphea ignea*), and they are available in a slightly bigger-flowered form, 'Dynamite', as well as in white, 'Kona White'. But if you like that smoking flower, you simply have to try the mammoth cigar plant, *C. micropetala*. Good grief, where has this been hiding all this time? In a single year, plants

MORE ☞

Cuphea 'Twinkle Pink'

Cuphea ignea 'Dynamite'

Cuphea ignea 'Kona White'

Cuphea hyssopifolia 'Charmar Pink'

Cuphea hyssopifolia 'Allyson'

Cuphea micropetala

Cuphea 'Firecracker'

Cuphea 'Firecracker', flower

will grow 3–5' tall, and when it flowers in September and October, it will be the dominant plant in the garden. The fact that it does not flower until the fall is looked upon too often as a detriment rather than a benefit. We need more autumn flowers, and this one is outstanding. Perhaps a balance between the dueling cigars is a plant that I like even more. Similar in shape to the cigar flower, 'David Verity' flowers all season long on 2–3' tall plants. When the smoke clears, this hybrid will be left in the cuphea arena. There is nothing bad about it.

Two other plants have really caught my attention and are likely included in the hybrid *Cuphea* ×*purpurea* group. I watched as a somewhat upright form with fire-engine-red flowers grew and thrived in hot, humid areas. The flowers form all summer and are relatively large for a cuphea. The plant is 'Firefly', and it looked outstanding in the ground and

MORE ☞

Cuphea micropetala, flowers

Cuphea 'Firefly', container

Cuphea 'David Verity'

Cuphea 'Firefly'

even more so when it fell out of one of our ginger containers. Plants grew all the way to the ground and then bent back up to greet passers-by. And then a year or so ago, we planted a low-growing free-flowering cuphea in the UGA Trial Gardens which turned out to be a hit for everyone passing by. The plant was called 'Firecracker', and it was fantastic. However, I recognized the plant from years past: it was first developed in Tifton, Georgia, under the name 'Georgia Scarlet'. A few years later I saw it in Australia called 'Tiny Mice', and then in America as 'Batface'; I love that name because if you pull a flower off and stare at it, that is what it looks like! Names notwithstanding, the plant by itself is a fabulous choice, but when it is put with other bright flowers like rudbeckias, you might consider sunglasses. Both 'Firefly' and 'Firecracker' are highly recommended. Full sun.

Curcuma

HIDDEN GINGER

Gardeners attach the name ginger to a number of genera, including *Asarum*, false ginger, and *Zingiber*, the true culinary ginger. The former is simple to find; the latter is available in specialty shops but mainly for eating, not for planting. The genus *Curcuma* is seldom seen in the local garden center, particularly in the North, but that may change as people discover its diversity and ease of growing. Warm temperatures are beneficial, but nowhere is it written that people in Michigan or Wisconsin cannot be successful with gingers. They may not be as dominant in the landscape in the North as in the South, but they will do just fine. Curcumas are increasingly produced as garden plants through tissue culture labs and are gaining a larger following in the landscape trade, so there is hope for us simple gardeners.

In choosing which gingers to include, I considered only a few whose garden attributes I had trialed as well as those that might be available, with some looking. There are dozens more, especially if you live in areas near the Gulf Coast or further south. I first tried a few tubers of the Siam tulip (*Curcuma alismatifolia*) many years ago and learned that buying the tubers might not be a good idea because

Curcuma zedoaria

Curcuma alismatifolia

Curcuma roscoeana

they need a good deal of heat to emerge. However, if germinated tubers are available, they quickly grow into upright plants with pink bracts, somewhat similar to a tulip. Place them close together as, like tulips, they do not branch. Flowers persist for months. Bigger gingers give more bang for the buck, however, and I enjoyed the habit, leaves, and the somewhat concealed flowers of the hidden ginger, *C. petiolata*. Plants are 3–5' tall and produce the pink flowers in the base of all those leaves. Quite stunning.

In many cases, certainly in the North, plants may not attain sufficient maturity to flower in a single season. We worked with *Curcuma roscoeana*, wonderfully named the jewel of Burma; its flowers are fabulous, but the foliage is also handsome, so this one is worth planting even if the flowers don't appear. If they can be flowered, inside or out, they will produce some of the neatest blossoms you have ever seen. The waxy basal flowers consist of shingled orange bracts surrounding the actual small flowers, and if picked, persist for weeks in a floral arrangement. It takes some bending to see those flowers, but it is well worth it. If I were to recommend one ginger to try, I would probably choose zedoary, *C. zedoaria*. The plant does have lovely basal flowers, almost as pretty as the previous species, but the foliage and habit are always outstanding. Plants are upright and statuesque, but the foliage, with the obvious purple midrib on each leaf, is what makes it number one in my book. We have placed it in containers and in the garden, and regardless, they look good. And as a potential bonus, they are winter hardy to zone 7b, perhaps a little colder. Bring in like caladiums if you want to save them for next spring. Full sun.

Curcuma petiolata

Curcuma roscoeana, flowers

Dahlia

While some people in some places can consider dahlias perennial, most of us must dig, store, and replant. For me, dahlias are one of the most difficult plants to love: too much heat, too many bugs, too many diseases, and far too much staking. But while I don't love them in my garden, I love them in other places where they put on their show. And what a show a good planting provides: short ones, tall ones, singles, doubles, pastels and flashy colors—no end to what a crazy person can plant. Like a number of other large plant groups (daylilies, roses,

Dahlia 'Caruso White'

MORE ☞

Dahlia, Swan Island Dahlias

Dahlia, staking at Anglesey Abbey

peonies), a garden "collection" is fairly common, and while such plantings are extremely impressive, as seen at Anglesey Abbey just outside Cambridge, England, or Swan Island Dahlias in Canby, Oregon, after a while dahlias are kind of boring. Like roses, they are at their best complementing, and being complemented by, other plants.

There are literally hundreds of registered cultivars, so where to start? Think about categories, then find cultivars you can't do without. Most dahlias are quite tall, hence the staking, but several dwarf ones that have been bred are similar in habit to bedding plants. Most of the smaller forms bear single flowers, and when I want a white, I search for 'Caruso White', and when I think of a mix, I first look for the clean singles of 'Bon Esperance', or the semi-double flowers of Figaro Mix.

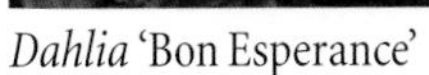

Dahlia 'Bon Esperance'

Dahlia 'White Queen'

Dahlia 'Rebecca Lynn'

Dahlia Figaro Mix

MORE ☞

With taller plants, there is a world of diversity out there. 'White Queen' is but one example of single flowers, and in the category of fully double flowers, lots of choice is available. I have always been impressed with 'Rebecca Lynn'; however, flower forms are like masks at Halloween: you never know what you will see next. Large bicolor flowers, such as 'Rutland Water' are common and eye-catching, but bicolor means different things to different people. 'Wheels' and 'Pooh' (what a great name!) are simply fun plants to have in the garden, with their semi-double multicolored flowers. More fun can be gained with examples of "spidery" flowers, such as 'Herbert Smith' and 'Red Devil'; such forms are wonderful in good weather but look like wet dogs after rain or high humidity.

Interest in flower color and form are not all that the genus can offer; foliar

Dahlia 'Rutland Water'

Dahlia 'Pooh'

Dahlia 'Wheels'

Dahlia 'Herbert Smith'

Dahlia 'Red Devil'

color too is important, and in particular, dahlias with purple leaves have gained a significant following. The best known is 'Bishop of Llandaff', with bright red flowers and handsome purple leaves, but many others, like 'Rumby', are also available to North American gardeners.

So many cultivars, so much to choose from, have fun. Dig and clean tubers in the fall; store in peat or sphagnum moss in an unheated garage or other area that does not consistently freeze. Full sun.

Datura

THORN APPLE

Here is a great genus with great stories. A weed in Virginia was responsible for all sorts of headaches, as well as hallucinations, when native Indians fed its leaves to the colonists at Jamestown. This plant became known as jimson weed. And even though that species (*Datura stramonium*) is not used in gardening, it seems a shame to waste the story, so who has to know?

The daturas that are available for gardeners are also poisonous if eaten in sufficient quantity, but that is no reason not to grow them. Don't worry about pets, they are smart enough to avoid them. Plants are shrubby and usually no more than 2' tall, and mostly carry white upright or outward-facing trumpet flowers, which are wonderfully fragrant. They are sometimes called angel's trumpet, the same as for *Brugmansia*, but the flowers of *Brugmansia* point down, those of *Datura* point up.

Dahlia 'Bishop of Llandaff'

Datura 'Ballerina Purple'

Datura 'Ballerina White'

Dahlia 'Rumby'

Datura 'Grand Marnier'

MORE ☞

Datura metel, garden

Datura metel

Datura, fruit

I have seen daturas used in many settings, and the gray-green color of the foliage and the white flowers complement most other flowers well. At Blue Meadow Farm in Massachusetts, they are simply part of the handsome mixed garden; at the Butchart Gardens in Victoria, they provide a nice background for variegated geraniums. Most gardeners grow the common white single-flowered datura, *Datura metel*, which is uncomplicated and as good as any other choice. The hybrid Ballerina series has thick flowers, often with a purple throat and purple underside to the flowers; 'Ballerina White' has semi-double clean white flowers. Most people like the singles better, and if I had my choice and I could find it, I would grow 'Grand Marnier' in a heartbeat. Her single soft yellow flowers are outstanding in every way. The common name, thorn apple, comes from the look of the fruit, which are covered in bristles and look somewhat like small green apples. Ornamental in their own right. Full sun.

Dianella caerulea

Dianella

FLAX LILY

I am including these plants (*Dianella tasmanica*, *D. caerulea*) because I have noticed that they are being sold in the American market, and most people have no idea what they even look like. They are annuals for most of us, perhaps hardy with good mulching to zone 7b. Plants have leaves much like an iris, rather forgettable, somewhat messy, and not much to write home about. The flowers are about 1" across at best, blue and yellow and quite disappointing if you are waiting for an iris flower. In and of themselves, they are handsome but can be overlooked if you walk by too quickly. However, the plant does have a nice habit, and its claim to fame, if you are lucky, is the dark blue berries that follow the flowers. They make a striking

Dianella caerulea, fruit

MORE ☞

Dianella tasmanica

Dianthus barbatus 'Cinderella Pink'

showing, and the fruit alone are worth the time. Best in containers. Overwinter in a warm area; they are too difficult to find to allow them to freeze. Full sun.

Dianthus

PINK

Annual China pink (*Dianthus chinensis*) and its hybrids, as well as the biennial sweet william (*D. barbatus*), are almost as popular as the perennial species. Sweet william doesn't fit neatly into categories like annual or perennial and, in general, requires a winter to provide the cold needed for flowering. Supposedly, it should be replaced after it flowers, but many biennial forms need replacing simply because they tire out, not because of their life cycle. Numerous cultivars have been selected; some like 'Cinderella Pink' are used exclusively for cut flowers because of their strong, lengthy stems. Plants in the Messenger series are also strong of stem and useful for cut flowers, but the shorter plants fit into a garden setting a little easier. Most sweet williams simply come as mixes and provide pastels and bright colors all spring. Cultivars can be located, but if you are going to the effort of searching, you might want to search for the dark flowered 'Sooty', one of the favorite stopping points at the Missouri Botanical Garden and also in Athens. A persistent, unique performer in both places.

China pinks are hardly seen at all in North American gardens because, in most parts of the country, they are wimpy and seldom live up to the picture found on the seed package. Let it not be said that they are not beautiful: I have trialed and seen beautiful examples, such as 'Parfait' and 'Rosemarie'; however, they simply didn't stay beautiful long enough. I think 'Snowfire', although old (it was an All-America Selection in 1978!), is the best of the China pinks, and it is still available.

The hybridization of sweet williams and China pinks, with the idea of combining the weather tolerance of the former with the long-flowering tendencies of the latter, has been accomplished, and the resulting hybrids (*Dianthus* ×*heddewigii*), such as 'Ideal Peace', have become immensely popular, being heartily embraced by gardeners and landscapers alike. In the South, combinations of white dianthus and purple pansies are planted in the fall, flower their heads off in March, and continue throughout the spring and into the summer. In the North, they can be planted in the fall as well, but most wait until early spring. In cool summers, they flower all summer. They look equally at home in large containers

Dianthus barbatus Messenger series

Dianthus chinensis 'Parfait'

Dianthus barbatus, garden

Dianthus chinensis 'Rosemarie'

Dianthus barbatus 'Sooty'

Dianthus chinensis 'Snowfire'

MORE ☞

showing off the architectural beauty of a fan palm, setting off the base of cold stonework, or showing off a warm picket fence. Colors and named forms are abundant, some of the better known being the Ideal series ('Ideal Red' makes a fine base to evergreen hedges on Sea Island, Georgia), and the timeless Telstar series, including 'Telstar Picotee', seen growing opposite in a garden in Swarthmore, Pennsylvania. We have conducted countless row trials of the hybrids in Georgia, and as uncreative as they are, 'Princess White', 'Festival Picotee', and others certainly illustrate the ample choices. The Diamond series

Dianthus hybrids with fan palm

Dianthus 'Ideal Red'

Dianthus hybrids with pansies

has become a favorite because of excellent performance throughout the country, and 'Diamond Purple' falling out of a bed is as good as any. So many of the hybrids have become available, it is difficult to find one that stands out from others, but 'First Love' probably fits that moniker. Flowers are of different colors and perform brilliantly almost everywhere I have seen them. In the Deep South (zone 8 and warmer), perhaps plants may need removal to make way for more heat-tolerant species, but in most of the country, they can remain and will flower well most of the season. They do prefer cool to hot, however. Full sun.

Dianthus hybrids with stonework

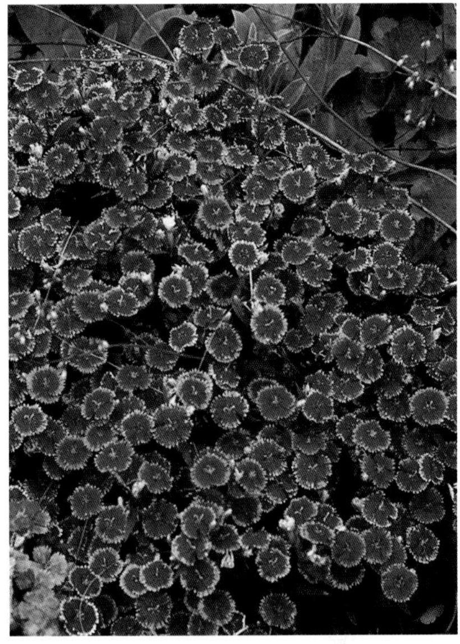
Dianthus 'Telstar Picotee'

Dianthus hybrids with picket fence

MORE ☞

Dianthus 'Ideal Peace'

Dianthus 'Diamond Purple'

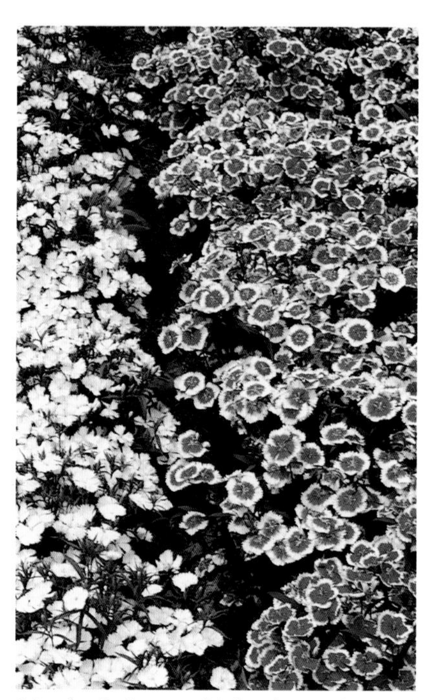

Dianthus 'Princess White', *D.* 'Festival Picotee'

Dianthus 'First Love'

Diascia

TWINSPUR

I enjoy teaching plant identification to students of all ages, and I especially love to show them how to teach a plant to someone else. The common name for this genus comes from the two appendages or spurs on the back of the petals, and once you point them out, nobody forgets the name twinspur. They may not remember the name diascia, but who cares?

Twinspurs have long been a fixture in the British Isles, and when I traveled to that area, I was blown away with the confident indifference twinspurs demonstrated in that climate. I saw many species, including the spectacular rigid diascia, *Diascia rigescens*. I came home eager to experiment, and even yelled at our breeders to get some diascias in the country so we could trial them! They are doing just that, and

Diascia rigescens

Diascia hybrid, basket

Diascia 'Kate'

Diascia 'Rupert Lambert'

Diascia 'Emma'

Diascia 'Lilac Mist'

MORE ☞

Diascia 'Little Charmer'

Diascia 'Ruby Field'

Diascia 'Sun Chimes Red'

Diascia 'Coral Belle'

Diascia 'Red Ace', flowers

Diascia 'Whisper Dark Apricot'

Diascia 'Sun Chimes Coral' with bacopa

diascias in this country just keep getting better. North American companies are making a slow but concentrated effort to make twinspur a mainstream annual, and although it has a way to catch up to petunias and begonias, progress is being made. In Athens, hardly a hotspot for twinspurs, we row out these hybrids and enjoy flowers in the spring, then let them fill in so we can enjoy them again in the fall. We put 'Rupert Lambert' by the brick walkway and other hybrids in hanging baskets around the gazebo. Who said research had to boring?

The problem for much of the country is that the heat in the summer sucks the flower power out of many diascias. None have the weather tolerance of a begonia, but if they don't have to be perfect, there are some wonderful forms out there right now, and they're getting better every year. I planted a couple of ladies some years ago, and both 'Kate' and

MORE ☞

Diascia 'Red Ace'

'Emma' provided strong colors on short stems. Red and rose are common colors, but 'Lilac Mist' has proven to be a favorite because of its upright habit and unique color. 'Little Charmer' also provided handsome color but grew only 3–4" tall. One of the oldest of available twinspurs is 'Ruby Field', a so-so cultivar that looks far better in Portland than in Cincinnati; she doesn't have the weather tolerance needed for inclement places. Equally old but a marvelous performer in all weather is 'Coral Belle', number one in our cultivar trials a few years ago in Athens. Tough, available, and beautiful to boot.

When pots of 'Sun Chimes Red' first appeared on the scene, they made people's heads turn. In the garden, they lose that "flash" but still do well. A combination of 'Sun Chimes Coral' and white bacopa is pleasing to the eyes and can stay looking good for a long time. Outdoors, I have been most impressed with the performance of the Whisper series, and 'Whisper Dark Apricot' takes a backseat to none. One of the problems with twinspurs has been their relative lack of vigor. The cultivars I have included here, for the most part, perform with sufficient vigor to overcome the difficulties of warm, humid summers; however, if you decide to plant 'Red Ace', do it quickly and get out of the way. This thing grows and grows, swallowing up all other poor diascias in its path. Plants flower well in the spring, grow all summer, and kick butt again in the fall. Most twinspurs show reasonable cold tolerance as well, often overwintering if sufficient snow cover is received but usually hardy to zone 7b. Full sun.

Duranta erecta

GOLDEN DEWDROP

I have admired golden dewdrop (*Duranta erecta*) ever since somebody pointed out the verbena-like blue flowers many years ago. And there I was in Perth, Australia, minding my own business when I rounded a corner and was greeted by a 30' high specimen; it blew me away! Of course, under cover of the darkness of night, I clipped a few branches, rooted them, and brought them back to Athens. The plant is pretty impressive even in Georgia; though it is only about 5' tall, it bears hundreds of flowers and fruits.

In Florida and the Gulf Coast, plants are considered shrubs and will be perennial perhaps as far north as zone 7, but the rest of us should think of them as annuals. The species itself is the most

Duranta erecta, flowers

common, bearing many small but handsome blue flowers all summer. If you have a long summer, or if you have a hot season, clusters of round golden fruit will begin to form in late summer; and if frost does not come too early, the plant will be laden with these golden clusters of grapes. Unfortunately, the fruit doesn't want to form until August, and many northern gardeners may not enjoy the late color. Still, the plant, even without the fruit, is well worth growing.

Several interesting cultivars have hit the marketplace in the last few years. Probably the one that has elicited the most interest is 'Sapphire Showers', a wonderful upright form with dark blue flowers bearing a white stripe. This should become quite popular. A couple of variegated forms provide a wonderful contrast of colors, depending on which form you can find. 'Variegata' brings a riot of green and white leaves. This form remains more prostrate and looks particularly good falling over itself, falling out of a container. 'Gold Edge' is very striking with its green and yellow foliage and upright habit. Neither are as large as the species, nor do they produce signifi-

MORE

Duranta erecta, fruit

Duranta erecta, Australia

Duranta erecta 'Variegata'

Duranta erecta var. *aurea*

Duranta erecta 'Gold Edge'

cant flowers or fruit. Another new form, with golden foliage and a dwarf habit (var. *aurea*), should become quite popular, perhaps even as an edging plant.

A word of warning. Depending on where the plants came from, they may bear some serious thorns. In nature, the species has a long thorn at each node, but cultivated forms are often thornless and should be sought out. The variegated forms are also armed and dangerous, but 'Sapphire Showers' is not. Don't poke your head in the middle of any of them. Full sun.

Echium

BUGLOSS

The echiums are most famous for the rocketship-looking plants with such wonderful names as pride of Tenerife (*Echium simplex*) or pride of Madeira (*E. candicans*), which you may discover on your fantasy trip to the Canary Islands or in gardens in southwest England. But not here, at least not outside conservatories. Great fun to visit, see them in such exotic places, but not a snowball's chance in hell that they would be gardened here. However, that doesn't mean we have to ignore the whole genus, because there is at least one terrific plant, and another may be worth a try.

Finding started plants of annual bugloss, *Echium vulgare*, will be difficult, but seeds are easily available. The grow only about 1' tall but are full of flowers. They are categorized as biennials, and the first year they may flower a little but won't be terribly exciting. Next year, however, they will be chock-full of blue to violet flowers, particularly in the spring and early summer. They are tough and provide a nice show with little effort.

We planted the species to greet visitors as they walked into the garden, but if I had it to do again, I would choose its much nicer selection, 'Blue Bedder'. They will tolerate full sun but have no

Echium vulgare 'Blue Bedder'

Echium candicans

Echium vulgare

problem in the midst of shade lovers like hostas. Another form I have tried, although for the most part quite unsuccessfully, is the red bugloss, *Echium amoenum*. I first saw it at Kew Gardens in England and was determined to find some seeds (which I did) and then revel in its beauty, which I did not because it was not. Probably Georgia was not to its liking. But that is no excuse for you: try some so you can do some reveling. Full sun to partial shade.

Emilia

TASSEL FLOWER

A little-known wildflower of India, Polynesia, and tropical Africa, tassel flower finds its way to gardens here and there

MORE ☞

Echium amoenum

Emilia javanica, flowers

Emilia sonchifolia

Emilia javanica, UGA Trial Gardens

for its flowers, which are useful as fillers in the garden and in the vase. The common species are the scarlet-flowered *Emilia javanica* and its closely related cousin, *E. sonchifolia*, better known for its orange flowers. They are similar in habit and ease of gardening. We grew what seemed like a ton of them in our cut flower trials, but maybe it seemed like that because we cut every stem and those we missed reseeded to make more, and more and more. It took us less than four weeks to fuel a major dislike of this weed; however, it was impossible not to admire its tenacity and color. And plants do make wonderful additions to the garden. The golden yellow forms were much more beloved than the red. They will reseed, so finding the seed should only be a one-time necessity. Full sun.

Erysimum

WALLFLOWER

The genus is probably best known for short-lived perennials, but without doubt the best and most colorful of the group are the wallflowers, all now classified under *Erysimum*, which used to be part of the genus *Cheiranthus*. Plants are technically biennials, although some flowering may occur the first year from seed. Nothing is brighter and fresher in the spring than a well-grown planting of wallflowers, either overwintered in a cool greenhouse prior to being sold at the garden center or overwintered in the garden. Unfortunately, for many gardeners the former is necessary, because plants don't overwinter much above zone 6.

When gardeners think of wallflowers, mostly they think of orange or yellow flowers, and hybrids (*Erysimum* ×*marshallii*) like 'Orange Bedder' and 'Yellow Bedder' are popular for good reason, whether complementing spring iris or planted on a wall for passers-by. 'Gold Bedder' provides softer color but with similar habit and vigor, and the flowers of 'Golden Gem' are equally handsome but on much shorter stems. A number of rainbow cultivars have also been developed, and while I am partial to the soft mauve of 'Constant Cheer', which only grows about 9" tall, I welcome the brighter, feistier colors of 'Warlock Beauty' as well. Not for the faint of heart, but they sure make spring more interesting.

In hot-summer climates, they should be removed after flowering. If the seeds are allowed to fall, they will germinate in late summer, and, if seeds are not killed by the cold, the plants should reappear next spring. Full sun.

Erysimum, United Kingdom

Erysimum 'Orange Bedder'

Erysimum 'Golden Gem'

Erysimum 'Yellow Bedder'

Erysimum 'Constant Cheer'

Erysimum 'Gold Bedder'

Erysimum 'Warlock Beauty'

Eschscholzia

CALIFORNIA POPPY

The name of this genus is a good example of why gardeners don't always embrace the joy of learning botanical nomenclature. Where did all those sch's come from and why? Well, turns out the plant was named for German physician and naturalist Johann Friedrich Eschscholtz, whose family had settled in Russia and whose original name "Escholtz" picked up another "sch" on the retranslation, back from Cyrillic to German. So now you know the rest of the story. By the way, the genus is pronounced "esh *olts* ee a."

The stunning orange flowers of California poppies (*Eschscholzia californica*) have became extraordinarily popular all over the country, not only for their brilliant color, but also because they seed

Eschscholzia californica with wallflowers

Eschscholzia californica, naturalized

Eschscholzia californica 'Lilac Gleam'

easily into naturalistic plantings. They are tough enough to be planted by busy roadways but also look at home in gardens, complementing wallflowers. Where they are allowed to naturalize, the orange flowers and the ferny foliage truly make an eye-catching vista in May.

Although most of the California poppies are flaming orange, other colors have been selected. 'Lilac Gleam' bears flowers in shades of lilac and purple, and one of my favorites has to be the simple white-flowered 'Alba'. Not as brilliant—perhaps that is why I enjoy it so.

Euphorbia

SPURGE

The most popular member of this genus, by far, is the Christmas poinsettia, and although many gardeners are either too attached or too cheap to get

Eschscholzia californica, roadside

Euphorbia milii

Eschscholzia californica 'Alba'

Euphorbia cyathophora

MORE ☞

rid of them, they will never become a garden plant. However, several annual euphorbs are sufficiently interesting or beautiful to include in the garden. Some are classically handsome, others can be said to be weird, which means that we will see more of it in the future. One such weird member that is sneaking into gardens is *Euphorbia milii*, which cannot be said to be shy.

Some gardeners, yours truly not included, find fire-on-the-mountain, *Euphorbia cyathophora*, interesting. Perhaps it is the name, because the name is probably the best part. Like a poinsettia, bracts turn red in late summer and fall, but there is very little va-va-voom to the plant. Interesting is the best thing I can say. However, if it is interest you want, you have to love gopher spurge, *E. lathyris*. A biennial, this plant supposedly releases chemicals that repel your hungry gophers, moles, and voles. I have not tested the theory, but gopher spurge has always remained standing in the Armitage garden, so it must work. Regardless of its properties, gopher spurge is a fascinating plant in its own right. The plant has handsome gray-green foliage, and where the stems branch near the top of the plant you may find the small white flowers. They are nothing to get excited about, but they give way to lovely purple fruit in the summer. If allowed to ripen, the seeds will germinate, assuring the continued presence of plants in the garden.

Euphorbia lathyris, flowers

Euphorbia lathyris, fruit

Euphorbia marginata 'Kilimanjaro'

Euphorbia marginata, cut flowers

I have seen it growing in the middle of gardens or by rock walls; I am never sure just where it will appear next.

The best known of the garden annuals is snow-on-the-mountain, *Euphorbia marginata*. Planted in early spring, plants will grow rapidly, showing off variegated foliage as they mature. With sufficient heat, plants can grow 3–4' tall, and when they flower, they produce clean white bracts. The flowers are white as well, but it is the bracts and the leaves that provide the show. 'Kilimanjaro' is a handsome compact selection with many clean white bracts. Where heat is less prevalent, such as in the Portland area, plants are equally beautiful but not as tall. This snowy plant is also useful for its cut stems; after cutting put the stem in boiling water or sear it on a hot plate to stop the flow of latex. Remember, all euphorbs have milky sap, and it can be quite irritating, so keep it away from your face, particularly your eyes. Full sun to partial shade.

Eustoma grandiflorum

LISIANTHUS, PRAIRIE GENTIAN

Prairie gentians are, as one might surmise, native to the American prairies, yet the actual wildflower is nowhere to be seen in North American gardens. But plant breeders around the world have discovered its marvelous properties as a cut flower, and flowers have been bred into a myriad of colors, occurring as

Euphorbia marginata

Eustoma grandiflorum 'Blue Liza'

Eustoma grandiflorum 'Avila Purple'

Eustoma grandiflorum 'Yodel Lilac'

MORE ☞

Eustoma grandiflorum 'Forever White'

Eustoma grandiflorum 'Avila Deep Rose'

Eustoma grandiflorum 'Echo White'

Eustoma grandiflorum 'Sapphire Pink Rim'

Eustoma grandiflorum 'Sapphire Blue Chip'

Eustoma grandiflorum 'Florida Blue'

singles or doubles in florists' coolers across the country. Sad to say, the majority of our native plants come back home from production facilities overseas. Cultivars for cut flower use abound, and they are beautiful. Just look at the Avila series, sold throughout the world and including 'Avila Deep Rose' and 'Avila Purple'. Some of the tougher cut flower cultivars are also at home in the garden, particularly the Yodel series (single flowers) and the Echo series (double). 'Yodel Lilac' and 'Echo White' have performed quite well in outdoor beds in Athens.

Most cut flower forms are too expensive, too tall, or too scarce to ever use them in the garden, and breeders have come up with dwarfer forms that make more sense for smaller areas. An excellent choice is 'Blue Liza', with dozens of flowers covering a compact habit, but 'Florida Blue' is almost as good, and with a little more heat tolerance. I have always enjoyed the white-flowered forms of lisianthus in the garden, and 'Forever White' makes a nice clean selection. But look what they have done to our flower! I stared in awe or perhaps morbid fascination at the meatballing of our prairie flower. The Sapphire series is impossible to ignore, and 'Sapphire Blue Chip' and 'Sapphire Pink Rim' may be abominations for purists but are wildly fascinating to those who admire detail.

Most areas of the country will be successful with lisianthus in the spring and early summer. They tend to decline in the heat and humidity of a warm summer, never to be seen again. Enjoy them while you can, indoors and out. Full sun.

Evolvulus pilosus

BLUE DAZE

Blue daze (*Evolvulus pilosus*) is one of those plants you can pass by one day, then stop the next and wonder why you

MORE ☞

Evolvulus pilosus 'Blue Daze', groundcover, with lantana

Evolvulus pilosus 'Blue Daze'

Evolvulus pilosus, garden

hadn't noticed it before. The plants are excellent in baskets and containers and as a low-growing groundcover.

They are only about 6–9" tall and flower most of the season. From a distance or on miserable overcast days, the flowers may not be terribly noticeable, but they make a terrific show most of the time. At the University of Georgia, plants are often used with 'New Gold' lantana, and while they work together from a distance, the blue flowers must be seen close-up to be appreciated. In small beds, they stay low, peeking out from their neighbors, to provide months of white-centered blue flowers to enjoy. Full sun to partial shade.

Felicia amelloides

BLUE MARGUERITE

I have always admired the wonderful blue flower of *Felicia amelloides*, especially on the West Coast or in Europe, but it does not get a fair shake in the East. True enough, plants prefer cooler nights and less humid conditions than those found in parts of the East, but not to try this at least once is to overlook a great offering. Even in the South, they will look terrific until temperatures refuse to budge out of the 90s.

They stand only about 15" tall, and they can vary from the lightest to the darkest blue. In the Butchart Gardens, they were so pale that they were almost white, whereas in Santa Barbara, Cali-

Felicia amelloides, Butchart Gardens

Felicia amelloides, California

Felicia amelloides 'Santa Anita'

Felicia amelloides 'Variegata'

Felicia amelloides 'Read's Blue'

fornia, the bold blue flowers showed off their yellow centers to busy passers-by. They make excellent container plants or will color up the front of a garden without trouble and continue to flower for months on end.

A few cultivars have been selected, but a thorough search may be needed to procure them. I believe the dwarfer form, 'Read's Blue', is well worth the effort as plants can cavort with sages or reside in rock gardens with equal ease. 'Santa Anita' has larger flowers and is coarser than other forms, not particularly attractive where I have seen it. The most common, and by far the least handsome, is 'Variegata', whose yellow and white and blue all seem to get jumbled together. But there are so many people who love variegation of any kind—there is no reasoning with them. Full sun to partial shade.

Fuchsia

My grandmother loved her fuchsias. Living in a small house in Montreal, she drank tea under her catalpa tree, where she could admire her baskets of fuchsias. When I travel to Europe, especially Germany, there does not seem to be a bare piece of ground or empty container that half a dozen fuchsias have not been thrust into. California and the Northwest are hotbeds for the cool-loving plant, but Long Island and the Northeast also have their fair share of fuchsites. Living in the

Fuchsia corymbiflora

Fuchsia ×hybrida 'Annabelle'

Fuchsia ×hybrida 'Sonata'

MORE ☞

Fuchsia magellanica

Fuchsia ×*hybrida* 'Checkerboard'

Fuchsia magellanica 'Rosea'

Fuchsia ×*hybrida* 'Cascading Angel Earrings'

Fuchsia ×*hybrida* 'Beacon'

Fuchsia ×*hybrida* 'Golden Marinka'

South, I am able to grow only a few of these plants, and while I can grow countless other things, I still miss them when I see them in their glory.

Over 8000 cultivars of fuchsia have been listed, yet few of them ever see the light of day in our gardens. For the species and many of the cultivars, mail-order sources, specialty nurseries, and Internet garden rooms are your best bet. But then again, who needs 8000 when most of us are happy when we can select from half a dozen? For the hard-core fuchsite, a few species are sold, and if you can nurture them, have a go. The long pendulous flowers of *Fuchsia corymbiflora* are awesome, but you may die of old age looking for it in "normal" outlets. Magellan's fuchsia, *F. magellanica*, is quite common in Europe and South America, and is an important hybrid in the long-flowered hybrids. By themselves, the normal red type and the pink 'Rosea' are vigorous and handsome, and used as hedges where they are hardy. Many gardeners feel that the species is as cold hardy and heat-tolerant as any of the hybrids. Most of the fuchsias sold today are hybrids (*F.* ×*hybrida*), with a myriad of different parents. These are the selections you will find crammed into a 12" basket at your local garden center. They all start out beautifully, but they require attention to watering and feeding when you get them home. The more heat in the summer, the more attention must be paid.

Where to start for cultivars? 'Dark Ice' is nearly always used in baskets (many outlets offer all cultivars that way). I can heartily recommend 'Cascading Angel Earrings' as the most heat-tolerant

Fuchsia ×*hybrida* 'Dark Ice'

Fuchsia ×*hybrida* 'Mrs Lovell Swisher'

Fuchsia ×*hybrida* 'Thalia'

Fuchsia ×*hybrida* 'Gartenmeister Bonstedt', container

MORE ☞

selection we have trialed. Nothing fancy, but it works. There is no end to colors and shapes that breeders have created, and it is a losing argument to proclaim one more beautiful than the other; like politics and religion, there is no correct answer. Pinkish and plump-ish can describe the flowers of the popular 'Annabelle', pinkish and obese may be better descriptors for 'Sonata'. Probably more red fuchsias, such as 'Beacon', are sold than any other, but flowers with more than one color are also popular. 'Mrs Lovell Swisher' is one of the many bicolored fuchsias, in this case white (sepals) and red (petals), and she is not alone in her abstract art. 'Checkerboard', with its narrow white sepals, and the larger-flowered 'Loveliness' are but two examples. A half-dozen variegated forms may be grown as well, and they can be striking or strikingly awful. I enjoy 'Golden Marinka' and especially 'Pink Veins', perhaps because it is more subdued than others.

Fuchsia ×hybrida 'Loveliness'

Fuchsia ×hybrida 'Pink Veins'

Fuchsia ×hybrida 'Koralle'

Fuchsia ×hybrida 'Gartenmeister Bonstedt', garden

A group of fuchsias that has become immensely popular in the last ten years are the triphylla, or three-leaf, hybrids. As the number of gardeners continues to expand, so do the boundaries of trial and error. Everyone wants to take the fuchsia they grew in Winnipeg or Santa Barbara and try it out in Atlanta or Dallas. Young gardeners see a fuchsia in the store and without a second thought, buy it, ignore it, and kill it. The triphyllas were trumpeted as possible help for this intolerance-of-heat-and-abuse problem, which gets in the way of two-thirds of the population enjoying these fine plants. Has the hype worked? The answer is a definite maybe. The triphyllas are more tolerant of abuse, but they are still fuchsias and still need attention to keep them looking good. Look for 'Thalia' and 'Koralle', both excellent performers in containers or the garden. The most popular of this popular group is probably 'Gartenmeister Bonstedt', thankfully shortened to 'Gartenmeister'. Plants have enjoyed an excellent reputation for performance, and they are classically handsome in containers or complementing other annuals like ornamental tobacco. If you have all but given up on fuchsias, try this one. If it still does not make you happy, spend your money on wine, then look again.

All fuchsias need consistent water; if they dry out, they will seldom recover. They look fine planted in the garden just like other plants, and if you can find an upright standard, you will reduce the problems of drying out. If using baskets or containers, use as large a size as possible, cramping their style will only cramp yours. Fertilize with a liquid fertilizer two or three times a season. Cool weather is always preferred to heat, and afternoon shade will be appreciated.

Gaillardia

BLANKET FLOWER

Most people recognize the genus as a perennial; however, the main annual species (*Gaillardia pulchella*) flowers longer and provides more choice of color. Although they are native to the southern United States, the annual species are not easy to locate in the garden shop, but many and various cultivars of *G. pulchella* have arrived on the scene to add to our annual palette.

Many of the selections bear rounded double to semi-double flowers; some (but not all) cultivars may be unnamed. 'Yellow Plume' flowers profusely on 12–15" tall plants, and I consider 'Yellow Queen' equally beautiful, if not identical: they may in fact be the same thing under different names. The Lollipop series was a popular selection in the 1980s; however, it is a little tall and is knocked

Gaillardia pulchella cultivars

MORE ☞

down by rain or wind. The Sundance series is an improvement and provides a number of color choices; 'Sundance Bicolor' is quite wonderful, and more compact than the older forms. Grown easily from seed, and occasionally will reseed. Full sun.

In 1996, I happened across an unusual white-flowered gaillardia in Mercer Botanic Gardens in Humble, Texas. Plants were on the endangered list in Texas, but I was given permission to collect seeds and see what they did in Athens. The plant is *Gaillardia aestivalis*

Gaillardia pulchella 'Sundance Bicolor'

Gaillardia pulchella 'Yellow Plume'

Gaillardia aestivalis var. *winkleri*, Texas

Gaillardia pulchella Lollipop series

Gaillardia aestivalis var. *winkleri*, purple form, UGA Trial Gardens

Gaillardia pulchella 'Yellow Queen'

var. *winkleri*, otherwise called white firewheel. To make a long story short, they did extraordinarily well, provided rich shades of purple as well as white, and have been perennial in our zone 7b garden. They are beautiful in every way, and we are making selections with the seed that has formed. Plantsmen at Steven F. Austin State University in Nacogdoches, Texas, are also working on domesticating the plant, and with a little luck, seed of selected cultivars will be available through seed companies in the near future. Full sun, sandy soils.

Gazania

TREASURE FLOWER

These South African plants sport some of the most beautiful and wonderfully detailed flowers among all the daisies.

MORE ☞

Gaillardia aestivalis var. *winkleri*, purple and white forms, UGA Trial Gardens

Gazania rigens has been sold for years as a bedding plant and exceptional colors have been developed. In many areas of the country, however, the heat and humidity of normal summers take their toll, and plants often melt out by July. While this continues to be the case in warmer areas, gazanias are becoming a little tougher. Hybridization with other species has helped. Their flowers are so beautiful, it is difficult to walk by a well-grown specimen in the garden center

Gazania rigens 'Ministar White'

Gazania rigens 'Sundance Yellow'

Gazania rigens 'Chansonette Yellow'

Gazania rigens 'Chansonette Pink'

Gazania rigens 'Daybreak Bronze'

Gazania rigens 'Daybreak Red Striped'

Gazania 'Double Yellow'

without wanting to take it home and plunk it in the garden.

The breeders have been busy, providing a number of series, each one supporting numerous color choices and often handsome gray-green foliage. The Sundance series was one of the earlier ones, 'Sundance Yellow' providing gardeners an insight of the potential the genus held. The Chansonette series lent 'Chansonette Yellow' and 'Chansonette Pink' to the garden palette, and Daybreak series came along with even more colors, and somewhat shorter plants. 'Daybreak Bronze' and Daybreak Red

Gazania rigens Klondyke series

Gazania 'Variegated Orange'

Gazania 'Orange Beauty'

Gazania linearis

MORE ☞

Striped' became quite popular. One of the problems with many of these selections was that they were a little too tall, and rain or wind could wreak havoc in the garden. They already had problems with heat and humidity, so shorter selections were called for. The Ministar series, such as 'Ministar White', and the Klondyke series have provided some of the shortening needed.

Gazania 'Waterlily'

But numerous other hybrids, incorporating the linear-leaf gazania, *Gazania linearis*, and other species, have also been developed, often with more handsome foliage and shorter stature. 'Double Yellow' provides a double-flowered selection, while 'Orange Beauty' allows for clean yellow flowers on short plants. Even variegated foliage is available, as found in 'Variegated Orange'; such variegated plants will become more readily available in the future but probably as vegetative material only. 'Waterlily' is an outstanding white-flowered gazania; flowers were bred in Australia, I am not sure if it is available in North America.

I mentioned that *Gazania linearis* was incorporated into the hybrids. This low-growing prolific flowerer is an outstanding plant on its own, but perhaps the more abusive climates on this continent have kept it out of our stores, because I never see it offered. Selections of this fine plant include 'Peggy's Pet', a mounding cultivar with silvery foliage and handsome orange flowers. Full sun to afternoon shade. Well-drained soils a must.

Gazania linearis 'Peggy's Pet'

Gerbera jamesonii

TRANSVAAL DAISY

Gerbera jamesonii has come a long way from its humble beginnings as a South African daisy. Gerberas have been bred to within an inch of their lives in Europe and have become major cut flowers for florists and designers all over the world. And they are beautiful! Grown in the sensual conditions of a heated greenhouse, they are cut, wrapped, and shipped without a blemish to enjoy some neighborly camaraderie with other flowers in the vase. Mixes like Gigi provide long stems and dazzling colors.

Outdoors, however, they are not quite as impressive, suffering from heavy rain, heat, and humidity, which are common to most of our gardens. Breeders have concentrated most of their efforts on cut flower varieties, but several dwarf forms suitable for the landscape have been developed. One of the first successful introductions was 'Happipot', which provided white, yellow, and red flowers, looked good in a container, and only grew about 18" tall. Similar flowers were seen in 'Mardi Gras' and other old cultivars. The brighter colors were (and still are) all the rage, but flowers in Masquerade Pastel Mix provided soft pastels pinks, salmons, and whites. The Masquerade series was bred for outdoor performance and has looked quite good, particularly the bright colors of 'Masquerade Scarlet'. Recently the Festival series appeared with 3" wide flowers on 10–12" tall plants. Beautiful in the pot, but like most others, they decline if the weather becomes abusive in the garden. Breeding of new landscape cultivars has slowed down, mainly because efforts

Gerbera jamesonii 'Happipot'

Gerbera jamesonii 'Mardi Gras'

Gerbera jamesonii 'Masquerade Pastel White', *G. j.* 'Masquerade Pastel Pink'

Gerbera jamesonii 'Masquerade Scarlet'

Gerbera jamesonii Festival series

Gerbera jamesonii Wolfpack Country series

have been concentrated on breeding more lucrative cut flower types; however, series like Wolfpack Country pop up every now and then and brighten the landscape one more time. Regardless of the color or name, all gerberas make excellent long-lasting cut flowers and are useful for entertaining.

Plants are better in containers than in the garden. Full sun to partial shade.

Gilia leptantha

Gilia capitata

Gilia

Native to California, gilias are wildflowers in the Sierra mountains but seldom seen in gardens, certainly not in the East. I have seen gilias here and there, but to grow them in the garden requires searching through seed catalogs and germinating your own plants. Two species are available from seed, and both sport handsome blue flowers on short plants.

Fine-leaf gilia, *Gilia leptantha*, has fine, almost filigreed leaves and wonderful light blue flowers, whereas globe gilia, *G. capitata*, bears much more rounded flowers and less divided leaves. They are most at home in open ground where drainage is excellent. Don't expect long-lasting performance in hot, humid gardens. Seeds of both may be found by consulting wildflower or meadow-flower catalogs online. Full sun.

Gladiolus

I have difficulty getting excited about gladioli as garden plants. They remind me of orchids: fabulous flowers, ugly plants. The hybrids (*Gladiolus* ×*hybridus*) are grown from corms, which are removed each fall to be replanted in the spring. The hybrids have been intensely bred but mostly for cut flower use, and one can see acres of flowers meant for florists and designers everywhere. As beautiful as many flowers are, the plants are often isolated and banished to the "cut flower" area of the garden, which is probably a good thing. A bucket of cut glads can bring a lot of joy to a lot of friends. Even in the overbred hybrids, a number of beautiful forms are available to discerning gardeners, and the dwarf forms can actually be incorporated into the garden. I have always loved the white flowers of 'The Bride', and it is hard not to get excited by cultivars such as the brilliant 'Robinetta'.

Gladiolus, cut flower field

Gladiolus, cut flowers

Gladiolus 'Robinetta'

MORE ☞

While the great bulk of glads fall into the cut flower hybrid category, a couple of species are well worth growing. I have always been impressed with the Byzantine gladiolus, *Gladiolus communis* subsp. *byzantinus*, because of the ease of growth and the wonderful electric-burgundy flower color. They are at home everywhere in the country, looking good in the garden as well as the flower vase.

Another marvelous plant to try is the Abyssinian glad, *G. callianthus* (aka *Acidanthera*), whose white flowers with a purple center also have a wonderful fragrance. The only cultivar available is 'Muralis', and corms are easy to find and easy to grow.

All glads should be planted as soon as frost is past, all can be cut when the first flower has opened. Corms should be dug and stored north of zones 8 to ensure perenniality. Full sun.

Glaucium

HORNED POPPY

When people see horned poppies, they are as impressed with the blue-gray foliage as they are with the flowers and the long, horned fruit. The foliage is as much a reason to try these plants in the garden as any, and in particular, the leaves of the red horned poppy (*Glaucium corniculatum*) and the yellow horned poppy (*G. flavum*) are every bit

Gladiolus 'The Bride'

Gladiolus communis subsp. *byzantinus*

Gladiolus communis subsp. *byzantinus*, garden

Gladiolus callianthus

Glaucium corniculatum

Glaucium corniculatum in snow

Glaucium flavum

as handsome as the ubiquitous dusty miller. A colleague of mine said I should explain that "it's not a *real* poppy," so people wouldn't look for it under P in a catalog. I replied, "Anybody that dumb wouldn't be reading this book." Don't look under P.

Plants are quite winter hardy and reseed prolifically in cool locations. I have seen plants of the red horned poppy absolutely ecstatic in the late snow of a Denver spring, and the red flowers, which emerge in May and June, are quite marvelous. Yellow horned poppies are more common on the eastern side of the country and have equally beautiful foliage and bright yellow flowers. The flowers of both are produced throughout the season, but flowering is heaviest in the spring. The long narrow fruit are responsible for the common name, and seeds can be gathered for next year's plants. Well worth a try in cooler climates. Full sun.

Gloriosa superba

GLORY LILY

The first time I saw this weird but spectacular plant, *Gloriosa superba*, I assumed that no one would grow it outside conservatories and home greenhouses. The fact that it is expensive, somewhat finicky, and dislikes being transplanted would also have something to do with its absence from gardens. However, it is for sale in many catalogs, I see it imprisoned in bulb bags at the local box store, and, sure as heck, people do grow it.

The deciduous climber comes from a tuber; if possible, start it indoors in a peat container three to four weeks prior to placing into a larger container outdoors. It can scramble through shrubs, but most people prefer to put it on a trellis in a protected area of the patio. Plants will not flower until mid to late summer, depending on heat, but what a dazzling show they provide.

MORE ☞

Gloriosa superba 'Rothschildiana'

Gloriosa superba 'Citrina'

The most common form is 'Rothschildiana', an amazing combination of red and yellow on delightfully fashioned flowers. However, if you are not the gaudy sort, you might want to look for 'Citrina', a wonderful shade of yellow. Equally beautiful but without the flash. Full sun in the North, afternoon shade in the South. Bring in to a frost-free area after the first kiss of frost outdoors.

Gomphrena

"Want tough, try gomphrena!" That could make an advertisement on television to rival James Bond or Spiderman. Those guys have nothing on the globe amaranth (*Gomphrena globosa*). Starting out as a persistent weed in the tropics, it has been morphed into a bedding and landscape plant with few equals for perseverance. That does not mean that everyone likes it, or that it is the prettiest plant in the landscape, only that it spits out the heat of a southwestern summer, tolerates the rain in Portland, and thrives in the gardens of Boston. It is a common member in gardens, meandering through cosmos and other annuals, and it can fill in entire islands in busy downtown areas. Of course, any plant that is that tough will also be sought after as a cut flower, both fresh and dried, and in

Gomphrena globosa 'Buddy White'

combination with yellow craspedia and pink centaurea, it holds its own.

Gardeners can choose from low-growing forms such as the Buddy series, including 'Buddy White', or the Gnome series, such as 'Gnome Purple' and 'Gnome White', all of which stay around knee-high. One of the most popular forms for cut flowers and for landscapes is 'Strawberry Fields', possessing a brilliant strawberry color that does not fade throughout the summer. In the landscape or in a vase by itself, it is an outstanding choice. But numerous other choices are available, all of them tough

Gomphrena globosa, garden

Gomphrena globosa 'Gnome Purple'

Gomphrena globosa, landscape island

MORE ☞

as nails. 'All Around Purple' is a bright choice for the garden whose opposite might be 'Lavender', far more subdued but an equal performer. One of my favorites was the recently developed 'Bicolor Rose', whose flowers are like the Energizer Bunny, they just keep going and going. As a garden plant or cut flower, it is tough to beat. Other species are occasionally found in garden centers, such as Haage's amaranth, *Gomphrena haageana*, but plants are generally so similar there is little reason to choose one over the other. Some of the cultivars are likely hybrids anyway, but one selection that has pleasantly stood out for me was 'Apricot'. It was sufficiently different in color and form that I

Gomphrena globosa 'Gnome White'

Gomphrena globosa, cut flowers

Gomphrena globosa 'Strawberry Fields'

Gomphrena globosa 'Strawberry Fields', cut flowers

Gomphrena globosa 'All Around Purple'

Gomphrena globosa 'Lavender'

wanted to try it. Not quite the vigor of many of the others but pleasant nevertheless. Full sun.

Graptophyllum pictum

CARICATURE PLANT

Another plant that was hidden for years in the bowels of conservatories and tropical greenhouses, *Graptophyllum pictum* has arisen from obscurity and become a popular plant for containers and gardens. Caricature plants are grown for their wonderful leathery foli-

Gomphrena globosa 'Bicolor Rose'

Gomphrena haageana 'Apricot'

Graptophyllum pictum 'Chocolate'

MORE ☞

age; flowers are not often formed except in the winter in heated greenhouses. For hot, humid, and drought-stricken gardens, this is the ticket.

The three main cultivars provide architectural interest and long-season enjoyment. The most popular is 'Chocolate', with dark purple leaves bisected with pink veins. An easy plant for combination plantings. 'Tricolor' is just that, a kaleidoscope of colors, not harsh or brutal but easy on the eyes. And in keeping with the trend for dark purple and black in plants, 'Black Beauty' is perfect. All selections are upright and ridiculously easy to grow. They laugh

Graptophyllum pictum 'Chocolate', garden

Graptophyllum pictum 'Tricolor'

Graptophyllum pictum 'Tricolor', garden

at heat, look good wherever they are placed and then, like good annuals, fall apart when temperatures dip into the high 30s. Easily found in good garden shops. Full sun.

Hamelia patens

TEXAS FIREBUSH

The common name for *Hamelia patens* immediately tells us two things. If you guessed that the Texas part probably means it loves heat and that the firebush has to do with the color, you would be right on. When I saw the plants thriving in the hellish August heat and brutal sun of San Antonio and then equally at home

MORE ☞

Graptophyllum pictum 'Black Beauty'

Hamelia patens, fall color

Hamelia patens, hedge, Texas

Hamelia patens, flowers

as a hedge in the Mercer Botanic Gardens outside Houston, I knew this would be a tough sell for the folks in Minot. However, as summers around the country heat up, the call for such colorful figures becomes stronger, but fair warning: they are not particularly vigorous until temperatures consistently remain above 80°F. Where they are happy, they make a brilliant showing of fire-red flowers and handsome green foliage, which will turn a brilliant burgundy in the fall.

Cultivars are not available; plants are generally raised from cuttings. For most gardeners in most of the country, they are best in containers by concrete, brick, or asphalt—that is, as brutal a location as possible. Full sun.

Helianthus

SUNFLOWER

How can there be so many different sunflowers? Van Gogh had it right when he painted the yellow kind, that is all there should be. But my oh my, how crowded the field has become. With all the bigger, brighter, bolder, dwarfer, larger, and seemingly better cultivars appearing

Helianthus annuus 'Ring of Fire'

Helianthus annuus 'Music Box'

Helianthus annuus, field

Helianthus annuus 'Sonya'

Helianthus annuus, dyed flowers

Helianthus annuus with lantana

Helianthus annuus 'Big Smile'

Helianthus annuus 'Crimson Thriller'

Helianthus annuus 'Chianti'

MORE ☞

every day, why is it that an old-fashioned field of sunflowers, grown for their seed, is still one of the prettiest sights on earth?

The sunflower (*Helianthus annuus*) has become the flower child for everything from coffee mugs to aprons and appears in vases in the sitting room and the boardroom. It has become a part of Americana, and a lovely one at that. Beats the heck out of the Confederate flag. As a cut flower, dozens of cultivars have been bred, ranging from 'Ring of Fire' to 'Sonya', and they are beautiful. However, there are always some people who feel that the natural colors need enhancing, and they vandalize the poor flower with gruesome dyes.

As garden plants, there is no end to what is out there, and one can find them standing off by themselves or mixed in with lantanas in the garden. They are all raised from seed, and the limiting factor as to what to grow is the availability of seed. I have seen well over eighty different cultivars of sunflowers, but I bet I couldn't lay my hands on more than a dozen. But what a wonderful dozen they would be.

The dwarf forms are becoming more popular, simply because they don't need staking and don't fall over. 'Music Box' is a handsome 2' form, and 'Big Smile' is even grown in containers, so that the large flowers can really be seen. The short and tall of it must include some of the big guys, and I figure if I am going to grow a 7' plant, it had better be impressive. The shimmering flowers of 'Crimson Thriller' are beautiful, and everybody can admire the flowers of 'Chianti',

Helianthus annuus 'Valentine'

Helianthus annuus 'Italian White'

Helianthus annuus 'Sun Goddess'

Helianthus annuus 'Sunbright'

if they are tall enough to see them. It is obvious that there is more than yellow to a sunflower, as attested by the pale yellow of 'Valentine' and the small white flowers of 'Italian White'.

But yellow is the dominant color, and there seem to be enough shades and shapes to keep everyone looking. 'Sun Goddess' and 'Sunbright' are attractive yellow flowers with large dark centers and look every bit the part of a sunflower. But if you don't pay attention, you may miss the double forms, two of which are 'Helios' and the beautiful 'Goldburst'. They hardly look like sunflowers, but people really love them.

All the previous cultivars belong to a single species of annual sunflower, but more is yet to come. I believe we will see more of the marvelous silver-leaf sunflower, *Helianthus argophyllus*. It is fabulous even when not in flower, the silvery leaves always an eye-grabber in the

MORE ☞

Helianthus annuus 'Helios'

Helianthus annuus 'Goldburst'

Helianthus argophyllus, container

Helianthus argophyllus, flowers

ground or in a container. The flowers are nothing to write home about, but they provide the classic sunflower look, and that is certainly not all bad. This is a sleeper, about to become a winner.

All sunflowers, especially *Helianthus annuus*, decline rapidly after flowering. The further South, the more rapid and the earlier the deterioration. Simply place another seed beside the plant when it begins to bud up, and as it begins to decline, the new plant will be attaining maturity. Pull out the old one, and voilà, you can enjoy them all over again. Full sun, lots of water.

Helichrysum italicum

Helichrysum

With the removal of the main flowering species into the genus *Bracteantha* (which see), this genus is left with a higgledy-piggledy potpourri of annual goodies. Many have been around for years, while others are only now starting to be grown in gardens.

One of the best known is the curry plant, *Helichrysum italicum*, with a fragrance remarkably similar to curry. The silver leaves look fine all season, and for me, the fragrance is far more pleasant than the taste of the real thing. The flowers are pleasant enough, although if it never flowered, it would still be a sought-after addition to the garden. Best in rock gardens or where drainage is excellent, but also fine in containers. Full sun, good drainage.

Helichrysum italicum, rock garden

Most of the "helis" have silvery foliage and have been used to accent other plants in baskets and containers. One such plant that has been sold for many years is licorice plant, *Helichrysum petiolare*. The plant is grown strictly for the foliage, the flowers are nondescript and of little value. 'Limelight' is one of the best, complementing other plants in containers or poking out from the edge

Helichrysum petiolare 'Limelight'

of the garden. For a different look, 'Variegatum' provides all sorts of interest, although it is perhaps not as complementary to other plants as 'Limelight'. Best in containers, hates wet feet.

The other two plants hanging about the fringes are silver everlasting, *Helichrysum splendidum*, and silver spike, *H. thianschanicum*. The former has upright shoots, almost standing at attention, and bears lots of yellow daisy flowers in late summer. Grown for the foliage; flowers should be removed. The latter is a recent introduction, designed to be put in containers by itself, or as a complement to others. It is sold as 'Icicles' and 'Silver Spike'. Both behave poorly in wet soils and high humidity. Full sun.

Heliotropium

HELIOTROPE

Grown in far greater numbers in your grandmother's heyday than today, heliotrope is nonetheless making a comeback. Ask anyone why they include heliotrope (*Heliotropium arborescens*) in the garden and they will immediately

MORE ☞

Helichrysum petiolare 'Limelight' with geraniums and phormium

Helichrysum petiolare 'Variegatum'

Helichrysum splendidum

Helichrysum thianschanicum 'Silver Spike'

respond, "It's the smell, stupid." Well, perhaps not that, but it is obvious that while one can look for excellence in plant form and performance, it's the smell, stupid. Unfortunately, the cultivars in Grandmother's day didn't go through the vigorous seed and greenhouse selection necessary for today's cultivars, and many modern forms have lost most of the fragrance. They look better, for sure, but it requires a serious inhale to find the perfume.

People love heliotropes and will grow them almost anywhere, including in hanging baskets dangling from a conservatory roof. But it is in the garden

Heliotropium arborescens

Heliotropium arborescens 'Marine Light Blue'

Heliotropium arborescens 'Marine'

that heliotrope is the sweetest, especially in 'Light Eyes' and other light-flowered forms. They are less impressive and more rampant than the more compact forms, such as the Marine series, but they are also many times more fragrant. But perhaps fragrance should not be considered a limitation to planting when the habit is so much improved. 'Marine' can look outstanding in great drifts, and the combination with red geraniums improves the look of both. The lighter-colored 'Marine Light Blue' is also a great flowering plant and excellent in the garden or containers. One of the best new cultivars I have seen, however, is 'Iowa', which combines excellent (not yet great) fragrance with a fine habit. By it-

Heliotropium arborescens 'Light Eyes'

Heliotropium arborescens 'Iowa'

Heliotropium arborescens 'Marine' with geraniums

MORE ☞

self, or in containers with verbena and pentas, the plant performs well, and putting it near a garden bench where one can lean over and sniff is a great idea. Full sun. Plants persist longer in the North than in the heat and humidity of the South.

Not all heliotropes are created equal, that is for sure. In fact, just emerging from the wild is one of our native forms, creeping heliotrope, *Heliotropium amplexicaule*. It is surely winter hardy to at least zone 7, perhaps 6, but it is being sold as an annual, and cold tolerance is simply a bonus. The main cultivar is 'Azure Skies', which is grown for its flowing habit out of baskets and containers, or sliding down the edges of beds. It flowers most of the summer, but there is one drawback. No pleasant fragrance caresses your nostrils; in fact, some people say that the odor assails their nostrils. As for me, it is neutral, but the plant is so prolific, I can forgive its lack of perfume. Certainly worth a try. Full sun, good drainage.

Hemigraphis repanda

WAFFLE PLANT

I am not sure where the common name arose, but for small areas, rock gardens, or containers, waffle plant (*Hemigraphis repanda*) is as unique-looking as its name. They are small plants, never rising more than 6" in height, but the colorful purple foliage and the lovely white to pink flowers are always pleasing to the eye. They can be useful, flanking a

Heliotropium amplexicaule 'Azure Skies', garden

Hemigraphis repanda

Heliotropium amplexicaule 'Azure Skies'

Hemigraphis repanda, garden

marker but never hiding it, or in combination with other plants in the garden. The only drawback is that plants are slow-growing and can be overtaken by more vigorous neighbors. An overlooked winner. Full sun to partial shade.

Hibiscus acetosella

Hibiscus

MALLOW

Many of the hibiscus used in gardens today are the hardy hibiscus, *Hibiscus moscheutos*, and they are big and brilliant compared to many of the annual ones that are commonly grown outdoors. But times are changing, and tropical hibiscus, like many other plants of that ilk, are moving from the Florida nursery to the Michigan garden.

Perhaps the most common annual hibiscus of gardens is the red shield hibiscus, *Hibiscus acetosella*. Plants provide marvelous deep to rosy red foliage all season, occasionally peeking out with a small red flower or two before the frost knocks them down. They can grow 6–8' tall and are great architectural features or complements to other plants in the garden. 'Copper Leaf' is sometimes sold; it bears more subdued leaves of a coppery rather than red color. Regardless, the upright stature and vigorous habit make this hibiscus difficult to overlook.

Hibiscus acetosella 'Copper Leaf'

The diversity of the genus is best shown by having your eye drift from the heights of the red shield to ground level, where the dwarf flower-of-an-hour, *Hibiscus trionum*, resides. With its white flowers and dark centers, the plants bloom continuously and sneer at heat and humidity. Never attaining more than 1' in height, plants enjoy a position in the front of the garden or in containers.

The ascent of the tropical hibiscus (*Hibiscus rosa-sinensis*) into mainstream gardens has been slow but steady. Always thought of as a Florida plant, gardeners in more northerly

Hibiscus rosa-sinensis 'Jakarta'

MORE ☞

Hibiscus trionum

Hibiscus trionum, flower

Hibiscus rosa-sinensis 'Kona'

locales would admire them on their southern holiday but ignore them at home. A number of breeders and sellers are working at trying to provide plants with more weather tolerance, so they will bloom as well on 70°F days as on 85°F days. The colors are undeniably beautiful, and the dark green foliage can be handsome when well grown, but it will turn yellow if under stress. Many cultivars are being introduced, and the only way to know which are the best is to try a couple. Cultivars show up locally; few are nationally recognized, so no telling what might be for sale. I have enjoyed 'Jakarta' and 'Kona', but handsome cultivars are sold everywhere. Full sun for all.

Hypoestes phyllostachya

POLKA DOT PLANT

The polka dot plant is still produced by American growers, but it is not as popular as it was only ten years ago. Nothing wrong with the plant, it is simply inevitable that as more plants are put in front of the North American gardener, others lose some of their appeal. Such is the case with *Hypoestes phyllostachya*.

Plants grown in the greenhouse are compact and brilliant when placed on the retail shelf, and once planted in the garden tend to expand and grow out of that habit. They make excellent container and groundcover candidates,

Hypoestes phyllostachya 'White Splash'

Hypoestes phyllostachya, greenhouse

Hypoestes phyllostachya 'Confetti Carmine Rose', *H. p.* 'Confetti White'

Hypoestes phyllostachya 'Pink Splash'

Hypoestes phyllostachya 'Confetti Carmine'

providing vigorous low growth with interesting spotted foliage. Flowers are forgettable and minor. We have trialed many cultivars, and I find those with white markings, such as 'White Splash', don't get lost when grown with other plants. 'Confetti White' is superior, and shows up even more when planted near 'Confetti Carmine Rose'. The darker-colored leaves, like those found on 'Pink Splash', are too busy for me, but the interesting tones of 'Confetti Carmine' are not too dark and show up reasonably well in the landscape. Full sun in the North, afternoon shade in the South.

Iberis

CANDYTUFT

This is another genus dominated by a perennial species, in this case perennial candytuft, *Iberis sempervirens*. However, there is more to candytuft than one species, and some of the annual forms are much showier than the usual perennials.

The most common of these uncommon plants is the amazing rocket candytuft, *Iberis amara*. Plants look like they're on the launch pad at Cape Canaveral, noses pointed in the air.

MORE ☞

They look terrific in gardens with a few red dianthus keeping guard. A number of improved rockets are also sold, the most popular being 'White Pinnacle', a large-flowered rocket that can also be useful as a cut flower. Quite outstanding but perhaps a little too big. A shorter but no less handsome form is 'Iceberg Superior'; either one is fun to grow. They are not as weather-tolerant as I would like and may not look good in the middle of July, but so what?

A form that is much less of a rocket is common candytuft, *Iberis umbellata*, which has wonderful colors on low-growing plants, looking like an aggrega-

Iberis amara 'White Pinnacle'

Iberis amara 'Iceberg Superior'

Iberis gibraltarica

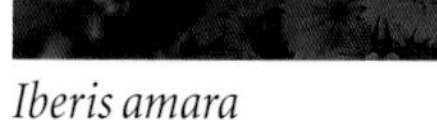

Iberis amara

Iberis umbellata 'Brilliant White'

Iberis umbellata 'Brilliant Rose'

Iberis linifolia

tion of candytuft and alyssum. The Brilliant series certainly works for me; I can't get enough of 'Brilliant White', which has a tinge of pink in the flowers, while the rosy pink flowers of 'Brilliant Rose' are outstanding.

A couple of other annual candytufts are floating around out there, with names like the Gibraltar candytuft and the narrow-leaf candytuft. The former (*Iberis gibraltarica*) is a low grower, not more than 6" tall, with light pink and white flowers. They grow rapidly and can fill in an area quickly. The latter (*I. linifolia*) is more upright, and while all the leaves of the annuals are narrow, these are the most so. Flowers are smaller and not as impressive as the others, but this species is perhaps worth a try if you find the seeds. All grown from seed; full sun, good drainage, cool temperatures.

Impatiens

From the balsam plant to busy lizzie, from jewelweed to impatiens, this genus has it all. From 6' tall weeds to the cheeky dwarf forms of the highly bred bedding plant to the brilliant flowers and foliage of the New Guinea plant, the

MORE ☞

Impatiens balfourii

Impatiens balsamina

Impatiens balsamina 'Tom Thumb'

Impatiens balsamina 'Blackberry Ice'

Impatiens balsamina 'Peach Ice'

Impatiens walleriana 'Variegata'

Impatiens glandulifera

Impatiens glandulifera, flowers

Impatiens walleriana, mix, UGA Trial Gardens

Impatiens walleriana 'Mini Variegated'

Impatiens walleriana 'Pixie Pink Border'

Impatiens walleriana 'Cheeky Spotted Orange'

Impatiens walleriana 'Fiesta Salmon with Blush'

MORE ☞

candy store is open and gardeners can choose their sweets. And choose they have been doing, making this genus the number-one-selling bedding plant in this country. Impatiens are without doubt the main choice for color in shady gardens. No other group of plants provides so much pizzazz for so long a time to so many shady areas.

However, there is more out there than simply the bedding impatiens or the New Guinea forms, albeit more is not always easy to find. Not that many years ago, one of the most common impatiens was rose balsam, *Impatiens balsamina*. It is slowly making a comeback but will likely not return to its former glory; the impatiens field is too crowded. However, the double-flowered species is easy to grow from seed and is readily available in seed packages. Often sold as "Camellia Flower," they are about 15" tall, but a dwarfer form, 'Tom Thumb', is also available. One of the best series I have grown is the Ice series, with double flowers and handsome variegated leaves. 'Blackberry Ice' has deeper rosy flowers, while 'Peach Ice' bears pastel pink blooms. They are outstanding for brightening up the shade.

While wandering around gardens here and there, one often finds the unusual among the plebeian. Such was the case when I first came across Balfour's impa-

Impatiens walleriana brightens a porch

Impatiens walleriana 'Dazzler Coral'

Impatiens walleriana, baskets

Impatiens walleriana 'Showstopper Picotee'

tiens, *Impatiens balfourii*, in a garden on Long Island. I have since grown it in Georgia and admired it in Vermont, but nobody seems to offer plants for sale. Plants attain about 18" and flower most of the season with pendulous white and pink blooms. Find it, grow it, enjoy it.

As beautiful as the genus is, many people consider some of the members awful weeds. Jewelweed and other tall forms inhabit moist areas and reseed themselves everywhere. They can become a bother, however. Policeman's helmet, *Impatiens glandulifera*, is at least beautiful before it becomes a nuisance; plants grow 5' tall but have beautiful large flowers of light to deep rose-pink. They tower over others and are not as weedy as some, but expect them to appear in a different area the next year.

Of course, the Big Two dominate the impatiens market. They are bedding impatiens, *Impatiens walleriana* (affectionately known as busy lizzie), and New Guinea impatiens, *I. hawkeri*. They are everywhere, and deservedly so. We have trialed hundreds of cultivars in Athens, and I can honestly say there are no "dogs," only differences in color, habit, or form that might impress one person more than another. They look outstanding dripping out of baskets, in combination with bedding plants like red salvia, or as simple porch plants planted in old strawberry pots. While the mainstream colors and form are most common, variegated culti-

Impatiens walleriana with red salvia

Impatiens walleriana 'Showstopper Flair'

Impatiens walleriana 'Accent Bright Eyed'

Impatiens walleriana 'Impulse Appleblossom'

MORE ☞

vars are sometimes available but don't seem as popular when so much else is out there. However, two other areas of breeding continue to expand the range. One is the dwarfing of impatiens, resulting in plants with smaller leaves and small (but seemingly hundreds of) flowers. They go under names like Mini series, such as the bicolor flowers of 'Mini Variegated', the Pixies, like 'Pixie Pink Border', or the impish Cheeky, one of the best being 'Cheeky Spotted Orange'. Outstanding performers, with quite a different look. The second area outside the main avenue of impatiens is the renaissance in double-flowered forms. A few cultivars have always been available, but the ascent of the Fiesta series, shown off by 'Fiesta Salmon with Blush', has brought the doubles out of hiding. Additional fine series are now available to gardeners.

While the previous forms and sizes enhance the usefulness of impatiens, it is the mainstream bedding plant that fills the garden centers and brightens the shade. And there's so much to choose from, it seldom matters if you read the label. The Dazzler series, such as 'Dazzler Coral' has been a terrific choice, but 'Super Elfin Blue Pearl' has probably had as many fans as any impatiens recently bred. For bicolored flowers, it is hard to beat 'Showstopper Picotee', and 'Showstopper Flair' is impressive also. I could go on forever about the diversity of color, but ending with an excellent "eyed" form, as in 'Accent Bright Eyes', and a beautiful pastel form, as shown by 'Impulse Appleblossom', may be enough. It is not hard to see why bedding impatiens holds onto

Impatiens walleriana 'Super Elfin Blue Pearl'

Impatiens hawkeri 'Trinidad'

Impatiens hawkeri 'Rosetta'

Impatiens hawkeri 'Pure Beauty Melissa'

Impatiens hawkeri 'Celebrette Wild Plum'

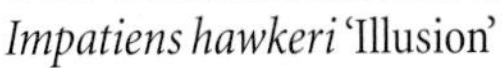

Impatiens hawkeri 'Illusion'

Impatiens hawkeri 'Petticoat Fire'

Impatiens hawkeri Painted Paradise series

Impatiens hawkeri 'Aztec'

the number-one spot in sales.

The bedding group may be leading the race, but New Guinea impatiens are rapidly making up ground. In tubs in Atlanta, Georgia, or in public gardens in East Lansing, Michigan, New Guineas are doing just fine, thank you. They tolerate more sun than the bedding forms and are able to be used in more areas of the garden. As with bedding impatiens, there is no end to the number of choices being bred and sold at the garden center and box store today. From the light flowers of 'Rosetta' to 'Pure Beauty Melissa' (one of over twelve cultivars in the Pure Beauty series) to the dark iridescent color of 'Celebrette Wild Plum' and the incredibly bright 'Petticoat Fire', there is something for every color combination and every taste. And yes, there are other horses in the race, and some beautiful variegated foliage forms of New Guineas are reemerging. The old 'Aztec' has given way to the spectacular Painted Paradise series. Handsome leaves and good flowers, they will almost be impossible not to put in your shopping cart come spring.

All impatiens favor at least afternoon shade; only the bedding forms require shade most of the day. Lots of water.

Ipomoea

MORNING GLORY

This is probably one of the most confusing genera in the garden, being represented by such different-looking flowers as the Spanish flag and morning glory. Most members of the group love to climb or at least romp around, and few remain well behaved, especially where they are happy.

And happiness is not all that difficult to attain for this vigorous group of happy-go-lucky well-known plants.

MORE ☞

Interestingly enough, however, not all are as well known as they should be. People are fascinated by the twisted flower buds of moon vine (*Ipomoea alba*); they can hardly wait to plant it themselves so they can watch the flowers open in late afternoon and evening. Moon vine is particularly appealing climbing over brick or stone walls, and the flowers are perfect at dusk. A great excuse for a walk in the garden with a glass of wine. But don't be too late—like many big-flowered vines, the flowers persist but a day.

Other lesser-known vines also make fabulous houseguests, and your own houseguests will believe you to be a master gardener. One of the weirdest is Spanish flag, *Ipomoea lobata*, with its elongated red and yellow flowers. Perhaps the common name resulted from the fact that red and yellow are the colors on the Spanish flag, but this plant is native to Mexico. Go figure. Plants are vigorous and can easily attain 15' in a single year. And I am seeing the cypress vine (*I. quamoclit*) more and more and beginning to appreciate the beautiful fern-like appearance of the foliage. Another of our southwestern natives, but plants look

Ipomoea alba, flower bud

Ipomoea alba

Ipomoea alba, flowers

Ipomoea tricolor 'Heavenly Blue'

Ipomoea ×*sloteri*

Ipomoea lobata, flowers

Ipomoea lobata

Ipomoea quamoclit

Ipomoea quamoclit, flowers

Ipomoea tricolor 'Pearly Gates'

MORE ☞

outstanding twining around posts in the Allen Centennial Gardens in Madison, Wisconsin—those fire-engine-red flowers almost require the use of polarized sunglasses. A hybrid of this species, *I.* ×*sloteri*, combines the dazzling flowers with fabulous frilly leaves.

As many people curse morning glory vines (*Ipomoea tricolor*) as love them. They curse them for their reseeding tendencies and persistent weedlike growth years after the original vine was removed. That characteristic alone has turned many gardeners off these vines, but let's not throw the baby out with the bath water. Beautiful plants are out there, and they may well be worth the future weeding. Many are hybrids with other species, and probably the all-time favorite is 'Heavenly Blue', a winner everywhere it is planted. The color seems perfect for nearly everyone. For a white, I love 'Pearly Gates'; it reminds me of a daytime moon vine but far more floriferous. Darker flower colors are also available, including 'Magenta', which is somewhat on the red side, and the ghoulish 'Kniola's Black', with small but almost black flowers. I think only people with hidden pierced body parts enjoy this one. And morning glories keep surprising people with the changes in their makeup. Who would have thought that variegated vines would have appeal, but 'Cameo Elegance' started off the movement, and the worker bees at our gardens just loved the combination of variegated foliage and red flowers of 'Good Morning Red' and the lavender-blue of 'Good Morning Blue'. Plants were bred in

Ipomoea tricolor 'Good Morning Red'

Ipomoea batatas 'Black Heart'

Ipomoea batatas 'Margarita'

Ipomoea batatas 'Margarita', containers

Ipomoea tricolor 'Magenta'

Japan, and the Good Morning series is a translation of the original unpronounceable Japanese names. They do not climb as well (they will need some help in twining) nor are they as vigorous as their non-variegated counterparts.

If you asked gardeners a few years ago what they thought of sweet potatoes (*Ipomoea batatas*), they would opine about their love or dislike of the taste of the yellow tuber. Who would have thought that this vegetable would become so popular as a garden plant? But it has, partly because the plants are almost indestructible, regardless of where in the country they are planted. 'Blackie' was one of the first introduced to the unsuspecting public, and it performed well in landscapes and baskets, spilling out of containers and adding a class of purple to the garden. 'Black Heart' (aka 'Ace of Spades') is similar in color but with heart-shaped leaves. It too looks great in containers, and between 'Black Heart' and 'Purple Majesty'

MORE ☞

Ipomoea tricolor 'Kniola's Black'

Ipomoea tricolor 'Good Morning Blue'

Ipomoea batatas 'Blackie'

Ipomoea tricolor 'Cameo Elegance'

Ipomoea batatas 'Pink Frost'

millet, containers are lush, full, and black as Mordor in Middle Earth. 'Pink Frost' adorns a few gardens as well, and although the rainbow colors are handsome, plants are far less vigorous (which is not necessarily a bad thing) than other cultivars on the market.

The all-time success story for this abused vegetable has to be the chartreuse 'Margarita', who can be found from Edmonton to Miami, brightening up landscapes and making gardeners feel like professionals. Whether falling out of beds in Athens or making cannas look even better in Niagara-on-the-Lake in Ontario, this is a no-brainer. And for even more fun, dig out the tubers in late fall—you will be amazed at the size of these things. Plant all ipomoeas in full sun, then get out of the way.

Iresine

BLOODLEAF

If we threw various types of iresine, coleus, acalypha, alternanthera, and amaranthus together and asked experts to properly identify them, there would be considerable head-scratching going on. While there are differences for those in the know, they all kind of look alike to the rest of us. *Iresine* has small flowers, similar to those acalyphas, and often painted foliage, like coleus and alternantheras. The beefsteak plant, *Iresine herbstii*, can attain 4–5' in the tropics but behaves more like a coleus in our gardens. There are a number of fine forms; unfortunately few are labeled, except as beefsteak plant. I love the upright rosy red form with dark red midribs and silvery veins, it seems to soften everything around it. For a dwarf selection, I have been most impressed with 'Purple Lady', a trailing dark purple form that has maintained the dark foliage and looked good all season. Well worth finding for baskets and containers. Full sun to afternoon shade.

Iresine herbstii

Iresine herbstii 'Purple Lady'

Kaempferia, Cornukaempferia

PEACOCK GINGER

Perhaps because I reside in an area of the country that is neither "in the North" nor "in the South" as far as plantings are concerned, I see many tropicals growing beside temperate plants. Obviously

Kaempferia pulchra var. *mansonii*

Athens is in the South, just walk by the beautiful antebellum homes on Milledge Avenue, but our relatively cold winter temperatures allow plantings of many temperate plants, while our hot summers invite more and more tropicals. That long introduction is my explanation of how hostas and peacock gingers came to be planted side by side in the shade garden at the University of Georgia. People from Florida and the Gulf Coast swear by the ornamental foliage and shade-loving characteristics of *Kaempferia*. They even call them southern hostas, since the true hosta does so poorly south of zone 7. And once I tried them at UGA, I fell in love with them and had to grow them in my shaded garden at home.

And they should be grown elsewhere. If you are trying any tropicals in the garden, include this in your wish list. There are over fifty species, but most available plants will be hybrids of various species such as *Kaempferia pulchra* or *K. gilbertii*. Don't worry about the parentage, look for named hybrids, as they all behave the same. Flowers look like phlox flowers, although they have only four petals. In general, they are light blue to

Kaempferia 'Alva'

Kaempferia 'Grande'

Kaempferia 'Bronze Peacock'

Cornukaempferia aurantiflora 'Jungle Gold'

MORE ☞

almost white, appear in the leaf axils, and flower on and off most of the summer. All selections grow from compact rosettes and remain 1–2' tall.

Manson's peacock ginger (*Kaempferia pulchra* var. *mansonii*) is a vigorous grower that flowers well but doesn't have the prized foliage of many of the others. One of my favorites is 'Alva', with large patterned leaves and light blue flowers; this also appears to be the most cold-tolerant, having come back, at least in zone 7b. 'Silverspot' has the most silvering on the leaves and is equally beautiful. 'Grande' is bigger than the others, with large wide silvery spotted leaves—excellent where the budget allows only one or two plants to be purchased. And for the bronze lovers, 'Bronze Peacock' is truly remarkable, with dark foliage that is an excellent contrast to the lavender-blue flowers.

Kaempferia 'Silverspot'

Kochia scoparia 'Acapulco Silver'

A close relative also known as the peacock ginger is *Cornukaempferia*. Plants behave identically to the kaempferias, but *Cornukaempferia aurantiflora*, the yellow peacock ginger, is even more beautiful, if that is possible. We have been growing 'Jungle Gold' for many years; the foliage is exquisitely patterned on the top and purple beneath. Add to that the bright golden yellow flowers, and this is pretty much a no-brainer.

These plants will not be easy to find through regular plant shops or normal catalogs. However they are being produced from tissue culture, and the only reason they are not more visible is that people don't ask for them. Like any member of the ginger family, they relish heat and are at their best in the hot, humid months. Place in deep shade (direct sun is a no-no), and wait until temperatures are consistently in the 50s before planting. Dig up after the first frost, and put in an area that doesn't freeze. They will emerge again when temperatures heat up. A heated cold frame works well, and the spring sun inside the frame will provide the extra heat needed to get them going again.

Kochia scoparia

BURNING BUSH

The woody plant lovers have their burning bush, *Euonymus alatus*, and the herbaceous plant people have their kochia. There is no comparison—in most parts of the country, the woody one wins the brightly burning contest hands down. The popularity of burning bush (*Kochia scoparia*) has declined in the last decade or so, perhaps because of its lack of flowers, and impatience of gardeners who didn't want to wait until the fall to see the bush burn.

However, it has an understated elegance even when in its green clothing.

And it is a really neat plant; it can be used in containers or as small "trees" in mixed landscapes. I think the planting at the Butchart Gardens, in which heliotrope bathed the floor while bushes of kochia stood at attention, was a classic. Along with cosmos and verbena and geraniums, the kochias held their own.

Several cultivars have been selected; the best known is 'Acapulco Silver', in which the tips of the branches are tinged in silver. Quite distinctive—provides color for those who miss flowers and burns quite nicely in the fall.

Full sun in the North, afternoon shade in the South. Grown from seed.

Kochia scoparia 'Acapulco Silver', fall color

Lablab purpureus

HYACINTH BEAN

Some plants have unpronounceable names, some have onomatopoeic names, others are simply fun to say. This great plant has one of those names you can drop at parties, as in "How is your lablab doing?" At best, somebody might engage you in conversation about this wonderful vine; at worst, they'll think you are stuttering about your dog.

Hyacinth bean (*Lablab purpureus*) will grow 10–15' in a single season, all the while producing wonderful flowers and great fruit. It can cover arbors, lathe houses, and entire sides of buildings when supplied with ample light and fertility. The "purpureus" comes from the fact that the plant sports purple leaves, deep pink flowers, and purple fruit. Fruit are edible, meaning you won't get violently ill, but far more tastier beans are out there.

MORE ☞

Kochia scoparia with heliotrope

Lablab purpureus

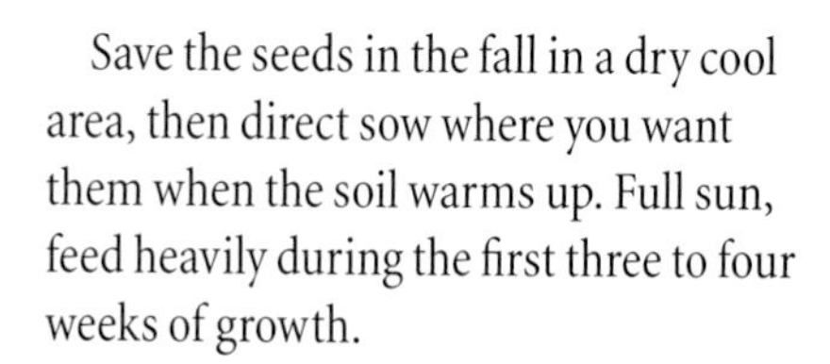
Save the seeds in the fall in a dry cool area, then direct sow where you want them when the soil warms up. Full sun, feed heavily during the first three to four weeks of growth.

Lantana

Lantanas have become a hot item in ornamental horticulture circles. Gardeners can choose from low-growing forms, upright bushes, many flower colors, those with variegated foliage, and even those with ornamental fruit. When temperatures are hot and cruddy and humidity is so thick you can cut it with a knife, lantanas will be standing strong and proud while many of their brethren will be cowering on the ground. Few plants can stand up to weather abuse as well as lantanas, and in many parts of the country, there is sufficient abuse to justify entire lantana gardens. Even in Europe, lantanas are making a lot of noise, and several cultivars, like 'Professor Raoux', are often seen as standards. Gardeners in the North have been ignoring this plant, but other than snobbery, I can think of no good reason why. Those in the South who are tired of it perhaps will be interested in the diversity of color and form.

Lablab purpureus, flowers

Lablab purpureus, fruit

Most lantanas seen in landscapes tend to be low-growing, usually no more than 2' tall. An underused species in this country is weeping lantana, *Lantana montevidensis*, which at the height of bloom is absolutely choking with purple flowers. Plants are more visible in areas with moderate temperatures and low humidity; they are mainly grown in the West.

Most lantanas used in gardens in the rest of the country belong to a single species, common lantana, *Lantana camara*, yet the variety is quite amazing. Choices among the dozens of low-growers include the deep colors of 'Radiation' and the calming hues of 'Silver Mound'. Probably the Patriot series contains the best diversity of lantanas, and seemingly dozens of varieties bear the Patriot name. I have been impressed with the orange-red hues of 'Patriot Firewagon', the mute yellow of 'Patriot Honeylove', the soft pink of 'Patriot Parasol', and the hot colors of 'Patriot Hot Country'. My guess as to the most popular low-grower is 'New Gold', whose golden flowers were so common between Athens and Atlanta during the 1996 Olympics that the passage between the two cities was known as "the pathway of gold." It flowers all season with absolutely no care and is still one of the leading sellers today. And like every other group of plants, a variegated form of lantana is also available, and this smart-looking one with yellow flowers and handsome foliage is 'Samantha'.

Not all lantanas are prostrate, weeping, or even low-growing. Tall-growing shrubs of common lantana are widely used in landscapes throughout the South and more and more in the North. The best known is 'Miss Huff', a plant that can grow 8' tall in a heartbeat and produces orange-yellow flowers all summer. She is probably the most cold hardy of all the lantanas, routinely coming back in the spring in zone 7, and often 6. However, two other upright forms have also shown

Lantana camara 'Professor Raoux'

Lantana camara 'Radiation'

Lantana montevidensis

Lantana camara 'Patriot Firewagon'

MORE ☞

Lantana camara 'Silver Mound'

Lantana camara 'Patriot Parasol'

Lantana camara 'Patriot Honeylove'

Lantana camara 'Patriot Hot Country'

Lantana camara 'Athens Rose'

Lantana camara 'Miss Huff'

considerable cold hardiness but have not been field tested for as long. 'Athens Rose' is about half the size of 'Miss Huff' and beautifully covered with rosy red flowers. Outstanding in gardens wherever it has been tested. A relative newcomer to the upright group is 'Deen Day Smith', with handsome pink flowers, larger than 'Athens Rose' but smaller than 'Miss Huff'. The plant recognizes a great lady and excellent gardener from Georgia.

Lantanas should always be functional, but who says we can't have a little fun as well? I named a particularly handsome hybrid, involving *Lantana trifolia*, 'Lavender Popcorn', and the moniker has stuck. The leaves are in threes and the small flowers are lavender. If that was all that could be said, I would have dismissed the plant as just another lantana; however, its true colors are shown around mid summer. At that time, small shiny balls of purple begin to appear; like an ear of corn, more and more "kernels" occur, and soon the long purple fruit are formed. At any one time, flowers and fruit are on the plant. Great fun, quite different. Plants are as tolerant of heat and humidity as all the others.

Any lantana can be cut back hard

Lantana camara 'New Gold'

Lantana camara 'Samantha'

Lantana 'Lavender Popcorn'

Lantana 'Lavender Popcorn', fruit

MORE ☞

during the growing season if it gets out of hand or needs a little shaping, but wait until spring to cut back dead limbs on perennial cultivars. Full sun.

Laurentia

ISOTOMA, PRATIA

The common name, isotoma, used to be the name of the genus, and people still tend to use the names interchangeably; the name pratia is also bandied about when discussing these plants. Not that any of the names are used that much, since plants are hardly known in North American gardens, an oversight that must be corrected.

The two species found in catalogs and garden centers are also confused. The

Lantana camara 'Deen Day Smith'

Laurentia axillaris

Laurentia axillaris 'Alba'

most common one is star flower, *Laurentia axillaris*, which bears somewhat prickly-looking foliage that gets covered up with handsome blue flowers in the shape of a star. Each arm of the star is long and narrow. Whether flowing out of baskets or brightening up a garden bed, plants are quite marvelous. The only cultivar I know is the white form, 'Alba'. We put it in a container with petunia and lantana and it held its own, but the blue is a better performer.

The second species, *Laurentia fluviatilis*, which is often sold under *Pratia*, is much smaller and lower to the ground. It bears many small light blue, almost white, flowers, which are also in the shape of a star but with much shorter arms. They are often used between rocks in rock walkways and can be shaped and trained to go where you want them. Both species have a milky sap and can cause skin irritation to sensitive people. Don't rub your eyes after handling the plants. Full sun to partial shade, excellent drainage.

Lavatera

TREE MALLOW

Lavateras became popular perennials with the introduction of 'Barnsley Pink' to North American gardeners. Others had been lurking in the shadow for years, including a few annual forms, but none has been particularly popular, at least in the east side of the country. The annual *Lavatera trimestris*, known simply as lavatera, is as beautiful as anything in the mallow family, and that is

Laurentia fluviatilis, rock work

Lavatera trimestris 'Tanagra'

Laurentia fluviatilis

Lavatera trimestris 'Loveliness'

MORE ☞

Lavatera trimestris 'Silver Cup'

Lavatera trimestris 'White Beauty'

saying something when you compare it to hibiscus, hollyhock, or rose-of-sharon.

However, being a member of the mallow family brings a few extras as well, like fungi and Japanese beetles, who seem to enjoy the plants as much as you do. Disease and bug problems are far less common where temperatures are cooler and the air is less humid.

The Armitage garden has had little success, but a number of choices await the rest of you. It is hard not to enjoy the iridescent pink flowers of 'Silver Cup', each flower measuring 4" across. 'Loveliness' is a tiny bit darker with slightly smaller flowers, but it looks terrific behind mealy-cup sage. The darkest flowers of them all appear to come with 'Tanagra', which sports deep red blossoms on 3–4' tall plants. For a white, 'White Beauty' does the job just fine.

All lavateras can be grown from seed, and they are not difficult to germinate or establish. Full sun. If they suffer in the heat of the summer and start to look particularly bad, sow additional seeds at their base, then pull out the old plants to be replaced by young ones; they will grow quickly and miss the worst of the heat.

Leonotis leonurus

Leonotis sibiricus

Leonotis

LION'S EAR

Approximately thirty species belong to this genus, but only one, *Leonotis leonurus*, is seen in North American garden centers, although others can probably be obtained through the Internet. The common name comes from the relative similarity of the individual flowers to a lion's ear. Since I have no intention of ever getting that close to a lion, who am I to argue?

As impressive as a lion is, its floral

namesake is no slouch either. Plants grow up to 5' in height and produce a swarm of eye-catching flowers. Each flower stem consists of whorls of a dozen or so brilliant orange flowers. There really are not that many orange flowers from which to choose—lots of yellows, golds, and scarlets, but after orange marigolds and California poppies, the cupboard is fairly bare.

Occasionally, I come across the Siberian lion's ear, *Leonotis sibiricus*, but not very often. It bears smaller, less vibrant flowers on even taller plants. But if you can find it, give it a try. It may overwinter for you as well. Full sun.

Limonium

STATICE

Statice is far more common in a florist's cooler than in a gardener's flower bed. I am always amazed at how little annual statice (*Limonium sinuatum*) I see in gardens. People buy it as a fresh cut

Leonotis leonurus, flowers

Limonium sinuatum 'Fortress Yellow'

Limonium sinuatum, cut flowers

Limonium sinuatum 'Fortress White'

MORE ☞

Limonium sinuatum 'Forever Gold'

flower or as part of a dried arrangement but believe that it, like milk, only comes from stores. Plants are generally obtained from seed; few retailers stock annual statice anymore, but if you enjoy cutting flowers from your garden, this is an easy plant to grow.

Not a great deal of choice is available, but you can't go too far wrong with the Fortress series, such as 'Fortress White' or 'Fortress Yellow', or the Forever series, like 'Forever Gold'. For fresh flowers, cut the stems when the first few flowers have opened (you can see the white centers, particularly in the darker colors), bunch them up, and enjoy their long vase life. If you are drying them, bunch up as before and hang them upside down in a dry warm room.

Occasionally, seeds of the rattail statice (*Limonium suworowii, Psylliostachys suworowii*) can be found in obscure seed catalogs, and if you enjoy cultivating the weird, give these a try. They produce long tails of light pink flowers and, common name aside, are really quite a delightful garden plant. An excellent cut flower, fresh or dried. Handle similarly to annual statice. Full sun, good drainage. All statice struggle in hot, humid summers.

Linaria

TOADFLAX

There must be something worth trying in this little-known genus, some of the species have such colorful common names. To be sure, many gardeners know the roadside flower, common toadflax, *Linaria vulgaris*, but few purposely plant it beside their roses. However, a number of annuals and reseeders are available to North American gardeners, some of which do well in the West and one or two in the East.

Probably *Linaria maroccana*, annual

Limonium suworowii, flowers

Linaria maroccana 'Fantasy Sparkling Pink'

Limonium suworowii

Linaria maroccana, Sea Island, Georgia

toadflax (aka bunny rabbits), is the best known of the species. Native to North Africa, plants have escaped and are quite common in the western half of the United States. They are closely related to snapdragons and have similar cultural requirements, that is, cool temperatures and full sun. I was impressed with the compact 9–12" height of a mixed planting at the Missouri Botanical Garden; however, the same planting on Sea Island, Georgia, although equally colorful, was almost 18" tall. Such height differences are quite common, as plants tend to stretch a little more in response to warm temperatures. A number of cultivars have been bred, but my choice is Fantasy, a modern series with vigor and many appealing colors. The mixture is fine in a wild setting, but single colors are more appropriate for the garden; 'Fantasy Sparkling Pink' has to be one of my favorites.

Linaria reticulata 'Crown Jewels'

Of the many species of toadflax, one of the prettiest is probably purple net toadflax, *Linaria reticulata*. As an early-season planting, 'Crown Jewels' more than holds its own, competing quite happily with poppies, snapdragons, and pinks.

MORE ☞

Linaria triornithophora, flowers

Linaria triornithophora

When I read about a plant called three birds flying (*Linaria triornithophora*), I had to give it a try. I grew it and noted the spurs (the wings) at the base of the flowers, but when the first flowers opened, I noticed there were four birds flying at each flower node. The flowers expanded and grew taller, and soon entire flocks were flying around. Handsome colors, upright stems, and excellent cut flowers as well—the plant needs to be seen in more of our gardens. One of its limitations (as in the entire genus) is its dislike of heat and humidity, but what else is new? They can be considered early spring candidates, planted along with nasturtiums and calendulas. Full sun.

Lobelia

Lobelias are as American as apple pie, and our red cardinal flower, *Lobelia cardinalis*, is probably the best known of them all. Perennial lobelias have been the hot item in the last number of years, while the old 1960s standby, annual bedding lobelia (*L. erinus*), has been relegated to the background of mainstream gardening, at least in the East and South. Not that it is any less useful or less colorful, it is simply that there are so many other plants to choose from that weren't there in the 1960s.

The fact is, bedding lobelia is better than it has ever been, with brighter colors and even heat-resistant cultivars that persist longer into the season. Having said that, it is no secret that plants do much better in cooler-summer climates than in hot, humid ones. Growing up in Montreal, I remember lobelia edging every garden bed in the entire city. And hanging around

Lobelia erinus 'Palace Blue with Eye'

Lobelia erinus, edging

Lobelia erinus 'Cascade Blue'

Lobelia erinus 'Cascade White'

all summer as well. Boring, but effective with marigolds and alyssum. I grow lobelia in Georgia, but it must be put in early and, if grown as an edging, is probably best removed by late June. While I was in Auckland, New Zealand, where the thermometer seldom sees 85°F, the baskets of 'Cascade Blue' lobelia were among the best I had ever seen.

Most cultivars have flowers in blue or purple, but a few bicolors are available, such as 'Palace Blue with Eye', and even an occasional white form ('Cascade White'). They are difficult to maintain in baskets, but large patio containers suit them just fine, and plants persist far longer. The most heat-tolerant cultivar I have ever trialed in Athens was 'Periwinkle Blue', which mixed well with double impatiens and white bacopa. Plants looked great all the way to August. Full sun in the North, afternoon shade in the South.

Lobularia maritima 'Wonderland White'

Lobularia maritima 'Wonderland Deep Purple'

Lobularia maritima

SWEET ALYSSUM

Sweet alyssum (*Lobularia maritima*) really is sweet: on a warm summer evening, the fragrance from the flowers

Lobularia maritima Easter Bonnet Mix

Lobelia erinus 'Periwinkle Blue'

Lobularia maritima 'Snow Crystals'

MORE ☞

is unmistakable, not overwhelming like hyacinths, but ephemeral and less obnoxious. The flowers and plants have been a mainstay for years, used as edging and anywhere low-growing plants with lots of flowers were needed.

I wonder how many beds have been edged with the white flowers of 'Snow Crystals' or covered by the snowfall of 'Wonderland White' over the years? Everyone thinks that alyssum comes only in white, but 'Wonderland Deep Purple' quickly puts that myth to rest. And mixtures can also find a place in gardens; the best one I have seen is Easter Bonnet, made up of whites, purples, and pinks. My favorite single color is 'Easter Bonnet Deep Pink'. All alyssums need excellent drainage and are equally at home in containers or in the garden bed. Full sun in the North, afternoon shade in the South.

Lobularia maritima 'Easter Bonnet Deep Pink'

Lotus berthelotii 'Amazon Sunset'

Lotus berthelotii

PARROT'S BEAK

When gardeners are asked what they think about lotus and lotus flowers, nine times out of ten they will talk about the water plant known as sacred lotus. But as beautiful as that plant is, it belongs to the genus *Nelumbo* (which see). Few people have grown or appreciated the beauty of parrot's beak, *Lotus berthelotii*, probably because it is so little known.

The foliage of parrot's beak is beautifully blue-gray, soft, and compact. Most of the time I see plants used as fillers in mixed containers, because in much of this country they seldom flower. In our Athens garden, the basket did little more than look ornamental, but the foliage was highly effective. However, when it does flower, look out. The cultivar 'Amazon Sunset' was flowering in coastal California in April, and people were gawking at all the red beaks. Actually it is a little much, and I prefer the subtle foli-

Lotus berthelotii with torenia and lantana

Lotus berthelotii

age without the flowers. And for most of us, that's all we will get anyway. Full sun, best in containers.

Lychnis

CAMPION

The species that belong to this genus are both colorful and plentiful. Many are perennials, but a few of the more enjoyable ones happen to be used as annuals. The flowers are colorful, and many species are easy to grow.

The most colorful is a hybrid that goes under the name of Arkwright's campion, *Lychnis ×arkwrightii*. When it was first introduced, gardeners were told that it was a perennial, but plants have not shown a perennial tendency at all, perhaps hanging on for a second year but often succumbing after one season. However, the brilliance of their flowers is such that they cannot hide anywhere, regardless of the number of plants surrounding them. The main cultivar is 'Vesuvius', an apt name for its spectacular fleeting color, but what light it brings!

As much as I enjoy Arkwright's cam-

Lychnis ×arkwrightii 'Vesuvius'

Lychnis ×arkwrightii 'Vesuvius', flowers

Lychnis flos-cuculi

Lychnis flos-cuculi 'Rosea'

Lychnis flos-jovis, flowers

MORE ☞

Lychnis flos-cuculi 'Alba'

Lychnis flos-jovis

pion, it has frustrated me more often than not. That is not the case with one of my favorite little jump-ups, known to all as ragged robin, *Lychnis flos-cuculi*. It "jumps up" every spring, returning from seeds thrown off during the past summer. The petals seem to be all beat up, and ragged it does appear. But they are undemanding and unpretentious, flowering away all spring and well into the summer. Since all are grown from seed, a good deal of variability occurs, and flowers from white ('Alba') to deep rose ('Rosea') can occur. However, for most of us, the light pink flowers are sufficient, growing where they feel comfortable and soon finding their own space. Put in some plants this spring, and within three years, you will have lots to share with friends.

Another charmer, although not nearly as cooperative, is flower of jupiter, *Lychnis flos-jovis*. Plants are native to mountain areas, mostly the European Alps, and are not as happy in areas of warm temperatures and high humidity. However, they are colorful, particularly the rose-colored form. Plants grow no taller than 1' but are covered with flowers in early summer. Not recommended for southern gardeners, but that leaves many others, particularly in the Northwest and Canada. Full sun.

Lysimachia congestiflora

LOOSESTRIFE, GOLDEN GLOBES

Few annuals of loosestrife are grown; the big sellers are all perennials. However, if you have been told that gooseneck loosestrife or some other perennial form is worthy of consideration, it is time to meet golden globes, *Lysimachia congestiflora*.

Plants grow in anything, anywhere. I have seen them falling out of hanging

Lysimachia congestiflora 'Variegata'

baskets at a garden center in Strongsville, Ohio, as well as planted at the base of a lantana standard in Columbus. The most common cultivar, 'Eco Dark Satin', has a darker eye than the species and looks terrific as a container plant. The green foliage always contrasts well with the golden yellow flowers, which tend to stay in bloom almost all season. For even more contrast, try 'Variegata'; it does not flower as prolifically, but the variegated foliage is sufficiently handsome to give it some space in the garden anyway. Full sun.

Mandevilla sanderi

BRAZILIAN JASMINE

Every year I drive past a modest home in Athens, and every year I say to myself, "I have to do that." For years now, a beautiful rose-colored mandevilla (*Mandevilla sanderi*) flowers in the front yard by the sidewalk of the house, and every year I notice it around June. Plants twine around a pole of some kind, and although the glossy green leaves are pleasant enough, all I see are flowers, flowers, and more flowers. Finally, when the first hard

MORE ☞

Lysimachia congestiflora, basket

Lysimachia congestiflora 'Eco Dark Satin'

Lysimachia congestiflora with lantana standard

frost comes, the plant crumples and goes to bed. Athens is in zone 7, yet this sucker comes back; that's all I need to know to become a believer in global warming.

But I see people in Michigan and Wisconsin putting plants in containers and letting them climb on their porches and patios. Cultivars have definitely left the tropics, and plants like 'Leah', with her blush-white flowers, and 'Janell', with rosy red blooms, are becoming more available. And why not? They grow perfectly well at 70–75°F, and while they won't grow as quickly as in Florida, they will provide months of pleasure nevertheless.

They are expensive, so after the first frost, cut them back and put them either in a cold frame or in a garage where temperatures stay above freezing.

Mandevilla sanderi 'Leah'

Mandevilla sanderi, Athens, Georgia

Mandevilla sanderi 'Janell'

Matthiola incana

STOCK

Stocks have so long been the domain of florists and cut flower growers, we seem to have forgotten that their origins were in the garden. Long admired for its fragrance and persistent vase life, stock (*Matthiola incana*) can more often be found by the acre in cut flower fields than by the plant in our gardens. As gardeners, we can never duplicate the job that cut flower producers do; we don't have the facilities or expertise, nor do we have access to cultivars specific to the cut flower trade. But that should not dissuade us from adding a few plants to the garden. Not to do so is a shame, because if part of the joy of having a garden is to cut flowers from it, then why not have a few plants of stocks to sweeten the arrangement?

Stocks can be bought as seed, and if put in the garden early enough, they will germinate and do well if you live in an area of cool summers. However, for the many of us who live where summer heats up rather quickly, started plants should be put in the ground as soon as possible after the last frost. The only forms you will find will be shorter than those grown commercially but can still be quite useful in the vase. 'Legacy Pink', at about 15" tall, is outstanding, while white forms, such as 'Column White', are standouts in the garden.

Dwarf forms have been all the rage, and perhaps they will catch on. While they are a little too short for my taste,

Matthiola incana, cut flower field

Matthiola incana 'Legacy Pink'

Matthiola incana 'Harmony Purple'

Matthiola incana 'Column White'

MORE ☞

others treat them as bedding plants and are quite content. The Cinderella series provides several colors, but 'Cinderella Lavender' is the hit. 'Harmony Purple' is but one of many colors available from the emerging midgets. One of the problems inherent in seed-propagated stocks is that a certain percentage will be single, such as with 'Midget Lavender', rather than the more favored double forms. All cultivars are supposed to be double, but in some cases up to 40 percent may be single (10 percent is more common). The singles simply are not what stocks are supposed to look like, but there is little that a gardener can do to determine if the seedlings going into the garden will be single or double. Some people enjoy them just as much. Full sun, cool temperatures only. They will likely perish when temperatures remain above 75°F and humidity gets high.

Melampodium paludosum

MEDALLION FLOWER

It was around 1985 that I first received some seeds of medallion flower (*Melampodium paludosum*) and reluctantly put them in the trial garden. After all, we had already trialed enough yellow daisies, most of which wussed out after a few weeks of hot weather, so I was hardly primed to be impressed. Six

Matthiola incana 'Cinderella Lavender'

Melampodium paludosum 'Medaillon', lining stairs

Matthiola incana 'Midget Lavender'

Melampodium paludosum 'Medaillon', Texas

Melampodium paludosum, framing bench

months later, I was telling others they had to try this thing, it really worked.

I had received a cultivar called 'Medaillon', which we soon put all over the campus at the University of Georgia. In our trial garden, I was so impressed that we lined the stairs with these wonderful starry flowers. Why was I providing such high praise? Simply because they grew well, flowered constantly, and did not suffer from heat and humidity in the way usually seen with marigolds or rudbeckias. Soon plants were being

MORE ☞

Melampodium paludosum 'Million Stars' with celosia

Melampodium paludosum 'Million Stars'

Melampodium paludosum with salvia

Melampodium paludosum 'Lemon Delight'

combined with acalyphas along paths at the Mercer Botanic Gardens in Humble, Texas, and later I was tripping on it planted with celosias and alternantheras and all sorts of plants. Each time, however, the melampodium was the showstopper. As a combination with velvet sage, or by itself, used as a backdrop for a small, very uncomfortable bench, the plants looked good nearly all season. And if they got tired or overgrown, all they needed was a serious haircut, and they would be in flower two weeks later.

Other yellow cultivars have come along, mainly to reduce the problem of stretch that plants were prone to. 'Million Stars' is one such introduction and probably my first choice. The excitement about the plant has died down considerably, and even I was walking by without a second look, until we received some seeds of a gorgeous lighter yellow form called 'Lemon Delight'. It was different enough for me to exclaim, "You have to try this thing, it really works!"

Full sun. Plants can reseed and become a nuisance; cut back hard about mid July in the South.

Mimulus

MONKEY FLOWER

A good deal of effort has gone into turning this average-looking flower into a big-time bedding plant. The hybrids (*Mimulus* ×*hybridus*) consist of parents native to the West Coast and high elevations. That computes into plants that do well in northern Europe, northern states, and coastal areas but generally do rather poorly in hot, humid areas.

Flowers often have spots on their faces, as shown by 'Highland Orange', but breeders have also provided clear faces. I have seen beautiful window boxes of the Magic series, whose clear faces were unusually bright, in Ireland. The Mystic series was also well received; 'Mystic Wine' and 'Mystic Yellow' certainly were impressive, but they still have problems with heat and humidity. Additional cultivars have been bred to overcome some of the heat problems, and better times are ahead.

Mimulus ×*hybridus* 'Highland Orange'

Mimulus ×*hybridus* 'Mystic Wine'

Mimulus ×*hybridus* Magic series

The best of the recent material is probably the Jellybean series (do you think the people who name plants must be smoking something?). We dutifully trialed a number of them; they were better, but they have a long way to go before they will be as mainstream here as in Europe.

Mimulus are best planted in window boxes or containers where soil, fertility, and water can be better controlled. Full sun.

Mirabilis

FOUR O'CLOCK FLOWER

Yes, they do. The common name is not a lie—perhaps not Rolex-accurate but close enough to show the kids. Flowers don't open until mid afternoon during the summer and are usually closed in the morning. People still enjoy these plants but perhaps not as much as they used to. Plants like *Mirabilis jalapa* and portulaca (which see) have the annoying habit of sleeping when we are awake, and plant breeders have been trying to add a few more hours to their day. And barely succeeding.

However, the plants are easy to grow from seed, and they form good-sized bushes in eight weeks or so, making sturdy garden plants with lots and lots of closed flowers (I guess I have never seen a four o'clock earlier than two o'clock, which may explain my frustration). However, some of the newer cultivars are full of flowers, which is obvious even at noon. 'Broken Colors' consists of

Mimulus ×hybridus 'Mystic Yellow'

Mirabilis longiflora

Mirabilis jalapa 'Tea Time Red'

Mirabilis jalapa 'Broken Colors'

MORE ☞

pastels of pink and off-white flowers; the Tea Time series (great name for this flower) is available in numerous colors, but I have been most impressed with 'Tea Time Red' and 'Tea Time Rose'.

Another species or two are also sold here and there; I tried long-tubed mirabilis, *Mirabilis longiflora*, which has long tubular white flowers and opens all day. Unfortunately, for me it was a waste of time and space, but its evening fragrance may entice you to try it. Full sun.

Moluccella laevis

BELLS OF IRELAND

A number of plants started their careers in the garden but found fame elsewhere, as an herb or a houseplant, or in this case as a cut flower. Does anybody grow bells of Ireland (*Moluccella laevis*) as a garden plant anymore? While it is not as colorful as impatiens—what green flowers are?—neither should it be shunned just because we can find it cleaned and packaged at the florist.

Bells of Ireland actually looks pretty neat in the garden, generally grown in the front so the unique flowers can be appreciated. Plants grow about 2–3' tall, and in mid summer they produce the wonderful lime-green bells. If the flower stems get a little heavy, prop a Y-shaped branch underneath, so you can admire them. If you wish to take them in, they can be enjoyed for weeks as a fresh cut stem, or you can hang them upside down in a dry airy place, after which they can be viewed for years. Seed packages can be purchased; try a few—green flowers are always in. Full sun.

Mirabilis jalapa 'Tea Time Rose'

Moluccella laevis

Moluccella laevis, flower

Monopsis

I include this little-known genus for no other reason than to share it with you, and predict that it may become reasonably common in the next five years. It is a relative of lobelia and has many of the same characteristics. That is, plants are low-growing, look best falling out of containers, and prefer cool-summer climates to warm, humid ones.

Some selections of *Monopsis campanulata* have hit the American gardening market, but the choices are few. The foliage is variable and looks a little like common yarrow. I have been pleased with the coppery tones of 'Bronze Beauty' because the color is somewhat unique; however, the best performer has been 'Blue Papillo', with its many dark blue flowers. Plants appear to be better suited to containers than to the garden bed, at least in warm-summer climates, and will probably be more in demand in the North than in the South. They are not going to replace bacopa or lobelia, but they may find a place on the North American gardening stage. Full sun in the North, afternoon shade in the South.

Musa, Ensete

BANANA

Bananas . . . If you are reading this and are not thinking, "This guy is nuts!", then you are an open-minded gardener, and we can drink beer together. After that, you probably will think, "This guy is nuts!"—but at least not because of bananas. Most of the world's banana production depends on plants from the genus *Musa*, but some of the ornamental forms are from *Ensete*. It really doesn't matter: none will produce fruit outdoors, and they are both used in the same way.

Monopsis campanulata 'Bronze Beauty'

Monopsis campanulata 'Blue Papillo'

Musa acuminata

Ensete ventricosum 'Maurelii'

MORE ☞

It is amazing how many gardeners in the North, let alone the South, are incorporating bananas as an architectural feature in the landscape. They are relatively easy to find in catalogs and online, and the ornamental forms are quite beautiful. Forget the fruit, enjoy the foliage.

I am no connoisseur of bananas; I am only just learning of the great diversity that is available. Go to a tropical plant catalog or type in "ornamental banana" online, and you too will be amazed. In our garden in Athens, we stuck my favorite species, Sumatran banana, *Musa sumatrana* (aka zebra banana), right in the middle of the petunia trials. Looked great, although a little wind-rocked. Leaves of this species have wonderful purple markings and always look exotic. I was impressed with myself, but heck, turns out people figured bananas are no big deal. In southern Germany, not exactly the tropics, I loved the short squat form of the purple-leaved Abyssinian banana, *Ensete ventricosum* 'Maurelii', erupting out of some yellow creeping zinnia. Outstanding. And green-leaved bananas (*M. acuminata*) flanked a path at the famous Palmengarten in Frankfurt; protected from the wind, the leaves were relatively unscathed, and vigorous. But that was Europe, you say—how about this country?

In Washington, D.C., the hotspot of all things weird, I came across another lovely form of *Ensete ventricosum* growing out of 'Camilla' coleus. Since this was Washington, it did not seem out of place. It was only when I made a September visit to Olbrich Botanical Gardens, however, that I truly crossed into the Twilight Zone. There, in Madison, Wisconsin, was my old favorite, *Musa sumatrana*, along with Japanese banana, *M. basjoo*, magnificent in its wavy green leaves. This is said to be the hardiest of the bananas, perhaps overwintering to as low as zone 5 with protection.

Of course, the problem is no longer how to get them; in fact, many companies even sell seeds for the banana lover. The problem is what to do with these 6–10' things when winter arrives. If you have no place to overwinter them, consider them a fun but expensive summer

Musa basjoo

Ensete ventricosum with coleus

Musa sumatrana

toy. If you wish to overwinter them, plant them in containers; that way they will not grow excessively and they can be taken in, with effort, to the garage or greenhouse. Plants can be cut down after the first frost, but if you wish to keep the plant intact, you must have heat and light. A dark garage may work for cut-back tubers but not for ornamental bananas. Regardless, have fun. Full sun.

Mussaenda

This spectacular plant is actually a shrub, regularly growing 10–15' in its homeland in tropical Africa and the Philippines. Over 300 species have been identified, but outside of south Florida and perhaps some of the Gulf States, a mussaenda in a North American garden is a rare sight indeed. And for good reason: availability is almost nonexistent, plants are woody and need some heat to mature, and while they are really neat and interesting the first year, they are at their best only after a few years and therefore overwintering must be accomplished somewhere for best success. Perhaps we will see more of these fascinating plants in botanical gardens and public gardens in the future, and slowly they may seep down to hard-core gardeners around the country.

I planted white mussaenda (*Mussaenda incana*) many years ago, with no idea of what to expect. At first I was intrigued with the small yellow flowers and then really beguiled by the large expanded bract-like white sepal. A single sepal on each flower was three to four times larger than the others, and as the plants matured, they seemed to be covered with fluttering white wings (I was definitely beguiled). Plants grew only about 2' tall, but that just made them easier to bring in for the winter.

MORE ☞

Mussaenda incana

Mussaenda incana, flowers

Mussaenda frondosa

Mussaenda frondosa, flowers

Three or four years later I finally came across another mussaenda, this time at the Ripley Garden in Washington, D.C. Although it had similar white sepals, the flowers were red, and it was even more beautiful than the one I was growing back in Athens. I saw the same species a year later at Landcraft Environments on Long Island. The botanical names are not particularly well documented for this genus, but it was likely red mussaenda, *Mussaenda frondosa*. Both places had been growing the plants for a number of years and obviously had brought them in for the winter. They are easy to grow; there is no reason why they can't be grown in Minnesota or Calgary. It is just a matter of finding a source to get started. Plant in containers, full sun.

Nelumbo nucifera

SACRED LOTUS

Plants have been cultivated for over 5000 years, and is it not special to have such a valued piece of history in our gardens? In the world of water gardens, the sacred lotus (*Nelumbo nucifera*) is probably king, sharing its kingdom with water lilies and a few ugly carp. It seems every sunny water garden has all three, but lotus dwarfs the others in beautiful leaves, classical flowers, and useful fruit. Not to mention size—this is not a plant for the small backyard barrel.

From the Chicago Botanic Garden to the Zurich Botanical Gardens, lotus are at home. The large rounded leaves and the beautiful white to pink-flushed flow-

Nelumbo nucifera, Chicago Botanic Garden

Nelumbo nucifera, fruit

Nelumbo nucifera, Zurich Botanical Gardens

Nelumbo nucifera 'Chawan Basu'

ers lend a calmness to any garden vista. And once the flowers are finished, the large fruit capsules dominate the scene, each one containing a dozen or so rock-hard seeds. Over time, the seeds are dispersed, and the capsule turns bronze and starts to shrivel. The immature capsules with the seeds can often be found at farmers' markets or craft stores, sold as dry flowers for the vestibule washstand.

Lotus has not been around for fifty centuries without some selection, natural or otherwise, taking place. Hundreds of cultivars have been named and are quite easy to find. Many are truly outstanding. I have enjoyed only a few, but they include those with changeable flower colors, often starting yellow ('Mrs. Perry D. Slocum'), double red flowers ('Momo Botan'), and white flowers edged in pink ('Chawan Basu'). It really does not matter if cultivars or the species itself resides in the pond—sacred lotus is the perfect addition to the water garden.

Plants will overwinter as long as the water does not freeze around the roots, and that depends on the depth of the water. Just let them stay where you have them if your pond won't freeze to the bottom; if you house them elsewhere, be sure they stay immersed in water and don't keep them so warm that they think it is spring. If you see some leaf dieback, cut them off close to the tuber, then leave the plant alone. Full sun.

Nelumbo nucifera 'Momo Botan'

Nelumbo nucifera 'Mrs. Perry D. Slocum'

Nemesia strumosa

I must admit, I never really had a lot of use for the nemesias I saw in retail centers or in neighborhood gardens. They were all a little washed out, rather leggy and did not show up particularly well. The flowers are relatively small, but to be fair, when plants are at their best, they produce dozens and dozens of them.

The new selections in the past few years have gone a long way to changing my opinion about *Nemesia strumosa*, and I can recommend a number of them to gardeners in the Midwest, northern states, and to most Canadian gardeners. They do far better during cool-weather times and may struggle when temperatures are hot and humid. The longer the hot, humid weather persists, the more they struggle. Even so, those I would recommend are a great deal better than most of what was out there ten years ago.

One of the older forms but still lovely is the bicolored 'Woodstock', with flowers of purple and yellow. Plants stay nicely upright, and flowering continues for many months. The best of the pinks is 'Shell Pink', growing about 15" tall and absolutely covered with light pink flowers. If I was to select a white for my daughters' gardens, I would tell them to look for 'Compact Innocence', which we have watched flower most of the season even in Georgia. 'Aromatica Lavender' is equally good and even overwinters in zone 7. A number of other selections have been bred and with a little search-

Nemesia strumosa 'Woodstock'

Nemesia strumosa 'Shell Pink'

Nemesia strumosa 'Compact Innocence'

Nemesia strumosa 'Aromatica Lavender'

ing, they are well worth trying. 'KLM' is a beautiful bicolor, from Dutch breeding, of course, and seems to cover itself with small gray-blue and white flowers. And for large flowers that look more like primroses than nemesias, I recently discovered Sundrops series, from an excellent American firm. I have not seen them outdoors, so cannot comment on their garden performance, but they sure catch the eye while in pots.

Full sun in the North, afternoon shade in the South.

Nemophila

Plants are native to California, and prefer moist soils and cool nights. They are not well known on the eastern side of the country, and even less known in the southern portion of that half. However, they make wonderful groundcover plants as one progresses north. Plants tend to flower heaviest in spring, and taper off significantly if conditions deteriorate. They are useful for naturalizing large areas, as they come back readily from seed. They are fanciful little plants, as can be seen by their fanciful common names.

Baby-blue-eyes may be the nickname of your favorite friend or pet, but it also refers to the magnificent blue flowers of *Nemophila menziesii*. The flowers usually have a clean white center, which makes the outer blue of the flower even more spectacular. In some cases everything gets turned around; the center becomes purple and the outer edges are white, as is the case with 'Pennie Black'.

Nemesia strumosa 'KLM'

Nemophila menziesii 'Pennie Black'

Nemophila maculata

Nemesia strumosa Sundrops series

Nemophila menziesii

MORE ☞

Five spot refers to the five dark spots on the end of the petals of *Nemophila maculata*. The plants stand only about 12" tall and are a little leggy, but they can be covered with white flowers throughout the spring and into the summer if weather is not too hot and soils don't become too dry. Full sun if moisture is consistently available, partial shade if not.

Nicotiana

TOBACCO

I get a little upset whenever I read that global warming and air pollution are the result of "greenhouse gases." Even though it sounds unbelievable, many people out there now look at greenhouses suspiciously and feel they must be partly to blame for some of these problems. It would be laughable if not so ignorant. The same argument can be heard from anti-smoking zealots who want to plow under all tobacco plants, as if the plant itself was making them cough. Fortunately for us all, many plants in the tobacco family are terrific ornamentals. So if you find yourself in the same room with the anti-smoking and the anti-gas people, it may be wise not to mention that your favorite flowering tobacco plant was raised in a greenhouse.

At least three species of tobacco make great garden plants. One of them, *Nicotiana sylvestris*, looks ostensibly like a "real" Virginia Slim tobacco plant. But it

Nemophila maculata, flowers

Nicotiana sylvestris with pennisetum

Nicotiana sylvestris

is not, and would not smoke well. It is a large plant, and when it is growing vigorously, the wavy leaves look like big green paddles. Plants can stand alone or can be the main feature in a mixed bed of purple-leaved lobelias and pink impatiens. In Chicago, plants were growing in a small fenced corner, appearing to ward away the evil spirits of the pennisetum grass. The flowers are quite beautiful, seemingly exploding from the top of the plant, perhaps accounting for its common name, white shooting stars. However, all is not Camelot in the tobacco plot; if aphids are within a mile of the plant, they will find it. As long as you know this will happen, it is a nonproblem. When you see them, wash

Nicotiana sylvestris with aphids

Nicotiana langsdorffii

Nicotiana ×*sanderae* with conifers

Nicotiana sylvestris with lobelia and begonias

MORE ☞

them away with a garden hose. You can douse with chemicals if that is your thing, but that is seldom necessary if you inspect your plants every now and then.

The plant that all people seem to enjoy but often do not recognize as a tobacco is the lime tobacco, *Nicotiana langsdorffii*. In most plantings, the flowers are almost hazy, not really standing out from the surroundings. Maybe this is why it is so seldom used in mixed plantings. But where plants are grown well, and when the dark green leaves contrast with the lime-green flowers, they are impossible to ignore. Lime tobacco has to be grown for a while to be appreciated; it is not going to be an impulse item at the corner garden store.

By far the most common plant in the

Nicotiana alata

Nicotiana ×*sanderae* 'Nikki Red'

Nicotiana ×*sanderae* 'Prelude Salmon'

Nicotiana ×*sanderae* 'Perfuma Lime'

ornamental tobacco family is the bedding form, the hybrid flowering tobacco, *Nicotiana* ×*sanderae*. They are unbelievably beautiful, and much of their beauty come from one of the main parents in the breeding, the winged tobacco, *N. alata*. Seldom seen for sale in containers anymore, winged tobacco is still available from seed. The plants are 3–4' tall, with numerous flowers of different colors, often red, and highly fragrant. In June Collin's garden in Portland, Oregon, the plant was reaching for the sky and perfuming all around it. Asked what she did to make it look so wonderful, she commented, "That old weed, I just threw it in there for the smell." Oh, to garden in Portland.

The hybrids are gorgeous, far shorter, and easier to grow. The color range is outstanding, but unfortunately, breeding for dwarfness resulted in the loss of fragrance. Such a shame, for now only the eyes can enjoy the planting. Oftentimes, plants won't even be labeled but can be seen from a football field away, flowering away in and among junipers and other plants in the garden. So many fascinating colors are available as well. A planting of Nikki Mix shows off many of the colors in the hybrids, and who would have thought to put a specimen of 'Nikki Red' in a container on the step going up to the house? Salmon colors have been quite popular as well. The light salmon color of 'Prelude Salmon' is quite wonderful, whereas 'Avalon Salmon' provides a darker color and holds up even in hot summer temperatures.

But for me, there are two plantings I recall the most. One was when someone was complaining that they had to have the lime-green color found in lime tobacco but couldn't find that plant anywhere. I showed her the brilliant lime-green color of 'Perfuma Lime', and voilá, a perfect substitute was made. The other perfect use was at a perfect place, Banff, Alberta, where the cool mountain air made everything perfect. A simple container planting of lobelia and rudbeckia, topped with white flowering tobacco, was as wonderful as the scenery surrounding it. Who says simplicity is not the best thing? Full sun.

Nicotiana ×*sanderae* Nikki Mix

Nicotiana ×*sanderae* 'Avalon Salmon'

Nicotiana ×*sanderae*, white form, Banff

Nierembergia

CUPFLOWER

The cupflowers belong to the same family as petunia (Solanaceae) and have similar wide open flowers and spreading habit. Plants are much stringier and more woody than petunias, and a bit more temperamental. They can be used as edging, but well-drained soils, such as a rocky area, a raised bed, or a container, are necessary for best performance, particularly in southern climes.

All cupflowers are cold hardy to about zone 7 or 8, but most people treat them as annuals. The most cold hardy is probably whitecap, *Nierembergia repens*, often sold under the name *N. rivularis*. The flowers are large relative to the plant and can be used to line a driveway or just to provide some beautiful shiny white flowers. Not terribly common, but once established, they will reseed if they find an area to their liking.

I seldom see one of my favorites, tall cupflower, *Nierembergia scoparia*. I came across this plant many years ago, and noticed that, unlike the more compact forms, this one liked to spread out more and grow a little taller. I also noticed that while some plants looked spectacular, too many others struggled. Inconsistent performance seems to be common, at least to my eyes, for many members of the genus. However, in areas where they have a little time to grow and overwinter, their second-year show is out of this world, with white flowers often blushed with lavender. If nierembergias do well in your area, this is a must-try plant.

Nierembergia repens

Nierembergia scoparia, flowers

Nierembergia scoparia

Nierembergia frutescens 'Purple Robe' with lotus and geraniums

The most common forms are two species that are inconsistently labeled and probably all mixed up. Both *Nierembergia frutescens* and *N. hippomanica* are called cupflower and are similar in appearance. The latter is less woody than the former and has shorter leaves and larger flowers. Both perform about the same and require similar conditions to do well, so it is not really all that important to know which one you are purchasing. 'Purple Robe' is the most common cultivar, and I have enjoyed it in a mixed container or by itself in a hanging basket. The deep color of a meandering planting of 'Purple Robe' was united with brightly colored florist hydrangeas in the conservatory at Longwood Gardens. A beautiful combination.

Plants sold as *Nierembergia hippomanica* var. *violacea* were perfect in the wonderful Old Westbury Gardens on Long Island, New York; this variety has some of the prettiest and largest flowers in the group. I most enjoy the white-flowered forms, such as 'White Star' or the even-better 'Mount Blanc'. Both have large clean white flowers and grow well if provided with well-drained conditions. If they overwinter, they will be some of the best and biggest plants in the spring garden, providing color to complement the pansies and violas. Full sun.

Nierembergia frutescens 'Purple Robe', basket

Nierembergia frutescens 'Purple Robe' with hydrangeas

Nierembergia hippomanica var. *violacea*

Nierembergia hippomanica 'Mount Blanc'

MORE ☞

Nierembergia hippomanica 'White Star'

Nierembergia hippomanica 'Mount Blanc', overwintered in Athens, Georgia

Nigella damascena, field for cut fruit

Nigella damascena, garden with fruit

Nigella

LOVE-IN-A-MIST

Between puffs and mists—loving must have enjoyed fascinating venues back when these names were first penned. When I look at love-in-a-mist (*Nigella damascena*), I see a nice blue-flowered plant with lacy leaves and interesting fruit, but I don't see love or the mist. Plant people will never be accused of being unimaginative.

This annual has been used for years as a simple and rather ordinary addition to the garden. However, if you examine a flower, you will find the structure is anything but ordinary. At the base of the flowers can be seen the long thin leafy structures (involucres) that supposedly account for the "mist," and with the pistil and stamens sticking up above a full skirt of sepals and petals, the flower looks like it is growing upside down. Seed is often available in packages at the local garden store; a mixture of white and blue flowers may result, with the white flowers generally having only a single row of petals.

The most common form is 'Miss Jekyll', named after the famed English gardener and writer, with full lavender to blue flowers above fennel-like foliage. A number of good double white forms are available; 'Albion' is as good as any. If all that nigella did was produce flowers, that would be quite sufficient, but the fruit is as interesting as the blooms. Each flower gives rise to a strange pod that stands above the foliage in mid to late summer. They start green and essentially dry on the plant, turning to a dull bronze. If the summer

Nigella damascena 'Albion'

Nigella damascena, mix with single white flowers

Nigella damascena 'Miss Jekyll'

Nigella damascena, flower

Nigella hispanica 'Exotic'

Nigella hispanica, fruit

MORE ☞

is dry and not too hot, they stay quite ornamental for a long time. They are harvested by cut flower growers who sell them at farmers' markets and to wholesalers for dried arrangements for the home.

Certainly, common love-in-a-mist is the most popular form of nigella; however, some people like to try a few of the other oddballs. Fennel flower, *Nigella hispanica*, commonly available in the selection 'Exotic', is also handsome but lacks the involucres and has single flowers only. But the finger-like appendages on the fruit make them even more bizarre than those of the common form. What better excuse to try some? Full sun.

Odontonema strictum

FIRESPIKE

This is not a plant for every gardener, especially impatient ones. In fact, I would hazard that this is a plant only for those fortunate few with long autumns and calm dispositions. Firespike (*Odontonema strictum*) is cold hardy to about zone 7b, but a hard winter will take it out. Because it is a slow grower in the spring, it is best to buy started plants, even if you live in a moderately mild climate. For people in the Gulf States and those with hot, long summers, this is a no-brainer.

The glossy deep green leaves are outstanding, and for some people that is reason enough to have it in the garden. But most of us would like a flower or two as well, and therein lies the problem for the impatient gardener. Plants don't begin to flower until October, even in the South, and if snow is already falling, this plant is not for you. But when it flowers, the spikes truly are on fire, and if the plant is happy, half a dozen spikes may be flaming at once. A great plant to reverse the summer blahs and to rejuvenate the fall garden. A variegated form, 'Variegata', is also available; although the leaves are interesting, flowering is very sparse. Full sun.

Odontonema strictum, flowers

Odontonema strictum 'Variegata'

Odontonema strictum

Orthosiphon stamineus

CAT'S WHISKERS

I have never been much of a fan of cats, and at the risk of losing readers, I must admit I just don't get it. Independence is a great thing, but give me a tail-wagging, tongue-drooling, can't-wait-to-greet-me yellow lab any day. So when a cat-loving gardener introduced me to a plant called cat's whiskers (*Orthosiphon stamineus*), I wasn't as enthusiastic as I might have been. However, the plant is not half bad, and the name is indeed descriptive.

Cat's whiskers are whiskered, that is for sure, and the whiskers are the result of the long stamens protruding from the individual lavender flowers. The most

Orthosiphon stamineus

common color, however, appears to be white, 'Albus', which is more floriferous than the lavender and contrasts better with the light green leaves. The opening flower spike is a beautiful study in plant function, the bottom flowers opening first, while the others patiently await their turn.

But two problems, other than the name, keep me from embracing this plant. Normally, only a few flowers appear at any one time, and the leaves always appear to be washed out and in need of fertilizer. When many flowers do open at once, however, they make a dramatic sight. Full sun.

Orthosiphon stamineus 'Albus'

Osteospermum

CAPE DAISY

Cape daisies, one of the many daisy flowers native to Cape province of South Africa, have been domesticated, bred, and morphed into an incredible number of colors and shapes. In their native setting, they receive cool weather in the winter and flower in the spring, then essentially are leafy plants during the hot summer. The same is true for the majority of the cultivars we see for sale in the spring on this continent: they flower profusely in the spring, then

Orthosiphon stamineus 'Albus', flowers

Osteospermum, variegated form

MORE ☞

become little shrublets through most of the summer. That is not to say they are not beautiful or worthy of inclusion in the garden, it simply means that they are spring flowerers, and for most of us, they will provide very little color during the summer. The same can be said for *Argyranthemum* (which see). The many species may occasionally be found in botanic gardens, but gardeners have little choice except for the hybrids.

But are they beautiful! A planting at the Paul Ecke Ranch in Encinitas, California, is an incredible sight and makes you want to buy every one of them. Bred in Australia, Germany, and Scandinavia, they are quite remarkable. A few variegated forms can be found, but they have a ways to go. Others cultivars, however, are striking. The whirligig pattern in the flowers of 'Nisinga Cream' is unique; the open daisy flowers of 'Seaside' and 'Brightside' provide a much calmer look. In western Washington state, the creamy flowers of 'Lubutu'

Osteospermum 'Nasinga Cream'

Osteospermum 'Seaside'

Osteospermum, California trials

Osteospermum 'Lubutu'

Osteospermum Passion Mix

Osteospermum 'Brightside'

Osteospermum 'White Flash' with bidens

Osteospermum 'Sparkler'

Osteospermum 'Lemon Symphony'

were also outstanding. In southern Germany, osteos are everywhere, and cultivars like 'White Flash' are routinely combined with other annuals like bidens. It might seem clear that most of the places where these blow-me-away plants are prettiest are areas where day and night temperatures hover between 50 and 75°F during the summer. However, those areas are simply where the plants will flower the longest; they can be attractive anywhere. At Longwood Gardens, a planting of 'Sparkler' looked lovely in May, and even at the Park Seed Company in warm South Carolina, the seed-propagated Passion Mix was outstanding in the spring. In our trials in Georgia, numerous cultivars have looked good in spring, such as the yellow 'Lemon Symphony', but flowering finished by early June.

Therefore, everyone can enjoy osteos, it is simply the expectations that disappoint some gardeners. Most of us will enjoy them in the spring; a few in the North, the mountains, or the West Coast can have them longer, perhaps even flowering through the summer.

The cultivars I have mentioned are but a small sampling of what is presently offered. There is far too much beauty not to try a few of them; buy them in flower and as large as the budget will allow. The foliage is quite handsome and at worse, you will end up with some nice little shrubs. Place them in well-drained areas of the garden or in large containers. Full sun.

Otacanthus caeruleus

BRAZILIAN SNAPDRAGON

If you can't get enough blue in the garden, Brazilian snapdragon (*Otacanthus caeruleus*) may be a plant worth considering. The leaves are clean, seldom attracting insects or diseases, and they grow reasonably vigorously, neither taking over the garden nor getting buried by a neighbor.

The lavender-blue flowers have a white eye, and three or four flowers are whorled around the end of the stem. Unfortunately, they don't begin to flower well until mid to late summer but, once in bloom, remain colorful for months. They are excellent for cutting as well and will persist in the vase for a week to ten days. Full sun.

Papaver

POPPY

The annual forms of this popular genus are not nearly as common in the garden as the perennial Oriental poppy, but at least one of them, the Flanders poppy, is at least as well known. Most of the poppies are short-lived perennials or biennials, and they self-sow so readily that it is sometimes difficult to characterize their growth cycle. For example, the Iceland poppy is perennial in northern climates, but an annual or biennial in most other areas of the country. All of these, however, are marvelous garden plants and provide stunning color.

I can never look at a Flanders poppy, *Papaver rhoeas*, in a field or garden without thinking of the destruction of life and the ability of one poem to capture the carnage, futility, and sacrifices of war. As a result of John McCrae's poem, the poppy became the visible means for nations to remember the

Otacanthus caeruleus

Otacanthus caeruleus, flowers

Papaver rhoeas, roadside

Papaver rhoeas Shirley series

Papaver rhoeas, field, Belgium

Papaver somniferum, flower

Papaver somniferum, single and double flowers

Papaver somniferum 'Paeoniflorum'

MORE ☞

Papaver somniferum 'Double Pink'

Papaver somniferum 'Single Puce'

Papaver somniferum 'Fringed Red'

Papaver somniferum 'Album'

Papaver somniferum, fruit

Papaver nudicaule with pansies

price of freedom. Fortunately, the flowers we use for roadside plantings and in the garden are too beautiful for such sobering thoughts to linger in our minds, and now we can simply enjoy their fleeting color. The choices for color are few, however, with the exception of the poppies in the Shirley series. Most of the time, seeds will yield plants with flowers of intense red or scarlet. Plant a lot of seeds, and if you are lucky, the planting may bring to mind the field of poppies in Belgium that so inspired the young Canadian physician and poet.

Just as the Flanders poppy evokes stories in my head, I can't help but imagine Toto sleeping in the field of flowers whenever I see the beautiful opium poppy, *Papaver somniferum*. I much prefer to think of the girl and her dog than of the despair and misery that have

Papaver nudicaule, Palmerston North, New Zealand

Papaver nudicaule 'Champagne Bubbles'

Papaver nudicaule, Chicago Botanic Garden

MORE ☞

Papaver nudicaule 'Party Fun'

Papaver nudicaule Wonderland series

Papaver nudicaule Constance Finnis Group

Papaver nudicaule, double form

resulted from abuse of its by-products. And as with the Flanders poppy, the deep scarlet flowers are too beautiful not to enjoy: planting some seeds in the fall results in some beautiful forms and colors the next spring. The main forms of opium poppy are the single and doubles, which often grow side by side. The double form, called 'Paeoniflorum' for obvious reasons, is quite spectacular. But spectacular is not the only color in this great plant; a mix of seed may yield single puce and double pink and white flowers, a calming influence on the riot of scarlet. If outrageous is your shtick and for sheer immodesty, try a few plants of 'Fringed Red'; people may think you have been sampling the juice. The fruit capsule, which has been the root of so much misery, is also quite beautiful and is cut for dried arrangements in the house. Break open the capsule and gather the seeds for next year's show.

Papaver nudicaule, the Iceland poppy, evokes images of flowers rising from melting ice packs, but in truth, as a garden plant, it is seldom used as a perennial. It has gained popularity in many regions because of its tendency to flower in the early spring and is often seen in the company of pansies and nasturtiums. Plants can stay in the ground until night temperatures begin to remain in the 70s. There is no hard and fast rule; simply remove them when they look tired, or when you want the space for something else. I have seen wonderful plantings at the State Botanical Garden of Georgia in which the Iceland poppies were interspersed with blue and white pansies, and in Chicago, a mixed panorama greeted walkers in the botanic garden there. One thinks of exotic plants when one thinks of New Zealand, but a mixture of white and yellow Iceland poppies in July provided a magnificent vista at the Victoria Esplanade in Palmerston North. A vista may be a marvelous sight from a distance, but the flowers of Iceland poppies should be appreciated up close; they are quite marvelous. Numerous cultivars have been bred, like 'Champagne Bubbles', 'Party Fun', and those in the Wonderland series. There are few differences between them, and all should do just fine. Occasionally, a single color may be available, as in the white poppies of the Constance Finnis Group, seen in England; and if you are a glutton for punishment, give the double forms a try. They are gruesome, the breeder should be imprisoned, but to each their own. Full sun, cool temperatures.

Passiflora

PASSION FLOWER

Passion flower vines and passion fruit were not even in my Canadian vocabulary as a boy growing up in Montreal. Much later, when I moved to the States, people would talk about what they called maypops as an obnoxious weed; I thought they were beautiful. I saw more passion flower vines in botanic gardens and conservatories, but they never seemed to get outside. In the last few years, however, I have admired the

Passiflora citrina

Passiflora coccinea

Passiflora violacea

MORE ☞

Passiflora serratifolia

Passiflora caerulea

Passiflora 'Sunburst'

Passiflora 'Amethyst'

Passiflora 'Little Orchid'

Passiflora 'Debbie'

yellow flowers of *Passiflora citrina* and the blue blossoms of *P. caerulea* in European gardens, and in this country, I reveled in a gorgeous planting of *P. violacea* at the Ripley Garden in Washington, D.C. Plantings are popping up further north as well, and other than the cost, there is no reason not to include them on an arbor or trellis.

Some of our better mail-order nurseries offer a wonderful variety of passion flower vines, including both species and named hybrids. The species are numerous, and easiest to think of by color; for example, the red flowers are brilliant in *Passiflora coccinea*. Marvelous small yellow flowers can be found on the hybrid 'Sunburst', hidden in the white-veined leaves. While multiple colors are the norm on passion flowers, blue and lavender is the most common combination. 'Amethyst' has beautiful blue flowers, while 'Little Orchid' provides some of the prettiest shades of orchid on any of the vines. Much of the beauty of passion flowers is due to the slender filament-like structure called the corona. They are particularly obvious in 'Debbie' and appear to be doubled in the flowers of *P. serratifolia*. All are wonderful; some flower more persistently than others, but all will transform your old trellis into something quite spectacular.

If placed in pots, plants can be cut back and brought into a heated garage to overwinter, or cuttings may be taken in the fall. Full sun.

Pavonia

Pavonias are known around the world, but American gardeners have not yet discovered them. Plants belong to the mallow family, the same as hibiscus, flowering maple, and cotton, and few members of that family do not have ornamental value.

The only species I can recommend is Brazilian firecracker, *Pavonia multiflora*, mainly because that is the only one most of us will have any chance of obtaining. Selection is under way, and this plant should be much more available to gardeners in a few years' time. Plants send up straight stems with leathery green leaves, and the unique blossoms are blood red. The weird flowers consist of thin bracts and red petals, which surround multicolored stamens protruding from within. Another weird thing is the alternative botanical name this plant sometimes goes under, *Triplochlamys*. Arguments have been made for both generic names, but until the dust settles, I vote to use the one I can pronounce.

Plants have been grown in conservatories and in tropical areas for years, and gardeners might want to try one or two in the patio container. Full sun.

Pelargonium

GERANIUM

The interest in geraniums rises and falls from one generation to the next, but they are always among the top five in annual sales of all flowers in North America. To the uninitiated, there does not seem to be all that much variety in geraniums; most of them are red, with a few whites and pinks thrown in every now and then. But, from my perspective, seeing what breeders have introduced to the greenhouse trade, there must be over three hundred different cultivars available, albeit many quite similar to each other. I have been studying, evaluating, and appreciating the beauty of geraniums for years. We had baskets by the front stairs in Guelph, Ontario, when my daughter Laura was six years old, and recently I trialed over 120 cultivars at the University of Georgia. Of those 120 geranium cultivars of all colors, probably no more than half a dozen existed more than three years ago. A lot of plants have

MORE ☞

Pavonia multiflora

Pavonia multiflora, flowers

Pelargonium ×*hortorum*, Guelph, Ontario

Pelargonium ×*hortorum*, UGA Trial Gardens

Pelargonium ×*hortorum* with verbena and pocketbook plant

gone under the bridge in the past twenty-five years, but not geraniums—they are as beloved as ever. Except perhaps by the people who have to maintain them. The constant deadheading is a long and tedious job. Still, it does not seem to matter what other flowers are on the market: landscapers and gardeners always want good old geraniums, and usually good old red geraniums.

In the garden, geraniums fall into two main categories, zonal geraniums (*Pelargonium* ×*hortorum*), by far the most common, and ivy-leaf geraniums (*P. peltatum*), always grown in hanging baskets. Martha Washington geraniums (*P. domesticum*) are only now starting to be seen again in garden containers, and few at that. Numerous other species geraniums, such as fancy-leaf forms and scented geraniums, can be found, but few of these find their way into outdoor gardens in this country.

I think most everybody knows what geraniums look like, so I will simply share a few creative settings and handsome cultivars. Red geraniums seem to make everything better, and mixed beds are the perfect setting for these colorful plants. The most beautiful use was at the

Pelargonium ×*hortorum* in a window box with bidens and Cape daisies

Pelargonium ×*hortorum* in a window box

Pelargonium ×*hortorum* with verbena and marigolds

Pelargonium ×*hortorum* with heliotrope

MORE ☞

Butchart Gardens in British Columbia, where the combination of red geraniums, lavender verbena, and pocketbook plant was the illustrated definition of awesome. Then I saw them combined with the same verbena but highlighted with yellow marigolds. The lowly marigold had never been in such exquisite company. And the bed of red geranium and 'Marine' heliotrope looked so good that I had to wait for about twenty minutes to take the picture because admiring people kept getting in the way!

Plantings don't have to be so grandiose or large to provide pleasure. Window boxes have always been an ideal setting for geraniums; a mixed box of light yellow Cape daisies, purple petunias, yellow bidens, and red geraniums made a wonderful scene in a mountain village. On paper, a mixed planting of rose and red geraniums sounds rather gruesome, but it sure worked for me.

Geraniums come in all Kodak hues, but approximately 80 percent of those sold are red; the next most popular color is pink. Heliotrope looks almost as good combined with pink geraniums as it did with red, and white alyssum has always been a good edging plant, helping to render the pink flowers even pinker. The next most sought-after color is white. In a combination setting or filling in an area between clipped yew hedges, white ('Pinto White') will always be popular. The zonal geraniums have it all, and it would be remiss of me not to add that orange, lavender, rose, salmon, and bicolor flowers can also be purchased. And just when I thought I had seen it all, I looked behind a solemn green bench, and there was a magnificent planting of 'Wilhelm Languth', arguably the best variegated geranium on the market. There is no doubt that zonal geranium performance is significantly enhanced in areas with cool nights.

In our trials in Athens, Georgia, we

Pelargonium ×*hortorum* with heliotrope

Pelargonium ×*hortorum* with sweet alyssum

Pelargonium ×*hortorum* 'Pinto White'

find that geraniums are one of the most time-consuming plants to maintain: spent flowers must be removed (deadheaded) or plants stop blooming and become susceptible to numerous fungal diseases, requiring constant attention. Maintenance is still a chore in the North, but not as much so. They are at their best in the North, Far West (where they are often perennial), and at higher elevations.

The ivy-leaf geranium is also highly popular and becoming even more so, for good reasons. The performance of the new cultivars is outstanding throughout the country. The preference for hanging baskets mirrors the trends to containers and smaller gardens, and many fine colors are now available to gardeners. They have handsome foliage and even when not in full flower, as in a container positioned on the stairs at Old Westbury Gardens on Long Island, the plants still looked good. Red is the dominant color in the ivies, and it was pretty difficult to argue with the large basket at the Montreal Botanical Garden. A basket of salmon-pink in Sydney, Australia, also looked magnificent, but we had only to step outside the door here at the University of Georgia to admire a mixed basket of rose and red ivies. Our baskets impressed and stopped people all summer, demonstrating another reason for the popularity of this group of geraniums: they tolerate heat and humidity better and deadheading is much less of an issue.

I am starting to see a few more Martha Washington geraniums, mostly in containers, in North American gardens. They still have problems with heat tolerance, so they are always going to be more popular in cooler areas. They can be grown in warm temperate areas, but

Pelargonium ×hortorum 'Wilhelm Languth'

Pelargonium peltatum, Old Westbury Gardens

Pelargonium peltatum, Montreal Botanical Garden

Pelargonium peltatum, Sydney

MORE ☞

Pelargonium domesticum 'My Choice'

Pelargonium domesticum 'Carnival'

Pelargonium peltatum, UGA Trial Gardens

Pelargonium domesticum 'Hollywood Lady'

much like osteospermums, they will seldom flower once night temperatures rise above 75°F. However, cultivars with flowers of red ('Carnival'), rose ('My Choice'), and white ('Hollywood Lady') might make any gardener with a little money decide to try a couple anyway. They are best in containers, they will do poorly in the ground.

All geraniums, except the Martha Washington types (partial shade), perform better in full sun; be careful of overwatering, particularly as temperatures rise.

Pennisetum

As a general rule, most ornamental grasses used by gardeners are perennial, and plants in this genus are no exception. However, at least three species make excellent annuals, and they provide grasses that do go away, unlike some of the persistent, spreading perennial grasses out there.

The least common is feathertop, *Pennisetum villosum*, which is perennial in zone 7b and warmer, but for most of us, it is best used as an annual. It grows 2–3' tall and by late summer is topped with feathery plumes of flowers. They are excellent leaning over walkways or simply gently flowing with the wind. The foliage is handsome enough, but it is the flowers that gardeners enjoy.

For foliage, two excellent choices are available. The old-fashioned purple fountain grass, *Pennisetum setaceum* 'Rubrum', is used in containers which can be placed anywhere that purple color is needed, and the same plants, towering over begonias in Will Carlson's Michigan garden, showed that the flowers are as beautiful as the foliage.

Pennisetum villosum

Pennisetum setaceum 'Rubrum'

Pennisetum setaceum 'Rubrum' with pink begonias

Pennisetum glaucum 'Purple Majesty'

MORE ☞

Pennisetum glaucum 'Purple Majesty', stand

The nice thing about the grass is even when not in flower, it is a terrific plant.

The latest and perhaps the one that may be even more popular is ornamental millet, *Pennisetum glaucum*. No kidding, these are the seeds usually found in your birdfeeder mix, hardly something you would ponder in the plant center. We grew a beautiful purple-leaved, purple-flowered cultivar for years, even before it had a name, and so I can highly recommend 'Purple Majesty', the name it bears today. As the dominant feature in a container or as a dense planting, a wonderful show is assured. The flowers not only attract birds but also make fine persistent cut flowers. Some people find the malodorous aroma of the cut stems outweighs the vase life. Regardless, this is a must-have grass for the garden. All pennisetums perform best in full sun.

Pentas lanceolata 'Orchid Illusion'

Pentas lanceolata 'Nova', flowers

Pentas lanceolata

STAR FLOWER

Star flowers (*Pentas lanceolata*) have been sold as ornamental plants for many years, but it is only in the last decade or so that they have attracted gardeners around the country. That they are good flowerers is a given, but with more attention being paid to garden form, and better breeding material, they have simply caught on with more people. As well they should—excellent color choices are available, and once temperatures warm up, plants will flower the entire season.

For many years, pentas hung around garden centers and on the periphery of gardeners' thoughts, never really enjoying stellar popularity. The cultivars were pretty enough but did not display sufficient vigor or flower power. Selections like 'Orchid Illusion' and 'Pearl White' were difficult to locate and were disappointing in most areas of the country after a month or so in the garden. I had trialed a lot of star flowers, and the only one I considered worthy of being included in my daughters' gardens was

Pentas lanceolata Butterfly series

Pentas lanceolata 'Pearl White'

Pentas lanceolata 'Nova'

Pentas lanceolata 'New Look Pink'

Pentas lanceolata 'New Look Violet'

MORE ☞

'Nova', a vigorous grower with many rose-colored flowers on 2' tall plants. The individual stems carry exquisite flowers, which are useful as cuts for the house and patio.

But the late 1990s and early 2000s have seen the renaissance of pentas from a once-in-a-while plant to one that is in constant demand, particularly as summers seem to be warming up. The New Look series is a seed-propagated form with excellent flowering on dwarf 1½' tall plants. Its fine flower colors and good vigor (plants don't get too big, however) renewed interest in the plant. 'New Look Pink' and 'New Look Violet' are among the many colors available in the series. The vegetatively propagated Butterfly series came on the heels of New Look and provided bigger, even more vigorous plants with flowers in numerous colors. We found they all flowered well, but 'Butterfly Pink' and 'Butterfly Red' were even better than the others. Hot temperatures won't reduce their flowering or vigor, but under such conditions, they may need a haircut in mid summer. The most eye-catching of all the star flowers is 'Stars and Stripes', the first available variegated leaf form, which has spurred interest even further. Both the variegation and the flowers remain all season. And another wonderful characteristic: almost every publication about butterfly or hummingbird gardens suggests pentas as an attractant. Need I say more? Go get some and get dirty. Full sun.

Pentas lanceolata 'Stars and Stripes'

Perilla frutescens

There is very little reason for including perilla (*Perilla frutescens*) as a garden annual; for many gardeners, it is nothing more than a green weed that reseeds everywhere. However, the purple-leaved form (var. *atropurpurea*) has benefitted from the interest in plants with purple foliage and is fairly common and easy to find. Its reseeding tendencies, its ease of growth, and the contrast it provides to green-leaved plants are a few good reasons to include it. Similar plants, like purple basil, seem to taste better, and purple coleus seems to perform better, but what do I know? A number of cultivars are available, including 'Nanking',

Pentas lanceolata 'Butterfly Red', *P. l.* 'Butterfly Pink'

Perilla frutescens 'Nanking'

which goes well with white salvias and other light-colored plantings. But be careful: plants reseed with great abandon, and you may be inundated with little purple things for many years. Full sun.

Petunia

It is a toss-up to determine which bedding annual takes the most verbal abuse in gardening, the marigold or the petunia. There are always lots of garden snobs who would rather eat horse dung than actually have a petunia in their garden. However, every endeavor has its snobs, who need be given no more thought than one would extend to a balloon expelling gas.

Without doubt, petunias are one of the all-time great success stories in horticulture. In the 1980s, petunias were the number one seller in American horticulture, but as other plants became available they lost popularity, mostly because breeders rested on their laurels a little too long. That is not to say that older cultivars were not good; in fact, many have been tweaked here and there and still are sold today. However, dozens more have been bred in the last ten years, revitalizing interest in this fine genus. At the UGA Trial Gardens, I am sure I have seen every one, row after row, after row, after row. I mean every last one of them! Of course, the interest by breeders simply reflects the interest of gardeners. While they have always been popular in gardens, today they are also poked and prodded into every available nook and cranny in containers across this country.

Perilla frutescens var. *atropurpurea*

Petunia 'Primetime Rose'

Petunia hybrids, UGA Trial Gardens

Petunia 'Surfina Rose Veined'

MORE ☞

Flower size differs from cultivar to cultivar; the large flowers, such as found in the Primetime series, are still common but not nearly as popular as they once were. The Surfinia series has been highly popular because of its better performance, cascading habit, and striking colors. 'Surfinia Rose Veined' is one of the brighter colors in the series; 'Surfinia White' is a clean white. Smaller-flowering forms have truly been the rage in recent years, because they are more weather-tolerant; when it rains, for example, flowers rebound more quickly. 'Supertunia Blushing Princess' provides handsome pastels. 'Carpet White' is part of the low-growing Carpet series, and the Fantasy series, such as 'Fantasy Ivory', has always been one of the best low-growing forms in our trials in Athens. However, even more compact forms, sometimes called petitunias or pocket petunias, are hitting the marketplace. Members of the Suncatcher series, such as 'Suncatcher Pink Vein', will be excellent additions to the garden, and 'Happy Dreams' and 'Bright Dreams' are outstanding and more in demand every year. It seems that of all the traditional bedding plant genera, petunias have held their place in the marketplace by constant renewal of cultivars that better reflect our need for good performance, not bigger flowers.

I suppose that it is impossible to suggest that one petunia is more important than another, but one series has nearly become a household name. The Wave series started with 'Purple Wave', which combined beautifully with everything,

Petunia hybrids, container

Petunia 'Surfina White'

Petunia 'Supertunia Blushing Princess'

Petunia 'Carpet White'

Petunia 'Fantasy Ivory'

Petunia 'Suncatcher Pink Vein'

Petunia 'Happy Dreams'

Petunia 'Bright Dreams'

Petunia 'Purple Wave' with coleus and sweet potato

Petunia 'Misty Lilac Wave'

Petunia 'Pink Wave'

MORE ☞

even plants like 'Amazon' coleus and 'Margarita' sweet potato. Its excellent performance all season long, everywhere in the country, soon spawned other colors in the series. 'Misty Lilac Wave' provides wonderful pastel flowers, and the lovely shade of 'Pink Wave' was not far behind. On the UGA campus they provided color from May to October. I thought I had seen all the pink I could stand until I discovered some small pots of 'Pink Wave Variegated' on a small patio table in Long Island. In that setting, they were quite wonderful—in the garden, well, not my cup of tea. Once the Wave series caught on, it seems that a new wave is introduced every year. Double-flowered forms were only a matter of time, and sure enough, 'Double Misty Lilac Wave' and others appeared in the early 2000s. With all the breeding for smaller flowers, and smaller plants, who would have believed that a group of plants called hedgifloras would be created? But created they were, and the Tidal Waves were almost as big as a hedge, a small one anyway. Certainly impressive.

With all the hybrids out there, species petunias have essentially gone the way of the ivory-billed woodpecker, but occasionally gardeners can find seeds of *Petunia integrifolia*, whose small flowers, heat tolerance, and long cascading habit still have a place in today's hybridized garden. The white form 'Alba' is my favorite.

All petunias perform better in raised beds or containers and in full sun. If some cultivars get too leggy by mid summer, give them a bit of a haircut, but don't be abusive. Plants will reflower in about two weeks.

Petunia 'Tidal Wave Rose'

Petunia 'Double Misty Lilac Wave'

Petunia 'Pink Wave Variegated'

Petunia integrifolia 'Alba'

Phlox

These plants are everywhere in the perennial garden—tall stately garden phlox to low-growers like creeping phlox and woodland phlox. Some of the prettiest flowers in the genus, however, reside in the much overlooked annual phlox, Drummond's phlox, *Phlox drummondii*. That it is so seldom used is a shame, because when people see it in full bloom, they stop and ask about it, wondering why they hadn't seen it before. The problem is that the plant is not particularly weather-resistant, breaking down under extremes of heat, humidity, and rain. Therefore I won't recommend that my daughters go out and buy half a dozen, but I can tell them to try one or two in a container. I have seen marvelous plantings in Calgary and Riverhead, Long Island; in Athens, they are marvelous only until mid June.

Traditional phlox flowers can be seen in Globe Mix, a mix of common colors on plants growing about 1' tall. I recall minding my own business in a Long Island garden, then being assailed with questions about an "unknown beauty" there. It was the annual phlox 'Phlox of Sheep', which, if for no other reason than the great name, should be more widely grown. I much prefer the single flowers over some of the other forms that the hand of man has obviously touched. I can put up with the star-shaped flowers of 'Petticoat Pink Shade' (they are cute and at least attractive), but I cannot

MORE ☞

Phlox drummondii Globe Mix

Phlox drummondii 'Promise Pink'

Phlox drummondii 'Phlox of Sheep'

Phlox drummondii 'Petticoat Pink Shade'

stomach the double flowers of some selections, such as 'Promise Pink'. Many people love them, I am simply not one of them. Full sun. Plants and seed may be found in the garden center.

Plectranthus

SWEDISH IVY

Here is a group of plants that has truly gone through a remarkable renaissance! To the interior landscaper, this was a mainstay plant, and basket after basket of Swedish ivy would hang in offices and malls. If someone said "Plectranthus" in a crowd, however, someone else might reply "Gesundheit," and if a gardener said he had plectranthus, others would wish him a speedy recovery and move away in an attempt not to catch it. Such was the depth of understanding of this group of plants.

Nearly all plectranthus are grown for their foliage. Some species have variegated or purple leaves and are quite handsome, but beware the odor: more than a few people have been turned off by the nasty smell of some of the species. The odor is only a problem if you get your nose too close, otherwise it's not an issue.

The other problem with this group of plants is, they look so much like other plants, such as coleus, perilla, and even basil, that often retailers are not even sure of the genus they are selling, let alone the species or cultivar. The number of common names provides a hint to the confusion. Flowering bush coleus, Chinese basil, prostrate coleus, country borage, French thyme, Indian mint, Mexican mint, soup mint, and Spanish thyme are only some of the names heard

Plectranthus forsteri 'Marginatus', Minnesota

Plectranthus forsteri 'Marginatus', Georgia

Plectranthus madagascariensis 'Variegatus'

Plectranthus ornatus

in a plectranthus discussion group. Smelling the leaves helps a lot in your identification sleuthing: basil smells like basil, coleus has no particular smell, and plectranthus, well, enough said.

Some of the old-fashioned forms have made a significant impact in the marketplace, such as *Plectranthus forsteri* 'Marginatus', whose white-margined, oval to rounded leaves make a nice show. When I saw the plants in Minnesota, they were rather small, but the margins were white and distinct; in Georgia plants were more robust, but the variegation was not the clean white it was in the North. A relatively hard-to-find plant is a beautiful small-leaved trailer, Madagascar variegated mintleaf, *P. madagascariensis* 'Variegatus'. Plants grow vigorously and are at their best bungee-jumping off a wall. Numerous other forms can be found, such as the green ornate mint, *P. ornatus*, although I am not sure there is a good reason to spend your money on it. I prefer to spend mine on the free-branching gray-leaved form, Cape mint, *P. oertendahlii*. The leaves are most unique, not flashy, but people often do a double take, especially when they are combined with purple-leaved plants, as here with purple shamrock. I have also been impressed with the potential of the low golden hybrid 'Troy's Gold', which seems to hold its color in abusive conditions. Nice in combination with darker foliage.

The most popular forms are probably those whose leaves mix well with other plants, such as silver plectranthus, *Plectranthus argentatus*, which is often used as a substitute for dusty miller. Plants grow too well at times and can be pruned at least once to provide a branched habit. Any variegated plant with a pleasant fragrance that can grow

Plectranthus oertendahlii

Plectranthus 'Troy's Gold'

Plectranthus argentatus

Plectranthus amboinicus 'Variegatus'

MORE ☞

in all climates will have a great following. Such is the case with oregano mint, *P. amboinicus* 'Variegatus', whose white and green leaves are excellent garden companions to sedum and can also be found in baskets complementing red verbena. A closely related selection with similar oregano-like fragrance but with yellow and green foliage is 'Athens Gem'. Both are tough as nails and provide season-long pleasure.

The assortment of plectranthus just mentioned are grown for the foliage alone; the flowers, if any, are secondary. However, a couple of new plants are quite beautiful in the fall when the lavender-blue flowers appear. They belong to either *Plectranthus ciliatus* or *P. zuluensis*, and, of the several forms, 'Mona' and 'Zulu Wonder' are worth a second look The former I thought was all right, the latter was terrific. Both have dark green foliage, and quite truthfully, do very little to pay back the money you spent until the fall, perhaps late September or October. At that time plants of 'Zulu Wonder' (and to a lesser degree 'Mona') are transformed into eye-catching beauties by the lovely lavender-blue flowers, which continue until temperatures hit 40°F. All plectranthus flower as days get shorter, some require such a short daylength that they flower only in the winter greenhouse. 'Mona' and 'Zulu Wonder' are

Plectranthus amboinicus 'Athens Gem'

Plectranthus ciliatus 'Mona'

Plectranthus ciliatus 'Zulu Wonder' in flower

Plectranthus amboinicus 'Variegatus' with verbena

Plectranthus ciliatus 'Zulu Wonder'

excellent additions to the garden because the absolute length of day is not as critical as with other cultivars. The only recommendation I have for northern gardeners is to try only one or two to determine if plants flower sufficiently before cold weather sets in. Otherwise, I am excited by any flowering plant that spruces up the fall. Full sun, good drainage.

Plumbago auriculata, Australia

Plumbago auriculata

CAPE LEADWORT

A visitor from the Midwest traveling to south Texas or south Florida cannot help but be impressed with the number of plantings of Cape leadwort (*Plumbago auriculata*): it seems to be the Official Plant of the Gulf States. If one also adds the number of plants used in California and in other parts of the world, that same visitor can't help but wonder why so few of these handsome plants are available in his part of the world. If gardeners ever mention leadwort, they are usually referring to the common perennial, *Ceratostigma*. In the southern Gulf States, plumbago is a shrub, much like caryopteris and salvia when they are

MORE 

Plumbago auriculata 'Escapade White'

Plumbago auriculata, Germany

Plumbago auriculata 'Imperial Blue'

perennial; elsewhere it acts like a vigorous annual. The plants eat up heat and humidity and flower throughout the season once temperatures rise above 70°F. The flowers resemble those of phlox and are generally light to dark blue. Not only do they look good in Texas, but they shone in containers in southern Germany and were hedge-like in Perth, Australia. This is a plant for all places.

There is not a lot to choose from in plumbago, although a white form, 'Alba', has been around for years. 'Royal Cape' and 'Imperial Blue' both have more vibrant, darker flowers than the species and seem to be used interchangeably; both are propagated from cuttings and are quite easily available. The Escapade series, introduced from seed, has done well in trials across the country. The plumbagos can be highly recommended for containers, and particularly in areas where heat and humidity are becoming more of a problem. Full sun.

Polygonum

Some polygonums are awful weeds, always present in the garden, and obnoxious as can be. Of the dozens of species worthy of actually spending money on, nearly all are used as perennials. Wouldn't it be nice if there was a plant with vigorous growth and nice flowers that did not threaten to take over everything around it? A plant known as magic carpet, *Polygonum capitatum*, perfectly fills the bill.

Plants are produced from seed and are seen only occasionally at garden centers. That is unfortunate, as they are easily grown in almost any climate and provide small but handsome, round pink flowers and excellent dark green to bronze foliage. All this on a spreading plant no more than 6" tall. The small dark leaves have a distinctive red V-shape pattern, which adds to the interest of the plant. In the summer, dozens of flowers form and continue to open throughout the season.

Magic carpet is well worth growing but is unlikely ever to be a mainstream item. It is difficult to talk people into an annual groundcover: after all, who wants to keep recovering the same ground year after year? However, as a short, vigorous garden plant, it really should be tried more often than it is. Plants may reseed in subsequent years, but that can't always be counted on. Full sun to afternoon shade.

Polygonum capitatum in flower with begonias

Polygonum capitatum

Portulaca

PURSLANE

I always marvel at the ability of plant breeders to take a genus of what most people consider weeds and create plants that are nothing short of beautiful. There are still plenty of weeds in this genus, but moss rose (*Portulaca grandiflora*) is not one of them. Over the years, a number of ornamental plants have been bred, including the Sunglow series, with half a dozen colors on low-growing plants. But the real breakthrough was with the Sundial series, which brought

Portulaca grandiflora 'Sundial Peppermint Stick'

Portulaca grandiflora Sunglow series

Portulaca grandiflora 'Sundial Mango'

Portulaca grandiflora 'Sundial Peach'

Portulaca grandiflora 'Sundial Mix'

MORE ☞

the moss rose out of the shadows and into the bright light of high demand.

A planting of some old 'Sundial Mix' shows off the many colors, but over the years the palette was widened. Some, like 'Sundial Peppermint Stick', were basically weird, but taste notwithstanding, there seemed to be a color for everyone. 'Sundial Mango' and 'Sundial Peach' were different and outstanding, 'Sundial Gold' was brilliant, and 'Sundial Fuchsia' was hot. Plants look good in the ground, in containers, or in baskets, but they are susceptible to a number of diseases that can cause problems in late summer. Be sure drainage is adequate, they do not like wet feet.

As much as I enjoy the colors of moss rose, I find them disappointing as temperature and humidity rise. However, I am seldom disappointed with ornamental purslane, *Portulaca oleracea*. Every

Portulaca grandiflora 'Sundial Gold'

Portulaca grandiflora 'Sundial Fuchsia'

Portulaca oleracea 'Yubi Rose'

Portulaca oleracea, UGA Trial Gardens

time I look at these plants, I cannot help but remember tearing purslane-the-weed from the lawn and even from cracks in the driveway; they were awful things that belonged in the rubbish. So what was I thinking when I said I would trial some purslane for a breeding company? It is good to keep an open mind, and in this case, I was so impressed that I became a big fan of this tough, colorful group of plants.

At Georgia, we evaluated rows of ornamental purslane, and I began to appreciate the color mix available. They can be used in baskets, in mixed containers, or as groundcovers. A number of cultivars are produced, including the Yubi series, which became the standard for ornamental purslane. Dark colors like 'Yubi Scarlet' and 'Yubi Rose' are impossible not to see from fifty yards away, but hot colors are not always appreciated in the middle of a sizzling summer. 'Yubi Light Pink' has always been my favorite; its soft colors and ability to combine with other plants keep it on my A list. For most gardeners, the way to use purslane is in mixed containers. The Summer Joy series also provides excellent colors, and we cram as many plants as possible into mixed containers. I am sure followers of the color wheel would disagree, but in our containers, it is a free-for-all, and, usually, the purslanes come out just fine. 'Summer Joy White' softens the verbena and ornamental grass in a container, and 'Summer Joy Scarlet' nicely complements some marguerite daisies and mussaenda in another mixed planting.

Portulaca oleracea, basket

Portulaca oleracea 'Yubi Scarlet'

Portulaca oleracea 'Yubi Light Pink'

Portulaca oleracea 'Summer Joy White'

MORE ☞

The recent addition of double forms really pushed the purslane envelope, and they were bred in the hopes that the flowers would stay open a little longer. The Fairytale series was developed, and even if the plants don't turn you on, the names would make Walt proud. Both 'Sleeping Beauty' (yellow, seen here with verbena) and 'Snow White' look good falling down the sides of patio pots, but the most interesting is probably 'Cinderella', with orange and red bicolor flowers. I said interesting, not necessarily beautiful. Look for other Fairytales coming your way, they are certainly different.

All is not perfect in the world of portulaca. The biggest complaint continues to be that flowers are closed early in the morning and after about 5:00 p.m. In this age, where the whole family is often out working or schooling during the day, being greeted by closed flowers entering and exiting the home does not do a great deal to endear these plants to gardeners. The double flowers of moss rose are better at staying open, and the purslanes are the worst; even the double forms are open only slightly longer than the singles. That is a bit of a bummer, so purchase with your eyes wide open, and enjoy them as you enjoy the rest of your garden: on the weekends. Full sun, good drainage.

Portulaca oleracea 'Summer Joy Scarlet'

Portulaca oleracea 'Sleeping Beauty'

Portulaca oleracea 'Snow White'

Portulaca oleracea 'Cinderella'

Pseuderanthemum

Here is yet another plant hardly anyone above the 30th parallel has ever heard of, but one that can provide excellent foliar color and reasonably good flower show with minimal effort. The hardest part will be to find the silly thing; be prepared for blank stares when you ask, "Do you have any pseuderanthemums?" One of the common names is chocolate soldier, which won't help much with the blank looks but will roll off your tongue a lot easier.

Chocolate soldier (*Pseuderanthemum alatum*) is grown for the Toblerone color of the leaves with their white-chocolate midveins. They grow vigorously, particularly as temperatures increase, and fill in areas of the garden rapidly. The pink flowers are a bonus, and are another reason for trying them, but it is the foliage and ease of maintenance that will make you come back for more. Plants are equally comfortable in full sun in the North or afternoon shade in the South.

Red pseuderanthemum (*Pseuderanthemum atropurpureum*), a relatively new addition to the garden palette, produces large, vigorous, shiny red-purple leaves. It is the sheen that makes it different from other upright purple-leaved plants. No flowers but quite a noticeable feature in the summer garden. Full sun everywhere.

Pseuderanthemum alatum

Pseuderanthemum atropurpureum

Reseda odorata

SWEET MIGNONETTE

Boy, trying to find some sweet mignonette anywhere in this country is a battle. It will be almost impossible to find plants for sale at your local garden center, and finding seeds is not that easy either. A quick search of the Internet yielded only a couple of companies selling mignonette seeds; there are others for sure, but suffice it to say, you really must want this plant in your garden.

And it is eminently want-able, particularly if you live in a cool climate, where summer temperatures of 80°F are uncommon. The green-tinged white blossoms are held like rockets, and plants flower for months at a time. This plant reeks of history, and yesterday's poets loved the plant. In the 1890s, in "The Old-Fashioned Garden," John Russell Hayes wrote what seems to be the

Reseda odorata

MORE ☞

precursor of "Where Have All the Flowers Gone?":

Foxgloves and marigolds and mignonette,
Dahlias and lavender and damask rose.
O dear old flowers, ye are blooming yet,
Each year afresh your lovely radiance glows:
But where are they who saw your beauty's dawn?
Ah, with the flowers of other years they long ago have gone!

Find some seeds. Plant them early. Pick a few for the vase. Don't bore people with bad nineteenth-century American poetry. Place in full sun in the North, afternoon shade in the South.

Rhodochiton atrosanguineus

PURPLE BELL VINE

This handsome annual vine is not used to advantage in American gardens. Purple bell vine (*Rhodochiton atrosanguineus*) climbs by twining its long petioles around structures and carries wonderful pendulous purple flowers. The name comes from *rhodo* ("red") and *chiton* ("cloak"), a reference to the sepals, which envelop the flower like a cloak. They are beautiful and should be admired up close.

No cultivars are available, so find some started plants or purchase some seeds and sow them in the house about six weeks before you want to put them outside. Be sure you place them by a structure that allows plants to twine. Full sun.

Reseda odorata, mixed border

Rhodochiton atrosanguineus, flowers

Rhodochiton atrosanguineus

Ricinus communis

CASTOR OIL PLANT

This is the same plant whose oil was plied on unsuspecting children growing up in the 1940s and '50s for stomach and bowel problems. It was vile stuff and is still obtainable at the local pharmacist. *Ricinus communis* also yields the deadly toxin ricin, used by terrorists and murderers. However, the plants from which the oil and toxin are derived are among the "in" plants used by designers for architectural interest—that is, they are big and bold, and usually with burgundy- to bronze-colored leaves. In warm climates, plants can easily grow 6' tall in a single season; elsewhere, 2–3' may be all that is reached.

Their garden popularity comes from the colored foliage. 'Carmencita', the

Ricinus communis 'Carmencita'

Ricinus communis 'Scarlet Queen'

Ricinus communis 'Impala'

MORE ☞

most popular of the bronze-leaved forms, may be used as a great big solitary feature in the garden or combined with the riotous colors of red lobelias and orange Mexican sunflowers. 'Scarlet Queen' (aka 'Carmineus') is similar, and I particularly enjoyed them in France, where pink dahlias and yellow statice offset the bronze foliage. 'Impala' has a flush of red in the leaves but is not as colored as either of the aforementioned cultivars. Plants with bronze leaves will continue to be the most popular; however, some green forms are also part of the castor oil plant family. 'Gibsonii' has green foliage when young but bronzes as

Ricinus communis 'Carmencita' with lobelias and Mexican sunflowers

Ricinus communis 'Gibsonii'

Ricinus communis var. *cambodgensis*

Ricinus communis, fruit

it ages. It grows to only 4'. It is much prettier than another "in" form, var. *cambodgensis*, which bears large dark green foliage.

The prickly seed pods may be deep red to pink and contain beautiful gold, silver, and black seeds. However, admire them from a distance. As Karen Neill of North Carolina State University states, "These temptingly attractive seeds are quite poisonous, so you must be sure to keep them away from children and unknowing adults. Three seeds are sufficient to kill an adult. One seed may be fatal to a child." Plants will often reseed, and once planted may be in the garden year after year. Full sun.

Rudbeckia hirta

BLACK-EYED SUSAN

I have always loved black-eyed susans. The old-fashioned daisies (*Rudbeckia hirta*) are still available from seed packages in garden centers and are often part of a meadow-flower mix. There is absolutely nothing wrong with these "old" plants, and they are still a favorite for North American gardeners. Two of the best named varieties in the mid 1980s were 'Rustic Colors', with their multicolored flowers, and the unassuming 'Marmalade', as simple as the spread for which it is named. Both are still available today. Annual rudbeckias essentially disappeared from the radar screen with the blitzkrieg of perennial forms like *R. fulgida* var. *sullivantii* 'Goldsturm', but in the mid 1990s and early 2000s, a number of exciting new cultivars emerged from breeding programs.

Rudbeckia hirta 'Rustic Colors'

Rudbeckia hirta 'Marmalade'

Rudbeckia hirta 'Gloriosa Double Gold'

Rudbeckia hirta 'Goldilocks'

MORE ☞

Today we can choose from tall forms and dwarf ones, and many beautiful colors as well. I have fallen in love with these plants all over again.

How can so many cultivars be developed when the colors don't really change that much? To my eyes, regardless of whether there is red or green in the flower, the dominant color is nearly always yellow. No blues, no whites, no purples, but they seldom disappoint. Cut flower growers and gardeners who enjoy cutting can still find 'Gloriosa Double Gold', a 2–3' tall large-flowered double form. For those who cannot grow dahlias well, these look sufficiently similar to yellow dahlias in the vase that your non-plant friends may not know. If the full-bodied look is your cup of tea, you might still be able to find 'Goldilocks', a semi-double that has long been a favorite. However, the newest of the doubles

Rudbeckia hirta 'Cherokee Sunset'

Rudbeckia hirta Becky Mix

Rudbeckia hirta 'Sonora'

Rudbeckia hirta 'Cordoba'

is 'Cherokee Sunset', with beautiful bicolored flowers. In the early 1990s, the single-flowered Becky Mix became a favorite because of the excellent outdoor performance, and landscapers opted for her above other single yellow forms. Shorter than many cultivars, she became increasingly popular because plants do not fall over with rain or wind as badly as the taller forms.

The centers of the flowers are generally black or bronze, but large red centers have become in vogue. 'Sonora' gets my vote for the most outstanding bicolor, and while she led the way for flowers with large red centers, at least two others recently appeared. 'Cordoba' and 'Spotlight' can also light up the garden,

Rudbeckia hirta 'Prairie Sun'

Rudbeckia hirta 'Indian Summer'

Rudbeckia hirta 'Indian Summer', flowers

Rudbeckia hirta 'Toto'

MORE ☞

and if you have a chance to grow any of these, you cannot go too far wrong. In the world of the dwarf daisy, 'Toto' has become the benchmark for yellow forms of black-eyed susans.

Black centers, bronze centers, even large red centers are not uncommon, but 'Irish Eyes' become phenomenally popular because of its green eye. Its instant success spawned the latest of the green-eyed forms, 'Prairie Sun', with two shades of yellow around the green eye. It performed so well that it was an All-America Selection in 2002. However, the cultivar that spurred the annual rudbeckia market the most was not fancy, or double, and had no particularly weird center. It was simply an excellent performer with a short habit and large flowers. 'Indian Summer' was the hands-down favorite for the All-America Selection medal in 1995 and is still among the most popular daisies in the garden today. Not only that, it was voted best fresh cut flower for the year 2000 by the Association of Specialty Cut Flower Growers. When you walk by a handsome planting of simple black-eyed susans, perhaps beside some red petunias, you are probably admiring a superstar.

Rudbeckia hirta 'Spotlight'

The beauty of black-eyed susans is obvious; however, do not believe that they will look as good as the magazine photos all season. As the temperature and humidity rise, the quality of the plants declines. The warmer the summer, the faster the plants are pulled. In Athens, we usually replace the rudbeckias by mid July, although they can stumble through the entire season. To have the trials look as good as the images, we reseed more susans beside the original plants while they still look good, so that when we take them up, the new ones aren't far from flowering. The further north, the longer it takes to get an outstanding show, but the longer the plants will persist. Full sun.

Ruellia

I have been working with herbaceous plants for a good while, and living in the North didn't prepare me for some of the plants that were routinely used in warmer climates. When we looked at photos of plants like taro, peacock ginger, and Mexican petunia, gardeners in Montreal knew that, like Mickey and Donald, they were fictional characters. Boy, have times ever changed. The comic books have come to life, and those plants are real.

When I saw ruellia growing in Texas and Florida, I was not sure if they could grow in northern climes. While they are slowly creeping northward, heat is required to provide a season long show, and Cincinnati may be their northern limit. They are becoming much more available, and only time will tell if northern gardeners discover these neat plants.

The biggest one among them is Texas petunia (*Ruellia brittoniana*), which, where happy, can easily grow 5' tall and

Rudbeckia hirta 'Irish Eyes'

Ruellia brittoniana 'Alba'

4' wide in a single season. It is cold hardy to zone 7b, perhaps to 7. In the North, 3' will be more common, but the handsome blue flowers are produced all summer. Each flower persists but one day, but the black stems and the disease and insect resistance are great positives. They are better as annuals than perennials, because they can be invasive in warm climates and will self-seed everywhere. If the species is too big, try a few of the cultivars. 'Alba' is a little smaller and has white flowers; 'Chi Chi' is about half the size of the species and bears beautiful pink flowers. 'Katie's Dwarf' is really an outstanding cultivar, growing only 6–9" tall and bearing large blue flowers like the species. Plants are hardy to zone 7, but as perennials, at least in their northern range, they tend to flower sparsely. Grow as annuals.

Another fine addition to the field is the hybrid 'Groundhugger', which can make a reasonable groundcover but is better used in pots or baskets. Plants grow about 12" tall and send out long stems that hug the ground or dangle from containers. Blue flowers occur along the stems. Of all the ruellias, this one probably needs the most heat to sustain persistent flowering. Light blue flowers occur on *Ruellia humilis*, and I have seen it reseed all over the place, in gardens as far north as the Missouri Botanical Garden. However, if blue is getting a little tiresome, the red ruellia 'Ragin' Cajun' is

Ruellia brittoniana

Ruellia brittoniana 'Chi Chi'

Ruellia brittoniana 'Chi Chi', flowers

Ruellia brittoniana 'Katie's Dwarf'

MORE ☞

outstanding. Also only about 12" tall, this dwarf selection of the red Mexican petunia (*R. elegans*) flowers all season with bright fire-engine-red flowers.

Plants are not as restless as other forms and tend to stay where they are planted.

All in all, any ruellias that can be found are worth a try, first in containers (if they overwinter, they may not be worth keeping), then in the garden. Beware of self-seeding tendencies, particularly in the species; if insufficient heat is available, plants will be fine but flowering will be limited. Full sun.

Ruellia 'Groundhugger'

Russelia

CORAL PLANT

Coral plant has been residing in obscurity in most of the country for many years. It is a shrub in its native habitat of Mexico and southern California but seldom attains shrub-like proportions in other parts of the country. The most common form is the fountain plant, *Russelia equisetiformis*, in which the foliage resembles horsetails. I have seen them as shrubs at Leu Gardens in Orlando, Florida, but even in Long Island they were interesting when mixed in containers with parrot's beak. Not as big but still worth planting. The coral tubular flowers begin when temperatures consistently get above 75°F and will flower on and off all season. I personally don't have much use for it, but Alan

Ruellia elegans 'Ragin' Cajun'

Ruellia humilis

Russelia equisetiformis, Leu Gardens

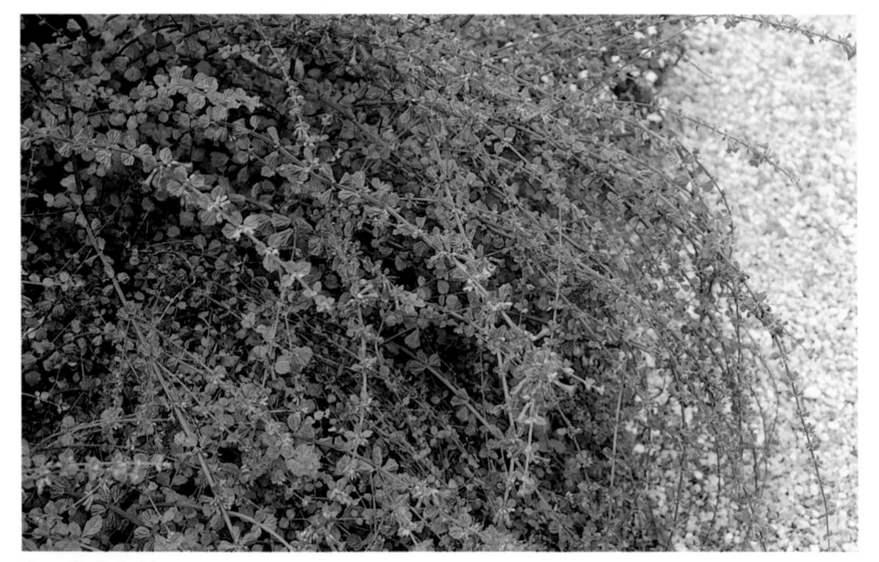

Russelia hybrid

Shapiro in Gainesville, Florida, grows it in his garden and loves it, and I never disagree with Alan. Hybrids involving running russelia, *R. sarmentosa*, have much more "normal" foliage and excellent flowers as well. It is unlikely the hybrids will ever be readily available outside of the Gulf States or California, but if you happen to find one, the beautiful shade of flowers and its disdain of heat and humidity may be worth a few dollars. Full sun.

Salpiglossis

PAINTED TONGUE

You are far more likely to see this plant in a conservatory or public greenhouse than you are in home gardens. In conservatories, these spectacular plants show off their flowers to the public for a few weeks, then are put back in the dusty corner. However, if you live in the mountains or on the northern edges of either coast, then perhaps you will also get to enjoy them for a few weeks in the garden or in containers. They are useless in the heat, humidity is not to their liking, they fall over with rain, and wind is not much good either. That is not to say you shouldn't try them, it is simply better if the public gardens waste their

Russelia equisetiformis with parrot's beak

Salpiglossis 'Splash Ivory'

MORE ☞

Salpiglossis 'Casino Royale'

money rather than you wasting yours. If their poor performance in any kind of inclement weather isn't enough to turn you off, then consider the common name. Enough said.

Of course, the fact that they are so fickle and wimpy means they must be gorgeous, and they are! Mixtures such as 'Casino Royale' and the Splash series bring many large petunia-like flowers in different shades to the table, and people, including myself, can't get enough of them. In spite of my less-than-enthusiastic recommendation, I still try a few every other year or so, even though I will only get to enjoy them for a heartbeat or two at most. They are better in containers than in the ground; if they flower for more than a month, buy every one of them. Seed is available from seed catalogs; have fun. Full sun in the North, afternoon shade in the South.

Salpiglossis 'Splash Purple'

Salpiglossis 'Splash Pale Yellow'

Salvia

SAGE

Having gone through the Salvia Stage of Life and survived, I can be both an advocate for and opponent against certain forms of this great genus. Many ornamental salvias, as well as the culinary sage, are perennials; however, the genus also sports many annuals. Salvias can be wonderful or just plain terrible, and the nice thing about the annual selections: if they do terribly, they will be put out of their misery over the winter.

I freely admit to confusion as to what species should be included in an annual book, because *Salvia*, as much as any genus, does not lend itself to being cubbyholed. Rather than spend time figuring out that it may live in zone 6b or 7a, I used this standard: if it is doubtful that

Salvia splendens, Michigan State University

Salvia splendens 'Carabiniere White'

Salvia splendens 'Hotline Red'

MORE ☞

someone in Oberlin, Ohio, can grow it as a perennial, I include it here. That leaves many fine forms, from the red bedding plants that paint the landscape to hybrids that are only now becoming available to salvia fanatics.

Let's start with the much maligned bedding salvia, *Salvia splendens*. Like most bedding, it is overused, overweight, and sometimes over the top. Gardens like the one at Michigan State University trial dozens of cultivars—very bright, but, after a while, they become, well, a

Salvia coccinea 'Snow Nymph'

Salvia splendens 'Sangria'

Salvia 'Faye Chapel'

Salvia darcyi

Salvia coccinea 'Lady in Red'

Salvia coccinea 'Hummingbird Forest'

Salvia coccinea 'Coral Nymph'

Salvia farinacea 'Victoria'

Salvia farinacea 'Argent'

Salvia farinacea 'Reference'

Salvia patens 'White Trophy'

Salvia farinacea 'Rhea'

Salvia greggii, Ireland

MORE ☞

Salvia patens

Salvia patens 'Cambridge Blue'

Salvia greggii 'Navajo Bright Pink'

Salvia greggii 'Coral'

Salvia greggii 'Desert Blaze'

Salvia 'Cherry Queen'

little boring. However, let's be honest, they work, and the planting of 'Hotline Red' looks as nice as any planting you will see in a landscape. Red is surely the dominant color of bedding salvia, but let's not forget the white flowers found on 'Carabiniere White', or the purple ones on 'Cleopatra Violet', to name just a couple of alternate colors. To make the point that there is no such thing as bad taste when it comes to breeding flowers, 'Sangria' is available to gardeners as well. Call it interesting, and leave it at that. A naturally occurring tall variant of bedding salvia is Van Houtt's salvia,

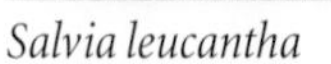
Salvia leucantha

Salvia leucantha 'Santa Barbara'

Salvia leucantha 'Midnight'

Salvia rutilans, unpruned

Salvia involucrata, flowers

MORE ☞

'Van-Houttei', which is normally a burgundy color, but I really enjoy its bright red sport, 'Faye Chapel', which flowers all season.

The red that dominates the genus is personified in Darcy's salvia, *Salvia darcyi* (*S. oresbia*). I saw some lovely plantings at the exquisite Chanticleer Garden, in Wayne, Pennsylvania, where plants had reseeded among the rocks around a pond. The bloody sage (*S. coccinea*) is aptly named; the blood-red flowers are reflected in its most famous cultivar, 'Lady in Red'. An even brighter red, if that is possible, is found in 'Hummingbird Forest', and yes, these red salvias really do attract hummingbirds, and butterflies and bees. But not all the bloody salvias are bloody, and selections such as 'Coral Nymph' and 'Snow Nymph' are some of the prettier forms of the species.

Blues, violets, and purples are the next most common shades, after red. The sage most often associated with this range is the mealy-cup sage, *Salvia farinacea*. Of all the mealy-cups you will pass by, the most common by far is 'Victoria', a handsome mid-blue form with time-tested excellence. 'Rhea', a darker form, was flowering in the Royal Botanical Gardens in Ontario at the same time as the snapdragons. Silver flowers are not uncommon in this species; the most common cultivar is 'Argent', which provides dozens of narrow silvery flowers most of the season. Not to be outdone by 'Sangria', the blue and white bicolored 'Reference' should be planted, perhaps in places where others can't see it. Lots of people love these bicolor salvias, but then lots of people love cats. Other blues in the genus include the gentian sage, *S.*

Salvia rutilans, pruned

Salvia 'Anthony Parker'

Salvia involucrata

Salvia regla

patens. The flowers are among the largest in the genus, but unfortunately, flowering is sparse most of the time. There are a few selections; 'Cambridge Blue' is probably the best known, and white-flowered forms, like 'White Trophy', can occasionally be found.

The Texas sage, *Salvia greggii*, has become quite popular, and with good reason. It does well in all conditions, and, although native to Texas, it flourishes in faraway places like Mount Usher Gardens in Ireland as well. The selections are reasonably short and, in the case of the Navajo series, also come in a number of colors. I have been most impressed with 'Navajo Scarlet' and 'Navajo Bright Pink'. Simple colors like 'Coral' are also easy on the eyes. A variegated-leaf form, 'Desert Blaze', has looked surprisingly good in trials, although it needs significant pruning if it grows too tall. Numerous hybrids with Texas sage have been bred. The best by far is 'Cherry Queen', which flowers the entire season and handles pruning well; the only maintenance sometimes required is a haircut. Texas sage is cold hardy to at least zone 7 and over a few years becomes quite shrubby.

A number of sages flower only in the fall. One of these is a tall vigorous blue-flowered species, known as velvet sage, *Salvia leucantha*. Hardy to about zone 7, it is being seen more and more throughout the country. The species itself, which has flowers of purple and white, is as good as any of the cultivars. Plants grow 4–5' tall and can be overwhelming, so a dwarf cousin, 'Santa Barbara', was selected as a better choice for smaller gardens. The most impressive cultivar, however, is 'Midnight', which bears totally purple flowers. Stunning from a distance, impressive close-up. A favorite red is pineapple sage, *S. rutilans*, whose leaves really do smell like pineapple and whose flowers are fire-engine red. Plants stand at least 4' tall and flower only in the fall, but they are worth waiting for. If not pruned in early summer, plants will produce only a few tall blooms; a hard pruning results in dozens of flowers. 'Anthony Parker' is a hybrid of velvet sage and pineapple sage. It is tall and interesting, but not as interesting as either of its parents. Another fall flowerer is the big, leggy, and altogether unmanageable rose-cup sage, *S. involucrata*. But the flowers are outstanding. The deep pink hue and the weird shape of the flowers, particularly the uppermost one, which

Salvia viridis 'Blue Bird'

Salvia viridis 'Rosea'

Salvia mexicana 'Limelight'

MORE ☞

Salvia viridis 'Rubra'

looks like a ball-peen hammer, keep people coming back for more. And finally, for the fall, if you can find the Hildago sage, *S. regla*, run out and buy it. The orange-scarlet flowers smother the plant and stop people in their tracks. The drawback to all these fall flowers is that the farther north one gardens, the more one worries that frost will take out the plants before the flowers have made a show. You take your chances, but the reward is worth the worry.

And to finish up, a couple of fun but unique salvias. Green sage, *Salvia viridis* (*S. horminum*), is not green but rather is distinguished by its colorful bracts. Pink ('Rosea'), purple ('Blue Bird'), and rose-colored bracts ('Rubra') make you look twice to determine that it really is a sage. Plants grow only 2' tall. If green is truly desired in the garden, you must try 'Limelight', a selection of Mexican sage, *S. mexicana*. Lots of flowers, mostly in the fall; people will hardly notice until you point them out, but then stand back for the chorus of enthusiasm. All salvias prefer full sun and reasonably good drainage. They are all fond of being cut back when needed.

Sanvitalia procumbens

CREEPING ZINNIA

Sanvitalia procumbens is an old-fashioned plant that has not changed a great deal since Victorian times. Plants do well in most areas of the country but become tired by mid summer in places where summers are hot and humid. Flowers really do look like zinnias but are smaller and occur in yellow and orange shades only. Plants are useful for edging and as a shiny groundcover, inserted among other annuals and perennials.

The most common form is 'Mandarin Orange', which can be used as a groundcover skirting blue salvias and crawling over rocks. People can't help but take any low-growing plant and make an edging plant out of it; creeping zinnia is no exception. However, most selections, are sufficiently well behaved to handle the edging duty well; here, 'Orange Sprite' holds back bamboo and heliotrope. Orange is probably the more popular color, but I also like the yellows, particularly when they can be incorporated among other plants. 'Yellow Sprite' can be used along with zinnias and marigolds to soften the edges on a brick walkway, while the combination of 'Yellow Carpet' with purple verbena

Sanvitalia procumbens 'Yellow Sprite'

Sanvitalia procumbens 'Yellow Carpet'

MORE ☞

Sanvitalia procumbens 'Mandarin Orange'

Sanvitalia procumbens 'Orange Sprite'

and black-eyed susans at the Butchart Gardens had cameras clicking and people stopping.

Full sun in the North, afternoon shade in the South.

Scabiosa

SCABIOUS

When one mentions scabiosa, most gardeners immediately think of the perennial forms that have become so popular, but annual pincushion flowers (*Scabiosa atropurpurea*) have always been around—they just haven't been able to compete with petunias or begonias for greenhouse or retail space. Plants are easily grown from seed and are sometimes used in a meadow-mix, and unless a cultivar is specified, it will likely consist of a mixture of colors including rose and scarlet flowers.

Scabiosa atropurpurea

Scabiosa atropurpurea 'Ace of Spades'

Scabiosa atropurpurea 'Chile Black'

Some purple forms have captured the imagination of gardeners. The most common, 'Ace of Spades', has become more widely available; plants grow about 18" tall and can be used as a black spot in the garden or brought in for the vase. A similar form but shorter and more compact is 'Chile Black', which I believe is going to be an excellent plant for North American gardeners. Full sun, good drainage.

Scaevola aemula

FAN FLOWER

Fan flower (*Scaevola aemula*) is one of the success stories in which a new plant became a garden favorite not because of marketing or promotion, but simply because it performed so well in gardens. Its fame spread by word of mouth, and soon various cultivars of fan flower were available in retail stores. Plants are native to Australia and are tolerant of heat but do just fine in temperate climates as well.

Many cultivars have emerged, most in the blue-lavender color range. They all look good in baskets, particularly 'Sapphire Blue', and are equally attractive in the garden. 'Mauve Clusters', an old-fashioned form, has small flowers

Scaevola aemula 'Outback Purple Fan'

MORE ☞

Scaevola aemula 'Outback White Fan'

Scaevola aemula 'Sapphire Blue'

Scaevola aemula 'Mauve Clusters'

Scaevola aemula 'Blue Flash'

Scaevola aemula 'Blue Ice'

Scaevola aemula 'Zigzag'

but is absolutely covered with them. Larger flower forms have since emerged, but many cultivars are essentially the same in appearance. The Outback series, especially 'Outback Purple Fan', has always been an excellent performer in our trials. 'Blue Flash' and 'Blue Ice' are both marvelous selections too, and oftentimes the choice is based solely on availability.

Blue-lavender is not the only color in this species, and breeders have been developing whites and bicolors. Whites are fairly common, and you can't go too far wrong with 'Outback White Fan'; many other whites and bicolors will soon be available, and I like the bicolor 'Zigzag' simply because it performs well and provides a little extra pizzazz. All fan flowers are excellent in patio containers, where they can be combined with other annuals. One thing I should add: whenever I talk about scaevola, at least one person in the audience tells me how much the rabbits enjoy it. If rabbits are a problem, you probably don't want to waste too much of your money. Full sun.

Senecio

The genus has over 10,000 members, and the vast majority are not particularly ornamental. In fact, most are shrubs, and few have been domesticated. There is a spattering of herbaceous species, but only one is a common denizen of gardens. The popular gray-leaved *Senecio cineraria*, dusty miller, is used as edging and in container plantings; other dusty millers are sometimes placed in the genus *Artemisia*.

Senecio cineraria is a beautiful plant,

Senecio cineraria with pansies

Senecio cineraria 'Cirrus' with red salvia

Senecio cineraria 'Cirrus' with purple salvia

Senecio cineraria 'White Diamond'

MORE ☞

and because of its ease of production and soft silver-gray color, it was probably overused in many landscapes. They were planted as solid sheets and after a while became quite tedious. However, let's give them their due: when they are combined with other flowers, they enhance everything around them. Even in containers, the pansies look brighter because of dusty miller's silvery foliage. The form I like best is 'Cirrus', whose deeply cut leaves on vigorous plants are outstanding. I love them combined with red salvia (together, both plants look better), and later when I noticed some plants among purple salvia, I was again taken with the contrast. Not only are the leaves terrific, very few flowers are produced, and this is a good thing. Lack of flowers is not a characteristic of all cultivars. 'White Diamond' has handsome oblong fluted leaves and performs just fine, but the flowers that form in mid summer do nothing for its appearance; this cultivar reminds me of another gray plant, lamb's ear, whose purple flowers also detract from what it is supposed to do.

Senecio viravira, also known as dusty miller, bears beautiful gray cut leaves. Plants fill in well and exhibit significantly more cold hardiness than the

Senecio viravira

Senecio confusus

Senecio confusus with sweet potato

Senecio confusus, flowers

common dusty miller. In this species, the flowers are also unremarkable. Full sun. Cut back in mid to late summer if they look tired.

While there are many plants in this diverse genus, one doesn't expect to come across a vine. I first saw the orangeglow vine (*Senecio confusus*) in the conservatory at Longwood Gardens, and while I really enjoyed it and made copious notes, I put it down as a greenhouse plant, and that was the end of that. When I visited one of my favorite nurseries, The Planters Palette in Winfield, Illinois, and saw it there, with its flowers artfully poking out of 'Margarita' sweet potato, I told myself that I had to get some. Unfortunately, all the visitors in the garden bought them while I was telling them how wonderful it was. Then on a chilly fall day, what did I walk under at Chanticleer Garden in Wayne, Pennsylvania, but two arbors of orangeglow. My friends all thought I was crazy as I traced and retraced my steps under the fiery orange daisies that complemented the plant. Even at that time of year, it was pretty darn neat. It may not be for everybody, but what is? How many daisies do you know that climb up trellises?

Some authorities have changed the botanical name to *Pseudogynoxys chenopodioides*. That's too confusing for me, and I'll keep it here until they all agree. Full sun.

Setcreasea pallida

PURPLE HEART

I can't help but chuckle when I see purple heart (*Setcreasea pallida*) growing proudly in the landscape. After all, this "dormitory plant," originally known as purple wandering jew, was purchased by students with the best of intentions to cozy up their dorm room. After a month or so, it would end up as one long decrepit stem, begging to be put out of its misery. Now it is favored by landscapers as if they just discovered it.

It is a terrific low-maintenance plant and can even take the abuse of University of Georgia students, who dangle their feet in it as if they were poolside.

Setcreasea pallida with cannas and lantana

MORE ☞

But as effective as it is as a monotone, it is even better when combined with plants like lantana and 'Bengal Tiger' canna lilies. It seems that it is only a plant for the South, but don't tell that to William Hoyt at the Allen Centennial Gardens at the University of Wisconsin. I visited this exceptional garden in September; Hoyt had combined purple heart with 'Aurora' coleus, and it was happily scampering over a few white petunias while still sporting colorful pink flowers. This is a plant that is in its glory anywhere in the country, and whether in containers or in the ground will not disappoint. Full sun.

Solanum

NIGHTSHADE

Plants that reside in this group are like Jekyll and Hyde: some are gentle and beautiful, while others are armed with sharp spines and dare you to grow them. Of course, give any gardener a dare, and that plant will be soon be in his garden.

Solanums are among the most sought-after plants these days. One of the most fashionable, which I hope is only a fad, is one of the most devious, purple solanum, *Solanum atropurpureum.* The green foliage is attractive, and the purple stems are handsome, if you can see them. I quickly found out that enthusiastically pulling apart the foliage to find the stems is not a good idea, as the stems are armed with sharp black thorns. However, after I pulled on thick gloves, I discovered the small orange fruit within, tasty but hardly worth the effort. Many of the solanums have excellent edible fruit, and some of these tropical vegetables are beginning to reside in our gardens. An example is naranjilla, *S. quitoense,* cultivated for fruit and juice production in South and Central America and now appearing in public gardens in Georgia and Washington, D.C. This plant is also ready for battle, but the foliage is really handsome, and the bright orange fruit are quite edible. Easy to grow from seed. Numerous little-known species are being grown only by solanum fanatics, including sticky nightshade, *S. sisymbriifolium,* grown for the prickly white flowers, cut leaves, and yellow fruit.

While thinking of fruit, I can't help but remark on the beautiful hanging baskets in a wonderful garden of Weihenstephan in southern Germany. The baskets were overflowing with fruit of

Setcreasea pallida, University of Georgia

Setcreasea pallida, University of Wisconsin

Solanum atropurpureum

Solanum atropurpureum, fruit

Solanum quitoense

Solanum quitoense, fruit

Solanum muricatum 'Pepino Gold'

Solanum sisymbriifolium

Solanum melongena 'Lavender Touch'

MORE ☞

pepino plant, *Solanum muricatum* 'Pepino Gold', and it was all we could do not to climb a ladder and pick them. From ornamental kale to ornamental sweet potato, vegetables will always have a place in the garden. If we can accept ornamental okra, then we surely will embrace ornamental eggplant, *S. melongena*. A number have been selected; I enjoy the handsome large leaves, purple flowers, and purple fruit of 'Lavender Touch'. Edible as well, if you are an eggplant person.

While most solanums are not overly large, they can certainly become so if properly grown or trained. Purple nightshade, *Solanum rantonnetii*, is a shrub that may not have sufficient time to grow and flower well in American gardens. However, if trained as a standard—as it was in the Royal Botanical Gardens in Ontario, behind some 'Illumination'

Solanum rantonnetii with amaranthus

Solanum rantonnetii, Zurich Botanical Gardens

Solanum wendlandii

amaranthus, and in the Zurich Botanical Gardens near a concession stand—these can be knockouts. The dark blue flowers are beautiful and open most of the summer. Growing and training your own standards may not be something you want to do, but they are occasionally sold, and if you can afford one, give it a try. Full sun.

Thorns, veggies, shrubs . . . there seems to be everything in this genus, including vines. It is difficult to include these vines in an annuals discourse, because unless they attain some maturity they will not produce a great number of flowers, and they are not hardy north of zone 7 or 8. However, I include them here so we can enjoy a few flowers if we get them. The easiest to find is the white form of the potato vine, *Solanum jasminoides*, which produces white tomato-like flowers on vigorous plants. This is a popular vine on the West Coast and in the Southeast, where it often overwinters. As an annual, it can be grown in a container and will still attain 5–6' the first year. Or, just let it roam over the ground, where it acts as a white groundcover. Flowers will be sparse the first year. Another vine that is worth a search is paradise flower, *S. wendlandii*, with beautiful large blue flowers on armed plants. Might be more appropriate to the conservatory than to the garden, but it is a beauty. Check your friendly Google-button for a source or two. Full sun.

Stachytarpheta

SNAKEWEED, FALSE VERVAIN

Too bad some of these botanical names are such a mouthful. People won't buy what they can't pronounce, and they certainly won't lay money down for anything that has "weed" in its common name. That is a shame, for while this is never going to be a mainstream plant, it has some interesting attributes. Plants in the genus should probably be called

Solanum jasminoides

Stachytarpheta jamaicensis, flowers

Stachytarpheta mutabilis

MORE ☞

the tease plant, because so few flowers open at any one time. The main species, *Stachytarpheta jamaicensis*, has blue-purple flowers and makes a wonderful plant in heat and humidity, but only three or four flowers open a day, until the entire length of the fifty or so flowers eventually opens. It is a long, painful process, but on the other hand, the flowers certainly continue blooming for a long period of time!

Pink snakeweed (*Stachytarpheta mutabilis*) is taller and lankier than its purple counterpart but is a much prettier color. It is another Mae West, teasing all the time, but the color is so nice, it doesn't seem to matter as much. Full sun.

Stachytarpheta jamaicensis

Stictocardia beraviensis

Stictocardia beraviensis

A plant that will be found only at the best of establishments; don't expect to find it at a box store but maybe at a specialty grower like GardenSmith, a wonderful, weird, and wacky place close to my home. The owner, Denise Smith, is the personification of her nursery, and between the two of us, we see who can surprise the other the most. She always wins. Like the time she gave me this marvelous vine, *Stictocardia beraviensis*, which we called braveheart vine. It grows about 3' a day, and has the most wonderful felty gray heart-shaped leaves and pleasant tropical orange flowers. It is useful as a screen for the side of a porch or to cover unsightly areas, like my garden. It's also a fun plant to simply watch grow.

The flowers are quite beautiful, but don't expect to see them unless you stick your face into the leaves; they are held close to the stems, and there are not that many anyway. Perhaps you have someone like Denise in your area; if so, try one. It is native to western Africa, and even though it looks like the next kudzu, it will not take serious frost.

Strobilanthes dyerianus

PERSIAN SHIELD

What a remarkable plant. Persian shield (*Strobilanthes dyerianus*) can be grown in almost any environment, in almost any part of the country. The bronze-purple coloring of the large leaves has been enjoyed in gardens for a long time, and when grown well, it is truly an architectural feature in the garden.

Plants can grow to 4' high and equally wide, even in a midwestern summer. They are as perfectly at home in the

Strobilanthes dyerianus

garden bed as they are in a large container. This is a large plant, so a small container simply will not do. We plant them intermingled with white petunias and nicotiana, or pink 'Aztec' verbena and purslane. Plants are easy to find at any decent retailer, but do not put plants out too early, or they may start forming flowers. The flowers are boring at best but worse than that, once flowering starts, the plant stops growing. Persian shield can handle afternoon shade, particularly in the South, where midday sun can cause premature wilting of the large leaves. Otherwise full sun.

Strobilanthes dyerianus with verbena and purslane

Sutera

BACOPA

When these small-flowering, trailing plants were first introduced, they were simply known as bacopa, both botanically and as a common name. The genus *Bacopa* consists of aquatic plants, somewhat similar in flower and more compact in habit. The bacopa of gardens is *Sutera grandiflora* or hybrids of the genus. That really doesn't matter a great deal, because wherever these are sold, they will be called bacopa, and that is that.

Strobilanthes dyerianus with verbena

Sutera 'Lavender Storm'

MORE ☞

Bacopas do not make particularly good garden plants, North or South, but are well suited to baskets and containers. We planted 'Lavender Storm', a well-known cultivar, among argyranthemum, purslane, and mussaenda, and the small flowers helped to fill out the container. I also enjoyed 'Snowflake' in our baskets, where they made a nice simple show. However, plants that remain in the greenhouse for a long time can really be impressive when they are placed in the garden. At the Missouri Botanical Garden, a basket of 'Snowstorm' essentially took over the entire corner of the garden, as well as the purple petunias trying to survive. Numerous cultivars have been bred, and differences are often slight, perhaps a little bigger flower here, or slightly different color there. Blues and lavenders are not uncommon, and 'Mauve Mist' is perhaps the best of them, with excellent color and rather large flower size. 'Lavender Showers' sports a large flower; 'Blue Showers' has flowers equally large and a bit more blue. I didn't think I would like the variegated form, 'Olympic Gold', but it mixed well with various plants and tumbled nicely out of the container. A genus closely related to bacopa is *Jamesbrittenia*, found as 'Penny Candy Violet' and 'Penny Candy Pink', which have flowers similar to bacopa but whose foliage is much more lacy and incised. Plants of *Jamesbrittenia* are not as vigorous as bacopa, at least in the heat, but still may appear under the bacopa name. They are sufficiently poorer in performance that it makes sense to check the leaves when buying.

Plants are much more vigorous in the North than in the South and outstanding in the West. In the South, they are more likely to struggle in the heat and humidity of July and August. Afternoon shade everywhere.

Sutera 'Snowflake'

Sutera 'Snowstorm'

Sutera 'Mauve Mist'

Sutera 'Lavender Showers'

Sutera 'Olympic Gold'

Jamesbrittenia 'Penny Candy Violet'

Tagetes

MARIGOLD

Comments about garden snobbery and the preferred diet of said snobs were mentioned under petunia, and similar comments could be made here. No doubt, the popularity of many bedding plants has faded with the introduction of so much new material to the gardener, and the marigold is certainly not as popular as it once was. Of all the bedding plants I work with, I believe I prefer marigolds the least, but part of that's because whenever I handle them, I start sneezing. Not a good plant for one who suffers from allergies. But my biases aside, they are highly functional plants.

Marigolds come in an assortment of sizes and colors; they are not all yellow. Many have been shown to provide nematode suppression and have been used in vegetable gardens as companion plants for years. For the gardener, there is no lack of choice.

The tallest forms, which at one time were referred to as hedge marigolds, are the African marigolds, *Tagetes erecta*. Standing 3–4' tall, they were the most popular in the heyday of bedding, in the 1960s through the 1980s. Cultivars like 'Orange Crush' would tower over plant-

Jamesbrittenia 'Penny Candy Pink'

Tagetes erecta 'Voyager Orange'

Tagetes erecta Inca series

Tagetes erecta 'Discovery Yellow'

MORE ☞

Tagetes erecta 'Disco Flame'

Tagetes 'Golden Gate'

Tagetes erecta 'Disco Marietta'

Tagetes tenuifolia 'Lemon Gem'

Tagetes tenuifolia 'Golden Gem'

Tagetes tenuifolia 'Lulu', flowers

ings of dianthus and other annuals. The tall forms were always popular, but when it rained or the wind blew hard, stems would invariably snap or plants would fall over. Newer, stronger African forms, such as 'Voyager Orange', were bred with large flowers on strong stems. The Inca series, in yellow and orange, remains one of the best for strength of stem, compact height, and persistent flowering. However, gardeners and landscapers still complained that plants were too tall, and as a result, the Discovery series was introduced. Compared to other African forms, it was far shorter and more weather-tolerant. African marigolds are easily found in retail stores; they are almost always yellow or orange and have round double flowers on reasonably sturdy plants.

While the African forms were always popular, the French marigold, *Tagetes patula*, was equally successful. Plants were shorter and better branched but had much smaller flowers. More diversity in flower color was available, and they were more weather-tolerant. French marigolds became the dominant form of marigold. Numerous cultivars appeared, classic double-flowered styles like 'Little Hero Yellow' or those with handsome

Tagetes patula 'Little Hero Yellow'

Tagetes erecta 'Durango Flame'

Tagetes tenuifolia 'Lulu'

MORE ☞

bicolored flowers, such as 'Durango Flame' and 'Disco Flame'. Single flowers also became available, cultivars like 'Disco Marietta', which were, and still are, quite popular. Many, many named varieties await you at the garden center. The genetic differences between the two species are significant, yet breeders found a way to bridge that gap and produced some exceptional hybrids. My favorite was 'Golden Gate', with excellent vigor and better disease tolerance, yet still compact. Other hybrids were bred, but difficulties in seed production have diminished the hybridization efforts and have made these increasingly difficult to obtain.

There is little doubt that when you walk into the garden center looking for marigolds, your choice will usually be limited to African or French forms. Hybrids may be available occasionally but are probably not labeled as such. However, approximately fifty species of marigolds are known, and a few of these may pop up every now and then at your favorite retail outlet.

Tagetes tenuifolia 'Ursula'

Tagetes lemmonii

The signet marigold, *Tagetes tenuifolia*, is my recommendation. The mounded habit, the fern-like leaves, and the small but numerous flowers provide welcome relief from the stiff upright forms of other marigolds, and breeders have provided us with some gardenworthy forms as well. The Gem series, including 'Lemon Gem' and 'Golden Gem', has been available for a number of years and stood the test of time. I also enjoy the look of 'Lulu', whose relaxed habit and persistent flowering allow it to combine well with petunias, amaranths, and zinnias. Excellent habit and flowering, even up close. 'Ursula' has also demonstrated excellent garden performance. There are parts of the country where other species may surface, such as *T. lemmonii*, native to Mt. Lemmon in Tucson, Arizona. Excellent for heat but rarely available. Fun to have as a native species but will do poorly in humidity and rain.

Marigolds have lost some of their luster in the gardening community for good reason. Among annuals, they are extremely high-maintenance, at least on my list. To ensure attractiveness, they must be deadheaded, a job that my nose and I detest, and they are susceptible to many insects, such as spider mites, leafhoppers, and thrips. For warm areas of the country, I recommend that they be planted early, removed in mid summer, and replanted in late summer for fall flowering. Seeds are cheap and germination is easy. Full sun.

Tecomaria

CAPE HONEYSUCKLE

I never am sure whether this genus should be placed under annuals, perennials, or shrubs, and I hesitate to get too enamored with it. I have tried Cape honeysuckle (*Tecomaria capensis*) several

Tecomaria capensis 'Scarlet'

times over the years in our gardens at Athens; one year I think it is terrific, the next it dies. To many people, it is perennial to zone 8, occasionally coming down to zone 7 territory as well.

I have seen them listed under various flower colors, including 'Scarlet' and 'Apricot', and they make handsome plants throughout the season; but, at least for us, they put out few flowers until the fall. In general, I have no problem with fall-flowerers; however, I was not pleased with the flower power of the plants. To be honest, I have seen some impressive specimens further south or in a greenhouse setting, but most of those have been perennial. I am not sure that the northern gardener would have sufficient growing time to enjoy ample flowering. However, if it is for sale, it is certainly worth a try; the plants are tough and not bothered by insects or diseases, and the flowers are gorgeous. Full sun.

Tecomaria capensis 'Apricot'

Thunbergia

This genus is full of surprises. All but one of its members have struggled in relative obscurity, but there is so much more fun yet to be had with the plants found within. Most are vines and require some support to climb, but once they start to grow, they can provide immense pleasure.

The best known is the black-eyed susan vine, *Thunbergia alata*, which has been decorating trellises for centuries. The most common black-eyed susans are orange with a black eye, which is what will result from the seed package you buy. They will be reasonably vigorous and can be trained around posts (tie some thick strands of rope from

Thunbergia alata 'Susie Orange'

Thunbergia alata 'White with Dark Eye'

MORE ☞

nails to allow the stems to twist around). They also are available in named cultivars, and the vigorous 'Susie Orange' would have climbed all over our pergola had we let it. I enjoy other colors as well; I loved the basket of white flowers with black eyes and the subtle hue of 'Red Shades'. These are often labeled by flower color only and can be obtained from seed catalogs. A vegetative form, the Sunny series, was bred with electric colors of lemon and orange. The tremendous growth displayed at Michigan State University gardens gives an indication of the vigor of 'Sunny Orange'.

Other lesser-known vines are equally beautiful. I can't get enough of sky vine, *Thunbergia grandiflora*, and grow it every year in our gardens at Athens. The dark green glossy leaves are themselves handsome, but the beautiful light blue flowers are to die for. Unfortunately, the flowers don't appear until late summer,

Thunbergia alata 'Red Shades'

Thunbergia alata 'Sunny Orange', Michigan State University

Thunbergia alata 'Sunny Lemon Star'

Thunbergia alata 'Sunny Orange', *T. a.* 'Sunny Lemon Star'

but then they continue to frost. They are winter hardy to about zone 7b. I first came across clock vine, *T. gregorii*, in Europe and was immediately taken with the vibrant orange flowers. I have had trouble locating the vine in this country but will continue to try, as it is worth the hunt. The previous two vines are somewhat uncommon, but when I saw Nilgari vine, *T. mysorensis*, in New Zealand, I about flipped out. It was so amazing that I asked for some seeds, ready to introduce the next great vine to America. Then a few months later, on a visit to Denise Smith, of GardenSmith Greenhouses, not forty minutes away, I saw the same vine in her greenhouse! Since Denise is always on the forefront of change, I knew I had a winner. Time will tell. All thunbergia vines need something that the stems can twine around. Large posts are too thick, wire and string may be too thin. A wire net on a fence works well. Full sun.

Not all species are vines, and bush thunbergia, *Thunbergia battiscombei*, wants to grow along the ground, yet will

Thunbergia grandiflora

Thunbergia gregorii

Thunbergia grandiflora, flowers

Thunbergia battiscombei

MORE ☞

also clamber over other plants in its way. It does not seem to know whether it wants to climb up, climb over, or simply be a bush. Regardless, the deep blue flowers with their orange eyes and white backs are quite beautiful. They may not put on a lot of flowers, but a few peeking out from the leathery foliage are common. They perform well in containers. Full sun.

Tibouchina

Glory bush or princess flower, *Tibouchina urvilleana*, is not uncommon in south Florida and the Gulf States, where it makes a stately shrub or small tree. It is only recently, however, that the attributes of the plants are being recognized in other parts of the country. The most common form, if tibouchina can ever be called common, is the large-flowered var. *grandiflora*, brought to the United States in 1985 from New Zealand. Plants were subsequently introduced as 'Athens Blue' and have been propagated for many years. They may or may not be called by that name any more, but the large blue to purple flowers and handsome disease-resistant, insect-resistant foliage are characteristic of the cultivar. They look terrific in containers or the garden; they start flowering in mid summer and continue on and off all season. They can carry dozens of flowers, but

Thunbergia mysorensis

Tibouchina urvilleana 'Jewel'

Thunbergia battiscombei, clambering

Tibouchina longiflora

four to six at a time is more common, depending on plant size. Plants will reach 3–4' in height, depending on locale, and become quite woody. They will often overwinter to zone 7b. Other forms of this species include the handsome but less vigorous smaller-flowered 'Jewel'.

The large-leaved tibouchina, *Tibouchina grandifolia*, has burst onto the landscape scene, at least in the southern states. This is one impressive plant, sporting huge velvety leaves on a 3–5' tall plant. It does not flower until late summer or fall, but even when not in flower, it adds that architectural feature to the garden. The purple flowers are smaller than 'Athens Blue' and are held in long inflorescences at the top of the plant. Truly a spectacular plant in and out of flower.

These two species are the best of the bunch, but others occasionally surface. I have grown long-flowered tibouchina, *Tibouchina longiflora*, but was disappointed with the lack of vigor and few flowers. This was a fall-flowerer only, and not really worth the wait. Full sun.

Tithonia rotundifolia

MEXICAN SUNFLOWER

This is a large, highly visible plant. It is amazing that such a small seed can produce such a colorful, giant plant in a single season. I see Mexican sunflower

MORE ☞

Tibouchina urvilleana var. *grandiflora* 'Athens Blue'

Tibouchina urvilleana var. *grandiflora* 'Athens Blue', flowers

Tibouchina grandifolia

Tibouchina grandifolia, flowers

(*Tithonia rotundifolia*) in many botanic gardens as well as private gardens, but it is usually too big for city lots. Most often I see it standing by itself, but when 'Torch' was combined with red dahlias, they made quite a sight. Even the fire-engine red of those dahlias was lost among the riot of orange in the bed. The most common of the Mexican sunflowers is 'Goldfinger', which can grow 6' tall in areas of warm summers and 3–4' tall elsewhere. The cultivar name is a little misleading, as the 2½" wide flowers are more orange than gold.

The best cultivar for smaller gardens is 'Fiesta del Sol', which grows about 3'

Tithonia rotundifolia 'Goldfinger'

Tithonia rotundifolia 'Goldfinger', flowers

Tithonia rotundifolia 'Fiesta del Sol'

Tithonia rotundifolia 'Torch' with dahlias

tall and equally wide. Its compact habit is a welcome sight after the bigger forms, which can get tall and leggy and snap off at various places. 'Fiesta del Sol' is not without problems; it tends to take a little longer to start flowering, but the shortness more than makes up for its laziness to flower. Full sun.

Torenia

WISHBONE FLOWER

I always enjoy teaching this genus in my herbaceous class, because I know it will always be readily identified (though perhaps not spelled correctly) as soon as the student looks inside the flower. There, two fused stamens look just like the wishbone from the Thanksgiving turkey. Simple stuff, this ID class.

The wishbone flower (*Torenia fournieri*) has historically been grown from seed and bred in many colors. Over the years, as the vigor improved and more cultivars became available, plants have become more visible, both indoors as houseplants and out. In the garden, I enjoy the Clown series, which offers many colors, including my favorite, 'Clown Blue'. The garden performance is excellent in spring and early summer but declines as hot temperatures occur. Plants persist longer in the North than in the South. Better in containers than in the garden bed.

A breakthrough in torenia breeding occurred with the appearance of 'Summer Wave Blue', a vegetatively propagated form. It has been an outstanding selection, and although flowering declines a little in the summer, the plant remains healthy. The flower color is excellent, and I highly recommend this flowering plant. 'Summer Wave

Torenia fournieri 'Clown Violet'

Torenia fournieri, wishbone

Torenia fournieri 'Clown Blue and White'

Torenia fournieri 'Clown Burgundy'

MORE ☞

Amethyst' followed that success and provided an additional color, then the Moon series came along, adding 'Blue Moon' and 'Pink Moon'.

Some people have tired of wishbone flower and even find it pedestrian. If this should happen to you, try the very different yellow wishbone flower, *Torenia flava* 'Suzie Wong'. She has bright yellow flowers with a deep throat. Mysterious and beautiful. The yellow wishbone has less vigor than the cultivars above, but it is fun to have her in the garden, even if that time is fleeting. All torenias do well in patio containers. Afternoon shade.

Torenia fournieri 'Pink Moon'

Torenia flava 'Suzie Wong'

Torenia fournieri 'Clown Blue'

Torenia fournieri 'Summer Wave Blue'

Torenia fournieri 'Summer Wave Amethyst'

Torenia fournieri 'Blue Moon'

Trachelium caeruleum 'Purple Umbrella'

Trachelium caeruleum 'Purple Umbrella', flower head

Trachelium caeruleum 'White Umbrella'

Tropaeolum speciosum

Trachelium caeruleum

THROATWORT

This annual is far more common in florists' shops and in vases than it is in the garden. Throatwort (*Trachelium caeruleum*) is usually produced in greenhouses and fields, and I have seen rows upon rows of these plants, which were thought to assuage ailments of the throat, ready for harvest. Flowers persist for well over a week in the vase. The flower head is beautiful, but it is not until you look at it closely that you realize it consists of hundreds of small individual flowers.

Although plants are usually greenhouse-grown, I have been asked to trial throatwort a number of times outdoors, but I can't say I have seen any breakthroughs for garden performance. In most gardens, they struggle in conditions of high heat and humidity, and heavy rain does not do them a lot of good either. Certainly they look better in the Northwest, Northeast, or in the mountains. Only purple flowers ('Purple Umbrella') and white ('White Umbrella') are available, and only occasionally at that. My feeling is that we will see a lot more throatworts in the vase, and few in the nursery. Full sun.

Tropaeolum

NASTURTIUM

The genus has been in gardens for centuries and takes on many faces. In the British Isles, hedges are often festooned with the flame nasturtium, *Tropaeolum speciosum*, which may succeed in half a

MORE ☞

dozen gardens in this country, but not yours or mine. Other species are absolutely fabulous, and equally difficult to grow, such as canary creeper, *T. peregrinum*, or the beautiful *T. polyphyllum* with blue-green leaves and vibrant yellow flowers. If you are really adventurous, try to find the vining multicolored nasturtium, *T. tricolorum*, purchased as a corm and trained in conservatories. All these magical plants can be found through diligent searching, all can be placed in the summer garden, all will be costly, and none will perform as well here as they do in England or Vancouver. But as long as the garden juices flow, we will always try plants the books tell us we can't grow. Just save a little money for the children's college fund.

The plant we are most familiar with is good old-fashioned *Tropaeolum majus*, and while these nasturtiums are kind of boring compared to the species just described, they have one characteristic that the others do not: they work! As many times as I have seen nasturtiums, I can't walk by these colorful plants as they flow out of window boxes or patio containers without admiring them. Perhaps nasturtiums have been superseded by newer introductions or other plants have better ad agencies—whatever, I don't really see a lot of nasturtiums anymore. Then again, maybe I am looking in the wrong gardens. All nasturtiums love cool temperatures; they are generally planted for the spring season and often removed as summer temperatures rise, for more heat-tolerant plants. That does not bother me at all—it is the lot of cool lovers like

Tropaeolum polyphyllum

Tropaeolum tricolorum

Tropaeolum peregrinum 'Canary Bird'

Tropaeolum majus Jewel series

calendula and viola, and they each have their place.

Nasturtiums come in many colors, and purchasing seeds will allow good selection. The Jewel series is a popular bright mixture of colors; 'Red Jewel' is particularly colorful. They are fine in the garden bed and useful in containers, and can be trained to climb as well. Orange and red are common, but lovely yellows like 'Moonlight' are worth seeking out. Many people are enamored with the variegated foliage forms, most often available in 'Alaska', which may bear yellow or orange flower. They are particularly handsome in containers. Fascina-

Tropaeolum majus 'Moonlight'

Tropaeolum tuberosum 'Ken Aslett'

Tropaeolum majus

Tropaeolum majus 'Red Jewel'

Tropaeolum majus 'Alaska'

Tropaeolum majus 'Darjean Gold'

MORE ☞

tion with variegation is one thing, yet when I heard about the double-flowered forms, I was definitely not interested. But when I saw 'Darjean Gold', I thought it was pretty neat, even if the flower color was not outstanding. However, I must have been fifty feet away when 'Hermine Grashoff' came into view. She had not yet reached her mature size, but she was already a 55-mph plant. The doubles are usually grown from cuttings and may not be all that easy to locate. Lastly, even harder to locate and more temperamental is the tuberous nasturtium, *Tropaeolum tuberosum*, which vines up walls with little effort. The only named cultivar I am aware of is 'Ken Aslett'. This is a teaser, don't get mad at me when Ken doesn't make it. All nasturtiums decline in the heat, so get them in early. Full sun.

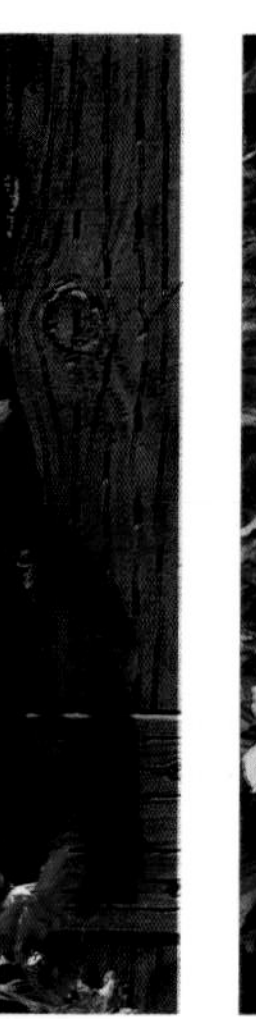
Tropaeolum majus 'Hermine Grashoff'

Turnera

One of my colleagues and friends in horticulture is Alan Shapiro, the owner of San Felasco Nurseries in Gainesville, Florida. I believe he feels that someone has to educate this poor foreigner, and he has taken on that difficult task himself. Whenever we talk plants, he always shows me species I have never heard of and helps me in spite of myself. A wonderful nursery, a great plantsman. It was Alan who introduced me to turneras, in particular to the buttercup flower, *Turnera ulmifolia*. To Floridians and Texans, this is a fairly common plant, reseeding and often becoming somewhat weed-like, but to the rest of the country, it is unknown.

Turnera ulmifolia 'Eldorado', flowers

Turnera ulmifolia 'Eldorado'

Turnera subulata

'Eldorado' is a selection that is available nationally, and time will tell if it succeeds above the 30th parallel. However, with its beautiful yellow flowers, handsome dark green foliage, and disdain of heat and humidity, this should be tried in Dubuque and Moose Bay as well as in Baton Rouge and Biloxi.

The genus is only now being trialed around the country, and another species that may have potential is *Turnera subulata*, with wonderful white flowers with a yellow eye. Plants are weedy, but selection is presently under way to improve the garden characteristics. Full sun.

Tweedia caerulea

Any plant with a name like tweedia can't be all bad, and I figured if I could get my hands on a few, I should surely like to try some. I did and I tried, and I found the ultimate in the color blue. *Tweedia caerulea* is surely not a common plant in retail stores, although more progressive growers may have some. It is also available through mail order and the Internet. So what's the deal? The flower color has been said to be the finest blue in the plant kingdom, and I cannot dispute that claim. Plants can be grown in containers or in the bed and have been used as cut flowers, the blue proving popular for weddings and corsages. When planting, put them where they will have protection from the wind and, if possible, from driving rain. They belong to the same family as milkweed, and they produce long narrow milkweed-like pods, which can get messy by the end of the season.

Tweedia caerulea

Tweedia caerulea, flowers

While people sometimes gush over the plant, they must also remember that rain can disfigure the flowers. And the plants themselves, well, they don't smell very good. Personally I love these things, but they are not particularly easy to grow, they set lots of messy fruit, and they have a disagreeable odor. Given those characteristics, and the enthusiasm of North American gardeners, I expect tweedia to become a bestseller. Full sun.

Verbena ×hybrida Olympia series

Verbena 'Fire King'

Verbena

VERVAIN

I am often asked what group of plants has seen the greatest explosion in the shortest amount of time. It is a good question to ponder and I have no absolute answer, but I would put verbenas close to the top, along with pansies, coleus, and sunflowers. As late as 1989, most annual verbena (*Verbena ×hybrida*) were seed-propagated, like the Olympia series, and although they were pretty, they lacked the vigor to withstand landscape rigors in many parts of the country. Good groundskeepers, like those at the University of Georgia, realized they needed something better and began to plant large beds of the pink Canadian verbena, *Verbena canadensis*. The perennial tall verbena did look much better with a dense planting of pink verbena at its feet, but landscapers needed additional choices. A few vegetative cultivars had always been kicking around, and in the late 1980s 'Homestead Purple' was introduced and enjoyed explosive popularity. It provided persistent flowering, excellent color, and exceptional vigor, and often overwintered in mild winters. Plants are still popular.

Armed with the knowledge that people would purchase verbena in large numbers, plant breeders got busy, and within five years, dozens of hybrid cultivars were introduced or simply reintroduced to fill the demand. At Athens, we tested dozens, trying to come up with reasons to recommend some over others. As of this writing, I bet there are over fifty cultivars vying for the gardener's dollar; some are fabulous, some are just good, but all are improvements over the old-fashioned seed items sold years ago. Some of the best include the cutleaf Tapien series, such as the beautiful

MORE ☞

'Tapien Pink' planted in a boxwood container by the side of a pool. Another excellent series is Temari, and 'Temari Bright Red' is indeed just that. Red-rose has always been a popular color in verbenas, and 'Fire King' proved to be an exceptionally good performer as well. 'Blue Princess' provided a nice lavender-blue color, and 'Denim Blue' also had many fans when it hit the retail stores.

We do a lot of verbena trialing in containers, and they combine well with anything. I love the terrific introductions in the Wildfire series. 'Wildfire Purple' is

Verbena canadensis with tall verbena

Verbena 'Blue Princess'

Verbena 'Homestead Purple'

Verbena 'Denim Blue'

Verbena, UGA Trial Gardens

Verbena 'Tapien Pink'

Verbena 'Temari Bright Red'

Verbena 'Wildfire Purple'

Verbena 'Wildfire Blush'

Verbena 'Tortuga Peach', *V.* 'Tortuga Red'

Verbena 'Ron Deal'

MORE ☞

certainly vigorous, but I didn't really mind that it ate up almost everything in the container except some white purslane. 'Wildfire Blush' provides outstanding but more subtle color as well. 'Tortuga Peach' and 'Tortuga Red' have large flowers and happily coexist with purslane and mussaenda. 'Aztec Red', but one of many colors of the Aztec series, flowered all summer in the containers and the garden. 'Turkana Scarlet' is one of the new generation of bright colorful verbenas, and I was also pleased with the Twilight series, such as 'Twilight Blue with Eye'. One of the brightest new verbe-

Verbena ×*hybrida* 'Peaches and Cream'

Verbena 'Aztec Red'

Verbena 'Turkana Scarlet'

Verbena 'Twilight Blue with Eye'

Verbena ×*hybrida* 'Sandy Rose'

Verbena ×*hybrida* Quartz series

nas is 'Ron Deal', with electric violet flowers and fine heat and humidity tolerance.

One of the best things that all this breeding did was make the seed-propagated cultivars of *Verbena* ×*hybrida* better, because seed breeders realized that they had to instill additional colors and vigor if people were going to use their cultivars. In a European garden, I noticed 'Peaches and Cream' used at the front of a large planting of marigolds and ageratum. It was handsome, but summer weather there is not as abusive as it is in the Midwest. Newer seed strains such as the Sandy series performed well, and many colors in the Quartz series have been developed. One of the seed series that was most popular before the onslaught of the vegetative forms was the Romance series, and even it has been improved for gardeners. 'Romance Violet with Eye' is one of the more vigorous colors.

The hybrids of these colorful verbenas dominate the annual verbena market, but our native cutleaf verbena, *Verbena tenuisecta*, is also a marvelous plant. It can be grown in all its purple glory as a groundcover, and it will flower from May to frost. Its white coun-

MORE ☞

Verbena rigida 'Polaris'

Verbena tenuisecta

Verbena ×*hybrida* 'Romance Violet with Eye'

Verbena tenuisecta var. *alba*

Verbena rigida 'Lilacina'

terpart, var. *alba*, is almost as good and equally vigorous. These plants have also been the backbone of some of the cultivars listed previously. The rigid verbena, *V. rigida*, is considered more of a perennial than annual, but it is often used as an annual in the Midwest or Northeast, where it will likely not overwinter. A common form is 'Lilacina', with purple flowers, but by far the most handsome selection is 'Polaris', with light mauve flowers used to perfection in a combination planting with red geraniums and yellow bidens. Full sun.

Vigna caracalla

Vigna

Whenever you eat bean sprouts in a sandwich or at a Chinese restaurant, you are eating sprouts from this genus. Moth bean, adzuki bean, mung bean, and cowpea are all important crops in India, Indonesia, and South and Central America. Gardeners are little interested in such facts but are fascinated with one of the members of this genus, the snail vine, *Vigna caracalla*.

Snail vines are easily grown from seed and consist of hairy leaflets and vigorous stems. They can grow 8–10' in a single season. However, it is not the leaves but the flowers that are unique, looking like pink to rose-colored snails' shells as they form later in the season. There are bigger vines, better vines, and more colorful vines, but none that will have people exclaiming as quickly as this one. Full sun.

Viola ×*wittrockiana*, UGA Trial Gardens

Viola

PANSY, VIOLET

Many of the literally hundreds of species of violets may be obnoxious weeds in your garden, but there are at least a bazillion well-behaved pansies and violas out there, waiting to be planted in early spring in the Midwest and North and in the fall in the South and Far West. Having resided in the South for the last twenty years, where pansies and violas are a landscape staple in winter and spring, I have been inundated with these plants and have trialed most of that bazillion. I have watched the trickle of cultivars become a torrent in a very short time. It has been a blast!

Pansies are not as popular in northern areas, where they are not normally planted out in the fall, but they are more cold hardy than many landscapers and gardeners give them credit for. They can be planted in early fall most anywhere, and if salt doesn't get them, they will flower at the first hint of spring. In areas of cool summers, they can remain in the ground the entire season. However, most pansies and violas are treated as winter annuals in the South (pulled out with the kale and Iceland poppies to make way for summer annuals) and as spring annuals in the North (removed with the nasturtiums for the same reason).

The pansies and violas sold in the garden center are referred to as *Viola* ×*wittrockiana*. In 1990, I was asked to help evaluate literally thousands of pansies in

Pansies with tulips and sign

Pansies, containers

Pansies high and low

Viola 'Medallion Yellow with Blotch' (pansy)

MORE ☞

trial fields in California; it was a daunting sight and, after the first fifty or so, an incredibly boring task. You would have thought I learned my lesson, but we were still doing the same thing in Georgia into the twenty-first century. And cultivars have evolved, not only in number but also in quality. I believe I can say there are no dogs out there anymore—buy the color you like, and it will more than likely perform just fine in your garden.

Pansies improve outdoor signage, fill baskets and containers high and low, and add early spring color to formal

Pansies in boxwood garden

Viola 'Accord Banner Yellow with Red Blotch' (pansy)

Viola 'Dancer Beaconsfield' (pansy)

Viola 'Maxim Marina' (pansy)

Viola 'Imperial Frosty Rose' (pansy)

Viola 'Ultima Yellow Beacon' (pansy)

Viola 'Atlas Blue' (pansy)

boxwood gardens, giving people an excuse to spend more than thirty seconds looking at boxwood gardens. Pansies come in two main color patterns, those with "faces" and those without. In the case of the former, the patterns are really quite fantastic. Those with big purple blotches are the most common, as in 'Medallion Yellow with Blotch', but blotches come in different colors, such as in 'Accord Banner Yellow with Red Blotch'. (Obviously, breeders' creativity in naming flowers died when they hit *Viola*!) Blues and purples combined with white also became popular. The

Viola 'Melody Red' (pansy)

Viola 'Padparaja' (pansy)

Viola 'Halloween' (pansy)

Viola 'Sorbet Coconut Swirl' (viola)

MORE ☞

purple color of 'Dancer Beaconsfield' is in sharp contrast to the more subtle blue in 'Maxim Marina'. One of the cultivars I thought was outstanding in our gardens was 'Imperial Frosty Rose', a color nearly everyone stopped to admire. When you walk into a garden center and see all these faces staring back at you, give one or two a home. However, landscapers realized that clear-face forms have the greatest visibility, and breeding those with clear faces (like 'Ultima Yellow Beacon'), which could be seen from a longer distance, became immensely popular. Blue will always have a place in gardens, and 'Atlas Blue' was a favorite to contrast with yellows. Reds are also reasonably popular; 'Melody Red' always showed up well in the landscape. Perhaps breeders got a little bored and went to work on eye-poppers and novelties. When the vibrant orange of 'Padparaja' was introduced, everybody did a double take; unfortunately it was a poor greenhouse performer and may be difficult to find these days. While that color was strikingly bright, black continues enormously popular. Black pansies like 'Halloween' are sold in the fall and must get gardeners into a ghostly spirit—how else can you explain such phenomenonal popularity? To be honest, they are fascinating, and like them or not, isn't it great to have such a choice?

Viola 'Princess Deep Purple' (viola)

Viola 'Jewel Blue' (viola)

Viola Sorbet series (viola), container

Viola 'Penny Azure Wing' (viola)

Viola 'Wink Purple and White' (viola)

A major trend in flower breeding in the '90s was to reduce flower size but increase flower number on big-ticket items like petunia, impatiens, and pansies. A viola is nothing more than a small-flowered version of the pansy. While there are numerous similarities, there are also numerous differences. Our data suggest that for best weather tolerance against snow, wind, and rain, violas rebound more quickly and are better garden performers—a generality but one that our trials have borne out. And breeders have not been sitting on their hands. The Sorbet series, a fabulous group of plants, is one of the most popular, showing up in gardens and in containers that welcome people to the front door. Containers of 'Princess Deep Purple' offer that deep color so desired by gardeners today, but I prefer calmer waters, such as those of 'Jewel Blue'. Violas also provide unique colors; 'Penny Azure Wing' is subtle and engaging, while the small flowers of 'Wink Purple and White' earned it many fans when we planted it in 2002. But my favorite of all the violas I have seen has to be 'Bilbo Baggins', part of the Hobbit series. Hundreds of small colorful flowers on 9" tall plants—J.R. would be proud.

The modern pansies and violas are difficult not to admire, but we should not forget one of the plants that made this happen, that is the good old johnny-jump-up, *Viola tricolor*. Jumping up everywhere, they became one of the main parents in the breeding revolution of this genus. It is always fun to have some of the old folks around, it puts things in perspective. Some of the johnnies also became transformed, and it is difficult to know where the violas leave off and the jump-ups begin. Of course, it does not matter, and if you can locate 'Irish Molly' or 'Penny Wood', two old-fashioned but handsome cultivars, your garden will be even richer.

Full sun. In the South, plant in October, fertilize heavily in February. In the North, plant in September or as soon as the melting snow in spring allows; fertilize when warm weather is forecast for three days in a row.

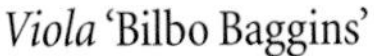

Viola 'Bilbo Baggins'

Viola 'Irish Molly'

Viola tricolor

Viola 'Penny Wood'

Xanthosoma

TANNIA

I had never even heard of *Xanthosoma* until a few years ago, when I was at a plant seminar and trade show. I was walking the floor when one of my plant friends asked, "Allan, what do you think of that golden xanthosoma?" I didn't have a clue what he was talking about, so I replied, "I must not have seen it yet, I don't recall it." "But it's right beside you, you were just looking at it." "Oh, that xanthosoma." So much for the expert.

Xanthosoma sagittifolium (tannia) is second only to *Colocasia* (eddo, taro) as a food crop; its edible corms are a staple carbohydrate throughout the tropics. Several ornamental forms of tannia have found their way into the garden, but unless somebody is giving you hints, you are unlikely to tell *Xanthosoma*, *Alocasia*, and *Colocasia* apart at first glance. I certainly did not (see *Alocasia*). While *Alocasia* and *Colocasia* have been gaining a foothold in gardeners' consciousnesses, *Xanthosoma* is a relative rookie to North American gardens.

In general, they are large plants, growing 4–5' tall and equally wide in a single season. They are not grown for their jack-in-the-pulpit type flowers but rather for their large foliage and architectural dominance. A couple of cultivars exist, and their foliar qualities are the only reason to grow this rather than the less expensive colocasias. The biggest is blue tannia, *Xanthosoma violaceum*, with deep green to purple-tinged foliage. My favorite is golden tannia, var. *muffafa*, whose lighter-colored leaves are outstanding. I have also seen this plant, or something very similar, labeled as 'Chartreuse Giant'. Regardless of the name, it can make a significant landscape feature. All require heat to get going, but they are more tolerant of drought and lower temperatures than their tropical cousins. All require a cold frame or greenhouse for overwintering. I have no doubt that as the tropical movement continues to grow, this group of plants will also grow in popularity. Full sun.

Xanthosoma violaceum

Xanthosoma violaceum var. *muffafa*

Xanthosoma violaceum 'Chartreuse Giant'

Xeranthemum annuum 'Lilac Stars'

Zea mays 'Bars and Stripes'

Zea mays 'Tiger Cub'

Xeranthemum

IMMORTELLE

Immortelle is one of the many plants known as everlastings, including relatives like strawflowers, *Bracteantha*. I have grown xeranthemums on a few occasions; they are easy to germinate from seed and grow well in the spring and early summer but decline with warm temperatures, high humidity, and summer rainfall. They are South African in origin and prefer hot, dry climates with excellent drainage. They are fun to grow and pick for the everlasting vase or for potpourri. *Xeranthemum annuum* 'Lilac Stars' is an available mixture, growing about 12–15" tall and providing handsome color early in the season. They can also be planted around mid to late summer, and they will flower well into the fall. Full sun.

Zea

CORN

I should not be surprised by anything I see in gardens anymore. Not by weird and worthless garden art, not by reflective mirrors, not by trains chugging back and forth, and certainly not by ornamental vegetables. In this book alone, I have described ornamental okra, kale, sweet potato, pepper, and eggplant, to name just a few, and so when I was told about some new cultivars of ornamental corn (*Zea mays*), I was somewhat prepared for the plants, which are now hitting the North American marketplace. After all, some of the prettiest sweet corn has white and yellow kernels, and Indian corn has always been pretty, but I was not prepared for the beauty of the plants themselves.

There have been many attempts at making corn more ornamental, but the two I saw at the Parks Seed trials in South Carolina were the best yet. The

MORE ☞

dwarfer form, 'Tiger Cub', has white bands running down the leaves and only stands about 3' tall. It was beautiful, and I was impressed. However, I was floored when I saw 'Bars and Stripes' around the corner; plants were 5' tall and had similar white markings on the foliage, but the stems and the fruit were purple. I did not taste the ears—I suspect there are tastier cobs out there—but their beauty was unsurpassed. Seed is being multiplied, so there will be enough to offer in 2004 or 2005. If you cultivate this in the middle of your garden, your vegetable gardening friends might finally consider you a "real" gardener after all. Full sun.

Zinnia

Johann Gottfried Zinn (1727–1759), a professor of botany at Göttingen, Germany, would have long faded from horticultural history had Linnaeus, the father of modern botany, not named a small daisy to commemorate his friend. Zinnias have been part of our gardens for as long as there have been gardens, and from that small daisy, many cultivars have been developed along the way. They have always been enjoyed by gardeners, and they have also been harvested for ages as cut flowers, complementing other cuts like statice, melampodium, and ornamental grasses. There are approximately twenty species, but only two or three contain most of the plants we garden with.

The most common and colorful group of plants belongs to the common zinnia, *Zinnia elegans*. These were probably a mainstay of your mother's garden and

Zinnia elegans 'Cherry Ruffles'

Zinnia elegans, Butchart Gardens

Zinnia elegans 'Big Top'

Zinnia elegans 'Silver Sun'

Zinnia elegans Dreamland series

Zinnia 'Profusion White'

Zinnia elegans 'Oklahoma Mix'

Zinnia 'Profusion Orange'

MORE ☞

her mother's garden before her. They are easy to germinate, easy to grow, and easy to love. They are used as colorful companions to a winding path at the Butchart Gardens, as a bold planting on the University of Georgia campus, as with 'Cherry Ruffles' here—in almost every conceivable situation. Zinnias first became popular as tall cut flower types; selections like 'Big Top' were used at the back of the bed so that their disease-ridden leaves would be hidden from the world. The tall cultivars were shortened a little, and much more garden-friendly forms, such as the Dreamland series, evolved. They are still 3' tall, with large flowers, but less needy of constant maintenance. Many other large-flowered tall cultivars have been bred. Oklahoma series was selected as the 2000 Cut Flower of the Year by the Association of Specialty Cut Flower Growers; 'Oklahoma Mix', growing 2–4' tall, is an excellent cut flower and handsome garden plant. I have always enjoyed the Sun series, particularly 'Silver Sun', as well as the 3' tall plants common in the Dahlia series, such as 'Dahlia Royal Purple'. Shorter upright forms are also available; Blue Point Mix provides many vibrant colors in a compact package. Foliar diseases are the

Zinnia, arrangement with statice, melampodium, and ornamental grass

Zinnia elegans 'Dahlia Royal Purple'

Zinnia elegans Blue Point Mix

Zinnia 'Profusion Cherry'

biggest problems with all cultivars of common zinnia, and if you eventually see enough plants shriveling up or leaves turning white or brown, the passion for zinnia lessens. To be sure, some cultivars are less susceptible than others, and if you are fortunate enough to be able to grow picture-perfect zinnias all season, go for it. If not, all is not lost. Some people resow seeds at the base of existing plants in June or July and lift the old plants as they tire, allowing the youngsters to mature in late summer and fall.

Another increasingly popular choice is to choose cultivars derived from more disease-resistant species. The Profusion series is a hybrid with common zinnia and other species and is the best zinnia for good performance, low maintenance, and color choice. 'Profusion Cherry' and 'Profusion White' were named All-America Selections in 1999 and 2001, respectively; 'Profusion Orange' is just as good.

Gardeners have long recognized the low-maintenance attributes of narrowleaf zinnia, *Zinnia angustifolia*. Plants grow only about 8–12" tall, but they flower and flower, normally in yellows and oranges; if they get a little leggy, simply cut them back. The Crystal series has performed very well in trials across the country, and both 'Crystal Orange' and 'Crystal White' provide months of color with few disease problems. That is not to say that disease will not rear its ugly head with these forms, but it will be far less obvious. Other low-growing forms include 'Persian Carpet', a selection of *Z. haageana*, with bicolored flowers and medium-grade maintenance.

All zinnias benefit from deadheading. Proper cultivar selection and ample spacing between plants reduces disease problems. Full sun.

Zinnia angustifolia

Zinnia 'Crystal Orange'

Zinnia 'Crystal White'

Zinnia haageana 'Persian Carpet'

PART TWO

Selected Plants for Specific Characteristics or Purposes

The following lists are for readers' convenience only, meant as guidelines for determining what plants fit what function. The plants are, for the most part, listed by genus only; the specific species or cultivar fitting the heading should be self-evident when reading that section.

FALL INTEREST

Many annuals provide outstanding interest in the fall, by virtue of their late flowers or fall leaf color. Plants that produce fruit in the fall are included under "Fruit."

Barleria (flowers)
Cuphea micropetala (flowers)
Kochia (foliage)
Odontonema (flowers)
Otacanthus (flowers)
Salvia (flowers)
Tecomaria (flowers)

SHADE

Some afternoon shade is necessary; most will tolerate filtered sun all day. Only *Cornukaempferia*, *Impatiens*, and *Kaempferia* tolerate deep shade.

Alternanthera
Begonia
Caladium
Coleus
Cornukaempferia
Impatiens
Kaempferia
Phlox

COOL SEASON

These plants perform best in the spring or fall, and do poorly in areas of hot summers and high humidity. Some are routinely used as winter annuals in the South.

Antirrhinum
Argyranthemum
Bellis
Brassica
Calendula
Clarkia
Consolida
Coreopsis
Dianthus
Erysimum
Felicia
Fuchsia
Heliotropium
Linaria
Lobelia
Matthiola
Osteospermum
Papaver
Pelargonium domesticum
Reseda
Salpiglossis
Viola
Xeranthemum

WINTER ANNUALS

These plants are usually planted in the fall and are often green during early winter, but flower or provide outstanding foliage in late winter and early spring.

Antirrhinum
Bellis
Brassica
Dianthus
Papaver
Viola

UNIQUE FLOWER OR FRUIT

Asclepias (fruit)
Bracteantha (flower)
Clerodendrum (fruit)
Lantana trifolia (fruit)
Nelumbo (fruit)
Nigella (fruit)
Ricinus (fruit)
Xeranthemum (flower)

EDIBLE PLANTS

These may not be on the menu of five-star restaurants, but each is enjoyed as a food crop somewhere in the world.

Abelmoschus esculentus
Abelmoschus manihot
Alocasia
Basella
Capsicum
Colocasia
Ipomoea batatas
Solanum

ARCHITECTURAL FEATURES

A nice way of saying that these are big plants that, when grown well, can dominate the garden.

Alocasia
Angelica
Basella
Brugmansia
Canna
Colocasia
Curcuma
Graptophyllum
Hibiscus acetosella
Leonotis
Musa
Mussaenda
Nelumbo
Solanum
Strobilanthes
Tibouchina
Tithonia
Xanthosoma

PRICKLY PLANTS

For the plant masochist, or lover of pain.

Argemone
Cirsium
Datura (fruit)
Duranta
Ricinus (fruit)
Solanum

FOR NATURALIZING

The following plants are often chosen for their ability to reseed and are tough enough to look good with minimal maintenance. Not all work as well as others, and plants must be chosen based on locale.

Coreopsis
Cosmos
Eschscholzia
Linaria
Lychnis
Nemophila
Polygonum

Portulaca
Rudbeckia
Sanvitalia
Scabiosa
Verbena

FOR FLORAL DESIGNS

These are plants for outdoor floral designs, such as floral clocks and formal floral settings. Essentially they are short, compact, and grown for their foliage, not their flowers.

Alternanthera
Begonia
Hemigraphis
Laurentia fluviatilis
Lobelia

FOR CONTAINERS AND BASKETS

Nearly all plants in this book perform well in containers or garden beds. This list contains those that, in general, perform better in containers than in the garden bed.

Abutilon
Acalypha
Alternanthera
Antirrhinum (trailing forms)
Asystasia
Ballota pseudodictamnus
Begonia (rex and tuberous groups)
Bidens ferulifolia
Brachycome
Calibrachoa
Cerinthe
Clerodendrum ugandense
Clerodendrum speciosissimum
Coleus
Dianella
Evolvulus
Gerbera
Heliotropium
Hemigraphis
Impatiens (doubles)
Iresine
Lobelia
Lotus
Mimulus
Monopsis
Musa
Mussaenda
Nierembergia
Pavonia
Pelargonium peltatum
Phlox
Portulaca
Scaevola
Sutera
Torenia
Verbena

FOR EDGING

These plants are generally short and provide season-long flowering.

Ageratum
Alternanthera
Begonia
Bellis
Calendula
Catharanthus
Erysimum
Evolvulus
Hemigraphis
Lobelia
Nierembergia
Sanvitalia
Verbena

FOLIAGE

Nearly all genera have a variegated member or two, but this list includes cultivars whose major ornamental asset is their foliage, either color, texture, or fragrance. Flowers may occur but are often secondary.

Abutilon
Acalypha
Alocasia
Alpinia
Alternanthera
Ballota
Basella
Begonia (rex group)
Breynia
Canna
Coleus
Colocasia
Curcuma
Euphorbia marginata
Graptophyllum
Helichrysum
Hypoestes
Impatiens (New Guinea)
Ipomoea batatas
Lotus
Pennisetum glaucum
Perilla
Plectranthus
Pseuderanthemum
Xanthosoma
Zea

FRAGRANCE

Fragrance is in the nose of the beholder, and not all of these are considered "bath-oil" fresh. However, they are fun to sniff.

Agastache
Cosmos
Datura
Helichrysum
Heliotropium
Lobularia
Nicotiana
Plectranthus
Reseda
Salvia
Tweedia
Viola

BIENNIALS

Some members of these genera require two years to flower, then either reseed or die.

Alcea
Angelica
Dianthus
Echium
Erysimum
Euphorbia
Glaucium

FRUIT

All of these provide fruit during the season, often quite ornamental.

Asclepias
Canavalia
Cardiospermum
Clerodendrum

Fruit, continued

Dianella
Duranta
Euphorbia lathyris
Lablab
Lantana trifolia
Nelumbo
Solanum
Tweedia
Zea

HERBAL PLANTS

Some medicinal, culinary, or fragrance use is contained in this group of plants.

Agastache
Acmella
Alocasia
Basella
Colocasia
Plectranthus
Salvia

NATIVES

Some members of these genera are native to North America.

Bidens
Centaurea
Coreopsis
Cosmos
Eustoma
Gaillardia
Gilia
Heliotropium
Ipomoea
Nemophila
Rudbeckia
Russelia
Salvia
Tagetes
Verbena

VINES

An absolute wonderful diversity of vines awaits the bold gardener.

Asarina
Basella
Canavalia
Cardiospermum
Clitoria
Cobaea
Gloriosa
Ipomoea
Lablab
Mandevilla
Passiflora
Rhodochiton
Solanum
Stictocardia
Thunbergia
Tropaeolum
Tweedia
Vigna

LOVE THE HEAT

Plants perform best when temperatures remain consistently above 75°F, and tolerate high humidity and heat well into the 90s. While they tolerate such abusive conditions, many perform well in moderate climates as well.

Alocasia
Alpinia
Catharanthus
Colocasia
Curcuma
Graptophyllum
Hibiscus
Lantana
Pentas
Plumbago
Ruellia
Russelia
Scaevola
Xanthosoma

LOVE THE WATER

These may do fine in regular garden beds, but they thrive in boggy soil or in garden ponds.

Canna
Colocasia
Nelumbo

BULBOUS ROOTS AND GRASSES

Alocasia
Caladium
Colocasia
Dahlia
Gloriosa
Ipomoea batatas
Pennisetum (grass)

POISONOUS

Be as smart as your dog, don't eat these things.

Alocasia
Brugmansia
Colocasia
Datura
Ricinus

CUT FLOWERS

Nearly all plants can be used as cut flowers, especially if vase life is not a consideration. This list contains an assortment of plants routinely used by florists, designers, and amateur flower arrangers.

Agastache
Ageratum
Antirrhinum
Bracteantha
Callistephus
Caryopteris
Celosia
Centaurea
Cirsium
Clarkia
Consolida
Curcuma
Dianthus barbatus
Euphorbia marginata
Eustoma
Gerbera
Limonium
Linaria
Moluccella
Nelumbo (fruit)
Nigella (fruit)
Otacanthus
Pennisetum glaucum
Pentas
Rudbeckia
Salvia
Scabiosa
Trachelium
Tweedia
Zinnia

U.S.D.A. Hardiness Zone Map

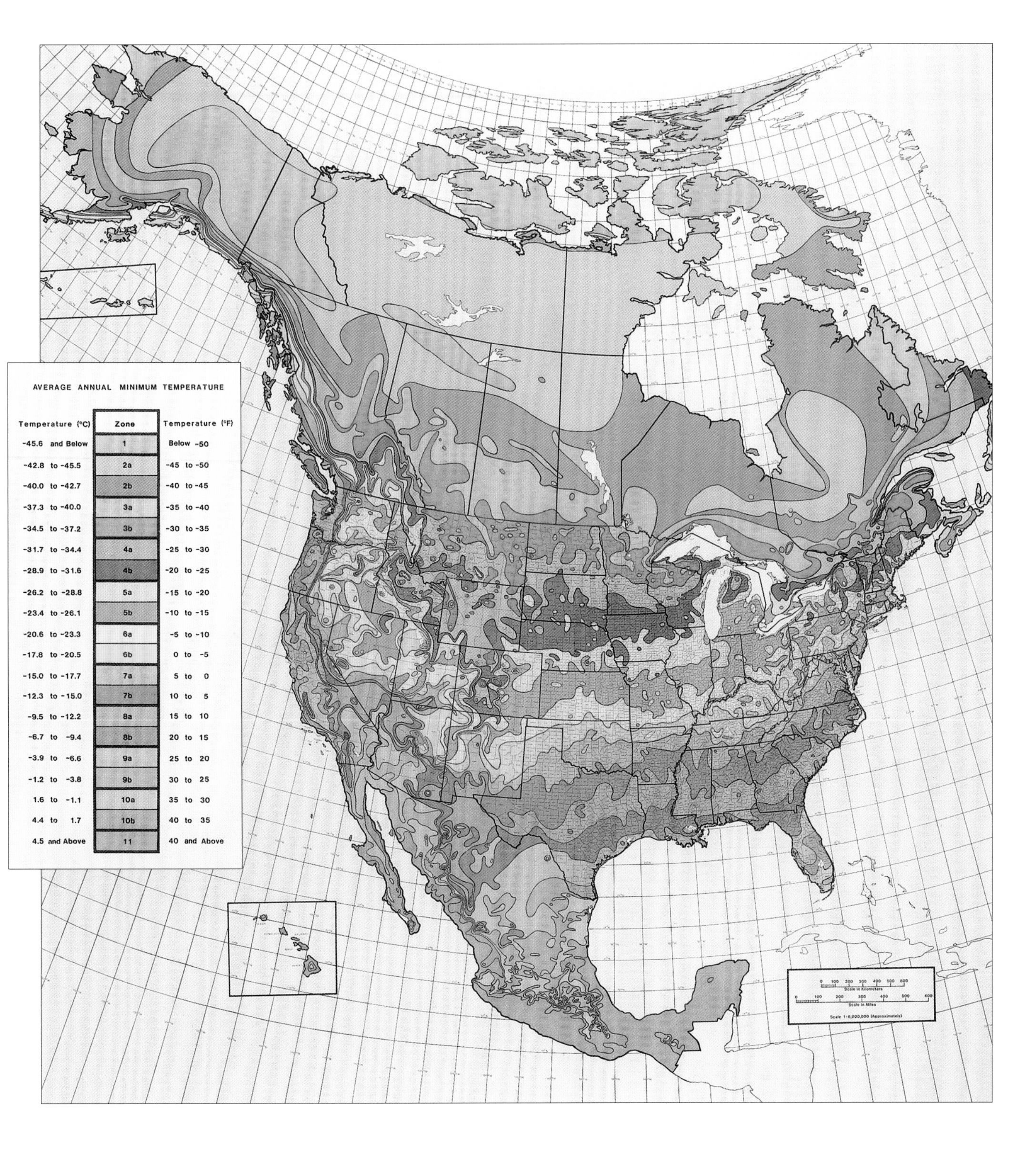

Index of Botanical Names

Index of Common Names

Armitage's Garden Perennials

ARMITAGE'S GARDEN PERENNIALS

A Color Encyclopedia

ALLAN M. ARMITAGE

Timber Press

All photographs are by Allan M. Armitage.

This book is dedicated to my children—

to newly married Laura, whose life keeps getting richer;
to hardworking Heather, whose spirit will never be broken;
to athletic Jonathan, who, without doubt, will capture his dream.

Susan and I have been blessed to watch them grow.

Contents

Preface

Some Thoughts of the Author

Gardening is one of those things that gets in one's blood—a thing that is difficult to explain, even to people who have been so transfused. Gardening is one of those abstract activities that means many things to many people. Rock gardens, alpine gardens, bog gardens, butterfly gardens, water gardens, and native plant gardens are nirvana to some and meaningless, to others. But all gardeners and their garden themes are tied together by the one glue that binds: the plants. And regardless of the real job they hold, when gardeners get together, the language of plants cuts through all other spoken bologna.

Plants are the common denominator of gardeners. Gardeners love plants, more than water features, or hummingbirds, or silly statues in their garden, and will go to incredible lengths—and expense—to secure them. By definition, gardeners are collectors. Numismatists and philatelists have nothing on gardeners! They encase their precious bounty in secure collections to be occasionally admired and evaluated. Not gardeners; they place their collections in abusive environments and dare them to live, but always with the hope of future glory, if not prosperity.

Gardeners love all plants, but perennials have a special place in the hearts of many, and oh boy, are they collectible! To talk about perennials often inspires passion, but to see them can incite lust and rioting among otherwise conservative, law-abiding citizens. So, to stir things up, I have provided in this book photos of some of my favorite perennials, hoping to share the diversity of plants that can make up a garden. If a picture is worth a thousand words, then I feel I have saved considerable forests.

Come join me as you turn these pages for a magical ride through some of the treasures of the perennial plant kingdom, and the joys of being a gardener. Simply remember the Armitage credo of gardening, "This is gardening, not brain surgery. On balance, gardening should always provide far more pleasure than pain." Have fun.

Acknowledgments

Many thanks to those around me who worked on this tome, especially Jessica Phillips and Amanda Miller. And special thanks to my editor, Franni Bertolino Farrell, whose attention to detail transformed incoherent writing into a readable, enjoyable experience.

Part One
Armitage's Garden Perennials
A to Z

Acanthus

BEAR'S BREECHES

Consider the common names of the plants we buy for our gardens: a bystander would be convinced that we are a bunch of zookeepers, not plantkeepers. Dogwood, pussy willow, and a few other woody plants provide links to the animal kingdom, but perennials are unabashedly animal-friendly. One can hardly grow herbaceous plants and not think animal: do pigsqueak, hogweed, leopard's bane, pussytoes, rattlesnake master, toad lily, and snakeroot ring any bells? Some of those names make sense because the plant actually resembles a particular fauna, but what in the world are the breeches of a bear? Who names these things anyway? I guess it really doesn't matter, since we are growing the plant, not the name. And certainly bear's breeches include some excellent garden plants.

The two common species are *Acanthus mollis*, common bear's breeches, and *A. spinosus*, spiny bear's breeches. Both have similar tall spikes of purple

Acanthus mollis

Acanthus spinosus

Acanthus mollis

Acanthus mollis

Acanthus mollis

MORE →

Acanthus mollis 'Holland's Lemon'

Acanthus spinosus

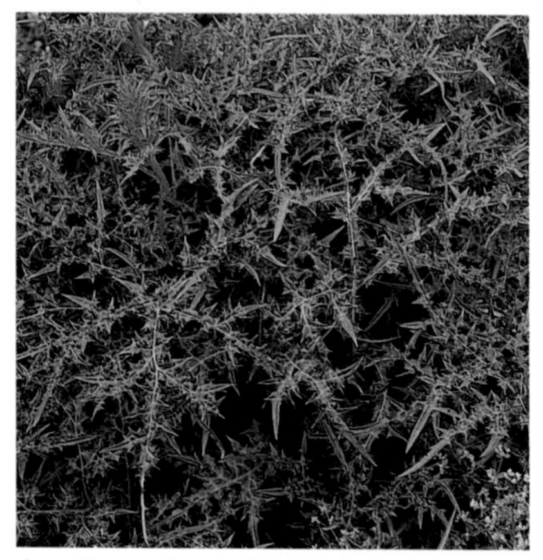
Acanthus spinosus 'Spinosissimus'

and white blossoms, which arise from the leafy plants in late spring. Each white flower on the flower stem is surrounded by a spiny purple bract, which provides color and—when mishandled—considerable pain. Mature clumps provide half a dozen to a dozen spikes of color in late spring, providing a wonderful contrast to the dark green foliage. The two species are best distinguished by their leaves. The leaf of *A. mollis* is much fuller and more rounded than that of *A. spinosus*, which is pointedly pinnately lobed. The common name of *A. spinosus*, spiny bear's breeches, misrepresents the species, as its spiny-looking leaves are not sharp at all.

A number of cultivars have been introduced. As a change from the green leaves of *Acanthus mollis*, golden leaves are the norm in *A. mollis* 'Holland's Lemon'. If you really want spiny in spiny bear's breeches, try *A. spinosus* 'Spinosissimus'. A true man- and woman-eater—it is a well-known fact that many a small pet has inadvertently wandered into a patch of breeches, never to be seen again. Now explain that common name one more time. Full sun, zones 6 to 10.

Achillea

YARROW

The genus *Achillea* is named for the Greek warrior Achilles; one species, *Achillea millefolium*, also known as woundwort, was said to have staunched the wounds of the great warrior's soldiers. The yarrows are a diverse group and provide many fine garden plants. Most are easy to grow, offering excellent foliage, years of color, and flowers useful for both fresh and dried arrangements.

Without doubt, *Achillea filipendulina* (fernleaf yarrow) and its hybrids are among the most welcome of all plants for the spring and summer garden. They are prized for their color and form, as an herbal plant for their fragrance, and as cut flowers for their outstanding longevity. Fernleaf yarrow has large (about 3" across), flat yellow flowers atop 3–4' tall plants. The compound leaves are somewhat fernlike, thus accounting for its common name. Several cultivars, such as 'Gold Plate' and 'Parker's Variety', have been developed, but few differences in appearance or garden performance are obvi-

Achillea 'Coronation Gold'

ous. All these yarrows can be cut and brought inside fresh or hung upside down for dried flower arrangements. Wait until the flowers are fully opened before cutting, otherwise they won't persist more than a single day.

Many yellow-flowered yarrows look alike, but several of the better cultivars offer the gardener additional choices. Most are hybrids, in which *Achillea filipendulina* is one of the main parents, and are vigorous and usually more compact. The grand dame is *Achillea* 'Coronation Gold', developed in 1953 to commemorate the coronation of Queen Elizabeth of England. Bearing large yellow flowers and handsome gray-green foliage on 2–3' tall plants, she has lost little of her original popularity with her subjects. As a garden plant or as a cut flower, 'Coronation Gold' is outstanding and should continue to be a mainstay among gardeners. Yellow-flowered hybrids that are shorter and more soft in tone than 'Coronation Gold' have also been popular. 'Moonshine', for one, has been a bright standby for many years. 'Anthea' is just a youngster compared to the previous cultivars but is rapidly being accepted by gardeners. The combination of full pale yellow to sulfur-yellow flowers on a 2' tall frame has made 'Anthea' one of my favorites. 'Martina' provides yet another excellent yellow

Achillea 'Moonshine'

Achillea 'Coronation Gold'

Achillea 'Anthea'

Achillea 'Coronation Gold'

MORE →

Achillea 'Anthea'

Achillea millefolium

Achillea 'Martina'

Achillea millefolium 'Colorado'

Achillea millefolium 'Rose Beauty'

and bears many flowers, but the flowering stems are not quite as erect as those of 'Anthea'. All cultivars are reasonably easy to locate in American nurseries. Full sun, zones 3 to 8.

Common yarrow, *Achillea millefolium*, is as plentiful as turf in some gardens and indeed can double as a ground cover. The plants spread like wildfire throughout the season, their finely cut green foliage quickly filling in large areas. Flowers occur as corymbs in spring and early summer, and although they can be used as fresh cut flowers, they persist for only two or three days, not nearly as long as the flowers of *A. filipendulina*.

The many selections of *Achillea millefolium* guarantee that the gardener will suffer no shortage of colors. 'Rose Beauty' provides lovely rosy hues; I love the deep desert reds and roses of 'Colorado', and for bright colors, 'Paprika' or 'Nakuru' work well. Some of the hybrids associated with *A. millefolium* also do well: both 'Appleblossom' and 'The Beacon' ('Fanal'), which have large pastel and bright rose-red flowers, respectively, spread quickly. Some of the newer hybrids are true breakthroughs in color: for oohs and aahs, nothing beats the earth tones of 'Terra Cotta' and 'Fireland'. They are similar, each rising to a height of 3' ('Fireland' may be a little taller). These

Achillea millefolium 'Nakuru'

should prove as popular as any of the cultivars already introduced. As cut flowers, the hybrid yarrows derived from *A. millefolium* are not quite as good as *A. filipendulina*, but I have seen outstanding arrangements with *Veronicastrum*, *Limonium*, and other perennials. All cultivars prefer good drainage and full sun. Hardy in zones 3 to 8.

As a substitute for snuff, *Achillea ptarmica*, sneezewort, probably works quite well, if one is still into that sort of thing; however, the flowers have myriad other uses. They are excellent cut flowers, acting as fillers in cottage bouquets, and the white double flowers are easy to use in the garden, combining well with almost any hue. Plants are generally at their best in northern areas or gardens where cool summer nights are the norm. The leaves are not

Achillea millefolium 'Paprika'

Achillea 'Appleblossom'

Achillea 'The Beacon' ('Fanal')

Achillea 'Terra Cotta'

Achillea arranged with *Veronicastrum* and *Limonium*

Achillea 'Fireland'

MORE →

Achillea ptarmica

Achillea ptarmica 'The Pearl' ('Boule de Neige')

Achillea ptarmica 'Ballerina'

Achillea ageratum 'W. B. Childs'

Achillea sibirica 'Kiku-San'

cut like other species but rather are thick and dark green, with entire margins. In general, plants are 1–2' tall but under good conditions can easily grow to 3' in height. Most selections of *A. ptarmica* have similar flowers, so using the old-fashioned 'The Pearl' ('Boule de Neige') or 'Perry's White' is about the same as choosing 'Angel's Breath' or 'Ballerina', except that these last two are somewhat more compact and shorter. Full sun, hardy in zones 3 to 7.

Achillea ageratum 'W. B. Childs', the white double-flowered Childs's yarrow, is a similar plant, with flowers that are almost identical to those of *A. ptarmica*; it differs from sneezewort, however, by having dissected leaves. Full sun, hardy in zones 2 to 8.

Tough as nails, with white to pink flowers and thick, lobed, dark green leaves, *Achillea sibirica*, the Siberian

Achillea sibirica leaf

Achillea sibirica 'Kiku-San'

yarrow, is beginning to find its way into American gardens. Plants are clump formers; unlike *A. millefolium*, they don't spread, nor do they have the girth and height of *A. filipendulina*. This outstanding yarrow will become a mainstream plant as people discover its ornamental and landscape attributes. Little has been done in the way of selection, however. 'Kiku-San' has creamy white flowers with the faintest pink in the blooms. Full sun, hardy in zones 2 to 8.

Aconitum

MONKSHOOD

Classic plants for the late summer and fall garden, the genus *Aconitum* adds bold accents to northern gardens. Flowers are usually in shades of blue or purple, but ivory, yellow, and bicolors can also be found. For certain, monkshood is poisonous (it is also known as wolfsbane), but for most intelligent people, that is not a problem. Simply don't eat the plants—any part of them. Don't worry about your pets: most dogs and cats are smarter than the average gardener. All monkshoods do far better in the northern United States and Canada than in the South.

One of the most popular of the purple- and blue-flowered species is *Aconitum carmichaelii*, azure monkshood, which grows 4–6' tall and has thick, dark green leaves that are divided about two-thirds of the way to the midrib. In late summer to early fall, dozens of individual hooded flowers make up each 5–6" long flower spike (the hood on the flower is responsible for the common name of the genus). Some cultivars of *A. carmichaelii*, also known as late-flowering monkshood, are among the latest of the genus to flower. They include the selection 'Arendsii', which I believe to be one of the finest. Its large deep blue flowers are held on compact well-branched 3' tall plants. For even more height (up to 6'), 'Barker's Variety', 'Kelmscott Variety', and variety *wilsonii* may also be planted.

Aconitum napellus, common monkshood, has handsome blue flowers that open a little earlier than those of *A. carmichaelii*, but as far as gardeners are concerned, there is little difference between the two species; 'Carneum' is

Aconitum carmichaelii 'Arendsii'

Aconitum carmichaelii var. *wilsonii*

Aconitum napellus

MORE →

Aconitum napellus 'Carneum'

Aconitum napellus

a beautiful pink-flowered selection. *Aconitum* ×*cammarum* is a wonderful strong-growing hybrid of *A. napellus*, with erect stems approximately 4' in height; its selection 'Bicolor' provides flowers in an exotic combination of azure blue and white. Place all monkshoods in partial shade and moist soils. Hardy in zones 3 to 7a.

How about a yellow wolfsbane? or white? There is more to this genus than blue and purple flowers. In yellow wolfsbane, *Aconitum lamarckii*, large racemes of yellow flowers are formed above light green, deeply divided leaves. Stems regularly fall over other plants, but so what? The soft yellows complement just about any other color and fit well into many gardens, even though they may be a little lanky. Cool temperatures, full sun, zones 3 to 6. *Aconitum lamarckii* is a native to Eu-

Aconitum lamarckii

Aconitum ×*cammarum* 'Bicolor'

Aconitum reclinatum

Aconitum septentrionale 'Ivorine'

rope, but our native species, *A. reclinatum*, white wolfsbane, provides the same effect with a little better weather-tolerance. Plants enjoy full sun and are hardy in zones 4 to 7.

The yellow and white wolfsbanes grow well in areas of cool summer temperatures, and West Coast gardeners can succeed with them all. A wonderful plant I always enjoy seeing is 'Ivorine', a selection of the little-known species *Aconitum septentrionale*, which bears white to light yellow flowers. It is well worth spending some time over the winter trying to locate this cultivar in catalogs. Hardy in zones 4 to 6 (occasionally 7).

Adiantum

MAIDENHAIR FERN

The realization that ferns are as garden-worthy as their flowering perennial counterparts has rekindled the love affair with the common green plant of grandmother's day. Of course, anyone interested in ferns quickly appreciates their remarkable diversity of color, size, and form. One of the most distinctive groups is the maidenhair family, consisting of the northern and southern maidenhairs.

Only gardeners who live in the southern third of the country are fortunate enough to appreciate the beauty of *Adiantum capillus-veneris*, the southern maidenhair fern, in their gardens. The light green fronds are doubly or triply divided and arch over on thin wiry stems. The stems appear in the spring in the form of thin horseshoes; however, the pinnae (individual "leaflets") are so numerous that a dense planting is achieved under favorable conditions. The pinnae are small, only about an inch long, and shaped like a fan. Plants require mild winters, basic soils, and excellent drainage and are not nearly as easy to grow as many of the coarser ferns commonly found at retailers. They are at their best tumbling from containers and raised beds, or arching over walls; they don't do well in acid conditions, and in areas of pine or oak growth, lime should be added. Native throughout the South Temperate Zone and subtropical regions in Europe, Africa,

Adiantum capillus-veneris

Adiantum capillus-veneris

Adiantum pedatum

MORE →

Adiantum pedatum

Adiantum pedatum subsp. *subpumilum*

Adiantum pedatum 'Imbricatum'

India, China, Japan, the Americas, and Australia. Reliably cold hardy in zones 7 to 10.

Southern maidenhair fern may be little known in the garden, but *Adiantum pedatum*, the northern maidenhair fern, does not suffer from any such lack of recognition. The wimpy looking fronds of the plant are put forth in the spring, but as temperatures rise, the grayish pinnae can be seen forming an almost perfect horseshoe on the ends of the unique black stems. As the plants mature, they top out at about 12" tall, and the half-inch-long pinnae change from gray to light green. The dark color of the stems is continued in the branches of the horseshoe, making this fern one of the most distinctive and easily recognized in American gardens. Plants move around freely in loose soils, and a few plants can quickly form significant colonies. The distinctive shape and garden "feel" of the lacy, airy fronds and black stems, combined with its toughness, have made this a most useful, must-have fern for the shady, moist woodland garden. As with *A. capillus-veneris*, lime is useful for best growth but seems to be less important for northern maidenhair fern than for its southern cousin.

It is hard to beat *Adiantum pedatum* for overall garden performance, but those who wish to walk on the wild side of maidenhair ferndom might want to try some of the variations on the theme of this species. 'Imbricatum' has crowded stiffly erect fronds that are rather blue-green; its long sweeping foliage make it appear almost shrublike. The opposite is true in subspecies *subpumilum*, in which the fronds are dwarf and congested; the plants grow in a 6–9" tall mound. Partial shade, good drainage, performs well in zones 2 to 7.

Ajuga

BUGLE WEED

Some plants simply perform too well for their own good, and bugle weed is one of them. Of the forty species known, only *Ajuga reptans* is used extensively, although a couple of others (*A. genevensis*, *A. pyramidalis*) are gaining momentum. Without doubt, common bugle weed is by far the most diverse, having undergone extensive breeding and selection. One of the strengths of bugle weed is its ability to colonize large areas of the garden. Many a gardener has started out tucking in a few plants only to turn around a few years later to find a sea of the stuff. Plants creep relentlessly into turf when positioned near it. A word has been coined to describe the result of such restlessness: "buglelawn."

Ajuga reptans, common bugle weed, is deservedly popular for its ability to settle large areas of the garden. Planted as small rosettes of foliage, it quickly searches out new ground. Not all selections of this ground cover are as fast growing, and intelligent cultivar selection can help curb the appetite for territory. Common bugle weed is grown mainly for the colorful foliage, but a large planting of the purple-blue flowers can be breathtaking in the spring.

Two of my favorite cultivars are 'Burgundy Glow', with multicolored foliage, and 'Catlin's Giant', with big dark green leaves and large spikes of blue flowers. Those desiring dark bronze leaves will be well satisfied by either the excellent 'Bronze Beauty' or 'Atropurpurea', while 'Silver Beauty' may be grown for its handsome variegation on the leaves. Partial shade, hardy in zones 3 to 9.

Another fine garden plant is Geneva bugle weed, *Ajuga genevensis*, with its light green wavy leaves and handsome

Ajuga reptans 'Burgundy Glow'

Ajuga reptans

MORE →

Ajuga reptans 'Bronze Beauty'

Ajuga reptans 'Catlin's Giant'

Ajuga reptans 'Atropurpurea'

Ajuga reptans 'Silver Beauty'

Ajuga genevensis 'Pink Beauty'

flowers. 'Pink Beauty' is the best available selection, producing good-looking flowers on moderately aggressive plants. Partial shade, hardy in zones 4 to 9.

Allium

ORNAMENTAL ONION

One of the reasons I enjoy gardening so much is that, having no self-imposed boundaries as to what plants may be deemed ornamental, I am free to welcome any and all comers, fruits and vegetables, sweet potatoes and herbs, to the ornamental landscape. Ornamental onions are not particularly tasty, but their beauty is seldom questioned, at least by the bold and inquiring gardener. Most members of the large genus *Allium* are bulbous and easily planted in spring or fall.

Allium christophii, Persian onion, produces deep purple flower heads 10–12" in diameter, among the largest of any onion. Each head consists of hundreds of star-shaped flowers suspended atop a 1–2' tall stem. Flowers open in the spring and persist for about three weeks. The flower is the most obvious part of the plant, not only because of its size but also because only two to three leaves are produced. This is a lovely onion, persist-

Cut flowers of *Allium giganteum* and *Achillea* 'Coronation Gold'.

ent and long-lived in many areas of the country. Full sun, not great in hot climates; performs best in zones 4 to 6 but is hardy in zones 4 to 8.

I have tried at least a dozen different onions in the Armitage garden, and *Allium* 'Globemaster' is absolutely one of the best. The three to four leaves emerge in early spring and soon a fat flower bud or two can be seen at the base. The flowers force their way through the foliage and emerge as 6" wide lavender softballs. Even the seed heads are ornamental, persisting for weeks after the flower has passed on. Great plants, about 3' tall, perennial as any onion I have grown. A couple of other interesting hybrids are out there; if you can't find 'Globemaster', give 'Beauregard' a try. Full sun to partial shade, hardy in zones 4 to 8.

Allium karataviense (Turkistan onion) and *A. giganteum* (giant onion) are the Mutt and Jeff of the onion world. These two species are obviously onions (just smell the leaves) but differ in flower color, leaf color, and height. The two gray-green leaves of *A. karataviense* lie on the ground and are mottled with purple. Through the base of the leaves emerge fat flower buds, which then give way to perfectly round silver-lilac flower heads on 4–6" tall scapes.

Compared to these dwarfs, the 6' tall *Allium giganteum* is an absolute behemoth. The gray leaves, which are themselves obvious, emerge early but die back even before the flowers are fully developed. The flowers consist of hundreds of purple flowers arranged in neat 4" wide globes, although interesting anomalies occur occasionally. Both species are excellent cut flowers; *A. giganteum* is a staple in the cut flower trade and may be purchased at all good flower shops.

Allium christophii

Allium christophii

Allium 'Globemaster'

Allium 'Globemaster' seed heads

Allium 'Beauregard'

MORE →

Allium giganteum with cowlick

Allium giganteum

Both *Allium karataviense* and *A. giganteum* are summer dormant, prefer full sun, and are cold hardy to zone 4; *A. giganteum* is more tolerant of heat and humidity. Persistent for about two years only.

Anemone

As a gardener, I admit to a certain degree of laziness. Okay, so sometimes I could admit to a lot. Being a tad lazy, I am always on the lookout for plants that can deliver good looks in as many seasons as possible. A few genera flower at different seasons, but one of the most rewarding has to be the genus *Anemone*. This great group of plants

Allium karataviense

Allium karataviense in bud

Allium giganteum

consists of spring flowerers, which arise from tubers (like a potato), and fibrous-rooted plants, which mostly flower in the fall, with one or two spring and summer bloomers thrown in. From the time the snow is melting to the time the snow is falling, anemones are a gardener's companion. Cut flowers, shade and sun lovers, and heights from ankle to waist, this fine genus offers something for everybody, especially lazy gardeners like me.

Often in the late fall, I have my trowel in one hand and the tubers of the Grecian windflower, *Anemone blanda*, in the other—and confusion as to which end is up. With real plants, any dummy knows to plant the green part up, but anemone tubers simply look like shriveled-up brown things. You could put them in a pail of water overnight and allow them to plump up to about four times their original size; this is fascinating to watch, but it will still be impossible to tell which way is up. Simply dig a shallow hole and throw the swollen things in. It doesn't really matter which end is up; the plants will find the proper orientation. Put about a hundred tubers around the garden, preferably in groups of at least twenty. They are so cheap, you can do this without spending your entire year-end bonus. Once you have tossed them in their respective trenches, you can expect wonderful springtime flowering—unless the squirrels, chipmunks, gophers, voles, or dogs get at them. That is why you plant a hundred. The flowers, consisting of 1–2" wide daisies in colors of blue, purple, red, white, and pink, are held over finely cut, ferny foliage. Single or double-flowered plants are available. They are only about 8" tall, but if they naturalize, they are outstanding components of the woodland garden. If they don't naturalize and become food for your garden fauna, you have not spent a great deal of money. Full sun is best, but woodland conditions are fine. Full sun to partial shade, hardy in zones 4 to 7.

The only real difference between cultivars is flower color, such as the blue flowers of 'Atrocaerulea' and 'Blue Star', the bicolors of 'Radar', and the white flowers of 'White Splendor', to name but a few.

Another tuberous species, even more ornamental than the Grecian windflower, is *Anemone coronaria*, the poppy anemone. Equally confusing as to head and tail, equally destined for a plunge in the water bucket, and equally tempting to hungry creatures, poppy anemones are nevertheless so beautiful that they have become an

Anemone blanda 'Atrocaerulea'

Anemone blanda 'Radar'

Anemone blanda 'Blue Star'

Anemone blanda 'White Splendor'

MORE →

Anemone coronaria 'Mona Lisa Red'

Anemone coronaria 'Mr. Fokker' (De Caen series)

Anemone coronaria 'Mt. Everest' (St. Brigid series)

important cut flower in the greenhouse and garden. Flowers are about 2" wide, and stems may be up to 18" long. Flowering occurs in early spring. Great garden show and a great cut flower. Plant in full sun, and protect from critters if possible. Hardy in zones 6 to 9.

Variety is available in the long-stemmed Mona Lisa and Cleopatra series; the shorter double-flowered De Caen series; and the semi-double- to double-flowered St. Brigid series. All selections are offered both in single colors and, more commonly, as mixes.

Regardless of how excited one gets about the spring flowerers, the crowning jewels of the anemone family are the fall-flowering Japanese species *Anemone hupehensis* and *A. tomentosa* and the hybrids of *A.* ×*hybrida*. When one thinks *Anemone*, one usually thinks of these. And with good reason! *Anemone hupehensis* includes some excellent 3–4' tall selections, such as the durable 'September Charm' and the rosy red semi-double flowers of 'Prinz Heinrich' ('Prince Henry'). Plants of *A.* ×*hybrida* are actually hybrids of several species, but they have become well adapted to American gardens, particularly those in the West and North. Provided with a little shade and ample moisture, plants can reach 5' in height and 3' across. The flowers begin to open in late summer to early fall and remain in color for three to five weeks, depending on temperatures. Single, semi-double, and double flowers in white, pink, rose, and lilac can be found. Some of my favorites are the semi- to fully double pink-flowered 'Kriemhilde' and the single pink 3" wide flowers of 'Max Vogel'. If I had but one to choose, however, I would probably show my true populist colors and go with the old-fashioned but timeless single white flowers of 'Honorine Jobert'. So much for keeping up appearances!

Southern gardeners who have had less success in establishing the hybrids should use the indestructible *Anemone tomentosa*, the grapeleaf anemone, with its pale pink or white flowers in late summer and early fall. The toughest of all its selections is 'Robustissima': handsome, adaptable to sun or shade, and disease and insect free. Plants bear fine 2" wide mauve-pink

Anemone coronaria 'Sylphide' (De Caen series)

flowers in late summer. I grow them in full sun in the University of Georgia Horticulture Gardens, where they remain in a fairly compact clump, but in the shady Armitage garden, plants move around with abandon and fill up space in no time. The hybrids are hardy in zones 4 to 7, *A. tomentosa* in zones 5 to 8.

Gardeners cannot live by tubers alone. Some of the finest garden plants are the fibrous-rooted species, such as

Anemone hupehensis 'Prinz Heinrich' ('Prince Henry')

Anemone ×hybrida 'Kriemhilde'

Anemone hupehensis 'September Charm'

Anemone ×hybrida 'Max Vogel'

MORE →

Anemone tomentosa 'Robustissima'

Anemone ×hybrida 'Honorine Jobert'

Anemone tomentosa 'Robustissima'

the spring-flowering snowdrop anemone, *Anemone sylvestris*. I love this plant for its habit of unfurling beautifully clean white flowers with yellow stamens in early spring. In fact, in areas of late winters, one can often see them piercing the snow, thus its common name. The 2" wide flowers are only part of the delight of this 1–2' tall

Anemone sylvestris

Anemone sylvestris

plant, since after flowering, the woolly fruit persists into the summer. On the downside, it can be outrageously aggressive, reseeding freely where it is happy. It is happier in the North than in the South, where inconsistent winters and hot summers take their toll. Some gardeners consider it a bit of a weed. Not me. I accept anyone's snowdrop anemone weeds with pleasure. Full sun, hardy in zones 4 to 7.

Aquilegia

COLUMBINE

Almost anywhere gardening is enjoyed, columbines are among the best-known and most popular garden plants. The Armitage garden would be but a shell of itself without columbines welcoming spring. Since we may choose from more than sixty-five different species of columbine and all sorts of named varieties, including one or two in the garden should not be difficult. The cultural requirements for all columbines, whether they originate from the East Coast, West Coast, Europe, or Asia, are essentially the same: partial shade and reasonably rich well-drained soils.

The plants are distinguished from most other genera by having petals with spurs, ranging from those with spurs over 4" long (*Aquilegia chrysantha*, the golden columbine) to those with spurs that are essentially nonexistent, such as some of the double-flowered and even triple-flowered cultivars of granny's bonnet, *A. vulgaris* ('Treble Pink'). Spur size and shape are helpful clues to the identity of many of the species. The spurs of the alpine columbine, *A. alpina*, and fan columbine, *A. flabellata*, are hooked (like a fishhook) while those on the Rocky Mountain columbine, *A. caerulea*, are

Aquilegia alpina

Aquilegia chrysantha var. *hinckleyana*

Aquilegia alpina

Aquilegia vulgaris 'Treble Pink'

Aquilegia flabellata 'Alba'

MORE →

Aquilegia flabellata 'Alba'

Aquilegia caerulea

Aquilegia caerulea

Leaf miner damage on *Aquilegia*

Aquilegia ×hybrida

Aquilegia ×hybrida 'Cardinal'

Aquilegia ×hybrida 'Blue Jay'

Aquilegia ×hybrida 'Lavender and White' (Biedermeier strain)

nearly always straight. *Aquilegia alpina* has some of the finest blue flowers and as a bonus—and even though it is native to the cool mountains of Austria—it tolerates heat as well as any species. *Aquilegia flabellata* normally has lavender flowers but is usually found in its white variant, 'Alba'; the blue cast to the foliage, the plump flowers, and the low stature make this selection a favorite among columbine lovers. The fine blue-and-white flowers of *A. caerulea* persist for years, especially in areas of cool summers. The leaves, which always occur in threes (ternate), are unfortunately susceptible to the bane of all columbines, the leaf miner. Leaf miners burrow just beneath the surface of the foliage, leaving scars like a crazed gopher. All species seem to be fair game for these marauding tunnelers, although some plants, in some years, fare better than others.

Columbine flower colors vary tremendously, especially in the selections of *Aquilegia ×hybrida*. As a seed-propagated mix, these hybrid columbines can be striking, providing a gala for the color-starved eye in the spring. The Song Bird series is particularly good, furnishing such choices as the brilliant red of 'Cardinal' and the fine

Aquilegia ×hybrida 'Music Yellow'

blue of 'Blue Jay'. The Biedermeier strain is far more compact and comes in single colors, bicolors ('Lavender and White'), and a mix. The Music series is outstanding, particularly 'Music Yellow'. *Aquilegia vulgaris* also provides a wide range of color, flower size, and flower shape; the double and triple flowers of its Barlow family, Pink, Blue, and Nora, are not only different from normal flowers but are flamboyant to boot. Speaking of which: while large gaudy columbines appear to be the norm, one of my favorites has always been the delightful red-and-yellow flowers of *A. canadensis*, the Canadian columbine. Just like citizens of that northern neighbor, the plants of this species are quiet, conservative, and do their job without bluster.

Columbines are notoriously promiscuous, and natural hybridization occurs with ease. The resulting seedlings are usually as handsome as any of the parents, leaving many a gardener puzzling over their provenance. Plants can remain in flower for three to six weeks, depending on how long the cool temperatures of spring persist. Partial shade, zones 3 to 8.

Aquilegia vulgaris 'Blue Barlow'

Aquilegia vulgaris 'Nora Barlow'

Aquilegia vulgaris 'Pink Barlow'

Aquilegia canadensis

Aquilegia canadensis

Arisaema ringens

Fruit of *Arisaema ringens*

Arisaema

JACK-IN-THE-PULPIT

Perhaps it's a guy thing: it seems that only men are intent on collecting plants in the genus *Arisaema*. I know I have always had a deep admiration for the foliage and flower details of our native Jack-in-the-pulpit, *Arisaema triphyllum*, but once I looked beyond the native Jack, a whole world of crazy collectibles opened before me. Of course, only other guys seem to be selling them. All the Jacks are terrific for shady spots and moist areas.

When confronted with *Arisaema ringens* (cobra Jack) or *A. sikokianum* (gaudy Jack), some people take a step back, walk around the plants, and mutter something intelligent about plant diversity. Most of us just say wow! The flowers of *A. ringens* consist of a thin but wide purple membrane, or spathe, that became known as the "pulpit." Within the pulpit hides the creamy white spadix (a narrow fleshy stalk), better known as Jack. This peculiar arrangement of flowers was dubbed by some observant fellow as Jack-in-the-pulpit, and that common name applies to nearly all plants in the genus. The 2–3' tall plants produce only two or three leaves, each made up of three glossy green leaflets.

Arisaema sikokianum bears much smaller leaves, often mottled or occasionally variegated, along with highly visible flowers. The spadix ends in a shiny white bulbous tip poking out of the maroon spathe. Not only is this a stunning species, but the hybrids involving *A. sikokianum*, such as the unnamed cross between it and *A. takedae*, are equally stunning.

These Japanese Jacks—*Arisaema ringens*, *A. sikokianum*, and *A. takedae* —all require shady, moist conditions and flower in early spring, much ear-

Arisaema sikokianum

Arisaema sikokianum

Arisaema ringens

lier than our native Jack. All perform well in zones 5 to 7.

The specific epithet of *Arisaema triphyllum* refers to the three ("tri") leaflets ("phyllum") found on the plant; however, plants are highly variable, often consisting of five or occasionally four leaflets. The same variability occurs in the average height (1–3') of the plants. The flowers, which occur in spring to early summer, consist of a spadix surrounded by a purple spathe. The plants multiply by small corms, which, if planted in the spring, will flower the second year. The corms, which can become quite large, were cooked and eaten by Native Americans; early settlers knew the plant as Indian turnip. Partial shade, hardy in zones 4 to 8.

Other *Arisaema* species are being offered by mail-order nurseries for collectors and shade gardeners. Little needs to be said about the makeup of these other Jacks; they differ only in the size, shape, and color of the spathe and in the overall dimensions of the plants. I think that the candy Jack, *Arisaema candidissimum*, with wonderful white spathes blushed in pink,

Arisaema sikokianum × *A. takedae*

Arisaema triphyllum

Arisaema candidissimum

Arisaema triphyllum

Arisaema candidissimum

MORE →

Arisaema consanguineum

and bloody Jack, *A. consanguineum*, a huge member with deeply cut leaves and blood-red spathes, are outstanding. But as soon as I recover from their beauty, I fall in love with the deep purple spathes of *A. fargesii* and the elegant long-necked *A. japonicum* (*A. serratum*). I am content with my regular Jack-in-the-pulpits, but I was fortunate to have planted *A. sazensoo*, the Japanese cobra Jack, in the Armitage garden. I was in seventh heaven, until I saw the unbelievable elegance of *A. tortuosum* in Kew Gardens in England. Arisaemas should not be planted or viewed by people with heart problems—one touch, one glimpse of any of these is enough to give one cardiac arrest. Plant them shallowly in moisture-retentive yet well-drained soils, rich in organic matter, in the shade garden. Hardy in zones 5 to 8.

Arisaema fargesii

Arisaema japonicum

Arisaema sazensoo

Arisaema tortuosum

Fruit of *Arisaema tortuosum*

Artemisia

Many members of the genus *Artemisia* are great plants, their gray hues providing a cool contrast to a sea of green or calming down neighboring (not to say "screaming") colors. Not all artemisias are long-lived perennials; a few often leave us after two or three years. The good selections, however, are worth every square inch of space.

Artemisia ludoviciana (white sage), a mainstay in older gardens, was the most commonly used large artemisia for gray foliage. Seldom is the species sold, but the main selection, 'Silver King', may become an unwelcome guest in gardens. Although they look terrific the first few years, plants are aggressive and difficult to remove. This vigorous nature makes them one of the most popular cut stems for fillers in arrangements, but in the garden, they develop into dozens of in-laws who bring the great aunts and second cousins with them for a visit and never go away. The leaves are almost entire, not cut like *Artemisia* 'Powis Castle'. Flowers are few and insignificant. They grow 3–5' tall and 3–4' wide and combine well with almost everything. Other than their roaming tendencies, they are fine plants. Full sun, hardy in zones 4 to 9.

Many other cultivars of *Artemisia ludoviciana* are out there, including 'Latiloba', whose similar entire leaf margins are distinctly lobed near the ends. Plants grow about 2' tall and as wide. Much more obedient. Another low grower is 'Valerie Fennis', whose silvery gray entire foliage, although absolutely wonderful in the spring, often melts out in the summer, partic-

Artemisia ludoviciana 'Latiloba'

Artemisia ludoviciana 'Silver King'

Artemisia ludoviciana 'Valerie Fennis'

Artemisia ludoviciana 'Valerie Fennis'

MORE →

Artemisia 'Powis Castle' trained as a standard

ularly in the South. She looks great again in the fall. The ugly yellow flowers put forth only detract from the foliage. Remove them or ignore them. Full sun to partial shade, hardy in zones 4 to 8.

Artemisia 'Powis Castle' is a terrific plant in many parts of the country. The evergreen, deeply cut gray leaves impart an airiness to the garden, and the plants provide a focal point for the eye. In fact, it is probably one of the first plants to draw one's eye—a garden designer's blue ribbon winner. Plants may be used to define a wall or introduce a garden bed and may even be trained as a small upright Powis tree. Left to its own devices, this hybrid grows 2–3' tall and equally wide. As it matures, the stems become woody (like a shrub) and may get lanky and untidy. If necessary, cut back in spring as new growth becomes active. Don't cut back in the fall. Full sun, hardy in zones 6 to 8.

Artemisia 'Huntington Gardens', a closely related plant with divided gray

Artemisia 'Huntington Gardens'

Artemisia 'Powis Castle'

Artemisia schmidtiana 'Nana' ('Silver Mound')

Artemisia 'Powis Castle'

Artemisia schmidtiana 'Nana' ('Silver Mound') as a container plant

leaves, can reach 3' in height. I find that it is more persistent than 'Powis Castle' but has the same look. Full sun, hardy in zones 6 to 8.

One of the best-sellers in the perennial trade, *Artemisia schmidtiana* has been a mainstay in northern gardens for years. The only available cultivar is 'Nana', a dwarf selection known as the silvermound artemisia (it is also sold as 'Silver Mound'). Plants produce tightly compact 1' tall mounds in the spring and early summer, making it a gardener's dream. In rock gardens and in containers, they are beautiful; however, in many gardens, in the South as well as in the North, plants often melt out in the centers as temperature and humidity rise. This is a rather ugly scene after hard summer rains. Plants are woody, like *Artemisia* 'Powis Castle', and evergreen in milder climates. I recommend this beautiful plant in the northern tier of States and southern Canada but not in the South. Full sun, hardy in zones 3 to 8.

Aruncus dioicus

Aruncus

GOATSBEARD

Consisting of only two species, and few cultivars, the genus *Aruncus* could hardly be commended for its wide diversity, but both its species are highly ornamental and useful garden plants, which, once established, live to ripe old ages. Male and female flowers occur on separate plants (that is to say, plants are dioecious), but garden performance is not affected by gender.

With a grand explosion of upright flower stems consisting of hundreds of small white flowers in late spring, *Aruncus dioicus*, common goatsbeard, tops out at 4–6' in height. Diminutive fruit may be formed on female plants, but their slight size and show are not missed if male plants are used. The alternate leaves are bipinnately compound and doubly serrated. I have always enjoyed the vigor and sheer size of the plant, and I admire plants in the Northeast, Midwest, and Northwest. Unfortunately it languishes in the South, so the Armitage garden is beardless. Full sun, zones 3 to 7.

Aruncus dioicus

Aruncus dioicus

MORE →

Aruncus dioicus 'Kneiffii'

Aruncus dioicus 'Kneiffii'

The deeply filigreed dark green leaves of 'Kneiffii', a smaller cutleaf selection, render it a far more delicate plant. Its flowers are less showy, however, and although horticulturally interesting, the plant is not nearly as eye-catching as the species. I also like the feathery flowers of 'Zweiweltenkind' ('Child of Two Worlds'), which is not quite as coarse and a little easier to use.

Aruncus aethusifolius, dwarf goatsbeard, is the antithesis of its grand and, some would say, overbearing cousin. Similarities between the two species include the dark green compound leaves and tiny white flowers, which are held above the plant. *Aruncus aethusifolius*, however, is far more useful for small areas and rock gardens, attaining but 1–2' in height. One to three flower stems are produced in late summer, and although the flowers are reasonably handsome, they don't provide a long-lasting show, persisting only for two to three weeks. Even worse, they brown out quickly after flowering. Actually, the foliage is the best part of the plant, handsome throughout the

Aruncus aethusifolius

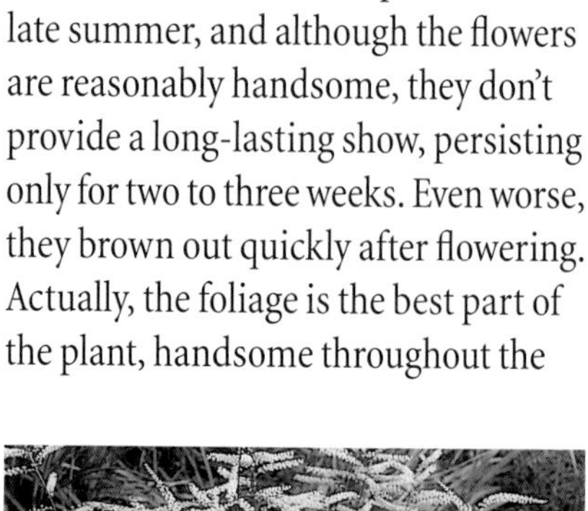

Aruncus 'Southern White'

Aruncus 'Southern White'

Aruncus dioicus 'Zweiweltenkind' ('Child of Two Worlds')

Aruncus aethusifolius

season regardless of the presence or absence of flowers. Full sun to partial shade, well-drained soils, zones 3 to 7.

A wonderful hybrid between the two species was given to me recently by Richard Lighty of the Mount Cuba Center for the Study of Piedmont Flora in Greenville, Delaware. I placed it in the trial gardens at the University of Georgia (zone 7b)—where goatsbeard has always done poorly at best—and it thrived. Plants are intermediate in height and demonstrate remarkable hybrid vigor, performing well in both heat and humidity. I believe it should be listed as *Aruncus* 'Southern White'. Full sun to partial shade, zones 3 to 7.

Asarum arifolium in bud

Asarum arifolium in flower

Asarum

WILD GINGER

Wild gingers occur throughout the world, but most of those that enliven our gardens hail from Asia and North America. They are handsome, ornamental, and a great deal of fun: handsome and ornamental for their deep green and mottled leaves and fun because of the "little brown jugs" (and some not-so-little jugs) of flowers borne beneath the foliage. All the gingers grow well with woodland species, such as *Mertensia*, *Trillium*, and *Podophyllum*. New species and selections are rapidly filling in shady, moist areas of American gardens.

Great variability occurs in our native *Asarum arifolium*, arrowleaf ginger. The dark leaves are in the shape of an arrow and may be mottled or entirely green, even evergreen, although the winter foliage looks dull and somewhat beaten up. In spring, well before the new leaves emerge, tan flower buds form, providing a glimpse of the fun to come. Fresh, light green spring leaves then emerge, and the silver mottling, if present, shows up as they mature. Finally, the buds give way to the jugs themselves. Crawl around on your hands and knees and peak under the leaves to find these elusive flowers—it's great fun. This belly crawl is a great equalizer of plant explorers, young and old, rich and poor. Shade and moisture are necessary, hardy in zones 4 to 8.

Asarum canadense, Canadian ginger, is a wonderful spreader, covering the ground with great enthusiasm. Its light green kidney-shaped leaves, 3–5" wide, are totally deciduous, disappearing in the fall and reappearing in early spring. They unfurl at the same time as the brownish red flowers, which

Flowers of *Asarum canadense* (left), *A. arifolium* (middle), and *A. shuttleworthii*, another wild ginger native from Virginia to Alabama and Georgia

Asarum arifolium

MORE →

Asarum splendens

Asarum yakushimanum

Asarum yakushimanum in flower

occur at the base of the leaf stems. The three sepals on the flowers are almost red and curled back on the jug. Arguably the best ground cover of the available gingers, and while it can become a bit of a nuisance, it is easy enough to divide and pass along to neighbors. Leaves are larger and plants more aggressive in the North than in the South. With shade and moisture, plants are excellent wherever they are grown. Hardy in zones 3 to 7.

Two relatively new gingers from the Orient provide yet more choice for collectors of the genus: *Asarum splendens* and *A. yakushimanum*, the Japanese gingers. *Asarum splendens* has silver-speckled green foliage and the usual flower jugs. The leaf variegation is cleaner than on some of our native species and immediately draws the eye. Plants are slow to grow compared to *A. arifolium* or *A. canadense* but eventually form a compact colony. Outstanding—and available. Hardy in zones 6 to 8.

Asarum yakushimanum bears shiny dark green leaves and extraordinarily large (up to 2" wide) brown flowers. The leaves can be 6" long with short petioles, and plants make a tight compact clump in the Armitage garden. They are slow to get going, but once established, grow reasonably quickly. Different, and a must for the collectors and lovers of this group of plants. Shade and moisture needed, hardy in zones 6 to 8.

Asarum canadense in flower

Asarum canadense

Asarum canadense

Aster

I love the fall, but I must admit, both my garden and I are a little tired by mid September. I mean, gardening is great and all that, but people who tell me how lucky I am that I can garden almost the entire year must be from Connecticut. The coolness of fall rejuvenates me after enduring the heat and humidity of the summer: the annuals are pooping out, the hostas are starting to turn yellow, and I just want to go hiking in the mountains. Then, just when I'm ready to plow up the whole place, the asters explode.

The genus *Aster* is immense, bearing species from China, Japan, and Europe, but it is best known for those species from the eastern United States, in particular our native species, the New England aster, *Aster novae-angliae*, and the New York or Michaelmas aster, *A. novi-belgii*. A couple of other natives are also well worth trying, such as the white wood aster, *A. divaricatus*, and the climbing aster, *A. carolinianus*. Some people still look upon asters as weeds? What are they thinking?

Most asters behave rather normally, for asters—sprawling over, growing up, or making big clumps of flowers. But what about one that climbs all over everything? *Aster carolinianus* doesn't actually climb over anything, but it has so many stems, going in so many different directions, that it can be trained to scale the highest wall or, with its own kudzu-like cunning, can totally obliterate your marigolds, which is probably a good thing. Get a strong trellis, a reinforced wall, or a circle of 4' tall galvanized steel fencing to support this wonder, which can grow 9–15' tall and 3–4' wide. The pink to lavender flowers open in mid October and can be cut down to the ground in the spring if it gets too rollicky for its own good. Hardy in zones 6 to 9.

While the asters named after New England are perhaps the best known, many other fine asters hook me on fall gardening just as much. I love our native wood aster, *Aster divaricatus*, with its small white flowers and 1–2' long purple stems. This is one of the few asters for which partial shade is desirable, so tuck it in with astilbes, hostas, or bergenias, or under baptisias. It does not want to stand up tall; in fact, it looks much better sticking out from under these other plants, where its September flowers can be shown off but its lanky stems are hidden. Even though the plants can look rather weedy in the summer, they are well worth the wait. Plants may be cut back in midsummer, but no later than 15 July. Full sun to partial shade, zones 4 to 8.

Aster novae-angliae and *A. novi-belgii* started out as ditch weeds and

Aster divaricatus

Aster carolinianus

Aster carolinianus

MORE →

Aster divaricatus

pasture plants and may still be enjoyed as such, but they are also valued for their persistent flowering, tough garden demeanor, and outstanding performance in a flower arrangement. Horticulturally speaking, little separates the two species: the New England asters do have rougher, hairier leaves than the New York asters, but extensive breeding has made even these slight

Aster novae-angliae 'Alma Potschke'

Aster novi-belgii 'Professor Kippenburg'

Aster novae-angliae 'Alma Potschke'

Aster novi-belgii 'Winston S. Churchill'

Aster novi-belgii 'Winston S. Churchill'

differences even more subtle. Both of these native plants had to go to England and Germany in the early 1900s for "finishing" before they were acceptable to American gardeners. They came back with names like 'Alma Potschke' (3–4'), 'Professor Kippenburg' (9–12"), and 'Winston S. Churchill' (2–3'). But the aster craze has not been dormant in this country. Selections such as 'Harrington's Pink' (3–5'), 'Purple Dome' (18–24"), 'Wood's Purple' and 'Wood's Pink' (9–12"), and 'Hella Lacy' (3–4') were all developed by American gardeners. Dozens of cultivars, in a rainbow of colors, are available, ranging from 8" to 6' tall and generally growing 2–4' wide. But I recommend only those that are of short to medium height (less than 4') for most gardens. The tall cultivars are beautiful but require support—unless sprawling is a desired trait in your garden. Asters also make fine cut flowers; for example, 'Elta', an *A. novi-belgii* hybrid, persists for five to seven days when a preservative is used. Full sun or afternoon shade; if plants are shaded, even medium forms will need support. Hardy in zones 4 to 8.

Some asters, like the wood asters, are sprawly wonderful things, but if you are not into sprawl, you might want to try *Aster tataricus* (Tatarian aster), a tall late-flowering aster from Siberia. Flowering at the same time as the fall sunflowers and toad lilies (*Tri-*

Aster novae-angliae 'Harrington's Pink'

Aster novae-angliae 'Purple Dome'

Aster novae-angliae 'Purple Dome'

Aster novae-angliae 'Hella Lacy'

Aster 'Elta' arranged with anemones

MORE →

cyrtis spp.), they are the dominant element in the late September and early October garden. The leaves, which emerge in the spring, look like big bunches of green chard and remain so until late in the summer, when the 7' tall stems begin to erupt with hundreds of light lavender flowers with yellow centers. The good thing about this species is that plants multiply rapidly; the bad thing is that plants multiply rapidly. If you feel kind, give a gift that keeps on giving.

A smaller offspring of this big mama, called 'Jin-Dai', is only about 4' tall, but I like Big Mama just the way she is. Full sun is best; plants in partial shade will be taller and sprawl more. Stake, or plant them through *Vernonia*, *Baptisia*, or some other large specimen for some neighborly support. Hardy in zones 4 to 8.

Astilbe

How useful does a group of plants have to be to make it a must-have for all gardeners? Some would argue that the moist, partially shady conditions needed for *Astilbe* eliminate it from such a list. I would argue, however, that the great choice of species and the impressive collection of cultivars put the genus on the must-try list, at the

Aster tataricus

Astilbe ×arendsii 'Venus'

Aster tataricus

Astilbe ×arendsii 'Cattleya'

very least. As landscapes and gardens mature, shade becomes more of an issue, and plants that offer colorful flowers in shady conditions will continue to be in high demand.

The choice of cultivars in the hybrid group *Astilbe* ×*arendsii* is almost endless, making choosing an astilbe only slightly less daunting than choosing a hosta, daylily, or peony. All require soils rich in organic matter and should be planted in areas that remain consistently moist. They are comfortable on streambanks but do not want to be in standing water. Many a scene at Longstock Water Gardens in England, where carex and *Astilbe* ×*arendsii* 'Venus' share the edge of the pond, remain well etched in my mind. Since most of our gardens are not crisscrossed by ponds or creeks, the next best thing is irrigation. Find a spot under high shade, provide organic matter if necessary, and water as needed. It is impossible to say which cultivars are best—to each his own! In my travels, I have always been impressed with 'Cattleya', a 3' tall pink-rose flowerer that also brings the Armitage shade alive. Great red color comes from 'Bonn' and 'Montgomery'; 'Gladstone' and 'Bridal Veil' provide handsome whites. 'Europa' and 'Elizabeth Bloom' are excellent soft pinks, while 'Rheinland' and 'Amethyst' are rosy to deep pink.

Astilbe ×*arendsii* 'Gladstone'

Astilbe ×*arendsii* 'Bridal Veil'

Astilbe ×*arendsii* 'Montgomery'

Astilbe ×*arendsii* 'Cattleya'

Astilbe ×*arendsii* 'Bonn'

MORE →

Astilbe ×arendsii 'Europa'

All these hybrids are terrific, but I am also truly enamored with our wonderful but little-known native *Astilbe biternata*, whose large white flowers

Astilbe ×arendsii 'Elizabeth Bloom'

and dark foliage some people have confused with *Aruncus*. Why such a superb native plant is so difficult for gardeners to obtain is baffling. Partial shade, hardy in zones 4 to 8.

Astilbe chinensis, the Chinese astilbe, has always seemed a rather staid cousin of the more flashy hybrids in the family. The common selection 'Pumila' is only about 1–2' tall, and its deep purple compact flowers don't contrast particularly well with the dark green leaves. It has many fans, however, including this fellow. Plants perform much more like ground covers than the *A. ×arendsii* hybrids and are great low-maintenance plants. Lots

Astilbe ×arendsii 'Rheinland'

Astilbe ×arendsii 'Amethyst'

Astilbe biternata

Astilbe chinensis 'Pumila'

of moisture is necessary for good growth, although they are quite tolerant of temporary drought. The stodgy image of 'Pumila' has been chipped away with the appearance of other good cultivars. 'Finale' has light pink flowers, and 'Visions', an outstanding selection, sports a little more rose color in the flowers.

Astilbe chinensis var. *taquetii* has been grown in American gardens for years. The common selection is 'Superba', the hairy plants of which rise to 5' in height and produce long columnar panicles of purple flowers. A great plant for early summer flowering, sure to catch the eye. The rich gene pool of the variety can be found in newer cultivars such as 'Purple Lance', with purple-red flowers, growing 4–4½' tall. All prefer moisture with a little shade—lots of shade in the South. Hardy in zones 4 to 8.

The most ornamental foliage of the astilbes occurs in *Astilbe simplicifolia*, the star astilbe, which offers dark glossy green leaves arranged in compact clumps. Never reaching more than 2' in height, plants are perfect for

Astilbe simplicifolia 'Sprite'

Astilbe simplicifolia 'Sprite' seed heads

Astilbe chinensis 'Visions'

Astilbe chinensis var. *taquetii* 'Superba'

Astilbe chinensis 'Finale'

Astilbe chinensis var. *taquetii* 'Purple Lance'

MORE →

Astilbe simplicifolia 'Dunkellanchs'

Astilbe simplicifolia 'Hennie Graafland'

Astilbe simplicifolia 'Willy Buchanan'

Astrantia major

the front of the garden or around a small pond. The inflorescences are much more open than other astilbes, providing a light, airy look when in flower. Even the final stage of seed production is ornamental, providing another few weeks of pleasant viewing. The best-known cultivar is 'Sprite', whose shell-pink flowers have proven outstanding for many years. Other cultivars, such as 'Hennie Graafland' and 'Dunkellanchs', are similar to 'Sprite', but 'Willy Buchanan' is set apart by its dwarf habit (less than a foot tall) and light pink flowers. As with other astilbes, moisture and partial shade are conducive to good performance. Hardy in zones 4 to 8.

Astrantia

MASTERWORT

A few plants have such nonsensical names that I cannot wait to get a look at the thing to see what part of it inspired the choice. If sneezewort has to do with sneezing, then what about masterwort? Gardeners are unlikely to be enamored with the name, nor are they likely to find the name attached to a plant at their local garden center. Common name aside, however, the genus *Astrantia* can do great things for partially shaded areas, particularly if water can be provided regularly.

The large, rather weird, 2–3" wide, white to pink flowers of *Astrantia*

Astrantia major

major, great masterwort, occur in early to mid spring. Short papery bracts stick out beneath the flowers, like rounded collars on a shirt. The deep green leaves are shallowly parted into three to seven divisions. Spreading by seed and stolons, the 2–3' tall plants, where comfortable, form an impressive display. Unfortunately for many gardeners, they are only comfortable in cool climates and abhor hot, humid summers. Several outstanding cultivars have been collected, however, and should be tried by adventurous gardeners. My favorite for sure is 'Margery Fish', a.k.a. 'Shaggy' for its greatly elongated collar of bracts, a truly shaggy mane. I first saw 'Ruby Wedding' many years ago and was pleased to see rosy red flowers had been selected from the species. 'Lars' is even darker and makes an impressive garden display. Those who enjoy weird flowers on variegated leaves should try 'Sunningdale Variegated'; the variegation disappears with summer temperatures, which is just as well. Astrantias are best for the West Coast or in zones 5 to 7a.

The good news is that the pink-flowering species *Astrantia maxima*, large masterwort, is the most handsome of all the masterworts. The bad news is that very few nurseries offer it for sale. The flowers are rose-pink, and the leaves are usually only three-parted. It is more difficult to propagate, and not enough gardeners have tried it to have any confidence in its hardiness limits. Find a few (they are out there), plant them, and let's get this plant in more gardens. Plants perform best in partial shade and are probably hardy in zones 5 to 7a as well as on the West Coast.

Astrantia major 'Margery Fish' ('Shaggy')

Astrantia major 'Sunningdale Variegated'

Astrantia major

Astrantia major 'Ruby Wedding'

Astrantia major 'Ruby Wedding'

Astrantia maxima

Astrantia maxima

Athyrium

Having grown up in Montreal in a garden-challenged family, I thought that everyone used ferns simply to cover the dirt. Wherever he could around our little semi-detached, Dad stuck in ferns—boring, never-changing green things that blackened at the first touch of frost. Nevertheless they were great for us boys, whose interest in hockey and baseball far exceeded our interest in garden maintenance. My eyes have opened, however, and my mind has expanded. Eureka, I like ferns. Age does have some value.

Athyrium filix-femina, lady fern, is a boring, never-changing green thing. Ah, but this is a boring, never-changing green thing with style and class, and better than that, this lady is tough as nails. She is deciduous, blackening at the second touch of frost, but her early croziers (ferns have such neat words associated with them—makes one sound intelligent) give rise to beautiful feathery fronds. The rachis (midrib) and stipe (petiole) are often pink or red, providing wonderful contrast to the green pinnae (see what I mean?). Plants stand upright and make handsome airy clumps. This is probably the most variable of all the ferns. I rather like the plumose feathery cultivars ('Plumosum', for instance), but others have been selected because they are, among other miscellaneous atrocities, crested ('Linearis'), both crested and plumose ('Plumosum Cristatum'), dwarf ('Minutissimum'), and round-pinnae'd, like a necklace ('Frizelliae'). Their main function is to provide curiosity, like a car wreck. Although these aberrations do reduce the boredom factor a little, they don't hold a candle to the species. Provide shade and moisture, hardy in zones 4 to 8.

The antithesis of a boring green thing, *Athyrium nipponicum*, the Japanese painted fern, provides toughness, style, and technicolor fronds. This plant makes fern growing a lot

Athyrium filix-femina

Athyrium filix-femina

Athyrium filix-femina 'Linearis'

Athyrium filix-femina 'Linearis'

more exciting. The colors on the main cultivar, 'Pictum', are indescribable—that is, I don't know how to describe them. Someone else took a stab, calling it "a metallic gray suffused with reddish or bluish hues"—which hardly narrows the field. Suffice it to say the fronds are a pastel blend of many lovely colors. Where conditions are to their liking, plants routinely spread themselves around. They tolerate heavy shade but are at their best in morning sun and prefer moist, rather than wet conditions. 'Ursala's Red' describes a selection with more red on the rachis, but it is not so different that one could consider it any better than the species itself. Hardy in zones 3 to 8.

Athyrium filix-femina 'Minutissimum'

Athyrium filix-femina 'Plumosum Cristatum'

Athyrium filix-femina 'Frizelliae'

Athyrium nipponicum 'Ursala's Red'

Athyrium nipponicum 'Pictum'

Athyrium nipponicum 'Pictum'

Baptisia australis with *Heuchera* 'Raspberry Regal'

Baptisia australis seed heads

Baptisia

FALSE INDIGO

I always enjoy a good story, and the history of the blue false indigo, *Baptisia australis*, makes for good reading. This blue-flowered species was one of the very first plants to be subsidized by the English government: the farmers in the colonies of Georgia and South Carolina grew it as a row crop to supplement the true indigo plant (*Indigofera*) for the British empire. The false indigos come in three main colors—blue, white, and yellow—but new hybrids and selections are bringing this fine plant into mainstream gardening. Great plants, great stories, great fun.

Baptisia australis is an excellent "last forever" plant; yet much to the chagrin of retailers, it looks like a stick in a pot when first purchased. Don't fret: plant that stick and soon enough, your friends will no longer be laughing. Plants take time to establish, but after a couple of years in the garden, they flower profusely and take on their classic form and substance. Plants, 3–4' tall and equally wide, look terrific by themselves or towering over other spring flowerers, such as *Heuchera* 'Raspberry Regal'. Flowers make excellent, albeit rather ephemeral, cut flowers for local occasions. After flowering, fat brown pods are formed. As the seeds within them mature, they come loose from the pod walls, and the whole pod becomes a miniature tambourine. Few insects and diseases bother the plant; however, they do collapse in the late fall, and the first frost turns everything about them black and mushy. Plants will continue to perform for at least ten years. Full sun is necessary for best performance; keep them out of poorly drained soils. Hardy in zones 3 to 8.

Several cultivars and hybrids can be found. A hybrid involving *Baptisia*

Baptisia 'Purple Smoke'

Baptisia australis

Baptisia 'Purple Smoke'

australis is 'Purple Smoke', whose smoke-colored stems and flowers make it truly unique. This is a winner. The dwarf (2' tall) species, *B. minor*, is outstanding and resembles its big brother in every way except size.

The Armitage garden is a mecca for *Baptisia*, and several representatives of the genus fight for recognition among the oaks and weeds. Unfortunately, the oaks are not interested in the garden below, and more and more shade covers the site. Fortunately, *Baptisia alba*, the white false indigo, is far more tolerant of partial shade than the blue false indigo. Plants are ornamental from early spring, when the black stems emerge, and on through the spring and summer, with their many clean white flowers and light green foliage. In late summer and fall, the upward-facing "pea pods" are the legacy of the spring and summer flower fling, but in 'Pendula', the pods are (you guessed it) pendulous. I don't recommend shade, although these plants certainly brighten it up. Well-drained soils are necessary, hardy in zones 5 (perhaps 4) to 8.

Blues and whites are wonderful, but the yellow indigos cannot be ignored.

Baptisia minor

Baptisia alba

Baptisia alba in the Armitage garden

MORE →

Baptisia alba 'Pendula'

Baptisia alba 'Pendula' seed heads

Baptisia viridis

Brightening up the sunny garden, forming interesting fruit, and offering decent foliage, they are sort of the lost sisters of the more popular white and blue versions of *Baptisia*. Their flowers were no less important to Native Americans, who also used them for coloring and dye. I enjoy the small foliage and flowers of *Baptisia tinctoria* (wild yellow indigo) and the bright bold foliage and flowers of *B. viridis*, while the creamy yellow color of *B. sphaerocarpa* provides subtlety seldom seen in this bold genus. Full sun, hardy in zones 4 to 8.

Baptisia sphaerocarpa

Baptisia tinctoria

Bergenia

PIGSQUEAK

Slow to become embraced in the mainstream American garden, pigsqueak is nevertheless offered by most perennial plant catalogs, so somebody must be buying it. If you want to impress your garden friends, rub a leaf of this plant between your thumb and index finger. If you are talented, everyone will soon hear the pig squeak. Be sure to practice on your own before you make a fool of yourself in public.

Bergenia ciliata, fringed bergenia, is a wonderful little-grown plant that can make even a nonbeliever like me want to take home a pigsqueak. Like other bergenias, the light green leaves are the best part of the plant, the organs that make it unique. They are densely pubescent (hairy) with small hairs

Bergenia ciliata

Bergenia ciliata

(cilia) surrounding the leaves. Plants look best in rock gardens or where the leaves can be admired close up. Consider the white flowers, flushed with rose, a bonus; the plants don't flower as well or grow as vigorously as common bergenias. Plant in partial (preferably afternoon) shade and protect from drying winds. Hardy in zones 5 to 7.

In my opinion, making the pig squeak is the best reason to purchase *Bergenia cordifolia* (heartleaf pigsqueak) and its hybrids, but thankfully for the breeders and sellers of bergenia, my opinion doesn't count for much. The 12" tall plants have glossy green leaves that can act as ground covers where shade and slightly moist conditions are found. The early spring flowers rise 8–12" above the leaves in early spring and persist for weeks if temperatures remain cool. Flowers are generally red or pink, but white is also available. The early flowers are often damaged if late freezes occur. In warmer areas of the country, plants are evergreen (actually "ever-bronze") but get badly battered in subfreezing temperatures. In the North, snow mercifully puts them out of view. On the West Coast, they are as perfect as bergenia can be, which is not saying too much. The bronze foliage in the fall and spring is one of the main selling points for gardeners. Partial shade, hardy in zones 4 to 8.

Amply demonstrating the diversity of bergenias are the many cultivars and hybrids of *Bergenia cordifolia*; *B. purpurascens*, purple pigsqueak, with its outstanding deep purple foliage; and others. 'Abendglocken' ('Evening

Bergenia 'Abendglocken' ('Evening Bells')

Bergenia cordifolia

Bergenia 'Ballawley'

Bergenia cordifolia in winter

Bergenia purpurascens

Bergenia 'Ballawley'

MORE →

Bells') and 'Bressingham Ruby' provide almost equally dark foliage in the early spring. 'Ballawley' and 'Pugsley Purple' (is that not an appropriate name for a pigsqueak?) have fine green foliage, while the flowers of 'Distinction', 'Morning Red', and 'Profusion' provide a strong hint as to why some people absolutely love this group of plants. That I am not one of them does not diminish my appreciation when I see *Bergenia* growing well.

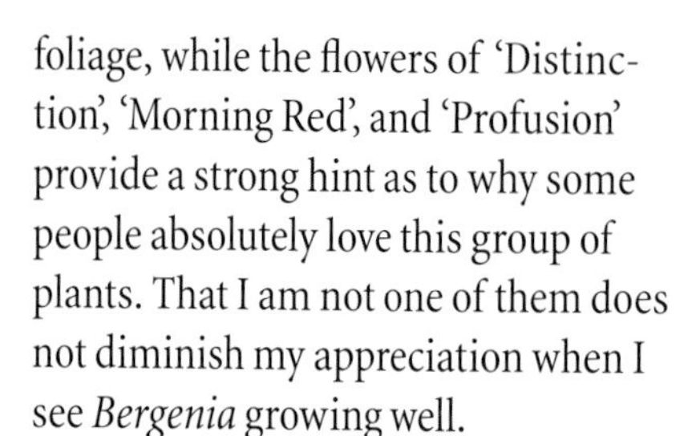

Bergenia 'Bressingham Ruby'

Bergenia 'Distinction'

Bergenia 'Profusion'

Bergenia 'Morning Red'

Boltonia

Late summer can be a bit of a low time in the garden, sandwiched as it is between the fireworks of summer and the last hurrahs of autumn. Several transition plants, including the ubiquitous yellow daisies, are up to the challenge; one of the best of these is yet another daisy, white as snow and persistent from year to year.

When you put *Boltonia asteroides* in the garden in the spring, plant its selection 'Snowbank'. You might want to add some orange zinnias or some dwarf red cannas at its feet to provide a little contrast, although the flowers comport comfortably with almost any-

Boltonia asteroides 'Snowbank'

Boltonia asteroides 'Snowbank'

Boltonia asteroides 'Pink Beauty'

thing. And since it grows 3–4' in height and equally wide, give it plenty of room. The small bluish green leaves are sufficiently handsome even when no flowers are present, but when the one-inch-wide white flowers appear in late summer and fall, the appropriateness of the cultivar name is readily apparent. Plants persist for years if placed in full sun and given reasonable drainage; in too much shade, they will require support and do not flower as freely. Full sun, hardy in zones 4 to 8.

'Pink Beauty' is a cousin of 'Snowbank', with many pale pink flowers in late summer and fall. More open and lanky, and not as good a plant, but worth a try for its flowering time and color.

Brunnera macrophylla

HEARTLEAF BRUNNERA

I thought the only place I would see outstanding plantings of *Brunnera macrophylla*, heartleaf brunnera, would be in places like Ireland or England, where such plants seem to grow in woodlands and stream banks like weeds. Not true, as a trip to Old Westbury Gardens on Long Island or Gardenview Horticultural Park in Strongsville, Ohio, will attest.

"Look at the forget-me-nots" is probably the first thing you'll think when you see the plants in flower. The wonderful little blue flowers with small yellow centers look for all the world like forget-me-nots, but the deep green heart-shaped leaves give away the plant's true identity. Where summer temperatures are cool, leaves can be 3" long or more, and plants make a beautiful ground cover in moist, shady soils, holding their own against real forget-me-nots in the same site. Together the plants look like two youngsters holding hands on a pleasant afternoon. *Brunnera macrophylla* is not for everybody—consistent moisture is essential, otherwise the margins of the leaves turn brown. But for the somebodies, it is terrific. The rest of us will continue to plant, pamper, and enjoy its brief visits to our gardens. Plants do well in zones 3 to 7a.

Trying to collect some of the outstanding cultivars of this species is a challenging and occasionally expen-

Brunnera macrophylla

Brunnera macrophylla

Brunnera macrophylla 'Variegata'

Brunnera macrophylla 'Variegata'

MORE →

Brunnera macrophylla 'Langtrees'

sive activity. Much of the variegated leaf of 'Variegata', the best of the available selections, is taken up with creamy white, and 'Langtrees' has silver white spots. 'Hadspen Cream' offers another variegated look and is highly sought after, a condition only intensified by low supply. The variegated forms are exceedingly difficult to propagate and difficult to establish, and therefore expensive to buy. Obviously, they must be good. Enjoy them if you can find them.

Campanula carpatica 'White Clips'

Campanula

BELLFLOWER

The genus *Campanula* offers so many species, cultivars, and varieties that any gardener, north or south, will never run out of plants to try. The species generally bear blue, lavender, or purple flowers, but many other hues, such as white, rosy red, and pink, have been selected. As to habit, the bellflowers offer something for almost every gardener, from upright 4' plants with large flowers to 6" rock garden subjects. The only drawback to the genus is that it is more appropriate for northern climates; southern gardeners have to struggle to find taxa that perform south of zone 6.

Among the low growers is *Campanula carpatica*, the Carpathian bellflower. Standing only 9–12" tall, this bellflower has some of the biggest, most colorful flowers, relative to the size of the plant, of any campanula. The bell-shaped flowers can be up to 2" across and are copiously produced in early to mid summer. Provide full sun and good drainage, and place them around some rocks or near the front of the garden. This species is native to eastern Europe, and plants are not tolerant of high temperatures and high humidity. I have had little success with them south of zone 6 in the eastern United States, but they can be produced in zones 7 and 8 on the West Coast. They are terrific in the northern Plains states, the Midwest, and Canada.

The Clips series ('Blue Clips', 'White Clips') and the Wedgewood series ('Wedgewood Blue', 'Wedgewood White') are excellent small-statured plants with large flowers. For some of the deepest blue flowers, try 'Kobalt

Campanula carpatica 'Kobalt Bell'

Campanula carpatica 'Blue Clips'

Bell'. *Campanula carpatica* var. *turbinata* is lower growing and produces large (again, relative to plant height) blue flowers; its selection 'Isabel' is an interesting plant with deep violet saucer-shaped flowers. She looks particularly good when growing among yellow flowers such as *Sedum*.

Both *Campanula portenschlagiana* (Dalmatian bellflower) and *C. poscharskyana* (Serbian bellflower) offer similar low-growing habits (6–9" tall), handsome blue to purple flowers, and absolutely unpronounceable botanical names. Both are exceptionally good plants for the rock garden or for tumbling over hillsides and containers. For the North American gardener, there is little to choose between them; usually one takes whatever can be found at the nursery or in the mail-order catalog. The bell-shaped flowers of *C. portenschlagiana* separate it from the star-shaped flowers of *C. poscharskyana*,

Campanula carpatica var. *turbinata*

Campanula carpatica var. *turbinata* 'Isabel' with *Sedum*

Campanula portenschlagiana

Campanula portenschlagiana

Campanula portenschlagiana 'Resholt's Variety'

Campanula portenschlagiana 'Resholt's Variety'

MORE →

but otherwise the species are similar in habit and color. The color ranges from lavender to purple, depending on location, and flowers open in late spring. When not in flower, the plants make good-looking clumps of dark green foliage, or they can be hidden by bigger plants as summer progresses. *Campanula portenschlagiana* performs well in zones 4 to 8, *C. poscharskyana* in zones 3 to 7. I find both species more heat tolerant than most others in the genus, having been successful in the Armitage garden.

The species are just fine in and of themselves, but for *Campanula portenschlagiana*, 'Resholt's Variety' is the best vivid blue, while the deeper purple flowers of 'Bavarica' provide a more somber effect. For *C. poscharskyana*, the range of choices is expanded by 'Blue Gown' and 'Stella', with blue-

Campanula portenschlagiana 'Bavarica'

Campanula poscharskyana

Campanula poscharskyana

Campanula poscharskyana 'Blue Gown'

Campanula lactiflora 'Alba'

Campanula lactiflora 'Loddon Anna'

Campanula lactiflora 'Loddon Anna'

Campanula lactiflora 'Pritchard's Variety'

and-white and vivid violet-blue flowers, respectively. The cultivars are more difficult to find and really no better than the species.

Campanula lactiflora (milky bellflower) and *C. latiloba* (delphinium bellflower) are totally different in habit than the low growers just mentioned, often reaching 4' in upright height, with flowers opening in mid to late summer. *Campanula lactiflora* produces hundreds of small lavender or white flowers on many-branched plants in midsummer. Among the best selections of it are 'Pritchard's Variety' and 'Superba', both with flowers in the lavender to purple range. 'Alba' is an excellent choice for clean white flowers, but my favorite is 'Loddon Anna', with soft pale pink flowers on sturdy 4' tall stems. But beware: all can reseed prolifically, and the resulting offspring may be any color. For best results, provide full sun or some afternoon shade and reasonably well-drained soils. Hardy in zones 5 to 7.

The delphinium bellflower, *Campanula latiloba*, is so named because the blooms are held close to the flowering stem, like the flowers of a delphinium. They are large (up to 2" long) and borne on the 3–5' tall plants in midsummer. The species itself is nowhere to be seen, but its variously hued selections 'Alba' (white), 'Hidcote Amethyst' (an interesting mauve-purple), and 'Highcliffe' (deep blue) provide some happy alternatives for the campanulite. They are most successful on the West Coast but may also be found growing in gardens in zones 5 to 7. Full sun or afternoon shade. Neither of these upright bellflower species do well in areas of hot summers and are seldom grown successfully in the southern half of the country. The low growers are more forgiving of heat and humidity than the upright forms.

Campanula lactiflora 'Pritchard's Variety'

Campanula lactiflora 'Superba'

Campanula latiloba 'Alba'

Campanula latiloba 'Hidcote Amethyst'

Campanula latiloba 'Highcliffe'

Canna

CANNA LILY

The cannas are back! Like an endangered creature slowly making its way back into the mainstream population, canna lilies have returned from relative obscurity to become a rising star in today's gardens and landscapes. In some communities, cannas are an important landscape plant for road medians or public parks, attesting to their toughness. The diversity in the genus had been limited to the point of being boring, with green-leaved, red-flowered plants dominating the choices. With the surging interest in cannas, however, all sorts of new (or rediscovered) leaf colors are finding their way to American gardens. The new cultivars are no more cold hardy or disease or insect resistant than their predecessors, but their new colors are readily embraced, and the need for large bold plants in the garden have made them more prominent in the landscape.

It took me a while to say nice things about the rather gaudy leaves of *Canna* 'Bengal Tiger' ('Pretoria'), but I have come around and actually like the plant. By themselves they are tough on the eye, but when they are sited in combination with other sun lovers, few complaints are ever heard. Two other new kids on the block are the

Canna leaves in a garden border

Canna 'King Humpert'

Canna 'Wyoming'

Canna 'Bengal Tiger' ('Pretoria')

stunning 'Tropicana' ('Phaison') and 'Panache', with foliage and flowers, respectively, to die for, while the variegated foliage of 'Stuttgart' is also becoming popular. 'Stuttgart' is an anomaly among cannas, preferring partial shade rather than full sun. The bicolored flowers of 'Cleopatra' are most interesting (some descriptions may not be so kind), but the plant is one of the toughest, growing through drought and flood. Others that I think are impressive are 'King Humpert', as well as good old 'Wyoming', whose bronze leaves and orange flowers continue to be popular. Yellow flowers can be found in 'Richard Wallace' and 'Independence'. All these hybrids are big, 3–5' tall, but 'Tropicana Rose' and 'Pink Sunburst' are genetic dwarfs, less than 3' tall. 'Pink Sunburst' grows much more robustly and wider than 'Tropicana Rose' and is an outstanding choice for the smaller garden.

I'm not sure the heated love affair with cannas will continue, but as long as new cultivars that perform well in the landscape are introduced, they should be around for a while longer.

Full sun, winter hardy in zones 7 to 10; the addition of winter mulching may allow overwintering into the southern end of zone 6 as well. Further north, treat them like dahlias: lift in the fall and replant in the spring.

Canna 'Richard Wallace'

Canna 'Panache'

Canna 'Tropicana' ('Phaison')

Canna 'Cleopatra'

Canna 'Pink Sunburst'

Canna 'Stuttgart'

Canna 'Pink Sunburst'

Centaurea cyanus

Centaurea dealbata 'Steenbergii'

Centaurea hypoleuca 'John Coutts'

Centaurea hypoleuca 'John Coutts'

Centaurea

CORNFLOWER, KNAPWEED

If Julie Andrews were walking the highways of America rather than the hills of Switzerland, she undoubtedly would have broken into song about the roads being alive with the blue of bachelor's buttons, or something equally euphonious. Well, maybe not... But the annual bachelor's button, *Centaurea cyanus*, does so consistently paint the roadsides (invasively so in the Midwest) that it seems to be a perennial, even though it in fact reappears annually from seed. But other fine members of the genus are perennial and, the bachelor part notwithstanding, well-behaved members for the garden. The base of the flowers of all cornflowers consist of shingle-like papery structures called involucre bracts, whose orientation and color often account for a significant part of the flower's beauty.

With 2" wide rosy purple flowers held above the mid-green cut leaves, *Centaurea dealbata*, the Persian cornflower, makes an impressive display from early to mid summer. Place the 2–3' tall plants in full sun in front or near the middle of the garden. They dislike hot, humid conditions and therefore perform better in the North than in the South. Flowers can be cut when just a little color is showing and will persist inside for an additional five to seven days. Cultivars of different parentage have appeared on the market, including selections of a similar species, *C. hypoleuca*. From the gardener's perspective, they are similiar in garden habit, garden performance, and even color. Full sun, zones 3 to 7.

'Steenbergii' is one of the many rose-purple selections of *Centaurea dealbata* found in mail-order catalogs and garden centers. The plants are more compact and often have a white center in the flowers. Another well-known cultivar (which may in fact be a hybrid with other species) is *C. hypoleuca* 'John Coutts'; its flowers are produced more readily and are more compact than other offerings. All are similar in appearance, but if I had a choice, I'd recommend John for your garden.

With a common name like Armenian basketflower, *Centaurea macro-*

Centaurea dealbata 'Steenbergii'

cephala cannot be all bad. I first saw the cut flowers of the species in the window of a Dutch florist shop, alongside stems of lilies and baby's breath, and was immediately impressed. The 3" wide yellow flowers, which are produced on 3–4' tall plants in late spring and early summer, are bright and beautiful but kind of messy-shaggy. In fact, they can look terrific one day and awful the next. (It is apparent that I am easily impressed.) Even the flower buds are handsome, surrounded by brown, papery bracts that add ornamental value to the flower. Not very good in the South. Plant in full sun, zones 3 to 7a.

Centaurea macrocephala

Centaurea macrocephala

Centaurea macrocephala

Centaurea montana

Centaurea montana

Centaurea montana 'Alba'

Centaurea montana, mountain bluet, offers fine blue flowers and almost black involucre bracts. Very aggressive in the North, where many an unsuspecting gardener has planted a couple of them only to see them become legion. The 2" wide flowers produce long petals around the outside of the bracts, and weedy as they may be, they are amazingly handsome.

Three cultivars of *Centaurea montana*, though difficult to find, are worth looking for. 'Alba' produces many white flowers; the larger blue flowers of 'Grandiflora' and the creamy white blossoms of 'Ochroleuca' are sufficiently different to make the search worthwhile. Full sun, zones 3 to 7.

Centaurea montana 'Grandiflora'

Centaurea montana 'Ochroleuca'

Cephalaria gigantea

Cephalaria gigantea in bud

Cephalaria gigantea

TATARIAN CEPHALARIA

A well-grown clump of *Cephalaria gigantea* is a "come-hither" planting. Sited at the center or back of the garden, with lesser subjects at its feet, this 6–8' plant dominates center stage. The large (4–8") compound leaves are usually light to mid green; however, as large as the plants are, blooms are the main reason for its inclusion. The primrose-yellow flowers, which begin as great meaty flower buds, are about 2" across and held on wiry stems well above the foliage. They look suspiciously like the yellow-flowered scabious, *Scabiosa ochroleuca*, only much taller and coarser. Plants do poorly in hot, humid climates and are best suited to the North and Far West. Full sun, well-drained soils, zones 4 to 7.

Cephalaria gigantea

Cephalaria gigantea

Cerastium

SNOW-IN-SUMMER

When the landscape plan calls for plants that supposedly look like snow in the summer, some people roll their eyes and scratch their heads over the intelligence of landscape designers. Such plants do exist, however, and the one that answers that call best is *Cerastium tomentosum*, whose combination of leaves, flowers, and habit have made it a popular plant in many gardens. In the spring (not the summer), the silvery gray leaves flow over rocks, making marvelous foils for more colorful plants at the front of the garden. The plants, covered with half-inch-wide white flowers, may not be quite like a snowbank but at least come close to snow-in-spring. Flowers occur as temperatures warm up and daylengths lengthen, persisting for four to six weeks, depending on temperature. In areas of little snowfall, the plants are "ever-gray" and quite handsome in the off-season. The foliage, like that of artemisias and lamb's ears, are excellent softeners of the garden border.

Cerastium tomentosum

Drainage becomes more important the further south one gardens. With poor drainage, plants melt out south of zone 7a, but are still useful in that area in raised beds or containers. Full sun in the North, afternoon shade in the South, excellent drainage required. Hardy in zones 3 to 7.

A couple of other species, such as *Cerastium buisseri* (also known as snow-in-summer), may be found, but they offer few obvious differences. Plants have similar white flowers but are less vigorous, which may be a plus for gardeners in places where *C. tomentosum* becomes too aggressive. Hardy in zones 3 to 6.

Cerastium buisseri

Cerastium tomentosum

Ceratostigma willmottianum

Ceratostigma willmottianum

Ceratostigma willmottianum 'Forest Blue'

Ceratostigma

LEADWORT

I was taught that the term "wort" means "to heal": liverwort heals the liver, lungwort heals the lung, and so forth. Obviously something went wrong here. All the same, the leadworts—healers or not—provide excellent plants for the late summer and fall garden.

The two species seen in American gardens are remarkably different. *Ceratostigma plumbaginoides* (trailing leadwort) is only 6–9" tall. Plants produce blue flowers, a half-inch to an inch across, in late summer and fall, and are one of the toughest little ground covers available. Without flowers, one hardly even notices the plants most of the year, but as days shorten and temperatures start to cool down, they perk up and put on their best blue dresses. The leaves are small (less than an inch in length) and are dark green most of the year, turning reddish as plants get older. They grow best in full sun and, with good drainage, are almost indestructible. This species performs well in zones 5 (4 with protection) to 8.

Neither well known nor widely grown, *Ceratostigma willmottianum* (Chinese leadwort) is certainly worth a try as more plants become available. Growing to 2' in height, it puts forth its handsome blue flowers for about six weeks in late summer. Chinese leadwort is not as tough and adaptable as trailing leadwort, but it has its compact habit to recommend it, and the blue flowers do well with anything white or yellow. 'Forest Blue' is widely adaptable and provides an excellent upright habit. Full sun to partial shade, hardy in zones 7 (perhaps 6) to 9.

Ceratostigma plumbaginoides

Ceratostigma plumbaginoides

Chrysanthemum

What this noble name has been subjected to! The genus, which represented dozens of fine garden plants throughout the world, was unceremoniously stripped of its name and thrown out on the street with but a few family members still clinging to its legs. *Chrysanthemum*—which had included the pot chrysanthemum, fall garden mum, Marguerite daisy, yellow and gold, pyrethrum daisy, ox-eye daisy, nippon daisy, and the ubiquitous shasta daisy—ended up with a couple of annual plants after the smoke had cleared. What a debacle. And now that people and the industry have finally accepted the change in some of the names, it appears as if the names will revert to the originals.

Some of the flowers of *Chrysanthemum coccineum* (*Tanacetum coccineum*) are so bright, it appears as if new paint were applied to the flowers, hence the common name, painted daisy. The 2–3" wide flowers appear in late spring and early summer over the light green, deeply cut, fetid foliage, which last property makes this species, also known as pyrethrum daisy, an excellent pest repellent. Plants may grow 3' tall and are notorious for their need for support. If cut back after flowering, they may return a second flush.

Some wonderful selections of *Chrysanthemum coccineum* exist, but they are not terribly easy to come by. 'James Kelway' is an old favorite, with bright red flowers atop 3' stems; 'Brenda' is similar in color but shorter, usually around 2' in height. 'Eileen May Robinson' is another terrific old-fashioned daisy with single pink flowers. Double flowers can be admired in 'Shirley Double', while other cultivars such as 'Bressingham Red' add color, handsome leaves, and cut flowers to this diverse group of plants. They are cold hardy in snow-covered zone 4 (occasionally to zone 3) but are not happy in the heat and humidity of a zone 7 summer. Full sun, good drainage.

Fall is the time for pot mums, sold by the dozen for a buck and a half each

Chrysanthemum coccineum 'James Kelway'

Chrysanthemum coccineum 'James Kelway'

Chrysanthemum coccineum 'Eileen May Robinson'

Chrysanthemum coccineum 'Eileen May Robinson'

MORE →

at the local box store. Colorful, cheap, useful, and boring. They perform better in the pot at K-Mart than they do in the garden. *Chrysanthemum* ×*koreanum* (*Dendranthema* ×*grandiflorum*) and other late-flowerers are outstanding, however, and ought to be used more. They are known as Korean hybrids or by their cultivar names, such as 'Ryan's Daisy', 'Hillside Sheffield', and 'Apricot Single'. 'Ryan's Daisy' is about 18–24" tall; 'Hillside Sheffield' and 'Apricot Single' are only about 12" high. Gazillions of flowers in late fall, before frost. Can be propagated by the shovelful, any time. Save your dollar and a half and buy something useful. Great plants! Full sun, zones 3 to 8.

The handsome variegated evergreen foliage of a well-grown specimen of silver and gold, *Chrysanthemum pacificum* (*Ajania pacifica*) always brings praise. The white margins are clean and crisp. Under satisfactory growing conditions, plants of the small slightly serrated leaves make a 3–4' wide clump in a single growing season. Height is only about 15", but its leaf color combines well with many neighbors, such as artemisias or dusty miller. Its other claim to fame is the appearance of dozens of round fuzzy balls of yellow flowers late in the season. Very late—as in November in the Armitage garden, hopefully before frost in more northern sites. Not really being a fan of small fuzzy round flow-

Chrysanthemum coccineum 'Brenda'

Chrysanthemum coccineum 'Brenda'

Chrysanthemum coccineum 'Shirley Double'

Chrysanthemum coccineum 'Bressingham Red'

ers, it took me a few years to think of them as something other than a distraction to the leaves. But now they are as anticipated as flowers of the spring and summer, with the added bonus of wondering if they will open before the frost gets them. Cut plants back if necessary in spring, not fall. Excellent drainage is an absolute requirement; site the plants on a slope if possible. Full sun, hardy in zones 5 to 9.

Chrysanthemum ×*superbum* (*Leucanthemum* ×*superbum*), commonly known as the shasta daisy, has been, is, and forever shall be one of the more popular perennials in the American landscape. They are in front of every gardener in every outlet in every spring—easy to grow, easy to pronounce, and as comfortable as an old shoe. That many of them fall apart in a year or two seems not to make the slightest difference. Nearly all shastas are clothed in white, whether in single, semi-double, or fully double attire.

All sorts of choices are available to the shasta connoisseur. The double fringed flowers of 'Aglaia' are absolutely gruesome; those of 'Wirral Supreme', not nearly as scary. Personally,

Chrysanthemum ×*superbum* 'Aglaia'

Chrysanthemum 'Ryan's Daisy'

Chrysanthemum 'Hillside Sheffield'

Chrysanthemum 'Apricot Single'

Chrysanthemum pacificum with *Artemisia* 'Powis Castle'

Chrysanthemum pacificum

Chrysanthemum pacificum

MORE →

Chrysanthemum ×*superbum* 'Wirral Supreme'

Chrysanthemum ×*superbum* 'Becky'

Chrysanthemum ×*superbum* 'Snow Cap'

I'll take single-flowered shastas any day—perhaps 'White Knight', with its lovely single white petals around a yellow center, or 'Snow Lady', an All-American award winner that flowers the first year from seed. 'Polaris' is large, and 'Snow Cap' is the best of the compact forms. If you are having problems with foliage falling apart after flowering, try 'Becky'. She bears fine white single flowers, but unlike the fine lady she was named for, she has the toughest demeanor of any shasta I have tried. In general, plants stand 18–30" tall and require full sun and well-drained soils. Rainy, humid climates are not to their liking. They do reasonably well in zones 4 to 9. Cut back after flowering in warmer areas of the country.

Chrysanthemum ×*superbum* 'Becky'

Chrysanthemum ×*superbum* 'Snow Lady'

Chrysanthemum ×*superbum* 'Polaris'

Chrysanthemum ×*superbum* 'White Knight'

Clematis

A large group of ornamental vines and a few non-viners make up this popular genus. The incredible popularity of the vines is due to their relative ease of culture and diversity of color, flower size, and form. Many a postal carrier has cursed a clematis while trying to wedge mail into a mailbox surrounded by a beanstalk that could support a young Jack. However, a couple of non-vining forms are equally satisfying, if not quite as spectacular, and deserve to be used much more widely.

Big and sprawling, *Clematis heracleifolia* (tube clematis) is non-vining and shrublike in its habit. The ends of the stems produce dozens of tubular flowers, making for showy inflorescences in late spring and summer. The large compound leaves are up to 12" long, and if the plant is overfertilized, the leaves will almost obscure the flowers. Flowers range from light to dark blue. The plant's main drawbacks are ranginess and leafiness; support tends to make the plant less rangy. Plants may be cut back in late summer if the foliage declines. *Clematis heracleifolia* can be more weedy than useful—but when in its prime, it is a showstopper. Full sun, zones 3 to 7.

'Côte d'Azur' and 'Wyevale Blue' are the most common offerings and differ only slightly from the species. 'Robert Briden' has a touch of blue on the mostly creamy white flowers.

Clematis integrifolia (solitary clematis), one of the big-time sleepers in herbaceous perennials, is a non-vining member that produces solitary flowers of deep blue and opposite entire leaves. A definite must-have plant, it has been obscured in the marketplace by the omnipresent vines but is well worth a place in the sunny garden. The numerous thin, 3' tall stems should be supported as they grow, otherwise they flop on the ground. The flowers begin in late spring and continue for six weeks, then off and on throughout the season. Under good garden condi-

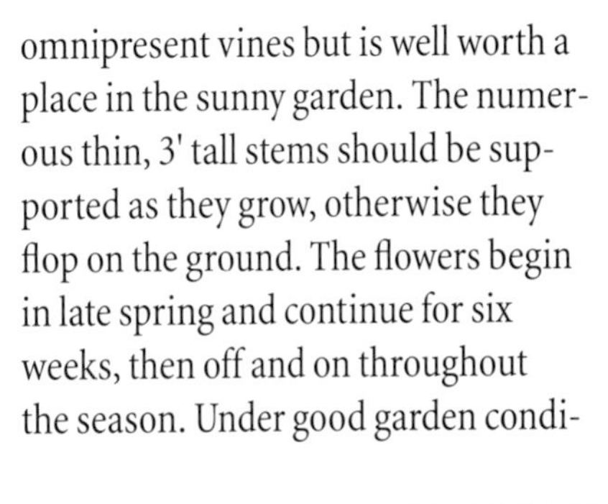

Clematis integrifolia

Clematis heracleifolia (right) and *C. integrifolia*

Clematis heracleifolia 'Robert Briden'

Clematis integrifolia

Clematis heracleifolia 'Côte d'Azur'

Clematis heracleifolia 'Wyevale Blue'

Clematis integrifolia seed heads

MORE →

Clematis integrifolia 'Alba'

Clematis integrifolia 'Rosea'

Clematis "mailboxensis"

tions, flowers go on to produce fluffy seed heads into the fall. Plants offering white ('Alba') and rose-colored ('Rosea') flowers are occasionally seen—they provide a nice splash of color, but I'll take the wonderful deep blue of the species any day. Full sun, zones 3 to 7.

Vining *Clematis* species and hybrids are everywhere—and with good reason. Where their roots are cool and their foliage is in sunshine, they can be as vigorous and colorful as any plant in the garden. The best support for many of the vines is through shrubs and trees, where they can climb to their heart's content and, in general, make any woody plant look better. In the Armitage garden, nary a shrub escapes from this twining nightmare.

The hybrids are most easily found, but let's not totally ignore the species. I love the tubular flowers of *Clematis texensis*, the Texas clematis, one of the best species for southern gardeners, replete with rose-red blossoms in the spring and summer and stunning fruit later on; 'Duchess of Albany', the most popular selection, has similar flowers but is even more vigorous. I plant the winter clematis, *C. cirrhosa*, for its combination of glossy evergreen leaves, small-flowering chalices, and cottony fruit. I have learned my lesson about planting the beautiful but self-seeding thug *C. terniflora* (*C. maximowicziana*; sweet autumn clematis): one needs to experiment with such explosive plants. After a few springs of removing seedlings from all over the place, I practice the creed of "rip out and replace" with this species.

Interspecific hybridization has re-

Clematis ×*jackmanii*

Clematis texensis seed heads

Clematis texensis 'Duchess of Albany'

sulted in a number of well-known hybrids that many gardeners prefer to the large-flowered hybrids. Most gardeners have heard of Jackman's clematis, *Clematis ×jackmanii*, which is as good as ever. When I can find *C. ×durandii*, with its deep blue leathery flowers, I jump at the opportunity.

But regardless of my obvious preference for more subtle forms, it is the large-flowered hybrids that attract the attention of most gardeners. With flowers 1–4" wide, and in sufficient colors for everyone, the 8–15' tall vines can cover trellises, holly bushes, clotheslines, and mailboxes with ease. I intensely dislike hybrids with double flowers, such as 'Duchess of Edinburgh' and 'Proteus' (I plant them in the Horticulture Gardens for others to see), but most others can be quite ornamental. The choice depends on color desired and the number of woody plants one can find to grow

Clematis cirrhosa

Clematis cirrhosa seed head

Clematis texensis 'Duchess of Albany'

Clematis cirrhosa in winter

Clematis ×durandii

Clematis terniflora

MORE →

Clematis terniflora

them over. So few shrubs, so many cultivars. 'Nellie Moser' is one of the most popular, available in almost any garden shop, but the hybrids also bring blues ('Elsa Spath', 'Madame Chalmondeley', 'Pearl d'Azure'), pinks ('Pink Champagne'), whites ('Huldine', 'Miss Bateman'), and rose-colored flowers ('Madame Julie Correvon', 'Ville de Lyon'). They all have their moments, and these moments don't end with the flowers. The fuzzy fruit of the hybrids is highly ornamental and provides almost as much value as the flowers—a better reason than ever to buy a few more hollies and spireas and slap a few vines over them. Full sun, zones 3 to 8.

Clematis 'Duchess of Edinburgh'

Clematis 'Nellie Moser'

Clematis 'Huldine'

Clematis 'Proteus'

Clematis 'Elsa Spath'

Clematis 'Miss Bateman'

Clematis 'Madame Chalmondeley'

Clematis 'Ville de Lyon'

Clematis 'Pink Champagne'

Clematis 'Pearl d'Azure'

Hybrid *Clematis* seed heads

Clematis 'Madame Julie Correvon'

Colchicum autumnale with *Rudbeckia fulgida*

Colchicum autumnale

Colchicum

AUTUMN CROCUS

The autumn-flowering genus *Colchicum* is known as the autumn crocus, but unlike *Crocus*, its members have six stamens rather than three. The corms can be quite large (up to 4" long) and need to be planted as soon as they are received from the mail-order nursery. They are expensive, relative to many other bulbous plants, but once established, they provide exotic entertainment in the garden for many months. Many a head has been scratched in the spring when straplike leaves emerge, only to disappear in a few weeks. Then, in late summer and fall, the single or double flowers appear, only about 6" tall and in cloaks of pink and rose. Colorful though they are, they can also be unkempt and uncooperative. Albeit handsome, few flowers stand upright for any length of time, and a single rainfall can make them look like wet mangy dogs. Pink dogs, of all things.

Colchicum autumnale, *C. speciosum*, and *C. byzantinum* are the most common species, but most of the garden plants are hybrids. Although colchicums often disappoint gardeners by

Colchicum speciosum

Colchicum naturalized

having too rapid a flowering time in the fall and too short a life span, cultivars like 'Autumn Queen' and 'Waterlily' can be outstanding, particularly when planted with *Rudbeckia* and other fall flowerers. Plant in shady areas and in well-drained soils. Hardy in zones 4 to 7 (8 on the West Coast).

Colchicum byzantinum

Colchicum 'Autumn Queen'

Colchicum 'Waterlily' with *Rudbeckia hirta*

Coreopsis

No matter how hard we try to abuse this group of native plants, they seem to come back for more, in every box store, catalog, and garden center each spring. Along with shasta daisies and columbines, year after year, the genus *Coreopsis* remains one of the top ten perennials sold. The bright yellow flowers of most of its members, along with its willingness to put up with most any garden soil, have made it a favorite. That it is easy for producers to grow, looks good in a container, and appears in every gas station from coast to coast also tends to keep it around. Indeed coreopsis is common, but don't expect all plants that carry the coreopsis label to perform equally well.

One of my favorites is *Coreopsis auriculata* 'Nana', a 12–15" tall selection known as mouse-ear coreopsis. Tough and well behaved, it explodes with bright yellow flowers in early spring. Its small size is made up for by the intense color of the 2" wide blooms. The leaves are spoon-shaped—somewhat like a mouse's ear, I am told. It is a lovely plant in the front of the garden or in a container, and it looks particularly good with concrete frogs. Not long-lasting, perhaps three years if drainage is good, but most coreopsis are similarly disposed: good drainage is a must. Full sun, zones 4 to 9.

One of the mainstays of the beginning gardener and landscaper looking for something bright and easy to grow is *Coreopsis grandiflora*, common coreopsis. In full sun, plants can be spectacular for the first year or two, but by the third year they will usually need dividing or they crash on all sides. This is not a problem unless a person doesn't look forward to such fun. Which is most of us. The other chore

Coreopsis auriculata 'Nana'

Coreopsis auriculata 'Nana'

MORE →

in keeping these plants happy is to remove the dead flowers as soon as possible. The more seed produced, the shorter the useful life of the plant.

Numerous cultivars and hybrids have been selected—all yellow, all quite similar, all requiring removal of spent flowers to do their best. 'Early Sunrise' is relied on in the industry for its ease of production and propensity to stay in flower; plants are about 2' tall. 'Goldfink' bears 2" wide single flowers, and 'Sunray' provides double flowers; both are approximately 2' tall. A similar species, *Coreopsis lanceolata*, has been refined in such good cultivars as 'Brown Eyes', which plants are a little taller than the type but equally handsome. Full sun, good drainage, zones 4 to 9.

Yellow, yellow, yellow—is there any other color out there? With coreopsis, the answer—at least for northern gardeners—is yes, in the form of the pink-flowered *Coreopsis rosea*. More of a spreading plant than an upright grower, plants are only about 9–15" tall. Rose-pink flowers, three-quarters of an inch wide, cover the plants in the spring

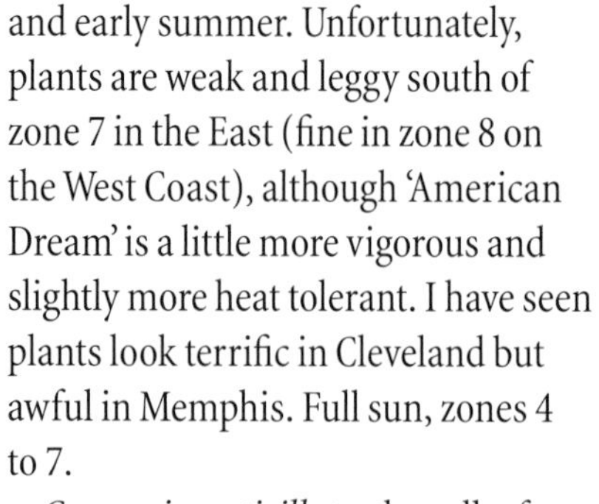

and early summer. Unfortunately, plants are weak and leggy south of zone 7 in the East (fine in zone 8 on the West Coast), although 'American Dream' is a little more vigorous and slightly more heat tolerant. I have seen plants look terrific in Cleveland but awful in Memphis. Full sun, zones 4 to 7.

Coreopsis verticillata, threadleaf coreopsis, is the tough guy of the group, providing classic yellow flowers, reasonably strong stems, and persistence of flower and plant in the sunny garden. The leaves are cut into "Edward Scissorhands" leaflets, and plants are almost as good-looking in

Coreopsis grandiflora 'Sunray'

Coreopsis grandiflora

Coreopsis grandiflora 'Sunray'

Coreopsis rosea

Coreopsis grandiflora 'Early Sunrise'

Coreopsis lanceolata 'Brown Eyes'

leaf as in flower. One of the brightest of the available cultivars is the large-flowered 'Golden Showers', but the best-performing selection is 'Zagreb', a 15–18" tough guy with golden yellow flowers. 'Zagreb' may be as good as it gets, but 'Moonbeam' is as popular as it gets. The number-one seller in many areas of the country, its soft light yellow flower color goes well with most other flowers in the garden. Full sun, zones 5 to 9.

Coreopsis verticillata

Coreopsis verticillata 'Golden Showers'

Coreopsis rosea

Coreopsis verticillata 'Zagreb'

Coreopsis verticillata 'Zagreb'

Coreopsis verticillata 'Moonbeam' with *Salvia*

Coreopsis verticillata 'Moonbeam'

Corydalis

So many corydalis, so few known! This genus is as diverse as any, including plants with white, yellow, and blue flowers. They are mostly thought of as rock garden subjects, but some species are quite common in any garden, rock or otherwise. The ferny leaves, one of their more enchanting characteristics, are charming even when no flowers are present. All require excellent drainage (as in rock gardens) and prefer partial shade or morning sun.

Corydalis cheilanthifolia, ferny corydalis, is seldom seen in American gardens, but it just might be worth a try. Plants are large, relative to other species in the genus, growing up to 15" tall. The pinnately cut leaves resemble the lip fern (*Chelianthes*—thus its specific name) with many yellow flowers arising from the blue-gray rosette. I have had no success with this plant in the Armitage garden, but what else is new. Gardeners in the Midwest have been luckier than I. Partial shade, excellent drainage, and cool summers are recommended. Hardy in zones 3 to 6.

Corydalis flexuosa, blue corydalis, is an extraordinary plant, and where it is happy, on the West Coast or in the Midwest, it rates the inevitable oohs and aahs. But the Armitage garden is like hell on earth for this plant, where the oohs and aahs are replaced by "where did it go?" (The guy who tends the Armitage garden is like a starving man salivating about food he can never have but wanting it all the same.) The fernlike foliage is often smoky gray, and the flowers are blue to purple. I have seen it look particu-

Corydalis flexuosa 'Blue Panda'

Corydalis cheilanthifolia

Corydalis flexuosa 'Blue Panda'

Corydalis cheilanthifolia

Corydalis cheilanthifolia

Corydalis flexuosa 'China Blue'

larly handsome in containers, where soil conditions can be more easily controlled. Plants go summer dormant, faster in warm summers than cool, but reemerge the next spring (except in my garden).

Several similar cultivars are offered. 'Blue Panda', the most common, is a good selection, being bluer than 'China Blue' or 'Père David', with their smoky blue and lavender-blue flowers, respectively. Partial shade, excellent drainage, zones 5 to 7.

The easiest, brightest, and most vigorous of the corydalis for most gardeners—*Corydalis lutea*, yellow corydalis—can be found bounding and jumping from rock to rock in gardens in the Northeast, Midwest, and Northwest. Small, plentiful yellow flowers cover the ferny green foliage on 9–15" tall plants. The bounding and jumping is the result of the copious viable seed produced; it flies everywhere, and where it lands on receptive soil, more yellow corydalis will soon emerge. Slightly better in the North than South. 'Alba', a white variant of the species, is worth a try if you get tired of yellow. Partial shade, good drainage, zones 5 to 7.

Crocosmia

Excellent plants for an exotic look, crocosmias boast many 8–15" long straplike leaves and colorful lily-like flowers. Up to a hundred flowers occur on stems held well above the foliage. Crocosmias have made the transition from the bulbous world to the mainstream garden world. Cultivars may be found in bulb catalogs as well as general plant catalogs, which speaks highly of the widespread performance and popularity of this group of plants.

Recent breeding and building up of material means numerous cultivars are now offered, all hybrids involving *Crocosmia crocosmiiflora*. The most popular is 'Lucifer', whose scarlet-red flowers blaze through the summer; she

Corydalis lutea

Crocosmia 'Lucifer'

Corydalis lutea

Corydalis lutea 'Alba'

Crocosmia 'Bressingham Blaze'

MORE →

Crocosmia 'Lucifer'

Crocosmia 'Spitfire'

Crocosmia 'Rowallane Yellow'

Crocosmia 'Citronella'

has been fashionable for years and her intense color combined with her vigor and ease of cultivation will keep her near the top of the crocosmia list for years to come. 'Bressingham Blaze' and 'Spitfire' are known by their large orange-red flowers and vigorous habit; they light up the flowers around them. Some of the better, brighter choices occur in the yellows; I like 'Citronella' but I really fancy 'Rowallane Yellow', from Rowallane Garden in Northern Ireland. All crocosmias are terrific for cut flowers as well.

Full sun for all cultivars. Wet soils result in rotting roots; container planting is useful to improve drainage. Spider mites are a common problem, especially if plants are stressed. Hardy in zones 5 to 8.

Crocus

"Hey Doc, which way is up on this bulb, anyway?" So wondered one of my brighter students after first being introduced to forcing crocus in the greenhouse. I had obviously not taught him much, nor had I been successful in teaching him that the crocus was a corm, not a bulb. To this student and most gardeners, however—bulb, corm, rhizome . . . few really care. Planting crocus and other cormy things in the

Crocus chrysanthus 'Blue Pearl'

fall is part of the life cycle for all gardeners. It brings cool weather, dirty fingernails, and the anticipation of a new season, even before the old one has transpired. Crocus is one of those plants that everyone has heard of, but the marvelous diversity of the genus is little known.

The many cultivars of *Crocus chrysanthus*, golden crocus, provide a wide range of choices to gardeners who prefer a little subtlety in their crocus. They are lesser known and smaller than the common large-flowered selections of Dutch crocus, *C. vernus*, but equally colorful. If a dozen Dutch crocus are required to make a show, then plan on massing at least twenty-five corms of *C. chrysanthus* among the plants in your garden. Corms may produce more than one flower, but in the Armitage garden, I find that most cultivars are not as long-lived as *C. vernus* cultivars. Where they are comfortable, however, they naturalize well.

Crocus chrysanthus 'Blue Bird' and 'Blue Pearl' are among the most lovely blues on the market; 'Moonlight' and 'Advance' provide handsome bright yellow flowers; 'Cream Beauty' provides a soft white in the garden; and 'Gypsy Girl' and 'Lady Killer', despite their obnoxious names, are multicolored and beautiful when you get close to them (from a distance, they kind of fade into the early spring landscape). Plant in full sun, although deciduous shade is also appropriate, zones 4 to 7.

A crocus is a crocus is a crocus, so I don't want to get too carried away with the numerous species, many of which need a magnifying glass to determine the differences between them. It is fun, however, to have some fall-flowering things to balance all those fast-disappearing spring bloomers. *Crocus speciosus* blooms in late summer and fall; it needs to be placed in full sun, unlike its ephemeral spring colleagues, which can tolerate deciduous shade. Nor is it particularly long-lived, perhaps persisting for two to three years, although such general statements invariably get me into trouble with gardeners who have had them for decades. Put about a dozen in the ground as soon as you can get them from the mail-order bulb dealer (late summer) and enjoy the bloom, however fleeting.

The choice of *Crocus speciosus* cultivars is much more limited than for the spring crocuses. I have enjoyed the rich blues of 'Cassiope' and 'Conqueror', but 'Oxonian' and 'Albus'—with flowers in soft blue and white, respectively—are also worth a go. Full sun only, zones 5 to 7.

The large-flowering cultivars of *Crocus vernus* are the result of years of breeding, mostly accomplished in Holland. Corms produce many 2" long

Crocus chrysanthus 'Moonlight'

Crocus chrysanthus 'Advance'

Crocus chrysanthus 'Lady Killer'

Crocus chrysanthus 'Moonlight'

Crocus chrysanthus 'Cream Beauty'

Crocus speciosus 'Cassiope'

MORE →

Crocus speciosus 'Conqueror'

Crocus speciosus 'Oxonian'

Crocus vernus 'Jeanne d'Arc'

Crocus vernus 'Queen of the Blues'

flowers that open to 1–2" in width. These Dutch selections are the most vigorous and arguably the most persistent and useful for naturalization. Plant the nose about 2" below the surface in the fall, in groups of at least a dozen.

Generally, I favor single colors in the garden—the white of *Crocus vernus* 'Jeanne d'Arc' is outstanding—although I do love to plant the big yellow ('Yellow Mammoth', 'Yellow Bunch') and purple ones together. The striped blooms of 'Pickwick' catch the eye, and blues and purples may be found in 'Queen of the Blues' and 'Remembrance'. While I am not a big fan of mixed colors, I have been awed at naturalized areas of mixed crocus. Some people naturalize in lawns, but one must be a patient character. Naturalization in turf requires yearly replanting until a population is established, and you must wait while the foliage turns yellow and goes dormant before the area can be mowed. My wife

Crocus vernus naturalized

Crocus vernus naturalized

would go crazy looking at long grass and yellow leaves. Wouldn't work at our house, guaranteed!

Zones 3 to 8, full sun while the leaves are green. Deciduous shade is tolerable, as long as sufficient sun reaches the crocus leaves before the trees re-leaf.

Crocus vernus 'Remembrance'

Crocus vernus 'Pickwick'

Dahlia 'Royal Dahlietta Apricot'

Dahlia 'Parakeet'

Dahlia

If diversity of flower, form, and habit are criteria for special garden plants, then hybrid dahlias are indeed in that special category. These are plants to either love or dislike with passion (hate should be saved for plants that are more deserving). In some areas of the country, they are true no-brainer plants, the mainstays of the summer and fall garden; in others, they require the weekly maintenance chores of stalking, spraying, deadheading, and Japanese beetle–plucking. Yet their beauty is undeniable, and the diversity within the hybrids equals that of chrysanthemums or peonies. Offerings such as 'Coltness' Mix', 'Royal Dahlietta Apricot', and 'Single Salmon' are effective as low-growing bedding plants and beautiful to boot, while medium-sized cultivars like 'Scarlet

Dahlia 'Emory Paul'

Dahlia 'Coltness' Mix'

Dahlia 'Single Salmon'

Dahlia 'Scarlet Beauty'

MORE →

Dahlia 'Pink Michigan'

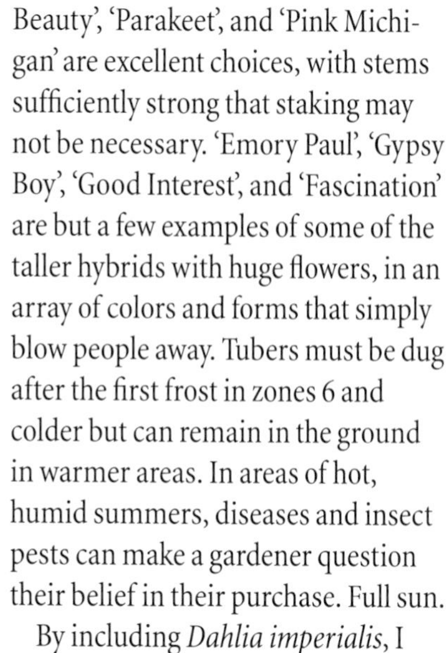

Beauty', 'Parakeet', and 'Pink Michigan' are excellent choices, with stems sufficiently strong that staking may not be necessary. 'Emory Paul', 'Gypsy Boy', 'Good Interest', and 'Fascination' are but a few examples of some of the taller hybrids with huge flowers, in an array of colors and forms that simply blow people away. Tubers must be dug after the first frost in zones 6 and colder but can remain in the ground in warmer areas. In areas of hot, humid summers, diseases and insect pests can make a gardener question their belief in their purchase. Full sun.

By including *Dahlia imperialis*, I

Dahlia 'Gypsy Boy'

Dahlia 'Good Interest'

Dahlia imperialis

Dahlia 'Fascination'

Dahlia imperialis

certainly am pushing the bubble to bursting: the tree dahlia is a plant that ninety-eight percent of gardeners in the United States cannot successfully grow, but let's pretend anyway. I first saw *D. imperialis* near Auckland, New Zealand, and therefore I resigned myself to the fact that it would seldom be seen over here. My next encounter was outside San José, Costa Rica, and at that time I decided that everyone should at least have a chance to see a photo of this magnificent plant, even if we can't grow it. Then I saw it used as an annual in gardens in California, where it cost the gardener about the same as a small car. The term "tree" is appropriate, as plants can reach 20' in height. The stems are woody and often tinged with a little red. The 2' long pinnately compound leaves are rather hairy above and have petioles about a foot long. Of course, foliage aside, it is the clusters of nodding pink flowers that keep people interested. Go for it, who needs another car anyway? Native to the Tropics, cold hardy to zone 9. Full sun.

Delphinium

My good friend Michael Dirr claims he never met a cheeseburger he didn't like. I have the same feeling about delphiniums, regardless of where I see them. I knew that plants in many colors, sizes, and flower types have been offered, but I never had the opportunity to see their forces aligned until I wandered into a cultivar trial at Wisley Gardens, England. It was almost enough to make me renew my vows to the Commonwealth and Queen. Unfortunately, we see about ten percent of the available taxa in the United States, but it is nice to know that interest in this Old World plant has not diminished. Delphiniums are also an outstanding cut flower and an important crop for the cut flower growers here and abroad. Cultivars such as *Delphinium* ×*belladonna* 'Volkerfrie-

Delphinium elatum hybrids on trial at Wisley

Delphinium ×*belladonna* 'Volkerfrieden'

Delphinium 'Barba Blue'

Delphinium 'Blue Bird'

MORE →

Delphinium 'Butterball'

den' and the *D. elatum* hybrid 'Barba Blue' have been selected for their cut flower attributes.

Delphiniums can be as beautiful in Atlanta as they are in Montreal, but the term "perennial" must be discarded if one is to grow them in the South. It is simply necessary to accept that delphiniums are annuals there (plant in October, enjoy in early spring, and pull out in June), and two- or three-year perennials elsewhere. In the South, plant at least a full one-gallon plant in October, otherwise insufficient rooting will occur by spring. In the North, plant either in the spring or in September.

A wide range of *Delphinium* species have been used in breeding; some of the more common hybrids, most often involving *Delphinium elatum*, are mixtures sold under the names of Round Table series, Mid Century hybrids, and Connecticut Yankee series. It is worth spending the time, however, trying to locate named cultivars in shades of deep blue ('Blue Bird', 'Molly Buchanan'), light blue ('Blue Dawn', 'Skyline'), lavender ('Ann Page', 'Blue Jade'), or yellow ('Butterball', 'Sun

Delphinium 'Blue Dawn'

Delphinium 'Blue Jade'

Delphinium 'Molly Buchanan'

Delphinium 'Skyline'

Delphinium 'Sun Gleam'

Gleam') for next spring's garden. Dwarf selections (*Delphinium grandiflorum* 'Tom Thumb') and those with outrageous scarlet flowers (*D. nudicaule*) are also great fun to try. All delphiniums, from dwarfs to six-footers, love cool summers and cold snow-covered winters for best perenniality.

The older cultivars are grown from seed and are tall and vigorous. With the many newer selections, there seems to be no end to the colors and sizes of this fine plant. Full sun, good drainage, zones 3 to 6 in the East, zone 8 on the West Coast.

Delphinium grandiflorum 'Tom Thumb'

Delphinium nudicaule

Dianthus

PINKS

I never realized that the plants I knew as dianthus were so closely linked to my wife's sewing hobby. Most of the pinks I had encountered were pink or red (a few were white), therefore the common name made perfect sense to me. I know very little about sewing, so when I learned that the common name had been granted because the petals of several species look like they were cut with pinking shears, I was cut down to size.

With about three hundred species of *Dianthus*, it should not come as any surprise that many people find a few of them better-than-average garden plants. By far the best-known member of this large genus is the carnation, *Dianthus caryophyllus*; millions of stems a year, of dozens of cultivars like 'Red Sims', are cut from farms in South America and shipped to your downtown florist. (They travel a long way to get to your table, so don't be too surprised if they are not as fresh as you would like.) But if you ask a hundred gardeners what their very favorite dianthus is, more than eighty of them would respond, without hesitation, "sweet William," *D. barbatus*. It's hard to understand how such a beautiful plant could be named after William, duke of Cumberland, best known for brutally crushing a handful of revolts against the English in the mid 1700s. "Sweet" is not exactly the name William would have chosen for himself. But these biennials have been around for a long time and will surely be popular for years to come. They are easy to identify by their unique flower buds and clusters of flowers in an array of colors. *Dianthus barbatus* blends like

Dianthus barbatus 'Indian Carpet' in bud

Dianthus barbatus 'Indian Carpet'

MORE →

Dianthus barbatus 'Messenger Mix'

'Messenger Mix' and 'Indian Carpet' are outstanding, and every now and then one can find a cute dwarf like 'Roundabout Picotee' to compare against cut flower selections such as 'Tall Cutting Mix'. Sweet Williams persist for only two years but occasionally reseed to provide some long-term guests. Provide full sun and well-drained soils. Hardy in zones 3 to 8.

The other plant that would come up in the aforementioned survey would be the maiden pinks, *Dianthus deltoides*, a much more perennial plant with hundreds of flowers over thin grasslike leaves. They initially flower in the spring, but if the flowers are removed when spent, blooms will continue into late spring and even early summer. 'Brilliant' and 'Red Maiden' are two fine selections with rose to red flowers, and 'Zing Rose' has deep scarlet flowers. All maiden pinks prefer full sun and hate wet soils. Hardy in zones 3 to 8.

Some of the most effective plants belong to the cheddar pinks, *Dianthus gratianopolitanus*. The cheddar pinks came from the Cheddar district of southern England, where the famous cheese is made in caves. An example is 'Bath's Pink', a wonderful pink-flowerer with blue-green foliage. In areas of mild winters, its leaves are evergreen and bring needed color to the winter scene. These pink cheese balls cover ground, hang over walls, and are almost indestructible; they flower their heads off in early spring, then simply look good the rest of the

Dianthus barbatus 'Roundabout

Dianthus deltoides 'Brilliant'

Dianthus deltoides 'Red Maiden'

Dianthus barbatus 'Tall Cutting Mix'

Dianthus deltoides 'Red Maiden'

Dianthus deltoides 'Zing Rose'

year. A similar and arguably better selection is 'Mountain Mist', with its pink flowers and even bluer leaves; it needs more cold than 'Bath's Pink' and won't flower in the deep South. Another fine plant is 'Firewitch', with rosy flowers over foliage more green than blue; it is much more rounded, not nearly as prostrate as the previous two cultivars, and also tends to flower on and off throughout the season, being one of the best return-flowerers in the genus.

The previous selections are terrific, but so are 'Tiny Rubies' and 'Baby Blanket', both of which offer deep pink

Dianthus gratianopolitanus 'Bath's Pink'

Dianthus caryophyllus 'Red Sims'

Dianthus gratianopolitanus 'Mountain Mist'

Dianthus gratianopolitanus 'Bath's Pink'

Dianthus gratianopolitanus 'Mountain Mist'

Dianthus gratianopolitanus 'Firewitch'

MORE →

double flowers topping out on 6–8" tall plants. Unlike 'Bath's Pink', they do not spread around at all but rather form small clumps. I can think of nothing better than eating cheese, drinking wine, and watching the cheddar pinks flower. Full sun is necessary. Hardy in zones 3 to 8.

Dianthus gratianopolitanus 'Tiny Rubies'

Dianthus gratianopolitanus 'Baby Blanket'

Dianthus gratianopolitanus 'Baby Blanket'

Dicentra

BLEEDING HEART

The genus *Dicentra* contains woodland, garden, and vining members, all shade tolerant, with flowers in shades of white, pink, red, or yellow—a popular old-fashioned group of plants that appeals to almost all gardeners.

Perhaps because our native fringed bleeding heart (*Dicentra eximia* in the East, *D. formosa* in the West) is a homeboy rather than a guest, people tend to consider it a little too common. Many novice gardeners look at it and don't see as romantic a plant as *D. spectabilis*, from Japan, but in fact, it offers the gardener a great deal more. First, our native species don't go summer dormant, and second, they offer much more diversity than the imports. If one visits the open glades of an eastern or western forest, fringed bleeding heart is likely much in evidence.

Green leaves with pink flowers are the norm, but breeders in Europe and the United States have provided us with leaves of green to bronze and flowers of white, purple, pink, and red; some may be selections of *Dicentra eximia* or *D. formosa*, or hybrids between the two species. 'Bacchanal' has deep rose flowers; 'Boothman's Vari-

Dicentra 'Bacchanal'

Dicentra 'Boothman's Variety'

Dicentra 'Luxuriant'

ety' and 'Luxuriant' are excellent plants with light rosy red flowers; and white flowers can be enjoyed on 'Langtrees' and 'Snowflakes'. Many other cultivars, equally handsome, are also available. Partial shade (that is to say, morning sun) is recommended, but too much shade results in few flowers. Hardy in zones 3 to 8.

Want a plant that stops people in their tracks? Try *Dicentra scandens*, a climber with hundreds of yellow lockets of flowers. They meander through shrubs or up a trellis, growing vigorously from dozens of twining stems. Plants grow about 10' tall, and starting in late spring or early summer, yellow flowers cover the vine. The leaves and flowers of this yellow climbing bleeding heart are much smaller than those of vines like *Clematis*, but the uniqueness and vigor of this plant will more than make up for the effort needed to find it. Plants require more sun than other species of bleeding heart; full afternoon sun should still be avoided. Hardy in zones 6 to 8.

Dicentra scandens 'Athens Yellow' came from seedlings of a plant brought to Athens, Georgia, from Ireland; it has brighter yellow flowers and is more vigorous than the type. Most plants sold are likely this cultivar.

Dicentra spectabilis, common bleeding heart, is a popular garden plant that undergoes a major metamorphosis each year, emerging early in the spring and going dormant in late summer. Gardeners sometimes wonder what they did wrong as they watch plants disappear between June and August, depending on summer temperatures and rainfall. This is a normal part of the growth cycle for this Japanese species. Annuals can be used to cover the soil left bare by plants that have died back. In early spring, plants push through the ground, their compound leaves and flowers already formed. They can make substantial specimens, growing 4' tall and equally wide on well established plantings. The pink to red lockets of flowers, whose hearts are no doubt bleeding, hang down from the flower stems in spring and persist for four to six weeks, depending on temperature.

Dicentra 'Langtrees'

Dicentra 'Snowflakes'

Dicentra scandens 'Athens Yellow'

Dicentra scandens 'Athens Yellow'

Dicentra spectabilis

MORE →

Dicentra spectabilis 'Alba'

The pink-flowered species itself is by far the most common. 'Alba', with its white rather than red hearts and slightly smaller plants, is different but no less beautiful. Place plants in friable, loose soil. Plants tolerate full sun in the North, but prefer afternoon shade in most other areas. The more sun, the more the soil dries out and the faster plants go dormant; on the other hand, too much shade results in few flowers. Hardy in zones 3 to 7.

Dicentra spectabilis

Dicentra spectabilis 'Alba'

Digitalis

FOXGLOVE

Best known for that wonderful old English weed, *Digitalis purpurea* (common foxglove), the genus includes some other outstanding members as well. All are characterized by many flowers held on long spike-like rods in spring or early summer, and slowly but surely, other lesser known members of the genus are strutting their stuff. All the same, at least ten times more *D. purpurea* is sold than all other foxgloves together, the result not only of its availability but also of its functionality and timeless beauty.

The "grandiflora" of *Digitalis grandiflora* (yellow foxglove) means "large-flowered"—a bit of a misnomer. Large they are compared to some foxgloves (such as *D. lutea*, another yellow-flowered species), but they are smaller than those of common foxglove and others. They do, however, have a couple of good characteristics going for them. First, the yellow flowers, with their brown spots within, are rather hand-

Digitalis grandiflora

some, and second, the plants are much more persistent than *D. purpurea* in the landscape. These true perennials should return for at least five years; eight- to ten- year stints are not uncommon. They grow 2–3' tall and tolerate partial shade and moist conditions. Hardy in zones 3 to 8.

The diversity of the genus *Digitalis* never ceases to amaze me, and when I first discovered strawberry foxglove, *Digitalis ×mertonensis*, I was charmed. The rosette of large leaves is darker green than common foxglove and far more ornamental. The large pink to rose-red flowers—like a ripening strawberry, not yet edible—are borne on one side of the flower stem only. Put about three plants together so that sufficient flowers are massed to catch the eye. These 2–3' tall hybrids persist for about two to three years, longer than *D. purpurea* but shorter lived than *D. grandiflora*. Place in partial shade and moist soils. Hardy in zones 3 to 8.

Most of the foxgloves we use in our gardens are native to the European continent and the United Kingdom. A native stand of *Digitalis purpurea*, common foxglove, in Ireland or Scotland is as breathtaking to the American traveler as our stands of asters are to the visiting European. As long as one remembers that *D. purpurea* is a biennial and needs to be purchased either as a one-year-old plant in the spring or planted in the fall to receive sufficient cold, then this species is a no-brainer. The need for a cold treatment is absolute, but since it is so popular, nobody seems to give it much thought. Plants may produce 4' long flower spikes in the spring in any number of colors. In flower, they are awesome, but leaves decline soon after, as

Digitalis grandiflora

Digitalis lutea

Digitalis lutea

Digitalis ×mertonensis in winter

Digitalis ×mertonensis

Digitalis ×mertonensis

MORE →

Wild stand of *Digitalis purpurea*

Digitalis purpurea with tulips

Digitalis purpurea 'Giant Shirley'

Digitalis purpurea 'Alba'

Digitalis purpurea 'Alba'

Digitalis purpurea 'Giant Shirley'

plants die back. In short, plant removal might as well be done sooner than later. All plants are raised from seed.

Separate colors of white, apricot, or yellow flowers can sometimes be found but most cultivars of *Digitalis purpurea* are available as a mixed bag of colors. Some of the best loved are the tall Excelsior Group, the shorter but equally brilliant Foxy Group, and 'Giant Shirley'. The admiration of these noble plants is shared by hundreds of gardeners and millions of bees, both of whom are ever present when the flowers open. While the pharmacological properties of common foxglove are well known, nobody but my hypochondriac friends tucks it in the garden for that reason. Place in partial shade; provide morning sun and moist organic soils. Hardy in zones 4 to 8.

Disporum

FAIRY BELLS

One of the many plants that separates a lover of gardening from a lover of garden design is fairy bells. *Disporum* consists of about fifteen species of shade tolerant woodland-residing plants, native to North America, China, and Japan. The plant I enjoy most is *Disporum sessile*, the Japanese sessile fairy bells. In particular, its yellow-flowered variety *flavum* ranks right up there in my great shade plant list, alongside some of the Jacks (*Arisaema*) and gingers (*Asarum*). In the spring, the plants—flowers already formed—rise up out of the ground with a mighty stretch, first unfurling their light green foliage, then showing off their butter-yellow flowers as they emerge from their leafy winter quarters. Sounds pretty impressive, until you realize I am referring to a plant that is only 2–3' tall and 12" wide. Many people who visit the Armitage garden quickly agree with me. Place three plants about 8" apart and you will be rewarded with a stunning sight. The flowers persist for many weeks, followed by round green fruit. Plant in

Emerging stems of *Disporum sessile* var. *flavum*

Disporum sessile var. *flavum*

Disporum sessile var. *flavum*

Disporum sessile 'Variegatum'

MORE →

partial shade; dense shade is tolerated but not appreciated. Avoid heavy clay soils. Hardy in zones 4 to 8.

'Variegatum', a selection of *Disporum sessile*, is not as tall or as vigorous, but its white-and-green variegated foliage is pleasing to the eye. Plants are more stoloniferous and thus spread around more easily than variety *flavum*, but they are only about 12" tall. The flowers tend to blend into the foliage because they too are variegated; the green fruit which follows continues to be ornamental. A fun plant—get down on your hands and knees to admire it fully. Partial to full shade, zones 4 to 8.

Disporum sessile 'Variegatum'

Fruit of *Disporum sessile* 'Variegatum'

Dryopteris

WOOD FERN

So much of the Armitage garden is in deep shade that at first I despaired of ever finding plants sufficiently tough for the area. I quickly realized, however, how lucky I was to have some dense shade because it allowed me to use all sorts of shade lovers, particularly the ferns. And in my research, I found that some of the wood ferns are among the toughest, adaptable, and versatile ferns available to the American grower.

Dryopteris erythrosora, autumn fern, has some excellent characteristics, including bronze to almost red new growth and an evergreen habit. They tolerate deep shade (where they can be united with other shade lovers like Solomon's seal, *Polygonatum*) but are also adaptable to areas of full morning sun. Plants can grow 2–3' tall and equally wide, making a significant impact in the shaded garden. The large fronds, up to 2' long and 10–12" wide, are the best part of the fern by far, emerging in the spring and tending to stay bronze throughout the summer, resulting in an subtle colorful look, and not just a filler for shade. One of the best selections from the stable of

Dryopteris erythrosora with *Polygonatum*

New growth of *Dryopteris erythrosora*

Dryopteris erythrosora

ferns available to gardeners. Plant in rich organic soils, zones 5 to 9.

Another outstanding tough fern is *Dryopteris filix-mas*, male fern. For years I have used male fern in the deepest shade and worst soil in the Armitage dungeon, and it is the one fern I can count on to return year after year, better than ever. For all its vigor, the planting remains in one spot and does not run all over the place. Nothing colorful, nothing flashy, just a good blue-collar plant. The several plants that have been selected by male fernites, such as 'Barnesii' and 'Polydactyla', generally differ in the shape of the pinnae (leaflets) and tips of the fronds. 'Cristata Martindale' is quite remarkable for a fern gone amok: plants have terminal crests, and the pinnae all curve toward the apex of the frond—it is distinctive and an eye-catcher. Shade, moisture, and reasonable soil help in the performance of the plant, but they are tolerant of drying out and poor soils. Hardy in zones 4 to 8.

Dryopteris marginalis, the marginal wood fern, is not as colorful as others but it is a hardy, useful plant for moderate to deep shade. The "marginal" part of its name comes from the arrangement of the spore cases on the margins of the undersides of the fronds. The fiddleheads (the unfolding fronds) are covered with a golden brown "fur," and the leathery fronds remain evergreen. Plants are about 2' tall and 2' wide. They are better ferns for the North than the South, preferring moist cool climes for best performance. Place in drifts of six to twelve plants in organically rich, moisture-retentive soils. Hardy in zones 4 to 7.

Dryopteris filix-mas

Dryopteris filix-mas 'Barnesii'

Dryopteris filix-mas 'Polydactyla'

Dryopteris filix-mas 'Cristata Martindale'

Underside of *Dryopteris marginalis*

Dryopteris marginalis

Echinacea

CONEFLOWER

"What can I put in the yard that even I can't kill?" I hear this a lot from husbands upon whom severe conjugal stress has been placed. Several correct answers present themselves, depending on the degree of stress or fright I see in the questioner's eyes. One is the coneflower, *Echinacea*, a group of plants for all gardeners, regardless of experience or ability. These purple, pink, and even yellow flowers from the great American midland are easy to recommend and almost indestructible.

Hardly one's idea of a full-size flower but certainly one that gets attention and a guaranteed second look is *Echinacea pallida*, the pale coneflower. The thin pale pink to purple ray flowers take a little getting used to; however, the combination of those flowers and the central disk is quite lovely. Deep green leaves are found at the base, and the flower stems rise to about 3' in height. Plants are not as popular or as persistent as their more famous cousin, *E. purpurea*, but they return for three to five years, asking little in the way of care. Plant in full sun, in almost any soil—include at least three plants, spaced a foot apart, to create a fuller looking group of flowers. Blooms occur in summer. Hardy in zones 4 to 8.

I first saw *Echinacea paradoxa*, yellow coneflower, in the great Missouri Botanical Garden, a must-see garden for anyone in the country. Plants look like common purple coneflower, although not as vigorous, but they have yellowish ray flowers rather than pale pink or purple ones. "This is a paradox," my guide said, and I nodded sagely—then quickly went to the library to look up the meaning of the word. Regardless of how much confusion this plant might elicit, it is handsome and well worth placing in a sunny area of the garden. Height is only 2–3', and the flowers range from light yellow to merest tinges of sunshine. Not as persistent as *E. purpurea*, but few plants are. Hardy in zones 4 to 7.

"Take your echinacea pill, dear" says my health-conscious wife as she presents me a tidy concoction of *Echinacea purpurea* (purple coneflower), ginkgo, and goldenseal to swallow. I no longer think of my stomach as a functioning organ of digestion but rather as my private botanical garden. On the other hand, after downing onion blossoms and ribs at the local restaurant, who am I to complain about healthy additives?

Medicinal uses aside, can you imagine Lewis and Clark first setting their eyes upon the majestic vistas of grasses and wildflowers and enormous populations of animal life in their journey across the American prairie? How I enjoy reading the accounts of their expedition! Even a trip to the great prairie garden at the Holden Arboretum outside Cleveland or to the natural Midwest area at the

Echinacea pallida

Echinacea paradoxa

Echinacea purpurea in a prairie

Chicago Botanical Garden fills me with joy and sadness—joy at the incredible diversity of plants that graced the land, mixed with sadness that so few of these areas exist any longer. I thank the visionary leaders of our arboreta and botanical gardens for preserving some of our natural history, and doing it so well.

This historical discourse does have a point, I think. One of the occupants of the great American prairie is *Echinacea purpurea*, the purple coneflower, which has made the transition to the backyard as well as any native plant and better than most. The ray flowers often droop downward off the black central cone, and plants rise in height from 3' in full sun to 4–5' in partial shade. They are best if planted in full sun in almost any soil. I love seeing them alone or together with lilies or loosestrife (*Lysimachia*).

Numerous selections of *Echinacea purpurea* have made for wider and more horizontally oriented ray flowers and various shades of purple. I don't believe that all these are a great deal better than what Lewis and Clark saw, but they are neater and fuller in flower than the original and so fit in better with current garden styles. Some of the purplish cultivars include 'Bright Star', with its rosier flowers; 'Bravado', with somewhat larger flowers; 'Magnus', in which the ray flowers are supposed to be more horizontal than

Echinacea purpurea 'Bright Star'

Echinacea purpurea 'Bravado'

Echinacea purpurea 'White Swan'

Echinacea purpurea 'White Lustre' with *Lilium*

Echinacea purpurea 'Magnus'

Echinacea purpurea 'Robert Bloom'

Echinacea purpurea 'White Lustre'

MORE →

those of the species; and 'Robert Bloom', with even larger flowers than most others. (In truth, if all purple cultivars were lined up, I doubt seriously whether one person in a hundred could tell you which cultivar was which; I would be in the group of ninety-nine, that is for sure.) White-flowered cultivars are shorter in habit but easier to mix and match in the garden. 'White Swan' and 'White Lustre', whose subtle differences are found in the color of the cone and orientation of the ray flowers, are both good. Full sun, zones 3 to 8.

Echinops ritro

GLOBE THISTLE

Blue flowers will always occupy an important place in gardens, perhaps because there never seems to be enough of them from which to choose. Provide a vigorous grower with interesting round blue flower heads, and a popular plant arises. I've always enjoyed *Echinops ritro* mixed in with other equally vigorous plants like the coneflowers and sea hollies. The flower heads and leaves are rather coarse and prickly to the touch, thus the common name. They make excellent cut flowers, fresh or dried, but picking them is not a lot of fun. Plants grow to 5' in height and 3–4' across. They attract swarms of bees, so check the flowers before you put your nose too close. They also attract aphids, which can disfigure both leaves and flowers.

A few selections are offered, but they are all similar to each other and if truth be told, similar to the species itself. 'Taplow Blue' is the main listing in catalogs and nurseries and grows 2–3' tall; 'Taplow Purple' is, well, a little more purple. 'Blue Cloud' has somewhat bluer flowers. Plant in full sun, in any reasonable garden soil, zones 3 to 7.

Echinops ritro

Echinops ritro 'Taplow Blue'

Echinops ritro 'Taplow Purple'

Echinops ritro 'Blue Cloud'

Aphid damage on *Echinops ritro*

Echinops ritro 'Taplow Blue'

Epimedium grandiflorum 'Rose Queen'

Epimedium grandiflorum 'Lilafee'

Epimedium

BARRENWORT

A wonderful genus of low growers for the woodland and shaded area of the garden. A few years ago, only two or three species were available but recent explorations in Japan and China and excellent breeding efforts have brought additional species and more interest to this fine group of plants. If you have shade, you should have epimediums.

Epimedium grandiflorum, longspur barrenwort, is easiest to find in nurseries and one of the finest species sold. The deciduous plants have the typical oblique leaves of the genus; the tough good-looking foliage makes them excellent as ground covers under trees and in woodland environments. The flowers are among the largest in the available barrenworts, sporting long spurs on pale pink flowers in early spring. The flowers, which often emerge before or at the same time as the foliage, persist for four to six weeks. While tolerant of deep shade, they perform better in an area with morning sun and afternoon shade. Similarly, provide moisture when needed, especially if plants are competing with tree roots. They are drought tolerant but not that tolerant.

'Rose Queen' is the most common cultivar of *Epimedium grandiflorum* offered, with outstanding rosy red flowers. The lilac flowers of 'Lilafee' are not quite as large, but they are outstanding when they stand above the foliage. Subspecies *koreanum* has long spurs, like 'Rose Queen', but its flowers are much less pink. Hardy in zones 5 to 8.

The small white flowers of Young's barrenwort, *Epimedium* ×*youngianum*, found in cultivars like its 'Niveum' and 'Milky Way', are the opposite of the splash and size of *E. grandiflorum*

Epimedium grandiflorum subsp. *koreanum*

Epimedium grandiflorum as a ground cover

MORE →

Epimedium ×*youngianum* 'Milky Way'

Epimedium ×*youngianum* 'Roseum'

Epimedium ×*youngianum* 'Niveum'

'Rose Queen'. The light rose flowers of *E.* ×*youngianum* 'Roseum' also have leaves with rosy red margins in the spring. Smaller in every respect than *E. grandiflorum*, but equally handsome and carefree.

I love *Epimedium* ×*rubrum*, red barrenwort, for a couple of reasons. In the Armitage potpourri I call a garden, the plants remain evergreen and are even reasonably handsome in the winter, not just plants with leaves that refuse to fall off. The new leaves, which emerge in early spring, are suffused with red, both around the margins and splotched on the bronzy leaf blades. The red flowers are not large, but they appear in numbers and persist as well as any other barrenwort. *Epimedium* ×*rubrum* is easy, undemanding, and colorful. For tolerance to shade, it has few equals. As with *E. grandiflorum*, providing an area of morning sun results in even better performance. Hardy in zones 5 to 8.

Let's face it. All barrenworts share many similarities: they are low growing, work well in the shade, and are seldom noticed by those admiring some noble beech or elegant elm. The comments that accompany the other barrenworts mentioned can be dittoed

Epimedium ×*youngianum* 'Niveum'

Epimedium ×*rubrum*

Epimedium ×*rubrum*

here for *Epimedium* ×*versicolor*, the bicolor barrenwort, but with a few exceptions. The flowers are the earliest to emerge, appearing before the foliage. The old leaves are also evergreen but should be removed as soon as you spy the first flower. They only detract from the wonderful yellow flowers, and additional foliage will appear to take the place of what you remove. An exceptionally good plant, tough as nails and reliable. Full to partial shade, moisture is appreciated. Hardy in zones 4 to 8.

Of the several selections of *Epimedium* ×*versicolor* offered, the main one is 'Sulphureum', with flowers ranging from soft yellow to almost butter-yellow. While we are talking about yellow-flowered epimediums, I cannot in all conscience omit one of the most vigorous and reliable of the worts, *E.* ×*perralchium* 'Frohnleiten', with its dark green leathery leaves and wonderful bright flowers. Not only is it outstanding when it is supposed to be, it is the best epimedium for winter foliage. A winner in all respects!

Epimedium ×*rubrum* in winter

Epimedium ×*rubrum*

Epimedium ×*versicolor* 'Sulphureum'

Epimedium ×*perralchium* 'Frohnleiten' in winter

Epimedium ×*versicolor* 'Sulphureum'

Epimedium ×*perralchium* 'Frohnleiten'

Epimedium ×*perralchium* 'Frohnleiten'

Eremurus aitchisonii

Eremurus aitchisonii

Eremurus

FOXTAIL LILY

Eremurus is not a plant for people checking out the petunias at K-Mart but rather a plant for the daring and curious. This most wonderful bulbous specimen is available mainly through mail-order catalogs and specialty nurseries. To see it is to become a believer, and viewing the tall stately candles of white, orange, yellow, and pastels is a great treat. Plants range 3–8' in height, poking through the soil in spring and reaching up and up to flower in late spring and summer. Like a grand fireworks show, the foxtail lilies rocket with momentary greatness, then totally disappear, nothing but an explosive memory. One doesn't usually think of light flowers as an exploding fireworks show, but when the creamy pink-white candles of *Eremurus aitchisonii* and the pure white missiles of *E. himalaicus* or pastels like the Highdown hybrids of *E.* ×*shelfordii* (*E.* ×*isabellinus*) are alight, you may change your definition of fireworks. The yellows of *E. stenophyllus* can easily be categorized as flaming. In most gardens, plants seldom return for more than a year or two, but if they are protected and luck is with you, a few more years of fireworks may be yours. Plant the tentacle-like rhizomes in a large hole, so that the tentacles are not cramped up. They must not be allowed to dry out before planting, and moisture is necessary after planting. Place other plants around them so once they disappear, they will not be missed. Enjoy the show. Full sun, hardy in zones 5 to 7.

Eremurus ×*shelfordii* Highdown hybrids

Eremurus himalaicus

Eryngium

SEA HOLLY

Live near the sea, plant sea oats. Or sea kale, or sea thrift, or simply enjoy the seaside with sea urchins. If you love the salt spray but don't live near the sea, importing sea holly from the Mediterranean coast to the suburban garden may help a little. A number of fine *Eryngium* species can be found, and while not all are even remotely native to a coastline, they are all colorful (usually silver or bluish) and interesting. Many make long-lasting cut flowers, but beware of the prickly blooms—they are much better to look at than to handle.

Some of the largest flowers and most colorful plants in the genus belong to *Eryngium alpinum*, the alpine sea holly. Certainly in northern climes, a blue tinge will appear on the stems and flowers of this species in mid to late summer, when the flowers are at their peak. Even when not at their peak, the immature flowers can be as handsome as the finished product. The plants grow about 2–2$^{1}/_{2}$' tall, and soft bracts extend from the flowers. Soft is relative, however, and even these bracts can provide some unwanted pain. The leaves are coarse and dull green.

Eryngium alpinum 'Amethyst', with lighter blue flowers and stems, is a popular cultivar; 'Blue Star' is probably the most common, with lavender-blue bracts. 'Superbum' has the largest flowers and is an excellent selection. Place in well-drained soils and full sun. Their maritime upbringing makes alpine sea hollies more comfortable in sand than clay. Hardy in zones 4 to 7.

Eryngium giganteum, or Miss Willmott's ghost, is the plant for people who have everything. Named for an eccentric English gardeness, it provides history, surprise, and ornamental value, with large flowers of steely silver rather than blue. These 3–4' tall

Immature flowers of *Eryngium alpinum*

Eryngium giganteum in a border

Eryngium alpinum

Eryngium alpinum 'Blue Star'

MORE →

biennials tend to disappear after flowering, but in areas where the Lady is happy, she will return from seed—if not the next year, then the year after, sneaking up on you like the ghost she is. Unfortunately, Miss Willmott's ghost is not happy in the South and is not often seen even in the East; but she haunts the Northwest with glee.

Eryngium giganteum 'Silver Ghost' is shorter (about 2' tall) and has large heads of gray-white flowers—not quite as ghostly but otherwise differing little from the species. Plant in well-drained soils, or sandy soils in full sun. Hardy in zones 4 to 8.

The genus *Eryngium* is remarkable in its ability to confuse gardeners with flowers and foliage that to most of us look like anything but sea holly. The eastern native *Eryngium yuccafolium*, rattlesnake master, supposedly cures rattlesnake bites or even drives the snakes away. My kind of plant in snake country. The leaves are narrow (like those of yucca), and the small flowers are creamy white and almost without bracts. Plants grow about 3–4' tall.

The foliage of *Eryngium agavifolium*, agave sea holly, looks like an agave and is similar to the rattlesnake tamer, only much more spiny. Both *E. agavifolium* and *E. yuccafolium* are heat tolerant and more amenable to poor soils than other more exotic species. The best part about them is that they are fun to have in the garden: they keep people guessing as to just what those plants want to be when they grow up. Full sun, reasonable soils. Both hardy in zones 5 to 9.

Eryngium giganteum

Eryngium giganteum 'Silver Ghost'

Eryngium agavifolium

Eryngium yuccafolium

Eryngium yuccafolium

Eupatorium

JOE-PYE WEED

To see some of our native plants glowing on their own and complementing other ornamentals makes you proud to be an American; too bad you often have to go overseas to appreciate the glow. This was brought home most clearly when I took a fall trip to the British Isles and admired the Joe-pye weeds towering over our asters and black-eyed Susans. I knew I would see asters and Susans, but I wasn't prepared for all the Joes. About half a dozen species are found in American gardens, and as a group they are attracting converts. Particularly good for the autumn, but some are impressive all season.

"Where did these fall-flowering ageratums come from? That is some bedding plant variety!" That was the first thing I thought when I came upon *Eupatorium coelestinum* (*Conoclinum coelestinum*; hardy ageratum) in a Midwest garden. Since I was supposed to be the expert, I kept quiet and listened as the real expert, the gardener, cursed this "darn weed." That is why experts are experts: they keep their mouths shut and learn from gardeners. The darn weed is pale blue to lavender and grows about 2–3' tall. The lanky growth makes it a little weedy, and more people enjoy it at the edge of the woods rather than in the middle of the garden. It is essentially unnoticed until the flowers appear in late summer and fall, and then it is everywhere. A terrific plant, much more tolerant of heat than most other members of the genus. A white selection, 'Album', is also available. 'Wayside' is a bit more compact and shorter, and does not appear to be as weedy as the species. Partial shade, good moisture. Hardy in zones 6 (perhaps 5) to 10.

Native in much of the eastern half of the country, *Eupatorium purpureum* (Joe-pye weed) is particularly impressive in the Smoky and Appalachian ranges. In the garden, where a little fertilizer and water are provided, I have seen 10' tall backdrops provided by half a dozen plants, each topped with large inflorescences of claret-colored flowers in the fall. They are best in areas with cool summers and consistent rainfall, so unfortunately, the Armitage garden in north Georgia can only offer some puny 3' tall excuses for the species. But when happy Joe-pyes are complementing the asters, the rudbeckias, and the daylilies in the fall, the yard is magically transformed into a garden. Butterflies, bees, and birds swarm about, and they look

Eupatorium purpureum with *Pennisetum*

MORE →

Eupatorium coelestinum

Eupatorium coelestinum 'Album'

Eupatorium coelestinum 'Wayside'

Eupatorium purpureum

Eupatorium purpureum

Eupatorium maculatum 'Gateway'

Eupatorium maculatum 'Gateway'

almost as good as they did when Joe Pye discovered them in the mountains.

Nurseries and catalogs offer similar plants, such as *Eupatorium maculatum*, spotted Joe-pye weed. The main difference is that *E. maculatum* has purple-spotted stems; otherwise, the habit and flowers of the two species are nearly the same. 'Atropurpureum', a purple-leaved selection, provides stunning purple hues from soil level to flower top. If the thought of 8' tall plants in the garden is a little overwhelming, *E. maculatum* 'Gateway', smaller but still a robust 4–5' tall, is otherwise similar to the type. Provide full sun and well-drained soils for both species, hardy in zones 4 to 7.

A fine native plant, *Eupatorium rugosum* (white snakeroot) is beginning to attract a loyal following among adventurous gardeners. Plants grow to 5' in height and are topped by white flowers in summer and early fall. I have seen excellent specimens in European and American gardens, but some of the best were in the outstanding display gardens at Blue Meadow Nursery in the Berkshires of western Massachusetts. Cold temperatures are no problem, but heat is not appreciated. A most useful cultivar, 'Chocolate', is admired more for its bronze to purple foliage than for its flowers. Plants are only 2' tall and are more shade tolerant than the species. White flowers also appear in late summer. Full sun and reasonable soils are needed. Hardy in zones 3 to 7.

Eupatorium rugosum

Eupatorium rugosum 'Chocolate'

Euphorbia characias subsp. *wulfenii*

Euphorbia

SPURGE

So many spurges, so little time! In a genus of nearly two thousand species, where does one start? A glance through some catalogs may get one off the starting block. I certainly have tried a good number, with occasional success, but have killed my fair share as well.

The handsome 4–5' tall upright plants of *Euphorbia characias*, Mediterranean spurge, have blue-green foliage and yellow bracts that are outstanding in early spring. That the species is native to the Mediterranean region should provide a hint as to its range of cold and moisture tolerance, but where winters are reasonably mild (zone 7 south) and soils not waterlogged, plants thrive and reseed with abandon. Although they persist for only two years, another population generally is starting up while others are dying down.

The most common variant, subspecies *wulfenii*, is shorter (3–4' tall) but otherwise quite similar. 'John Tomelson' bears showy bright yellow bracts, and 'Lambrook Gold' has

Euphorbia characias subsp. *wulfenii*

MORE →

Euphorbia characias 'John Tomelson'

Euphorbia characias 'Lambrook Gold'

bracts so yellow that one is advised to put on sunglasses before viewing them. 'Ember Queen', a variegated selection of the species, is simply a must-have plant. Full sun to partial shade, well-drained soils are essential. Hardy in zones 6 (perhaps 5) to 8.

A relative newcomer to the spurge scene, *Euphorbia dulcis* (chameleon spurge) is represented by the purple-leaved cultivar 'Chameleon', thus its common name. Growing in mounds rather than upright or spreading, it can be beautiful in combination with green or white plants around it. Unfortunately its range of adaptability is rather narrow: it looks poor where too warm and dies where too cold. Worth a try, however, if loose change is rattling around in your pocket. Full sun, reasonable soils, hardy in zones 5 to 7.

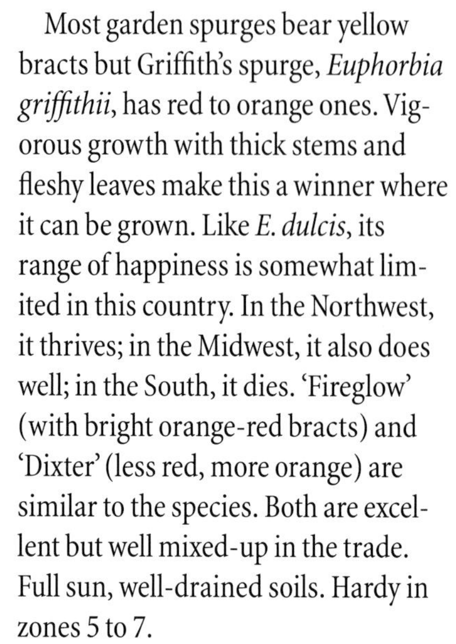

Most garden spurges bear yellow bracts but Griffith's spurge, *Euphorbia griffithii*, has red to orange ones. Vigorous growth with thick stems and fleshy leaves make this a winner where it can be grown. Like *E. dulcis*, its range of happiness is somewhat limited in this country. In the Northwest, it thrives; in the Midwest, it also does well; in the South, it dies. 'Fireglow' (with bright orange-red bracts) and 'Dixter' (less red, more orange) are similar to the species. Both are excellent but well mixed-up in the trade. Full sun, well-drained soils. Hardy in zones 5 to 7.

Euphorbia myrsinites, the myrtle spurge, is probably the most reliable of the ornamental spurges. The stems are covered in whorled blue-green leaves and terminate in sulfur-colored

Euphorbia characias 'Ember Queen'

Euphorbia dulcis 'Chameleon'

Euphorbia dulcis 'Chameleon'

Euphorbia griffithii 'Fireglow'

bracts. A great plant, but in areas of the Southeast and Southwest, where it reseeds with abandon, it may be considered both a handsome 6–9" ground cover or a pernicious weed. On the other end of the height spectrum is *E. lathyris*, caper spurge, a fun-to-grow plant with an upright habit, wonderful green flowers, and bluish fruit that resembles capers. Its reputation of discouraging gophers and voles is suspect, but it certainly attracts attention. Great fun! Full sun to partial shade, moist soils. Myrtle spurge is hardy in zones 5 to 9, caper spurge in zones 6 to 9.

Euphorbia myrsinites

Euphorbia myrsinites

Euphorbia lathyris

Euphorbia myrsinites

Euphorbia lathyris

Euphorbia griffithii 'Dixter'

Euphorbia lathyris

Gaillardia ×grandiflora

BLANKETFLOWER

Gaillardia ×grandiflora is one of those plants that doesn't get much respect even though it is tough, colorful, and easily available. Perhaps it is the lack of challenge that makes gardeners shrug their shoulders when asked about blanketflower. Like the good masochists we are, it may simply be too simple. Plants may grow up to 3' tall, but most available cultivars are shorter and more compact, usually extending only 12–18". The daisy flowers are made up of many colors (thus the "blanket" in blanketflower) and may be up to 2½" wide. The drawback to *G. ×grandiflora* is that it is not particularly long-lived: four years is an excellent run, two years is frustratingly normal.

A good many cultivars have been developed. Particularly popular are 'Goblin' and 'Golden Goblin', two dwarf selections. I think 'Goblin' is exceptional, but I have no use for the hideous double flowers of the Lollipop series. Flowers of *Gaillardia ×grandiflora* all have multicolored blooms consisting of crimson, yellow, and burgundy. Hardy in zones 2 to 9.

One of the parents of blanketflower is *Gaillardia pulchella*, an agreeable half-hardy (zone 8) species with multicolored flowers. Its selection 'Yellow Plumes' is a great improvement on the species. Full sun and well-drained soils are necessary. Good drainage is essential, otherwise plants rot overnight.

Gaillardia ×grandiflora 'Goblin'

Gaillardia ×grandiflora 'Goblin'

Gaillardia ×grandiflora 'Golden Goblin'

Gaillardia ×grandiflora Lollipop series

Gaillardia pulchella 'Yellow Plumes'

Gaura

The generic name comes from the Greek *gauros* ("superb"), a probable reference to the flowers of this genus, which consists of about twenty species; but only *Gaura lindheimeri*, our Texas native, has made its way into American gardens. The plants have become popular because they are tough as nails, putting up with blistering sun, terrible soils, and parking lot abuse. The foliage is handsome enough, although half a dozen plants are needed to make a full planting. It is, however, those superb white flowers suffused with pink that entrance gardeners. They are held well above the foliage and wave in the breeze like a swirl of butterflies.

An exciting addition is 'Siskiyou Pink', introduced by Baldassare Mineo of Siskiyou Rare Plant Nursery in Medford, Oregon. The pink to rosy red flowers of this selection make a handsome contrast to the leaves and remain colorful even during the heat of summer. 'Corrie's Gold' is a variegated cultivar with yellow-and-green foliage and white flowers. Full sun is necessary, otherwise no particular needs. Hardy in zones 5 to 8.

Gaura lindheimeri 'Siskiyou Pink'

Gaura lindheimeri 'Siskiyou Pink'

Gaura lindheimeri

Gaura lindheimeri

Geranium ×cantabrigiense 'Biokovo Karmina'

Geranium ×cantabrigiense 'Biokovo'

Geranium ×cantabrigiense 'Biokovo'

Geranium cinereum 'Ballerina'

Geranium

CRANESBILL

Geraniums are a collector's dream, so diverse that they can be collected like fine silver. From prostrate dwarfs to those that scramble through shrubs, from purple to rosy red flowers, geraniums provide something for everyone. As a gardener, I have gone through my "geranium stage of life" and no longer have to try every new (or old) geranium that finds its way into a catalog or the garden center. Now I can waste my money on other groups of plants, trying to find a single good one in a hundred tries. (Finding that one plant is the holy grail of the gardener—the ninety-nine others are quickly forgotten.) All geraniums have palmate (shaped like a hand) leaves, five-petaled flowers, and fruit reminiscent of a crane's bill, hence the common name.

A hybrid from England between the ground cover *Geranium macrorrhizum* and the European native *G. dalmaticum*, the Cambridge geranium (*Geranium ×cantabrigiense*) provides aggressive growth with handsome flowers. The purple-violet flowers persist longer than many species because little seed is produced, so the plants remain in flower for many weeks. Plants seldom grow taller than 12", 6–8" being more common.

Geranium ×cantabrigiense 'Biokovo', with white flowers tinged pink, is the best-known selection—an excellent cultivar that has done well in many parts of the country. 'Biokovo Karmina' bears raspberry-red flowers. Both are about 10" tall and bear little seed. Full sun to partial shade, hardy in zones 5 to 7.

Geranium cinereum, the grayleaf geranium, is the plant for rock gardeners or those who simply enjoy the more subtle aspects of plant composition. The small leaves of this species are gray-green, and the flowers may be rose-red or pink, usually with a fine pattern of colorful veins in the petals. Given their propensity to die in wet soils and hot weather, they should be placed in areas of exceptional drainage, that is to say rock gardens, where they will fare much better. I think 'Ballerina', with its lilac-pink flowers, and 'Splendens', with deep magenta, dark-centered blossoms, are outstanding. Both stand 4–6" tall and flower early in the spring. 'Laurence Flatman' is similar to 'Ballerina' and has deep venation to the pink flowers. Full sun, excellent drainage. Hardy in zones 5 to 7.

Without doubt, one of the best geraniums for both hot and cool climates is Endress's geranium, *Geranium endressii*. 'Wargrave Pink', the only selection offered, has enjoyed consistently good reviews throughout the country. Plants can grow up to 18" tall and are covered in spring by one-inch-wide, notch-petaled, salmon-pink flowers. One of my choices for the beginning geranium collector. Partial shade, good drainage, zones 4 to 7.

Geranium psilostemon, the Armenian geranium, is a plant that can't figure out whether it should be a vine or a normal plant—and therefore has become a scrambler. Its long stems, if properly maintained, form shrublike mounds of light green foliage, 3' tall and equally wide. Like a kid after a playground fight, each magenta flower sports a large black eye. This is a big

Geranium cinereum 'Splendens'

Geranium cinereum 'Laurence Flatman'

Geranium endressii 'Wargrave Pink'

Geranium endressii

Geranium endressii

MORE →

Geranium endressii 'Wargrave Pink'

Geranium psilostemon 'Bressingham Flair'

Geranium psilostemon

Geranium psilostemon

Geranium 'Ann Folkard' with *Alchemilla*

lanky plant, but if supported, it is a people stopper. 'Bressingham Flair' is similar but not quite as big and a little easier to use.

'Ann Folkard', a natural hybrid involving *Geranium psilostemon*, is a true scrambler, growing through and over small shrubs. The leaves are almost chartreuse, and the flowers have similar rose-red to magenta flowers. Where happy, 'Ann Folkard' takes the form of the plant it is growing through. It seems to be happiest on the West Coast, but gardeners in the Midwest and Northeast are claiming success. The South has not been as friendly. Full sun to partial shade, good drainage, zones 5 to 7.

Geranium sanguineum, bloody cranesbill, is the toughest species in the genus. Plants thrive in the North and the South, from the West Coast to the East. When other geraniums let you down, try the bloody cranesbill. The common name sounds like a medieval battle, and it alone makes plants worthy of a little space. Growing about 12" tall, they are covered with magenta flowers beginning in the spring and continuing for six to eight weeks. The leaves are among some of the smallest in this large genus. This cranesbill is not nearly as sexy as many others but makes up for it by its reliability. Selections 'Alan Bloom' and 'Cedric Morris' offer larger flowers than the species

Geranium 'Ann Folkard'

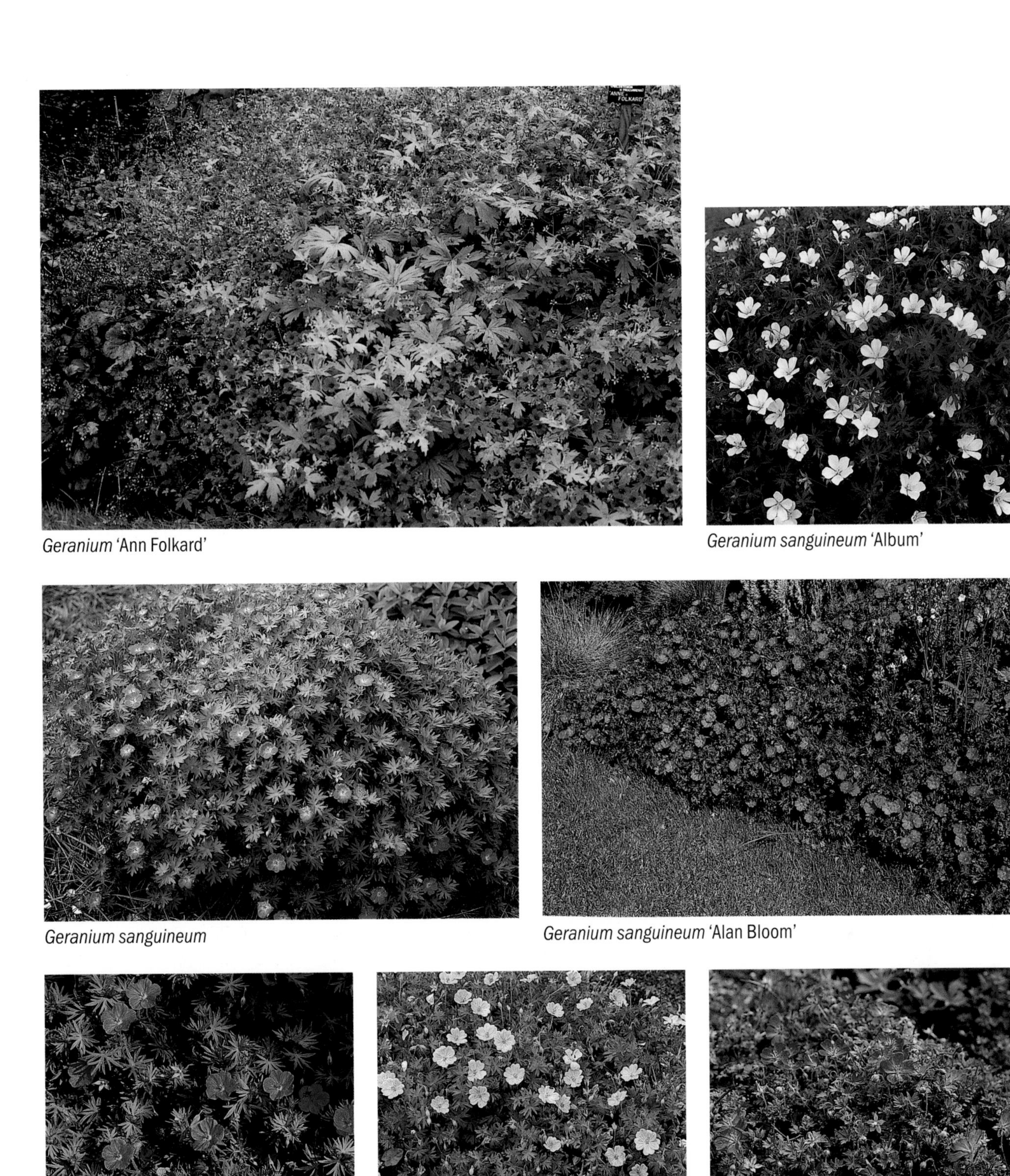

Geranium 'Ann Folkard'

Geranium sanguineum 'Album'

Geranium sanguineum

Geranium sanguineum 'Alan Bloom'

Geranium sanguineum 'Cedric Morris'

Geranium sanguineum 'Glenluce'

Geranium sanguineum 'Minutum'

MORE →

and excellent vigor; 'Minutum' is more dwarf and better suited to sunny rock garden situations.

For me, the magenta flowers of *Geranium sanguineum* are a little hard to take, therefore the white flowers of 'Album', the veined pink flowers of 'Striatum', and the lovely pink flowers of 'Glenluce' are among my favorites. Full sun, reasonable drainage. Hardy in zones 3 to 8.

Geranium sanguineum 'Striatum'

Geranium sanguineum 'Striatum'

Geum

AVENS

Indian chocolate, chocolate root, lion's-beard, old man's whiskers, grandfather's-beard, prairie smoke, cloveroot, and herb bennet are some of the more descriptive common names for members of the genus *Geum*, suggesting that some of them may be hallucinogenic. Regardless, they all beat the heck out of avens (whatever an avens is). At least fifty species of this venerable genus are known but only three or four are consistently offered. The most popular is the Chilean avens, *Geum chiloense*, which is colorful but overrated. A few other species, although more subtle, are outstanding plants for the appropriate situation; I enjoy the orange flowers and compact habit of *G. coccineum* 'Werner Arends', especially around *Hakonechloa* and other bright grasses.

Since the plants of *Geum chiloense* are so popular, they must be much better than most of the specimens I have seen. The main cultivars have been in commerce for many years and provide colorful flowers held high above the hairy compound leaves. The excesses of the American climate are tough on most of them, resulting in lots of leaves, few flowers, and short-lived plants. Better performance can be expected in areas of cool summers; the record for these plants is not so good in the heat and humidity of the South and lower Midwest. To be fair, they can look stunning in well-drained but consistently moist soils and cool climes.

Geum coccineum 'Werner Arends'

Geum chiloense 'Lady Stratheden'

Geum chiloense 'Fire Opal'

Geum chiloense 'Mrs. Bradshaw'

I have been more a critic than a fan of some of the *Geum chiloense* cultivars for many years. Many people love them, however. The most common selections are 'Lady Stratheden', an 18" plant with buttercup-yellow semi-double flowers, and 'Mrs. Bradshaw', with its scarlet semi-double blossoms. 'Fire Opal' is a brilliant scarlet. Full sun to partial shade, well-drained soils. Hardy in zones 4 to 7.

Geum rivale (Indian chocolate, water avens) is particularly suitable for gardeners who have a boggy area and like the taste of dilute chocolate—although I have a feeling that the chocolate part won't gain the plant many fans. (The thick, brown rootstock may be boiled in water, yielding a brownish liquid that tastes faintly like chocolate.) Regardless of its confectionary appeal, the plant is wonderful in a cool, moist, partially shaded area. The foliage has seven to thirteen leaflets, and the bell-shaped nodding flowers are usually reddish purple. Even the flower buds are ornamental. I like the white-flowered 'Album', but it is difficult to locate; 'Leonard's Variety' and 'Leonard's Double' are the most common taxa, bearing mahogany-red nodding flowers and deeply cut foliage, in single or double forms, respectively. Terrific in the Northeast and Northwest, but performs poorly in hot, humid summers. Consistent moisture is essential. Partial shade to full sun, hardy in zones 3 to 7.

Geum triflorum is a native American. Its common name, prairie smoke, is derived from the distinctive feathery fruit, which arises from drooping purplish red inflorescences, each made up of two to seven flowers. The 6" long leaves are softly hairy and consist of approximately thirty leaflets. Native to the prairies and the mountains of the West, this 9–12" tall species is icy cold hardy. The flowers of variety *campanu-*

Geum rivale

Geum chiloense 'Mrs. Bradshaw'

Geum rivale

Geum rivale 'Album'

Geum chiloense 'Mrs. Bradshaw' in winter

Geum rivale in bud

Geum rivale 'Leonard's Variety'

MORE →

latum, one of several natural varieties that occur, are more bell-shaped than those of the type. Full sun, consistent moisture, zones 2 to 7.

Geum triflorum

Geum triflorum var. *campanulatum*

Hakonechloa macra 'Aureola' with *Hosta*

Hakonechloa macra

HAKONE GRASS

What a terrific sight! *Hakonechloa macra* (rolls off the tongue, doesn't it?) is a shiny green-and-yellow dwarf grass from Japan that sparkles in the late afternoon sun, bringing alive whatever corner of the garden it calls home. It is only about 9–15" tall, consisting of layers of 4–6" long leaves. The fall flowers, while not colorful, are showy nevertheless; but it is this slow-growing grass's cascading habit, fresh look, and pinkish red fall color that give it its season-long appeal. One of the few colorful grasses at home in partial shade, it consorts freely with the likes of astilbes, hellebores, and hostas.

The golden variegated *Hakonechloa macra* 'Aureola' is particularly handsome, but 'Alboaurea', with white margins on its green leaves, is no slouch either. I like all the cultivars, in fact; I only wish they were a little quicker to grow and more tolerant of the abuse heaped upon them in the Armitage garden. Partial shade, consistent moisture, and compost-laden soils are best. Hardy in zones 6 to 8.

Hakonechloa macra 'Alboaurea'

Hakonechloa macra 'Alboaurea' in flower

Hakonechloa macra 'Aureola'

Helenium

SNEEZEWEED

Obviously someone with hayfever coined the common name for this North American genus. When I am snuffling and sneezing in the fall, I direct my sniffily wrath toward whatever is in flower at the time. Sneezeweed would make me sneeze, which I could verify if I stuck my nose in the middle of a flower, but at that time of year, sticking my nose in the middle of my Hannah dog's coat works just as well. Regardless of its name, *Helenium* offers some fine fall-flowering plants that are real color-makers at that time of year.

Although the genus consists of over thirty species, the cultivars associated with *Helenium autumnale*, common sneezeweed, provide the greatest color and diversity. Its selection 'Rubrum' provides hues in the burnt-orange curve of the rainbow, but it is the hybrids involving this and other species that are special. 'Brilliant' and 'Coppelia' offer additional burnt oranges and other fall tints, while 'Butterpat', 'Gartensonne', 'Riverton Beauty', 'Wyndley', and 'Zinnaeflora' have flowers in various shades of yellow to light orange. With heights approaching

Helenium 'Riverton Beauty'

Helenium 'Zinnaeflora'

Helenium autumnale 'Rubrum'

Helenium 'Gartensonne'

Helenium 'Butterpat'

Helenium 'Wyndley'

MORE →

3–5', the more vigorous cultivars often require staking to keep them from falling over in heavy weather. Cutting them back once during the summer makes them shorter and stronger. Full sun, well-drained soils are best. Hardy in zones 3 to 8.

Helenium 'Brilliant'

Helenium 'Coppelia'

Helianthus angustifolius

Helianthus

SUNFLOWER

A frequent trick question in trivia games: where does a Jerusalem artichoke come from? The surprising answer: from a sunflower. Gets them every time. Jerusalem artichoke, *Helianthus tuberosum*, is a perennial, but by far the best-known species in the genus is the annual sunflower, *H. annuus*, which Kansans adopted as their state flower. That state flower provides oil for cooks and seeds for birders but mainly contributes sunshine to gardens throughout the world. The perennial sunflowers for the garden are equally sunny and beautiful but not nearly as well known. All require full sun, and most are large.

Helianthus angustifolius, the swamp sunflower, is a big plant, growing 5–8' tall and lighting up the fall garden like a spotlight in the night. Plants produce dozens of 1–1½" wide flowers in September and October and continue to do so until frost. The 5–7" long narrow leaves are opposite, entire, and seldom troubled by bugs or fungi. Full sun is an absolute must, resulting in strong stems and many flowers. If grown in shade, plants will stretch to over 8' tall, then fall over. Not a pretty sight. The other drawback to the species is its aggressive nature: it will spread and may soon become a nightmare, a bright, happy-face nightmare, requiring fibbing to friends about why they should be thanking you for the basket of white roots you are a little too eagerly providing. Drainage is not as important as it is to many other perennials. Hardy in zones 6 (with protection) to 8, with reasonably rich soils.

Another large plant, not for the faint of heart, is *Helianthus giganteus* (giant sunflower), a seven-to-twelve-footer that seems to grow about a foot a day. It doesn't spread like *H. angustifolius*, but the clump gets bigger and bigger. The prettiest selection is 'Sheila's Sunshine', with primrose-yellow flowers. Great plant, but get the metal stakes out—it will topple like a pine tree in a storm if not supported. Hardy in zones 5 to 9.

Helianthus ×*multiflorus*, the "many-flowered" sunflower, is another excellent perennial—admittedly without

Helianthus angustifolius

the knockout power of *H. angustifolius* but also without its wandering ways. Flowers appear in summer and into the fall, held above dark green opposite foliage. Unfortunately, Japanese beetles, aphids, and other goodies feel comfortable on this plant. The 3" wide flowers are often double, yellow, and numerous. I enjoy 'Capenoch Star' and 'Morning Sun', both of which offer single yellow flowers; double and semi-double flowers shine on 'Corona Dorica' and 'Loddon Gold'. All are about 3–5' tall. Full sun and well-drained soils are necessary for best performance. Hardy in zones 4 to 8; disease and insect pressure are greater in the South.

Helianthus giganteus 'Sheila's Sunshine'

Helianthus ×multiflorus 'Capenoch Star'

Helianthus ×multiflorus 'Corona Dorica'

Helianthus ×multiflorus 'Morning Sun'

Helianthus ×multiflorus 'Loddon Gold'

Heliopsis helianthoides 'Goldgreenheart'

Heliopsis helianthoides 'Goldgreenheart'

Heliopsis helianthoides

SUNFLOWER HELIOPSIS

Like the late great John Denver said, "Sunshine on my shoulder makes me happy." So does sunshine in my garden, and I enjoy *Heliopsis helianthoides* for the sunny disposition it brings to the garden. Plants grow about 3' tall, and the dark green serrated leaves provide good value even when not in flower. The yellow to golden daisy flowers, 2–2½" wide, are produced at the end of every stem. The good part is their brightness and ease of culture. The bad part is that Japanese beetles, aphids, and other chewing things also enjoy that brightness; however, since gardeners like to share so much, we might as well share with the bugs as well.

Many of the selections of *Heliopsis helianthoides* are hybrids between the species and its variety *scabra*, which provides the coarse feel to the leaves.

Heliopsis helianthoides 'Incomparabilis'

Heliopsis helianthoides 'Summer Sun'

Heliopsis helianthoides 'Mars'

Heliopsis helianthoides 'Ballerina'

Heliopsis helianthoides 'Golden Plume'

The most popular is 'Summer Sun', a 2–3' tall plant with excellent credentials in the North and South. Many other single and semi-double flowerers, such as 'Ballerina' and 'Mars', look similar. My favorite is 'Goldgreenheart', whose green heart is surrounded by golden petals. A little gaudy, but we all need a little shtick. Doubles like 'Golden Plume' and 'Incomparabilis' are useful for those who prefer fuller flowers. Full sun, well-drained soils. Hardy in zones 3 to 9, but better in the North than the deep South.

Helleborus

HELLEBORE, FALSE ROSE

Flowering long before the calendar date of spring, the hellebores come in an assorted mix of flower color, leaf size, and vigor. Although two species dominate the scene, many other fine hellebores are available through specialty nurseries. They are evergreen and produce dozens of flowers with white, purple, or green sepals (their petals are actually inconspicuous nectaries). I couldn't imagine my garden without hellebores; they are as much a part of the coming of spring as the melting of snow.

We are starting to see *Helleborus foetidus* (bearsfoot hellebore), a recently awakened sleeper in the land of hellebores, throughout gardens and landscapes. The compound leaves, which consist of narrow fingerlike leaflets, provide some outstanding foliage, and the small greenish flowers provide a show from February to June. Even the fruit, which forms after flowers have lost their color, provides garden value into late spring or early summer. Planted with small-flowering

Helleborus foetidus

Helleborus foetidus

Helleborus orientalis

MORE →

daffodils, Virginia bluebells, and hepaticas, this hellebore is a no-brainer. 'Wesker Flisk', a selection of the species, has more of a red tint to many of the petioles and leaflets. Even its yellow-green flowers have a slight rouge appearance. Do not fret if you cannot find it, however, as it is not significantly different from the type. Provide afternoon shade and well-drained soils. Hardy in zones 5 to 9.

All the positive statements just made can be repeated in spades for the Lenten rose, *Helleborus orientalis*, the most popular of all false roses. The leaves are much bigger than *H. foetidus*, and the leaflets are not as fingerlike. The flower stems arise from the ground, forming many white, green, or mauve to purple flowers in late winter and early spring, and providing more flower power than *H. foetidus* but not as subtly. I can think of a few problems that beset the bearsfoot hellebore, but I am hard-pressed to come up with any for the Lenten rose. They persist for years, reseed easily, welcome spring even in the snow, remain in flower and fruit for months, and blend in to the rest of the landscape once their day in the sun is complete. No wonder the supply cannot keep up with demand.

New cultivars of *Helleborus orientalis* appear more and more frequently, but most are seed-propagated and offered as a mix or series. Among the finer selections are 'Dusk' and 'Dark Burgundy', which produce dark purple to almost black flowers; the Party Dress series has some of the most perfect double flowers in the genus. Partial shade and reasonably well-drained soils boost longevity and their ability

Helleborus foetidus 'Wesker Flisk'

Helleborus foetidus 'Wesker Flisk'

Foliage of *Helleborus foetidus* (left) and *H. orientalis*

Helleborus orientalis Party Dress series

Helleborus orientalis

Helleborus orientalis

Helleborus orientalis 'Dusk'

Helleborus niger

to produce seedlings. Hardy in zones 4 to 9.

The white flowers of *Helleborus niger*, the Christmas rose, provide a beautiful sharp contrast to the dark green foliage, making it the "cleanest" looking of the hellebores. More difficult to establish than the previous two species, it nevertheless thrives where conditions are to its liking. Unfortunately, those conditions are more demanding than needed for most other hellebores sold in the country. Try them in different moist, shady locations and leave them alone. Once established, they will reseed and the colony will be well on its way.

A few cultivars have been introduced, but the variations on the species are slight indeed, and *Helleborus niger* itself is equal to any of them. On the other hand, a few outstanding hybrids have been produced using Christmas rose as a parent. Although none are easy to find, that never stopped intrepid gardeners before. *Helleborus* ×*nigristern*, a handsome cross between *H. niger* and *H.* ×*sternii*, provides dark green foliage and a pink tinge to the flowers. The finest of all is the Blackthorn Group, which strain stops people in their tracks—an example of what can be achieved by dedicated hellebore breeders. Partial shade and well-drained soil with plenty of organic matter. Hardy in zones 3 to 8.

Helleborus niger

Helleborus ×*nigristern*

Helleborus Blackthorn Group

Hemerocallis

DAYLILY

All the world's a garden and all the players are daylilies. At least it seems that way. Wherever the sun shines, there resides another daylily. One daylily after another muscles into the gardens of America, each trying to outdo the other; each daylily breeder adds a little pinch of this or a big dollop of that. That daylilies are so popular obviously point to the obvious: they are colorful, available, and essentially trouble-free. They have been bred to within an inch of their lives, providing gardeners with a vast panorama of options: singles, doubles, rebloomers, dwarfs, giants, diploid, tetraploid—the beat goes on and the beat is good. In our pursuit of the next great daylily, however, do not trample upon some of the fine species that parented the hybrids. Species such as *Hemerocallis dumortieri* and *H. fulva*, with the brownish backs to their tepals, and *H. minor*, which helped tame the vigor of the hybrids, are still gardenworthy plants.

Hemerocallis fulva

MORE →

Hemerocallis dumortieri

Hemerocallis minor

Hemerocallis hybrids are categorized into various heights (dwarf, low, medium, and tall) and a dizzying array of flower shapes and colors. When I see dwarfs like 'Eenie Weenie' and 'Stella d'Oro', I am more impressed with the long flowering time than the compact habit. The classic selections of 'Hyperion' and 'Golden Chimes' provide tall, vigorous plants in shades of yellow, and another old-fashioned selection is still one of the best deep yellows of all, 'Mary Todd'. But that is just the beginning! I bounce from the pure white of 'Ice Carnival' to whites with yellow centers such as 'Gentle Shepherd' and 'Luminous Jewel', and then to bicolors like 'Pandora's Box' and 'Lady Diva', to reds ('Red Joy', 'Scarlet Tanager'), pinks ('Benchmark', 'China Bride'), pastels ('Tender Shepherd'), and even almost black ('Black Ruffles'). But before I crawl away, exhausted by this DNA tinkering, my eye spies even more unworldly shapes. I see the fringed tepals of 'Atlanta Irish Heart', the obnoxious double flowers of 'Heather Harrington', and the spidery tepals of hybrids like 'Kindly Light' and 'Red Rain'! I run for cover under a stately beech, panting in the shade of a classic, never-changing hardwood. (How did this beech get purple leaves?)

Hemerocallis 'Eeenie Weenie'

Abundant blooms are produced when daylilies are planted in soils

A hillside of *Hemerocallis*

amended with manure or leaf mold. When plants first emerge in the spring, provide a well-balanced fertilizer to give them a kick start. Plants are heavy feeders and require consistent moisture to be at their best. Of course, they don't appreciate boggy soils, and good drainage is important. So is full sun; too little sun results in few buds, and in some cultivars, buds may not open at all. In essence, when planning a site for your daylilies, choose an area of full sun, provide some fertilizer and moisture in a well-drained area, and get out of the way. Aphids can be a problem, but in general, choosing the right daylily is simply a matter of taste. Hardy in zones 3 to 9.

Hemerocallis 'Gentle Shepherd'

Hemerocallis 'Stella d'Oro'

Hemerocallis 'Hyperion'

Hemerocallis 'Luminous Jewel'

Hemerocallis 'Mary Todd'

Hemerocallis 'Ice Carnival'

Hemerocallis 'Pandora's Box'

Hemerocallis 'Golden Chimes'

Hemerocallis 'Lady Diva'

MORE →

Hemerocallis 'Red Joy'

Hemerocallis 'Black Ruffles'

Hemerocallis 'Scarlet Tanager'

Hemerocallis 'Tender Shepherd'

Hemerocallis 'Heather Harrington'

Hemerocallis 'Benchmark'

Hemerocallis 'Atlanta Irish Heart'

Hemerocallis 'Red Rain'

Hemerocallis 'China Bride'

Hemerocallis 'Kindly Light'

Hepatica

LIVERLEAF

I finally found a nursery that was propagating liverleaf, not just digging it out of the wild. I was ecstatic; I had studied up on this wonderful wildflower and had long lusted after our two wonderful eastern natives, *Hepatica acutiloba* and *H. americana*. My getting excited over diminutive hepaticas often causes eyes to glaze over, especially when I have to get down on all fours just to admire them. Even my dog has no respect; she walks over them and even lies down on top of them. Never growing more than 6" tall and as wide, liverleaf nonetheless can carpet a woodland area once established. Both species have small white or light blue flowers that are among the earliest to flower in the spring. In the Armitage garden, they emerge in late February and flower through April. They differ mainly in the shape of the three-lobed leaves: the lobes of *H. americana* are rounded, whereas those of *H. acutiloba* are pointed. Foliage is usually bronze to purple in the spring and green by and throughout summer. Most available plants are grown from seed, therefore leaves may be spotted or entirely green. Similarly, flower color ranges from deep blue to white.

Several non-native species have also generated a good deal of interest but are even more difficult to locate. *Hepatica nobilis* is native to northern Europe and is similar to *H. americana*. The plants have larger, bluer flowers, and selections of it have been offered

Hepatica americana

Hepatica americana

Hepatica acutiloba

Hepatica americana

Hepatica nobilis

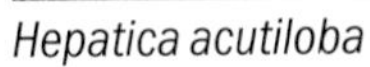

Hepatica acutiloba

Hepatica nobilis 'Light Blue'

Hepatica nobilis 'Rubra'

MORE →

with red ('Rubra') or light blue flowers. There is something fascinating about hepaticas with atypical flower colors; unfortunately, the effort to stabilize the colors of our native species has not received the same attention. If you can find *H. nobilis* or its selections and live in the North, go for it: they may be expensive, but if they live, they will have been worth every dollar. Similar wallet shedding should be done without a second thought if the blue-flowering *H. transsilvanica* comes up for sale; its numerous handsome large flowers occur in early spring. Outstanding and eye-popping.

Hepaticas are among the many ephemerals that grace our garden in early spring. They are best placed in deciduous shade (under oaks or beeches, for instance) where they can enjoy full sun while flowering, then disappear in the vegetation of later emerging shade plants once the canopy fills in. They enjoy the company of rue anemone (*Anemonella thalictroides*), Virginia bluebells, and trilliums. Hardy in zones 3 to 7.

Hepatica transsilvanica

Heuchera

CORAL BELLS

Every time I open a catalog, I see that someone has developed a new heuchera. If it is not the best coral bell ever, then it would never have been developed, or so the catalog says. But after reading a dozen catalog descriptions, it is apparent that some of them belong in the fiction section of the library. Coral bells are best known for the clusters of small coral bell-shaped flowers atop long stems. They have been around for many years, favorites of our grandmothers. But how many of these things do we really need? I

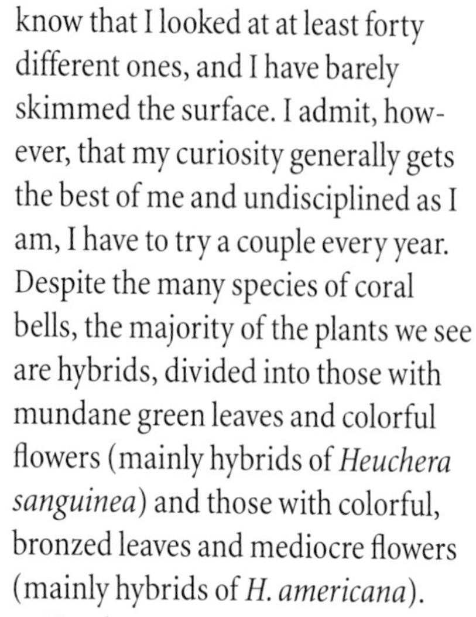

know that I looked at at least forty different ones, and I have barely skimmed the surface. I admit, however, that my curiosity generally gets the best of me and undisciplined as I am, I have to try a couple every year. Despite the many species of coral bells, the majority of the plants we see are hybrids, divided into those with mundane green leaves and colorful flowers (mainly hybrids of *Heuchera sanguinea*) and those with colorful, bronzed leaves and mediocre flowers (mainly hybrids of *H. americana*).

Heuchera americana, the American alumroot, is an excellent garden plant all by itself, reveling in rich soils and moist, shady spots. Growing to about

Heuchera americana

Heuchera americana with *Hosta*

12" tall when not in flower and up to 3' when the small greenish flowers appear, plants are always noticed by native plant enthusiasts but usually overlooked by everyday gardeners. The evergreen bronze leaves, which are often lined with darker veins, are always more colorful in the cooler months of early spring and fall. In areas of little snow, they even look good when cloaked in ice. They are outstanding in combination with other shade tolerant plants such as hostas; both genera have their moments of beauty and complement each other well.

Breeders have taken advantage of the vibrant leaves of *Heuchera americana* and other species with distinctive foliage, such as *H. micrantha*. With all the hybridization going on, however, we are getting closer to plants with the winning combination of good leaf and good flower. It was difficult to get too excited about the older hybrids, although several cultivars bred for their fine leaves, such as 'Dale's Selection', were immediately accepted by gardeners. Then along came the wonderful bronze-leaved 'Palace Purple', the finest bronze-leaf in its heyday and still an excellent plant; 'Palace Purple' fertilized the heuchera business and soon, like weeds after a rain, all sorts of new hybrids appeared.

A comparison of 'Palace Purple' with cultivars like the shiny dark 'Bressingham Bronze' shows some of the obvious leaf differences. As can be seen in the hybrid names, the breeders are as good at providing interesting names as they are in providing interesting plants. How can you resist 'Smokey Rose', 'Amethyst Mist', 'Chocolate Veil', 'Plum Pudding', 'Whirlwind', or 'Persian Carpet'—all almost as exciting as their names promise. As a group, the Veils ('Chocolate Veil', 'Pewter Veil') are excellent, and 'Whirlwind' has some of the finest foliage of any of them. In areas of little snow, plants like 'Pewter Veil' are nearly as good in the winter as they are in the

Leaves of *Heuchera* 'Palace Purple' (left) and 'Bressingham Bronze'

Heuchera 'Palace Purple'

Heuchera 'Smokey Rose'

Heuchera 'Dale's Selection'

Heuchera 'Amethyst Mist'

Heuchera 'Chocolate Veil'

MORE →

summer. Hard to ask for more. And yet even more choices for the gardener are in the offing, and it is unlikely that the throng will lessen in the coming years.

Plants do well in moist soils and partial shade. Although they will grow well in heavy shade, leaf colors are more vibrant with two to three hours

Heuchera 'Pewter Veil'

Heuchera 'Pewter Veil' in winter

Heuchera 'Bressingham Bronze'

Heuchera 'Whirlwind'

Heuchera 'Plum Pudding'

Heuchera 'Canyon Pink'

Heuchera 'Persian Carpet'

Heuchera 'Fireglow'

Heuchera 'Huntsman'

of direct sun. In general, the flowers of bronze-leaved plants are less exciting than other coral bells and should be removed when they emerge. They will not be missed, and the energy involved in seed production is redirected to foliage production. Plants are generally 2–3' tall and 2' wide, hardy in zones 4 to 9.

Heuchera sanguinea itself can be a little boring. No question that some fine cultivars involving this species are available, but there are now enough corals, reds, pinks, cherries, bicolors, and whites to fill most gardens in America, and it takes a confident fibber to distinguish one named introduction from another. But when they flower in the spring, several can be quite captivating. That I am not a big fan of coral bells does not mean I don't appreciate the rosy flowers of 'Canyon Pink', 'Fireglow', 'Huntsman', and 'Oakington Jewel', or the white blooms of 'June Bride' and 'White Cloud'. But the best of them all is 'Raspberry Regal', the tallest coral bell I have encountered in my trials, with strong stems terminating in dozens of raspberry-red flowers. It is terrific as a garden plant and equally good when the flower stems are cut and used as fillers for larger flowers. Full sun is just fine for this vigorous grower, but some shade is also tolerated. Many flowering coral bells persist only a few years, but 'Raspberry Regal' seems to return year after year. As much as I admire some of the flowering hybrids, I think variegated coral bells like 'Snowstorm' ought to be trashed. I am constantly told how wonderful they are. I don't listen. To each his own.

Plant in partial shade, or in an area with two to three hours of direct light. Consistent moisture is necessary for best flower production. Remove flower heads after blooms are finished to reduce seed production. Plants are about 3–5' tall, hardy in zones 3 to 8.

This brief discussion on *Heuchera* would not be complete without mention of *Heuchera villosa* (hairy alumroot), a little-used native of the southeastern United States. Both

Heuchera 'Oakington Jewel'

Heuchera 'Oakington Jewel'

Heuchera 'Raspberry Regal'

Heuchera 'June Bride'

Heuchera 'White Cloud'

MORE →

the heart-shaped leaves and the small white flowers are hairy, accounting for the common name. The purple-leaved 'Purpurea' is excellent, and one of the newest up-and-comers is 'Autumn Bride'. It has wonderfully wide (6") lime-green leaves, and the white flowers occur in the fall, not the spring as with most of its cousins. Another choice, for the undisciplined in us all. *Heuchera villosa* requires shade to thrive; too much sun results in a constant wilted look, and any stress to the plant can also cause spotting on the leaves or leaf margin burn. Doesn't sound quite as good as other species, but I still enjoy its fresh foliage and late-flowering tendencies. Plants grow 1–3' tall, hardy in zones 6 to 9.

Heuchera villosa 'Autumn Bride'

Heuchera villosa 'Purpurea'

Heuchera villosa 'Autumn Bride'

Hibiscus

MALLOW

These excellent perennials are thought of as plants for southern gardens, but they grow well into zone 5. The greenhouse hibiscus (*Hibiscus rosa-sinensis*), in all its many colors, is best known as a houseplant and conservatory specimen—probably the reason these plants are believed to have such poor cold hardiness. Garden hibiscus have also been selected in numerous colors and heights, and sufficient choice is available. For this fellow from Montreal, where hibiscus was something only seen in a botanical garden, and a novelty at that, being able to grow a couple outside is indeed a treat.

Hibiscus coccineus

Hibiscus coccineus

Hibiscus coccineus, swamp hibiscus, is a marvelous little-known plant whose 3" wide blood-red flowers are as colorful as any greenhouse hibiscus seen in florist shops. The many stout woody stems are clothed in dark green leaves, and their erect, stiff habit provides see-through architecture throughout the summer. The many narrow-petaled flowers occur at the top of the 5–6' stems in early summer and continue opening for about six weeks. The leaves are palmately compound and handsome in their own right. After a hard frost, the entire plant dies to the ground in the winter.

Plant in full sun, as shade retards growth and flowering. Constant moisture encourages the flowering and growth of this great plant, but plants grow just fine in normal garden soils. One does not require a swamp to be successful. Hardy in zones 7 to 10.

Hibiscus moscheutos, common rose mallow, is the hibiscus for the North, at least to zone 5, bringing the look of the Tropics to Baltimore and Chicago, with woody stems and many summer flowers. Patience is needed for the plants to emerge in the spring; they are often among the last to arise. Once they do, they produce many woody stems and grow 3–4' tall. Everyone loves the flowers, including a squadron of flying pests. In particular, hordes of Japanese beetles flock to its yummy leaves.

Many cultivars (likely hybrids of this species and two or three others) are available, representing nearly all the colors of the rainbow. Some of my favorites are 'Lord Baltimore' and 'Lady Baltimore', an older couple with red and pink flowers, respectively. Others, such as the wonderful pink-flowered 'Anne Arundel', are also handsome. Cultivars with the Disco name, such as 'Disco Belle' and 'Disco White', have enormous flowers (easily 8" across) and are also hardy as far north as Chicago (zone 5b). Garden hibiscus should be placed in full sun; shade results in lanky, tall plants. Most cultivars are hardy in zones 5 to 10.

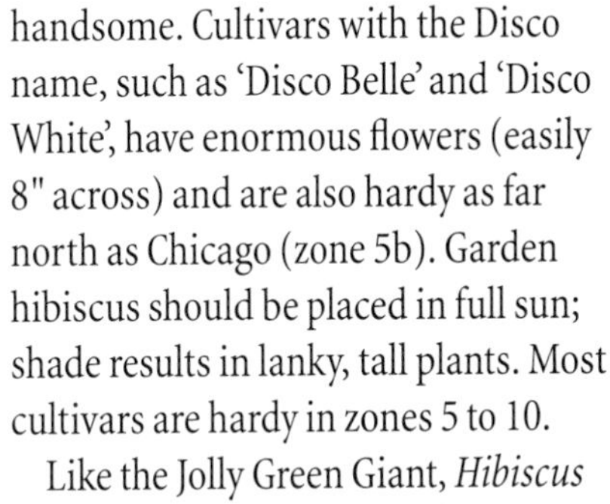

Like the Jolly Green Giant, *Hibiscus mutabilis* (Confederate rose) rises 8–10' in height in a single year and makes everyone smile. Plants produce multiple strong (an inch in diameter) woody stems with large velvety, lobed leaves. But it is the 2–3" wide flowers that provide the entertainment. They open in the fall, starting in early October and

Hibiscus 'Lord Baltimore'

Hibiscus 'Disco Belle'

Hibiscus 'Anne Arundel'

Hibiscus 'Disco White'

Hibiscus mutabilis

MORE →

Hibiscus mutabilis 'Flore Plena'

continuing for as long as two months, or until frost. In the species, the flowers open white or pink, then change to deeper red by the evening (the specific epithet, *mutabilis*, means "changing"). The most common selection is 'Flore Plena', with large double pink flowers; cultivars with red or rose flowers ('Raspberry Rose') can also be found. Place in full sun; partial shade results in even taller plants with a minimum of flowers. Hardy in zones 7 (occasionally 6) to 10.

Hibiscus mutabilis 'Flore Plena'

Hibiscus mutabilis 'Raspberry Rose'

Hosta

What does one do with shade? You can either curse your misfortune or celebrate your good luck. If shade is attributable to the presence of mature hardwoods or conifers, then feel blessed not to have your house in a clear-cut subdivision. If however the shade is cast by a Joe Camel billboard or something equally obnoxious, get rid of whatever stands between you and the sun. Simple Armitage rule of thumb: trees stay, tree products go.

If daylilies are the kings of sun, hostas are the kings, queens, princes, and princesses of shade: they are enjoying an unprecedented period of popularity in American gardens. For some gardeners, they are a gift to brighten up the darkness here and there; for others, they are obsessions, collected like baseball cards, resulting in a crop rather than a garden. I really like hostas, and every now and then I must stop myself from buying the next chartreuse or variegated one, lest my shade become a hosta nursery. In the Armitage garden, however, I have the unwelcome help of deer, voles, bugs, and my Hannah dog, who joyfully chases squirrels indiscriminately. Hostas are noted for their foliage (and visits from Hannah and Bambi certainly result in notable foliage). The

Emerging leaves of a hosta

flowers, reminiscent of lilies, are handsome and quite useful as cut flowers. In fact, some of the most fragrant flowers belong to the fragrant hosta, *Hosta plantaginea*.

As the new leaves push from the soil and begin to unfurl, hosta time begins. Vistas of greens, whites, yellows, and blues appear before one's eyes, color to challenge any garden plant. Hostas differ in habit, and their mature size helps decide their use. Plants may be categorized as small (*Hosta venusta*), ground covers (*H.* 'Francee'), edging (*H.* 'Gold Edger'), background (*H.* 'Sun Power'), and specimen plant (*H. sieboldiana* 'Frances Williams', *H. fluctuans* 'Variegata'). Foliar choices are abundant: from species hostas to selections to hybrids with names like 'Red Neck Heaven' and 'Royal Standard', there is no lack of choice. From leaves that may be described as green (*H.* 'Invincible'), bluish (*H.* 'Blue Cadet'), and chartreuse (*H.* 'Sum and

Hosta 'Francee'

Hosta 'Sun Power'

Hosta venusta

Hosta 'Gold Edger'

Hosta fluctuans 'Variegata'

A vista of hostas

Hosta 'Red Neck Heaven'

MORE →

Hosta sieboldiana 'Frances Williams' in a border

Hosta 'Royal Standard'

Hosta 'Blue Cadet'

Hosta 'Invincible'

Hosta 'Sum and Substance'

Substance') to the variegations of white-and-green (*H.* 'Antioch'), yellow-and-green (*H.* 'Bright Lights', 'Spritzer'), and white-and-yellow (*H. montana* 'Aureomarginata'), the hosta collector is in his glory. The challenge offered by this plant is to choose one or two cultivars among the hundreds that bombard you each year.

Hosta 'Antioch'

Hosta 'Bright Lights'

Hosta 'Spritzer'

Although the number of cultivars and their population has risen astronomically, hostas are not trouble-free. They are attacked by insects, voles, moles, slugs, and deer. Nothing is more frustrating than watching a plant disappear because voles have eaten the roots or slugs have torn up the leaves, or walking out in the morning to discover a favorite hosta has been decimated by marauding deer. Such is life in the hosta world.

Plant hostas in partial shade; they tolerate more sun than most people believe. The further north one gardens, the more sun hostas can tolerate. Few do not benefit from some afternoon shade. Keep plants consistently moist or leaf margins become brown. Hardy in zones 3 to 8.

Hosta montana 'Aureomarginata'

Woolly aphid on a hosta bloom

Slug damage on a hosta

A hosta decimated by deer

Hypericum

SAINT JOHN'S WORT

Along with *Echinacea*, Saint John's wort is as often found in the medicine cabinet as in the garden. Its antidepressant properties have long been a part of herbal dosings in Europe, and our stressed-out society has also come to embrace *Hypericum* with a vengeance. The species that is helping to calm and placate is *Hypericum perforatum*, which is seldom grown as a garden plant; however, a number of others are widely planted for their large yellow flowers or ornamental fruit.

Hypericum androsaemum (tutsan) can be a terrific plant in zones 5 to 7 for its upright habit, small flowers, and

Hypericum androsaemum

Hypericum androsaemum

MORE →

Hypericum androsaemum

Hypericum androsaemum 'Albury Purple'

Hypericum androsaemum 'Variegatum'

Hypericum calycinum

Hypericum calycinum

ornamental fruit. They grow to about 3' in height and bear small bright yellow flowers, which are somewhat hidden by the foliage. The flowers are far less noticeable than those of most of its cousins, but the colorful fruit, a deep red, is used as a filler in upscale arrangements. The fruit-laden stem is so much in demand that plants are also grown commercially by cut flower growers throughout the world. Plants do poorly in the deep South but are a great addition in much of the rest of the country. An excellent selection for the garden is 'Albury Purple', which provides good purple foliage and interesting fruit on the same plant. 'Variegatum' has wishy-washy creamy white margins on the leaves, but the variegation is neither crisp nor clean, resulting in a plant that looks like it

Hypericum 'Hidcote'

Hypericum 'Hidcote'

isn't sure what it really wants to be. Plant in full sun to partial shade, zones 5 to 7.

The long stamens in the 2–3" wide flowers of *Hypericum calycinum* (Aaron's beard) look a lot like, well, long stamens, but perhaps Aaron's beard was unusually scraggly. In any case, the bright, beautiful flowers cover the plants in spring and early summer. They are best used as ground covers and can spread rapidly in areas of cool summers and mild winters. The glossy green leaves cover large berms and hillsides, making a splendid carpet. Plants in the South do not withstand the difficult summer heat and humidity and often look ragged by August, but they do return fresh in the spring.

A hybrid involving *Hypericum calycinum* arose at Hidcote Gardens in England and is appropriately known as *H.* 'Hidcote'. Each 2" wide yellow flower is sterile and persists for days on the 2–3' tall plants. Beautiful, but a little temperamental in much of this country. Plant in full sun to afternoon shade, hardy in zones 5 to 7.

Ipheion uniflorum 'Wisley Blue'

Ipheion uniflorum

SPRING STARFLOWER

Blooming their little heads off in early spring, a planting of a few dozen bulbs of *Ipheion uniflorum* today produces hundreds of bluish star-shaped flowers in February to March in a couple of years. The flowers, which are held on 4–6" stems, are slightly fragrant; however, the narrow grasslike, pale green leaves give off the scent of garlic when handled. It is this slightly unpleasant smell that limits more widespread use of this fine species. If you admire them with your eyes rather than your hands, I can think of no reason not to include a few of these inexpensive plants.

Most of what is offered through catalogs is *Ipheion uniflorum* itself, with light blue flowers; however, several selections of the species are available. The most common is the darker blue 'Wisley Blue', which is the best of the easy-to-find cultivars. 'Rolf Fiedler' has larger petals and clear blue flowers on 4" stems, but Rolf does not produce nearly as many flowers as the others. For a surprise, try the white 'Album'. Plant in full sun, zones 5 to 9.

Ipheion uniflorum

Ipheion uniflorum 'Rolf Fiedler'

Ipheion uniflorum (left), *I. uniflorum* 'Wisley Blue' (middle), and *I. uniflorum* 'Rolf Fiedler'

Iris danfordiae

Iris reticulata 'J. S. Dijt'

Iris xiphium hybrids

Iris

So many choices, such a small garden! The Armitage lament about so many wonderful perennials, but never more true than with this immense genus of ornamental plants. From America to Siberia, with stops in Europe, Japan, and China, no place, it appears, has failed to send us irises that have not been welcomed to our gardens with open arms. Most are grown from rhizomes or regular fibrous roots, but a few arise from bulbs or corms. The bulbous irises tend to be early-flowering and short (4–9"), while the bearded irises and other more common forms flower later and are more robust. From Brainerd, Minnesota, to Lafayette, Louisiana, there is an iris that wants to be there.

All the bulbous species (*Iris danfordiae, I. reticulata, I. xiphium*) and their cultivars tend to be early, short, and ephemeral. The Danford iris (*I. danfordiae*) is only about 4" tall, but its bright yellow flowers stand out at a time when few other plants are in flower. I love to plant them as an annual by my rocks by the pond, since they seldom come back after the first year. Combining them with *Chionodoxa*, *Pushkinia*, and other early bulbs makes the yellow flowers even brighter. Full sun to partial shade, hardy in zones 5 to 9.

The small bulbs of reticulated iris, *Iris reticulata*, belie the large flowers produced on the 4–6" plants. Occurring in various shades of purple and blue, the flared petals and small standards appear in February and March, before the short leaves expand. After flowering, the leaves shoot up to about 12" long. Some excellent selections of reticulated iris include 'Harmony', 'Cantab', and 'J. S. Dijt'. Individual bulbs may not persist more than about three years, although once established, some may continue to flower for four to five years. Full sun, hardy in zones 5 to 8.

The Dutch irises (hybrids involving *Iris xiphium*) send up their foliage early, but the 12–18" tall flower stems open later than the other bulbous species. In fact, this tall flower is a common and popular cut flower, often seen in your local florist or grocery store, and is excellent for cutting out of your own garden. The Dutch hybrids may be planted in the fall as far north as zone 6b, and persist for two to three years. Foliage appears in late winter or early spring, and flowers of white, blue, purple, and yellow provide rainbows of bloom—beautiful or gaudy,

Iris reticulata 'Harmony'

Iris reticulata 'Cantab'

depending on one's outlook. Cultivars include 'Blue Dream', with dark blue and yellow flowers; the lighter blue 'Ideal' (one of the best for cut flowers and also one of the easiest to obtain); and an outstanding white, 'White Wedgewood'. Full sun, hardy in zones 6b to 9.

If an award were presented to "most popular perennial with too many choices," the bearded iris would be the winner. The "bearded" part refers to the band of hairs on the falls (the drooping petals), and with all colors of the rainbow available and dwarf to tall cultivars for sale, the gardener is hard-pressed to know which one to choose. The leaves are about 2" wide and often tinged with blue. Depending on cultivar, flowers are produced as early as very early spring to mid summer. Although leaf diseases and insects are creating more problems in the bearded irises than in the Siberians or Japanese, bearded iris will no doubt continue to be popular, if only by virtue of sheer numbers available.

I was at the Royal Botanical Garden in Hamilton, Ontario, when the beardeds were doing their thing, and what a thing it was! That garden is well worth a visit any time, but the panorama of color during iris time is outstanding. Some of my favorite hybrids are 'All Aglow', 'Chensled', 'Cozy Calico', and 'Ecstatic Night', but 'Glittering Amber', 'Lynn Hall', and 'Wild Ginger' aren't half bad either. Full sun, hardy in zones 3 to 10.

The American gardener has lately embraced the flat-topped large-flowering *Iris ensata* (Japanese iris) and its

Cut stems of *Iris* 'Ideal'

Iris 'White Wedgewood'

Iris 'All Aglow'

Iris 'Chensled'

Iris 'Cozy Calico'

Iris 'Glittering Amber'

Iris 'Wild Ginger'

MORE →

hybrids with abandon: the popularity of Japanese irises has increased threefold in the 1990s. The flowers are among the biggest in the genus, and sufficient color choice exists for any combination. Large leaves and immense fruit are also characteristic of this fine group of iris. They tolerate swampy conditions, but normal garden soils are fine assuming they are irrigated in dry times.

The numerous Japanese introductions ('Aichi', 'Aka-fururin', 'Kigari Bi') sound like a cross between someone suffering from a bad cold and samurai battle cries; those bred by American hybridizers have more prosaic names. Japanese-American relations are always enhanced when consumers can choose among such diverse cultivars as 'Pink Frost', with its tinge of pink on creamy white flowers; 'Moonlight', whose purple and white petals always catch the eye; 'Regal', a deep lavender with white streaks on its falls; and

Iris 'Ecstatic Night'

Iris 'Lynn Hall'

Iris 'Pink Frost'

Japanese iris vista

'Rikki-Pikki', the cleanest white of all. Each brings the typical large flat shot of color on 3–4' tall stems. Full sun, hardy in zones 4 to 9.

Iris louisiana, the Louisiana iris, is making a good deal of noise in the iris world, no longer simply content to be an interesting group of plants from the bayous of Louisiana and the Gulf Coast. In fact, the Louisiana irises are actually a complex made up of about five species and the hybrids between them. Narrow leaves on 3–5' tall plants and smooth (not bearded) flowers with drooping standards (the upright petals) typify this group. They love water and require it in serious amounts; however, bayous are not necessary as long as irrigation can be applied. 'Sun Chaser' and 'Sun Fury' are hybrid crosses of such species as *I. fulva*, with its copper-colored flowers; the dixie iris, *I. hexagona*; and the red to purple flowers of *I. nelsonii*. They are all worth a try. Northern hardiness has not been established, but they are more cold tolerant than they are credited with being. Probably zones 4 to 9. Full sun and consistent moisture are recommended.

Their dozens of colors—all with clean, narrow dark green foliage—make the Siberians a favorite among iris lovers. The leaves are among the

Iris fulva

Iris hexagona

Iris 'Regal'

Iris nelsonii

Iris 'Moonlight'

Iris 'Rikki-Pikki'

Iris 'Butter and Sugar'

MORE →

Iris 'Sun Fury'

best in the iris family, seldom exhibiting disease or insect problems. But of course most gardeners don't purchase irises for their leaves, and choosing among flowers in hues of white, blue, lavender, and yellow should satisfy most of us. Plants grow 2–3' tall and quickly form significant colonies.

Of the many cultivars listed in catalogs, one of the most popular is 'Caesar's Brother', with dark velvet flowers; I also enjoy the whites found in 'Butter and Sugar' and 'White Swirl'. 'Pansy Purple', 'Llewelyn', and 'Sally Kerlin' bring blues and purples to the table, and 'Ruffled Velvet' is just as the name implies. Full sun translates into the most flowers per plant; plants grow well in areas of partial shade but produce few flowers. Hardy in zones 3 to 9.

Siberian iris at Longwood Gardens in Pennsylvania

Iris 'Pansy Purple'

Iris 'Ruffled Velvet'

Iris 'Llewelyn'

Iris tectorum, the Japanese roof iris, offers large flowers of purple or white on short (12–15" tall) plants, making this easy-to-grow roof iris a favorite for the front of the garden. The short raised bristles borne along the midrib of the falls help to identify this species as a member of the crested iris group. The small standards are the same color as the falls. The light green leaves are wider than most of the other irises in the garden, but because they are shorter, they don't take up as much room when flowering is complete. Plants move by above-ground rhizomes and can form a significant colony in two to three years.

The best cultivar of *Iris tectorum* is the white-flowering 'Album'. The yellow streak along the falls contrasts subtly yet effectively with the clean white of the rest of the flower. Variegated foliage and lavender-blue flowers can be found on 'Variegatum'. Partial shade and consistent moisture help performance. Hardy in zones 4 to 8.

Iris 'Sally Kerlin'

Iris tectorum

Iris 'White Swirl'

Iris tectorum 'Album'

Iris tectorum

Kalimeris

JAPANESE ASTER

With persistent double white flowers, cut leaves, and excellent weather tolerance, *Kalimeris pinnatifida*, the Japanese aster, is on the Armitage list of no-brainers for new gardeners. Other than its outstanding performance, I suppose there is nothing particularly remarkable about the plant. It consorts with all sorts of neighbors, including shade tolerant astilbes and sun loving verbena. The 1–2' tall plants start flowering in late spring or early summer and continue to do so until frost. A small piece obtained from a friend will fill out into a wide colony within a year or two.

Another species, *Kalimeris yomena*, is best known for its green-and-yellow selection, 'Variegata'. It is handsome, I suppose, but does not possess the outstanding performance of *K. pinnatifida*. Full sun to partial shade, zones 4 to 8.

Kalimeris pinnatifida

Kalimeris yomena 'Variegata'

Kirengeshoma palmata

YELLOW WAXBELLS

This unique species from Japan provides all sorts of subjects for lively conversation: leaves, flowers, fruit, and, not least, debate over how to pronounce the name of the genus. The

Kalimeris pinnatifida with *Verbena*

Kirengeshoma palmata

Kirengeshoma palmata

opposite palmately lobed leaves are light green, and the yellow drooping flowers are thick and waxy, thus the common name. The interest in the plant continues after flowering, with the appearance of fruit that might have been dreamed up by Stephen King: two to three pointed horns are borne on the inflated capsule. Plants are not the easiest to establish, needing protection from winds and an abundance of organic matter. Moist soils are recommended, but boggy conditions should be avoided. Place in partial shade, or at least shaded from afternoon sun; not recommended for the hot, humid summers of the South. Hardy in zones 5 to 7.

Kirengeshoma palmata

Fruit of *Kirengeshoma palmata*

Kniphofia

RED-HOT POKER

Ever wonder how the various vowels and consonants got together to make up a name like *Kniphofia*? It is one genus I consistently misspell, never remembering if it is "ph" or "f," and in what order. The name begins to make sense, however, when one learns that it was discovered by the German botanist, J. H. Kniphof. (I'm just glad my friend Billy Goidehlpht didn't discover any plants.) Red-hot pokers are so called because the tall spires of flowers are often scarlet or fire-engine red; however, yellows, greens, and pinks are also part of this plant's palette. The sword-shaped leaves form a large tuft of foliage, giving rise to the upwardly mobile spires in late spring or early summer. The most common species is the old-fashioned *Kniphofia uvaria*, whose many flowers still provide good value for the money. Often the flowers at the top are scarlet; the older ones at the bottom of the spike are chartreuse-green, providing a bicolor effect.

The assortment of colors offered to the public has exploded, and the gardener may now choose from selections of *Kniphofia uvaria* or hybrids involving several other species. The vigorous spires of 'Bressingham Comet' and the smaller spikes of 'Atlantia' are among

Kniphofia 'Bressingham Comet'

Kniphofia 'Shining Scepter'

Kniphofia 'Atlantia'

MORE →

my favorites in the red to scarlet range. I have recently become a convert from the red, hot part of the poker to the beauty of the yellow pokers. I love the bright yellows of the large fat pokers of 'Shining Scepter', the smaller 'Sally's Comet', and the classical shape of 'Sunningdale Yellow', which is outstanding even in containers. For a more subdued look, I add the softer yellow of 'Sulphur Gem'. Torn between the "red hot" colors and the yellows? How about burnt orange? 'Kingston Flame' (4–5' tall) and the luminous 'Catherine's Orange' (3' tall) both provide a good number of bright, eye-catching blooms. Full sun, zones 5 to 8.

Kniphofia 'Sally's Comet'

Lamium

DEAD NETTLE

The lamiums are closely related to the stinging nettles (*Urtica* spp., which are never forgotten by those who have meandered too close to them), but since lamiums lacks the stinging hairs, they were dubbed dead nettles. Low-growing plants for shade, lamiums provide variegation of foliage and reasonable flowers. Two main species are found in landscapes, and both are quite useful for specific uses.

Lamium galeobdolon (*Lamiastrum galeobdolon*; yellow archangel) is one of the finest species for deep, deep shade that I have come across. Its selection 'Variegatum' bears opposite green-and-silver leaves on square stems. Plants are only about 9" tall. The distance between the leaves is considerable, resulting in long stems that cover the ground like a speed skater. The variegated leaves combined with deep yellow flowers brighten up even the darkest location. This is the kind of aggressive plant I like: it takes over areas that no

Kniphofia 'Sulphur Gem'

Kniphofia 'Kingston Flame'

Lamium galeobdolon

Kniphofia 'Sunningdale Yellow'

Kniphofia 'Catherine's Orange'

other plant wants to battle. Several other cultivars have been selected, but for covering ground, 'Variegatum' is the best bet. The compact 'Herman's Pride' has more refined silver markings and the same bright yellow flowers; plants don't spread but rather form handsome clumps of colorful foliage. I have great fun growing yellow archangel in tubs, letting the plants boil over to start another drifting puddle of color at the base. Partial to deep shade, consistent moisture. Hardy in zones 4 to 8.

Many selections of *Lamium maculatum*, spotted nettle, are offered for sale to the American gardener, and while each claims to be better than the one before, they all do the same job: they slowly fill in with astonishing variability of leaf and flower, though they don't trip over themselves in their exuberance to do so. The 6–9" tall plants have opposite multicolored leaves and flowers in shades of pink, mauve, and white. Better in the North than the South, where the humidity often results in leaf spotting problems.

Some of the variation in the species can be seen in 'Chequers', a popular cultivar with green-and-white leaves and deep pink flowers. For mauve to pink flowers and bleached foliage, 'Beacon Silver' has proven tough and popular; the same foliage and white flowers may be found on the aggressive 'White Nancy'. Partial shade, zones 3 to 7.

Lamium maculatum 'Beacon Silver'

Lamium galeobdolon

Lamium maculatum 'White Nancy'

Lamium galeobdolon 'Herman's Pride'

Lamium maculatum 'Chequers'

Liatris borealis

Liatris scariosa 'White Spires'

Liatris

GAYFEATHER

The habit of flowering from the top down on erect spikes makes gayfeathers unique among garden plants. The 3–5' tall, mid to late summer spike of *Liatris spicata* consists of individual button-shaped, aster-like flowers, usually mauve in color but sometimes white or rosy red. There is not a lot of "body" to liatris, and the plant grows much like a lily, with thin grasslike leaves surrounding the central stem. Putting three to five plants together provides a more immediate picture than scattering them.

The commercial cut flower industry long ago discovered that liatris makes an excellent cut flower. Cut the stems when the flower is about a third of the way open and place immediately in a solution of floral preservative for many days of enjoyment. The gayfeathers are native to the midwestern United States and are particularly prevalent in the Great Plains and the Midwest; gardeners in these regions are advised to plant them and get out of the way.

Several other species are also available. I enjoy the full flowers of *Liatris scariosa* and particularly its white selection, 'White Spires'. The short *L. borealis* may not be very tall (approximately 1'), but it is an excellent performer; its opposite in size, *L. pycnostachya*, at 6' tall, is large enough to be used as a weapon. And for something quite un-liatris like, try *L. graminifolia*, whose grasslike leaves demand a double take.

All have their moments in the sun. but it is the common gayfeather, *Liatris spicata*, that is the most available and the most widely grown. Its white-flowered selection 'Floristan White' stands out well, and the slightly shorter, more compact 'Kobold' is also worth a spot in the garden. Full sun, zones 3 to 9.

Liatris graminifolia

Liatris spicata

Liatris spicata

Ligularia

Most species in the genus *Ligularia* work best in a large garden where the daring gardener has lots of room for experimentation. Ligularias take front stage with their large leaves and impressive yellow and orange flowers. They are all moisture lovers and in fact do best, under all circumstances, where water is readily and consistently available. If water is lacking, the plant that looks so plumb and beautiful in the cool morning air looks like a limp rag doll in the warm afternoon sun. I wouldn't plant any ligularia if I didn't have a wet space for it. Not all species are big, brash, and bold; some are rather common looking.

The large rounded dark green leaves of *Ligularia dentata*, bigleaf ligularia, make it a favorite, particularly on the edge of water features such as streams and ponds. The bright flowers are secondary in appeal; it is the attractive

Liatris spicata 'Kobold'

Ligularia dentata 'Desdemona'

Liatris spicata 'Floristan White'

Ligularia dentata 'Desdemona'

MORE →

Ligularia sibirica

foliage that is the charm. Provide consistent moisture and, if possible, keep out of the afternoon sun. It is almost impossible not to have the leaves wilt on warm days, even though the wilting does not seem to cause any permanent damage. Looks lousy, though. Slugs account for shot holes in the leaves, adding to the gardener's dismay. Several cultivars are sold, the best being 'Desdemona', although 'Othello' is similar. Whenever I go to a nursery, they look too similar, making me believe the original plants have since been mixed-up at the production level.

Ligularia stenocephala, narrow-spiked ligularia, offers a much different look: its leaves are triangular to heart-shaped, above which the long slender flower stalks arise. Dozens of small yellow flowers open along the 1–2' long raceme in late spring. An excellent architectural plant where abundant, consistent moisture levels can be maintained. Without consistent moisture, leaves look wilted much of the time.

The only selection of *Ligularia stenocephala* to be found in most nurseries is 'The Rocket', which hoists lemon-yellow flowers on 18–24" long stems. Absolutely outstanding plants where the environment consists of cool nights, warm days, and plenty of moisture. Not recommended for the South. Full sun to partial shade, zones 5 to 8.

Other interesting species of *Ligularia* include *Ligularia macrophylla*, with large, wide sword-like leaves like no other species, and *L. sibirica* (cold hardy to zone 3), with silver backs to its large round green leaves.

Ligularia stenocephala 'The Rocket'

Ligularia stenocephala 'The Rocket'

Ligularia macrophylla

Lilium

LILY

Trying to choose a few lilies is like trying to choose a few daffodils: with so many to choose from, where does one begin? That the choice is so difficult, however, is testament to the beauty and diversity of the genus *Lilium*. From little-known species to the dozens of hybrids, no gardener can complain about a lack of options. All prefer full sun and good soil drainage.

If I had to choose but five species to grow, I could probably get down to about seven or eight—and then pick the final five names out of a hat. I hope that I would choose the gold band lily, *Lilium auratum*, with its prominent gold bands down the length of each white petal. Other variants of this upright lily include the white-flowered 'Opala' and the larger-flowered variety *platyphyllum*. Hardy in zones 4 to 9. I think that if I could grow the Canada lily, *L. canadense*, I would have an entire garden full of them. The pendant golden flowers stop everybody in their tracks with their classic beauty. Unfortunately, they are difficult to find and do poorly in warm climates. Hardy in zones 3 to 7. Would I pick the orange, nodding flowers of *L. henryi*, Henry's lily? The scarred face (actually raised projections called papillae) and the reflexed petals of the flowers make an impressive picture. They tower to about 6' in height and return year after year. Hardy in zones 4 to 7. As I stuck my hand in the lily hat yet again, fingers crossed, I would hope to choose the fragrant, exotic regal lily, *L. regale*. On a still evening, nothing can match the sweet smell emanating from the regal lily in the garden. The buds are a soft wine color, and the flowers retain that hue on the outside of the petals but are beautifully white when they open. The combination of buds and flowers is indeed a wonderful picture.

Lilium auratum

Lilium auratum 'Opala'

Lilium auratum var. *platyphyllum*

Lilium canadense

MORE →

Lilium canadense

Lilium regale

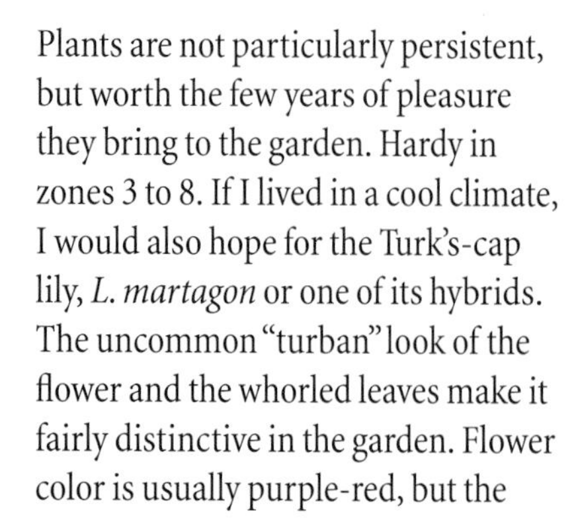

Plants are not particularly persistent, but worth the few years of pleasure they bring to the garden. Hardy in zones 3 to 8. If I lived in a cool climate, I would also hope for the Turk's-cap lily, *L. martagon* or one of its hybrids. The uncommon "turban" look of the flower and the whorled leaves make it fairly distinctive in the garden. Flower color is usually purple-red, but the

Lilium henryi

Lilium regale

Lilium henryi

Lilium martagon

Lilium martagon 'Album'

Lilium Backhouse hybrid

white 'Album' is especially handsome. Of the many hybrids involving *L. martagon*, the Backhouse hybrids are among the toughest, and handsome as well. Hardy in zones 3 to 7.

The number of Asiatic and Oriental hybrids now available to the gardener is mind-boggling. From large upright trumpet flowers to graceful nodding blooms, from ten-foot giants to two-foot pixies, the choices are seemingly endless. In general, the flowers and

Lilium 'Amourette'

Lilium 'Campfire'

Lilium 'Apollo'

Lilium 'Vivaldi'

Lilium 'Enchantment'

Lilium 'Dandy'

Lilium 'Acapulco'

Lilium 'Casa Blanca'

Lilium 'Imperial Gold'

MORE →

the leaves of the Oriental hybrids are larger and plants flower a little later than the Asiatics, but all are worth a try in the garden when the lily fever is upon you. A few of my favorites in the Asiatic group include the bronze-orange color found in 'Amourette'; the virgin white of 'Apollo'; the fiery orange of 'Campfire'; the subtle peach hues of 'Dandy'; the ever-popular 'Enchantment'; and 'Vivaldi', a warm yellow. In the Oriental group, I enjoy the red-pink 'Acapulco' and the white 'Casa Blanca' and have been impressed with 'Imperial Gold'. The soft color of 'Soft Moonbeam' and the short stature of 'Trance' have provided immense enjoyment in the Armitage garden, but my all-time favorite has to be 'Olivia', who returns year after year to lighten up the garden.

Linum

FLAX

Entire oceans of blue can be seen in European farmfields, where annual blue flax, *Linum usitatissimum*, is still grown for the fiber and linseed oil the plants yield, but only a few species of flax are used for gardens. One of the most handsome but seldom seen is yellow flax, *L. flavum* (zones 5 to 7),

Lilium 'Soft Moonbeam'

Linum flavum

Lilium 'Olivia'

Lilium 'Trance'

Linum perenne

with its 2" wide butter-yellow flowers. *Linum perenne*, the perennial flax, is the most common species and with good reason. The tough stems terminate in nodding flower buds, which then turn up to the viewer their beautiful blue hue. 'Album' is a good white selection. A good plant for edges; prefers partial shade in the South, full sun in the North. Great drainage is necessary. Hardy in zones 4 to 8.

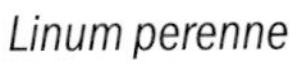

Linum perenne

Linum perenne 'Album'

Linum usitatissimum by the acre

Lobelia

Lobelia tupa

Lobelia ×speciosa 'Bee's Flame'

From brilliant reds to handsome blues and purples, lobelias can be impressive. Red is their classic color, found in *Lobelia cardinalis* (cardinal flower), *L. tupa*, and in the red and scarlet hybrids. A good deal of selection and breeding has produced garden choices, only a few of which are improvements on *L. cardinalis* itself.

Ask anyone about *Lobelia cardinalis*, and they will tell you about a beautiful plant, probably growing near some water, with brilliant red flowers. To see dozens growing together in a colony is to have an out-of-body experience. The lipped flowers are held on a long flower stem, and the hummingbirds and butterflies will love them as much as you. Provide full sun if sufficient moisture can be provided, partial shade if plants are growing in normal garden soils. Hardy in zones 2 to 9. Blood lobelia, *L. tupa*, has large matte-red flowers combined with handsome foliage. Plants prefer full sun to partial shade, zones 7 to 8. The hybrids, known as *L.* ×*speciosa*, include 'Bee's Flame', 'Compliment Scarlet', and 'Scarlet Fan'. All sport brilliant red to scarlet flowers on 3–4' tall plants. Cultural recommendations are similar to *L. cardinalis*. Hardy in zones 5 to 8.

Blue, lavender, and purple are also found in the genus. One common blue lobelia is known botanically as *Lobelia siphilitica* for its supposed efficacy in treating that disease. If the Latin label is difficult for bashful gardeners to ask for by name, they may simply inquire about big blue lobelia. Plants grow 2–3' tall, flower later than cardinal flower, and tolerate partial shade to full sun. Hardy in zones 4 to 8. Several hybrids bear lavender to purple flowers; the best known are other excellent hybrids of *L.* ×*speciosa*, such as 'Compliment Purple'. The least-known hybrid is probably *L.* ×*gerardii*, which has many lavender to purple flowers on unbranched stems; 'Vedrariensis' is similar to the hybrid but with dark green leaves tinged with red and dark violet flowers. Long-lived, good looking, and hardy in zones 4 to 8. Full sun to afternoon shade recommended; provide plenty of moisture.

Lobelia ×speciosa 'Compliment Scarlet'

Lobelia cardinalis

Lobelia siphilitica

Lobelia ×speciosa 'Compliment Purple'

Lobelia ×gerardii 'Vedrariensis'

Lunaria

MONEY PLANT, HONESTY

Lunaria annua is a most common biennial (a plant that takes two years to flower, then dies), with a a common name that refers to the silver-dollar shape of the fruit. The fruit turns translucent over time and may be dried for long-lasting indoor decorations. Where the plants do well, they are lovely, but they also seed every-

Lunaria annua fruit

Lunaria annua

Lunaria annua 'Alba'

MORE →

Lunaria annua 'Variegata'

Lunaria annua 'Variegata'

Lunaria rediviva

where, so that your small plot, conceived as a place to grow a plant or two for dried fruit, soon resembles the Franklin Mint. Their propensity for self sowing results in large colonies in the spring, but if most flowers are removed before the seed is released, the advance can be controlled. The common flower color is lavender, but 'Alba' is even prettier and reseeds true. 'Variegata', with variegated leaves and lavender flowers, is outstanding. Partial shade is best. Hardy in zones 4 to 8.

Another species of *Lunaria* is the shrubby money plant, *Lunaria rediviva*. Much more perennial than its biennial counterpart, *L. rediviva* has finely toothed leaves and fragrant flowers. Other than size, however, the most notable difference between the two species is the fruit. In *L. rediviva*, it is elliptical rather than round as in the more common *L. annua*. They are more difficult to grow, but certainly worth a try if you are already a fan of this genus. Provide partial shade to full sun, well-drained soils. Hardy in zones 4 to 8.

Lunaria rediviva

Lupinus

LUPINE, BLUEBONNET

Seldom is heard a discouraging word about lupines when one sees them in their flowering glory—they are that perfect. "Discouraged" is the word, however, for many gardeners who try to reproduce the Texas bluebonnets in their eastern yard or the English lupines in their Midwest garden. But even two or three fall-planted lupines are a source of sheer delight in the spring garden and can be enjoyed even though they don't look like the planting at Chatsworth in England. The genus is certainly variable; from the awesome light yellow flowers of the California tree lupine, *Lupinus arboreus*, to the blue-flowered northwesterner *L. polyphyllus* and its white-flowered cousin, 'Albus'. Throw in the roses of the annual Mexican lupine, *L. hartwegii*, and it becomes obvious that nature has provided a well-set table.

Of course, sitting at the head of the table are the hybrids, a potpourri of species first popularized by George

Lupinus 'Russell Hybrid Pink'

Russell, an English plantsman, who bred the famous Russell hybrids. Numerous crosses followed including the ivory flowers of 'Blushing Bride', the pink of 'Gina Lombaert', and the wonderful mixtures found in the Gallery hybrids. Additional cultivars are being offered more and more, but the Russells are still the most readily available and therefore continue to be the main game in town. Regardless of the lupine chosen, remember that they love cool weather, hate the combination of heat and humidity, and except for fortunate gardeners in the Northwest and perhaps the Northeast, they will not be as handsome the second or third year as they were the first. Many are easily grown from seed, and nurseries often carry substantial containers of well-grown plants that may be planted out in the fall. If you can find them, go for it. Plant in full sun, well-drained soils. Hardy in zones 3 to 7.

Lupinus arboreus

Lupinus 'Russell Hybrid Mix'

Lupinus 'Blushing Bride'

Lupinus 'Gina Lombaert'

Lupinus 'Gallery Mix'

Lychnis ×*arkwrightii* 'Vesuvius'

Lychnis flos-cuculi

Lychnis flos-cuculi 'Alba'

Lychnis

CAMPION

I was scratching my head the other day, wondering what in the world a name like campion has to do with anything. Except for one of my students, whose last name was Campion and who saw no problem with the name, the rest of us couldn't figure out why anybody would hang that moniker on a plant. Turns out some of these plants grew wild outside Roman stadiums, used for athletic events, like Christians vs. Lions, and garlands of them were used to crown the champion (usually a lion), hence the common name. Several fine annual species are offered, such as the little-known *Lychnis* ×*arkwrightii* (better known in the hybrid 'Vesuvius') and the wild, ragged *L. flos-cuculi*, ragged robin, and its white variant 'Alba'.

Without doubt, two species of *Lychnis* and their selections reign supreme in American gardens. A native of eastern Europe, *Lychnis chalcedonica*, the Maltese cross, has been a garden favorite for many years. Opposite leaves, swollen nodes, and the five-petaled flowers—with petals shaped like a cross—show its affiliation with the dianthus family, and indeed the

Lychnis chalcedonica

Lychnis chalcedonica

Lychnis chalcedonica 'Flore Plena'

genera are closely related. The common form and color of the flowers is single and scarlet, but double flowers ('Flore Plena'), rose-colored blooms ('Carnea'), and even flowers of puce ('Murky Puce'—now who would name anything "murky puce"?) are occasionally seen. New hues for an old-fashioned plant. Full sun, decent soils, zones 3 to 7.

The other reigning species is the short-lived but explosive *Lychnis coronaria*, rose campion, characterized by magenta to rosy red flowers and gray woolly leaves. It reseeds itself with abandon: individual plants may disappear, but in general, gardeners will find this plant returning year after year. The species has gaudy purple flowers, but several hybrids, in particular 'Abbotsford Rose', subdue the magenta and replace it with bright rose. For more conservative gardeners, a white selection ('Alba') and a bicolor ('Angel Blush') help to make the garden an even more pleasant place for champions. Full sun to afternoon shade, zones 4 to 7.

Lycoris

RESURRECTION FLOWER

Oh, that the fine genus *Lycoris* would have a little more tolerance to cold: its members may presently be enjoyed only by those who garden south of zone 6, although one species goes into zone 5. The foliage of the plants, known as resurrection flowers, emerges in the late winter and spring, then goes dormant in the summer, leaving nothing but bare ground and despondent gardeners, sure that their plants have died. Like magic, however, in late summer and fall, naked stems emerge, as if resurrected, topped with brilliant amaryllis flowers. The stems have given rise to another common name, naked ladies, and some gleeful gardeners like to plant them with *Or-*

Lycoris albiflora

Lychnis chalcedonica 'Carnea'

Lychnis coronaria 'Abbotsford Rose'

Lychnis coronaria 'Alba'

Lychnis coronaria 'Angel Blush'

Lychnis coronaria 'Angel Blush'

MORE →

Lycoris aurea

Lycoris radiata in bud

nithogalum umbellatum—which enjoys many common names. Who says creativity is dead in America?

Brilliant flowers of white (*Lycoris albiflora*) and yellow (*L. aurea*) can occasionally be found, but the large mauve flowers of *L. squamigera* and the fire-engine red of *L. radiata* are the most common. The latter two can multiply rapidly, and passing bulbs

Lycoris squamigera

Lycoris radiata

across the fence is a common occurrence. *Lycoris squamigera* is hardy to zone 6, the others to zones 7 or 8. Full sun to partial shade. All are outstanding.

Lysimachia

LOOSESTRIFE

At last a genus for people who don't want challenges and who enjoy the prospect of plants that live. Loosestrifes are the worst of thugs to the best of plants, and they all bring beauty, character, and the chance of allowing you to shower your neighbors with plants they will have forever. The usual flower color is yellow, but white is common with several species as well. When you plant *Lysimachia*, you are planting the future. Line up your friends now.

An aggressive member of the clan, *Lysimachia ciliata* (hairy loosestrife) has lots of small cilia or hairs along its stem and beneath its leaves, and many yellow flowers are borne at the nodes above the foliage as plants mature. The running root system of this green-leaved species provides plants all over the place. In recent years, the boring green species has been superseded by

Lycoris squamigera

Lycoris radiata with *Nicotiana*

'Purpurea', which is equally aggressive but much more handsome. I can even put up with its traveling ways because its purple-leaved foliage provides terrific contrasts with other plants in the garden—it even makes my bishop's weed (*Aegopodium*) look good. In hot, humid summers, the purple leaf fades somewhat but still remains a muted dark green. In the winter and early spring, it provides color in an otherwise barren landscape. Full sun to partial shade, zones 5 to 8.

Lysimachia clethroides (gooseneck loosestrife) is the reigning king and queen of the roamers, but it is nevertheless a beautiful plant in the right place. The right place simply happens to be an island bed surrounded by concrete. While I can make light of its traveling tendencies, gooseneck is a wonderful plant for filling in large areas and providing handsome white flowers. The many half-inch-wide flowers are arranged on a long, undulating (like a goose's neck) inflorescence. Excellent for cut flowers. That it is a roamer is simply testament to its success. Grows in full sun to partial shade; moist soils are to its liking. Hardy in zones 3 to 8.

A closely related plant but without the roaming habit is another white flowerer, *Lysimachia ephemerum*, upright loosestrife. I thought this would be the cat's meow when I first discovered its existence, to have a plant with flowers similar to gooseneck (without the neck) but without worrying that it would take over. It does well in areas of the Northwest, not too bad on Long Island, only fair in the Midwest and Southeast. Still a plant worth trying if you're a frustrated gooseneck lover. Hardy in zones 5 to 7.

The common name of *Lysimachia nummularia*, creeping Jenny, includes a strong hint as to what the plant wants to do. Happily, this first-rate plant is a creeper that most gardeners enjoy and encourage. Particularly

Lysimachia ciliata 'Purpurea'

Lysimachia ciliata 'Purpurea' with *Aegopodium*

Lysimachia clethroides

Lysimachia ciliata

Lysimachia clethroides

MORE →

Lysimachia ephemerum

Lysimachia ephemerum

Lysimachia nummularia

Lysimachia nummularia spilling over a window box

Lysimachia japonica 'Minutissima'

Lysimachia japonica 'Minutissima'

good for filling in areas around steps, rocks, or places where people routinely traverse, as stepping on it every now and then does no harm whatsoever. The yellow flowers add a little color, particularly to the green-leaved species; this contrast is lost when one grows the best selection, gold-leaved 'Aurea', whose golden color brightens the spring then fades a little in the heat of summer. Fewer flowers are produced but they are lost in the foliage anyway. Rooting at the nodes between the leaves allows *L. nummularia* to be fairly aggressive, but it is easily pulled out if it gets too rambunctious. I love this plant but am still trying to figure out who Jenny is. Partial shade, zones 3 to 9.

Another wonderful creeping member of the genus is probably my favorite, the short Japanese loosestrife, *Lysimachia japonica* 'Minutissima'. This 1" tall plant, with its tiny leaves and small yellow flowers, is growing between the stones in my little walkway and puts up with the abuse of gullywashers, drought, and the heavy boots of my visitors. Great plant for a specific area. Partial shade, zones 5 to 8.

Macleaya cordata

PLUME POPPY

Macleaya cordata is a plant that needs lots of room—it's perfect for the unsqueamish gardener for whom space is not a problem. I have seen outstanding displays of plume poppies in large containers, on either side of an entrance, where their growth can be controlled. Their lobed leaves, light green above and gray-green beneath, have gained plume poppies quite a following. They are particularly handsome

Lysimachia nummularia 'Aurea'

Lysimachia nummularia 'Aurea'

Macleaya cordata

Macleaya cordata

Macleaya cordata

MORE →

when plants are young, fluttering in the breeze. The small cream-colored flowers are held in long plumes at the top of the plants in early to mid summer. Plants are 6–10' tall, spreading quickly by rhizomes to form large colonies. In fact, they are thugs and a nightmare to remove. When broken, they bleed a yellow sap, a characteristic common to the poppy family. No cultivars are available. Full sun to partial shade, hardy in zones 3 to 8.

Mertensia virginica

Mertensia virginica 'Alba'

Mertensia asiatica

Mertensia

BLUEBELL

Spring is the time of great promise in the garden, with many of us frantically scraping the soil, hoping to rediscover our favorite prizes. I know that spring has sprung when the light green leaves and the blue flowers of *Mertensia virginica*, Virginia bluebell, show themselves in late winter and early spring. I love watching the pink buds evolve from being coiled up like a scorpion's tail to opening to deep pink or blue flowers. Lavender and blue are the normal flower colors, but some plants retain their rose-pink flower color until nearly the end of bloom time. The big floppy leaves look a little like donkey ears and get larger as spring progresses. Finally, in early summer, normal summer dormancy is reached and the plants decide to go to bed, leaving the area bare—but that usually presents no problem because by that time neighboring plants have grown over the area. *Mertensia virginica* is a woodland plant, best grown at the edge of a woodland path or by a shaded pond. Few cultivars have been isolated; occasionally a rose-pink ('Rosea') occurs, which looks very nice with other small bulbs such as

Mertensia virginica 'Rosea' with *Ipheion*

Mertensia asiatica

Mertensia sibirica

Ipheion. A white-flowered 'Alba' also turns up, but who wants a white bluebell? Partial shade, zones 3 to 8.

Other interesting species of *Mertensia*, although less vigorous and more secretive, are the compact Asian bluebell, *Mertensia asiatica*, with incredible blue leaves and light blue flowers, and the full-bodied, tall Siberian bluebell, *M. sibirica*, which does not go dormant.

Miscanthus

EULALIA GRASS

Of all the grasses used in ornamental horticulture, save those for turf, the grasses of the genus *Miscanthus* are far and away the most popular. An explosion of interest in foliage and an emphasis on low maintenance has drawn the grasses into the mainstream of American gardening. They are particularly useful in commercial and institutional landscapes, where low maintenance is much more important than in the urban or suburban garden. Other species can be obtained, but the main species is common miscanthus grass, *Miscanthus sinensis*.

All eulalia grasses should be grown in full sun, although plants will tolerate some shade. In partial shade, plants are taller and more floppy, requiring a cage to keep them from staggering over everything. They may be enjoyed all winter but should be cut back to the base in spring, as soon as new growth has commenced. Do so with heavy shears or a chain saw—these are not wimpy plants, and in fact are considered invasive in the Northeast, Southeast, and Midwest.

Miscanthus sinensis itself provides a handsome planting in the summer and wonderful bronze foliage and flowers in the winter—indeed, good fall color is a given for all species and cultivars of *Miscanthus*. It is the summer foliage, however, that is the raison d'être of this particular species, and wonderful combinations of foliage and flowers abound. 'Adagio', 'Arabesque', and 'Yaku Jima' are examples of selections with mainly green foliage; for variegated foliage, one can choose 'Cabaret', an introduction with wide

Miscanthus sinensis in winter

Miscanthus sinensis 'Adagio'

Miscanthus sinensis 'Arabesque'

Miscanthus sinensis

MORE →

bands of white, or the narrow-banded, narrow-leaved 'Morning Light', both of which are quickly superseding 'Variegatus', the old variegated standby. Banded foliage is found on cultivars like the upright-growing 'Strictus'. Large flowers and good-looking foliage combine in 'Malepartus' and 'Silberfeder' ('Silver Feather'). Full sun, hardy in zones 5 to 9.

Miscanthus sinensis 'Morning Light'

Miscanthus sinensis 'Malepartus'

Miscanthus sinensis 'Variegatus'

Miscanthus sinensis 'Yaku Jima'

Miscanthus sinensis 'Cabaret'

Miscanthus sinensis 'Strictus'

Monarda

BEEBALM

How much *Monarda* have I given away in the last few years? Fragrant, handsome, and colorful the beebalms may be, but well behaved they are not. Three plants will form a large colony the first year, surround their neighbors the next, and be pulled out the third. In areas where such multiplication is not a problem, however, and where powdery mildew does not make its host too unsightly, beebalm sports many beautiful colors and offers excellent performance. I am not sure where this place is or where these plants are, but I am assured they exist.

Miscanthus sinensis 'Silberfeder' ('Silver Feather')

Monarda 'Blue Stocking'

Monarda 'Squaw'

MORE →

Monarda 'Cambridge Scarlet'

Monarda 'Talud'

Monarda 'Croftway Pink'

Monarda 'Petite Delight'

Several species may be found, but the main player, and one that moves around the garden so well, is *Monarda didyma*, also known as Oswego tea because plants were first collected around Oswego, New York, and used to brew a tea-like concoction. Many cultivars may be purchased, or more likely you will find a gardener who will welcome the opportunity to share some with you. Cultivars vary from each other in color and height, and in their susceptibility to powdery mildew. All breeders claim to have found the cleanest introduction, but until you actually try them in the garden, no one truly knows for sure.

I find that all *Monarda* hybrids grow well, in colors ranging from pink and red to blue and lilac. 'Blue Stocking' has violet-blue flowers and grows like a blue streak; it is reliably mildew resistant. Both 'Cambridge Scarlet' and 'Talud' provide bright red-scarlet flowers. 'Croftway Pink' and 'Beauty of Cobham' are a couple of older cultivars but are still popular, presumably because their flowers blend so well with other garden plants. 'Squaw' is a large plant with flowers of a rosy scarlet; 'Donnerwolke' has handsome lilac flowers; and white blooms can be found in 'Snow White'. I have grown many of them, and all have their moments, all are invasive, and none are absolutely resistant to mildew, no matter what is claimed. Most are about 3' tall, but a breakthrough in beebalm hybridizing, 'Petite Delight', offers pink flowers on an 18" tall frame—with little mildew, at least in my trials. All prefer full sun, hardy in zones 3 to 7.

Monarda 'Beauty of Cobham'

Monarda 'Donnerwolke'

Monarda 'Snow White'

Narcissus

DAFFODIL

I can't think of an easier way to obtain color in the spring garden than to plant bulbs in the fall, and narcissus are almost foolproof. Nature—and the Dutch—have already done the hard work, providing us with a self-contained flowering unit that allows us to expend a minimum of effort to reap the maximum benefit. The perenniality of daffodils is outstanding: from the deep South to the frozen North, they come back year after year.

So much hybridization has been accomplished with the major bulbs—and daffodils are certainly one—that they have been classified into different groups. For hybrid daffodils, twelve divisions have been identified, based on the size of the perianth (petals) and the corona (cup), resulting in daffodil terms like trumpet, large-cupped, small-cupped, and double. The single-flowered trumpet and large-cupped daffodils are probably the most popular harbingers of spring, but let us not ignore the many colorful cultivars that produce flowers in clusters. *Narcissus bulbocodium*, the hoop petticoat daffodil, and *N. cyclamineus*, cyclamen daffodil, are small but interesting species daffodils (a thirteenth division) useful for naturalizing and rock garden work. These species, less vigorous than the hybrids, are seen more on the West Coast than in the rest of the country. Full sun, zones 3 to 8.

Narcissus bulbocodium 'Primrose' (bulbocodium group)

Narcissus 'Biscayne' (large-cupped group)

Narcissus cyclamineus

Narcissus 'February Gold' (cyclamineus group)

MORE →

Narcissus 'Foresight' (trumpet group)

Narcissus 'Unsurpassable' (trumpet group)

Narcissus 'Ice Follies' (large-cupped group)

Narcissus 'Carlton' (large-cupped group)

Narcissus 'Barrett Browning' (small-cupped group)

Narcissus 'Flower Drift' (double group)

Narcissus 'Stint' (triandrus group)

Narcissus 'Bridal Gown' (double group)

Narcissus 'Susy' (jonquilla group)

Narcissus 'Hillstar' (jonquilla group)

Narcissus 'Pipit' (jonquilla group)

Narcissus 'Jenny' (cyclamineus group)

Narcissus 'Garden Princess' (cyclamineus group)

Narcissus 'Baby Moon' (misc. group, miniatures)

Narcissus 'Tuesday's Child' (triandrus group)

Narcissus 'Actaea' (poeticus group)

Narcissus 'Hawara' (misc. group, miniatures)

MORE →

Narcissus 'Avalanche' (tazetta group)

Narcissus 'Tête-à-Tête' (misc. group, miniatures)

Narcissus 'Geranium' (tazetta group)

Narcissus 'Belcato' (split-corona group)

Narcissus 'Cum Laude' (split-corona group)

Nepeta

CATNIP

Nepeta is one of those genera that gardeners learn to appreciate but find difficult to define. That it consists of more than 250 species suggests a genus with a good deal of diversity; for most gardeners, however, it is difficult to get past the fact that it is some kind of catnip. *Nepeta* is in the mint family, whose members may be recognized by their square stems, opposite leaves, and whorled flowers. One helpful way to discriminate between *Nepeta*, *Salvia*, and other minty plants is by using your nose. Nepeta, in general, smells like—well, smells like nepeta! Pick a leaf of nepeta, one of salvia, and one of mint, and let your nose do the walking. Of course, when I do this, my nose does more running than walking, as well as sneezing. All species of *Nepeta* are excellent for the edge of garden beds or even along a pathway, where their fragrance is released when one touches the leaves in passing.

The main species in the trade is Faassen's hybrid, *Nepeta* ×*faassenii*,

Nepeta ×*faassenii*

Nepeta ×*faassenii*

with numerous short cultivars such as 'Blue Dwarf' and 'Blue Wonder'. The highly popular *N.* ×*faassenii* 'Six Hills Giant', sometimes referred to as *Nepeta gigantea* because of its large leaves and 3' height, is a terrific plant for cooler climates but tends to be weedy in warm summers.

A wonderful low grower (1–2' tall) with the boldest flowers of the genus is the veined nepeta, *Nepeta nervosa*. The veins on the leaves are easily visible, thus the common name. A tall species, with only the faintest catnipy odor, is the very cold hardy (to zone 3) Siberian nepeta, *N. sibirica*. This is a beautiful plant, not as floppy as *N.*

Nepeta ×*faassenii* 'Six Hills Giant'

Nepeta nervosa

Nepeta sibirica

Nepeta ×*faassenii* 'Six Hills Giant'

MORE →

×*faassenii* and others and much more classic in habit. Probably the most un-nepeta-like species is the light yellow-flowered *N. govaniana* (zones 4 to 7). Growing 2–4' tall with mild catnip odor, it is more curious than useful. All require full sun, although afternoon shade is useful in the South. Most are hardy in zones 5 to 7, often to zone 4.

Nepeta sibirica

Nepeta govaniana

Oenothera

EVENING PRIMROSE, SUNDROPS

Many plants go under the name of evening primrose (those that open during the evening) or sundrops (those that show their colors during the day). With the introduction of new species and hybridization among species, the distinction has become blurred, and the common names are used interchangeably. The flowers of *Oenothera* have four petals; the sepals are pink to purple, particularly in bud; and the distinctive pistil is in four parts. A good number of species are weeds, but half a dozen better ones are offered in the trade. All enjoy full sun and require good drainage.

Oenothera fruticosa, common sundrops, is the species most often offered. The bright yellow flowers are held well above the 15–18" tall plants. The flowers are 1–2" wide and open most of the day, even if the sun is not shining. The sepals are red, and often the foliage is spotted red as well. Differences are not always obvious among available cultivars. I like 'Sonnenwende', for its pink flower buds and large bright yellow flowers; 'Lady Brookborough', with dozens of smaller flowers; and 'Yellow River', which stands about 18" tall and is covered with yellow blooms. I would be hard-pressed, however, to tell the difference between the three without a correct label. Full sun, hardy in zones 4 to 8.

Oenothera missouriensis, Ozark sundrops, has the largest flowers relative to the size of the plant in the genus. The yellow flowers are up to 5" across (although 3" is more common) and are held on 6–12" tall plants. Sepals are also tinged pink, and leaves are long, narrow, and entire. They are excellent plants for the rock garden, enjoying the extra drainage found there, but do not cope particularly well with heat and humidity. Few cultivars have warranted naming; one, 'Greencourt Lemon', has pale yellow flowers and slightly grayer leaves. Full sun, hardy in zones 4 to 7.

Oenothera fruticosa 'Sonnenwende'

Oenothera fruticosa 'Lady Brookborough'

Oenothera fruticosa 'Yellow River'

Another large-flowered yellow species is known as beach evening primrose, *Oenothera drummondii*. Large (3–4" wide) flowers on long stems mark this plant. It will grow in sand and prefers well-drained soils. Full sun, hardy in zones 7 to 10.

Easily discernible from most other species is the southcentral native, *Oenothera speciosa* (showy evening primrose), which bears pink rather than yellow flowers. The flowers are about 2" across, and the linear leaves are about 2–3" long. Plants can easily become weeds, taking over entire counties in a single growing season. A dream plant at first glance, a bit of a nightmare after a few years. The white-flowered 'Alba' is equally aggressive; 'Ballerina Hot Pink' is a brighter selection but is difficult to locate. Full sun, zones 5 to 8.

A similar species is Mexican evening primrose, *Oenothera berlandieri*, na-

Oenothera missouriensis

Oenothera speciosa

Oenothera speciosa 'Alba'

Oenothera missouriensis 'Greencourt Lemon'

Oenothera speciosa 'Ballerina Hot Pink'

Oenothera berlandieri 'Woodside White'

Oenothera drummondii

Oenothera speciosa

MORE →

tive to the Southwest and the Pacific Coast. Differing only slightly in appearance from *O. speciosa*, it is a bit less aggressive. Available in several cultivars; 'Siskiyou', with 2" wide pink flowers, and 'Woodside White', the white entry, are worth looking for. Full sun, zones 6 to 8.

Oenothera berlandieri 'Siskiyou'

Osmunda cinnamomea fiddleheads coming up through *Epimedium*

Osmunda

FLOWERING FERN

"Flowering fern" is a misnomer for sure: *Osmunda* has no flowers at all, much less pretty flowers. Rather, its common name is a reference to the conspicuous spore cases and fertile fronds of some of the species. These are some of the largest and most vigorous ferns, and coarser than many others. After all, the genus was named for Osmunder, the Saxon god of war, and what self-respecting Saxon would choose anything but a gung-ho fern. Although obvious differences distinguish the species, all prefer moist conditions and shade.

The cinnamon fern, *Osmunda cinnamomea*, is the most versatile species in the genus, easy to grow from North to South while still providing the classic fern habit. The fiddleheads are most beautiful when they unfold in the spring, whether by themselves on the woodland floor or coming through shade tolerant ornamentals like mayapples or epimediums. The base of each frond bears scattered tufts of cinnamon-colored hairs, hence the common name. The spores are found in the handsome cinnamon-colored fertile leaves. Too much heat and humidity yields stunted plants; shade and consistent moisture is required. An excellent fern for the beginning gardener, useful in zones 3 to 7, zone 8 on the West Coast.

Osmunda claytoniana is known as the interrupted fern, a perfect fit for the plant. The arrangement of the spore cases in the middle of many of the fronds is unique to this species, and I have yet to meet anyone who isn't fascinated with this interrupted arrangement. Plants are large (up to 3' tall and equally wide), and they eat up significant portions of woodland floor where they are established. The green fronds, apart from their being interrupted, are like those of most other ferns. Once the spores are shed in early summer, the interrupted area becomes bare. It is the most common fern in the Berkshires of western Massachusetts and easily established in areas of cool temperatures and moist soils. Best for woodland gardens; does poorly in the South, as lots of shade and moisture

Osmunda cinnamomea

are necessary for best growth. Too aggressive for formal borders. Good for zones 3 to 6, zone 8 on the West Coast.

Osmunda regalis, the royal fern, is the most classic of this classic group of ferns. Where happy, they are some of the largest, most robust plants in the fern family. The light green fronds are compound, unlike the simple fronds of *O. claytoniana*. The fertile spores of the plant are borne on the ends of the fronds, rather than separately as in the cinnamon ferns. Plants can be up to 6' tall and 4' across, eventually producing a huge tussock of roots, the source of osmunda fiber, long used as an amendment for growing orchids. Absolutely stunning in areas of partial shade and heavy moisture. Needs copious organic matter and cool nights to look its best. Zones 3 to 7, zone 8 on the West Coast.

Osmunda claytoniana

Osmunda claytoniana

Osmunda cinnamomea

Osmunda regalis

Osmunda regalis

Osmunda regalis reflected

Paeonia

PEONY

"The colder the winter, the better the blooms." Thus was I taught the First Law of Peonies by my grandmother as a young boy in Montreal, and sure enough, every now and then, winters would be milder than usual, and the peonies would produce half the number of usual flowers. The scraggly old plants in that Montreal yard were as ugly as could be—except for a two-week period when they put on their springtime flowers. One does not have to be a zone 3 Montrealer to enjoy peonies: they are excellent south to zone 5, satisfactory to zone 6, but only marginal in zone 7. Since peony performance also declines with high heat in the summer, southern gardeners are

Paeonia 'Balliol' (single bush form)

Paeonia 'Nadin' (single bush form)

Paeonia 'Zu Zu' (semi-double bush form)

Paeonia 'Rose Garland' (single bush form)

Paeonia 'White Cockade' (semi-double bush form)

Paeonia 'First Lady' (double bush form)

always on the cusp as they cheer their peonies on. West Coast-ers benefit from moderate summers and usually enjoy excellent flowering.

Peonies come in two shapes, the bush form and the tree form. Most of my preceding comments refer to the incredibly popular and highly bred bush peonies, which are classified as early-, mid-, and late-flowering, with single, semi-double, and double blooms. As a general rule of thumb, the further south one gardens with bush peonies, the more early, single to semi-double forms should be selected. The tree peony, although much more expensive, is increasing in popularity and availability. Most are hybrids of *Paeonia suffruticosa*. They can grow 6–7' tall and are more handsome when not in flower than the bush peonies. The massive blooms are usually double, although singles are occasionally found. Flowers grow to 5" across and

Paeonia 'Red Imp' (double bush form)

Paeonia 'Argosy' (semi-double tree form)

Paeonia 'Honey Gold' (double bush form)

Paeonia 'Banquet' (semi-double tree form)

Paeonia 'Golden Hind' (semi-double tree form)

Paeonia 'Souvenir de Maxime Cornu' (double tree form)

Paeonia 'Daffodil' (double tree form)

Paeonia 'Red Moon' (double tree form)

MORE →

are so heavy, they have to be lifted to be admired. Hardiness zones of 4 to 7 are most appropriate. Full sun in the North; afternoon shade is tolerated in the South.

All the clinical information just offered belies the lure and emotion associated with this fine flowering plant. Everybody loves peonies. They are hugely popular as cut flowers, and displaced Northerners struggle to find at least one cultivar for their new homes in Tucson, Atlanta, or New Orleans. Hundreds of cultivars are available through specialty growers, better garden centers, and mail-order catalogs, and collecting peonies can quickly become an expensive obsession.

Papaver rhoeas

Papaver

POPPY

From Flanders Field to the Wizard of Oz, from fresh rolls and bagels to blighted city streets, poppies have been woven into our poetry, literature, and social structure for many years. That they have been memorialized and cursed with equal vigor underscores the longevity and the beauty of some of the species. Both the Flanders poppy, *Papaver rhoeas*, and the opium poppy, *P. somniferum*, are considered annuals in most American gardens but will occasionally reseed to produce a "perennial" show. The Flanders poppy is easy and colorful, and to see a European field in full finery can bring tears of joy or sadness to the eyes, depending on how quickly John McCrae's poem comes to mind. ("In Flanders fields the poppies blow / Between the crosses, row on row.") It is definitely an age thing. The opium poppy is so handsome that it cannot be ignored as a garden plant, drugheads be damned. The scarlet flowers of the species are beautiful on their own, but 'Album' (a white selection) and the peony-flowered variety *paeoniflorum* are happy to

A field of *Papaver rhoeas*

make the choosing more difficult. Add to that handsome blue-green foliage and the everlasting seed capsules, and we have a plant that can be enjoyed both in the garden and in the vase. What a shame that poeple have messed up such a great plant.

All poppies love cool climates, as their common names make pretty obvious. For example, the Iceland poppy, *Papaver nudicaule*, does not suggest sunny beaches and outdoor picnics, but its colorful crepe paper flowers make it worthwhile no matter where you garden. The best thing is that it can be used as a fall-planted complement to the trillions of pansies that are set out in southern and western American landscapes each autumn. Numerous cultivars are offered, usually in mixed colors and nearly always grown from seed. 'Champagne Bubbles' and 'Party Fun' can be found in both single colors and as a mix; occasionally double-flowered cultivars ('Flore Pleno') are available, but they do not have the simple classic beauty of the singles. The Iceland poppy will not make it through summers in about seventy percent of the country, but so what?

Papaver somniferum

Papaver somniferum

Papaver somniferum seed heads

Papaver somniferum 'Album'

Papaver somniferum var. *paeoniflorum*

Papaver nudicaule 'Champagne Bubbles'

Papaver nudicaule with pansies

MORE →

As long as you know what to expect, plant and enjoy.

By far the most popular perennial species is the Oriental poppy, *Papaver orientale*, whose bold, colorful flowers enliven late spring. The dark green, coarse leaves appear prickly (they are not), but as tough as they look, they are wimpy, going dormant as temperatures warm up in the summer. The most common color is red, but cultivars are offered in salmon-pink ('Cedric Morris'), pink ('Lighthouse'), crimson ('Avebury Crimson', 'Goliath'), and bicolors ('Picotee'). From the extraordinarily garish singles of 'Suleika' to the warped double flowers of 'Fireball' to the dainty colorful blooms of 'Ladybird', nobody ever accused an Oriental poppy of being subtle.

Oriental poppies do poorly in the heat and should be avoided south of

Papaver nudicaule 'Party Fun'

Papaver orientale

Papaver orientale 'Cedric Morris'

Papaver nudicaule 'Flore Pleno'

Papaver orientale 'Avebury Crimson'

Papaver orientale 'Fireball'

Papaver orientale 'Ladybird'

Papaver orientale 'Lighthouse'

Papaver orientale 'Goliath'

Papaver orientale 'Picotee'

Papaver orientale 'Suleika'

zone 6, although some zone 7 gardeners will be successful for a few seasons. Where they do well, however, they are spectacular. All poppies are most comfortable in zones 3 to 5 (occasionally zone 6 for the Oriental poppy), zone 8 on the West Coast. Full sun, good drainage.

Patrinia

This plant emerged like a lightning bolt when first introduced and continues to be popular for its ability to shrug off inclement weather. Hot or cool, dry or wet, one patrinia or another continues to do its thing. Of the approximately fifteen species, only three are real choices for the garden and landscape, the differences among them attributable more to height and stature than overall appearance. The shortest of the available taxa is *Patrinia triloba*, which is the least showy of the group but useful where small garden spaces don't lend themselves to the larger members of the clan. Partial shade, morning sun. Hardy in zones 5 to 7 (maybe 8). I also enjoy the foliage of another relatively small member, the white patrinia, *P. villosa*. The foliage can act as a bright ground cover and to me is prettier than the flowers. Full sun, zones 5 to 8.

The most common species is also the tallest. The scabious patrinia, *Patrinia scabiosifolia*, bears large leaves of deep green and hundreds of bright yellow flowers. Plants will grow 3–6'

Patrinia villosa

Patrinia triloba

Patrinia scabiosifolia

Patrinia scabiosifolia

MORE →

tall and should not require staking if placed in full sun. Initially, when in flower, this species looks like an overgrown mustard, but as you learn to appreciate its resiliency and lack of maintenance requirements, it grows on you. Plants will reseed, but if that is not in the garden plan, simply whack them down before the fruit forms. If cut when flowers are about half open, however, the blooming stems may be brought inside as a wonderful filler for other cut flowers. The most popular of the smaller introductions is 'Nagoya', whose full-blown stature is usually around 3'. Full sun, zones 5 (4 with protection) to 8.

Patrinia scabiosifolia 'Nagoya'

Penstemon

BEARDTONGUE

The genus *Penstemon* is one of the more interesting groups of plants to use in the garden, not only for its diversity of form and color but also for the botanizing you can enjoy on your own. The name "penstemon" refers to the five stamens in the flower; however, if one looks inside, only four stamens are obvious. The fifth one is there, but looks quite different from the other four; it is properly referred to as a staminode, in case anybody really wants to know such things. In

Penstemon cardwellii

Penstemon barbatus 'Skylight'

Penstemon barbatus 'Hyacinth'

many species and cultivars, this thin, narrow tongue-like structure is hairy, accounting for the common name. I guess you have to be there . . .

Penstemons create blocks of colorful flowers and/or foliage, and nearly all are native to the United States. They are among the most versatile of plants, ranging from short ground-covering species hardly known at all (*Penstemon cardwellii*) to a handful of well-known upright selections (*P. digitalis* 'Husker Red') to the dozens of garden hybrids. Flowers are mostly in the white, red, purple, and pink range; however a few species, such as *P. confertus*, also bear quite dramatic yellow flowers.

The most cold tolerant species is common beardtongue, *Penstemon barbatus*, whose large wide-lipped flowers are slightly bearded on the lower lip. They are easy to grow, provide numerous colors, and persist for many years. Many cultivars have been selected, including 'Hyacinth', with large rosy pink flowers, and 'Skylight', which produces handsome rose-and-white bicolor blooms. The species has also been included as a parent to many hybrids, passing on its larger flowers and additional cold tolerance. Full sun, zones 2 to 8.

Three native species have proven their worth: *Penstemon digitalis*, *P. pinifolius*, and *P. smallii*, native to the Southwest, Southeast, and East, respectively. Smooth white penstemon, *P. digitalis*, is probably the best known, mainly due to the breeding efforts of

Penstemon confertus

Penstemon digitalis 'Husker Red'

Penstemon digitalis 'Husker Red'

Penstemon barbatus 'Hyacinth'

Penstemon digitalis

MORE →

Penstemon pinifolius

Dale Lindgren at the University of Nebraska, where the purple-leaved cultivar 'Husker Red' was developed. The species itself is terrific, with large deep green leaves and wonderful white flowers held well above the foliage. The leaves of 'Husker Red' are the reddest during cool weather, but when temperatures remain over 85°F for a period of time, they tend to lose much of their red pigment. Still and all, a great plant in much of the country. Full sun, zones 4 to 8.

The pineleaf penstemon, *Penstemon pinifolius*, with thin green leaves and wonderful tubular, rosy salmon blooms, comes alive with flower power in the late spring and summer. It welcomes full sun but does not appreciate areas of high humidity and summer rain. Hardy in zones 7 to 9. On the other hand, heat, humidity, and rainfall do not bother Small's penstemon, *P. smallii*, nearly as much. Its flowers are pink-purple on the outside and white on the inside. This species also tolerates shade better than most penstemons, although some direct sun

Penstemon pinifolius

Penstemon smallii

Penstemon smallii

Penstemon 'Port Wine'

Penstemon 'Schönholzeri' ('Firebird')

builds stem strength. Partial shade, zones 6 to 8.

The numerous species of *Penstemon* are quite lovely, but it is the hybrids that are stealing the show in American gardens. Although the parentage of most of them may be traced to North American species, they had to go to Europe, especially the British Isles, for gentrification. They are finally returning home and have been strutting their stuff in many locations. Most are hardy in zones 4 to 7 (8 on the West Coast) and prefer full sun, but in the South they appreciate a little afternoon shade if possible. Some of the red- to wine-colored cultivars I enjoy are 'Port Wine', 'Ruby', and 'Schönholzeri' ('Firebird'). They differ in flower size and vigor, but all are eye-catching. Purples and blues include 'Sour Grapes' and 'Stapleford Gem'; white flowers can be found in 'White Bedder' and 'Snowstorm'. 'Hidcote Pink' is a wonderful pink, while the bicolors

Penstemon 'Sour Grapes'

Penstemon 'Hidcote Pink'

Penstemon 'Stapleford Gem'

Penstemon 'Snowstorm'

Penstemon 'Ruby'

Penstemon 'White Bedder'

MORE →

are represented by the outstanding 'Thorn' and 'Mother of Pearl'. The list goes on and on, and a good deal of money will be spent before your short list of favorites can be determined. Full sun to a little afternoon shade, zones 5 (sometimes 4) to 8.

Penstemon 'Mother of Pearl'

Perovskia atriplicifolia

RUSSIAN SAGE

I used to enjoy telling the story of how *Perovskia atriplicifolia*, Russian sage, got its common name—that the foliage was so pungent it was said to smell like the feet of marching Russian soldiers. But with the Cold War over and political correctness rampant, I apologize to all the Russian soldiers whose feet I maligned. (The foliage actually smells like my son's feet, on a good day, but enough of that.) The genus was in fact named for Russian general V. A. Perovsky, and this species is tough and reliable throughout the country. In northern gardens, the flowers are an intense blue and remain that way all summer; in southern gardens, the intense blue tends to fade as summer temperatures increase. Plants grow tall, up to 5' in height, and tend to flop over no matter the intensity of sun or summer temperatures. A good haircut in late spring encourages branching and reduces height. Regardless of the problems, the silver foliage is handsome, and its fragrance is an additional bonus for those with sinus problems.

A few cultivars are listed, but I don't see a great deal of difference from one to the other. 'Longin' does have darker blue flowers, and 'Filagran', with its deeper cut foliage, provides a more lacy appearance. Full sun, zones 5 to 9.

Penstemon 'Thorn'

Perovskia atriplicifolia

Perovskia atriplicifolia 'Longin'

Phlomis

JERUSALEM SAGE

I am sure that all gardeners go through various stages of plant fixations in their gardening years, and people have embraced trilliums, campanulas, saxifrages, and salvias with the zeal of philatelists and numismatists. I have gone through my "salvia stage of life" but am presently enamored of another sage, *Phlomis*. Fortunately, Jerusalem sages are not nearly as numerous as salvias, and I can't find that many for sale anyway, so my present affliction is much easier to control. Jerusalem sages occur in two main flower colors, yellows and lavender-pinks. All have hairy foliage, with some silvering to it, and the flower buds are almost as beautiful as the flowers themselves. *Phlomis* is a useful companion to almost all plants in the garden, regardless of season or stage of flowering.

The yellow forms are bigger but also more compact in habit. They are best represented by *Phlomis fruticosa*, the most popular species, and *P. russeliana*, both known as Jerusalem sage. *Phlomis fruticosa* has 2–4" long silvery green leaves and is handsome throughout the season in the North, throughout the year in the South. The green flower buds occur in whorls up the stem, then give way to bright yellow flowers, like lights on a candelabra. Outstanding in leaf, terrific in bud and flower, and as a bonus, wonderful in fruit. The fruit remains on the plants for many weeks, adding yet another ornamental charm to an already interesting plant. Plants get woody at the base; a hard prune in the spring every two to three years rejuvenates them. Full sun, hardy in zones 4 to 8. Plants tend to reseed, so get ready to share them with others.

Phlomis russeliana is bigger in every way, with larger leaves and habit, but

Phlomis russeliana in bud

Phlomis fruticosa in winter

Phlomis fruticosa

Phlomis fruticosa

MORE →

Phlomis russeliana

Phlomis russeliana

the leaves are much more dull green than silver green, and the flowers are a softer yellow. Not quite as hardy, nor as compact of habit. Full sun, zones 5 to 8.

The lavender-pinks are well represented by *Phlomis bovei*, the Moroccan sage, and *P. italica*, the Italian sage. In general, the plants and leaves are smaller than the yellow-flowered species just described, but the flower color is equally arresting. Plants stand about 2–4' and appear rather lanky. It is more difficult to find nurseries selling lavender-pink *Phlomis*, likely because they are cold hardy only to zone 8 (7 with protection). Provide full sun and well-drained soils.

Phlomis bovei

Phlomis italica

Phlomis russeliana

Phlomis fruticosa (left) and P. russeliana

Phlox

In 1745 the American botanist John Bartram sent a specimen of *Phlox* to England, billing it as "a fine creeping Spring Lychnis." No sooner did it land than it became a hit in that land of gardens, and the English embraced it as their own. The genus enjoyed such popularity there that in 1919 Reginald Farrar enthusiastically wrote of it, "The day that saw the introduction, more than a century since . . . ought indeed to be kept as a horticultural festival." So many good garden plants are now available that Messrs. Bartram and Farrar would probably have no trouble at all drumming up support for a phlox festival.

I enjoy all the low growers, but I think some of the finest garden plants have to belong to the woodland phlox, *Phlox divaricata*, with its handsome coat of lavender flowers and thin dark green leaves, 1½–2" in length. The species is a denizen of woodland edges, allowing the gardener to fill in many partially shaded areas in a rock garden or shaded spot. Woodland phlox are more substantial than many other low-growing phlox, growing 12–15" tall and harmonizing well with other low growers; it also combines beautifully with plants with colorful foliage, like golden spirea. If the plants reseed, various shades of blue, lavender, and light purple are sure to appear. Some wonderful cultivars are available. Try the clean white of 'Fuller's White', the outstanding icy cold blue of 'Dirigo Ice', and the regal

Phlox divaricata with golden spirea

Phlox divaricata

Phlox divaricata 'Dirigo Ice'

Phlox divaricata 'Fuller's White'

Phlox divaricata 'Louisiana Blue'

MORE →

Phlox divaricata 'Clouds of Perfume'

Mildew damage on *Phlox paniculata*

Phlox paniculata 'David'

purple of 'Louisiana Blue'. I also enjoy the pale blue blossoms of 'Clouds of Perfume', which is neither like a cloud nor particularly fragrant, but I like the name. Place in partial shade, hardy in zones 5 to 8.

Phlox paniculata is a tough perennial, tolerating late freezes, droughts, and hot summers for five to eight years; dozens of flowers, averaging about an inch across, are held at the top of each plant in 8" wide clusters. Their classic habit and reliability make them the choice for the gardens of many houses, from my daughter's fixer-upper to those of Frank Lloyd Wright. These are plants that turn the summer garden into a veritable rainbow, flowering in June through August. Unfortunately, in many cultivars, one of those veritable colors is the white of powdery mildew. This disease starts on the bottom leaves and can rapidly disfigure the entire plant. I have seen much worse cases of mildew in Montreal than in Athens; however, on highly susceptible cultivars, it matters very little where the plants reside. Providing good circulation and thinning the emerging plants to four or five strong stems in the spring can help.

With hundreds of *Phlox paniculata* cultivars from which to choose, gardeners can afford to be picky: color

Mixed display of *Phlox paniculata*

Phlox paniculata 'Robert Poore'

Phlox paniculata 'Bright Eyes'

of flower, vigor of plant, and susceptibility to mildew are all characteristics to be considered. Two vigorous selections that have enjoyed immense popularity are the white-flowered 'David' and 'Robert Poore', with large trusses of iridescent purple flowers on 5' tall plants. I have seen very little mildew on either. Other handsome cultivars include the beautiful 'Prospero', whose white flowers with blushes of pink stand out in the summer garden. I also enjoy the popular 'Bright Eyes', with pale pink flowers and a crimson eye, and 'Franz Schubert', with light pink flowers on 3' tall plants. 'Red Indian' is a rosy pink; 'Starfire' is a brilliant scarlet; 'Red Eyes' provides exactly that in the middle of light pink flowers; and 'Fairest One' has many trusses of rose-colored flowers with a darker red eye. For lavender hues, 'Blue Boy' is a useful addition. Those after variegated foliage will find 'Norah Leigh' striking, if not particularly easy to grow, with her green-and-white leaves and pink to lavender flowers. Place in full sun; plants grow 3–5' tall. Hardy in zones 4 to 8.

The neat thing about the genus *Phlox* is the number of low growers that justify Reginald Farrar's obsession. One is creeping phlox, *Phlox stolonifera* (6–12" tall), which creeps around rapidly and is an excellent ground cover to boot. The leaves are about 2" long, and plants bear 1–1½"

Phlox paniculata 'Fairest One'

Phlox paniculata 'Norah Leigh'

Phlox paniculata 'Prospero'

Phlox paniculata 'Red Indian'

Phlox paniculata 'Franz Schubert'

Phlox paniculata 'Starfire'

Phlox paniculata 'Red Eyes'

MORE →

Phlox stolonifera 'Bruce's White'

Phlox stolonifera 'Sherwood Purple'

Phlox stolonifera 'Variegata'

wide flowers. They do well in light shade and should not be planted in full sun, except in the far North. Creeping phlox gets around in various colors: 'Bruce's White' is the best white of the group, and one of the better darker selections is 'Sherwood Purple'. If I must have a pink-flowering creeping phlox in the Armitage garden, I would choose 'Homefires'. Last but not least is 'Variegata', a slow grower whose variegated foliage makes a lovely contrast to the other green-leaved cultivars in this fine group of plants. Partial shade, zones 2 to 8.

All species of *Phlox* are native to the United States. Bartram could have sent any one of them, so why was such a commotion made over *Phlox subulata*, a plant we call the gas station plant, the outhouse plant, and other ghastly names—properly known as moss phlox? Let there be no doubt: scorned as it is, this is a great plant. It covers grand hillsides, sneaks under picket fences, grows beside driveways, and makes festive gas stations and trailer parks everywhere. It may be faulted for its short bloom time, but how extraordinary that time is. Dense carpets of pink appear in early spring, obscuring the leaves; when the blooms have faded, carpets of green leaves, each an inch long and an eighth of an inch

A drift of *Phlox subulata*

Phlox stolonifera 'Homefires'

Phlox subulata on a smaller scale

wide, simply blend into the landscape. These 4–6" tall mats come in an astonishing range of colors. Some of my favorites include 'Oakington Blue', with flowers of light blue, and 'Candy Stripe', an outstanding white-and-pink bicolor. I think I stopped maligning moss phlox when I stumbled across the indescribable pastel flowers of 'Coral Eye' and the starry white flowers of 'Snowflake', which is so white in flower that the foliage all but disappears. I also can't help but single out 'Scarlet Flame', whose names describes its effect, and 'Maiden's Blush', with the lightest of pinks on its dozens of flowers. Great plants, easy to grow in full sun and well-drained soils. Full sun, hardy in zones 2 to 8.

Phlox subulata 'Candy Stripe'

Phlox subulata 'Coral Eye'

Phlox subulata 'Scarlet Flame'

Phlox subulata 'Maiden's Blush'

Phlox subulata 'Oakington Blue'

Phlox subulata 'Snowflake'

Physosostegia virginiana 'Bouquet Rose' ('Pink Bouquet')

Physostegia virginiana

OBEDIENT PLANT

If gardeners were ever to compile a list of misnomers in common names, obedient plant would be near the very top. *Physostegia virginiana*, a native of the eastern United States, is many things, but obedient is not one of them. It is an elegant plant, with opposite leaves, square stems, and handsome pink flowers on a spiky flower head, but its beauty and elegance belie its land-grabbing proclivity. If you don't have sufficient space to allow for a little roaming, don't plant obedient plant. If room is available, however, the 12–18" plants are excellent companions for yellow evening primroses and blue asters. Dozens of one-inch-long lipped flowers open from the bottom to the top, and when about a third of the flowers are open, they are perfect for picking and bringing in the house. As a cut flower, they persist for at least a week in tap water, longer if a flower preservative is used.

Some excellent selections of *Physostegia virginiana* can be found in nurseries and mail-order catalogs. The pink-flowered 'Bouquet Rose' ('Pink Bouquet') grows 3–4' tall and is an excellent choice, differing only slightly from the species. 'Vivid', with darker flowers, grows only 2–3' tall and may be the best choice for the smaller garden. The white-flowered cultivars are probably the prettiest; they are a little more dwarf than the pink-flowered

Physostegia virginiana 'Vivid'

Physostegia virginiana 'Alba'

Physostegia virginiana 'Summer Snow'

Physostegia virginiana 'Alba'

Physostegia virginiana 'Variegata'

selections and flower a few weeks earlier. 'Alba' and 'Summer Snow' are similar in flower color, but 'Alba' is a little shorter. The most interesting selection is 'Variegata', which sports pink flowers and outstanding white-and-green variegated foliage. The plant is probably more handsome when flowers are absent. Plant in full sun in well-drained soils, hardy in zones 2 to 9.

Pinellia

The genus *Pinellia* will never enjoy a large following, partly because so few gardeners and growers know about it. The requirements of these plants are similar to others in the Jack-in-the-pulpit family (Araceae), that is, shade and consistent moisture. Also similar to other members of the family, they are appreciated for their deep green foliage and the long lazy tongues (Jacks) that protrude from the small purple pulpits.

Two useful species are *Pinellia pedatisecta*, with its four to five compound leaves, and *P. tripartita*, with only three leaves. Both have long tongues and are similar in flower. Plants can reseed with abandon, particularly if the shade is airy (as under tall pines), not dense (as under oaks or maples). These are plants for plant lovers who enjoy a quiet stroll through the garden to admire the less obvious. Hardy in zones 6 to 8.

Pinellia pedatisecta

Pinellia tripartita

Physostegia virginiana 'Variegata'

Pinellia pedatisecta

Pinellia tripartita

Platycodon grandiflorus in bud

Platycodon grandiflorus

Platycodon grandiflorus 'Shell Pink'

Platycodon grandiflorus 'Mariesii' with *Hemerocallis*

Platycodon grandiflorus

BALLOONFLOWER

Although *Platycodon grandiflorus* is native to the Far East, these plants have become American favorites, thanks mostly to their curious swollen buds and chalice-shaped blue to purple flowers, which open wide in mid to late summer. Slow to emerge, even given up for dead by rookie ballooners, they grow rapidly into sizeable 3' plants. The flower buds swell and swell, just like a balloon, finally popping open to reveal beautiful five-petaled flowers with dark blue veins. They are particularly useful growing with lilies or other summer-flowering white or yellow plants.

The diversity in the genus is seen in cultivars with white ('Albus'), pink ('Shell Pink'), double ('Plenus'), and occasionally even spotted ('Florovariegatus') flowers. One of the problems with balloonflower is that stems are weak, and staking is often required, particularly in inclement weather. Because of this, two shorter selections have been bred: 'Mariesii' is 1–2' tall and 'Sentimental Blue' is only 6–9" tall. Both require less maintenance but are not as classy as the real thing. Plants require full sun, or they will flop over. Hardy in zones 3 to 7.

Platycodon grandiflorus 'Albus'

Platycodon grandiflorus 'Plenus'

Platycodon grandiflorus 'Sentimental Blue'

Platycodon grandiflorus 'Florovariegatus'

Platycodon grandiflorus 'Sentimental Blue'

Polemonium

JACOB'S LADDER

The genus *Polemonium* is diverse, ranging from 3' tall plants to dwarf runners, and all are happier in cool rather than warm summers. The blue, white, or pink flowers generally present themselves in early to mid summer. Of the twenty-five or so species, one or two are quite endearing, if not enduring, and a few others are well worth trying.

Polemonium caeruleum and *P. foliosissimum*, common upright species, have about twenty leaves climbing the stem, each leaf representing a rung of the Jacob's ladder we are climbing. They stand 2–3' tall and produce masses of lavender-blue flowers in the spring and early summer. I have seen excellent stands in Franklin Park, Columbus, Ohio, and in Trois Rivières, Quebec, where they grow like weeds. The two species are fine plants in their own right; however, several excellent cultivars of *P. caeruleum* have been developed.

The white-flowered *Polemonium caeruleum* 'Album' is also upright, and the white flowers make a nice contrast to the dark green leaves. Subspecies *himalayanum* ('Himalayanum') is a little taller and probably more cold tolerant. Lower growers, such as 'Dawn Light', have emerged; their shorter stature is their main claim to fame. The newest and most unique is the variegated 'Brise d'Anjou', with clean green-and-white leaves and blue flowers. The foliage is the best part of this plant, as the open flowers tend to be lost in the leaves. All cultivars are cold hardy to at least zone 4, and heat tolerant to

Polemonium caeruleum

Polemonium caeruleum 'Album'

Polemonium caeruleum subsp. *himalayanum* ('Himalayanum')

Polemonium foliosissimum

Polemonium caeruleum 'Brise d'Anjou'

MORE →

about zone 6 east of the Rocky Mountains, zone 8 west of the Rockies. Full sun, well-drained soils.

Polemonium caeruleum 'Dawn Light'

Polemonium carneum

Both *Polemonium carneum*, salmon Jacob's ladder, and *P. reptans*, creeping Jacob's ladder, are much lower growing than *P. caeruleum* and *P. foliosissimum* and therefore are perfect for the front of the garden bed. The salmon-flowered *P. carneum*, native to the western United States, is beautiful but less adaptable than the blue-flowered species. Plants are also more difficult to obtain, but if your local nursery carries the plant, give it a try. It is only about 18–24" tall, with pink to salmon flowers. *Polemonium reptans* is native to the eastern United States and—although it does not run fast—can be a pest in gardens it takes a liking to; its selection 'Blue Pearl' grows about 8–10" tall, with bright blue flowers. The type provides excellent greenery and numerous flowers throughout the season; it is easy to grow and makes a nice filler in partially shaded to sunny areas. Neither species does well in hot summer climates, and zone 6 is about as far south as they want to be. *Polemonium carneum* is only cold tolerant to zone 6 (perhaps 5), but *P. reptans* can tolerate temperatures in zone 2. Well-drained soils, partial shade to sun.

Polygonatum

SOLOMON'S SEAL

The genus *Polygonatum* provides a wonderful store of shade tolerant plants for the woodland, many of them among our finest natives. The common name has many a good yarn associated with it; one is that, during the times of the great kings, the roots acted as a glue to heal broken bones, and it was this sealing property that begat the name Solomon's seal. (I don't believe it either.) Of the many closely related species, three have a definite place in the woodland or garden.

Both *Polygonatum commutatum*, great Solomon's seal, and *P. odoratum*, fragrant Solomon's seal, are upright species (at least 2' tall) and bear lovely dangling white flowers at the leaf nodes. I love the way the stems of *P. commutatum* burst through the spring ground, the leaves tucked in and the entire stem resembling a fat green shish-kabob skewer. As the leaves unfurl, the small floating flower buds break open to reveal clean white flowers dangling from each node. Plants look good even

Polemonium reptans 'Blue Pearl'

Emerging stems of *Polygonatum commutatum*

after the season is finished, the amber leaves and old flowers a study in nature's beauty. So common in the Northeast and Midwest that it is hardly even noticed, this plant richly deserves a place in the shaded woodland.

The fragrant Solomon's seal, *Polygonatum odoratum*, is the European version of the great one but is a pretender compared to it. Similar in habit, with green leaves and white flowers, the stature of the species itself is less imposing and its performance not as good. Hope is offered, however, by the main offering in the garden catalogs, the excellent selection 'Variegatum'. Now this is a marvelous plant, its white flowers adding to the beauty of the variegated leaves, which turn an outstanding bronze by autumn. It is obvious, at least to me, why this is a favorite Armitage plant in the oak forest I call a garden.

Both *Polygonatum commutatum* and *P. odoratum* require partial shade with two to three hours of bright light to be their best. Hardy in zones 3 to 8.

As robust and grand as the previous two species are, *Polygonatum humile*, dwarf Solomon's seal, is refined and charming. Plants grow only 6–9" tall, still with the characteristic small white flowers formed at the nodes. A rich full planting can be obtained in two to three years, and a better ground cover

Polygonatum commutatum

Polygonatum commutatum in fall

Polygonatum odoratum 'Variegatum'

Polygonatum commutatum

Polygonatum odoratum 'Variegatum'

Polygonatum odoratum 'Variegatum' in fall

MORE →

for a small area is hard to imagine. Plants prefer partial shade, but not as much as the upright Solomons. One of the problems with its size is that other plants quickly overgrow it, resulting in too much shade and moisture and a subsequent loss of plants. While I admire and use the upright species, I lust after this one. Partial shade, hardy in zones 5 to 7.

Polygonatum humile

Polygonatum humile

Polygonum affine 'Hartford'

Polygonum

KNOTWEED, SMARTWEED, FLEECEFLOWER

The knotweeds are probably more cursed than loved, bringing a mixture of beauty and downright belligerence. That the best-known plants are weeds like Pennsylvania smartweed, lady's thumb, and common knotweed tells us that the genus *Polygonum* is indeed adaptable. Several species are widely planted and don't share the overly aggressive behavior of their impolite cousins. All polygonums have red to pink flowers on thin inflorescences, and the petioles of their leaves clasp the stem, a telltale characteristic of the genus. Some taxonomists insist that the genus *Polygonum* should be changed to *Persicaria*, but some do not. Until consensus is reached, I will continue to talk about polygonums and the quite wonderful common names associated with them.

When conditions suit it, the low-growing *Polygonum affine* (*Persicaria affinis*; Himalayan fleeceflower) can be considered a ground cover. The small leaves emerge purple-green in the spring. As the plants mature, spikes of rosy red flowers appear, covering the planting by early summer. They do well in cool summers; I have had no success in north Georgia but have seen terrific stands in the Northeast, Midwest, and Northwest. Available cultivars include 'Hartford' and the more aggressive 'Superbum'. Excellent drainage is essential. Plants perform better in full sun to partial shade; too much shade results in sparse plantings. Hardy in zones 3 to 7.

Probably the best known and most planted of the garden species, *Polygonum bistorta* (*Persicaria bistorta*;

snakeweed) can be found doing well everywhere but in the deep South. The plants consist of wavy green leaves, each with a white midrib, and above them, looking something like pink bottlebrushes, are 4–5" spikes of pink flowers. They look particularly good combined with purple flowers, such as ornamental onions. Plants do very well where moisture accumulates, although they are not bog plants. The flowers are highly prized as cut flowers and persist for about a week in a bouquet. Excellent plantings may be found from Pennsylvania to Chicago to Den-

Polygonum affine 'Superbum'

Polygonum bistorta with *Allium*

Polygonum affine

MORE →

ver. Subspecies *carneum* has cherry-red flowers; variety *regelianum* bears creamy white flowers. All pink-flowering offerings are likely 'Superbum'. Full sun is appropriate if consistent moisture can be provided, otherwise some afternoon shade is useful. Hardy in zones 3 to 7.

Polygonum bistorta 'Superbum'

Polygonum bistorta 'Superbum'

Polygonum bistorta subsp. *carneum*

Primula

PRIMROSE

Oh, to live in primrose country! When I visit my gardening friends on the West Coast or overseas, I revel in the magic of spring primroses. Not that the Armitage garden is entirely bereft of this wonderful genus, but the primrose path is easier trodden in climates where extremes of cold and heat are uncommon. Of the four hundred or so species, we in the States are lucky to find two or three different kinds for sale, even in quality garden centers, and must instead peruse the mail-order seed and plant sources for any satisfaction. Seed is generally not difficult to germinate, and many species may be obtained through specialist

Primula denticulata

Polygonum bistorta var. *regelianum*

seed sources. Essentially all primroses perform better with mild winters, mild summers, partially shaded areas, and consistent moisture in the soil. Some require boggy soils to do well and wimp out at the first hint of drought or heat, while others are much tougher than they look.

Both *Primula denticulata*, the drumstick primrose, and *P. veris*, cowslip, require similar growing conditions—that is, shady, moist, and not too cold—but cowslips tolerate heat much better. Looking at the flower of *P. denticulata* reaffirms its common name; these drumsticks occur in shades of lavender, rose-blue ('Rosea'), and white ('Alba'). They flower early, in February or March, then succumb to the rigors of heat in much of the country. They are beautiful when in flower, and their foliage simply disappears into the plants that grow up around it. Hardy in zones 5 (4 with protection) to 7.

The common cowslip, *Primula veris*, is a terrific, adaptable, and functional primrose that works well in American gardens. The dark green leaves are in perfect contrast to the deep yellow flowers, which continue to open for four to six weeks in the spring. One of the best primroses for southern gardeners—heat is not a problem, assuming water is available, and plants reseed easily. A primrose path is almost possible. Hardy in zones 5 (4 with protection) to 8.

Some of the most beautiful and architectural primroses of all fall into the candelabra group. The flowers of these several species are arranged on long flower stems, like lights on an exquisite candelabra. They all require copious amounts of water and in fact are best suited for water gardens, sides of streams, or boggy soils. If such conditions are provided, then plants can tolerate full sun, but afternoon shade is usually appreciated. The best known of the candelabras, the Japanese primrose, *Primula japonica*, is usually seen in a mixture of flower colors. Some monochromatic selections can also be found occasionally, such as 'Postford White' and the rosy pink 'Splendens'.

Primula denticulata 'Rosea'

Primula denticulata 'Alba'

Primula veris

Primula japonica

Primula japonica 'Postford White'

MORE →

Primula japonica 'Splendens'

The American gardener doesn't have access to as many of the candelabras as their European colleagues; however, if you are successful with Japanese primrose, then all sorts of primrose doors open. I would be like a kid in a candy store and try some that look impossible, such as Bulley's primrose, *Primula bulleyana*, with its vibrant orange flowers. Even the name is terrific. For a more refined effect, I would plant some florinda primroses, *P. florindae*, by the side of my pond. With its dangling yellow flowers and classic habit, it is a plant well worth trying. My candelabra collection would be incomplete without a few plants of the butter-yellow *P. heladoxa*, the rosy flowers of *P. pulverulenta* 'Bartley's Strain', or my all-time favorite from Ireland, *P.* 'Rowallane Rose'. These may not take you, your garden, and your neighborhood miles along that primrose path—still, half the fun is in the trying. All are probably hardy in zones 5 to 7, prefer the Northwest, and

Primula bulleyana

Primula florindae

Primula heladoxa

Primula heladoxa

need lots of water and partial shade.

Almost everyone who sees Vial's primrose, *Primula vialii*, has to look twice to even recognize it as a primrose, but once the synapses click, the next thoughts are "I must have it" and "Where do I get it?" The purple flowers extend nearly 2' into the air and are only vaguely primrose-like. A good deal of interest in establishing this plant in American gardens is underway, and they soon may be more readily available. Success requires mild summers and winters, moisture, and a protected area. Partial shade, hardy in zones 5 to 7.

Primula 'Rowallane Rose'

Primula pulverulenta 'Bartley's Strain'

Primula vialii

Primula pulverulenta 'Bartley's Strain'

Primula vialii

MORE →

The common English primrose, *Primula vulgaris*, is not all that common in the United States but very common in Europe, where many selections have been made. Short in stature but frost and heat tolerant, they are usually available in yellows and whites. 'Alba' has creamy white flowers with yellow centers; 'Atlantia' has the cleanest white blooms I have seen. The most common variations on the theme are 'Gigha White' and subspecies *sibthorpii*, which are white or off-white and pink, respectively. The English primrose is also known for the old-fashioned highly bred double-flowerers, such as 'Double Burgundy' and 'Double Yellow', which were mostly grown for exhibition and not the garden. Still available, but not nearly as popular as in Queen Victoria's time. Partial shade, hardy in zones 5 to 8.

Primula vulgaris 'Gigha White'

Primula vulgaris subsp. *sibthorpii*

Primula vulgaris 'Alba'

Primula vulgaris 'Double Burgundy'

Primula vulgaris 'Atlantia'

Primula vulgaris 'Double Yellow'

Pulmonaria

LUNGWORT

A favored shade plant, lungwort can be counted on to produce a blend of handsome foliage and wonderful blue, lavender, red, or white flowers. I love the earliness of leaves and flowers, the beauty of the foliage, and the flowers. They are tougher than they look, asking only for some shade and well-drained soils. Lungworts occur in different guises: those with plain green leaves and flowers in the blue to lavender range (*Pulmonaria angustifolia*); those with plain green leaves and flowers of pink to red (*P. rubra*); those with spotted leaves that are long and narrow (*P. longifolia*); and those with spotted leaves that are relatively short and wide (*P. saccharata*). Noting the differences in leaf shape and spotting is the easiest way to sort out the spe-

Leaves of *Pulmonaria saccharata* (left), *P. longifolia* (middle), and *P. angustifolia*

Pulmonaria angustifolia

cies. A good deal of breeding and selection occurred in the 1990s, and the number of cultivar choices has risen exponentially.

There is little to choose between *Pulmonaria angustifolia*, common lungwort, and *P. rubra*, red-flowered lungwort, as far as leaf shape and leaf color are concerned. They both have hairy unspotted green leaves that poke out of the soil early in the spring, either at the same time as the flowers or a little after. The plainness of the foliage makes these lungworts less popular among gardeners; however, they offer some of the finest flowers in the genus. Some of the biggest and bluest flowers can be found in selections of *P. angustifolia*, such as 'Mawson's Variety' and 'Munstead Blue', respectively. They also possess good heat tolerance, performing well in our trials at the University of Georgia. Happy and hardy in zones 3 to 7 in the East, to zone 8 in the West.

The selections of *Pulmonaria rubra* are a bit more complex than others. The nonspotted leaves are similar to those of *P. angustifolia*, although they may be a little larger. The pink to red flowers open as the new leaves emerge. Plants are not as vigorous or as tough as others, and we had more losses in this group of lungworts than in any other. Still, their color guarantees them popularity, and some of the selections are interesting, including 'Bowles' Red', the toughest of the group we tested, and 'David Ward', by far the most ornamental but least robust, with its red flowers and variegated foliage. Perform well in zones 3 to 6 in the East, to zone 8 in the West.

The species *Pulmonaria longifolia* makes up many of the lungworts in American gardens, probably because the spotted foliage is handsome long after the flowers have come and gone. The common name, long-leaved lungwort, describes the long, narrow leaves, which are quite distinct from all other lungworts. The flowers are usually lavender to blue. The best-

Pulmonaria angustifolia 'Mawson's Variety'

Pulmonaria angustifolia 'Munstead Blue'

Pulmonaria rubra 'Bowles' Red'

Pulmonaria rubra 'Bowles' Red'

Pulmonaria rubra 'David Ward'

Pulmonaria rubra 'David Ward'

MORE →

Pulmonaria 'Roy Davidson'

Pulmonaria saccharata 'Berries and Cream'

known selection is 'Bertram Anderson', with its long narrow leaves and striking blue flowers. Several others have shown excellent promise. The selection sold both as subspecies *cevennensis* and 'Little Blue' has some of the most ornamental foliage in the entire genus, while the hybrid between *P. longifolia* and *P. saccharata*, *P.* 'Roy Davidson', possesses some of the leaf characteristics of *P. longifolia* but bears light blue flowers. All the long-leaved selections and hybrids are excellent performers, tolerating hot, humid summers better than other lungworts and providing excellent foliage and habit in most of the country. Hardy in zones 3 to 7.

Selections of spotted lungwort, *Pulmonaria saccharata*, are by far the most easily available and popular. The foliage is wider than those of *P. longifolia*, and spotting patterns are highly variable. In fact, they are like fingerprints, no leaf being exactly the same as another. Flowers range from pink to lavender to deep blue. So many fine selections have been produced that you should have no problem finding one for the shade. Try 'Benediction', with its fine light blue flowers, or 'Berries and Cream', a favorite in the Armitage garden for its pink flowers and beautiful spotted pattern. 'Excalibur' is almost white; 'Spilled Milk' is an apt description; and the lightly spotted 'Highdown' is among the best of them all, providing excellent ornamental value, good flowering, and a tough disposition. 'Mrs. Kittle' has clean spots and feels at home in the shade of small shrubs like golden spirea, and the light

Pulmonaria saccharata 'Berries and Cream'

Pulmonaria longifolia 'Bertram Anderson'

Pulmonaria saccharata 'Benediction'

Pulmonaria longifolia 'Bertram Anderson'

Pulmonaria longifolia subsp. *cevennensis* ('Little Blue')

blue flowers and good leaves of 'Mrs. Moon' have made her a longtime favorite. Finally, the white flowers of 'Sissinghurst White' are always a welcome addition in the spring. Given the depth and range of offerings, describing lungworts is becoming as difficult as describing coral bells, daylilies, or hostas. All the better for us gardeners! Hardy in zones 3 to 7 in the East, to zone 8 in the West.

Pulmonaria saccharata 'Excalibur'

Pulmonaria saccharata 'Mrs. Kittle'

Pulmonaria saccharata 'Highdown'

Pulmonaria saccharata 'Spilled Milk'

Pulmonaria saccharata 'Sissinghurst White'

Pulmonaria saccharata 'Mrs. Moon'

Pulsatilla pratensis

Pulsatilla vulgaris

Pulsatilla

PASQUEFLOWER

Except to the hard-core alpine and rock garden enthusiasts, the diversity of the genus *Pulsatilla* is largely unknown. Those in the know grow pasqueflowers for the beauty of their dissected foliage and their handsome purple to white flowers in early spring. Flowers emerge before the foliage in most cases, followed by the leaves, but the waving seed heads are the most striking part of the plants, persisting for many weeks after the ephemeral flowers have disappeared. Because they flower in late winter and early spring when snow may still be on the ground, the flowers and seed heads persist for as long as the cool weather holds up. I have seen absolutely stunning plantings in the Denver Botanic Gardens (there the pasqueflowers are seeding everywhere) and have grown them in north Georgia with reasonable success. If one lives in an area where alpines do well, then it is worth chasing down plants of *Pulsatilla halleri* or *P. pratensis*, both of which flower early and often. But most gardeners don't have the time or money to find such gems and will usually be limited to the common pasqueflower, *P. vulgaris*. That certainly is not all bad: the plant provides excellent foliage and dozens of deep purple flowers. And the seed heads persist for many weeks, giving another dimension to the plant. A few cultivars have been selected, but I have been most impressed with the white-flowered 'Alba', which forms similar

Pulsatilla halleri

Pulsatilla vulgaris

Pulsatilla vulgaris seed heads

Pulsatilla vulgaris 'Alba'

seed heads and whose white flowers contrast well with the foliage. Provide full sun, excellent drainage. Hardy in zones 4 (3 with protection) to 7.

Ranunculus

BUTTERCUP

Buttercups are a study in diversity, for sure. Plants may develop from a tuber, like a potato, or from fibrous roots, like most other perennials. Although most people think of buttercups as yellow, their flowers appear in a full spectrum of hues, including white. Some species turn over and die at the first feel of frost; others are tough as nails through all kinds of inclement weather, elbowing-out any other plant in their proximity.

The most colorful and the most persnickety is the tuberous-rooted Persian buttercup, *Ranunculus asiaticus*. Usually seen as a pot plant from the greenhouse or as a cut flower grown in cool summer areas, it produces some of the prettiest flowers in the genus. They are favorites among bulb aficionados, but they seldom act as a perennial, being frost tolerant only to about 28°F. Tubers should be soaked in water and put in the garden in the fall in mild areas, and in the spring in areas of cold winters and cool summers. Coolness is necessary for best performance, and plants will produce many double flowers in the spring, then go dormant in the summer. Selections may be purchased as single ('Bloomingdale Yellow') or mixed ('Sunningdale Mix') colors. Full sun and excellent drainage are necessary. Hardy in zones 7 to 9.

Another little tuberous species is

Ranunculus asiaticus 'Sunningdale Mix' with dusty miller

Ranunculus ficaria

MORE →

Ranunculus asiaticus 'Bloomingdale Yellow'

Ranunculus ficaria, which if conditions are to its liking can become terribly invasive. One selection of the plant that is not at all invasive (I continue to hope it will grow faster) is 'Brazen Hussy', who lives up to her name in March when the shamelessly brash yellow flowers sit atop the small deep purple leaves. Plants are only about 6" tall, but they shine like brass in an otherwise drab garden. They flower for weeks on end, and the foliage remains richly bronze until plants go dormant in midsummer. They will reseed; the little hussies that appear the following spring will produce flowers in a couple of years. A wonderful plant, hardy in zones 6 to 8.

Ranunculus aconitifolius is a lovely white-flowered double, whose leaves resemble those of wolfsbane (*Aconitum*). Seldom seen, but worth a try; it is not as aggressive as some of the yellows. Hardy in zones 5 to 8.

The common yellow buttercups are represented by numerous species. The

Ranunculus aconitifolius

Ranunculus ficaria

Ranunculus ficaria 'Brazen Hussy'

Ranunculus bulbosus 'Flore Pleno'

Ranunculus bulbosus 'Flore Pleno'

Ranunculus repens 'Susan's Song' ('Buttered Popcorn')

double yellow flower of the invasive *Ranunculus bulbosus* 'Flore Pleno' is quite lovely, but note the thuggery in its eyes. Creeping buttercup, *R. repens*, is equally invasive. If one is going to use these plants as a ground cover, then being invasive is a good quality. One of the prettiest selections of *R. repens* is the white-and-green variegated 'Susan's Song' ('Buttered Popcorn'). In mild winters, the foliage is as pretty in the winter as in the summer. It looks terrific with bronze foliage of *Ajuga* and *Oxalis*. My favorite, but be warned—she gallops!

Ranunculus repens 'Susan's Song' ('Buttered Popcorn') with *Ajuga*

Rehmannia angulata

Rehmannia

CHINESE FOXGLOVE

Rehmannia elata and *R. angulata* (Chinese foxglove) are marvelous plants that never fail to elicit all sorts of favorable comments, as well as the all-too-common "What are they?" and "Where did you find them?" They belong to the same family (Gesneriaceae) as African violets and gloxinias and are also characterized by hairy stems and alternate leaves, which in the case of both species are light green and deeply lobed or toothed, like an oak leaf. *Rehmannia angulata* is smaller (about 2' tall) than *R. elata* (2–4' tall) and not as hairy. The flowers of *R. angulata* bear orange dots inside the lower lip; the flowers of *R. elata* have yellow throats and red dots. It is hard to tell the two apart unless they are growing side by side. Although plants stand only about 2' tall, they present a handsome look in late spring and midsummer, when the large flower buds open. Indeed, the plants are grown for their beautiful flowers, usually of a bright rose-purple. The flowers are bunched together in terminal clusters, and when in flower, the plants are similar to foxglove, only shorter. They spread rapidly by seed and even in the same season, seedlings will grow and flower, quickly resulting in a reasonably large colony. Although they are native to China, these two species are not cold hardy north of zone 7, and even there, cold winters can take them out. They should be planted in partial shade in a protected area sheltered from the worst of the winter winds. Winter wetness can be a serious problem, therefore a raised bed is best for longer lasting stands.

Rehmannia elata

Rodgersia aesculifolia

Rodgersia

People are forever looking for foliar character in their gardens, wanting large bold plants with flowers secondary to the foliage. It is not easy to find such plants, and in fact, the desire for foliage accounts for much of the recent turn to ornamental grasses. *Rodgersia* is such a plant: its foliage provides wonderful contrast to all sorts of flowering plants. That the foliage is outstanding is only part of the appeal; the flowers, like giant astilbes, are also enchanting in midsummer. The leaves of most of the species are bronze or become so later in the season. The flowers are borne in large panicles well above the foliage and are found mainly in whites, pinks, and reds.

Alas, the tale is not fully told. Beautiful as they are, rodgersias have serious intimate needs. They are not at all

Rodgersia aesculifolia

Rodgersia sambucifolia

Rodgersia pinnata 'Rubra' (left) and 'Superba Alba'

Rodgersia pinnata 'Superba'

comfortable when temperatures are warm, and once temperatures consistently reach 80°F or more, their foliage looks a little tatty. Furthermore, they are plants best suited for a bog or streamside condition: placing these plants in dry soils is like potting up primroses in Miami. They prefer shady conditions, and a combination of moist soils, cool summers, and partial shade will ensure your chance for success with them. They do well on the West Coast but with proper attention to moisture and shade, they can be wonderful additions to gardens in zones 5 and 6, even though they will be a challenge. Additional mulching is necessary in zone 5; keep out of the worst winter winds.

Four species are occasionally offered, all bearing many similarities. *Rodgersia aesculifolia* and *R. sambucifolia* have leaves that look surprisingly like those of horsechestnut (palmate) and elderberry (pinnate), respectively, and lovely pink flowers to boot. The flowers of *R. pinnata* can be white ('Alba'), tall and white ('Superba Alba'), red ('Rubra'), or the best of all, tall, brassy, and rose-red ('Superba'); its leaves are pinnate and bronze through most of the growing season. The most commonly offered species is *R. podophylla*, with wonderful bronze palmate leaves and creamy white flowers.

I am not sure if any one species is easier than the others, but given the dearth of architectural plants, any one is worth a try. What else do you know that is big, bold, and beautiful and wants to be planted in a bog?

Rodgersia pinnata 'Alba'

Rodgersia podophylla

Rudbeckia

CONEFLOWER, BLACK-EYED SUSAN

Of all the genera in the daisy family, *Rudbeckia* is one of the best known and popular. Gardeners who couldn't tell an astilbe from an aster have no trouble confidently inquiring after your rudbeckias. For a long visual show with a minimum of upkeep and maintenance, the coneflowers fit just about everybody's idea of a good perennial.

By far the most popular of the coneflowers, *Rudbeckia fulgida*, an orange species, has smothered summer and fall gardens in the selection *R. fulgida* var. *sullivantii* 'Goldsturm'. In every garden from Dallas to Duluth, from every spit of land, wherever the sun shines, 'Goldsturm' is there. The species itself, which does not differ greatly from this ubiquitous representative, is only to be found occasionally in botanical gardens and herbaria specimens. 'Goldsturm' originated in 1937 at Foerster's Nursery in Germany, described as a late summer- to fall-flowering perennial with persistent orange ray flowers surrounding a rounded black disk. Plants grow 2–3' tall and large colonies form rapidly, complementing everything from ornamental grasses

Rodgersia podophylla

Rudbeckia fulgida var. *sullivantii* 'Goldsturm'

MORE →

Rudbeckia laciniata

to white lilies. Although they are overplanted, it is with good reason. I admit I am tired of seeing this thing in every garden and gas station in the country, but I am equally pleased that a plant with this much beauty can please so many people who would otherwise have planted five geraniums and watched them die. Full sun, heavy feeder, adequate moisture. Plants hate shade and don't do well in drought. Hardy in zones 3 to 8.

Rudbeckia laciniata 'Goldquelle'

Both *Rudbeckia laciniata* and *R. nitida*, cutleaf coneflowers, are tall (4–7') and have pinnately compound or pinnately cut leaves and yellow flowers with a greenish disk. The species are quite dramatic, especially when one comes across a sole specimen, standing like a sentinel. A few excellent cultivars are so large that one plant is sufficient for a good show; they make good eye-popping fall-flowering specimens. They may be listed as selections of one species or another, but similarities to both species may be found upon close observation.

One of the finest is the double-flowered *Rudbeckia laciniata* 'Goldquelle', which is only 3–4' tall and forms significant clumps in a year or two. The double yellow flowers are terrific when they first open, and for a few days thereafter, but can look scruffy when they start to decline. This is a more serious problem in hot, humid climates than in those with cool nights. I really

Rudbeckia fulgida var. *sullivantii* 'Goldsturm'

like the tall (up to 7') *R. nitida* 'Herbsonne' ('Autumn Sun'). Dozens of long drooping sulfur-yellow petals surround a cylindrical green disk, making a glorious show from September through November, dwarfing red dahlias or red cannas. Both require full sun, good drainage, and protection from winds. Too much shade or exposure to high winds results in the need for staking. Zones 3 to 8 for 'Goldquelle', zones 5 (perhaps 4) to 8 for 'Herbsonne'.

Rudbeckia triloba, the three-lobed coneflower, is another native of the Great Plains. This prairie species provides plants absolutely covered with small (1½" across) flowers on 3–5' tall plants. The bottom leaves are trilobed, thus accounting for the common name. Plants are not as perennial as other species, generally flowering themselves to oblivion after two or three years; but they reseed and reappear with abandon, never going away entirely. The yellow to orange ray flowers surround a black to purple disk. A great plant, even when not in flower. Full sun, good drainage, zones 3 to 10.

Rudbeckia nitida 'Herbsonne' ('Autumn Sun')

Rudbeckia triloba

Rudbeckia triloba

Rudbeckia triloba

Salvia guaranitica

Salvia guaranitica 'Argentina Skies'

Salvia guaranitica 'Purple Knight'

Salvia

SAGE

I went through my "salvia stage of life" a few years ago, and fortunately I emerged reasonably unscathed. Going through the SSOL is like going through the teenage years: out of control and out of money. Salvias are perfect for the plant collector, but putting the first new salvia in newly prepared ground is like putting the first tropical fish in a newly purchased aquarium. It is impossible to stop at one. It is such a large genus, replete with species, selections, and hybrids, that just when you think you have seen the end of them, someone comes along with another. For the beginner, common sage, *Salvia officinalis*, with its numerous variations, is enough to get one hooked; it is then a simple matter to move on to more beautiful and more robust specimens. Many species of *Salvia* are native to South America, southern United States, and Mexico, so cold tolerance is not one of their better attributes. Cold tolerance only to zone 5 is not uncommon; zone 7 is typical for many species and cultivars.

Want a big, bold salvia in blooming color for at least twelve weeks, from early summer on? The 4–6" long dark

Salvia guaranitica

Salvia guaranitica 'Black and Blue'

Salvia guaranitica 'Purple Splendour'

green opposite leaves of *Salvia guaranitica*, blue anise sage, provide a subtle contrast to the deep blue flowers, which open all over the 4–6' tall plants. At the University of Georgia Horticulture Gardens, this has been such an outstanding and long-lived plant that it was designated a "Georgia Gold" winner, a plant that is almost foolproof. This no-brainer also has a few selections of its own. Probably the most popular is the light blue–flowered 'Argentina Skies', which is as beautiful as the species but not as floriferous. Several old-fashioned cultivars are out there, but few have found common acceptance. 'Black and Blue', 'Purple Knight', and 'Purple Splendour' are big (up to 7' tall) and possess large flowers, but they are somewhat weedy. Full sun, good drainage, zones 7 (sometimes 6) to 10.

Salvia involucrata, bulbous pink sage, and *S. koyamae*, yellow sage, are about as different as plants can be in the same genus, but both are coveted for the qualities they deliver to the gardener. The bulbous pink sage is actually cherry pink, and the flowers terminate in a swollen knob—not exactly useful for a common name. Plants are large (4–5' tall stems) and are very lax and open. In most gardens they'll need at least one pinch, but since they don't flower until late summer and fall, two pinches may be required. A more compact selection of *S. involucrata*, although still large, is 'Bethellii', a much better choice for the gardener than the species. Weedy, lanky, and lax it may be, but people love the color and the weird-looking flowers. Useful in the vase as a cut flower as well as in the garden. Full sun, zones 8 (perhaps 7) to 10.

Salvia koyamae has much less exciting flowers but fits in many gardens. Plants can spread rapidly and the 6–8" long green leaves make an outstanding show throughout the season. Plants are only about 2' tall, therefore no staking or pinching is required. The short light yellow flower stems may not be as eye-catching as others, but I think they are wonderful. The other wonderful characteristic of this species is its tolerance to shade—in the Armitage garden, it grows and flowers well with only about three hours of sunlight a day. Partial shade, good drainage, zones 6 to 8.

While its virtues are well known to lovers of spice and good food, sage

Salvia koyamae

Salvia koyamae

Salvia involucrata

Salvia involucrata 'Bethellii'

Salvia involucrata

MORE →

(along with the others in the Simon and Garfunkle line-up of "parsley, sage, rosemary, and thyme") is now recognized as a fine ornamental, one of the more vigorous and robust of the culinary herbs. *Salvia officinalis*, common sage, historically sat in the herb garden, waiting for an alchemist, monk, or Victorian lady to wander by and pull off its leaves for some medicinal or culinary use, like kids pulling wings from butterflies. In these more enlightened times, however, it doubles as a fine garden plant, by itself or interplanted among roses and other ornamentals. The beautiful whorled light purple flowers are the highlight of the species.

White flowers make *Salvia officinalis* 'Albiflora' come to life, and the foliar selections of the species hardly qualify the plant as "common" anything. They produce few blooms, but their lack of flower color is more than compensated for by their diversity of foliage. 'Icterina' has light and darker green splashed on the leaves; 'Purpurescens' bears purple leaves and looks terrific on its own but really shines when placed with brighter colors. 'Tricolor' looks like my son was painting nearby and spilled a mixed palette of paint on the leaves. Full sun, excellent moisture required. Hardy in zones 4 to 7 in the East, but plants do well in West Coast zone 8 as well.

Hybrid purple sage goes under numerous botanical names, including *Salvia nemerosa*, *S.* ×*superba*, and *S.* ×*sylvestris*. Given cool nights and good

Salvia officinalis 'Purpurescens'

Salvia officinalis 'Purpurescens'

Salvia officinalis

Salvia officinalis 'Albiflora'

Salvia officinalis 'Icterina' with *Felicia*

moisture, hybrid purple sage can make an outstanding display. Plants grow about 2–2½' tall and flower throughout the summer. They do poorly in hot summers and high humidity, but elsewhere they are wonderfully eye-catching. Common hybrid cultivars in the American nursery trade are confused in nomenclature, offered variously as selections of *S. nemerosa* and *S. ×sylvestris*. 'East Friesland' ('Ostfriesland') and 'Lubecca' are marvelous hybrids, with their deep purple to blue, compact full flowers. 'Tanzerin', 'Blue Hill', and 'Blue Queen' ('Blaukönigin') are probably hybrids, with *S. nemerosa* as the dominant parent, but regardless of parentage are just as useful as *S. ×sylvestris* hybrids, if not quite as vigorous. Full sun, good drainage, zones 4 to 7.

Salvia 'Indigo Spires' grows 4–5' tall but flowers all season long. Outstandingly tough in heat and humidity, it is often one of the few plants flowering

Salvia nemerosa 'Blue Queen' ('Blaukönigin')

Salvia nemerosa 'Blue Hill'

Salvia officinalis 'Tricolor'

Salvia ×sylvestris 'East Friesland' ('Ostfriesland')

Salvia nemerosa 'Tanzerin'

Salvia ×sylvestris 'Lubecca'

MORE →

even when summer heat approaches the unbearable. Its drawback is its gangly growth, and a spring pinch is a good idea. Also beautiful in the fall.

Salvia 'Indigo Spires' with *Phlomis*

Salvia 'Indigo Spires'

Santolina

The plants themselves cannot take credit for the popularity of *Santolina*; rather it is what the gray-green foliage does for their neighbors that makes them so desirable. Not particularly tolerant of hot summers and high humidity, and absolutely intolerant of poor drainage, *Santolina* is not for everybody. But if you are designing a garden stroll through fragrant foliage, be sure to include this herb. The fragrance is not soon to be forgotten—not awful, but very pungent, a great identification feature.

Santolina chamaecyparissus, lavender cotton, is the most common of the species encountered in gardens. Its many finely divided leaflets are a soothing gray-green with a white sheen beneath, a very effective softener of the intense greens and bright flower colors of summer. When well grown, they make loose leafy balls in the landscape and later in the summer produce rather forgettable yellow daisy flowers. They are often sheared and used as an edging, which is cruel and unusual punishment for any plant. They become woody at the base after a year or so in the garden and may require a hard pruning of old wood for

Santolina chamaecyparissus

Santolina pinnata

Santolina pinnata 'Edward Bowles'

rejuvenation. Full sun, excellent drainage, zones 6 to 8.

A closely related species is *Santolina pinnata*, also with gray-green to silver foliage but with lovely off-white flowers. 'Edward Bowles', with large primrose flowers, is its excellent selection. Plants are winter hardy only to zones 7 or 8.

Santolina virens, green lavender cotton, is grown as much for its yellow flowers as its bright green foliage, which resembles that of rosemary (the plant is also known as *S. rosmarinifolia*). The leaflets are quite small (less than half an inch), resulting in more stick-like foliage. Plants do not have the powerful smell of the common species, but rather a sanitized aroma. Not nearly as much fun or exercise for the nose. Full sun, excellent drainage, hardy in zones 7 to 9.

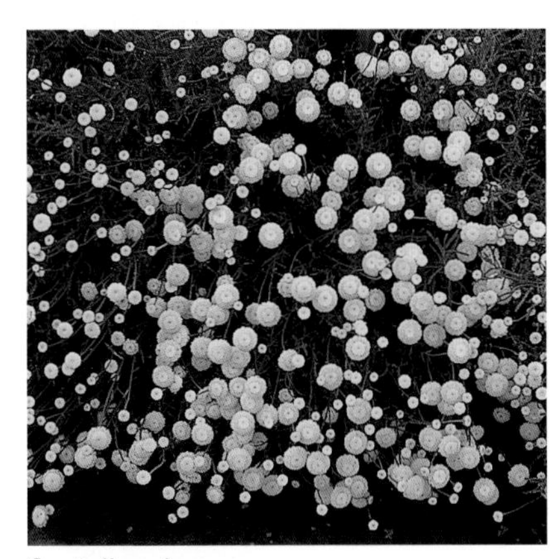

Santolina virens

Saponaria ocymoides

Saponaria

SOAPWORT

Plants of *Saponaria ocymoides*, rock soapwort, are far better falling off rocks or running through a sunny rock garden than they are planted in the "common" garden ground. In the spring, flowers cover the plants like pink lava. The one-inch-long leaves are flat and olive green. Great plants, but they do roam. Once established, they reseed vigorously and stay around for years. They are less heat tolerant than *S. officinalis*, and don't do well in areas of hot summers and high humidities. Full sun to partial shade, good drainage, zones 2 to 7.

The leaves of *Saponaria officinalis*, soapwort, "yeelde out of themselves a certain juice when they are bruised, which scoureth almost as well as soap." This was written in 1597, when real soap was quite expensive and used only sparingly (perfumes and washing in lavender water were far more common). But there was a drawback to boiling the leaves of *S. officinalis* and lathering up with the result—the itchy problem of dermatitis, which occurred quite regularly. Otherwise this weak challenger to Irish Spring makes a wonderful, rambunctious garden

Saponaria officinalis

Saponaria officinalis 'Alba'

Saponaria ocymoides

MORE →

plant. "Rambunctious" is a nice word; "aggressive," "weedy," and "invasive" are apt descriptions as well, especially in the West. It is a plant usually found in cottage gardens, where its romping and bouncing around are appreciated. Plants are effective setting off a white picket fence or roaming by a streambank. The opposite leaves occur on 2–3' tall plants, topped with pink flowers all summer. Single white-flowered cultivars, such as 'Alba', are also available, but double-flowerers, such as 'Rosea Plena' (pink), are probably the most common of all soapworts. Full sun, moderate drainage, zones 2 to 8.

Scabiosa

SCABIOUS, PINCUSHION FLOWER

Not many people have pin cushions in their sewing drawers anymore (most people don't have sewing drawers anymore), but as one looks at the flower head of scabious, one appreciates immediately how apt the common name is. (The genus name, on the other hand, is Latin for "scabies," the disease the plant was incorrectly thought to cure.) Three species of scabious are found in gardens: the mostly cool-toned *Scabiosa caucasica* and *S. columbaria* and the less frequently encountered yellow-flowering *S. ochroleuca*.

Both *Scabiosa caucasica*, common scabious, and *S. columbaria*, pincushion flower, grow 2–3' tall and are similar in their garden look, environmental response, and availability. Historically, *S. caucasica* has been a mainstay for lilac to purple flowers for the summer garden. The plants consist of pinnately lobed opposite leaves and form large mounds with light blue to purple flowers. Many variations of the species occur, from larger lavender ('Denise', 'Perfecta'), deeper blue ('Moerheim Blue'), and taller cut flower selections ('Fama') to plants with handsome white flowers ('Bressingham White', 'Miss Willmott'). We anxiously await the flowers, but let us not ignore the

Scabiosa caucasica 'Fama'

Scabiosa caucasica 'Denise'

Scabiosa caucasica 'Moerheim Blue'

Scabiosa caucasica 'Perfecta'

Scabiosa Scabiosa caucasica 'Miss Willmott'

wonderful clean-looking pinwheel fruit. Like an architect's model of a futuristic domed restaurant revolving on a giant leg, such is the fruit of scabious.

Shorter, more compact, and more floriferous plants are the claims to fame for selections of *Scabiosa columbaria*. For the most part, the two cultivars that took the gardening world by storm were worthy of the hype. 'Butterfly Blue' provides persistent flowering on 2' tall plants nearly all summer and is the best scabious to hit the market in many years. Its companion, 'Pink Mist', is not as colorful as 'Butterfly Blue' but is a good plant nevertheless.

Both *Scabiosa columbaria* and *S. caucasica* require full sun and good drainage and are hardy in zones 3 to 7.

Most gardeners believe that blue, lavender, and purple are the only colors available in the genus *Scabiosa*. While those hues are common, the wonderful primrose-yellow flowers of *Scabiosa ochroleuca*, cream scabious, should not be overlooked. Plants are much taller (3–4') than *S. caucasica*, and although its flowers are similar in

Scabiosa caucasica 'Bressingham White'

Fruit of *Scabiosa caucasica*

Scabiosa columbaria 'Butterfly Blue'

Scabiosa columbaria 'Butterfly Blue' with *Knautia*

Scabiosa columbaria 'Pink Mist'

Scabiosa ochroleuca

Scabiosa ochroleuca

MORE →

form and size (1–2" wide) to *S. caucasica*, they provide a much more muted color in the summer garden. The pinnate leaves are divided into eleven to thirteen lobes and blend well with other garden plants. It is not as tolerant of heat and humidity as the blue pincushions but is effective in the Midwest, Northeast, and Northwest. Plants are often mistaken for the closely related *Cephalaria gigantea*, which is larger in every way, including height, leaves, and flowers. Full sun to partial shade, good drainage, zones 5 to 7.

Sedum

STONECROP

I love the sedums for their amazing diversity of foliage, flower, and plant habit. Many of the more than three hundred species are succulent and may be upright or low growing, as useful for rock gardens as they are for borders. All sedums perform best in full sun and have moderate water requirements and persistent flowers. Hardiness differs from species to species, but in general plants do well in zones 4 to 7.

Botanically the low-growing sedums (*Sedum acre*, *S. kamtschaticum*, *S. spathulifolium*, *S. spurium*, *S. reflexum*, *S. ternatum*) differ from each other in many ways, including their flower form, rootstock development, and foliar characteristics. From the gardener's point of view, however, they are used in the same manner. They are all best for rock gardens, ground covers, or simply as low-growing border or edging plants. While they broadly prefer similar conditions, the choice of low growers may be further narrowed when performance, flower color, aggressiveness, or disease tolerance are taken into consideration.

Goldmoss stonecrop, *Sedum acre*, is one of the most aggressive and best-known species in American gardens. "Goldmoss" is descriptive indeed: when the plants are in flower, the golden yellow flowers entirely cover the mossy foliage. The small quarter-inch-long leaves overlap like shingles, and the leaves appear scaly. Only 2–3" tall, plants will move in and around anything in their path, and a wonderful soft green ground cover often results. Over time, if Lady Luck is smiling, one finds themselves digging out rather than planting *S. acre*, and the Lady may not be quite as welcome anymore. Hardy in zones 3 to 8.

Another popular ground cover is

Sedum acre

Sedum acre

Sedum spurium 'Green Mantle'

Sedum spurium 'Fuldaglut'

two-row stonecrop, *Sedum spurium*, whose foliage can look awful much of the time. Luckily, many cultivars sport arresting bronze foliage or flowers, as well as a few good green-leaved sedums that can occasionally be discovered. One such green selection is 'Green Mantle', which looks unusually good in leaf. I also enjoy the bronze 'Fuldaglut', which combines earthy leaves and flowers and reaches a height of 2–6". Hardy in zones 3 to 7.

The choice of aggressive low growers also extends to stone orpine, *Sedum reflexum*, which looks like a tiny evergreen with bluish green needle-like leaves. Plants spread like stoloniferous junipers, filling in areas with blinding speed—at least for a sedum. One of the finest choices is 'Blue Spruce', outstanding but aggressive, with plants about 6–10" tall. Hardy in zones 5 to 8.

For some of the most beautiful foliage and handsome flowers to boot, particularly for gardeners in the West, try *Sedum spathulifolium*. Plants have blue-green spatulate (shaped like a spatula) leaves and short trailing stems. I love the silvery leaves of 'Cape Blanco' and its dozens of yellow flowers, each three-quarters of an inch wide. Plants are up to 6" tall. Hardy in zones 6 to 8.

Yet one more low grower is the whorled stonecrop, *Sedum ternatum*. The light green leaves are whorled around the stems, and plants grow about 6" tall. Above the foliage, many small starry white flowers are produced in spring. A bonus for these plants is their higher tolerance of shade compared to other ground-covering species. Partial shade, zones 4 to 8.

Finally, to round out the low growers, from the Kamchatka peninsula comes *Sedum kamtschaticum*, a diminutive clumper rather than an aggressive ground cover. The 1½" long leaves and purple buds and yellow flowers provide an outstanding display in spring and early summer. With its large number of bicolored buds and flowers, 'Diffusum' is even more eye-catching. The most popular cultivar, from the Weihenstephan Test Gardens near Tubingen, Germany, is the unpronounceable 'Weihenstephaner Gold', with golden yellow flowers over a ground-hugging plant. Full sun, good drainage, zones 3 to 8.

The upright *Sedum* species and cultivars grow 1–3' tall, with the many branches growing up instead of out.

Sedum reflexum 'Blue Spruce'

Sedum spathulifolium 'Cape Blanco'

Sedum ternatum

Sedum kamtschaticum

Sedum kamtschaticum 'Diffusum'

Sedum kamtschaticum 'Weihenstephaner Gold'

MORE →

The best-known example of this group by far is *Sedum* 'Autumn Joy' ('Herbstfreude'), one of the toughest and best-known perennials in American gardens. Other sedums can easily challenge 'Autumn Joy' for beauty if not for persistence. The 12–15" tall aizoon stonecrop, *Sedum aizoon*, has flat 2" long leaves and dozens of yellow flowers in early summer. Variety *aurantiacum*, with its red stems and deep yellow to orange flowers, is even showier. Full sun, zones 4 to 8.

Many fine upright hybrids have recently been selected with various parents in the progeny, including the showy stonecrop, *Sedum spectabile* (*Hylotelephium spectabile*), and *S. telephium*, among others. *Sedum* 'Autumn Joy' seems to be grown in every garden in the entire universe, but how can one complain about such success? Large succulent leaves, pink flower buds that darken as they age, and bronze-red flowers in late summer and fall have made this sun-loving plant a desirable addition. Some people even find its spent flowers ornamental in the winter. I don't. *Sedum spectabile* 'Meteor' is equally beautiful, but I for one cannot find a great deal of difference between it and 'Autumn Joy'. Other close relatives of 'Autumn Joy' are *S. spectabile* 'Carmen', with large rosy pink flowers; *S.* 'Ruby Glow', with ruby red flowers; *S.* 'Sunset Cloud', which bears dozens of rosy red flowers; and the fabulous *S.* 'Strawberries and Cream'. I enjoy all these colored hybrids, but none is as foolproof, throughout the

Sedum aizoon var. *aurantiacum*

Sedum 'Autumn Joy' ('Herbstfreude') in flower

Sedum 'Autumn Joy' ('Herbstfreude') in winter

Sedum 'Autumn Joy' ('Herbstfreude')

Sedum 'Autumn Joy' ('Herbstfreude') in bud

country, as 'Autumn Joy'. They all flower in mid to late summer and early fall. Full sun, zones 3 to 8.

For darker foliage, *Sedum* 'Atropurpureum' has outstanding bronze-red foliage on a 2–3' upright plant; *S.* 'Vera Jameson', similar but with better flowers, is probably more readily available than 'Atropurpureum' and is frequently mixed-up with it at nurseries. *Sedum* 'Mohrchen' came to us from Germany. Its large glossy purple leaves are gaudy, and the plant performance has been a disappointment to me. To each his own—some people simply gush over the plant. The upright cultivars, green- or purple-leaved, are highly useful garden plants and combine well with a wide assortment of other perennials, annuals, and shrubs. Full sun, zones 4 to 8.

Sedum spectabile 'Meteor'

Sedum spectabile 'Carmen'

Sedum 'Ruby Glow'

Sedum 'Sunset Cloud'

Sedum 'Strawberries and Cream'

Sedum 'Atropurpureum'

Sedum 'Vera Jameson'

Sedum 'Mohrchen'

Silene virginica

Silene regia

Silene polypetala

Silene

CAMPION

The campions provide low-growing species for containers, rock gardens—any place where colorful spots of color are welcome. Leaves are entire; the flowers may be notched or fringed, often with an inflated calyx that looks like a small bladder. Some of the most brilliant red colors can be seen in our native fire pink, *Silene virginica*, whose flowers dare you to pass them by without comment. The 10–20" tall plants do well in cool climates and are occasionally offered to the gardener who must have native plants in the garden, but truth be told, enjoying them in their native habitat makes far more sense. The western relative of the eastern fire pink is called wild pink, *S. regia*. Plants are taller (2–3') but bear the same stunning scarlet flowers. Both species require partial shade and good drainage, and do well in zones 4 to 7.

A wonderful eastern native is fringed campion, *Silene polypetala*. Plants are only 4–6" tall, with light green leaves, but the fringed pink flowers are unlike any others in the eastern woodland. They are not easy to grow: even when it appears that a population has been established, the colony may disappear the next year. If nursery-grown plants are available, however, they are worth a try because of their unique beauty. They are on some state endangered lists and absolutely must not be shorn for the wild. An interesting hybrid between *S. polypetala* and *S. virginica* is 'Longwood', bearing

Silene 'Longwood'

Silene caroliniana 'Millstream Select'

Silene uniflora

Silene fimbriata

deeper pink flowers with the same fringed look (partial shade, zones 6 to 8). Unfortunately, plants don't appear to be any longer lived than either of the parents when domesticated.

Silene caroliniana, Carolina campion, is another low-growing species, with slightly notched pink flowers on 4–8" tall plants. 'Millstream Select' (full sun to partial shade, zones 5 to 8) is an example of one of the selections from the garden at Millstream House, the home of the much-missed H. Lincoln Foster. In our haste, let us not ignore the Mutt and Jeff of the whites: the 6" seaside campion, *S. uniflora*, with swollen calyces and off-white flowers, and the little-known 2–3' tall white fimbriated campion, *S. fimbriata*. *Silene fimbriata* has panicles of few, large, white fringed flowers, but since it is seldom grown in American gardens, it is difficult to know where it will thrive (I'd hazard full sun to partial shade, probably zones 5 to 8).

Sisyrinchium

BLUE-EYED GRASS

It is only recently that American gardeners noticed these All-American plants. Perhaps because the genus name has so many syllables, people would just as soon not have to tell anybody about it. The common name is simple enough, however, and quite descriptive of the native species.

In the spirit of horticultural nomenclature, it should be noted that blue-eyed grass is not a grass at all but actually belongs to the iris family. In spring the tufted grassy leaves of southeastern native *Sisyrinchium angustifolium* are interspersed with small (half-inch-wide) rounded blue flowers, arising from the base. The white flowers of 'Album' are similar in shape and size and are easier to see in the dark green leaves. From the eastern United States comes *S. atlanticum*, quite similar to *S. angustifolium* but with larger, darker flowers, often with a yellow center. They are lovely plants, quite popular among gardeners who enjoy something a little different, but I have trouble getting excited about them—perhaps because in the Armitage garden they become overgrown with weeds every year. Both species are quite prostrate, occasionally rising up to 12–18" tall. Partial shade; *S. angustifolium* is hardy in zones 3 to 8, and *S. atlanticum* in zones 5 to 9.

The outstanding large-flowered species of the western United States can take your breath away. My favorite is *Sisyrinchium idahoense*, which is a stand-alone plant when properly grown. Plants have 2' tall linear leaves and marvelous 1–1½" dark blue flowers with a yellow eye. 'California Skies' is outstanding, and for a fine white, try 'Album'. Plants are not vigorous in heat and humidity and are not often successful in the eastern part of the country. Full sun to partial shade, excellent drainage, zones 4 to 7.

Sisyrinchium angustifolium

Sisyrinchium angustifolium 'Album'

Sisyrinchium atlanticum

Sisyrinchium idahoense 'California Skies'

Sisyrinchium idahoense 'Album'

MORE →

Sisyrinchium striatum 'Aunt May'

Sisyrinchium striatum

Sisyrinchium striatum, yellow blue-eyed grass, is native to Argentina and Chile. This fine upright grower is well known to gardeners on the West Coast but, like many of the more ornamental forms, struggles in the East. The one-inch-wide leaves grow 1–3' tall, but without the flowers, the plant is rather nondescript, like an iris without flowers. The creamy yellow flowers, on the other hand, are quite distinctive, much different from our native species. They are up to an inch wide and striped with purple on the backsides, thus the term *striatum*. Plants will reseed if grown in suitable conditions and can be a bit of nuisance for lucky gardeners. I am not among the lucky ones, having killed this and its variegated cousin at least half a dozen times. I am nothing if not persistent! This variegated cousin is 'Aunt May', whose combination of handsome green-and-white leaves and yellow flowers won me over immediately. I bought this wonderful plant at a small nursery in England, washed its roots in the hotel toilet (not a good idea), and waited in line to present my treasure to the fine inspectors of the U.S. Department of Agriculture. After much head-scratching, book-searching, and root-probing, Aunt May and I were off to the Armitage garden. Alas, it wasn't to be, and Aunt May and I parted company for the last time two years later. Plants are now available in the United States, and such efforts are no longer necessary for me to kill the plant. I can do it all locally. Full sun to partial shade, good drainage, zones 5 to 8.

With the plethora of *Sisyrinchium* species and cultivars, it is not surprising that hybrids, man-made or natural, would be promoted to American gardeners. A few have such outrageous names that curious gardeners simply must have them. The best name is probably 'Quaint and Queer'; it simply demands attention. 'Biscutella' isn't far behind. 'Quaint and Queer' is small and has dull purple flowers with yellow centers. The biscuit one is quite similar, with dusky purple flowers and yellow centers, but is taller and more vigorous, except in my garden, where they both perish with equal vigor. Another lovely hybrid that has escaped the Armitage survival test is 'E. K. Balls', with dark mauve flowers and gray-green foliage. All hybrids perform well in the North and West. Full sun to partial shade, good drainage, zones 5 to 7, zone 8 on the West Coast.

Sisyrinchium 'Biscutella'

Sisyrinchium 'Quaint and Queer'

Sisyrinchium 'E. K. Balls'

Smilacina racemosa

FALSE SOLOMON'S SEAL

False Solomon's seal is a common native plant in almost any eastern woodland, and although it cavorts well with *Mertensia*, *Polygonatum*, and all sorts of other natives, this species is lovely in its own right when spied in the shade of oaks or poplars. While making your way through the woods, look for creamy white flowers, alternate leaves, and fruit changing from dull green to mature red. Such woodland walks are indeed good for the soul, but that does not mean *Smilacina racemosa* will not positively shine when placed under garden conditions. Flowers open in early spring, and foliage remains handsome until late fall. Shade, cool nights, and well-drained soils are needed for best performance. Buy two or three nursery-grown plants, place them side by side, and bring a little woodland home. Zones 3 to 7.

Fruit of *Smilacina racemosa*

Smilacina racemosa

Smilacina racemosa

Stachys byzantina

Stachys byzantina

Stachys byzantina 'Countess Helene von Stein'

Stachys

BETONY

The last time most of us felt the ear of a lamb was probably the last time most of us milked a cow. But if I can't on short notice feel the ear of a lamb, I can at least caress the sheepskin we bought in New Zealand. (You know New Zealand: the country that has a population of ten million, three million of them people.) When I caress that skin, then run outside and caress the leaves of lamb's ears (*Stachys byzantina*), they both feel wonderful. Nothing alike, but wonderful nevertheless. The handsome gray foliage of *S. byzantina* looks good from a distance and is used effectively both to soften harsh colors and edge brick walkways. But get up close and you will see that the lamby feel comes from soft hairs, easily visible on the upper and lower sides of the leaves. The purple flowers shoot up in late spring to early summer, but I think they detract from the foliage. Plants look great anywhere in the spring, but leaves can melt out in areas of high heat and humidity.

'Countess Helene von Stein' is the best selection of *Stachys byzantina* for most of the country; she has significantly larger leaves and fewer flowers than the species, but she is also more tolerant of heat and humidity, her true raison d'être. 'Sheila Macqueen' is more compact; the leaves are less hairy than the type, and the flowers are sterile. The most colorful cultivar is 'Primrose Heron', whose primrose-yellow leaves are most beautiful in the spring even though they revert to the normal gray color in the summer. My favorite, at least in the spring. Excellent drainage necessary, partial shade, zones 4 to 7.

Stachys byzantina 'Sheila Macqueen'

Stachys byzantina

Most weekend gardeners know about lamb's ears, but the numbers fall way off when you ask the same group to name another species of *Stachys*. Actually there are about three hundred of them, but let's not get too picky. *Stachys macrantha*, big betony, has 1½–2" long dark green leaves with scalloped edges; the foliage is roughly hairy, not soft like that of its gray cousin. But whatever the leaves lack is more than made up for by the dozens of violet-pink flowers in late spring and early summer. Plants grow up to 2' tall and when in flower can be seen a football field away. Big betony is seen much more in European gardens than in this country, which may be attributed to its dislike of temperature extremes. The only cultivar ever seen is 'Robusta', which is a bit more robust than the species. Both selection and species prefer full sun and good drainage, and do well in zones 2 to 7.

Stachys byzantina 'Primrose Heron'

Stachys macrantha

Stachys macrantha 'Robusta'

Stachys macrantha 'Robusta'

Stokesia laevis

STOKES'S ASTER

Stokesia laevis, Stokes's aster, is a native of the eastern United States, with small one-inch-wide lavender flowers; but the original native has undergone a significant transformation through selection and breeding. Native plant lovers enthusiastically embrace this meadow dweller, while mainstream gardeners use the new and improved models with equal enthusiasm. The 6–8" long entire leaves have a pronounced white midrib and are evergreen in milder locations. The flowers open in early to mid summer and consist of two rows of ray flowers up to 4" across, although 2–2½" is normal. Plants are 1–2' tall and equally wide. They are tough, do well in full sun to partial shade, and persist for many years as long as winter drainage is good.

The selections of *Stokesia laevis* for the garden are many, the most common being 'Blue Danube', with compact habit and 2–2½" wide lavender flowers. Others in the blue to lavender range include 'Klaus Jelitto', with even larger flowers; 'Wyoming', with its deeper blue flowers; and the perfectly named upright form of 'Omega Sky-

Stokesia laevis 'Blue Danube'

MORE →

rocket', whose strong flower stems head straight into the air, giving it a unique appearance, interesting as a garden plant and highly useful as a cut flower. Last but not least, an off-white flowerer, 'Alba', is also available. Full sun, good drainage, zones 5 to 9.

Stokesia laevis 'Alba'

Stokesia laevis 'Blue Danube'

Stokesia laevis 'Omega Skyrocket'

Stokesia laevis 'Klaus Jelitto'

Stokesia laevis 'Wyoming'

Stylophorum diphyllum

WOOD POPPY, CELANDINE POPPY

Native from Tennessee to Missouri, *Stylophorum diphyllum* is simply a terrific species for the woodland garden, providing bright yellow spring flowers even in heavy shade. It comports well with Virginia bluebells and other early spring woodland plants: the blue and yellow flowers go together like apples and strudel. Early in the spring, as the poppies emerge from their winter rest, light green deeply cut basal leaves and 1½–2" wide flowers unfold. A yellow sap exudes from cut parts of the plant, providing great fun for any face- and fingerpainters who happen by. Keep it out of your eyes. Plants reseed, which means that two or three plants can become a significant colony in three to five years. No cultivars are available; the Chinese native *Stylophorum lasiocarpum* bears a similar flower and has larger coarser foliage. Partial to heavy shade, zones 4 to 8.

Stylophorum diphyllum with *Mertensia*

Stylophorum diphyllum

Stylophorum lasiocarpum

Symphytum

COMFREY

Plants of the genus *Symphytum* were once used as a poultice, believed, among other things, to speed the setting of broken bones. With such an important healing property, boneset (as it was also known) became a staple of monastic and herb gardens. About thirty-five species are counted in the genus, and that is about thirty-three too many for most gardeners. Essentially, they have the same look, fill the same shady spaces, and bear similar pendulous bell-shaped flowers on long one-sided inflorescences. But they are loved by many. Whether one goes with the 5–6' tall prickly comfrey, *Symphytum asperum*; the low-growing blue-flowered *S. caucasicum* or light blue *S. grandiflorum*; or the variable *S. officinale*, the differences in plant habit and flower color are only slight.

Symphytum offers some highly ornamental variegated plants. Most sought after are the variegated cultivars of the hybrid between *Symphytum asperum* and *S. officinale*, known as *S.* ×*uplandicum*. They include 'Variegatum' and 'Axeminster', an extraordinarily vigorous introduction from Canada. Another excellent variegated cultivar is *S. officinale* 'Variegatum'. *Symphytum* 'Goldsmith' has yellow-and-white foliage and has become quite popular but does not seem as vigorous or as tough as the others. The variegated plants are eye-catching and

Symphytum caucasicum

Symphytum asperum

Symphytum grandiflorum

MORE →

must-have plants for many gardeners. Unfortunately, they are very difficult to propagate and thus difficult to locate and quite expensive.

All comfreys require good drainage. They do best in partial shade and burn up in full sun in many areas of the country. Hardy in zones 4 to 7 in the East, to zone 8 on the West Coast.

Symphytum officinale

Symphytum officinale

Symphytum officinale 'Variegatum'

Symphytum ×*uplandicum* 'Variegatum'

Symphytum ×*uplandicum* 'Variegatum'

Symphytum 'Goldsmith'

Symphytum ×*uplandicum* 'Axeminster'

Tanacetum

TANSY

Several plants that long resided under the *Chrysanthemum* umbrella have been repositioned under cover of *Tanacetum*. These interesting garden plants are all fetid of foliage; they are also fairly temperamental, not much liking cold winters, hot or humid summers, wet feet, or drought. Other than that, they are good garden plants.

Tanacetum vulgare has to be one of the most aromatic herbs available to the gardener. To touch it is to be tansied for an hour or more. I avoid planting herbs in the Armitage garden as I have determined that I am not an herb kind of a guy. Tansy is my exception, however, and I enjoy the deeply cut dark green foliage, its smell, and its sturdy stature. Plants may grow up to 4' tall (although 2–3' is more common), but seldom need support. The yellow flowers are small, buttonlike, and entirely forgettable. Though it is smaller in height, the best selection by far is 'Crispum', with its fabulous finely cut foliage. Plants seldom flower, also a plus. The species is considered invasive in parts of the West. Full sun, excellent drainage, hardy in zones 5 to 7.

Thalictrum

MEADOW RUE

Thalictrum species are natural inhabitants of damp, shady areas, flowering in early summer, with lacy foliage that presents a fernlike appearance. In general, the ornamental parts of the flowers consist of colorful stamens and sepals. About 130 species of meadow rue have been identified, and the gardener may choose, with difficulty, from upright clumpers to 6–9" ground covers.

Prostrate meadow rues, most suitable to rock gardens and alpine environments, can sometimes be found in specialty nurseries. The maidenhair fern–like appearance of *Thalictrum minus* 'Adiantifolium' is the best part of the plant and can be enjoyed even if flowering is sparse. Plants grow in 1–2' tall clumps and perform well in zones 3 to 7. The deeper green foliage and numerous lavender flowers of China meadow rue, *T. ichangense*, are outstanding in late spring and early summer. Plants are only 6–9" tall and fill in rocky outcrops or other well-drained areas in zones 5 to 7. Neither of these low growers does well in areas of hot summers and high humidity.

Thalictrum ichangense

Tanacetum vulgare

Tanacetum vulgare 'Crispum'

MORE →

The most common of the upright meadow rues is the columbine meadow rue, *Thalictrum aquilegiifolium*. The foliage is blue-tinted and similar to that of columbine, thus the common and botanical names. Plants are generally 2–3' tall, but well-satisfied plants can grow 5' tall and 3' wide. The normal flower color, provided by sepals and long stamens in the spring, is lavender; but the species itself is generally seed-propagated and flower color can be quite variable, deeper or lighter lavender. Unfortunately, flowers are not persistent and tend to shatter after a week or so. Sometimes the flowers are dioecious (male or female only); however, the fruit is especially handsome on plants that have female, or perfect, flowers. Cultivars include the white-flowered 'Album' (sometimes sold as 'White Cloud'), which discolors to creamy white over time; the darker 'Atropurpureum'; the pink 'Roseum'; and the rose-purple 'Thundercloud' ('Purple Cloud'). Partial shade, good drainage, zones 5 to 7.

Thalictrum minus 'Adiantifolium'

Thalictrum aquilegiifolium

Thalictrum aquilegiifolium 'Album' ('White Cloud')

Another upright species is *Thalictrum flavum*, yellow meadow rue, a robust grower that bursts out of the ground like John Glenn's Discovery rocket, with smooth divided foliage and thick stems. Plants grow tall and thin and are best planted in clumps of three or four. Single plants grow too tall for their width and easily outgrow the space provided. Clumps form rapidly, and panicles of small yellow flowers appear in late spring. Flowers consist mainly of long stamens, which fall like yellow confetti within a few days of opening. Height is generally 4–6', and plants are used to great advantage as a backdrop to shorter plants. 'Glaucum', the most popular selection of this plant, presents a winning combination of blue-green foliage and yellow flowers that is even better than the species. Full sun, good drainage, zones 5 to 8.

Thalictrum lucidum is another tall (5–7') grower with light yellow flowers and fine green divided foliage. The leaves do not have the blueness of 'Glaucum', but these outstanding plants grow rapidly and quickly fill in a large area. Full sun, zones 4 to 7.

Thalictrum rochebrunianum, lavender mist, is my favorite upright meadow

Thalictrum aquilegiifolium 'Atropurpureum'

Thalictrum aquilegiifolium 'Roseum'

rue, tall and thin, producing dozens of small lavender-purple flowers atop 4–6' tall stems. Although many small compound leaves are formed, the plant can be considered a see-through plant: one that reduces but does not block vistas behind it. As with *T. flavum*, plants look better in groups than they do a plant at a time. Plants are a little better in the North than the South, but they look terrific anywhere. Little diversity occurs within the species—the common name is also used for the cultivar 'Lavender Mist'. Partial shade, good drainage, zones 4 to 7.

Thalictrum flavum

Thalictrum flavum

Thalictrum flavum

Thalictrum flavum 'Glaucum' with *Delphinium*

Thalictrum rochebrunianum 'Lavender Mist'

Thalictrum flavum 'Glaucum'

Thalictrum lucidum

Thalictrum rochebrunianum 'Lavender Mist'

Thermopsis montana

Thermopsis

FALSE LUPINE

The native false lupines are well named because both the leaves and the flowers resemble the much more appreciated European lupines. In general, the foliage of *Thermopsis* is palmately compound, and the early spring flowers are yellow. Few differences occur from species to species; the eastern and western natives, *Thermopsis caroliniana* (*T. villosa*) and *T. montana*, respectively, are particularly similar. They flower in very early spring, providing bright color often before other plants have even started to expand. White selections ('Alba') of both species have also been offered, but they are much less common than those with yellow flowers. The foliage can remain handsome for a long time, but eventually the garden is better served by hiding plants with late-flowering perennials or annuals. *Thermopsis fabacea*, native to Kamchatka and the Kurile Islands, bears larger leaves, flowers in summer, and tends to be more vigorous. Full sun, good drainage, zones 3 to 8 (sometimes 9).

Thermopsis montana 'Alba'

Thermopsis caroliniana

Thermopsis fabacea

Thermopsis montana

Thymus

THYME

Thymus is an immense genus of more than 350 species, best known for their culinary and ornamental properties. All thymes available to gardeners are low-growing spreading plants and, without a label, are incredibly difficult to tell apart. The best way to distinguish thyme from other herbs is to sniff the fragrance of its opposite leaves; remember, however, that thyme not only smells like thyme but also, in some selections, like caraway or lemon. Most taxa are native to the Mediterranean, and therefore excellent drainage and full sun are necessary. Plants lend themselves well to rock, trough, and alpine gardens.

One of the most handsome species is woolly thyme, *Thymus pseudolanuginosus*, whose common name comes from the long hairs on the prostrate stems. Although pink flowers are produced, the plant's fuzziness is its best attribute in dry climates. In warm areas that receive a good deal of summer rain, however, it is a detriment, because water does not evaporate easily from the leaves and plants may melt out badly. Full sun, zones 5 to 8.

A couple of common species with lavender-purple flowers are *Thymus praecox*, creeping thyme, and *T. serpyllum*, wild thyme. They both form thick mats under conditions of cool nights and good drainage. *Thymus vulgaris*, common thyme, is the culinary thyme of the grocery aisle; it forms purple or white flowers on 12–15" tall plants. Several selections of these species are available, including the variegated *T. vulgaris* 'Silver Posie'. All cultivars do poorly in rainy and humid summers and must be planted where drainage is excellent. Full sun, zones 5 to 8.

Thymus vulgaris

Thymus pseudolanuginosus

Thymus vulgaris 'Silver Posie'

Thymus praecox

Thymus serpyllum

Tiarella cordifolia

Tiarella cordifolia 'Oakleaf'

Tiarella cordifolia var. *collina*

Tiarella

FOAMFLOWER

Many excellent selections and hybrids of *Tiarella cordifolia*, an outstanding native plant, have been developed recently, attracting keen interest in the entire genus. Particularly useful for shady gardens, these plants are generally 6–12" tall, forming slow-growing colonies that bear white or pink flowers in the spring. One of the earlier introductions, *T. cordifolia* 'Oakleaf', with dark green leaves and pink flower buds and flowers, is still a favorite. Variety *collina* is similar to the species but is more of a clumper than a colonizer. The leaves of both the type and the variety are heart-shaped and are evergreen in most climates.

Flowers are similar in most foamflowers, and the newer hybrids of *Tiarella* have been mainly selected for their foliage characteristics, giving the gardener greater choices than ever before. 'Dunvegan' has marvelous foliage, each leaf consisting of five lobes with the central one long and narrow; excellent flowering in the spring as well. 'Skeleton Key' is equally fresh-looking in the spring, with dozens of white flowers and light green lobed leaves. Other hybrid entries are 'Brandywine' and 'Snowflake', each with vigorous shiny green leaves and creamy white flowers. Interest in leaf coloration and leaf mottling resulted

Tiarella 'Dunvegan'

Tiarella 'Brandywine'

Tiarella 'Skeleton Key'

Tiarella 'Snowflake'

in cultivars such as 'Ink Blot', 'Dark Star', and 'Tiger Stripe', to name but a few. The genus provides outstanding characteristics for the garden and has been unfairly stuck in the "shady native" category for too long. It should be a mainstream plant. Partial shade, good drainage, zones 3 to 8.

Tiarella 'Ink Blot'

Tiarella 'Dark Star'

Tiarella 'Tiger Stripe'

Tradescantia

SPIDERWORT

The genus *Tradescantia* commemorates the family Tradescant, in particular the father and son, known as Tradescant the Elder and Tradescant the Younger. As gardeners to Charles I of England in the early 1600s, they received many plants from the colonies. The Younger also traveled to America, bringing back to the Empire such treasures as Virginia creeper and Michaelmas daisies.

Although our native species *Tradescantia virginiana* has gone through significant changes, it remains a staple in American gardening. The light green straplike foliage is common to all the selections, and all produce dozens of flowers, each opening for a single day. Breeding has concentrated on flower colors, and many are available. Flower color, flower persistence, and compact habit make many of the newer cultivars interesting. 'Bilberry Ice' has a cool lavender look; 'Bluestone', 'Zwanenburg Blue', and 'Purple Dome' have good blue-lavender flowers; 'Concord Grape', 'Purewell Giant',

Tradescantia virginiana 'Bilberry Ice'

Tradescantia virginiana 'Bluestone'

Tradescantia virginiana 'Zwanenburg Blue'

Tradescantia virginiana 'Purple Dome'

Tradescantia virginiana 'Concord Grape'

MORE →

Tradescantia virginiana 'Purewell Giant'

Tradescantia virginiana 'Joy'

Tradescantia virginiana 'Pauline'

Tradescantia virginiana 'Innocence'

and 'Joy' provide deeper rose-purple flowers; 'Pauline' has the best pink flowers in the group; and white flowers can be found in 'Innocence'. Afternoon shade and moisture is essential for good performance, but spiderworts don't do well in boggy soils. Hardy in zones 4 to 8.

Tricyrtis

TOAD LILY

It's obvious that the common name for the genus *Tricyrtis* was not chosen with commercial sales in mind. Just try to talk someone into buying a toad lily—not an easy task. That the flowers tend to be spotted and brownish maroon like a toad is simple bad luck, because no matter how shamelessly one promotes the plant and flower, it is not until you see it in its glory that it can be appreciated. A good deal of effort in breeding has brought toad lilies out of obscurity, and although they all still look "kind of the same" to my students, the world of toad lilies is just unfolding. Gardeners know they have reached the highest possible gardening plateau when they ask for cow manure for their birthday and peruse catalogs in search of toad lilies. No turning back then. Spouses beware!

Tricyrtis formosana, Formosa toad lily, is one of the easiest toad lilies to grow for much of the United States and is reasonably easy to obtain. The leaves are softly hairy and ascend the 2–4' tall stem like those of a real lily. The green leaves sort of fade into the garden for most of the season, then flower buds begin to form in late summer and early fall. Even in flower, nothing about it will knock your socks off, as the maroon color of the flowers is not one the eye locks on. But the flowers, with their spotted petals and sepals, are a study in subtlety and complexity, and will reward notice—once one takes the time to look (turn the flower over and note the warts). Plants are both clump formers and stoloniferous, meaning that they move around the garden and increase in number over

Tricyrtis formosana

Tricyrtis formosana

Tricyrtis formosana 'Alba'

the years, but they are certainly not invasive. 'Alba', a white variant, occasionally appears from a population, and the few I have seen are even more handsome than the species.

Tricyrtis formosana differs from common toad lily, *T. hirta*, by being more upright and having most of its flowers on the upper third of the stem. It is an excellent plant for late summer and fall flowering. The species is not without problems, however, the most serious being the tendency of the leaf tips to turn brown under stress, such as drought or excessive heat. This results in terrible-looking plants that even the weird flowers cannot overcome. Some years they are almost perfect, others perfectly awful. Partial shade, moist soils, zones 4 to 9.

Tricyrtis hirta, the most common species of toad lily, is a plant of classic beauty—leaf tip burn notwithstanding. The flowers and foliage are similar to those of *T. formosana*, but plants differ by being pendulous rather than upright, and the flowers tend to be a little larger and occur along at least half of the 2–3' long stem. The spotted flowers are maroon to purple (occasionally lighter) and occur in late summer and fall. I love seeing them arching gracefully over rocks by a pond or other water feature. 'Miyazaki' is a popular selection of the species.

Numerous toad lily cultivars have been offered to the gardening public, and while response among the general populace has not been overwhelming, veteran gardeners cannot get enough. Most are hybrids between *Tricyrtis hirta* and *T. formosana*; the differences between them are often subtle, but that should not be surprising in this subtle genus. The hybrids, despite their sometimes unpronounceable names, are generally vigorous growers and somewhat pendulous in form, with lighter, often larger flowers. 'Kohaku' is large and popular, while the

Flowers of *Tricyrtis hirta* (left) and *T. formosana*

Tricyrtis formosana 'Alba' with *Salvia*

Tricyrtis hirta

Tricyrtis hirta 'Miyazaki'

Tricyrtis 'Kohaku'

Tricyrtis 'Lemon Glow'

MORE →

chartreuse leaves distinguish 'Lemon Glow' from the others. I also really enjoy the shrubby habit and the dozens of spotted flowers of 'Shirohotogisu', which is neither pendulous nor upright but somewhere in between. Partial shade, moist soils, zones 4 to 8.

Tricyrtis 'Shirohotogisu'

Trillium

Rose trillium, nodding trillium, great white trillium, wake-robin, showy trillium, snow trillium, wood lily, stinking Benjamin, sessile trillium, toad trillium, yellow trillium—these are but a few of the names describing members of this great genus. That trilliums prefer woodland conditions, that their flowers appear in early spring and are gone soon thereafter, that plants disappear entirely in the summer—all this doesn't make the trillium sound particularly enchanting. But don't tell a trillium fan that. It is a truth universally acknowledged that if trilliums were native to England, the War of the Roses would have been known as the War of the Trilliums. Trillium lovers are passionate. All reason seems to have left them, and heaven forgive the unsuspecting novice who digs a trillium from the wild. The game of "what trillium is that?" can still get violent among trillites. I must admit to such tendencies, but I am now reformed, I think.

Passions aside, trilliums have a place in the shade garden, and like any other genus, some species are more adaptable than others in a given environment. The easiest way to describe members of this large genus is by describing how the flower is held: either by a short flower stem called the pedicel (pediceled), or attached directly to the top of the plant (sessile), like a king perched on his throne. Each has its own special beauty and charm, but making definite identification is best left to the taxonomists. Exacting propagation techniques make wide distri-

Trillium cuneatum

Trillium sessile

Trillium cuneatum 'Eco Silver'

Trillium sessile 'Eco Strain'

Trillium stamineum

bution of many trilliums difficult, although tissue culture should soon help to overcome some of the problems. Meanwhiile, if you can't find trilliums in the nursery, take a walk in the woods and enjoy nature's treasures. Take a photo, not a plant.

The sessile species include *Trillium cuneatum*, *T. sessile*, *T. decipiens*, *T. stamineum*, *T. luteum*, and *T. discolor*. The first three species are similar to the non-trillium eye. Regardless of their exact identity, all are equally ornamental, bearing maroon-brown flowers on top of the three leaves, which vary immensely in their degree of mottling. The flowers of *T. cuneatum* (toad trillium; zones 5 to 9) are usually longer and more narrow than those of *T. sessile* (sessile trillium; zones 4 to 7). The leaves of *T. cuneatum* are also narrower than those of *T. sessile*, which tend to be rhomboidal in shape. *Trillium cuneatum* and *T. decipiens* (zones 6 to 9) are more southern in habitat than *T. sessile*. The nice thing about many of the sessile trilliums is that the foliage is actually more handsome than the flowers, although if they don't flower, gardeners are a little disappointed. Every now and then, selections of some of the sessile trilliums will be offered, and differ from the various species by having a different leaf or flower color. For instance, the mottled leaves of *T. sessile* 'Eco Strain' and the dull silvery leaves of *T. cuneatum* 'Eco Silver' are interesting and subjectively showy.

Trillium decipiens

Trillium luteum

Trillium discolor

After so many remarkably similar trilliums, *Trillium stamineum* (twisted trillium) is easily recognized by the twisted purple petals which lie flat, showing off the large conspicuous stamens. Quite lovely, certainly different.

Two sessile species sport yellow flowers. The long pointed petals of *Trillium luteum* (yellow trillium; zones 5 to 7) vary from deep butter-yellow to the more common light yellow. While the purple to maroon flowers of the others can sometimes get lost in the woodland canopy, no such problem with *T. luteum*. Outstanding. But for classical pale yellow flowers, I much prefer the look of the primrose trillium, *T. discolor* (zones 6 to 8). The petals are spatula-shaped, and even in bud, the plant is eye-catching.

Pediceled species include *Trillium catesbaei*, *T. cernuum*, *T. erectum*, *T. grandiflorum*, and *T. vaseyi*. The flowers of *T. catesbaei* (rose trillium; zones 6 to 9) and *T. cernuum* (nodding trillium; zones 3 to 7) have a similar characteristic, that is, they nod. They nod below the leaves, and it is easy to pass them by without ever glimpsing the flower. That would be a shame because the light to deep rose flowers of *T. catesbaei* and the white blooms of *T. cernuum* are really quite lovely. Another

Trillium discolor in bud

MORE →

characteristic the two species share is their flared-back petals; when you are bending down and looking up, the stamens and pistil can be appreciated, even as you slip a disc.

The flowers of *Trillium erectum* (stinking Benjamin; zones 4 to 7) have a subtle mangy smell to them, but their beauty cannot be denied. The flower is held on a long pedicel and points slightly downward. The petals are usually red to maroon, but a good deal of diversity occurs in the wild, where whites and pale yellows may occasionally be seen. The leaves are about as wide as they are long and seldom mottled.

Trillium vaseyi (Vasey's trillium; zones 5 to 7) has the same purple flower color as *T. erectum* but that is about as similar as it gets. The flower is among the largest in the genus. They are carried on a pedicel but are held beside rather than above the leaves. An absolutely stunning plant, although not particularly easy to find commercially or to establish.

The granddaddy, aunt, and uncle of all North American trilliums is *Trillium grandiflorum* (great white trillium; zones 4 to 7). Carpeting open woods and regaling all those who view it, whether en masse or one at time, the white trillium is the epitome of native woodland plants. As the flowers decline, they often turn a rosy red color, yet another charm to this quite marvelous plant. Plants are so revered in Canada that it was adopted as the provincial flower of Ontario. With its successful carpeting of the northern woodland and its stunning beauty, this species has probably been subjected to more abuse from picking, gathering, and digging than any other trillium. It puts up with humans anyway, making our springtimes even brighter. Garden cultivars have been developed such as the double-flowered 'Flore Pleno' and the rosy-flowered 'Roseum'.

Trillium catesbaei

Trillium cernuum

Trillium catesbaei

Trillium erectum

Trillium cernuum

Trillium erectum

Trillium vaseyi

Trillium vaseyi

Trillium grandiflorum

Aging flowers of *Trillium grandiflorum*

Trillium grandiflorum 'Flore Pleno'

Trillium grandiflorum 'Roseum'

Uvularia grandiflora 'Sunbonnet'

Uvularia perfoliata

Uvularia

BELLWORT, MERRY BELLS

Subtlety is the hallmark of this genus of woodland plants. Not particularly showy, but admired by those who do not equate beauty with showmanship. Five species are known, all shade tolerant and moisture loving and all native to eastern North America. The bellworts are remarkably similar in makeup and garden performance, bearing small pale yellow flowers, which hang from the nodes of the upper leaves. It is the leaves that differ among the species, and although not particularly striking, the differences are notable. In *Uvularia grandiflora* (large-flowered bellwort) and *U. perfoliata* (perfoliate bellwort), the stem appears to pierce and pass through the leaves—a unique arrangement described by the term "perfoliate." The flowers of *U. grandiflora* are significantly larger than those of *U. perfoliata*, and on the whole it is a more visual plant. *Uvularia perfoliata* appears to spread throughout the garden more rapidly, which is either good or bad, depending if you like the thing. A few cultivars are occasionally offered by mail-order specialists, such as 'Sunbonnet', a bigger, brighter selection of *U. grandiflora*.

The leaves are sessile (that is, no leaf

Uvularia grandiflora

Uvularia perfoliata

Uvularia sessilifolia

Uvularia sessilifolia

stem or petiole) in the third common species, *Uvularia sessilifolia*. An even more vigorous plant under shady, moist conditions, plants can quickly colonize an area. The flowers are similar to those of *U. perfoliata*. All require shade and moisture and are hardy in zones 4 (3 with protection) to 9.

Veratrum

FALSE HELLEBORE

Veratrum was the ancient name of *Helleborus*, thus accounting for this genus's common name. From a stout black rhizome emerges a plant grown for the wonderful pleated leaves and unique branched flower heads. I love *Veratrum viride* (American false hellebore) but have a difficult time finding it for the Armitage garden. That all parts of the plant are poisonous may tend to limit its use somewhat, but only mad dogs and Englishmen would ever think of putting that fact to the test. The flowers rise from within the plant to form otherworldly branched green panicles. Plants grow 3–6' tall and when in flower, are guaranteed to elicit all sorts of oohs and aahs and a concluding "what is it?" from any and all passers-by. Plants go dormant in the heat of the summer. Partial shade and moisture are needed. Hardy in zones 3 to 7.

Two species from Europe and Asia are equally outstanding. The European false hellebore, *Veratrum album*, differs from *V. viride* only in its native setting and flower color, being whitish on the inside and greenish yellow outside. The other difference is that it is even more difficult to locate than its American counterpart. Plants are only about 2–4' tall but, like their American cousins, are knockouts. The black false hellebore, *V. nigrum*, is similar in habit and foliage but the black-purple flowers, which occur in dense racemes, are incredible. Plants are about 4' tall. To locate any of these fine plants is to willingly go into debt, no questions asked! Partial shade, moisture, zones 4 to 7.

Veratrum viride

Veratrum nigrum

Veratrum album

Veratrum viride

Verbena peruviana

Verbena tenuisecta

Verbena tenuisecta 'Imagination'

Verbena

VERVAIN

Verbenas have been a mainstay of perennial gardens since great grandmother's time and will continue to be one of those plants that comes and goes from the horticultural stage. Colorful annual bedding verbenas are offered every spring, vying with the many perennial offerings for attention. Perennial verbenas are extremely diverse, varying in height from upright-growing *Verbena bonariensis* and its dwarfer twin, *V. rigida*, to low growers like *V. peruviana* and hybrids of *V. canadensis* and *V. tenuisecta*. All require full sun and exceptionally good drainage.

Verbena peruviana, *V. tenuisecta*, and *V. canadensis* are low-growing species. From hugging the ground to romping over large areas of terrain, these species are outstanding for gardens, containers, and patio planters. *Verbena peruviana*, Peruvian verbena, is the most compact of the three, bearing deep red flowers on spreading mats of green, 2–4" tall. Full sun, zones 7 to 9.

The most handsome leaves are to be found in the fernlike foliage of cutleaf verbena, *Verbena tenuisecta* (zones 7

Verbena tenuisecta

Verbena 'Tapien Blue'

Verbena 'Tapien Pink'

to 10). Dozens of small lavender-blue flowers cover the foliage in midsummer and throughout the season. This species is probably the most heat tolerant of the three low growers. 'Imagination' is a seed-propagated selection of the type and variety *alba* is equally floriferous. Recent breeding using *V. tenuisecta* resulted in 'Tapien Blue' and 'Tapien Pink', both highly recommended cultivars. Full sun, hardy to zone 7.

Verbena canadensis, rose verbena, is native to North America and occurs naturally in the form of rose flowers. The most common verbena offered commercially, it is hardy to zone 7, perhaps zone 6 if snow cover is sufficient. Hybrids between it and other species have exploded. 'Homestead Purple' is an excellent vigorous early flowerer that paved the way for many others. 'Taylortown Red' is a good red-flowered hybrid, while 'Sissinghurst' and 'Abbeville' provide handsome rosy pink and lavender flowers, respectively. 'Carrousel' provides bicolor flowers, and 'Silver Anne' is always a popular, tempering color. All require full sun and excellent drainage and can occasionally be cut back if the plants grow too vigorous or the stems become spindly. Hardy in zones 7 (perhaps 6) to 10.

Upright species of verbena include

Verbena tenuisecta var. *alba*

Verbena 'Taylortown Red'

Verbena 'Carrousel'

Verbena 'Sissinghurst'

Verbena 'Abbeville'

Verbena 'Tapien Pink'

Verbena 'Homestead Purple'

MORE →

Verbena bonariensis

Verbena rigida 'Polaris'

Verbena bonariensis, tall verbena, and *V. rigida*, rigid verbena. Being upright is not the only characteristic these South American natives share. Both are square-stemmed, bristly hairy, and bear small rosy purple flowers for a long period of time. *Verbena bonariensis* is 3–6' high and flowers from early

Verbena 'Silver Anne'

Verbena rigida 'Lilacina'

Verbena bonariensis

Verbena rigida

summer throughout the season. Like *Thalictrum*, it is a see-through plant, which even when densely planted remains open enough to allow one to see what is on the other side. Mildew is a serious problem if plants are in wet conditions or too much shade. Few cultivars of *V. bonariensis* have been developed, although since many are raised from seed, various shades of flower color occur. Full sun, zones 6 to 9.

Verbena rigida is similar in texture and color but only about 2' tall. The leaves are opposite, also bristly, and likewise susceptible to powdery mildew. Its selection 'Lilacina' has blue-purple flowers; 'Polaris' is vigorous and lavender-flowered. Both *V. rigida* and *V. bonariensis* reseed prolifically, but the resulting plants seldom flower as well as the parents. Full sun, zones 7 to 9.

Veronica

SPEEDWELL

The genus *Veronica* provides a wide range of height, color, and texture. The low growers work well in rock gardens and raised beds, and benefit from cool nights and good drainage; taller species are used in perennial borders, and some enjoy a well-deserved reputation as cut flowers. Many prostrate low growers have been made available to gardeners, even though the scientific names keep changing. It is likely that nobody has a clue what species gardeners are using anyway, and telling them that the names have been changed is not only confusing but more often than not, absolutely useless information. I figure if a plant is named after a saint (in this case, Saint Veronica), it can't be all bad.

One of the ways to tell the low growers from the upright speedwells (other than height) is that the flowers on the low growers are always produced in the lateral leaf nodes. That is, they arise from the leaf nodes near the top of the stem, instead of being terminal as in the case of tall species like *Veronica spicata* or *V. longifolia*. The low growers are often bright blue, and the carpets of foliage may be totally hidden by the many flowers in late spring and early summer. Some of the more floriferous of the low growers are selections of *V. austriaca* subsp. *teucrium* ('Blue Fountain', 'Shirley Blue'), but plants with golden leaves ('Aurea') are also available to those who enjoy chartreuse foliage. Full sun, zones 4 to 7.

Veronica austriaca

Veronica austriaca subsp. *teucrium* 'Shirley Blue'

Veronica incana

Veronica austriaca subsp. *teucrium* 'Blue Fountain'

Veronica austriaca subsp. *teucrium* 'Aurea'

MORE →

Veronica prostrata 'Trehane'

Veronica incana, another prostrate species, generally has blue flowers and gray foliage, a contrast that works well in the Armitage garden. 'Silver Carpet' is a good representation of the species. I also enjoy the bright yellow-green foliage of *V. prostrata* 'Trehane', which makes an excellent ground cover even when not in flower. When plants start flowering in spring, the blue and gold are outstanding together. Both species need excellent drainage and full sun. Hardy in zones 3 to 7.

While many veronicas are useful for the front of the garden, the upright *Veronica longifolia*, long-leaved speedwell, is generally sufficiently tall to be viewed when placed in the middle or even in the back of a garden. Plants bear upright spikes of flowers on 3–4' long stems, each terminal spike consisting of dozens of small quarter- to half-inch-wide flowers. Plants are strong enough and tall enough to be used as a cut flower and are grown as such throughout the world. Mainte-

Veronica prostrata 'Trehane'

Veronica longifolia 'Blauriesen'

Veronica longifolia 'Blauriesen'

Veronica longifolia 'Schneeriesen'

nance is minimal in full sun, but plants require staking if placed in too much shade. Evidence of good breeding can be found in blue cultivars such as 'Blauriesen'—one of the most popular cut flower speedwells in the world—while white and rosy flowers, respectively, have been raised in 'Schneeriesen' and 'Rosalinde'. All selections of *V. longifolia* perform best in full sun in normal soils. Hardy in zones 4 to 8.

The best-known species of the entire genus is the upright *Veronica spicata*, spiked speedwell. It comes in many colors (blue and lavender are the main colors) and heights, the normal height range being 1–3'. The 2" glossy green leaves are usually serrated in the middle. The terminal upright flowers begin to open in early summer and often continue for two months or more, especially if spent flowers are deadheaded. The dozens of cultivars of *V. spicata* perform well in full sun and well-drained soils. Blue-flowered selections are most common, including the glossy-leaved 'Blue Bouquet' and the compact 'Blue Spires'. While I enjoy the blue flowers, the palette is expanded by selections such as 'Lili Corinna', which is about 2' tall with handsome lavender flowers. 'Barcarolle' and 'Erika' have upright pink flowers, and 'Heidekind' bears deep rosy red flowers in spring and summer. Hardy in zones 3 to 7.

Veronica spicata 'Barcarolle'

Veronica spicata 'Erika'

Veronica spicata 'Heidekind'

Veronica spicata 'Blue Spires'

Veronica spicata 'Blue Bouquet'

Veronica spicata 'Lili Corinna'

Veronicastrum virginicum 'Roseum'

Veronicastrum virginicum

CULVER'S ROOT

This native species is a fairly recent darling of American gardeners. Plants grow up to 5' tall and can be 3–4' wide. Whorls of three to six leaves occur along the stems, and it is this arrangement that is the easiest way to distinguish *Veronicastrum* from the closely related *Veronica*. The flowers of the two are similar, but the inflorescences are generally more narrow and longer in culver's root. There is some disagreement among eggheads as to whether the species is strictly lavender or both lavender and white. I prefer to agree with the lumpers rather than the splitters: white or lavender, I love this plant. The white-flowered variant is the most available color, and it not only makes an excellent garden plant but is highly prized as a cut flower. Put the flower stems together with yarrows and statice in a vase, and the effect is most dramatic. They are best when grown in full sun and provided with

Veronicastrum virginicum

Veronicastrum virginicum

Veronicastrum sibiricum

sufficient water and fertilizer. Occasionally the pink-flowered 'Roseum' may be found, and it too can be quite dramatic. The lavender variant of the type as well as *V. sibiricum* (zones 3 to 7), a European species, have blue to lavender flowers but are more difficult to locate. *Veronicastrum virginicum* requires full sun and is hardy in zones 4 to 8.

Viola

VIOLET

Over five hundred species of this old-fashioned plant have been documented—a genus sufficiently diverse to cause the same gardener to enthusiastically embrace some species while considering others obnoxious weeds. In fact, I find the latter to be more common than the former. In the Armitage garden, I yank and toss the fast-moving marsh violet, *Viola cucullata*, but carefully cultivate Labrador violet, *V. labradorica*, and birdsfoot violet, *V. pedata*. The genus *Viola* includes the fragrant sweet violet, *V. odorata*, sold as a cut flower since Roman times, as well as our modern pansies and violas. All species perform better in cooler climates than in hot weather: in the North, violets do well in the summer; in the South, in the winter. All ornamental violets are excellent in the spring in most locales.

Viola cornuta, the horned violet, is not as commonly seen in American as in European gardens, possibly the proliferation of bedding pansies and violas has smothered this species. A shame, because it offers wonderful diversity of color and form. The flowers, each 1–1½" across, are somewhat star-shaped and have a long slender spur, accounting for its common name. It is not as accommodating of weather extremes as other species, but plants generally flower well in the spring, and if cut back after flowering, may bloom again, at least in cooler summers. In the South, plants have a more difficult time surviving the summer and may have to be treated as winter annuals. Dozens of cultivars have been bred in Europe, some well worth seeking. I love the deep 'Jersey Gem' and the light 'Lilacina', both vigorous in growth and in flowering. The white flowers of 'Alba' brighten the garden, and the lavender-pink blossoms of 'Rosea' are also excellent. Full sun, good drainage, zones 6 to 9.

One of the best, easiest, and finest of the violets—the dark-leaved Labrador violet, *Viola labradorica*—can nevertheless be as aggressive as any other

Viola cornuta 'Lilacina'

Viola cornuta 'Jersey Gem'

Viola cornuta 'Alba'

MORE →

weed. Native to northern climates, plants are outstanding in the North and almost as good in the South. The mauve quarter-inch-wide flowers may be small but can almost cover up a plant in the spring. The plant essentially sits around in the summer but is outstanding in the fall, winter (in the South), and spring. The best part of this violet is the purple foliage: almost black in early spring, it lightens only slightly when the plant is in flower. Plants form nice clumps but also spread rapidly. No cultivars are available, but since they reseed themselves, variations of leaf and flower color can sometimes be spotted. An Armitage favorite! Partial shade, zones 3 to 8.

Probably the best known, at least to native plant enthusiasts, of the native eastern violets, *Viola pedata*, birdsfoot violet, is also the easiest species to identify. The leaves are palmately compound (like the foot of a bird?), and bluish flowers with orange stamens are formed in the spring. As a garden member, birdsfoot violet is also one of the more difficult to establish, but that never stopped anyone from trying. Plants must be placed in partial shade, in extremely well-drained soil, or they will be difficult to establish. Several seed-raised colors occur naturally, and a few cultivars, such as 'Artist's Palette', have also been selected and propagated.

Viola cornuta 'Rosea'

Viola labradorica

Viola labradorica

Viola pedata

Waldsteinia

BARREN STRAWBERRY

Waldsteinia is a relatively unknown ground-covering genus, consisting of about five species, most of which are native to the United States. Plants are not vigorous growers, which limits the ability of these ground covers to cover ground. They do, however, produce strawberry-like foliage, consisting of

Viola pedata

Viola pedata 'Artist's Palette'

Waldsteinia fragarioides

three leaflets, often 1–2" long, which are rounded or wedge-shaped. In the summer, leaves are often glossy green, and in areas where little snow cover occurs, the foliage turns a handsome purple. They grow over each other to form a thick mat, and in the spring, light to deep yellow half-inch-wide flowers occur. The flowers are interesting if not dramatic. I have seen *Waldsteinia fragarioides* and *W. ternata* look good in the cooler climates, while *W. lobata* and *W. parviflora* handle warm summers well. Plants thrive in moist, shaded conditions. *Waldsteinia fragarioides* and *W. ternata* are hardy in zones 4 to 7, *W. lobata* and *W. parviflora* in zones 6 to 8.

Waldsteinia lobata

Waldsteinia parviflora

Yucca

Yuccas are popular for their bold architectural form and strong upright, often spine-tipped leaves. The dense spikes of pendulous tulip-shaped blooms are also impressive. In long, warm summers, flowers occur in midsummer, and when summers are cool, flowers still occur but may be quite late. Yuccas have a reputation of being frost tender; however species such as *Yucca filamentosa*, Adam's needle, are cold hardy to about 5°F. Not exactly Winnipeg, but more hardy than most people think. The margins of the upright leaves vary dramatically in their amount of filaments, but some plants can be quite "filamentous" indeed.

Waldsteinia ternata

Yucca filamentosa

Waldsteinia ternata in winter

Yucca filamentosa 'Gold Band'

MORE →

Selections of *Yucca filamentosa* with multicolored foliage have become popular in recent years, and the yellow- and white-variegated leaves have become part of town and garden landscape plantings. 'Gold Band', 'Golden Sword', and 'Bright Edge' are but three examples that have caught my eye. The diversity in the genus is incredible, and hybrids with *Y. filamentosa* are also becoming more numerous; I find myself admiring these much more living in the South than I ever did when I was gardening in the North. Full sun, good drainage, zones 5 to 9.

Yucca filamentosa

Yucca filamentosa 'Golden Sword'

Yucca filamentosa 'Golden Sword'

Yucca filamentosa 'Bright Edge'

Zantedeschia

CALLA LILY

My fondest visual memory of the time I spent in New Zealand is the image of callas strewn like white lollipops over the green landscape. As a kid buying the occasional flower to assuage my guilt over some transgression, I thought these flowers were incredibly beautiful but rather artificial. Not to mention far more expensive than my guilt or transgressions dictated. Just as kids believe that milk comes from cartons, so did I think that callas came from florist shops. These flowers of the New Zealand fields changed all that.

The most common of these uncommon lilies is the white calla lily, *Zantedeschia aethiopica*. It is the embodiment of erotic cleanliness, with a large pure white spathe around an upright spadix. The wavy lustrous green leaves, which can be 8" wide and a foot long, are borne on plants which themselves can easily reach 3½' in height. In American gardens, the white calla is often planted in the spring, enjoyed

Zantedeschia aethiopica 'Green Goddess'

all summer, and dug up in the fall to be stored in a cool garage, like a dahlia. They usually grow about 3' tall and form three to five flowers in a year. They make exceptionally good cut flowers, persisting such a long time that the New Zealanders routinely ship the cut stems around the world. Plants are best suited for wet areas and naturalize well in moist grassy pockets or even in shallow ponds. In the Armitage garden, they are outstanding in the corners of the pond, where splashing water keeps them constantly moist.

A few cultivars of *Zantedeschia aethiopica* have been selected, the best known being 'Crowborough', which is hardier than the species and perhaps a little more refined. 'Green Goddess' has a spathe that can't decide to be white or green, so it is somewhere in between—a hideous thing. 'Little Gem' is one of my favorites, with many more flowers than the species and only about 2' tall.

Several colorful *Zantedeschia* hybrids have been developed in New Zealand, California, and Europe. Most have large colored spathes and spotted leaves. The best and most hardy is 'Black Magic', which easily grows 3–4' tall and produces myriad golden yellow flowers with black throats. Another favorite is 'Majestic Red', a tall

Zantedeschia 'Black Magic'

Zantedeschia aethiopica 'Little Gem'

Zantedeschia 'Majestic Red'

Zantedeschia aethiopica

Zantedeschia aethiopica 'Crowborough'

MORE →

hybrid suitable for cut flowers, as well as the more dwarf 'Pacific Pink', whose flowers differ only slightly in color but are smaller than the others. The hybrids are more shade tolerant and do not need or want the moist conditions required by the white callas. I like them all: it is difficult to beat a well-grown calla. Still, few gardeners want to dig them each year. Full sun to partial shade, moist conditions, zones 8 (7 in moisture) to 10.

Zantedeschia 'Pacific Pink'

Zauschneria

CALIFORNIA FUCHSIA

The genus *Zauschneria* has gardeners either very passionate or very frustrated. The scarlet to red flowers of *Zauschneria californica* (*Epilobium canum*; California fuchsia) are magnets to hummingbirds, thus accounting for its other common name, the hummingbird trumpet. They grow about 2' tall, making little shrublets that are rather woody at the base. The leaves are green and can be almost smothered by flowers in midsummer. To visit the garden of my friends Panayoti and Gwen Kelaidis in Denver, Colorado, is to immediately become a zauschneria convert. A beautiful sight. To visit my garden in Athens, Georgia, is to immediately understand the meaning of heat-stressed California fuchsias. A gruesome scene. Taxonomists are arguing the nomenclature of *Zauschneria*. Many believe that the entire genus should be folded into the genus *Epilobium*, while others argue that it should remain where it is. Until the dust settles, I vote to leave it alone.

The most common cultivar came from the Irish National Botanical Garden at Glasnevin; it is properly called 'Dublin', although it is also distributed as 'Glasnevin'. Full sun, well-drained soils, zones 6 to 9.

Zauschneria californica

Zauschneria californica

Part Two
Selected Plants for Specific Characteristics or Purposes

Aggressive Plants

The following plants tend to grow more rapidly than "normal" perennials, often squeezing out their competitors in a year or two. Aggressiveness is often thought of as a negative trait, but when an area requires rapid filling, this tendency is much appreciated. Many of these plants could also be used as ground covers.

Ajuga genevensis
Ajuga reptans
Anemone sylvestris
Anemone tomentosa
Aster tataricus
Corydalis lutea
Eupatorium coelestinum
Helianthus angustifolius
Ipheion uniflorum
Lamium galeobdolon
Lamium maculatum
Lychnis coronaria
Lysimachia ciliata
Lysimachia clethroides
Lysimachia nummularia
Macleaya cordata
Monarda didyma
Oenothera berlandieri
Oenothera drummondii
Oenothera speciosa
Osmunda claytoniana
Physostegia virginiana
Ranunculus bulbosus
Ranunculus ficaria
Ranunculus repens
Salvia koyamae
Saponaria officinalis
Sedum acre
Stachys byzantina

Plants for Wet and Boggy Places

The following perennials perform better in consistently moist conditions.

Brunnera macrophylla
Canna hybrids
Geum rivale
Geum triflorum
Iris ensata
Iris fulva
Iris hexagona
Iris louisiana
Iris nelsonii
Ligularia dentata
Ligularia macrophylla
Ligularia sibirica
Ligularia stenocephala
Lobelia cardinalis
Lobelia tupa
Osmunda regalis
Polygonum bistorta
Primula bulleyana
Primula florindae
Primula heladoxa
Primula japonica
Primula pulverulenta
Ranunculus bulbosus
Ranunculus ficaria
Ranunculus repens
Rodgersia aesculifolia
Rodgersia pinnata
Rodgersia podophylla
Rodgersia sambucifolia
Zantedeschia hybrids

Cut Flowers

Everybody loves bouquets. It may be argued that every plant in the garden can be cut and brought indoors to enjoy, but the following plants are considered cut flowers because of their reasonably strong stems and good vase life. Always cut stems in the morning or evening, place immediately in water, and use a cut flower preservative in the vase.

Acanthus mollis
Acanthus spinosus
Achillea filipendulina
Achillea millefolium
Achillea ptarmica
Aconitum carmichaelii
Aconitum napellus
Allium christophii
Allium giganteum
Allium karataviense
Allium 'Beauregard'
Allium 'Globemaster'
Anemone coronaria
Artemisia ludoviciana
Aster novae-angliae
Aster novi-belgii
Aster tataricus
Astilbe ×arendsii
Astilbe chinensis var. *taquetii*
Astrantia major
Astrantia maxima
Baptisia alba
Baptisia australis
Baptisia sphaerocarpa
Baptisia viridis
Boltonia asteroides
Campanula lactiflora
Campanula latiloba
Centaurea macrocephala
Chrysanthemum coccineum
Chrysanthemum ×superbum
Crocosmia hybrids

Cut Flowers, continued
Dahlia hybrids
Delphinium elatum
Delphinium nudicaule
Dianthus barbatus
Dianthus caryophyllus
Digitalis purpurea
Dryopteris erythrosora (foliage)
Echinacea purpurea
Echinops ritro
Eremurus himalaicus
Eremurus stenophyllus
Eryngium alpinum
Eupatorium maculatum
Eupatorium purpureum
Gaillardia ×grandiflora
Geum triflorum
Helenium autumnale
Helianthus angustifolius
Helianthus ×multiflorus
Heliopsis helianthoides
Helleborus orientalis
Heuchera sanguinea
Hibiscus moscheutos
Hypericum androsaemum (fruit)
Iris ensata
Iris louisiana
Kniphofia hybrids
Liatris spicata
Lilium auratum
Lilium regale
Lupinus polyphyllus
Lycoris albiflora
Lycoris aurea
Lycoris radiata
Lycoris squamigera
Lysimachia clethroides
Macleaya cordata
Miscanthus sinensis
Monarda didyma
Nepeta ×faassenii
Nepeta sibirica
Paeonia hybrids
Papaver nudicaule
Papaver somniferum
Patrinia scabiosifolia
Penstemon barbatus
Penstemon digitalis
Phlox paniculata
Physostegia virginiana
Platycodon grandiflorus
Polemonium caeruleum
Polemonium foliosissimum
Polygonatum odoratum
Primula vialii
Scabiosa caucasica
Stokesia laevis
Thalictrum aquilegiifolium
Veronica longifolia
Veronica spicata
Veronicastrum sibiricum
Veronicastrum virginicum

Drought Tolerance

The following plants tolerate drought well, but remember: no plant "likes" to be grown under drought conditions, and performance is always better when some irrigation is provided.

Aster novae-angliae
Aster novi-belgii
Aster tataricus
Epimedium grandiflorum
Epimedium ×perralchium
Epimedium ×rubrum
Epimedium ×youngianum
Eryngium agavifolium
Eryngium yuccafolium
Yucca filamentosa
Zauschneria californica

Flower Color

The human eyeball is a mysterious thing, and the interpretation of a color is always somewhat subjective, so be warned: the following lists of plants of a particular flower color are guidelines only. For instance, "white," to me, is a range, including the creamy whites, perhaps with a hint of pink.

WHITE
Achillea ageratum 'W. B. Childs'
Achillea millefolium 'Nakuru'
Achillea ptarmica
Achillea ptarmica 'Ballerina'
Achillea ptarmica 'The Pearl' ('Boule de Neige')
Achillea sibirica
Aconitum septentrionale 'Ivorine'
Allium karataviense
Anemone blanda 'White Splendor'
Anemone coronaria
Anemone coronaria 'Mt. Everest'
Anemone coronaria St. Brigid series
Anemone ×hybrida 'Honorine Jobert'
Anemone sylvestris
Aquilegia flabellata 'Alba'
Arisaema candidissimum
Arisaema sikokianum
Arisaema sikokianum × A. takedae
Aruncus aethusifolius
Aruncus dioicus
Aruncus dioicus 'Kneiffii'
Aruncus dioicus 'Zweiweltenkind' ('Child of Two Worlds')
Aruncus 'Southern White'
Aster divaricatus
Astilbe ×arendsii 'Bridal Veil'
Astilbe ×arendsii 'Gladstone'
Astilbe ×arendsii 'Rheinland'
Astilbe biternata
Astilbe simplicifolia 'Dunkellanchs'
Astilbe simplicifolia 'Willy Buchanan'
Astrantia major 'Margery Fish' ('Shaggy')
Astrantia major 'Sunningdale Variegated'
Baptisia alba

Baptisia alba 'Pendula'
Boltonia asteroides
Boltonia asteroides 'Snowbank'
Campanula lactiflora 'Alba'
Campanula latiloba 'Alba'
Centaurea montana 'Alba'
Cerastium buisseri
Cerastium tomentosum
Chrysanthemum ×*superbum* 'Aglaia'
Chrysanthemum ×*superbum* 'Becky'
Chrysanthemum ×*superbum* 'Polaris'
Chrysanthemum ×*superbum* 'Snow Cap'
Chrysanthemum ×*superbum* 'Snow Lady'
Chrysanthemum ×*superbum* 'White Knight'
Clematis integrifolia 'Alba'
Clematis terniflora
Clematis 'Huldine'
Clematis 'Miss Bateman'
Corydalis lutea 'Alba'
Crocus chrysanthus 'Cream Beauty'
Crocus vernus 'Jeanne d'Arc'
Dicentra spectabilis 'Alba'
Dicentra 'Langtrees'
Dicentra 'Snowflakes'
Digitalis purpurea 'Alba'
Disporum sessile 'Variegatum'
Echinacea purpurea 'White Lustre'
Echinacea purpurea 'White Swan'
Epimedium ×*youngianum*
Epimedium ×*youngianum* 'Milky Way'
Epimedium ×*youngianum* 'Niveum'
Eremurus aitchisonii
Eremurus himalaicus
Eryngium agavifolium
Eryngium yuccafolium
Eupatorium coelestinum 'Album'
Eupatorium rugosum
Eupatorium rugosum 'Chocolate'
Gaura lindheimeri
Gaura lindheimeri 'Corrie's Gold'
Geranium sanguineum 'Album'
Geum rivale 'Album'
Helleborus niger
Helleborus niger Blackthorn Group
Helleborus ×*nigristern*
Helleborus orientalis
Helleborus orientalis Party Dress series
Hemerocallis 'Gentle Shepherd'
Hemerocallis 'Ice Carnival'
Hemerocallis 'Luminous Jewel'
Heuchera villosa
Heuchera villosa 'Autumn Bride'
Heuchera villosa 'Purpurea'
Heuchera 'June Bride'
Heuchera 'White Cloud'
Hibiscus mutabilis
Hibiscus 'Disco White'
Hosta montana
Hosta montana 'Aureomarginata'
Hosta sieboldiana
Hosta sieboldiana 'Frances Williams'
Hosta 'Bright Lights'
Hosta 'Invincible'
Hosta 'Royal Standard'
Hosta 'Spritzer'
Hosta 'Sum and Substance'
Iris tectorum 'Album'
Iris xiphium 'White Wedgewood'
Iris 'Butter and Sugar'
Iris 'White Swirl'
Kalimeris pinnatifida
Kalimeris yomena
Kalimeris yomena 'Variegata'
Lamium maculatum 'White Nancy'
Liatris spicata 'Floristan White'
Lilium auratum
Lilium auratum 'Opala'
Lilium martagon 'Album'
Lilium regale
Lilium 'Apollo'
Lilium 'Casa Blanca'
Lilium 'Olivia'
Linum perenne 'Album'
Lunaria annua 'Alba'
Lunaria rediviva
Lupinus polyphyllus 'Albus'
Lychnis coronaria 'Alba'
Lychnis flos-cuculi 'Alba'
Lycoris albiflora
Lysimachia clethroides
Lysimachia ephemerum
Macleaya cordata
Mertensia virginica 'Alba'
Miscanthus sinensis
Miscanthus sinensis 'Adagio'
Miscanthus sinensis 'Arabesque'
Miscanthus sinensis 'Cabaret'
Miscanthus sinensis 'Malepartus'
Miscanthus sinensis 'Morning Light'
Miscanthus sinensis 'Silberfeder' ('Silver Feather')
Miscanthus sinensis 'Strictus'
Miscanthus sinensis 'Variegatus'
Miscanthus sinensis 'Yaku Jima'
Monarda 'Snow White'
Narcissus 'Actaea'
Narcissus 'Avalanche'
Narcissus 'Barrett Browning'
Narcissus 'Bridal Gown'
Narcissus 'Flower Drift'
Narcissus 'Geranium'
Narcissus 'Ice Follies'
Oenothera berlandieri 'Woodside White'
Oenothera speciosa 'Alba'
Paeonia 'White Cockade'
Papaver nudicaule 'Party Fun'
Papaver somniferum 'Album'
Penstemon digitalis
Penstemon digitalis 'Husker Red'
Penstemon 'Mother of Pearl'
Penstemon 'Snowstorm'
Penstemon 'White Bedder'
Phlox divaricata 'Dirigo Ice'
Phlox divaricata 'Fuller's White'
Phlox paniculata 'David'
Phlox stolonifera 'Bruce's White'
Phlox subulata 'Snowflake'
Physostegia virginiana 'Summer Snow'
Platycodon grandiflorus 'Albus'
Polemonium caeruleum 'Album'
Polygonatum commutatum
Polygonatum humile
Polygonatum odoratum
Polygonatum odoratum 'Variegatum'
Primula denticulata 'Alba'
Primula vulgaris 'Alba'
Primula vulgaris 'Atlantia'
Primula vulgaris 'Gigha White'
Pulmonaria saccharata 'Sissinghurst White'
Pulsatilla vulgaris 'Alba'
Ranunculus aconitifolius
Rodgersia pinnata 'Alba'
Rodgersia pinnata 'Superba Alba'
Rodgersia podophylla
Rodgersia sambucifolia
Salvia officinalis 'Albiflora'

White, continued
Saponaria officinalis 'Alba'
Sedum reflexum
Sedum reflexum 'Blue Spruce'
Sedum spurium
Sedum ternatum
Silene fimbriata
Silene uniflora
Sisyrinchium angustifolium 'Album'
Sisyrinchium idahoense 'Album'
Smilacina racemosa
Stokesia laevis 'Alba'
Thalictrum aquilegiifolium 'White Cloud'
Thermopsis montana 'Alba'
Tiarella cordifolia
Tiarella cordifolia var. *collina*
Tiarella cordifolia 'Oakleaf'
Tiarella 'Brandywine'
Tiarella 'Dunvegan'
Tiarella 'Ink Blot'
Tiarella 'Snowflake'
Tiarella 'Tiger Stripe'
Tradescantia virginiana 'Innocence'
Tricyrtis formosana 'Alba'
Trillium cernuum
Trillium grandiflorum
Trillium grandiflorum 'Flore Pleno'
Veratrum album
Verbena tenuisecta var. *alba*
Veronicastrum virginicum
Yucca filamentosa
Yucca filamentosa 'Bright Edge'
Yucca filamentosa 'Gold Band'
Yucca filamentosa 'Golden Sword'
Zantedeschia aethiopica

LAVENDER/BLUE
Acanthus mollis
Acanthus mollis 'Holland's Lemon'
Acanthus spinosus
Acanthus spinosus 'Spinosissimus'
Aconitum carmichaelii
Aconitum carmichaelii 'Arendsii'
Aconitum carmichaelii var. *wilsonii*
Aconitum napellus
Aconitum reclinatum
Ajuga reptans
Ajuga reptans 'Atropurpurea'
Ajuga reptans 'Bronze Beauty'
Ajuga reptans 'Burgundy Glow'
Ajuga reptans 'Catlin's Giant'
Ajuga reptans 'Silver Beauty'
Allium christophii
Allium giganteum
Allium 'Beauregard'
Allium 'Globemaster'
Anemone blanda
Anemone blanda 'Atrocaerulea'
Anemone blanda 'Blue Star'
Anemone coronaria
Anemone coronaria 'Mr. Fokker'
Anemone coronaria 'Sylphide'
Anemone coronaria St. Brigid series
Aquilegia alpina
Aquilegia caerulea
Aquilegia flabellata
Aquilegia flabellata 'Alba'
Aquilegia ×hybrida 'Blue Jay'
Aquilegia ×hybrida Biedermeier strain
Aquilegia vulgaris
Aquilegia vulgaris 'Blue Barlow'
Aster novae-angliae 'Hella Lacy'
Aster novae-angliae 'Purple Dome'
Aster novi-belgii 'Professor Kippenburg'
Aster tataricus
Baptisia australis
Baptisia minor
Baptisia 'Purple Smoke'
Brunnera macrophylla
Brunnera macrophylla 'Langtrees'
Brunnera macrophylla 'Variegata'
Campanula carpatica
Campanula carpatica 'Blue Clips'
Campanula carpatica 'Kobalt Bell'
Campanula carpatica var. *turbinata*
Campanula carpatica var. *turbinata* 'Isabel'
Campanula lactiflora 'Pritchard's Variety'
Campanula lactiflora 'Superba'
Campanula latiloba
Campanula latiloba 'Hidcote Amethyst'
Campanula latiloba 'Highcliffe'
Campanula portenschlagiana
Campanula portenschlagiana 'Bavarica'
Campanula portenschlagiana 'Resholt's Variety'
Campanula poscharskyana
Campanula poscharskyana 'Blue Gown'
Centaurea cyanus
Centaurea dealbata
Centaurea montana
Centaurea montana 'Grandiflora'
Ceratostigma plumbaginoides
Ceratostigma willmottianum
Ceratostigma willmottianum 'Forest Blue'
Clematis ×durandii
Clematis heracleifolia
Clematis heracleifolia 'Côte d'Azur'
Clematis heracleifolia 'Robert Briden'
Clematis heracleifolia 'Wyevale Blue'
Clematis integrifolia
Clematis ×jackmanii
Clematis 'Elsa Spath'
Clematis 'Madame Chalmondeley'
Corydalis flexuosa
Corydalis flexuosa 'Blue Panda'
Corydalis flexuosa 'China Blue'
Crocus chrysanthus 'Blue Pearl'
Crocus chrysanthus 'Lady Killer'
Crocus speciosus
Crocus speciosus 'Cassiope'
Crocus speciosus 'Conqueror'
Crocus speciosus 'Oxonian'
Crocus vernus 'Pickwick'
Crocus vernus 'Queen of the Blues'
Crocus vernus 'Remembrance'
Delphinium ×belladonna 'Volkerfrieden'
Delphinium grandiflorum 'Tom Thumb'
Delphinium 'Barba Blue'
Delphinium 'Blue Bird'
Delphinium 'Blue Dawn'
Delphinium 'Blue Jade'
Delphinium 'Molly Buchanan'
Delphinium 'Skyline'
Echinops ritro
Echinops ritro 'Blue Cloud'
Echinops ritro 'Taplow Blue'
Echinops ritro 'Taplow Purple'
Epimedium grandiflorum 'Lilafee'
Eryngium alpinum
Eryngium alpinum 'Blue Star'
Eryngium giganteum
Eupatorium coelestinum

Hepatica acutiloba
Hepatica americana
Hepatica nobilis
Hepatica nobilis 'Light Blue'
Hepatica transsilvanica
Hosta venusta
Hosta 'Antioch'
Hosta 'Blue Cadet'
Hosta 'Francee'
Hosta 'Gold Edger'
Hosta 'Red Neck Heaven'
Hosta 'Sun Power'
Ipheion uniflorum
Ipheion uniflorum 'Rolf Fiedler'
Ipheion uniflorum 'Wisley Blue'
Iris hexagona
Iris reticulata
Iris reticulata 'Cantab'
Iris reticulata 'Harmony'
Iris tectorum
Iris xiphium
Iris 'Ideal'
Iris 'Llewelyn'
Iris 'Lynn Hall'
Iris 'Regal'
Iris 'Sally Kerlin'
Linum perenne
Linum usitatissimum
Lobelia siphilitica
Lunaria annua
Lunaria annua 'Variegata'
Mertensia asiatica
Mertensia sibirica
Mertensia virginica
Monarda 'Blue Stocking'
Monarda 'Donnerwolke'
Nepeta ×*faassenii*
Nepeta ×*faassenii* 'Six Hills Giant'
Nepeta nervosa
Nepeta sibirica
Penstemon cardwellii
Perovskia atriplicifolia
Perovskia atriplicifolia 'Filagran'
Perovskia atriplicifolia 'Longin'
Phlox divaricata 'Clouds of Perfume'
Phlox divaricata 'Louisiana Blue'
Phlox paniculata 'Blue Boy'
Phlox stolonifera
Phlox stolonifera 'Sherwood Purple'
Phlox subulata 'Oakington Blue'
Physostegia virginiana 'Alba'
Platycodon grandiflorus
Platycodon grandiflorus 'Florovariegatus'
Platycodon grandiflorus 'Mariesii'
Platycodon grandiflorus 'Plenus'
Platycodon grandiflorus 'Sentimental Blue'
Polemonium caeruleum
Polemonium caeruleum 'Brise d'Anjou'
Polemonium caeruleum 'Dawn Light'
Polemonium caeruleum subsp. *himalayanum*
Polemonium foliosissimum
Polemonium reptans
Polemonium reptans 'Blue Pearl'
Primula denticulata
Pulmonaria angustifolia
Pulmonaria angustifolia 'Mawson's Variety'
Pulmonaria angustifolia 'Munstead Blue'
Pulmonaria longifolia
Pulmonaria longifolia 'Bertram Anderson'
Pulmonaria longifolia subsp. *cevennensis* ('Little Blue')
Pulmonaria saccharata
Pulmonaria saccharata 'Benediction'
Pulmonaria saccharata 'Excalibur'
Pulmonaria saccharata 'Highdown'
Pulmonaria saccharata 'Mrs. Moon'
Pulmonaria saccharata 'Spilled Milk'
Pulmonaria 'Roy Davidson'
Rodgersia aesculifolia
Rodgersia pinnata
Salvia guaranitica
Salvia guaranitica 'Argentina Skies'
Salvia guaranitica 'Black and Blue'
Salvia guaranitica 'Purple Knight'
Salvia guaranitica 'Purple Splendour'
Salvia nemerosa 'Blue Hill'
Salvia nemerosa 'Blue Queen' ('Blaukönigin')
Salvia nemerosa 'Tanzerin'
Salvia officinalis
Salvia officinalis 'Icterina'
Salvia officinalis 'Purpurescens'
Salvia officinalis 'Tricolor'
Salvia ×*sylvestris*
Salvia ×*sylvestris* 'East Friesland' ('Ostfriesland')
Salvia ×*sylvestris* 'Lubecca'
Salvia 'Indigo Spires'
Scabiosa caucasica
Scabiosa columbaria
Scabiosa columbaria 'Butterfly Blue'
Sisyrinchium angustifolium
Sisyrinchium atlanticum
Sisyrinchium idahoense
Sisyrinchium idahoense 'California Skies'
Sisyrinchium 'Biscutella'
Sisyrinchium 'E. K. Balls'
Sisyrinchium 'Quaint and Queer'
Stachys byzantina
Stachys byzantina 'Countess Helene von Stein'
Stachys macrantha
Stachys macrantha 'Robusta'
Stokesia laevis
Stokesia laevis 'Blue Danube'
Stokesia laevis 'Klaus Jelitto'
Stokesia laevis 'Omega Skyrocket'
Stokesia laevis 'Wyoming'
Symphytum asperum
Symphytum caucasicum
Symphytum grandiflorum
Symphytum officinale
Symphytum officinale 'Variegatum'
Symphytum ×*uplandicum*
Symphytum ×*uplandicum* 'Variegatum'
Symphytum 'Goldsmith'
Thalictrum aquilegiifolium
Thalictrum aquilegiifolium 'Atropurpureum'
Thalictrum ichangense
Thalictrum minus 'Adiantifolium'
Thymus praecox
Thymus pseudolanuginosus
Thymus serpyllum
Thymus vulgaris
Thymus vulgaris 'Silver Posie'
Tradescantia virginiana
Tradescantia virginiana 'Bilberry Ice'
Tradescantia virginiana 'Bluestone'
Tradescantia virginiana 'Concord Grape'
Tradescantia virginiana 'Purewell Giant'
Verbena bonariensis
Verbena rigida
Verbena rigida 'Lilacina'
Verbena rigida 'Polaris'
Verbena tenuisecta
Verbena tenuisecta 'Imagination'

Lavender/Blue, continued
Verbena 'Abbeville'
Verbena 'Homestead Purple'
Verbena 'Tapien Blue'
Veronica austriaca
Veronica austriaca subsp. *teucrium*
Veronica austriaca subsp. *teucrium* 'Aurea'
Veronica austriaca subsp. *teucrium* 'Blue Fountain'
Veronica austriaca subsp. *teucrium* 'Shirley Blue'
Veronica incana
Veronica longifolia
Veronica longifolia 'Blauriesen'
Veronica prostrata
Veronica prostrata 'Trehane'
Veronica spicata
Veronica spicata 'Blue Bouquet'
Veronica spicata 'Blue Spires'
Veronica spicata 'Lili Corinna'
Veronicastrum sibiricum
Veronicastrum virginicum
Viola cornuta
Viola cornuta 'Jersey Gem'
Viola cornuta 'Lilacina'
Viola cucullata
Viola labradorica
Viola pedata
Viola pedata 'Artist's Palette'

YELLOW
Achillea filipendulina
Achillea millefolium 'Paprika'
Achillea 'Anthea'
Achillea 'Coronation Gold'
Achillea 'Martina'
Achillea 'Moonshine'
Aconitum lamarckii
Aquilegia canadensis
Aquilegia chrysantha
Aquilegia chrysantha var. *hinckleyana*
Aquilegia ×*hybrida* 'Music Yellow'
Artemisia ludoviciana
Artemisia ludoviciana 'Latiloba'
Artemisia ludoviciana 'Silver King'
Artemisia ludoviciana 'Valerie Fennis'
Artemisia 'Huntington Gardens'
Baptisia sphaerocarpa
Baptisia tinctoria
Baptisia viridis
Canna 'Cleopatra'
Canna 'Richard Wallace'
Centaurea macrocephala
Centaurea montana 'Ochroleuca'
Cephalaria gigantea
Chrysanthemum pacificum
Clematis cirrhosa
Coreopsis auriculata
Coreopsis auriculata 'Nana'
Coreopsis grandiflora
Coreopsis grandiflora 'Early Sunrise'
Coreopsis grandiflora 'Sunray'
Coreopsis lanceolata
Coreopsis lanceolata 'Brown Eyes'
Coreopsis verticillata
Coreopsis verticillata 'Golden Showers'
Coreopsis verticillata 'Moonbeam'
Coreopsis verticillata 'Zagreb'
Corydalis cheilanthifolia
Corydalis lutea
Crocosmia 'Citronella'
Crocosmia 'Rowallane Yellow'
Crocus chrysanthus 'Advance'
Crocus chrysanthus 'Moonlight'
Delphinium 'Butterball'
Delphinium 'Sun Gleam'
Dicentra scandens
Dicentra scandens 'Athens Yellow'
Digitalis grandiflora
Digitalis lutea
Disporum sessile
Disporum sessile var. *flavum*
Echinacea paradoxa
Epimedium ×*perralchium*
Epimedium ×*perralchium* 'Frohnleiten'
Epimedium ×*versicolor*
Epimedium ×*versicolor* 'Sulphureum'
Eremurus stenophyllus
Euphorbia characias
Euphorbia characias 'Ember Queen'
Euphorbia characias 'John Tomelson'
Euphorbia characias 'Lambrook Gold'
Euphorbia characias subsp. *wulfenii*
Euphorbia dulcis
Euphorbia dulcis 'Chameleon'
Euphorbia lathyris
Euphorbia myrsinites
Gaillardia ×*grandiflora*
Gaillardia ×*grandiflora* 'Goblin'
Gaillardia ×*grandiflora* 'Golden Goblin'
Gaillardia ×*grandiflora* Lollipop series
Geum chiloense 'Lady Stratheden'
Helenium autumnale
Helenium 'Butterpat'
Helenium 'Riverton Beauty'
Helenium 'Wyndley'
Helianthus angustifolius
Helianthus giganteus
Helianthus giganteus 'Sheila's Sunshine'
Helianthus ×*multiflorus*
Helianthus ×*multiflorus* 'Capenoch Star'
Helianthus ×*multiflorus* 'Corona Dorica'
Helianthus ×*multiflorus* 'Loddon Gold'
Helianthus ×*multiflorus* 'Morning Sun'
Heliopsis helianthoides
Heliopsis helianthoides 'Ballerina'
Heliopsis helianthoides 'Golden Plume'
Heliopsis helianthoides 'Goldgreenheart'
Heliopsis helianthoides 'Incomparabilis'
Heliopsis helianthoides 'Mars'
Heliopsis helianthoides 'Summer Sun'
Hemerocallis dumortieri
Hemerocallis fulva
Hemerocallis minor
Hemerocallis 'Atlanta Irish Heart'
Hemerocallis 'Eeenie Weenie'
Hemerocallis 'Golden Chimes'
Hemerocallis 'Heather Harrington'
Hemerocallis 'Hyperion'
Hemerocallis 'Kindly Light'
Hemerocallis 'Mary Todd'
Hemerocallis 'Stella d'Oro'
Hypericum androsaemum
Hypericum androsaemum 'Albury Purple'
Hypericum calycinum
Hypericum 'Hidcote'
Iris danfordiae
Iris 'All Aglow'
Iris 'Butter and Sugar'
Iris 'Moonlight'
Iris 'Sun Fury'
Kirengeshoma palmata
Kniphofia 'Sally's Comet'
Kniphofia 'Shining Scepter'
Kniphofia 'Sulphur Gem'
Kniphofia 'Sunningdale Yellow'
Lamium galeobdolon
Lamium galeobdolon 'Herman's Pride'

Ligularia dentata
Ligularia dentata 'Desdemona'
Ligularia macrophylla
Ligularia sibirica
Ligularia stenocephala
Ligularia stenocephala 'The Rocket'
Lilium auratum var. *platyphyllum*
Lilium canadense
Lilium Blackhouse hybrid
Lilium 'Imperial Gold'
Lilium 'Soft Moonbeam'
Lilium 'Vivaldi'
Linum flavum
Lupinus arboreus
Lycoris aurea
Lysimachia ciliata
Lysimachia ciliata 'Purpurea'
Lysimachia japonica
Lysimachia japonica 'Minutissima'
Lysimachia nummularia
Lysimachia nummularia 'Aurea'
Narcissus bulbocodium
Narcissus bulbocodium 'Primrose'
Narcissus cyclamineus
Narcissus 'Baby Moon'
Narcissus 'Belcato'
Narcissus 'Biscayne'
Narcissus 'Carlton'
Narcissus 'Cum Laude'
Narcissus 'February Gold'
Narcissus 'Foresight'
Narcissus 'Garden Princess'
Narcissus 'Hawara'
Narcissus 'Hillstar'
Narcissus 'Jenny'
Narcissus 'Pipit'
Narcissus 'Stint'
Narcissus 'Susy'
Narcissus 'Tête-à-Tête'
Narcissus 'Tuesday's Child'
Narcissus 'Unsurpassable'
Nepeta govaniana
Oenothera drummondii
Oenothera fruticosa
Oenothera fruticosa 'Lady Brookborough'
Oenothera fruticosa 'Yellow River'
Oenothera missouriensis
Oenothera missouriensis 'Greencourt Lemon'
Paeonia 'Argosy'
Paeonia 'Daffodil'
Paeonia 'Golden Hind'
Paeonia 'Honey Gold'
Patrinia scabiosifolia
Patrinia scabiosifolia 'Nagoya'
Patrinia triloba
Patrinia villosa
Penstemon confertus
Phlomis fruticosa
Phlomis russeliana
Primula florindae
Primula heladoxa
Primula veris
Primula vulgaris
Primula vulgaris 'Double Yellow'
Ranunculus asiaticus 'Bloomingdale Yellow'
Ranunculus bulbosus
Ranunculus bulbosus 'Flore Pleno'
Ranunculus ficaria
Ranunculus ficaria 'Brazen Hussy'
Ranunculus repens
Ranunculus repens 'Susan's Song' ('Buttered Popcorn')
Rudbeckia fulgida
Rudbeckia fulgida var. *sullivantii* 'Goldsturm'
Rudbeckia laciniata
Rudbeckia laciniata 'Goldquelle'
Rudbeckia nitida
Rudbeckia nitida 'Herbsonne'
Rudbeckia triloba
Salvia koyamae
Santolina chamaecyparissus
Santolina pinnata
Santolina virens
Scabiosa ochroleuca
Sedum acre
Sedum aizoon
Sedum aizoon var. *aurantiacum*
Sedum kamtschaticum
Sedum kamtschaticum 'Diffusum'
Sedum kamtschaticum 'Weihenstephaner Gold'
Sedum spathulifolium
Sedum spathulifolium 'Cape Blanco'
Sisyrinchium striatum
Sisyrinchium striatum 'Aunt May'
Stachys byzantina 'Primrose Heron'
Stachys byzantina 'Sheila Macqueen'
Stokesia laevis 'Mary Gregory'
Stylophorum diphyllum
Stylophorum lasiocarpum
Tanacetum vulgare
Thalictrum flavum
Thalictrum flavum 'Glaucum'
Thalictrum minus 'Adiantifolium'
Thermopsis caroliniana
Thermopsis fabacea
Thermopsis montana
Trillium discolor
Trillium luteum
Uvularia grandiflora
Uvularia grandiflora 'Sunbonnet'
Uvularia perfoliata
Uvularia sessilifolia
Waldsteinia fragaroides
Waldsteinia lobata
Waldsteinia parviflora
Waldsteinia ternata

PINK/ROSE

Achillea millefolium
Achillea millefolium 'Nakuru'
Achillea millefolium 'Rose Beauty'
Achillea 'Appleblossom'
Aconitum napellus 'Carneum'
Ajuga genevensis 'Pink Beauty'
Anemone blanda 'Radar'
Anemone coronaria
Anemone coronaria St. Brigid series
Anemone hupehensis 'September Charm'
Anemone ×*hybrida* 'Kriemhilde'
Anemone ×*hybrida* 'Max Vogel'
Anemone tomentosa
Anemone tomentosa 'Robustissima'
Aquilegia vulgaris 'Nora Barlow'
Aquilegia vulgaris 'Pink Barlow'
Aquilegia vulgaris 'Treble Pink'
Aster carolinianus
Aster novae-angliae 'Alma Potschke'
Aster novae-angliae 'Harrington's Pink'
Aster novi-belgii 'Winston S. Churchill'
Astilbe ×*arendsii* 'Cattleya'
Astilbe ×*arendsii* 'Europa'
Astilbe ×*arendsii* 'Venus'
Astilbe simplicifolia
Astilbe simplicifolia 'Dunkellanchs'
Astilbe simplicifolia 'Hennie Graafland'
Astilbe simplicifolia 'Sprite'
Astilbe simplicifolia 'Willy Buchanan'
Astrantia major

Pink/Rose, continued
Astrantia major 'Margery Fish' ('Shaggy')
Astrantia major 'Sunningdale Variegated'
Astrantia maxima
Bergenia ciliata
Bergenia cordifolia
Bergenia purpurascens
Bergenia 'Abendglocken' ('Evening Bells')
Bergenia 'Ballawley'
Bergenia 'Bressingham Ruby'
Bergenia 'Distinction'
Bergenia 'Profusion'
Boltonia asteroides 'Pink Beauty'
Campanula lactiflora 'Loddon Anna'
Canna 'Cleopatra'
Canna 'Panache'
Canna 'Tropicana' ('Phaison')
Canna 'Pink Sunburst'
Canna 'Stuttgart'
Centaurea dealbata 'Steenbergii'
Centaurea hypoleuca
Centaurea hypoleuca 'John Coutts'
Chrysanthemum coccineum 'Eileen May Robinson'
Chrysanthemum coccineum 'Shirley Double'
Chrysanthemum 'Apricot Single'
Chrysanthemum 'Hillside Sheffield'
Chrysanthemum 'Ryan's Daisy'
Clematis integrifolia 'Rosea'
Clematis texensis
Clematis texensis 'Duchess of Albany'
Clematis 'Duchess of Edinburgh'
Clematis 'Pink Champagne'
Clematis 'Proteus'
Clematis 'Ville de Lyon'
Colchicum autumnale
Colchicum byzantinum
Colchicum speciosum
Colchicum 'Autumn Queen'
Colchicum 'Waterlily'
Coreopsis auriculata
Coreopsis rosea
Dahlia imperialis
Dahlia 'Good Interest'
Dahlia 'Gypsy Boy'
Dianthus barbatus
Dianthus barbatus 'Indian Carpet'
Dianthus deltoides
Dianthus gratianopolitanus
Dianthus gratianopolitanus 'Baby Blanket'
Dianthus gratianopolitanus 'Bath's Pink'
Dianthus gratianopolitanus 'Firewitch'
Dianthus gratianopolitanus 'Mountain Mist'
Dianthus gratianopolitanus 'Tiny Rubies'
Dicentra eximia
Dicentra formosa
Dicentra spectabilis
Dicentra 'Bacchanal'
Dicentra 'Boothman's Variety'
Dicentra 'Luxuriant'
Digitalis ×mertonensis
Digitalis purpurea
Echinacea purpurea 'Bright Star'
Epimedium grandiflorum
Epimedium grandiflorum subsp. *koreanum*
Epimedium grandiflorum 'Rose Queen'
Epimedium ×youngianum 'Roseum'
Gaillardia ×grandiflora
Gaillardia ×grandiflora 'Goblin'
Gaillardia ×grandiflora Lollipop series
Gaura lindheimeri 'Siskiyou Pink'
Geranium ×cantabrigiense
Geranium ×cantabrigiense 'Biokovo'
Geranium ×cantabrigiense 'Biokovo Karmina'
Geranium cinereum
Geranium cinereum 'Ballerina'
Geranium cinereum 'Lawerence Flatman'
Geranium cinereum 'Splendens'
Geranium endressii
Geranium endressii 'Wargrave Pink'
Geranium sanguineum 'Glenluce'
Geranium sanguineum 'Minutum'
Geranium sanguineum 'Striatum'
Helleborus orientalis Party Dress series
Hemerocallis 'Benchmark'
Hemerocallis 'China Bride'
Hemerocallis 'Pandora's Box'
Hemerocallis 'Tender Shepherd'
Heuchera sanguinea
Heuchera 'Canyon Pink'
Heuchera 'Fireglow'
Heuchera 'Huntsman'
Heuchera 'Oakington Jewel'
Heuchera 'Raspberry Regal'
Hibiscus mutabilis
Hibiscus mutabilis 'Flore Plena'
Hibiscus mutabilis 'Raspberry Rose'
Hibiscus 'Disco Belle'
Hibiscus 'Lord Baltimore'
Iris nelsonii
Iris 'Chensled'
Iris 'Glittering Amber'
Iris 'Pink Frost'
Lamium maculatum
Lamium maculatum 'Beacon Silver'
Lamium maculatum 'Chequers'
Lilium martagon
Lilium 'Acapulco'
Lilium 'Dandy'
Lilium 'Trance'
Lupinus polyphyllus 'Russell Hybrid Pink'
Lychnis chalcedonica 'Carnea'
Lychnis coronaria 'Abbotsford Rose'
Lychnis coronaria 'Angel Blush'
Lychnis flos-cuculi
Lycoris squamigera
Mertensia virginica 'Rosea'
Monarda 'Croftway Pink'
Monarda 'Petite Delight'
Oenothera berlandieri
Oenothera berlandieri 'Siskiyou'
Oenothera speciosa
Oenothera speciosa 'Ballerina Hot Pink'
Paeonia 'First Lady'
Paeonia 'Rose Garland'
Paeonia 'Souvenir de Maxime Cornu'
Papaver nudicaule 'Champagne Bubbles'
Papaver nudicaule 'Party Fun'
Papaver orientale 'Cedric Morris'
Papaver orientale 'Lighthouse'
Papaver orientale 'Picotee'
Penstemon barbatus
Penstemon barbatus 'Hyacinth'
Penstemon barbatus 'Skylight'
Penstemon smallii
Penstemon 'Hidcote Pink'
Penstemon 'Sour Grapes'
Penstemon 'Stapleford Gem'

Penstemon 'Thorn'
Phlomis italica
Phlox paniculata 'Bright Eyes'
Phlox paniculata 'Fairest One'
Phlox paniculata 'Franz Schubert'
Phlox paniculata 'Norah Leigh'
Phlox paniculata 'Robert Poore'
Phlox paniculata 'Starfire'
Phlox stolonifera 'Homefires'
Phlox stolonifera 'Variegata'
Phlox subulata 'Candy Stripe'
Phlox subulata 'Coral Eye'
Phlox subulata 'Maiden's Blush'
Physostegia virginiana
Physostegia virginiana 'Bouquet Rose' ('Pink Bouquet')
Physostegia virginiana 'Variegata'
Physostegia virginiana 'Vivid'
Platycodon grandiflorus 'Shell Pink'
Polemonium carneum
Polygonum affine
Polygonum affine 'Hartford'
Polygonum affine 'Superbum'
Polygonum bistorta
Polygonum bistorta subsp. *carneum*
Polygonum bistorta var. *regelianum*
Polygonum bistorta 'Superbum'
Primula denticulata 'Rosea'
Primula japonica
Primula japonica 'Splendens'
Primula pulverulenta 'Bartley's Strain'
Primula vialii
Primula vulgaris subsp. *sibthorpii*
Primula 'Rowallane Rose'
Pulmonaria rubra
Pulmonaria rubra 'Bowles' Red'
Pulmonaria rubra 'David Ward'
Pulmonaria saccharata 'Berries and Cream'
Pulmonaria saccharata 'Mrs. Kittle'
Ranunculus asiaticus
Rehmannia angulata
Rehmannia elata
Rodgersia pinnata 'Rubra'
Rodgersia pinnata 'Superba'
Salvia involucrata
Salvia involucrata 'Bethellii'
Saponaria ocymoides
Saponaria officinalis
Scabiosa columbaria 'Pink Mist'
Sedum spectabile 'Carmen'
Sedum spectabile 'Meteor'
Sedum spurium
Sedum spurium 'Fuldaglut'
Sedum spurium 'Green Mantle'
Sedum 'Atropurpureum'
Sedum 'Autumn Joy' ('Herbstfreude')
Sedum 'Mohrchen'
Sedum 'Ruby Glow'
Sedum 'Sunset Cloud'
Sedum 'Vera Jameson'
Silene caroliniana
Silene caroliniana 'Millstream Select'
Silene polypetala
Silene 'Longwood'
Thalictrum aquilegiifolium
Thalictrum aquilegiifolium 'Roseum'
Tradescantia virginiana 'Joy'
Tradescantia virginiana 'Pauline'
Tradescantia virginiana 'Purple Dome'
Trillium catesbaei
Trillium grandiflorum
Trillium grandiflorum 'Flore Pleno'
Trillium grandiflorum 'Roseum'
Verbena canadensis
Verbena peruviana
Verbena 'Carrousel'
Verbena 'Silver Anne'
Verbena 'Tapien Pink'
Veronica longifolia 'Rosalinde'
Veronica spicata 'Barcarolle'
Veronica spicata 'Heidekind'
Viola cornuta 'Rosea'
Zauschneria californica

ORANGE/RED

Achillea millefolium 'Colorado'
Achillea millefolium 'Paprika'
Achillea 'Terra Cotta'
Achillea 'The Beacon' ('Fanal')
Anemone coronaria
Anemone coronaria 'Mona Lisa Red'
Anemone coronaria St. Brigid series
Anemone hupehensis 'Prinz Heinrich' ('Prince Henry')
Aquilegia canadensis
Aquilegia ×*hybrida* 'Cardinal'
Astilbe ×*arendsii* 'Bonn'
Astilbe ×*arendsii* 'Montgomery'
Astrantia major 'Lars'
Astrantia major 'Ruby Wedding'
Bergenia 'Morning Red'
Canna 'Bengal Tiger' ('Pretoria')
Canna 'King Humpert'
Canna 'Wyoming'
Chrysanthemum coccineum
Chrysanthemum coccineum 'Brenda'
Chrysanthemum coccineum 'James Kelway'
Crocosmia 'Lucifer'
Crocosmia 'Spitfire'
Dahlia 'Pink Michigan'
Dahlia 'Royal Dahlietta Apricot'
Dahlia 'Scarlet Beauty'
Dahlia 'Single Salmon'
Delphinium nudicaule
Dianthus caryophyllus 'Red Sims'
Dianthus deltoides
Dianthus deltoides 'Brilliant'
Dianthus deltoides 'Red Maiden'
Dianthus deltoides 'Zing Rose'
Epimedium ×*rubrum*
Euphorbia griffithii
Euphorbia griffithii 'Dixter'
Euphorbia griffithii 'Fireglow'
Geum chiloense
Geum chiloense 'Fire Opal'
Geum chiloense 'Mrs. Bradshaw'
Geum rivale
Geum rivale 'Leonard's Variety'
Geum triflorum
Geum triflorum var. *campanulatum*
Helenium autumnale 'Rubrum'
Helenium 'Brilliant'
Helenium 'Coppelia'
Helenium 'Gartensonne'
Hemerocallis 'Red Joy'
Hemerocallis 'Red Rain'
Hemerocallis 'Scarlet Tanager'
Hepatica nobilis 'Rubra'
Hibiscus coccineus
Hibiscus moscheutos
Hibiscus 'Anne Arundel'
Iris fulva
Iris 'Wild Ginger'
Kniphofia 'Atlantia'
Lilium henryi
Lilium 'Amourette'
Lilium 'Campfire'
Lilium 'Enchantment'
Lobelia cardinalis

Orange/Red, continued

Lobelia ×speciosa
Lobelia ×speciosa 'Bee's Flame'
Lobelia ×speciosa 'Compliment Scarlet'
Lobelia tupa
Lupinus 'Gina Lombaert'
Lychnis ×arkwrightii
Lychnis chalcedonica
Lychnis chalcedonica 'Flore Plena'
Lycoris radiata
Monarda 'Cambridge Scarlet'
Paeonia 'Balliol'
Paeonia 'Banquet'
Paeonia 'Red Imp'
Paeonia 'Red Moon'
Paeonia 'Zu Zu'
Papaver nudicaule
Papaver nudicaule 'Party Fun'
Papaver orientale
Papaver orientale 'Avebury Crimson'
Papaver orientale 'Fireball'
Papaver orientale 'Goliath'
Papaver orientale 'Suleika'
Papaver rhoeas
Papaver somniferum
Papaver somniferum var. *paeoniflorum*
Penstemon pinifolius
Penstemon 'Ruby'
Penstemon 'Schönholzeri' ('Firebird')
Phlox paniculata 'Red Eyes'
Phlox subulata 'Scarlet Flame'
Primula bulleyana
Primula pulverulenta
Silene regia
Silene virginica
Trillium vaseyi
Verbena 'Sissinghurst'
Verbena 'Taylortown Red'

PURPLE

Arisaema consanguineum
Arisaema fargesii
Arisaema japonicum
Arisaema ringens
Arisaema sazensoo
Arisaema sikokianum
Arisaema sikokianum × A. takedae
Arisaema tortuosum
Arisaema triphyllum
Asarum arifolium
Asarum canadense
Asarum splendens
Asarum yakushimanum
Astilbe chinensis
Astilbe chinensis 'Finale'
Astilbe chinensis 'Pumila'
Astilbe chinensis var. *taquetii*
Astilbe chinensis var. *taquetii* 'Purple Lance'
Astilbe chinensis 'Visions'
Astilbe ×arendsii 'Rheinland'
Echinacea pallida
Echinacea purpurea
Echinacea purpurea 'Magnus'
Echinacea purpurea 'Robert Bloom'
Eupatorium maculatum
Eupatorium maculatum 'Gateway'
Eupatorium purpureum
Euphorbia dulcis 'Chameleon'
Geranium psilostemon
Geranium psilostemon 'Bressingham Flair'
Geranium sanguineum
Geranium sanguineum 'Alan Bloom'
Geranium sanguineum 'Cedric Morris'
Geranium 'Ann Folkard'
Helleborus foetidus
Helleborus foetidus 'Wesker Flisk'
Helleborus orientalis
Helleborus orientalis 'Dusk'
Helleborus orientalis Party Dress series
Hemerocallis 'Black Ruffles'
Heuchera villosa 'Autumn Bride'
Iris reticulata 'J. S. Dijt'
Iris 'Cozy Calico'
Iris 'Ecstatic Night'
Iris 'Pansy Purple'
Iris 'Ruffled Velvet'
Liatris borealis
Liatris graminifolia
Liatris spicata
Liatris spicata 'Kobold'
Lobelia ×gerardii
Lobelia ×gerardii 'Vedrariensis'
Lobelia ×speciosa 'Compliment Purple'
Lychnis coronaria
Penstemon 'Port Wine'
Pinellia pedatisecta
Pinellia tripartita
Primula vulgaris 'Double Burgundy'
Pulsatilla halleri
Pulsatilla pratensis
Pulsatilla vulgaris
Tricyrtis formosana
Tricyrtis hirta
Tricyrtis hirta 'Miyazaki'
Tricyrtis 'Kohaku'
Tricyrtis 'Lemon Glow'
Trillium cuneatum
Trillium cuneatum 'Eco Silver'
Trillium decipiens
Trillium erectum
Trillium sessile
Trillium stamineum

GREEN OR CHARTREUSE

Geum triflorum var. *campanulatum*
Hakonechloa macra
Hakonechloa macra 'Alboaurea'
Helleborus foetidus
Helleborus foetidus 'Wesker Flisk'
Helleborus orientalis Party Dress series
Heuchera americana
Heuchera 'Amethyst Mist'
Heuchera 'Bressingham Bronze'
Heuchera 'Chocolate Veil'
Heuchera 'Dale's Selection'
Heuchera 'Palace Purple'
Heuchera 'Pewter Veil'
Heuchera 'Plum Pudding'
Heuchera 'Smokey Rose'
Heuchera 'Whirlwind'
Veratrum viride

Fragrant Flowers/Foliage

The following perennials have fragrant flowers or leaves. Fragrance is an intensely personal thing. Some people believe a flower is marvelously scented, while other noses may detect a fetid odor for the same bloom.

Allium giganteum
Anemone sylvestris
Campanula lactiflora
Clematis heracleifolia
Dianthus caryophyllus
Dianthus gratianopolitanus
Hemerocallis fulva
Hosta sieboldiana
Ipheion uniflorum
Iris louisiana
Iris reticulata
Lilium auratum
Lilium regale
Lupinus polyphyllus
Narcissus hybrids
Phlox divaricata
Phlox paniculata
Primula bulleyana
Primula denticulata
Primula japonica
Primula pulverulenta
Primula vulgaris
Santolina chamaecyparissus
Santolina virens
Thymus praecox
Thymus pseudolanuginosus
Thymus serpyllum
Thymus vulgaris
Trillium luteum

Ground Covers

All plants cover the ground, but some plants do so more aggressively. The following plants, which generally spread by tubers, stolons, or runners, can be used to cover large areas reasonably quickly. As in all discussions, where you live—where the ground is!—will influence what plants you should select to cover the ground.

Achillea millefolium
Adiantum pedatum
Ajuga genevensis
Ajuga reptans
Asarum canadense
Astilbe chinensis
Astrantia major
Bergenia cordifolia
Bergenia purpurascens
Brunnera macrophylla
Campanula portenschlagiana
Campanula poscharskyana
Ceratostigma plumbaginoides
Dianthus deltoides
Epimedium grandiflorum
Epimedium ×perralchium
Epimedium ×rubrum
Epimedium ×versicolor
Geum rivale
Lamium galeobdolon
Lamium maculatum
Lysimachia japonica
Lysimachia nummularia
Macleaya cordata
Patrinia triloba
Patrinia villosa
Phlox divaricata
Phlox stolonifera
Phlox subulata
Polemonium reptans
Pulmonaria angustifolia
Pulmonaria longifolia
Pulmonaria saccharata
Ranunculus bulbosus
Ranunculus ficaria
Sedum acre
Stachys byzantina
Thymus praecox
Thymus pseudolanuginosus
Tiarella cordifolia
Viola labradorica
Waldsteinia fragarioides
Waldsteinia lobata
Waldsteinia parviflora
Waldsteinia ternata

Plant Height

Plant height varies tremendously with the climate in which you garden. Heat, cold, sun, shade, rainfall, and soils affect the mature height of any plant. While the absolute heights may differ from region to region, the relative heights in the following lists should be the same in most areas of the country.

One Foot or Less
Adiantum pedatum
Ajuga genevensis
Ajuga reptans
Allium karataviense
Anemone blanda
Anemone coronaria
Anemone sylvestris
Aquilegia flabellata
Arisaema sikokianum
Artemisia schmidtiana 'Nana' ('Silver Mound')
Aruncus aethusifolius
Aruncus 'Southern White'
Asarum arifolium
Asarum canadense

One foot or less, continued
Asarum splendens
Asarum yakushimanum
Athyrium nipponicum
Baptisia minor
Bergenia ciliata
Bergenia cordifolia
Bergenia purpurascens
Brunnera macrophylla
Campanula carpatica
Campanula portenschlagiana
Campanula poscharskyana
Cerastium buisseri
Cerastium tomentosum
Ceratostigma plumbaginoides
Ceratostigma willmottianum
Colchicum autumnale
Colchicum byzantinum
Colchicum speciosum
Coreopsis auriculata
Coreopsis auriculata 'Nana'
Coreopsis rosea
Corydalis cheilanthifolia
Corydalis flexuosa
Corydalis lutea
Crocus chrysanthus
Crocus speciosus
Crocus vernus
Dianthus deltoides
Dianthus gratianopolitanus
Disporum sessile
Epimedium grandiflorum
Epimedium ×perralchium
Epimedium ×rubrum
Epimedium ×youngianum
Euphorbia myrsinites
Geranium ×cantabrigiense
Geranium cinereum
Geranium sanguineum
Geum rivale
Hakonechloa macra
Hepatica acutiloba
Hepatica americana
Hepatica nobilis
Hepatica transsilvanica
Hosta venusta
Hosta hybrids
Ipheion uniflorum
Iris danfordiae
Iris reticulata
Lamium galeobdolon
Lamium maculatum
Linum flavum
Linum perenne
Lychnis ×arkwrightii
Lysimachia japonica
Lysimachia nummularia
Mertensia asiatica
Mertensia virginica
Narcissus bulbocodium
Narcissus cyclamineus
Oenothera berlandieri
Oenothera drummondii
Oenothera missouriensis
Oenothera speciosa
Patrinia triloba
Patrinia villosa
Penstemon smallii
Phlox divaricata
Phlox stolonifera
Phlox subulata
Pinellia pedatisecta
Pinellia tripartita
Polemonium reptans
Polygonatum humile
Polygonum affine
Primula denticulata
Primula veris
Primula vialii
Primula vulgaris
Pulmonaria angustifolia
Pulmonaria longifolia
Pulmonaria rubra
Pulmonaria saccharata
Pulsatilla halleri
Pulsatilla pratensis
Pulsatilla vulgaris
Ranunculus bulbosus
Ranunculus ficaria
Ranunculus repens
Saponaria ocymoides
Sedum acre
Sedum kamtschaticum
Sedum reflexum
Sedum spathulifolium
Sedum spurium
Silene caroliniana
Silene polypetala
Silene regia
Silene uniflora
Silene virginica
Sisyrinchium angustifolium
Sisyrinchium idahoense
Stachys byzantina
Stylophorum diphyllum
Stylophorum lasiocarpum
Thalictrum ichangense
Thalictrum minus 'Adiantifolium'
Thymus praecox
Thymus pseudolanuginosus
Thymus serpyllum
Thymus vulgaris
Tiarella cordifolia
Trillium catesbaei
Trillium cernuum
Trillium cuneatum
Trillium decipiens
Trillium discolor
Trillium erectum
Trillium grandiflorum
Trillium luteum
Trillium sessile
Trillium stamineum
Trillium vaseyi
Uvularia grandiflora
Uvularia perfoliata
Uvularia sessilifolia
Verbena canadensis
Verbena peruviana
Verbena tenuisecta
Veronica austriaca
Veronica incana
Veronica prostrata
Viola cornuta
Viola cucullata
Viola labradorica
Viola pedata
Waldsteinia fragarioides
Waldsteinia lobata
Waldsteinia parviflora
Waldsteinia ternata

One to Three Feet
Acanthus mollis
Acanthus spinosus
Achillea filipendulina
Achillea millefolium
Achillea ptarmica
Achillea sibirica
Allium christophii
Anemone coronaria
Anemone tomentosa
Aquilegia alpina
Aquilegia caerulea
Aquilegia canadensis
Aquilegia chrysantha
Aquilegia vulgaris
Arisaema candidissimum
Arisaema ringens
Arisaema sazensoo
Arisaema sikokianum
Arisaema sikokianum × A. takedae
Arisaema triphyllum
Aster novae-angliae
Aster novi-belgii
Astrantia major
Astrantia maxima
Athyrium filix-femina
Baptisia sphaerocarpa
Baptisia tinctoria
Baptisia viridis
Centaurea cyanus
Centaurea dealbata
Centaurea hypoleuca
Centaurea montana
Chrysanthemum coccineum
Chrysanthemum ×koreanum
Chrysanthemum pacificum
Chrysanthemum ×superbum
Coreopsis grandiflora
Coreopsis lanceolata
Coreopsis verticillata
Crocosmia hybrids
Dahlia hybrids
Delphinium nudicaule
Dianthus barbatus

Dicentra eximia
Dicentra formosa
Dicentra spectabilis
Digitalis grandiflora
Digitalis lutea
Digitalis ×mertonensis
Digitalis purpurea
Disporum sessile
Disporum sessile var. *flavum*
Dryopteris erythrosora
Dryopteris filix-mas
Dryopteris marginalis
Echinacea pallida
Echinacea paradoxa
Echinacea purpurea
Eryngium giganteum
Eupatorium coelestinum
Euphorbia characias
Euphorbia dulcis
Gaillardia ×grandiflora
Gaura lindheimeri
Geranium endressii
Geum chiloense
Geum triflorum
Helleborus foetidus
Helleborus niger
Helleborus ×nigristern
Helleborus orientalis
Hemerocallis dumortieri
Hemerocallis fulva
Hemerocallis minor
Hemerocallis hybrids
Heuchera sanguinea
Heuchera villosa
Hibiscus moscheutos
Hosta montana
Hosta sieboldiana
Hosta hybrids
Hypericum androsaemum
Hypericum calycinum
Hypericum 'Hidcote'
Iris ensata
Iris fulva
Iris hexagona
Iris louisiana
Iris nelsonii
Iris xiphium
Kalimeris pinnatifida
Liatris borealis
Liatris spicata
Lilium hybrids
Linum usitatissimum
Lobelia siphilitica
Lobelia tupa
Lunaria annua
Lunaria rediviva
Lupinus polyphyllus
Lychnis chalcedonica
Lychnis coronaria
Lychnis flos-cuculi
Lycoris albiflora
Lycoris aurea
Lycoris radiata
Lycoris squamigera
Lysimachia ciliata
Lysimachia ephemerum
Mertensia sibirica
Monarda didyma
Nepeta ×faassenii
Nepeta govaniana
Nepeta nervosa
Oenothera fruticosa
Osmunda cinnamomea
Osmunda claytoniana
Papaver nudicaule
Papaver orientale
Papaver rhoeas
Papaver somniferum
Penstemon barbatus
Penstemon cardwellii
Penstemon confertus
Penstemon digitalis
Penstemon pinifolius
Phlox paniculata
Platycodon grandiflorus
Polemonium carneum
Polygonatum odoratum
Primula bulleyana
Primula florindae
Primula heladoxa
Primula japonica
Primula pulverulenta
Ranunculus aconitifolius
Ranunculus asiaticus
Rehmannia angulata
Rehmannia elata
Rudbeckia fulgida
Salvia koyamae
Salvia officinalis
Salvia ×sylvestris
Santolina chamaecyparissus
Santolina pinnata
Santolina virens
Saponaria officinalis
Scabiosa caucasica
Scabiosa columbaria
Sedum aizoon
Silene fimbriata
Sisyrinchium atlanticum
Sisyrinchium striatum
Smilacina racemosa
Stachys macrantha
Stokesia laevis
Symphytum asperum
Symphytum grandiflorum
Symphytum officinale
Tanacetum vulgare
Tradescantia virginiana
Tricyrtis hirta
Verbena rigida
Veronica spicata
Zauschneria californica

Three Feet or More

Aconitum carmichaelii
Aconitum lamarckii
Aconitum napellus
Aconitum reclinatum
Aconitum septentrionale 'Ivorine'
Allium giganteum
Allium 'Beauregard'
Allium 'Globemaster'
Arisaema consanguineum
Arisaema fargesii
Arisaema japonicum
Arisaema tortuosum
Artemisia ludoviciana
Aruncus dioicus
Aster novae-angliae
Aster novi-belgii
Baptisia alba
Baptisia australis
Boltonia asteroides
Campanula lactiflora
Campanula latiloba
Centaurea macrocephala
Cephalaria gigantea
Chrysanthemum ×superbum
Clematis cirrhosa
Clematis ×durandii
Clematis heracleifolia
Clematis integrifolia
Clematis ×jackmanii
Clematis terniflora
Clematis texensis
Clematis hybrids
Crocosmia hybrids
Dahlia imperialis
Dahlia hybrids
Delphinium elatum
Dianthus caryophyllus
Dicentra scandens
Digitalis lutea
Dryopteris erythrosora
Echinops ritro
Eremurus aitchisonii
Eremurus himalaicus
Eremurus stenophyllus
Eryngium agavifolium
Eryngium alpinum
Eryngium yuccafolium
Eupatorium maculatum
Eupatorium purpureum
Eupatorium rugosum
Euphorbia griffithii
Euphorbia lathyris
Geranium psilostemon
Helenium autumnale
Helianthus ×multiflorus
Heliopsis helianthoides
Hemerocallis hybrids
Hibiscus coccineus
Hibiscus mutabilis
Hosta hybrids
Iris ensata
Iris louisiana
Kirengeshoma palmata

Three feet or more, cont.
Ligularia dentata
Ligularia macrophylla
Ligularia sibirica
Ligularia stenocephala
Lilium auratum
Lilium canadense
Lilium henryi
Lilium martagon
Lilium regale
Lilium hybrids
Lobelia cardinalis
Lobelia ×gerardii
Lobelia ×speciosa
Lunaria rediviva
Lupinus arboreus
Lupinus polyphyllus
Lysimachia clethroides
Macleaya cordata
Miscanthus sinensis
Miscanthus hybrids
Nepeta ×faassenii 'Six Hills Giant'
Nepeta sibirica
Osmunda cinnamomea
Osmunda regalis
Papaver somniferum
Patrinia scabiosifolia
Perovskia atriplicifolia
Phlomis fruticosa
Phlomis italica
Phlomis russeliana
Physostegia virginiana
Platycodon grandiflorus
Polemonium caeruleum
Rodgersia aesculifolia
Rodgersia pinnata
Rodgersia podophylla
Rodgersia sambucifolia
Rudbeckia laciniata
Rudbeckia nitida
Rudbeckia triloba
Salvia guaranitica
Salvia involucrata
Salvia 'Indigo Spires'
Santolina chamaecyparissus
Scabiosa ochroleuca
Symphytum asperum
Symphytum caucasicum
Symphytum ×uplandicum
Thalictrum aquilegiifolium
Thalictrum flavum
Thermopsis caroliniana
Thermopsis fabacea
Thermopsis montana
Tricyrtis formosana
Veratrum album
Veratrum viride
Verbena bonariensis
Veronica longifolia
Veronicastrum sibiricum
Veronicastrum virginicum
Zantedeschia hybrids

Interesting Foliage/Fruit

The following plants are often planted for the ornamental value of the foliage and fruit, rather than the flowers.

FOLIAGE
Acanthus mollis 'Holland's Lemon'
Acanthus spinosus 'Spinosissimus'
Achillea 'Coronation Gold'
Adiantum capillus-veneris
Adiantum pedatum
Ajuga reptans 'Atropurpurea'
Ajuga reptans 'Bronze Beauty'
Ajuga reptans 'Burgundy Glow'
Ajuga reptans 'Catlin's Giant'
Ajuga reptans 'Silver Beauty'
Allium karataviense
Artemisia ludoviciana 'Latiloba'
Artemisia ludoviciana 'Silver King'
Artemisia ludoviciana 'Valerie Fennis'
Artemisia schmidtiana 'Nana' ('Silver Mound')
Artemisia 'Huntington Gardens'
Artemisia 'Powis Castle'
Aruncus dioicus 'Kneiffii'
Astrantia major 'Sunningdale Variegated'
Athyrium filix-femina 'Frizelliae'
Athyrium filix-femina 'Linearis'
Athyrium filix-femina 'Minutissimum'
Athyrium nipponicum 'Pictum'
Athyrium nipponicum 'Ursala's Red'
Bergenia ciliata
Bergenia purpurascens
Brunnera macrophylla 'Langtrees'
Brunnera macrophylla 'Variegata'
Canna 'Bengal Tiger' ('Pretoria')
Canna 'Cleopatra'
Canna 'King Humpert'
Canna 'Panache'
Canna 'Tropicana' ('Phaison')
Canna 'Pink Sunburst'
Canna 'Stuttgart'
Disporum sessile 'Variegatum'
Dryopteris erythrosora
Dryopteris filix-mas 'Barnesii'
Dryopteris filix-mas 'Polydactyla'
Dryopteris marginalis
Eupatorium rugosum 'Chocolate'
Euphorbia characias 'Ember Queen'
Euphorbia dulcis 'Chameleon'
Gaura lindheimeri 'Corrie's Gold'
Hakonechloa macra
Hakonechloa macra 'Alboaurea'
Hakonechloa macra 'Aureola'
Heuchera villosa 'Purpurea'
Heuchera 'Amethyst Mist'
Heuchera 'Bressingham Bronze'
Heuchera 'Chocolate Veil'
Heuchera 'Dale's Selection'
Heuchera 'Palace Purple'
Heuchera 'Smokey Rose'
Heuchera 'Whirlwind'
Hosta montana
Hosta montana 'Aureomarginata'
Hosta sieboldiana
Hosta sieboldiana 'Frances Williams'
Hosta venusta
Hosta 'Antioch'
Hosta 'Blue Cadet'
Hosta 'Bright Lights'
Hosta 'Francee'
Hosta 'Gold Edger'
Hosta 'Invincible'
Hosta 'Red Neck Heaven'

Hosta 'Royal Standard'
Hosta 'Spritzer'
Hosta 'Sum and Substance'
Hosta 'Sun Power'
Kalimeris yomena 'Variegata'
Lamium maculatum 'Beacon Silver'
Lamium maculatum 'Chequers'
Lamium maculatum 'White Nancy'
Lysimachia ciliata 'Purpurea'
Lysimachia japonica 'Minutissima'
Lysimachia nummularia 'Aurea'
Macleaya cordata
Mertensia asiatica
Miscanthus sinensis 'Adagio'
Miscanthus sinensis 'Arabesque'
Miscanthus sinensis 'Cabaret'
Miscanthus sinensis 'Malepartus'
Miscanthus sinensis 'Morning Light'
Miscanthus sinensis 'Silberfeder' ('Silver Feather')
Miscanthus sinensis 'Strictus'
Miscanthus sinensis 'Variegatus'
Miscanthus sinensis 'Yaku Jima'
Osmunda claytoniana
Penstemon digitalis 'Husker Red'
Phlox paniculata 'Norah Leigh'
Phlox stolonifera 'Variegata'
Physostegia virginiana 'Variegata'
Polemonium caeruleum 'Brise d'Anjou'
Polygonatum odoratum 'Variegatum'
Pulmonaria longifolia
Pulmonaria longifolia 'Bertram Anderson'
Pulmonaria longifolia subsp. *cevennensis* ('Little Blue')
Pulmonaria rubra 'David Ward'
Pulmonaria saccharata
Pulmonaria saccharata 'Benediction'
Pulmonaria saccharata 'Berries and Cream'
Pulmonaria saccharata 'Excalibur'
Pulmonaria saccharata 'Highdown'
Pulmonaria saccharata 'Mrs. Kittle'
Pulmonaria saccharata 'Mrs. Moon'
Pulmonaria saccharata 'Sissinghurst White'
Pulmonaria saccharata 'Spilled Milk'
Pulmonaria 'Roy Davidson'
Ranunculus ficaria 'Brazen Hussy'
Ranunculus repens 'Susan's Song' ('Buttered Popcorn')
Salvia officinalis 'Icterina'
Salvia officinalis 'Purpurescens'
Salvia officinalis 'Tricolor'
Santolina chamaecyparissus
Santolina virens
Sedum reflexum
Sedum reflexum 'Blue Spruce'
Sedum spathulifolium 'Cape Blanco'
Sedum spurium 'Fuldaglut'
Sedum 'Atropurpureum'
Sedum 'Mohrchen'
Sedum 'Vera Jameson'
Sisyrinchium striatum 'Aunt May'
Stachys byzantina
Stachys byzantina 'Countess Helene von Stein'
Stachys byzantina 'Primrose Heron'
Stachys byzantina 'Sheila Macqueen'
Symphytum 'Goldsmith'
Symphytum officinale 'Variegatum'
Symphytum ×*uplandicum* 'Variegatum'
Thalictrum flavum 'Glaucum'
Thymus vulgaris 'Silver Posie'
Tiarella cordifolia 'Oakleaf'
Tiarella 'Brandywine'
Tiarella 'Ink Blot'
Tiarella 'Snowflake'
Tiarella 'Tiger Stripe'
Tricyrtis 'Lemon Glow'
Trillium cuneatum 'Eco Silver'
Trillium sessile
Uvularia grandiflora
Uvularia grandiflora 'Sunbonnet'
Veronica austriaca subsp. *teucrium* 'Aurea'
Yucca filamentosa 'Bright Edge'
Yucca filamentosa 'Gold Band'
Yucca filamentosa 'Golden Sword'

FRUIT

Baptisia alba
Baptisia alba 'Pendula'
Baptisia australis
Baptisia minor
Baptisia sphaerocarpa
Baptisia tinctoria
Baptisia viridis
Clematis ×*durandii*
Clematis integrifolia
Clematis ×*jackmanii*
Clematis terniflora
Clematis texensis
Clematis hybrids
Euphorbia lathyris
Geum triflorum
Geum triflorum var. *campanulatum*
Hypericum androsaemum
Hypericum androsaemum 'Albury Purple'
Kirengeshoma palmata
Lunaria annua
Lunaria annua 'Variegata'
Lunaria rediviva
Osmunda cinnamomea

Native Plants

The following plants are native to the United States.

Aconitum reclinatum
Aquilegia caerulea
Aquilegia canadensis
Aquilegia chrysantha
Arisaema triphyllum
Asarum arifolium
Asarum canadense
Aster carolinianus
Aster divaricatus
Aster novae-angliae
Aster novi-belgii
Astilbe biternata
Baptisia alba
Baptisia australis
Baptisia minor
Baptisia sphaerocarpa
Baptisia tinctoria
Baptisia viridis
Boltonia asteroides
Clematis texensis
Coreopsis auriculata
Coreopsis grandiflora
Coreopsis lanceolata
Coreopsis rosea
Coreopsis verticillata
Dicentra eximia
Dicentra formosa
Dryopteris marginalis
Echinacea pallida
Echinacea paradoxa
Echinacea purpurea
Eryngium yuccafolium
Eupatorium coelestinum
Eupatorium maculatum
Eupatorium purpureum
Eupatorium rugosum
Gaillardia ×grandiflora
Gaura lindheimeri
Geum triflorum
Geum triflorum var. *campanulatum*
Helenium autumnale
Helianthus angustifolius
Helianthus giganteus
Heliopsis helianthoides
Hepatica acutiloba
Hepatica americana
Heuchera americana
Heuchera villosa
Hibiscus coccineus
Hibiscus moscheutos
Iris fulva
Iris hexagona
Iris louisiana
Iris nelsonii
Liatris borealis
Liatris graminifolia
Liatris spicata
Lilium canadense
Lobelia cardinalis
Lobelia siphilitica
Mertensia virginica
Monarda didyma
Oenothera berlandieri
Oenothera drummondii
Oenothera fruticosa
Oenothera missouriensis
Oenothera speciosa
Osmunda cinnamomea
Osmunda claytoniana
Osmunda regalis
Penstemon barbatus
Penstemon cardwellii
Penstemon confertus
Penstemon digitalis
Penstemon pinifolius
Penstemon smallii
Phlox divaricata
Phlox paniculata
Phlox stolonifera
Phlox subulata
Physostegia virginiana
Polemonium reptans
Rudbeckia fulgida
Rudbeckia laciniata
Rudbeckia nitida
Rudbeckia triloba
Silene caroliniana
Silene polypetala
Silene regia
Silene virginica
Sisyrinchium idahoense
Smilacina racemosa
Tiarella cordifolia
Tradescantia virginiana
Trillium catesbaei
Trillium cernuum
Trillium cuneatum
Trillium decipiens
Trillium discolor
Trillium erectum
Trillium grandiflorum
Trillium luteum
Trillium sessile
Trillium stamineum
Trillium vaseyi
Uvularia grandiflora
Uvularia perfoliata
Uvularia sessilifolia
Veratrum viride
Verbena canadensis
Viola labradorica
Viola pedata
Waldsteinia fragarioides
Waldsteinia lobata
Waldsteinia parviflora
Yucca filamentosa
Zauschneria californica

Sun/Shade Tolerance

Perennials do not "like" sun or shade but tolerate conditions of sun or shade in varying degrees. Most species that tolerate heavy shade also tolerate dappled or partial shade. Plants that tolerate full sun seldom do well in heavy shade and vice versa.

A quick and dirty guide to determining the amount of sun or shade in a garden location: On a sunny day, with your back to the sun, hold a piece of white paper in your right hand, place your left hand about six inches in front of the paper. If a sharp shadow falls on the paper, consider the area in full sun; if a fuzzy shadow occurs, consider the area in partial shade; and if no shadow can be detected, then you are in heavy shade. Obviously, the amount of shade at a given location in the garden changes with the track of the sun. An area of full sun is generally considered five hours or more of direct sun; one in heavy shade is less than one hour; and partial shade/sun is somewhere in between.

Heavy Shade

Adiantum capillus-veneris
Adiantum pedatum
Ajuga reptans
Arisaema candidissimum
Arisaema consanguineum
Arisaema fargesii
Arisaema japonicum
Arisaema ringens
Arisaema sazensoo
Arisaema sikokianum
Arisaema sikokianum × *A. takedae*
Arisaema tortuosum
Arisaema triphyllum
Asarum arifolium
Asarum canadense
Asarum splendens
Asarum yakushimanum
Athyrium filix-femina
Brunnera macrophylla
Disporum sessile
Dryopteris erythrosora
Dryopteris filix-mas
Dryopteris marginalis
Epimedium grandiflorum
Epimedium ×*perralchium*
Epimedium ×*rubrum*
Epimedium ×*versicolor*
Epimedium ×*youngianum*
Hepatica acutiloba
Hepatica americana
Hepatica nobilis
Hepatica transsilvanica
Hosta montana
Hosta sieboldiana
Hosta venusta
Hosta hybrids
Osmunda cinnamomea
Osmunda claytoniana
Osmunda regalis
Pinellia pedatisecta
Pinellia tripartita
Viola pedata

Partial Shade/Sun

Acanthus mollis
Achillea ageratum
Aconitum napellus
Adiantum capillus-veneris
Adiantum pedatum
Ajuga genevensis
Ajuga reptans
Allium 'Globemaster'
Anemone blanda
Anemone sylvestris
Anemone tomentosa
Aquilegia alpina
Aquilegia caerulea
Aquilegia canadensis
Aquilegia chrysantha
Aquilegia flabellata
Aquilegia vulgaris
Arisaema candidissimum
Arisaema consanguineum
Arisaema fargesii
Arisaema japonicum
Arisaema ringens
Arisaema sazensoo
Arisaema sikokianum
Arisaema sikokianum × *A. takedae*
Arisaema tortuosum
Arisaema triphyllum
Aruncus aethusifolius
Aruncus 'Southern White'
Aster divaricatus
Astilbe ×*arendsii*
Astilbe biternata
Astilbe chinensis
Astilbe chinensis var. *taquetii*
Astilbe simplicifolia
Astrantia major
Astrantia maxima
Athyrium filix-femina
Athyrium nipponicum
Baptisia alba
Bergenia ciliata
Bergenia cordifolia
Bergenia purpurascens
Brunnera macrophylla
Campanula portenschlagiana
Campanula poscharskyana
Canna 'Stuttgart'
Cerastium buisseri
Cerastium tomentosum
Clematis cirrhosa
Clematis heracleifolia
Clematis integrifolia
Colchicum autumnale
Colchicum byzantinum
Colchicum speciosum
Corydalis cheilanthifolia
Corydalis flexuosa
Corydalis lutea
Dicentra eximia
Dicentra scandens
Dicentra spectabilis
Digitalis grandiflora
Digitalis lutea
Digitalis ×*mertonensis*
Digitalis purpurea
Disporum sessile
Disporum sessile var. *flavum*
Dryopteris filix-mas
Dryopteris marginalis
Epimedium grandiflorum
Epimedium ×*perralchium*
Epimedium ×*rubrum*
Epimedium ×*versicolor*
Epimedium ×*youngianum*
Eupatorium coelestinum
Euphorbia dulcis
Euphorbia lathyris
Euphorbia myrsinites
Geranium cinereum
Geranium endressii
Helleborus foetidus
Helleborus niger
Helleborus ×*nigristern*
Helleborus orientalis
Hepatica acutiloba
Hepatica americana
Hepatica nobilis
Hepatica transsilvanica

Partial Shade/Sun, cont.

Heuchera sanguinea
Heuchera villosa
Hosta montana
Hosta sieboldiana
Hosta venusta
Hosta hybrids
Iris tectorum
Kalimeris yomena
Kirengeshoma palmata
Lamium galeobdolon
Lamium maculatum
Ligularia dentata
Ligularia macrophylla
Ligularia sibirica
Ligularia stenocephala
Lobelia cardinalis
Lobelia siphilitica
Lobelia ×speciosa
Lobelia tupa
Lunaria annua
Lunaria rediviva
Lysimachia ciliata
Lysimachia japonica
Lysimachia nummularia
Mertensia asiatica
Mertensia sibirica
Mertensia virginica
Nepeta govaniana
Osmunda cinnamomea
Osmunda claytoniana
Osmunda regalis
Penstemon digitalis
Penstemon smallii
Phlox divaricata
Phlox stolonifera
Pinellia pedatisecta
Pinellia tripartita
Polemonium reptans
Polygonatum humile
Polygonatum odoratum
Polygonum affine
Polygonum bistorta
Primula bulleyana
Primula denticulata
Primula florindae
Primula heladoxa
Primula japonica
Primula pulverulenta
Primula veris
Primula vialii
Primula vulgaris
Pulmonaria angustifolia
Pulmonaria longifolia
Pulmonaria rubra
Pulmonaria saccharata
Ranunculus ficaria
Ranunculus repens
Rehmannia angulata
Rehmannia elata
Rodgersia aesculifolia
Rodgersia pinnata
Rodgersia podophylla
Rodgersia sambucifolia
Salvia koyamae
Sedum ternatum
Silene fimbriata
Silene polypetala
Silene regia
Silene virginica
Smilacina racemosa
Stachys byzantina
Stylophorum diphyllum
Stylophorum lasiocarpum
Symphytum asperum
Symphytum caucasicum
Symphytum grandiflorum
Symphytum officinale
Symphytum ×uplandicum
Thalictrum aquilegiifolium
Thalictrum ichangense
Thalictrum minus 'Adiantifolium'
Tiarella cordifolia
Tricyrtis formosana
Tricyrtis hirta
Trillium catesbaei
Trillium cernuum
Trillium cuneatum
Trillium decipiens
Trillium discolor
Trillium erectum
Trillium grandiflorum
Trillium luteum
Trillium sessile
Trillium stamineum
Trillium vaseyi
Uvularia grandiflora
Uvularia perfoliata
Uvularia sessilifolia
Veratrum album
Veratrum viride
Viola labradorica
Viola pedata
Waldsteinia fragarioides
Waldsteinia lobata
Waldsteinia parviflora
Waldsteinia ternata

Full Sun

Acanthus mollis
Acanthus spinosus
Achillea filipendulina
Achillea millefolium
Achillea ptarmica
Achillea sibirica
Aconitum carmichaelii
Aconitum lamarckii
Aconitum napellus
Aconitum reclinatum
Aconitum septentrionale 'Ivorine'
Allium christophii
Allium giganteum
Allium karataviense
Allium 'Beauregard'
Allium 'Globemaster'
Anemone coronaria
Anemone sylvestris
Anemone tomentosa
Artemisia ludoviciana
Artemisia schmidtiana
Aruncus dioicus
Aruncus 'Southern White'
Aster carolinianus
Aster novae-angliae
Aster novi-belgii
Aster tataricus
Baptisia alba
Baptisia australis
Baptisia minor
Baptisia sphaerocarpa
Baptisia tinctoria
Baptisia viridis
Boltonia asteroides
Campanula carpatica
Campanula lactiflora
Campanula latiloba
Campanula portenschlagiana
Campanula poscharskyana
Canna hybrids
Centaurea cyanus
Centaurea dealbata
Centaurea hypoleuca
Centaurea macrocephala
Centaurea montana
Cephalaria gigantea
Cerastium buisseri
Cerastium tomentosum
Ceratostigma plumbaginoides
Ceratostigma willmottianum
Chrysanthemum coccineum
Chrysanthemum ×koreanum
Chrysanthemum pacificum
Chrysanthemum ×superbum
Clematis ×durandii
Clematis heracleifolia
Clematis integrifolia
Clematis ×jackmanii
Clematis terniflora
Clematis texensis
Clematis hybrids
Coreopsis auriculata
Coreopsis grandiflora
Coreopsis lanceolata
Coreopsis rosea
Coreopsis verticillata
Crocosmia hybrids
Crocus chrysanthus
Crocus speciosus
Crocus vernus
Dahlia imperialis
Dahlia hybrids
Delphinium elatum

Delphinium nudicaule
Dianthus barbatus
Dianthus caryophyllus
Dianthus deltoides
Dianthus gratianopolitanus
Echinacea pallida
Echinacea paradoxa
Echinacea purpurea
Echinops ritro
Eremurus aitchisonii
Eremurus himalaicus
Eremurus stenophyllus
Eryngium agavifolium
Eryngium alpinum
Eryngium giganteum
Eryngium yuccafolium
Eupatorium coelestinum
Eupatorium maculatum
Eupatorium rugosum
Euphorbia characias
Euphorbia dulcis
Euphorbia griffithii
Euphorbia lathyris
Gaillardia ×*grandiflora*
Gaura lindheimeri
Geranium ×*cantabrigiense*
Geranium endressii
Geranium psilostemon
Geranium sanguineum
Geum chiloense
Geum rivale
Geum triflorum
Hakonechloa macra
Helenium autumnale
Helianthus angustifolius
Helianthus giganteus
Helianthus ×*multiflorus*
Heliopsis helianthoides
Hemerocallis dumortieri
Hemerocallis fulva
Hemerocallis minor
Hemerocallis hybrids
Hibiscus coccineus
Hibiscus moscheutos
Hibiscus mutabilis
Hypericum androsaemum
Hypericum calycinum
Hypericum 'Hidcote'
Ipheion uniflorum
Iris danfordiae
Iris ensata
Iris hexagona
Iris louisiana
Iris nelsonii
Iris reticulata
Iris tectorum
Iris xiphium
Kalimeris pinnatifida
Kniphofia hybrids
Liatris borealis
Liatris graminifolia
Liatris spicata
Ligularia dentata
Ligularia macrophylla
Ligularia sibirica
Ligularia stenocephala
Lilium auratum
Lilium canadense
Lilium henryi
Lilium martagon
Lilium regale
Linum flavum
Linum perenne
Linum usitatissimum
Lobelia cardinalis
Lobelia ×*gerardii*
Lobelia siphilitica
Lobelia ×*speciosa*
Lobelia tupa
Lunaria annua
Lunaria rediviva
Lupinus arboreus
Lupinus polyphyllus
Lychnis ×*arkwrightii*
Lychnis chalcedonica
Lychnis coronaria
Lychnis flos-cuculi
Lycoris albiflora
Lycoris aurea
Lycoris radiata
Lycoris squamigera
Lysimachia ciliata
Lysimachia clethroides
Lysimachia ephemerum
Macleaya cordata
Miscanthus sinensis
Miscanthus hybrids
Monarda didyma
Narcissus bulbocodium
Narcissus cyclamineus
Narcissus hybrids
Nepeta ×*faassenii*
Nepeta ×*faassenii* 'Six Hills Giant'
Nepeta govaniana
Nepeta nervosa
Nepeta sibirica
Oenothera berlandieri
Oenothera drummondii
Oenothera fruticosa
Oenothera missouriensis
Oenothera speciosa
Paeonia hybrids
Papaver nudicaule
Papaver orientale
Papaver rhoeas
Papaver somniferum
Patrinia scabiosifolia
Patrinia triloba
Patrinia villosa
Penstemon barbatus
Penstemon cardwellii
Penstemon confertus
Penstemon digitalis
Penstemon pinifolius
Perovskia atriplicifolia
Phlomis fruticosa
Phlomis italica
Phlomis russeliana
Phlox paniculata
Phlox subulata
Physostegia virginiana
Platycodon grandiflorus
Polemonium caeruleum
Polemonium carneum
Polemonium foliosissimum
Polygonum affine
Polygonum bistorta
Pulsatilla halleri
Pulsatilla pratensis
Pulsatilla vulgaris
Ranunculus aconitifolius
Ranunculus asiaticus
Ranunculus bulbosus
Ranunculus ficaria
Ranunculus repens
Rehmannia angulata
Rehmannia elata
Rudbeckia fulgida
Rudbeckia laciniata
Rudbeckia nitida
Rudbeckia triloba
Salvia guaranitica
Salvia involucrata
Salvia officinalis
Salvia ×*sylvestris*
Salvia 'Indigo Spires'
Santolina chamaecyparissus
Santolina pinnata
Santolina virens
Saponaria ocymoides
Saponaria officinalis
Scabiosa caucasica
Scabiosa columbaria
Scabiosa ochroleuca
Sedum acre
Sedum aizoon
Sedum kamtschaticum
Sedum reflexum
Sedum spathulifolium
Sedum spurium
Silene caroliniana
Silene uniflora
Sisyrinchium angustifolium
Sisyrinchium atlanticum
Sisyrinchium idahoense
Sisyrinchium striatum
Stachys macrantha
Stokesia laevis
Thalictrum aquilegiifolium
Thalictrum flavum
Thermopsis caroliniana
Thermopsis fabacea
Thermopsis montana

Full Sun, continued

Thymus praecox
Thymus pseudolanuginosus
Thymus serpyllum
Thymus vulgaris
Tradescantia virginiana
Tricyrtis formosana
Tricyrtis hirta
Verbena bonariensis
Verbena canadensis
Verbena peruviana
Verbena rigida
Verbena tenuisecta
Veronica austriaca
Veronica incana
Veronica longifolia
Veronica prostrata
Veronica spicata
Veronicastrum sibiricum
Veronicastrum virginicum
Viola cornuta
Viola cucullata
Yucca filamentosa
Zantedeschia hybrids
Zauschneria californica

Sprawling Habit/Vines

The following vines or plants tend to sprawl if not provided with support. Large sprawling plants can be trained to grow through and over small shrubs or can be supported by neighboring plants.

Campanula portenschlagiana
Campanula poscharskyana
Clematis cirrhosa
Clematis ×durandii
Clematis heracleifolia
Clematis ×jackmanii
Clematis terniflora
Clematis texensis
Dicentra scandens
Euphorbia myrsinites
Geranium psilostemon
Geranium 'Ann Folkard'
Oenothera speciosa
Silene polypetala

Evergreen/Winter Interest

Although much of the country is covered with snow in the winter, some plants still provide winter interest in the form of architectural features, seed heads, and persistent foliage.

Ajuga genevensis
Ajuga reptans
Asarum arifolium
Asarum splendens
Asarum yakushimanum
Bergenia cordifolia
Bergenia purpurascens
Clematis cirrhosa
Dryopteris erythrosora
Dryopteris marginalis
Epimedium grandiflorum
Epimedium ×perralchium
Epimedium ×rubrum
Helleborus foetidus
Helleborus niger
Helleborus ×nigristern
Helleborus orientalis
Hepatica acutiloba
Hepatica americana
Hepatica transsilvanica
Heuchera americana
Miscanthus sinensis
Phlomis fruticosa
Phlomis russeliana
Phlox stolonifera
Phlox subulata
Pulmonaria angustifolia
Pulmonaria longifolia
Pulmonaria saccharata
Ranunculus repens
Sedum acre
Sedum kamtschaticum
Sedum spathulifolium
Sedum spurium
Sedum 'Autumn Joy' ('Herbstfreude')
Tiarella cordifolia

Flowering Season

As far as a plant is concerned, the seasons depend on environmental changes such as soil warming, day and night temperatures, photoperiod, and frost—not calendar dates, as we are used to thinking. A spring-flowering plant simply means it is early to flower, not that it flowers in March, April, or even May. The flowering calendar offered here is therefore relative.

SPRING

Acanthus mollis
Acanthus spinosus
Achillea ageratum
Achillea millefolium
Adiantum capillus-veneris
Ajuga genevensis 'Pink Beauty'
Ajuga reptans
Allium christophii
Allium giganteum
Allium karataviense
Allium 'Beauregard'
Allium 'Globemaster'
Anemone blanda
Anemone coronaria
Anemone sylvestris
Aquilegia alpina
Aquilegia caerulea
Aquilegia canadensis
Aquilegia chrysantha
Aquilegia flabellata
Aquilegia vulgaris
Arisaema candidissimum
Arisaema consanguineum
Arisaema ringens
Arisaema sazensoo
Arisaema sikokianum
Arisaema sikokianum × *A. takedae*
Arisaema tortuosum
Arisaema triphyllum
Aruncus aethusifolius
Aruncus 'Southern White'
Asarum arifolium
Asarum canadense
Asarum splendens
Asarum yakushimanum
Astilbe ×*arendsii*
Astilbe chinensis
Astrantia major
Astrantia maxima
Baptisia alba
Baptisia australis
Baptisia minor
Baptisia sphaerocarpa
Bergenia ciliata
Bergenia cordifolia
Bergenia purpurascens
Brunnera macrophylla
Centaurea montana
Cerastium buisseri
Cerastium tomentosum
Chrysanthemum coccineum
Coreopsis auriculata
Corydalis cheilanthifolia
Corydalis flexuosa
Corydalis lutea
Crocus chrysanthus
Crocus vernus
Dianthus barbatus
Dianthus deltoides
Dianthus gratianopolitanus
Dicentra eximia
Dicentra spectabilis
Digitalis purpurea
Disporum sessile
Disporum sessile var. *flavum*
Epimedium grandiflorum
Epimedium ×*perralchium*
Epimedium ×*rubrum*
Epimedium ×*versicolor*
Epimedium ×*youngianum*
Euphorbia characias
Euphorbia myrsinites
Geranium cinereum
Geranium endressii
Geranium sanguineum
Geum chiloense
Geum rivale
Geum triflorum
Geum triflorum var. *campanulatum*
Helleborus foetidus
Helleborus niger
Helleborus ×*nigristern*
Helleborus orientalis
Hepatica acutiloba
Hepatica americana
Hepatica nobilis
Hepatica transsilvanica
Heuchera sanguinea
Ipheion uniflorum
Iris danfordiae
Iris reticulata
Iris tectorum
Iris xiphium
Lamium galeobdolon
Lamium maculatum
Lobelia cardinalis
Lobelia ×*gerardii*
Lobelia siphilitica
Lobelia ×*speciosa*
Lobelia tupa
Lunaria annua
Lunaria rediviva
Lupinus arboreus
Lupinus polyphyllus
Lychnis ×*arkwrightii*
Lychnis flos-cuculi
Lysimachia japonica
Lysimachia nummularia
Mertensia asiatica
Mertensia sibirica
Mertensia virginica
Narcissus bulbocodium
Narcissus cyclamineus
Narcissus hybrids
Nepeta ×*faassenii*
Nepeta ×*faassenii* 'Six Hills Giant'
Nepeta govaniana
Nepeta sibirica
Oenothera berlandieri
Oenothera missouriensis
Oenothera speciosa
Osmunda cinnamomea
Osmunda claytoniana
Osmunda regalis
Paeonia hybrids
Penstemon barbatus
Penstemon smallii
Phlox divaricata
Phlox stolonifera
Phlox subulata
Pinellia pedatisecta
Pinellia tripartita
Polemonium reptans
Polygonatum humile
Polygonatum odoratum
Polygonum affine
Polygonum bistorta
Primula bulleyana
Primula denticulata
Primula florindae
Primula heladoxa
Primula japonica
Primula pulverulenta
Primula veris
Primula vulgaris
Pulmonaria angustifolia
Pulmonaria longifolia
Pulmonaria rubra
Pulmonaria saccharata
Pulsatilla halleri
Pulsatilla pratensis

Spring, continued
Pulsatilla vulgaris
Ranunculus asiaticus
Ranunculus bulbosus
Ranunculus repens
Saponaria ocymoides
Saponaria officinalis
Scabiosa caucasica
Scabiosa columbaria
Sedum acre
Sedum aizoon
Sedum aizoon var. *aurantiacum*
Sedum kamtschaticum
Sedum reflexum
Sedum spathulifolium
Sedum spurium
Sedum ternatum
Silene caroliniana
Silene polypetala
Silene regia
Silene uniflora
Silene virginica
Smilacina racemosa
Stachys byzantina
Stachys macrantha
Stylophorum diphyllum
Stylophorum lasiocarpum
Symphytum asperum
Symphytum caucasicum
Symphytum grandiflorum
Symphytum officinale
Symphytum ×*uplandicum*
Thalictrum aquilegiifolium
Thalictrum flavum
Thalictrum ichangense
Thalictrum minus 'Adiantifolium'
Thermopsis caroliniana
Thermopsis montana
Thymus praecox
Thymus pseudolanuginosus
Thymus serpyllum
Thymus vulgaris
Tiarella cordifolia
Trillium catesbaei
Trillium cernuum
Trillium cuneatum
Trillium decipiens
Trillium discolor
Trillium erectum
Trillium grandiflorum
Trillium luteum
Trillium sessile
Trillium stamineum
Trillium vaseyi
Uvularia grandiflora
Uvularia perfoliata
Uvularia sessilifolia
Veratrum album
Veratrum viride
Verbena peruviana
Verbena tenuisecta
Veronica austriaca
Veronica austriaca subsp. *teucrium*
Veronica incana
Veronica longifolia
Veronica prostrata
Veronica spicata
Viola cornuta
Viola cucullata
Viola labradorica
Viola pedata
Waldsteinia fragarioides
Waldsteinia lobata
Waldsteinia parviflora
Waldsteinia ternata

SUMMER
Acanthus mollis
Acanthus spinosus
Achillea ageratum
Achillea filipendulina
Achillea millefolium
Achillea ptarmica
Achillea sibirica
Aconitum carmichaelii
Allium giganteum
Anemone sylvestris
Anemone tomentosa
Arisaema candidissimum
Arisaema consanguineum
Arisaema fargesii
Arisaema japonicum
Artemisia ludoviciana
Artemisia schmidtiana
Aruncus dioicus
Aster divaricatus
Astilbe ×*arendsii*
Astilbe biternata
Astilbe chinensis
Astilbe chinensis var. *taquetii*
Astilbe simplicifolia
Baptisia tinctoria
Baptisia viridis
Boltonia asteroides
Campanula carpatica
Campanula lactiflora
Campanula latiloba
Campanula portenschlagiana
Campanula poscharskyana
Canna hybrids
Centaurea cyanus
Centaurea dealbata
Centaurea hypoleuca
Centaurea macrocephala
Cephalaria gigantea
Chrysanthemum ×*superbum*
Clematis ×*durandii*
Clematis heracleifolia
Clematis integrifolia
Clematis ×*jackmanii*
Clematis texensis
Clematis hybrids
Coreopsis grandiflora
Coreopsis lanceolata
Coreopsis rosea
Coreopsis verticillata
Crocosmia hybrids
Delphinium elatum
Delphinium nudicaule
Dianthus caryophyllus
Dicentra scandens
Digitalis grandiflora
Digitalis lutea
Digitalis ×*mertonensis*
Echinacea pallida
Echinacea paradoxa
Echinacea purpurea
Echinops ritro
Eremurus aitchisonii
Eremurus himalaicus
Eremurus stenophyllus
Eryngium agavifolium
Eryngium alpinum
Eryngium yuccafolium
Eupatorium rugosum
Euphorbia dulcis
Euphorbia griffithii
Euphorbia lathyris
Gaillardia ×*grandiflora*
Gaura lindheimeri
Geranium ×*cantabrigiense*
Geranium endressii
Geranium psilostemon
Geum triflorum
Geum triflorum var. *campanulatum*
Helianthus ×*multiflorus*
Heliopsis helianthoides
Hemerocallis dumortieri
Hemerocallis fulva
Hemerocallis minor
Hemerocallis hybrids
Hibiscus coccineus
Hibiscus moscheutos
Hosta montana
Hosta sieboldiana
Hosta venusta
Hypericum androsaemum
Hypericum 'Hidcote'
Ipheion uniflorum
Iris ensata
Iris fulva
Iris hexagona
Iris louisiana
Iris nelsonii
Kalimeris pinnatifida
Kalimeris yomena
Kirengeshoma palmata
Kniphofia hybrids
Liatris borealis
Liatris graminifolia

Liatris spicata
Ligularia dentata
Ligularia macrophylla
Ligularia sibirica
Ligularia stenocephala
Lilium auratum
Lilium auratum var. *platyphyllum*
Lilium canadense
Lilium henryi
Lilium martagon
Lilium regale
Linum flavum
Linum perenne
Linum usitatissimum
Lobelia cardinalis
Lobelia ×*gerardii*
Lobelia siphilitica
Lobelia ×*speciosa*
Lobelia tupa
Lychnis chalcedonica
Lychnis coronaria
Lycoris albiflora
Lycoris aurea
Lycoris squamigera
Lysimachia ciliata
Lysimachia clethroides
Lysimachia ephemerum
Macleaya cordata
Monarda didyma
Nepeta ×*faassenii* 'Six Hills Giant'
Nepeta nervosa
Oenothera drummondii
Oenothera fruticosa
Paeonia hybrids
Penstemon cardwellii
Penstemon confertus
Penstemon digitalis
Penstemon pinifolius
Perovskia atriplicifolia
Phlomis fruticosa
Phlomis italica
Phlomis russeliana
Phlox paniculata
Physostegia virginiana
Platycodon grandiflorus
Polemonium caeruleum
Polemonium carneum
Polemonium foliosissimum
Primula bulleyana
Primula florindae
Primula heladoxa
Ranunculus aconitifolius
Ranunculus ficaria
Rehmannia angulata
Rehmannia elata
Rodgersia aesculifolia
Rodgersia pinnata
Rodgersia podophylla
Rodgersia sambucifolia
Salvia guaranitica
Salvia involucrata
Salvia koyamae
Salvia officinalis
Salvia ×*sylvestris*
Salvia 'Indigo Spires'
Santolina chamaecyparissus
Santolina pinnata
Santolina virens
Saponaria officinalis
Scabiosa caucasica
Silene fimbriata
Sisyrinchium angustifolium
Sisyrinchium atlanticum
Sisyrinchium idahoense
Sisyrinchium striatum
Stokesia laevis
Thalictrum aquilegiifolium
Thermopsis fabacea
Tradescantia virginiana
Veratrum album
Veratrum viride
Verbena bonariensis
Verbena canadensis
Verbena rigida
Verbena tenuisecta
Veronica spicata
Veronicastrum sibiricum
Veronicastrum virginicum
Yucca filamentosa
Zantedeschia hybrids
Zauschneria californica

FALL

Aconitum carmichaelii
Aconitum lamarckii
Aconitum napellus
Aconitum reclinatum
Aconitum septentrionale 'Ivorine'
Anemone tomentosa
Aster carolinianus
Aster divaricatus
Aster novae-angliae
Aster novi-belgii
Aster tataricus
Boltonia asteroides
Canna hybrids
Ceratostigma plumbaginoides
Ceratostigma willmottianum
Chrysanthemum ×*koreanum*
Chrysanthemum pacificum
Clematis terniflora
Colchicum autumnale
Colchicum byzantinum
Colchicum speciosum
Crocus speciosus
Dahlia imperialis
Dahlia hybrids
Eupatorium coelestinum
Eupatorium maculatum
Eupatorium purpureum
Eupatorium rugosum
Helenium autumnale
Helianthus angustifolius
Helianthus giganteus
Heuchera villosa
Hibiscus mutabilis
Lycoris albiflora
Lycoris aurea
Lycoris radiata
Miscanthus sinensis
Miscanthus hybrids
Rudbeckia fulgida
Rudbeckia laciniata
Rudbeckia nitida
Rudbeckia triloba
Salvia involucrata
Salvia 'Indigo Spires'
Santolina chamaecyparissus
Tricyrtis formosana
Tricyrtis hirta

U.S. Department of Agriculture Hardiness Zone Map

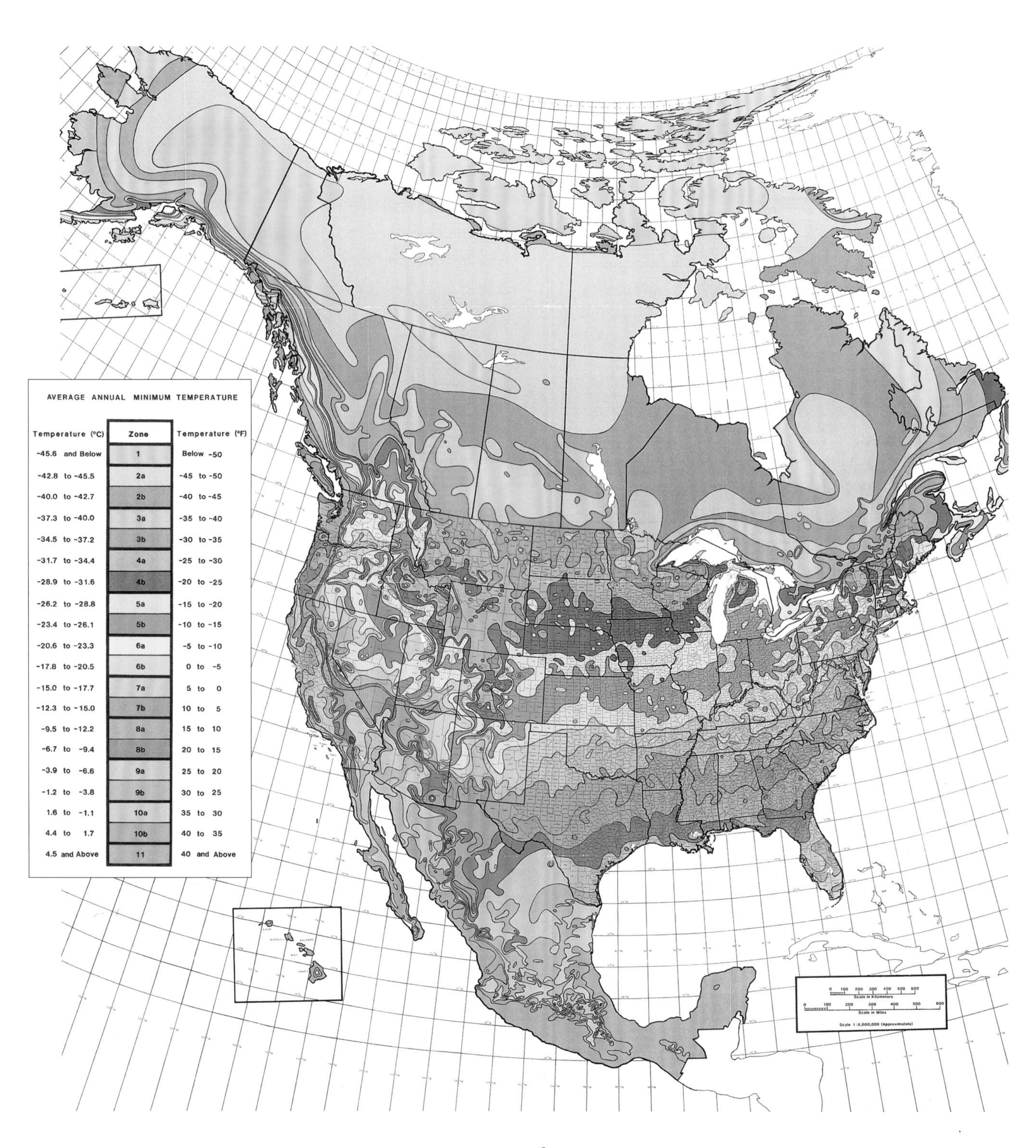

Index of Species and Cultivars

Index of Common Names